The New York Times

GUIDE TO

RESTAURANTS

IN

NEW YORK CITY

REVISED AND EXPANDED

The New York Times

GUIDE TO

RESTAURANTS IN NEW YORK CITY

REVISED AND EXPANDED

Bryan Miller

Times BOOKS

LIBRARY OF CONGRESS CATALOGING-IN-PUBLICATION DATA
Miller, Bryan.
The New York Times guide to restaurants in New York City.
Includes index.
1. Restaurants, lunch rooms, etc.—New York (N.Y.)—
Guide-books. 2. New York (N.Y.)—Description—1981–
—Guide-books. I. New York Times. II. Title.
TX907.3.N72N46   1988   647′.95′7471   88-40158
ISBN 0-8129-1735-9

Manufactured in the United States of America

9   8   7   6   5   4   3   2

REVISED EDITION

To my mother, Dorothy, who always cooks with gusto and love—and never demands a tip.

ACKNOWLEDGMENTS

Putting together a book like this is a painstaking exercise that requires an energetic and professional support team, with which I am blessed. Many thanks to the editors at Times Books for all their patience and help, especially Jonathan Segal, Ruth Fecych, and Beth Pearson; also to my editors at *The New York Times*— particularly Annette Grant, Myra Forsberg, Don Caswell and many others in the Weekend section—who make it happen week after week.

CONTENTS

(To locate the review and neighborhood map for each restaurant in this book, please consult the Restaurant Index.)

INTRODUCTION

"Eating in restaurants for a living—you must have the greatest job in the world!" is the usual response when I tell people what I do. Sure, it sounds glamorous, but there are plenty of hazards and pressures that go along with it, I point out, trying to sound professional. But every job has its tedious side: what's a little indigestion or a scorching soup in the lap, after all—when you got to do for a living what other people do for fun. Well, it's true. And there is no better place to do it than New York City.

According to the National Restaurant Association, about 40 percent of all food dollars are spent on meals eaten away from home—in New York City, where dining out is a near obsession, that figure is undoubtedly much higher.

Not only has the volume of restaurants in this city reached staggering proportions—there are about fifteen thousand in the five boroughs—but there also has the cost of whiling away several hours in some of the better known dining rooms. The average dinner tab for two in upper-echelon restaurants has surpassed the $100 plateau (including tax, tip, and a modest bottle of wine). This is all the more reason a guidebook like this is essential. Most people simply can't afford to make mistakes. I have run gastronomic interference for you, discovering what the best local chefs have to offer while at the same time enduring more gray slabs of meat substance and cardboard tarts than I care to remember. This book represents four years and nearly two thousand restaurant meals—not to mention enough antacid tablets to supply the Seventh Fleet—trying to sort it all out.

The definition of a good guidebook, I believe, is one that allows a reader to find precisely what he or she wants within three subway stops, assuming there are no track fires or stuck doors. For this reason the restaurant reviews are relatively short and to the point, and every entry in the book is easily identified on maps and thoroughly cross-referenced.

- If you're looking for a specific restaurant, see the Restaurant Index, beginning on page 469.
- If you're looking for a particular type of restaurant (Open Sunday, Broadway Theater, etc.) see Special Offerings, page 32.

- If you're looking for restaurants in a particular neighborhood, see the Maps, beginning on page 2.
- If you're looking for a particular dish, see Best Dishes, beginning on page 461.

The Diner's Journal selections, which appear every Friday in the Weekend section of *The New York Times*, grew out of a desire to fill the needs of younger and budget-minded readers. These are often restaurants that are too small or too narrowly focused to merit a full review, but for one reason or another are worth pointing out. Perhaps I found a place that makes a terrific couscous, or a storefront Italian spot that has a grandmother in the back turning out hand-rolled cannelloni that could bring tears to a Neapolitan's eyes. Also included is a comprehensive rundown of wine bars around town.

The section entitled "Best Dishes" offers a quick way to satisfy any food craving that takes you hostage, be it for chili or chocolate mousse.

A word about the *New York Times* system of restaurant reviewing is in order for those who may not be familiar with the newspaper's method. In the course of my work as food critic for *The Times* I visit restaurants anonymously every day. In the event I am known to the establishment—this is unavoidable in some cases—I reserve a table under a different name and send dining companions ahead of time to claim it. Frequently I send confederates to dinner before writing the review to determine how unknown patrons are treated.

Readers often ask me if it is possible to review a restaurant when the owner happens to know me. While it is always easier to work anonymously, such a circumstance does not obviate an honest assessment. I realized this during a year-long kitchen apprenticeship in a French restaurant seven years ago, during which time several local critics came in.

When the owners told me what was happening it became evident there was little we could do. By this time all our sauce stocks had been prepared, the fish, meat, and vegetables purchased, and the desserts made. We could have given the critic extra-large portions, but that might well have backfired and caused a negative reaction. On any given day a kitchen can perform only up to its level of competence (or incompetence, as the case may be); nothing magical can be done for a critic's sake on short notice.

Of course the service staff can pour on the white-glove treatment, but any professional reviewer can see through that by simply observing how others in the dining room are being treated.

TIPPING

One matter of constant confusion to diners is tipping. In some restaurants, not only is there a waiter to tip but there is also a captain, a maître d'hôtel, and perhaps a sommelier. There are guidelines, however.

Since waiters generally earn minimum wage, their income is derived primarily from tips, which average roughly 16 to 20 percent of the bill. Many New Yorkers find it convenient to double the sales tax of 8.25 percent to arrive at a 16.5 percent tip. In effect, the tip is paying the waiter's salary and is not necessarily a gratuity for satisfactory performance. My feeling is that, unless service is exceptionally poor, the standard tip is expected. If service is unacceptable, less can be left to signal displeasure. Extraordinary service could merit more than 20 percent.

A few restaurants, such as The Quilted Giraffe and Huberts, now add automatic gratuities of 15 to 18 percent to the bill, in the European tradition. This has not become widespread, however.

Payment for captains, who usually supervise teams of waiters, varies with the restaurants. In older and traditional restaurants, captains often receive substantial salaries and keep all their tips. In most newer restaurants, captains earn slightly more than waiters but, like them, still depend on tips for much of their income. In these establishments all tips are pooled. In either case, diners should remember that the rule of thumb for restaurants with captains is 16 to 18 percent of the pretax total for waiters plus 5 percent for captains.

If, however, you want to single out a particular captain or waiter for extraordinary work, you can hand him or her a supplementary cash gratuity upon leaving and say, "This is for you, thank you," to indicate that it is not intended for the tip pool. The amount should be commensurate with the bill, although the range is generally $5 to $20.

Maîtres d'hôtel seat guests and should keep things running smoothly in the dining room. They do not usually receive tips unless they have performed specific favors, such as finding you a table on a busy night. In that case, a cash gratuity is standard. The amount depends on the type of restaurant and the circumstances but could be as little as $5 or as much as $20 or more.

Sommeliers are an increasingly rare breed these days, an unaffordable luxury in this era of six-figure rents. If a restaurant has a sommelier and he or she is genuinely helpful, the rule of thumb is 10 percent of the cost of the wine. If the sommelier does little more than hand you the wine list and pour the first round, no tip is necessary.

SMOKING

The city's restaurants are now required by law to offer designated no-smoking sections (those with fewer than fifty seats are exempt). Some establishments are complying with the new regulations better than others; it's a tricky situation in places that have only one main dining room, where smoke can drift freely no matter where one sits. It's a good idea to make your seating preference known upon reserving a table.

THE COAT CHECK

One area of tipping that few diners think about but has been raised in letters from *New York Times* readers is that of the coat check. My colleague at the newspaper, Marian Burros, wrote an illuminating story about the confusion surrounding tips to coat checkers. In most cases, she found, $1 per coat is considered adequate—and many establishments are posting signs suggesting that. A coat checker at Quatorze, the French bistro on 14th Street near Eighth Avenue, was quoted as saying she is "stiffed" by one of every nine or ten customers. And one of every seven or eight customers gives her a dollar regardless of how many coats are checked. Jean-Claude Baker, owner of Chez Josephine on 42nd Street near Ninth Avenue, agreed that $1 per coat is sufficient. Of course, if you tote half of your office into a restaurant on the way home in shopping bags, as I often do, a bit more might be appropriate.

WHAT TO EXPECT FROM SERVICE

Here are thirteen points of good service that customers should expect in all so-called white tablecloth restaurants.

- *Personal appearance.* All service personnel should be clean and wear fresh clothes.
- *Attitude.* Courtesy and pleasantness are the cornerstones of customer relations. The greeting and good-bye are particularly important. There is nothing more uncomfortable than arriving at a restaurant and standing on the fringe of the dining room unnoticed by the staff.
- *Product knowledge.* Those who serve food should have basic knowledge of the ingredients and cooking techniques used in each dish on the menu. Once I had a waiter describe a dish as "Veal with some sort of brown sauce on top." Appetizing, isn't it?

- *Wine.* Those who serve wine should have at least minimal knowledge about grape varieties and general flavor characteristics.
- *Table setting.* The tableware should be clean and set in the proper fashion before customers are seated.
- *Watchfulness.* Waiters should always be within hailing distance of customers, close enough to respond to eye contact. This way, when guests are ready to order or need something, the waiter can come promptly. Diners, on the other hand, should never try to get a waiter's eye by snapping fingers or bellowing, "Waiter!"
- *Ashtrays.* Ashtrays should be cleared frequently, especially before food is brought to the table.
- *Table clearing.* The table should be cleared and crumbed between the serving of the entrée and the dessert.
- *Serving.* The old rule about serving on the left and removing on the right applies primarily to classic French-style presentation in which foods are served from platters. Having food arranged on plates in the kitchen has rendered that rule nearly obsolete. Food should be served on the side that is least disruptive to the diner.
- *"Everything okay?"* Waiters should never ask this question while customers are eating. It is annoying and reflects a lack of confidence about the food on their part. They should be nearby to respond to comments or complaints.
- *"Who gets the chicken?"* The service staff should never auction its food at tableside. It doesn't take a photographic memory to jot down on a pad who gets what.
- *"Freshly ground pepper?"* This is one of the most annoying habits I encounter in restaurants. The question invariably is asked before I have a chance to taste anything, usually by a waiter toting a peppermill the size of a Louisville slugger. Tell the waiter to come back after you have tasted the food.
- *The check.* Waiters should not present the check while guests are still drinking coffee unless it is requested. This gives diners the impression of being rushed. When diners ask for the bill, it should be presented promptly to the person who made the request.

RESERVATIONS

In fairness it must be pointed out that many problems in the flow of service can be attributed to inconsiderate diners who arrive late for their reservations without calling ahead and letting management know, or worse, fail to show up altogether. This has forced some restaurants to adopt the airline practice of overbooking to cover their losses. If everyone happens to show up, of course, a crisis ensues. Some top New York restaurants, including La Côte Basque and Le Cirque, report no-shows approaching 50 percent on weekends and holidays. Diners who change their plans should always give restaurants as much advance notice as possible.

GRIPES

If you have a complaint about the food, wine, or service, bring it up discreetly with the manager or owner. Too often diners vent their wrath on waiters, who may not be responsible for the problem—certainly not if the food is substandard. Never make a scene. That only exacerbates the situation and makes everyone defensive. You would be surprised how much more you can accomplish by talking to management in a polite but firm tone. If you still do not get satisfaction, find out if there is a higher-up, perhaps a major investor or absentee owner, and write a cogent, thoughtful letter. Take it from somebody who gets more than his share of irate letters, a smart-alecky tone only diminishes your chances of success.

If the problem involves sanitation in the dining room or kitchen, contact the New York City Department of Health (285-9503).

EDITOR'S NOTE

A few words about the system of alphabetization used in this book are in order. A strict letter-by-letter approach has been followed, and spaces between words as well as punctuation marks have been disregarded. For example, Barbetta comes before B. Smith's; China Grill precedes Chin Chin. English articles (*A*, *An*, *The*) have also been disregarded, though foreign articles such as *La* and *El*, have not, so that La Gauloise follows Lafayette. Numbers in restaurant names are alphabetized as if they were spelled out, so that Cafe 58 precedes Cafe 43.

The index at the back lists all restaurants in the book following the same letter-by-letter system.

The New York Times

GUIDE TO

RESTAURANTS
IN
NEW YORK CITY

REVISED AND EXPANDED

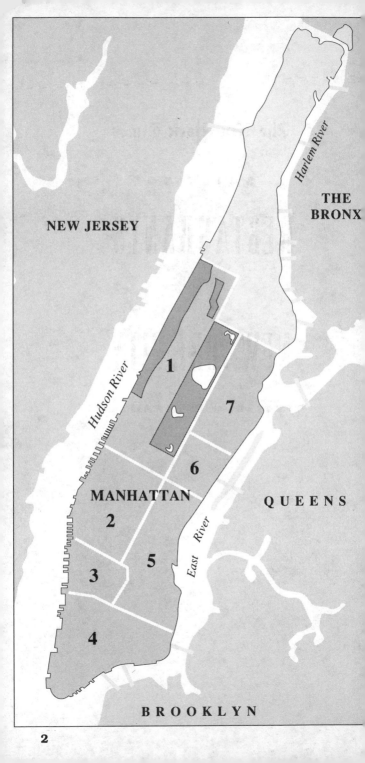

NEW JERSEY

THE BRONX

Harlem River

1

Hudson River

7

6

MANHATTAN

QUEENS

2

5

East River

3

4

BROOKLYN

MAPS

Every Manhattan restaurant in this guidebook appears on a map in this section. Those in the other boroughs of the city are listed on page 18. If you aren't sure which map carries the restaurant you are looking for, consult the restaurant index (see page 469). Each entry in the index is followed by a map number and the page(s) where the restaurant is described.

On the key facing each map, restaurants covered only in the Diner's Journal are followed by (DJ).

1. West 50s and north (includes Lincoln Center, Central Park, and the Upper West Side)

2. West 14th Street to West 49th Street (includes Chelsea and the Broadway Theater District)

3. Houston Street to West 13th Street, west of Broadway (includes the West Village)

4. Below Houston Street (includes SoHo, TriBeCa, Chinatown, Little Italy, Wall Street, and South Street Seaport)

5. Houston Street east of Broadway to East 49th Street east of Fifth Avenue (includes the East Village, Gramercy Park, and Murray Hill)

6. East 50s and 60s

7. East 70s and north (includes the Upper East Side)

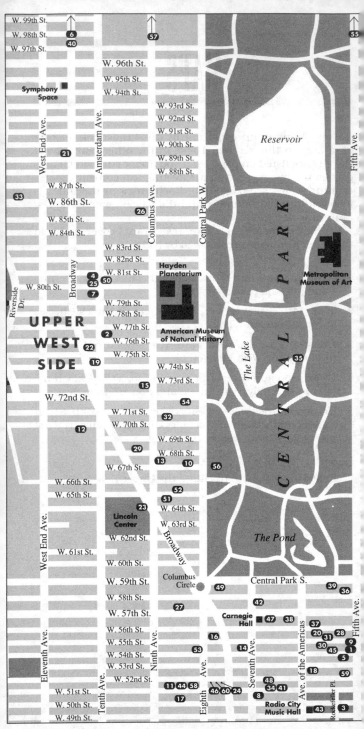

MAP 1

West 50s and North

(Includes Lincoln Center, Central Park, and the Upper West Side)

1. Adrienne, 700 Fifth Ave.
2. Alcala, 349 Amsterdam Ave.
3. American Festival Cafe, 20 W. 50th St. (DJ)
4. Amsterdam's Bar & Rotisserie, 428 Amsterdam Ave.
5. Aquavit, 13 W. 54th St.
6. Au Grenier Café, 2867 Broadway. (DJ)
7. Baci, 412 Amsterdam Ave. (DJ)
8. Bellini by Cipriani, 777 Seventh Ave.
9. Bistro d'Adrienne, 700 Fifth Ave. (DJ)
10. Café des Artistes, 1 W. 67th St.
11. Cafe des Sports, 329 W. 51st St. (DJ)
12. Cafe Luxembourg, 200 W. 70th St.
13. Cameos, 169 Columbus Ave.
14. Carnegie Deli, 854 Seventh Ave. (DJ)
15. Cavaliere, 108 W. 73rd St.
16. Chantal, 257 W. 55th St. (DJ)
17. Chez Napoleon, 365 W. 50th St. (DJ)
18. China Grill, 60 W. 53rd St.
19. Coastal, 300 Amsterdam Ave.
20. Darbar, 44 W. 56th St.
21. Docks Oyster Bar and Seafood Grill, 2427 Broadway.
22. Ernie's, 2150 Broadway. (DJ)
23. The Fountain Cafe in Lincoln Center, Broadway at W. 64th St. (DJ)
24. Gallagher's, 228 W. 52nd St.
25. Good Enough to Eat, 424 Amsterdam Ave. (DJ)
26. Grapes, 522 Columbus Ave. (DJ)
27. Indian Brasserie, 327 W. 57th St.
28. Kuruma Zushi, 18 W. 56th St.
29. La Boîte en Bois, 75 W. 68th St.
30. La Bonne Soupe, 48 W. 55th St. (DJ)
31. La Caravelle, 33 W. 55th St.
32. La Kasbah, 70 W. 71st St.
33. La Mirabelle, 333 W. 86th St.
34. Le Bernardin, 155 W. 51st St.
35. Loeb Boathouse in Central Park, near 75th St. (DJ)
36. The Manhattan Ocean Club, 57 W. 58th St.
37. Marie-Michelle, 57 W. 56th St.
38. Maurice, 118 W. 57th St.
39. Mickey Mantle's, 42 Central Park S. (DJ)
40. 107 West, 2787 Broadway.
41. Palio, 151 W. 51st St.
42. Petrossian, 182 W. 58th St.
43. The Rainbow Room, 30 Rockefeller Plaza.
44. René Pujol, 321 W. 51st St.
45. Restaurant Raphael, 33 W. 54th St.
46. Russian Samovar, 256 W. 52nd St.
47. The Russian Tea Room, 150 W. 57th St.
48. Sam's Restaurant, 152 W. 52nd St.
49. San Domenico, 240 Central Park So.
50. Sarabeth's Kitchen, 423 Amsterdam Ave.
51. Sfuzzi, 58 W. 65th St.
52. Shun Lee, 43 W. 65th St.
53. Siam Inn, 916 Eighth Ave.
54. Sidewalkers', 12 W. 72nd St. (DJ)
55. Sylvia's, 328 Lenox Ave. (DJ)
56. Tavern on the Green, Central Park West at W. 67th St.
57. Terrace, 400 W. 119th St.
58. Tout Va Bien, 311 W. 51st St. (DJ)
59. "21" Club, 21 W. 52nd St.
60. Victor's Café 52, 236 W. 52nd St.

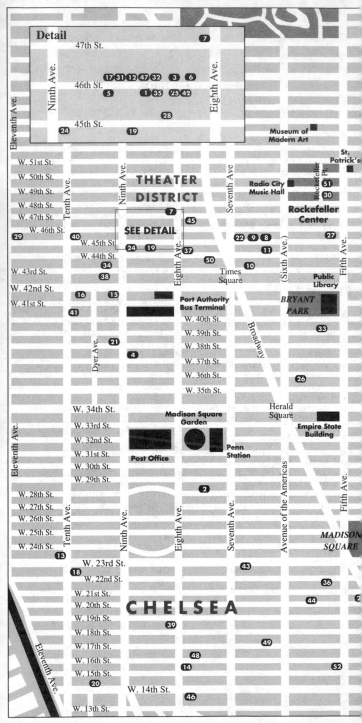

Detail

47th St.

Ninth Ave.

Eighth Ave.

7

46th St.

17 **31** **12** **47** **32** **3** **6**

5 **1** **35** **25** **42**

28

45th St.

24 **19**

Eleventh Ave.

Ninth Ave.

Tenth Ave.

Seventh Ave.

Rockefeller Pl.

Fifth Ave.

Museum of Modern Art

St. Patrick's

W. 51st St.

W. 50th St.

W. 49th St.

W. 48th St.

W. 47th St.

THEATER

DISTRICT

Radio City Music Hall

51

30

Rockefeller Center

7

W. 46th St.

29

40

SEE DETAIL

45

W. 45th St.

24 **19**

37

22 **9** **8**

27

W. 44th St.

34

50

11

(Sixth Ave.)

W. 43rd St.

38

Times Square

10

Public Library

W. 42nd St.

W. 41st St.

16

15

Broadway

BRYANT PARK

41

Port Authority Bus Terminal

33

W. 40th St.

W. 39th St.

Dyer Ave.

21

W. 38th St.

4

W. 37th St.

W. 36th St.

26

W. 35th St.

W. 34th St.

W. 33rd St.

Madison Square Garden

Herald Square

W. 32nd St.

Empire State Building

W. 31st St.

Penn Station

W. 30th St.

Post Office

W. 29th St.

Avenue of the Americas

2

Eleventh Ave.

Tenth Ave.

Ninth Ave.

Eighth Ave.

Seventh Ave.

Fifth Ave.

W. 28th St.

W. 27th St.

W. 26th St.

W. 25th St.

MADISON SQUARE

W. 24th St.

13

W. 23rd St.

18

W. 22nd St.

43

36

W. 21st St.

W. 20th St.

C H E L S E A

44

2

W. 19th St.

W. 18th St.

39

W. 17th St.

49

W. 16th St.

48

W. 15th St.

14

52

20

W. 14th St.

46

W. 13th St.

6

MAP 2

West 14th Street to West 49th Street

(Includes Chelsea and the Broadway Theater District)

① Audrone's, 342 W. 46th St. (DJ)
② The Ballroom, 253 W. 28th St.
③ Barbetta, 321 W. 46th St.
④ Bellevues, 496 Ninth Ave. (DJ)
⑤ Big Wok, 360 W. 46th St. (DJ)
⑥ Broadway Joe, 315 W. 46th St. (DJ)
⑦ B. Smith's, 771 Eighth Ave.
⑧ Cabana Carioca, 123 W. 45th St. (DJ)
⑨ Cabana Carioca No. II, 133 W. 45th St. (DJ)
⑩ Cafe 43, 147 W. 43rd St.
⑪ Café Un Deux Trois, 123 W. 44th St.
⑫ Carolina, 355 W. 46th St.
⑬ Chelsea Central, 227 Tenth Ave.
⑭ Chelsea Trattoria Italiana, 108 Eighth Ave.
⑮ Chez Josephine, 414 W. 42nd St.
⑯ Chita, 444 W. 42nd St. (DJ)
⑰ Crêpes Suzette, 363 W. 46th St. (DJ)
⑱ Empire Diner, 210 Tenth Ave. (DJ)
⑲ Encore Encore, 318 W. 45th St.
⑳ Frank's, 431 W. 14th St. (DJ)
㉑ Giordano, 409 W. 39th St. (DJ)
㉒ Hamburger Harry's, 145 W. 45th St. (DJ)
㉓ Indian Oven 2, 913 Broadway.
㉔ Jezebel, 630 Ninth Ave.
㉕ Joe Allen, 326 W. 46th St. (DJ)
㉖ Keen's, 72 W. 36th St.
㉗ Kitcho, 22 W. 46th St.
㉘ Kodama, 301 W. 45th St. (DJ)
㉙ Landmark Tavern, 626 Eleventh Ave. (DJ)
㉚ La Reserve, 4 W. 49th St.
㉛ Lattanzi, 361 W. 46th St. (DJ)
㉜ La Vieille Auberge, 347 W. 46th St. (DJ)
㉝ Lavin's, 23 W. 39th St.
㉞ Le Madeleine, 403 W. 43rd St. (DJ)
㉟ Le Rivage, 340 W. 46th St. (DJ)
㊱ Lola, 30 W. 22nd St.
㊲ Mamma Leone's, 261 W. 44th St.
㊳ Manhattan Island, 428 W. 43rd St.
㊴ Man Ray, 169 Eighth Ave.
㊵ Mike's American Bar & Grill, 650 Tenth Ave. (DJ)
㊶ Nicole's Capri, 442 Tenth Ave. (DJ)
㊷ Orso, 322 W. 46th St.
㊸ Ozeki, 158 W. 23rd St.
㊹ Periyali, 35 W. 20th St.
㊺ Pierre au Tunnel, 250 W. 47th St.
㊻ Quatorze, 240 W. 14th St.
㊼ The Red Blazer Too, 349 W. 46th St. (DJ)
㊽ Riazor, 245 W. 16th St. (DJ)
㊾ Ristorante da Umberto, 107 W. 17th St.
㊿ Sardi's, 234 W. 44th St. (DJ)
(51) The Sea Grill, 19 W. 49th St.
(52) Sofi, 102 Fifth Ave.

MAP 3

Houston Street to 13th Street, West of Broadway

(Includes the West Village)

1. Au Troquet, 328 W. 12th St.
2. Cafe de Bruxelles, 118 Greenwich Ave. (DJ)
3. Caffè Vivaldi, 32 Jones St. (DJ)
4. Caribe, 117 Perry St. (DJ)
5. Cent'Anni, 50 Carmine St.
6. Chez Jacqueline, 72 Macdougal St. (DJ)
7. The Coach House, 110 Waverly Pl.
8. Corner Bistro, 331 W. 4th St. (DJ)
9. Cuisine de Saigon, 154 W. 13th St.
10. Da Silvano, 260 Ave. of the Americas.
11. Fukuda, 61 Grove St. (DJ)
12. Gulf Coast, 489 West St. (DJ)
13. Harlequin, 569 Hudson St.
14. Il Cantinori, 32 E. 10th St.
15. Il Mulino, 86 W. 3rd St.
16. Jane Street Seafood Cafe, 31 Eighth Ave.
17. John Clancy's, 181 W. 10th St.
18. La Gauloise, 502 Ave. of the Americas.
19. La Métairie, 189 W. 10th St.
20. La Tulipe, 104 W. 13th St.
21. Melrose, 48 Barrow St.
22. Peculier Pub, 182 W. 4th St. (DJ)
23. Rakel, 231 Varick St.
24. Restaurant Florent, 69 Gansevoort St. (DJ)
25. Rio Mar, 7 Ninth Ave. (DJ)
26. Sabor, 20 Cornelia St.
27. Sevilla Restaurant and Bar, 62 Charles St.
28. Texarkana, 64 W. 10th St.
29. The Village Green, 531 Hudson St.
30. Ye Waverly Inn, 16 Bank St. (DJ)

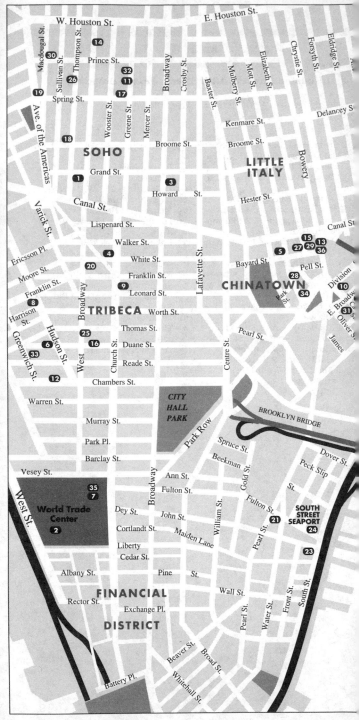

MAP 4

Below Houston Street

(Includes SoHo, TriBeCa, Chinatown, Little Italy, Wall Street, and South Street Seaport)

1. Abyssinia, 35 Grand St. (DJ)
2. American Harvest, 3 World Trade Ctr.
3. Amsterdam's Grand, 454 Broadway.
4. Arquà, 281 Church St.
5. Big Wong, 67 Mott St. (DJ)
6. Bouley, 165 Duane St.
7. Cellar in the Sky, 1 World Trade Ctr.
8. Chanterelle, 6 Harrison St.
9. Exterminator Chili, 305 Church St. (DJ)
10. Great Shanghai Restaurant, 27 Division St.
11. Greene Street Restaurant, 101 Greene St.
12. Hamburger Harry's, 157 Chambers St. (DJ)
13. HSF (Chinatown), 46 Bowery. (DJ)
14. I Tre Merli, 463 W. Broadway. (DJ)
15. King Fung, 20 Elizabeth St.
16. Le Zinc, 139 Duane St.
17. Manhattan Bistro, 129 Spring St. (DJ)
18. Manhattan Brewing Company, 40-42 Thompson St. (DJ)
19. Mezzogiorno, 195 Spring St.
20. Montrachet, 239 W. Broadway.
21. The Nice Fulton, 64 Fulton St.
22. The Nice Restaurant, 35 E. Broadway.
100. North Star Pub, 93 South St. (DJ)
24. Ocean Reef Grille, 11 Fulton St.
25. The Odeon, 145 W. Broadway.
26. Omen, 113 Thompson St.
27. Oriental Town Seafood Restaurant, 14 Elizabeth St.
28. Peking Duck House Restaurant, 22 Mott St. (DJ)
29. Phoenix Garden Restaurant, 46 Bowery.
30. Provence, 38 Macdougal St.
31. Say Eng Look, 5 E. Broadway.
32. SoHo Kitchen and Bar, 103 Greene St. (DJ)
33. Tommy Tang's, 323 Greenwich St.
34. 20 Mott Street Restaurant, 20 Mott St.
35. Windows on the World, 1 World Trade Ctr.
36. Yuet Tung, 40 Bowery. (DJ)

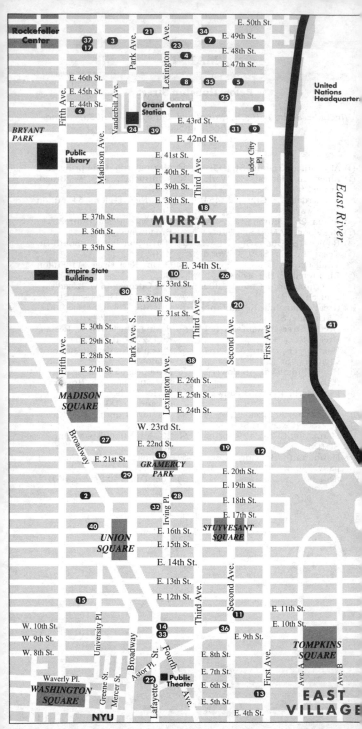

Rockefeller Center
37 17 3
21
34
7
23
4
8 35 5
25
1
United Nations Headquarters

E. 50th St.
E. 49th St.
E. 48th St.
E. 47th St.
E. 46th St.
E. 45th St.
E. 44th St.
6

BRYANT PARK

Public Library

Fifth Ave.
Madison Ave.
Vanderbilt Ave.
Park Ave.
Lexington Ave.

Grand Central Station
24 39
E. 43rd St.
31 9
E. 42nd St.
E. 41st St.
E. 40th St.
E. 39th St.
E. 38th St.
18

MURRAY HILL

E. 37th St.
E. 36th St.
E. 35th St.

Third Ave.
Tudor City Pl.

East River

Empire State Building
30
10 26
E. 34th St.
E. 33rd St.
E. 32nd St.
20
E. 31st St.

E. 30th St.
E. 29th St.
E. 28th St.
E. 27th St.
38
E. 26th St.
E. 25th St.
E. 24th St.

Fifth Ave.
Park Ave. S.
Lexington Ave.
Second Ave.
First Ave.

MADISON SQUARE

W. 23rd St.
E. 22nd St.
27
E. 21st St.
16
19 12
29
GRAMERCY PARK
E. 20th St.
E. 19th St.
2
E. 18th St.
32 28
E. 17th St.
40
STUYVESANT SQUARE
E. 16th St.
UNION SQUARE
E. 15th St.
E. 14th St.
E. 13th St.
E. 12th St.

Broadway
Irving Pl.

15
E. 11th St.
11
E. 10th St.
TOMPKINS SQUARE
W. 10th St.
W. 9th St.
W. 8th St.
14 33
36
E. 9th St.
University Pl.
Astor Pl.
Broadway
Third Ave.
Second Ave.
First Ave.
E. 8th St.
E. 7th St.
Waverly Pl.
22
Public Theater
E. 6th St.
13
E. 5th St.
WASHINGTON SQUARE
Greene St.
Mercer St.
Lafayette St.
Fourth Ave.
E. 4th St.
EAST VILLAGE
NYU
Ave. A
Ave. B

MAP 5

Houston Street east of Broadway to East 49th Street east of Fifth Avenue

(Includes the East Village, Gramercy Park, and Murray Hill)

① Ambassador Grill, 1 United Nations Plaza.
② America, 9 E. 18th St.
③ Aurora, 60 E. 49th St.
④ Bukhara, 148 E. 48th St.
⑤ The Captain's Table, 860 Second Ave.
⑥ Chikubu Restaurant, 12 E. 44th St.
⑦ Chin Chin, 216 E. 49th St.
⑧ Christ Cella, 160 E. 46th St.
⑨ Cinco de Mayo, 45 Tudor City Pl.
⑩ The Dolphin, 227 Lexington Ave.
⑪ The "11" Cafe, 170 Second Ave. (DJ)
⑫ First Avenue Restaurant, 361 First Ave. (DJ)
⑬ Gaylord, 87 First Ave.
⑭ Gelateria Siracusa, 65 Fourth Ave. (DJ)
⑮ Gotham Bar and Grill, 12 E. 12th St.
⑯ Gramercy Park Bistro, 2 Lexington Ave. (DJ)
⑰ Hatsuhana, 17 E. 48th St.
⑱ Hayato, 571 Third Ave. (DJ)
⑲ The Health Pub, 371 Second Ave. (DJ)
⑳ HSF, 578 Second Ave. (DJ)

㉑ Inagiku, 111 E. 49th St.
㉒ Indochine, 430 Lafayette St.
㉓ Ménage à Trois, 134 E. 48th St.
㉔ Oyster Bar and Restaurant in Grand Central Station.
㉕ Palm, 837 Second Ave.
㉖ Pasta Presto, 613 Second Ave. (DJ)
㉗ Pesca, 23 E. 22nd St.
㉘ Pete's Tavern, 129 E. 18th St. (DJ)
㉙ Positano, 250 Park Ave. So.
㉚ The Ritz Cafe, 2 Park Ave.
㉛ Ryan McFadden, 800 Second Ave. (DJ)
㉜ Sal Anthony's, 55 Irving Pl.
㉝ Siracusa, 65 Fourth Ave. (DJ)
㉞ Smith & Wollensky, 201 E. 49th St.
㉟ Sparks Steakhouse, 210 E. 46th St.
㊱ Sukhothai, 149 Second Ave.
㊲ Tandoor, 40 E. 49th St.
㊳ Tatany, 388 Third Ave.
㊴ Trumpet's, 109 E. 42nd St.
㊵ Union Square Cafe, 21 E. 16th St.
㊶ The Water Club, East River at 30th St.

MIDTOWN EAST

E. 69th St.
E. 68th St.
E. 67th St.
E. 66th St.
E. 65th St.
E. 64th St.
E. 63rd St.
E. 62nd St.
E. 61st St.
E. 60th St.
E. 59th St.
E. 58th St.
E. 57th St.
E. 56th St.
E. 55th St.
E. 54th St.
E. 53rd St.
E. 52nd St.
E. 51st St.
E. 50th St.
E. 49th St.
E. 48th St.
E. 47th St.
E. 46th St.
E. 45th St.
E. 44th St.
E. 43rd St.
E. 42nd St.
E. 41st St.

Fifth Ave.
Madison Ave.
Park Ave.
Lexington Ave.
Third Ave.
Second Ave.
First Ave.
Vanderbilt Ave.
Tudor City Pl.

Temple Emanuel

St. Patrick's Cathedral

Grand Central Station

United Nations Headquarters

Mitche Pl.

MAP 6

East 50s and 60s

1. Akbar, 475 Park Ave.
2. Alo Alo, 1030 Third Ave.
3. Arcadia, 21 E. 62nd St.
4. Arizona 206, 206 E. 60th St.
5. Arizona 206 Cafe, 206 E. 60th St. (DJ)
6. Auntie Yuan, 1191A First Ave.
7. Bice, 7 E. 54th St.
8. Brasserie, 100 E. 53rd St. (DJ)
9. Drive, 405 E. 50th St.
10. Café Europa, La Brioche, 347 E. 54th St. (DJ)
11. Café 58, 232 E. 58th St.
12. Cafe Nicholson, 323 E. 58th St. (DJ)
13. Café Pierre, Fifth Avenue at E. 61st St.
14. Cafe 212, 212 E. 52nd St. (DJ)
15. Chez Louis, 1016 Second Ave.
16. Contrapunto, 200 E. 60th St.
17. David K's, 1115 Third Ave.
18. David K's Cafe, 1115 Third Ave. (DJ)
19. Dāwat, 210 E. 58th St.
20. The Drake Bar, 440 Park Ave. (DJ)
21. Felidia, 243 E. 58th St.
22. 540 Park, 540 Park Ave.
23. The Four Seasons, 99 E. 52nd St.
24. Golden Tulip Barbizon Restaurant, 140 E. 63rd St. (DJ)
25. Huberts, 575 Park Ave.
26. Il Nido, 251 E. 53rd St.

15

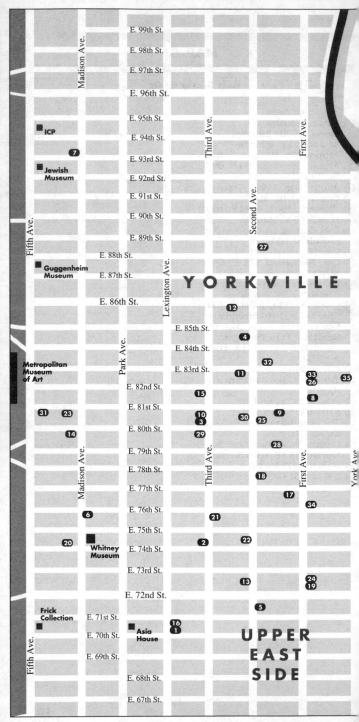

E. 99th St.
E. 98th St.
E. 97th St.
E. 96th St.
E. 95th St.
E. 94th St.
E. 93rd St.
E. 92nd St.
E. 91st St.
E. 90th St.
E. 89th St.
E. 88th St.
E. 87th St.
E. 86th St.
E. 85th St.
E. 84th St.
E. 83rd St.
E. 82nd St.
E. 81st St.
E. 80th St.
E. 79th St.
E. 78th St.
E. 77th St.
E. 76th St.
E. 75th St.
E. 74th St.
E. 73rd St.
E. 72nd St.
E. 71st St.
E. 70th St.
E. 69th St.
E. 68th St.
E. 67th St.

Madison Ave.
Third Ave.
First Ave.
Second Ave.
Fifth Ave.
Lexington Ave.
Park Ave.
Madison Ave.
York Ave.

ICP

7

Jewish
Museum

Guggenheim
Museum

YORKVILLE

Metropolitan
Museum
of Art

27

12

4

32

11

33
26
35

15

8

31 **23**

10
3

30 **25**

9

14

29

28

18

17

34

6

21

20

Whitney
Museum

2

22

13

24
19

5

Frick
Collection

Asia
House

16
1

**UPPER
EAST
SIDE**

MAP 7

East 70s and North

(Includes the Upper East Side)

1. An American Place, 969 Lexington Ave.
2. Anabelle's, 1294 Third Ave.
3. Anatolia, 1422 Third Ave.
4. Azzurro, 1625 Second Ave.
5. Café Greco, 1390 Second Ave.
6. Carlyle Restaurant, 35 E. 76th St. (DJ)
7. Devon House Ltd., 1316 Madison Ave.
8. Dieci X, 1568 First Ave.
9. Diva, 36 E. 81st St. (DJ)
10. East, 1420 Third Ave.
11. Erminia, 250 E. 83rd St.
12. Fleming's, 232 E. 86th St. (DJ)
13. Fu's, 1395 Second Ave.
14. The Gibbon, 24 E. 80th St.
15. La Métairie (East), 1442 Third Ave.
16. La Petite Ferme, 973 Lexington Ave.
17. Lion's Rock, 316 E. 77th St. (DJ)
18. Lusardi's, 1494 Second Ave.
19. Marcello, 1354 First Ave.
20. Metro, 23 E. 74th St.
21. Mezzaluna, 1295 Third Ave. (DJ)
22. Pamir, 1437 Second Ave.
23. Parioli, Romanissimo, 24 E. 81st St.
24. Petaluma, 1356 First Ave.
25. Pig Heaven, 1540 Second Ave.
26. Primavera, 1578 First Ave.
27. Rathbone's, 1702 Second Ave. (DJ)
28. Remi, 323 E. 79th St.
29. Sam's Café, 1406 Third Ave.
30. Sistina, 1555 Second Ave.
31. The Terrace, 995 Fifth Ave. (DJ)
32. Trastevere, 309 East 83rd St.
33. Violetta, 1590 First Ave.
34. Voulez-Vous, 1462 First Ave.
35. Wilkinson's Seafood Café, 1573 York Ave.

RESTAURANTS IN THE BOROUGHS

THE BRONX

Dominick's, 2335 Arthur Ave. (DJ)

BROOKLYN

De'Vine Restaurant and Wine Bar, 396 Seventh Ave. (DJ)
Gage & Tollner, 372 Fulton St. (DJ)
Monte's Venetian Room, 451 Carroll St. (DJ)
Moroccan Star, 205 Atlantic Ave. (DJ)
New Prospect Cafe, 393 Flatbush Ave. (DJ)
Peter Luger, 178 Broadway.
Raintrees, 142 Prospect Park West.
The River Café, 1 Water Street.
Tommaso, 1464 86th St. (DJ)

QUEENS

Cali Viejo, 84-24 Roosevelt Ave., Jackson Heights (DJ)
Cali Viejo II, 73-10 Roosevelt Ave., Jackson Heights (DJ)
La Fusta, 8-32 Baxter Avenue, Elmhurst (DJ)
Roumeli Taverna, 33-04 Broadway, Astoria.
Water's Edge at the East River Yacht Club, 44th Drive and
    East River, Long Island City.

STAR RATINGS

THE STAR SYSTEM

The Times's star system rates restaurants on the following scale:

★ ★ ★ ★	extraordinary
★ ★ ★	excellent
★ ★	very good
★	good
no stars	poor to satisfactory

Stars are intended as a quick visual clue to the overall quality of a restaurant. I assign the stars based on a formula that breaks down like this: roughly 80 percent for food quality, 20 percent for service and atmosphere. These factors are evaluated without regard to price. That means that an "excellent" restaurant costing $40 per person and an equally good one for $60 per person would receive the same three-star rating. This does not mean I am unconcerned about price. If I feel the food or wine is excessively costly, that is always pointed out in the review. Keeping price out of the star formula simply allows me to compare apples to apples without the complication of adding various price levels to the equation. (For a breakdown of restaurants by price, see page 23.)

RATINGS

★ ★ ★ ★

Chanterelle
Lafayette
Le Bernardin
Le Cirque
Lutèce
The Quilted Giraffe

★ ★ ★

Aurora
The Four Seasons
Gotham Bar and Grill
Hatsuhana
Huberts
La Côte Basque

(★ ★ ★)	(★ ★)
La Reserve	Il Nido
La Tulipe	Indochine
Le Cygne	Jezebel
Le Régence	John Clancy's
Maurice	Kitcho
Mitsukoshi	La Caravelle
Montrachet	Le Périgord
The River Café	Man Ray
San Domenico	Marcello
The Sign of the Dove	Marie-Michelle
	Melrose
	Metro
★ ★	Mezzogiorno
	The Nice Restaurant
Adrienne	Omen
Akbar	Orsini's
Alcala	Orso
Alo Alo	Oyster Bar and Restaurant
An American Place	in Grand Central Station
Anabelle's	Palio
Aquavit	Pamir
Arcadia	Parioli, Romanissimo
Arizona 206	Periyali
Arquà	Phoenix Garden Restaurant
Auntie Yuan	Pig Heaven
Au Troquet	Positano
Azzurro	Primola
Bouley	Provence
Brive	Prunelle
Cafe Greco	Quatorze
Cafe Luxembourg	The Rainbow Room
Cellar in the Sky	Rakel
Chelsea Central	Remi
Chelsea Trattoria Italiana	Restaurant Nippon
Chez Louis	Restaurant Raphael
Chikubu Restaurant	Rosa Mexicano
China Grill	The Sea Grill
Chin Chin	Sistina
The Coach House	Sofi
Coastal	Sparks Steakhouse
Darbar	Tatany
David K's	Terrace
Devon House Ltd.	Tommy Tang's
Dieci X	Toscana
The Dolphin	Trastevere
Fu's	"21" Club
Greene Street Restaurant	Union Square Cafe

(★ ★)

The Village Green
Violetta
Voulez-Vous
Wilkinson's Seafood Café
Zarela

★

Ambassador Grill
American Harvest
Amsterdam's Grand
Anatolia
The Ballroom
Bice
Bukhara
Café des Artistes
Café 58
Café Pierre
Café Un Deux Trois
Cameos
Carolina
Cavaliere
Cent'Anni
Chez Josephine
Cinco de Mayo
Contrapunto
Cuisine de Saigon
Da Silvano
Dāwat
Docks Oyster Bar and
  Seafood Grill
East
Encore Encore
Erminia
Felidia
Gaylord
The Gibbon
Great Shanghai Restaurant
Harlequin
Il Cantinori
Il Mulino
Inagiku
Indian Oven 2
Jane Street Seafood Cafe
Keen's
King Fung

(★)

La Boîte en Bois
La Grenouille
La Métairie
La Métairie (East)
La Mirabelle
La Petite Ferme
Lavin's
Le Chantilly
Le Zinc
Lola
Manhattan Island
The Manhattan Ocean Club
Maxim's
Ménage à Trois
The Odeon
Ozeki
Palm
Pesca
Petaluma
Peter Luger
Petrossian
Pierre au Tunnel
Primavera
René Pujol
Roumeli Taverna
Russian Samovar
The Russian Tea
  Room
Sabor
Sal Anthony's
Sam's Café
Sam's Restaurant
Sevilla Restaurant and Bar
Shun Lee
Siam Inn
Sukhothai
Tandoor
Tavern on the Green
Trumpet's
20 Mott Street Restaurant
Victor's Café 52
The Water Club
Water's Edge at East River
  Yacht Club
Windows on the World

SATISFACTORY

Barbetta
D. Smith's
Cafe 43
The Captain's Table
Christ Cella
Gallagher's
Indian Brasserie
Kuruma Zushi
Lusardi's
The Nice Fulton
Ocean Reef Grille
107 West
Oriental Town Seafood
    Restaurant
Raintrees
Ristorante da Umberto
The Ritz Cafe
San Giusto
Sarabeth's Kitchen
Say Eng Look
Smith & Wollensky
Texarkana

POOR

America
Bellini by Cipriani
Mamma Leone's

PRICE LISTINGS

The information box at the top of each review gives an idea of the restaurant's price range. Based on the cost of a three-course dinner with tax (excluding tip and drinks), the price range is as follows:

Inexpensive	**less than $25**
Moderate	**$25 to $35**
Moderately Expensive	**$35 to $45**
Expensive	**$45 or more**

EXPENSIVE

Adrienne
American Harvest
Aquavit
Arcadia
Aurora
Barbetta
Bellini by Cipriani
Bouley
Brive
Café Pierre
The Captain's Table
Cellar in the Sky
Chanterelle
Chez Louis
China Grill
Christ Cella
Devon House Ltd.
The Dolphin
Erminia
Felidia
540 Park
The Four Seasons
The Gibbon
Gotham Bar and Grill

Huberts
Il Mulino
Il Nido
La Caravelle
Lafayette
La Grenouille
La Métairie
La Reserve
La Tulipe
Le Bernardin
Le Chantilly
Le Cirque
Le Cygne
Le Périgord
Le Régence
Lutèce
Maurice
Ménage à Trois
Mitsukoshi
Montrachet
Orsini's
Palio
Palm
Parioli, Romanissimo
Petrossian
Primavera

Prunelle
The Quilted Giraffe
The Rainbow Room
Restaurant Raphael
The River Café
The Russian Tea Room
San Domenico
San Giusto
Sistina
Smith & Wollensky
Sofi
"21" Club
Water's Edge at the East
    River Yacht Club

*MODERATELY
EXPENSIVE*

Ambassador Grill
Anabelle's
Arizona 206
Arizona 206 Cafe
Auntie Yuan
Au Troquet
The Ballroom
Bice
B. Smith's
Café des Artistes
Cafe Luxembourg
Cafe Nicholson
Cameos
Cavaliere
Cent'Anni
Chin Chin
The Coach House
Coastal
Da Silvano
Dieci X
Diva
Fu's
Gallagher's
Greene Street Restaurant
Hatsuhana
Il Cantinori
Indochine
Jane Street Seafood Cafe

John Clancy's
Keen's
La Gauloise
La Métairie (East)
La Petite Ferme
Lavin's
Le Rivage
Le Zinc
Lola
Mamma Leone's
The Manhattan Ocean Club
Marcello
Marie-Michelle
Melrose
Metro
Mezzaluna
The Odeon
Oyster Bar and Restaurant
    in Grand Central Station
Pesca
Peter Luger
Pierre au Tunnel
Primola
Rakel
Remi
René Pujol
Restaurant Nippon
Ristorante da Umberto
Sal Anthony's
Sardi's
The Sea Grill
Sfuzzi
Sidewalkers'
The Sign of the Dove
Siracusa
Sparks Steakhouse
Tavern on the Green
Terrace
Texarkana
Toscana
Trastevere
Trumpet's
Union Square Cafe
The Village Green
Violetta
The Water Club
Wilkinson's Seafood Café
Windows on the World

MODERATE

Akbar
Alcala
Alo Alo
America
American Festival Cafe
Amsterdam's Grand
Anatolia
Arquà
Audrone's
Au Grenier Café
Azzurro
Baci
Bellevues
Bistro d'Adrienne
Brasserie
Broadway Joe
Bukhara
Café 58
Cafe 43
Cafe Greco
Cafe 212
Café Un Deux Trois
Carnegie Deli
Carolina
Chantal Café
Chelsea Central
Chelsea Trattoria Italiana
Chez Jacqueline
Chez Josephine
Chez Napoleon
Chikubu Restaurant
Chita
Cinco de Mayo
Contrapunto
Crêpes Suzette
Cuisine de Saigon
Darbar
David K's
David K's Cafe
Dāwat
De'Vine Restaurant and
   Wine Bar
Docks Oyster Bar and
   Seafood Grill
Dominick's
East
Encore Encore

Ernie's
Frank's
Fukuda
Gage & Tollner
Great Shanghai Restaurant
Gulf Coast
Harlequin
Hayato
The Health Pub
HSF
HSF (Chinatown)
Inagiku
Indian Oven 2
I Tre Merli
Jezebel
Joe Allen
King Fung
Kitcho
Kodama
Kuruma Zushi
La Boîte en Bois
La Fusta
La Kasbah
La Mediterranée
La Mirabelle
Landmark Tavern
Lattanzi
La Vieille Auberge
Le Madeleine
Loeb Boathouse
Lusardi's
Manhattan Bistro
Manhattan Island
Man Ray
Mezzogiorno
Mickey Mantle's
Mike's American Bar & Grill
New Prospect Cafe
The Nice Fulton
The Nice Restaurant
Ocean Reef Grille
Omen
107 West
Oriental Town Seafood
   Restaurant
Orso
Ozeki
Pamir
Pasta & Dreams

Peking Duck House
  Restaurant
Periyali
Petaluma
Pig Heaven
Positano
Provence
Quatorze
Raintrees
The Red Blazer Too
Restaurant Florent
The Ritz Cafe
Rosa Mexicano
Roumeli Taverna
Russian Samovar
Sabor
Sam's Café
Sam's Restaurant
Sarabeth's Kitchen
Say Eng Look
Sevilla Restaurant and Bar
Shun Lee
SoHo Kitchen and Bar
Sukhothai
Sylvia's
Tandoor
Tatany
Terrace Five
Tommaso
Tommy Tang's
Tout Va Bien
20 Mott Street Restaurant
Victor's Café 52
Voulez-Vous
Zarela

INEXPENSIVE

Abyssinia
Big Wok
Big Wong
Cabana Carioca
Cabana Carioca No. II
Cafe des Sports
Cali Viejo
Cali Viejo II
Caribe
Corner Bistro
The "11" Cafe
Empire Diner
Exterminator Chili
Gaylord
Good Enough to Eat
Gramercy Park Bistro
Hamburger Harry's
Indian Brasserie
La Bonne Soupe
Les Délices Guy Pascal
Manhattan Brewing
  Company
Monte's Venetian Room
Moroccan Star
Pasta Presto
Phoenix Garden Restaurant
Riazor
Rio Mar
Siam Inn
Yuet Tung

TYPES OF CUISINE

AMERICAN

America
American Festival Cafe
American Harvest
An American Place
Amsterdam's Grand
Arcadia
Arizona 206
Arizona 206 Cafe
Broadway Joe
B. Smith's
Cafe 43
Cafe Nicholson
Cameos
The Captain's Table
Carolina
Chelsea Central
China Grill
Chita
Christ Cella
The Coach House
Coastal
Corner Bistro
De'Vine Restaurant and
    Wine Bar
Docks Oyster Bar and
    Seafood Grill
The Dolphin
Empire Diner
Encore Encore
Exterminator Chili
First Avenue Restaurant
Fleming's
The Fountain Cafe in
    Lincoln Center
The Four Seasons
Gage & Tollner
Gallagher's
Good Enough to Eat
Gotham Bar and Grill

Grapes
Greene Street Restaurant
Gulf Coast
Hamburger Harry's
The Health Pub
Hubert's
Jane Street Seafood Cafe
Jezebel
Joe Allen
John Clancy's
Keen's
Landmark Tavern
Lavin's
Lion's Rock
Loeb Boathouse in Central
    Park
Manhattan Brewing
    Company
Manhattan Island
The Manhattan Ocean Club
Melrose
Metro
Mickey Mantle's
Mike's American Bar and
    Grill
New Prospect Cafe
North Star Pub
Ocean Reef Grille
The Odeon
107 West
Oyster Bar and Restaurant
    in Grand Central Station
Palm
Peculier Pub
Pesca
Peter Luger
Pete's Tavern
P. J. Clarke's
The Quilted Giraffe
Raintrees
Rathbone's

The Red Blazer Too
Ritz Cafe
The River Café
Ryan McFadden
Sam's Café
Sam's Restaurant
Sarabeth's Kitchen
Sardi's
The Sea Grill
Sidewalkers'
The Sign of the Dove
Smith & Wollensky
Sofi
SoHo Kitchen and Bar
Sparks Steakhouse
Sylvia's
Tavern on the Green
Terrace Five
Texarkana
"21" Club
The Village Green
The Water Club
Water's Edge at the East
    River Yacht Club
Wilkinson's Seafood Café
Windows on the World
Ye Waverly Inn

HSF
HSF (Chinatown)
King Fung
The Nice Fulton
The Nice Restaurant
Oriental Town Seafood
    Restaurant
Peking Duck House
    Restaurant
Phoenix Garden Restaurant
Pig Heaven
Say Eng Look
Shun Lee
20 Mott Street Restaurant
Yuet Tung

CARIBBEAN / CUBAN

Caribe
Lola
Sabor
Victor's Café 52

CHINESE

Auntie Yuan
Big Wok
Big Wong
China Grill
Chin Chin
David K's
David K's Cafe
Fu's
Great Shanghai Restaurant

FRENCH

540 Park
Adrienne
Ambassador Grill
Anabelle's
Au Grenier Café
Aurora
Au Troquet
Bellevues
Bistro d'Adrienne
Bouley
Brasserie
Brive
Cafe de Bruxelles
Café des Artistes
Café Europa, La Brioche
Café 58
Cafe Greco
Cafe Luxembourg
Café Pierre
Café Un Deux Trois
Cellar in the Sky
Chantal Café
Chanterelle
Chez Jacqueline
Chez Josephine
Chez Louis
Chez Napoleon
Crêpes Suzette
Devon House Ltd.
The Drake Bar

The Gibbon
Golden Tulip Barbizon
  Restaurant
La Boîte en Bois
La Bonne Soupe
La Caravelle
La Côte Basque
Lafayette
La Grenouille
La Mediterranée
La Métairie
La Métairie (East)
La Mirabelle
La Petite Ferme
La Reserve
La Tulipe
La Vieille Auberge
Le Bernardin
Le Chantilly
Le Cirque
Le Cygne
Le Madeleine
Le Périgord
Le Régence
Le Rivage
Les Délices Guy
  Pascal
Le Zinc
Lutèce
Man Ray
Marie-Michelle
Maurice
Maxim's
Ménage à Trois
Montrachet
Petrossian
Pierre au Tunnel
Provence
Prunelle
Quatorze
The Rainbow Room
Rakcl
René Pujol
Restaurant Florent
Restaurant Raphael
Sofi
Terrace
Tout Va Bien
Trumpet's

The Village Green
Voulez-Vous

GREEK

Periyali
Roumeli Taverna

INDIAN

Akbar
Bukhara
Darbar
Dāwat
Gaylord
Indian Brasserie
Indian Oven 2
Tandoor

ITALIAN

Alo Alo
Arquà
Audrone's
Azzurro
Baci
Barbetta
Bellini by Cipriani
Bice
Cafe Greco
Caffè Vivaldi
Cavaliere
Cent'Anni
Chelsea Trattoria Italiana
Contrapunto
Da Silvano
Dieci X
Dominick's
Erminia
Ernie's
Felidia
Frank's
Gelateria Siracusa
Giordano
Il Cantinori
Il Mulino

Il Nido
I Tre Merli
Lattanzi
Lusardi's
Marcello
Mamma Leone's
Mezzaluna
Mezzogiorno
Monte's Venetian Room
Nicole's Capri
Orsini's
Orso
Palio
Parioli, Romanissimo
Pasta & Dreams
Pasta Presto
Petaluma
Positano
Primavera
Primola
Remi
Ristorante da Umberto
Sal Anthony's
San Domenico
San Giusto
Sfuzzi
Siracusa
Sistina
Tommaso
Toscana
Trastevere
Union Square Cafe
Violetta

JAPANESE

Chikubu Restaurant
East
Fukuda
Hatsuhana
Hayato
Inagiku
Kitcho
Kodama
Kuruma Zushi
Mitsukoshi
Omen
Ozeki

Restaurant Nippon
Tatany

KOSHER

Diva
La Kasbah

MEXICAN

Cinco de Mayo
Rosa Mexicano
Zarela

MIDDLE EASTERN

Anatolia
Moroccan Star
Pamir

RUSSIAN

Russian Samovar
The Russian Tea Room

SEAFOOD

The Captain's Table
Coastal
Docks Oyster Bar and
    Seafood Grill
The Dolphin
Gage & Tollner
Jane Street Seafood Cafe
John Clancy's
Le Bernardin
The Manhattan Ocean Club
Ocean Reef Grille
Oyster Bar and Restaurant
    in Grand Central Station
Pesca
The Sea Grill

Sidewalkers'
Wilkinson's Seafood Café

SOUTH AMERICAN

Cabana Carioca
Cabana Carioca No. II
Cali Viejo
Cali Viejo II
The "11" Cafe
La Fusta

SPANISH

Alcala
The Ballroom
Harlequin
Riazor
Rio Mar
Sevilla Restaurant and Bar

OTHER

Ethiopian
Polish
Scandinavian

STEAKHOUSES

Broadway Joe
Christ Cella
Keen's
Palm
Peter Luger
Smith & Wollensky
Sparks Steakhouse

THAI / CAMBODIAN

Siam Inn
Sukhothai
Tommy Tang's

VIETNAMESE

Cuisine de Saigon
Indochine

Abyssinia
Gramercy Park Bistro
Aquavit

SPECIAL OFFERINGS

BARGAINS

Abyssinia
Alcala
Alo Alo
Amsterdam's Grand
Anatolia
Audrone's
Au Grenier Café
Baci
Big Wong
Bistro d'Adrienne
Brasserie
Bukhara
Café 58
Café Un Deux Trois
Cali Viejo
Cali Viejo II
Caribe
Chelsea Central
Chelsea Trattoria Italiana
Chez Jacqueline
Corner Bistro
Crêpes Suzette
Cuisine de Saigon
Darbar
The "11" Cafe
Empire Diner
Exterminator Chili
Fukuda
Gaylord
Good Enough to Eat
Gramercy Park Bistro
Great Shanghai Restaurant
Hamburger Harry's
The Health Pub
HSF
HSF (Chinatown)
Indian Brasserie
Indian Oven 2
Jezebel

Joe Allen
King Fung
Kitcho
Kodama
La Bonne Soupe
La Fusta
La Kasbah
La Mediterranée
La Mirabelle
La Vieille Auberge
Manhattan Bistro
Manhattan Island
Mezzogiorno
Mickey Mantle's
Moroccan Star
New Prospect Cafe
The Nice Restaurant
Omen
107 West
Oriental Town Seafood
    Restaurant
Orso
Ózeki
Pamir
Pasta & Dreams
Pasta Presto
Peking Duck House
    Restaurant
Phoenix Garden Restaurant
Pig Heaven
Quatorze
Restaurant Florent
Riazor
Rio Mar
Roumeli Taverna
Sabor
Sevilla Restaurant and Bar
Siam Inn
Sukhothai
Sylvia's
Tandoor

Tommy Tang's
20 Mott Street Restaurant
Victor's Café 52
Voulez-Vous
Yuet Tung

BREAKFAST

American Festival Cafe
Brasserie
Café Pierre
Carnegie Deli
Empire Diner
Exterminator Chili
Frank's
Friend of a Farmer
Good Enough to Eat
Le Régence
Les Délices Guy Pascal
Restaurant Florent
Sarabeth's Kitchen
Sylvia's
Windows on the World

BROADWAY THEATER

American Festival Cafe
Audrone's
Barbetta
Bellini by Cipriani
Big Wok
Broadway Joe
B. Smith's
Cabana Carioca
Cabana Carioca No. II
Café 43
Café Un Deux Trois
Carnegie Deli
Chez Josephine
China Grill
Chita
Crêpes Suzette
Darbar
Encore Encore
Hamburger Harry's
Joe Allen
Kodama

La Bonne Soupe
La Caravelle
La Vieille Auberge
Le Bernardin
Le Madeleine
Mama Leone's
Manhattan Island
The Manhattan Ocean Club
Marie-Michelle
Maurice
Mike's American Bar & Grill
Orso
Palio
Petrossian
Pierre au Tunnel
The Red Blazer Too
René Pujol
Restaurant Raphael
Russian Samovar
The Russian Tea Room
Sam's Restaurant
San Domenico
Siam Inn
Victor's Café 52

BUSINESS ENTERTAINING

Adrienne
Ambassador Grill
American Harvest
Anabelle's
Aquavit
Arcadia
Arquà
Audrone's
Aurora
Au Troquet
Barbetta
Bistro d'Adrienne
Bouley
Café 58
Café Pierre
Carolina
Cavaliere
Chanterelle
Chelsea Trattoria Italiana
Chez Louis

Chikubu Restaurant
Chin Chin
Cinco de Mayo
The Coach House
Crêpes Suzette
David K's
Dāwat
Devon House Ltd.
The Dolphin
540 Park
The Four Seasons
Fu's
Gallagher's
Gaylord
The Gibbon
Gotham Bar and Grill
Great Shanghai Restaurant
Harlequin
Huberts
Il Nido
Inagiku
John Clancy's
Keen's
Kitcho
La Caravelle
La Côte Basque
Lafayette
La Gauloise
La Grenouille
La Métairie
La Reserve
La Tulipe
La Vieille Auberge
Lavin's
Le Bernardin
Le Chantilly
Le Cygne
Le Périgord
Le Régence
Le Rivage
Lutèce
Manhattan Island
The Manhattan Ocean Club
Maurice
Metro
Mitsukoshi
Montrachet
Orsini's
Orso

Palio
Periyali
Pesca
Petrossian
Pierre au Tunnel
Positano
Primavera
Primola
Prunelle
Quatorze
Remi
René Pujol
Restaurant Nippon
Restaurant Raphael
The Russian Tea Room
San Domenico
The Sea Grill
The Sign of the Dove
Sistina
Sofi
Sparks Steakhouse
Tandoor
Terrace
Texarkana
Toscana
Trumpet's
"21" Club
Union Square Cafe
Victor's Café 52
Violetta
Voulez-Vous
The Water Club
Water's Edge at the East
    River Yacht Club
Windows on the World

FUN FOR KIDS

Abyssinia
America
American Festival Cafe
Anatolia
Arizona 206
Arizona 206 Cafe
Auntie Yuan
Bukhara
China Grill

Chita
Cinco de Mayo
Contrapunto
David K's
David K's Cafe
Docks Oyster Bar and
  Seafood Grill
East
Exterminator Chili
Fu's
Gaylord
Good Enough to Eat
Hamburger Harry's
Hayato
HSF (Chinatown)
Jezebel
Keen's
King Fung
La Kasbah
Manhattan Island
Mezzaluna
Mezzogiorno
The Nice Restaurant
Pasta Presto
Peking Duck House
  Restaurant
Pig Heaven
Sam's Restaurant
Shun Lee
Sidewalkers'
Sylvia's
Tavern on the Green
Tommy Tang's
20 Mott Street Restaurant
The Water Club
Water's Edge at the East
  River Yacht Club
Windows on the World

LINCOLN CENTER AREA

Café des Artistes
Cafe Luxembourg
Cameos
The Fountain Cafe in
  Lincoln Center
La Boîte en Bois
La Kasbah

Sfuzzi
Shun Lee
Sidewalkers'
Tavern on the Green

LIVE MUSIC

Cameos
Chez Josephine
Cinco de Mayo
Encore Encore
Gaylord
Indian Oven 2
Jezebel
La Mediterranée
Lola
Maxim's
The Rainbow Room
The Red Blazer Too
Riazor
Rio Mar
Russian Samovar
The Sea Grill
Tavern on the Green
Victor's Café 52
The Village Green
Windows on the World
Zarela

NOTABLE WINE LIST

Adrienne
Alcala
Ambassador Grill
Aquavit
Arcadia
Arquà
Aurora
Barbetta
Bistro d'Adrienne
Bouley
Brive
Cellar in the Sky
Chanterelle
Chelsea Central
Chez Louis
Chin Chin
Coastal

De'Vine Restaurant and
  Wine Bar
Felidia
The Four Seasons
Harlequin
Huberts
Il Nido
Keen's
La Côte Basque
Lafayette
La Grenouille
Lavin's
Le Bernardin
Le Cirque
Le Périgord
Le Régence
The Manhattan Ocean Club
Maurice
Melrose
Mezzogiorno
Montrachet
New Prospect Cafe
Oyster Bar and Restaurant
  in Grand Central Station
Periyali
Provence
The Quilted Giraffe
The Rainbow Room
Raintrees
Remi
The River Café
Sal Anthony's
San Domenico
The Sea Grill
The Sign of the Dove
Siracusa
Smith & Wollensky
Sofi
SoHo Kitchen and Bar
Sparks Steakhouse
Terrace
Trumpet's
"21" Club
Union Square Cafe
The Village Green
The Water Club
Windows on the World

*OPEN SUNDAY**

Abyssinia
Adrienne
Alcala
Alo Alo
America
American Festival Cafe
Amsterdam's Grand
Anabelle's
Anatolia
Arizona 206
Arizona 206 Cafe
Auntie Yuan
Azzurro
Baci
Bellevues
Bellini by Cipriani
Bice
Big Wok
Big Wong
Bistro d'Adrienne
Brasserie
Broadway Joe
B. Smith's
Bukhara
Café des Artistes
Café 58
Cafe Greco
Cafe Luxembourg
Café Pierre
Café Un Deux Trois
Caffè Vivaldi
Cali Viejo
Cali Viejo II
Cameos
Carnegie Deli
Carolina
Cavaliere
Cent'Anni
Chelsea Central
Chez Jacqueline
Chez Louis
Chin Chin
Chita
The Coach House
Coastal

* Many restaurants close on the weekends during July and August.

Contrapunto
Corner Bistro
Crêpes Suzette
Cuisine de Saigon
Darbar
Da Silvano
David K's
David K's Cafe
Dāwat
De'Vine Restaurant and
  Wine Bar
Dieci X
Diva
Docks Oyster Bar and
  Seafood Grill
The Dolphin
Dominick's
East
The "11" Café
Empire Diner
Encore Encore
Erminia
Ernie's
Exterminator Chili
540 Park
Fu's
Fukuda
Gage & Tollner
Gallagher's
Gaylord
Gelateria Siracusa
Giordano
Good Enough to Eat
Gotham Bar and Grill
Great Shanghai
Greene Street Restaurant
Gulf Coast
Hamburger Harry's
Harlequin
Hatsuhana
The Health Pub
HSF
HSF (Chinatown)
Il Cantinori
Inagiku
Indian Brasserie
Indian Oven 2
Indochine
I Tre Merli

Jane Street Seafood Cafe
Joe Allen
John Clancy's
King Fung
Kitcho
Kodama
La Boîte en Bois
La Bonne Soupe
La Fusta
La Gauloise
La Kasbah
La Mediterranée
La Métairie
La Métairie (Paul)
Landmark Tavern
La Tulipe
Le Madeleine
Le Régence
Les Délices Guy Pascal
Le Zinc
Lola
Lusardi's
Mamma Leone's
Manhattan Bistro
Manhattan Island
The Manhattan Ocean Club
Man Ray
Marcello
Marie-Michelle
Maurice
Melrose
Mezzaluna
Mezzogiorno
Mickey Mantle's
Mike's American Bar & Grill
Moroccan Star
New Prospect Cafe
The Nice Restaurant
Ocean Reef Grille
The Odeon
Omen
107 West
Oriental Town Seafood
  Restaurant
Orso
Ozeki
Pamir
Pasta & Dreams
Pasta Presto

Peking Duck House
   Restaurant
Pesca
Petaluma
Peter Luger
Pete's Tavern
Petrossian
Phoenix Garden Restaurant
Pig Heaven
Primavera
Primola
Provence
Prunelle
Quatorze
Raintrees
The Red Blazer Too
Remi
Restaurant Florent
Riazor
Rio Mar
The River Café
Rosa Mexicano
Roumeli Taverna
Russian Samovar
The Russian Tea Room
Sabor
Sal Anthony's
San Domenico
Sarabeth's Kitchen
Sardi's
Say Eng Look
The Sea Grill
Sevilla Restaurant and Bar
Sfuzzi
Shun Lee
Siam Inn
Sidewalkers'
The Sign of the Dove
Siracusa
Sistina
Sukhothai
Sylvia's
Tandoor
Tatany
Tavern on the Green
Texarkana
Tommaso
Tout Va Bien
Trastevere

Trumpet's
20 Mott Street Restaurant
Victor's Café 52
The Village Green
Violetta
Voulez-Vous
The Water Club
Water's Edge at the East
   River Yacht Club
Wilkinson's Seafood Cafe
Windows on the World
Ye Waverly Inn
Yuet Tung

OPEN TILL MIDNIGHT

Abyssinia
America
Amsterdam's Grand
Arizona 206 Cafe
Auntie Yuan
The Ballroom
Bellevues
Brasserie
Broadway Joe
B. Smith's
Cabana Carioca
Cabana Carioca No. II
Café des Artistes
Café 58
Cafe 43
Cafe Luxembourg
Café Un Deux Trois
Caffè Vivaldi
Carnegie Deli
Cavaliere
Chelsea Trattoria Italiana
Chez Josephine
Chita
Contrapunto
Corner Bistro
David K's Cafe
De'Vine Restaurant and
   Wine Bar
Docks Oyster Bar and
   Seafood Grill
The "11" Cafe
Empire Diner

Encore Encore
Ernie's
Felidia
Fukuda
Fu's
Gallagher's
Gaylord
Greene Street Restaurant
Gulf Coast
HSF (Chinatown)
Indochine
I Tre Merli
Joe Allen
La Bonne Soupe
La Métairie (East)
Landmark Tavern
Le Madeleine
Le Zinc
Lola
Lusardi's
Mamma Leone's
Manhattan Bistro
The Manhattan Ocean Club
Man Ray
Marcello
Melrose
Mezzaluna
Mezzogiorno
Mickey Mantle's
Ocean Reef Grille
The Odeon
Pasta & Dreams
Peculier Pub
Petrossian
Petaluma
Pig Heaven
Primavera
Primola
Quatorze
The Red Blazer Too
Restaurant Florent
Rio Mar
Rosa Mexicano
Roumeli Taverna
Russian Samovar
The Russian Tea Room
Sardi's
Sevilla Restaurant and Bar
Sfuzzi

Shun Lee
Sistina
Smith & Wollensky
SoHo Kitchen and Bar
Tavern on the Green
Texarkana
Tommy Tang's
20 Mott Street Restaurant
"21" Club
Victor's Café 52
Violetta
Voulez-Vous
Yuet Tung

OUTDOOR CAFÉS

American Festival Cafe
Barbetta
Bice
Cafe Greco
Chez Josephine
Da Silvano
Empire Diner
La Bonne Soupe
La Petite Ferme
Le Madeleine
Manhattan Island
Ocean Reef Grille
Pete's Tavern
Provence
Restaurant Raphael
The River Café
Sal Anthony's
The Sea Grill
Tavern on the Green
Terrace Five
The Water Club

PRIVATE ROOMS

Adrienne
Alcala
American Harvest
Aquavit
Barbetta
Bistro d'Adrienne

Bouley
B. Smith's
Cafe 43
Cafe Nicholson
Cavaliere
Chez Josephine
Chikubu Restaurant
Chin Chin
The Coach House
Darbar
Devon House Ltd.
Indian Brasserie
John Clancy's
Keen's
Kitcho
La Fusta
La Mediterranée
La Reserve
Le Cirque
Le Périgord
Le Régence
Mamma Leone's
The Manhattan Ocean Club
Maxim's
Mitsukoshi
Montrachet
The Nice Restaurant
Orsini's
Palio
Pasta & Dreams
Periyali
The Quilted Giraffe
The Rainbow Room
Restaurant Nippon
The River Café
Sal Anthony's
Sam's Restaurant
San Giusto
Sardi's
The Sea Grill
The Sign of the Dove
Smith & Wollensky
Tandoor
Tavern on the Green
Toscana
"21" Club
Victor's Café 52
Violetta
The Water Club

Water's Edge at the East
   River Yacht Club
Windows on the World
Zarela

ROMANTIC

Adrienne
Ambassador Grill
Aquavit
Aurora
Au Troquet
Barbetta
Bistro d'Adrienne
Bouley
Brive
Café des Artistes
Cafe Nicholson
Café Pierre
Cellar in the Sky
Chez Josephine
Chin Chin
Devon House Ltd.
Erminia
The Four Seasons
The Gibbon
Gotham Bar and Grill
Greene Street Restaurant
Huberts
Jezebel
Keen's
La Caravelle
La Côte Basque
Lafayette
La Grenouille
La Métairie
La Petite Ferme
La Reserve
Le Bernardin
Le Cygne
Le Régence
Lutèce
Maurice
Maxim's
Metro
Orsini's
Palio
Petrossian

Positano
Prunelle
The Rainbow Room
Rakel
Restaurant Raphael
The River Café
The Sea Grill
The Sign of the Dove
Sofi
Terrace
Trastevere
The Village Green
The Water Club
Water's Edge at the East
   River Yacht Club
Windows on the World

TAKEOUT

Anatolia
Baci
Brasserie
David K's Cafe
Dāwat
De'Vine Restaurant and
   Wine Bar
Empire Diner
Frank's
Gramercy Park Bistro
The Health Pub
Indian Brasserie
Kodama
Les Délices Guy Pascal
Manhattan Island
The Nice Fulton
Oriental Town Seafood
   Restaurant
Prunelle
Restaurant Nippon
Riazor
Rio Mar
Roumeli Taverna
Say Eng Look
Sylvia's
Zarela

A TASTE OF NEW YORK CITY FOR OUT-OF-TOWN VISITORS

Alo Alo
American Festival Cafe
Café des Artistes
Carnegie Deli
Cellar in the Sky
The Coach House
The Four Seasons
Gage & Tollner
Keen's
La Côte Basque
Le Bernardin
Le Cirque
Loeb Boathouse
Lutèce
Oyster Bar and Restaurant
   in Grand Central Station
Palm
Peter Luger
The River Café
P. J. Clarke's
The Rainbow Room
The Russian Tea Room
The Sea Grill
Sylvia's
Tavern on the Green
Terrace
"21" Club
The Water Club
Windows on the World

WEEKEND BRUNCH

Adrienne
Ambassador Grill
America
American Festival Cafe
Amsterdam's Grand
Anabelle's
Au Grenier Café
Baci
Bice
Brasserie
B. Smith's
Café des Artistes

41

Cafe Greco
Cafe Luxembourg
Café Un Deux Trois
Cameos
Cavaliere
Chelsea Central
Chita
Coastal
Corner Bistro
Crêpes Suzette
Darbar
David K's
David K's Cafe
De'Vine Restaurant and
 Wine Bar
Docks Oyster Bar and
 Seafood Restaurant
The "11" Cafe
Empire Diner
540 Park
Fu's
Good Enough to Eat
Greene Street Restaurant
Hamburger Harry's
The Health Pub
Kuruma Zushi
La Bonne Soupe
La Gauloise
La Métairie (East)
Landmark Tavern
Le Madeleine
Les Délices Guy Pascal
Loeb Boathouse
Lola
Manhattan Island

Man Ray
Metro
New Prospect Cafe
The Nice Restaurant
Ocean Reef Grille
The Odeon
107 West
Peking Duck House
 Restaurant
Petaluma
Pig Heaven
Raintrees
The Red Blazer Too
Remi
The River Café
Rosa Mexicano
The Russian Tea Room
Sal Anthony's
Sarabeth's Kitchen
Say Eng Look
The Sea Grill
Sfuzzi
Shun Lee
The Sign of the Dove
Sylvia's
Tavern on the Green
20 Mott Street Restaurant
The Village Green
Voulez-Vous
The Water Club
Water's Edge at the East
 River Yacht Club
Windows on the World
Ye Waverly Inn
Yuet Tung

RESTAURANT
REVIEWS

ADRIENNE

★ ★

700 Fifth Avenue, at 55th Street, 247-2200.

Atmosphere: Plush, soft, and roomy.

Service: Efficient.

Price range: Expensive.

Credit cards: All major cards.

Hours: Breakfast, 7 to 10 A.M., daily; brunch, noon to 3:30 P.M., Sunday; lunch, noon to 2:30 P.M., Sunday through Friday; dinner, 6 to 10:30 P.M., Monday through Saturday.

Reservations: Required.

Wheelchair accessibility: Long stairway up to dining room.

🍐 It might seem that midtown Manhattan needs another $250-a-day hotel about as much as it needs another T-shirt shop, yet here is the lavishly renovated former Gotham Hotel, a dignified turn-of-the-century landmark on Fifth Avenue, rechristened Hotel Maxim's de Paris. The $100-million face-lift includes two restaurants that feature intriguing Mediterranean-style fare, one called Bistro d'Adrienne, the other a more formal setting called simply Adrienne.

The sunny and colorful cuisines from Mediterranean countries—particularly Italy, Greece, North Africa, and the Provence region of France—are featured at both. The chef at the more formal Adrienne (see BISTRO D'ADRIENNE, page 412) is Jean-Michel Diot, a twenty-nine-year-old French chef who trained under Jacques Chibois at the Royal Gray, a Michelin two-star restaurant in Cannes on the French Riviera. Mr. Chibois is the consulting chef to both restaurants in the hotel.

The food at Adrienne is light and vividly seasoned with Provençale herbs and spices, particularly garlic, thyme, and tarragon. Olive oil is the foundation for most sauces in place of butter and cream. Count on spending about $60 a person for dinner with tax and tip, a little less at lunch (the bistro runs about $40 a person at dinner). Service is refined and for the most part vigilant.

The preferred seats at Adrienne are near the tall arched windows that frame the view of Fifth Avenue. The room is soft and sophisticated, with salmon-pink walls, thick rugs, belle époque sconces, pale yellow tablecloths, and generously spaced tables. For all its elegance and attention to detail, the room was described by more than one diner as overly bright and "feeling like a hotel lobby."

One thing is for sure: this is not standard hotel food. You can start with an enticing combination of sautéed rouget, or red mullet, along with a lemony tabbouleh made with semolina, minced black olives, diced tomatoes, and olive oil. Equally arresting is the plate of grilled shrimp ringing thin pasta with a sauce of wild mushrooms, celery, truffles, fresh coriander, and a dash of cream.

Mediterranean food at its best is clean, subtle, and aromatic. One example among the entrées at Adrienne is the succulent roasted rabbit, simply but wonderfully emboldened with fresh thyme and ringed with baby turnips, carrots, and flageolets. Lobster benefits from the same approach, brushed with strong olive oil and roasted. The halved lobster—for $32 one would expect the whole creature—is ringed by couscous with raisins and a fresh coriander sauce. The seafood preparations tasted were stellar, such as the red snapper with braised cabbage and fennel, and the John Dory with eggplant confit and diced black olives.

Pastilla is a North African specialty not often encountered here, a phyllo pie filled with shredded squab, almonds, eggs, and spices. While this cinnamon-dusted rendition was brightly seasoned with ginger and mixed spices, the contents unfortunately were dry. Magret of duck is more reliable, the sliced breast meat deliciously rare and accompanied by buttered pommes de terre Maxim cooked in duck fat.

The Mediterranean theme follows through dessert with such offerings as le mendiant de chocolat, little football-shaped pastries with a thin dark chocolate lid and light pistachio-cream filling. Chicory coffee sauce adds a refreshing dry edge to the sweet pear crisp, and diced caramelized apples in puff pastry are fine if you have a sweet tooth. Adrienne has a sumptuous, and expensive, Sunday brunch.

AKBAR

★ ★

475 Park Avenue, between 57th and 58th streets, 838-1717.

Atmosphere: Dimly lit, comfortable, spacious.

Service: Somewhat slow and indifferent.

Price range: Moderate.

Credit cards: All major cards.

Hours: Lunch, 11:45 A.M. to 2:45 P.M., Monday through Saturday; dinner, 5:30 to 10:45 P.M., daily.

Reservations: Recommended.

Wheelchair accessibility: All facilities on one level.

❧ Akbar, an aristocratic-looking Indian restaurant on Park Avenue that is frequented largely by urban Moguls from the northeastern steppes of Manhattan, has surprising appeal for commoners as well—namely some beguiling food at reasonable prices. While the cooks here may not dazzle with inventive twists and impressive presentations, their straightforward, almost textbooklike approach to refined Indian cuisine almost always pleases. Vindaloos are appropriately hot, condiments are cool, curries are complex, and tandoor-roasted foods are succulent. One cannot ask for much more.

The long rectangular dining room is soothing and comfortable with its deep red rugs, white walls, beveled columns, backlit stained glass, and cozy alcoves. The phlegmatic service staff sometimes must be flagged down for water or other requests, and don't expect much help when it comes to explaining the menu.

A good way to start is with the assortment of vegetable appetizers that features two types of cleanly fried fritters, one stuffed with mild white goat cheese, the other with sweet wilted onions, peas, and cubed potatoes. A second mixed-appetizer platter, this one including meat, combines tasty lamb samosas redolent of cumin; dried-out nubbins of baked, yogurt-marinated chicken (tikka); battered cauliflower, and spicy ground lamb molded on roasting skewers called seekh kebabs.

The wondrous breads of India are well turned out here; best among them is the airy onion-filled nan called kulcha. Earthy whole-wheat chapatis and parathas go well with all the sauces, and dirigible-light puffed poori bread comes to the table all golden and pulsing as if ready for flight.

Fans of tandoori roasting will not be disappointed here, for the various chicken dishes are paragons of the art—mildly hot outside from a coating of mixed spices and succulent within. Only tandoori lobster seems ill-suited to this treatment; the meat tends to tighten and lose its characteristic flavor in the superhot oven.

One quizzical preparation is called chicken jalfrezi, described on the menu as a chicken casserole with homemade cheese, assorted vegetables, and spices. Upon failing to detect any cheese in it I asked the waiter what had happened. "Oh, we didn't put any cheese in tonight," he replied matter-of-factly, then walked away.

Lamb vindaloo, a smoldering dish from southwestern India, excels here because it has much more than mere BTU's going for it—the pulpy sauce is stratified with sensations of cumin, garlic, ginger, and cinnamon. A side dish of buttery lentils, called dal, is soothing but underseasoned. Another winning lamb dish is sag, cubed meat simmered slowly with creamed spinach and spices. One superb rice dish not to be missed is called chicken biryani, which melds nuggets of chicken, saffron rice, cashews, and almonds.

One weak spot on the menu is seafood. Prawns cooked in a subtle ginger and cumin-perfumed sauce were dry from overcooking, and fish begum bahar combined pieces of scrod in a bland cream sauce. Beer is the best beverage with this dynamic food, and it's just as well because the small, narrow wine card offers little of interest.

Standard Indian desserts are generally well made, such as the fried milk rounds in a pool of honey called galub jamun, and rasmalai, crumbly cheese flecked with pistachios and doused with rosewater. Mango ice cream is creamy and ripe-tasting; rosewater ice cream tastes like perfume to me, but several diners at my table enjoyed it.

Don't be intimidated by Akbar's pricey location—it offers good mileage for the dollar, in a colorful, alluring setting.

ALCALA

★ ★

349 Amsterdam Avenue, between 76th and 77th streets, 769-9600.

Atmosphere: Warm and inviting, with a long marble-topped tapas bar and brick-walled dining room.

Service: Pleasant and helpful; kitchen can be slow.

Price range: Moderate.

Credit cards: All major cards.

Hours: Dinner, 5:30 to 11 P.M. (tapas bar open until midnight), Tuesday through Saturday, 3 to 10 P.M., Sunday.

Reservations: Suggested.

Wheelchair accessibility: Bar-area tables on ground level; restrooms downstairs.

🍴 Centuries before the neologism *grazing* was coined to describe hit-and-run eaters, the Spanish were doing just that at their tascas, convivial restaurants where a copious display of appetizers, called tapas, were lined up along the bar. So it should be no surprise to Rufino Lopez, a native of Galicia in northwestern Spain, that nomadic nibblers are flocking to his inviting restaurant, Alcala.

The chefs, a pair of Americans who were trained by a Spanish consultant, produce a range of compelling dishes, from traditional stews and roasts to more contemporary creations. The elevated dining room has a warm, friendly feeling—polished wood floor, brick and whitewashed walls, gentle lighting, and a pretty little backyard garden café. A large dining area downstairs is for private functions.

It's fun to start off at the long marble-topped bar up front and choose from an assortment of cold and hot appetizers. If it is true, as some medical reports contend, that olive oil lowers cholesterol levels, then Alcala should accept Blue Cross/Blue Shield cards for payment, for nearly everything on the menu has some. Among the more intriguing tapas (the selection varies daily) are fresh anchovies in a vinegar-laced marinade, morsels of octopus in a similar dressing with pimientos; tender golden rings of fried calamari; rosy smoked trout over sliced cucumbers with dill; a zesty salad of artichoke hearts, sliced beef tongue, and chickpeas in a cumin-perfumed olive-oil dressing, and shellfish salad (tiny squid, scallops, shrimp) in a herby vinaigrette dressing.

The mussels under confetti of minced sweet peppers and capers are tasty, but can be marred by grit; marinated grilled tuna came out dry when I had it. Try a few slivers of serrano, the buttery cured Spanish ham, along with rough-textured bread and a glass of robust red wine.

Speaking of wine, the Spanish selection here is perhaps the best in New York, with many remarkable bargains to be had if you are adventurous. In white, you can't go wrong with the clean and crisp Ermita Despiells from the Penedès region, or the equally pleasing Marques de Griñon; more than forty reds are stocked, starting at less than $15. I enjoyed the Monte Real Reserva from Rioja, but there are many more the staff can recommend. The sherry selection is impressive, too.

If you don't go overboard with tapas, consider the roasted suckling pig as an entrée. A slab of pale, savory pork hides under a brittle, caramel-colored sheet of skin, all in a clear, rich broth perfumed with rosemary. A gutsy occasional special is the wide earthenware casserole holding morcilla (blood sausage), smoked pork, chicken, beef brisket, peas, and spinach. All the meats are well cooked and authoritatively seasoned.

Other alluring preparations include the pepper-dusted fresh grouper ringed by a tasty assortment of eggplant, zucchini, tomatoes, and squash; juicy broiled lamb chops with stewed vegetables; and crisply sautéed salmon steak, rosy rare in the center, flanked by two sauces: a lemony olive-oil-and-garlic emulsion and a faintly piquant granular purée of dried peppers and almonds.

It is puzzling how such a capable kitchen can fall flat when it comes to paella. Twice, the shellfish version featured perfectly good lobster, clams, and shrimp, but the rice was gluey and lacked character, as if it had been cooked separately and combined with the shellfish at the last minute.

The service staff here, mostly Spaniards, is as congenial and well meaning as one could ask, but sometimes the kitchen can't keep up with the rush of orders on a busy night.

For dessert, the thick, rich almond tart is splendid, if weighty, paired with apple purée vitalized with lemon zest. The Catalonian cream—a Spanish crème brûlée—is ultra-light and tinged with cinnamon. Pass up the flossy rum cream roll called brazo de gitano for the exhilarating orange flan ringed with crème anglaise and shredded coconut.

Whether you are "just grazing through" or settling in for a while, Alcala is a spot with considerable charm and Latin spirit.

ALO ALO

★ ★

1030 Third Avenue, at 61st Street, 838-4343.

Atmosphere: Grand café setting, colorful, convivial, and international.

Service: Young, casual waiters and waitresses who sometimes get overwhelmed at busy times.

Price range: Moderate.

Credit cards: All major cards.

Hours: Open daily. Lunch, noon to 3 P.M.; light dishes, 3 to 6 P.M.; dinner, 6 to 11:45 P.M.

Reservations: Suggested.

Wheelchair accessibility: All facilities on one level.

❧ Alo Alo is the kind of uplifting Italian restaurant that I go to for its lively scene and solid, undemanding fare. The whimsically chic dining room resembles a grand café. It has a towering ceiling supporting futuristic disk-shaped chandeliers, cartoonlike papier-mâché characters perched on ledges above the room, wraparound glass exterior walls and inside walls sporting dreamy pastel murals of forest scenes. The glass-fishbowl effect creates a bright and breezy ambiance during the day, and at night it becomes a glittery urban setting in which the boundaries between outside and inside blur.

The clientele is decidedly upscale and polyglot, and the after-work bar scene is colorful. It's fun to stop here for a glass of wine or a caipirinha, which is the Brazilian national cocktail made with fresh lime and sugarcane liquor.

Pastas here, in general, are intense and boldly seasoned, employing the freshest of ingredients. For starters, there are several glistening salads—arugula in a good vinaigrette, fresh endive with anchovies, and radicchio with Parmesan cheese slices.

The most interesting appetizer, though, is the swordfish salad. It is really a carpaccio of raw, fresh, glistening marinated swordfish sliced into translucent sheets and garnished with tiny juliennes of carrots, parsley, oregano, and lemon basil. The swordfish has a delicate oceanic flavor and a texture similar to very lean salmon.

Of the soups sampled—pasta e fagioli and a veal soup with vegetables—the former was the hands-down winner at my table. It was thick and rustic, heavy on the beans, with a pleasing balance of seasonings. The veal soup by comparison was pale and salty with strips of dry meat and leeks.

The stars of this menu's cast are the pastas. A good example is pennette with duck sauce, which features resilient little tubes of al dente pasta tossed with small cubes of fresh duckmeat in an earthy duck-stock-and-tomato sauce redolent of fresh rosemary. Another good bet is the spaghetti with arugula, anchovies, and butter. The tart arugula plays off the saline anchovy flavor beautifully.

If you crave a good risotto, try the one here, which is offered as a special in various guises. I had it mixed with radicchio. The rice, cooked in a good beef broth, had just the proper semifirm texture; the shreds of radicchio throughout imparted a pleasing sharp edge.

Pastas are not the only crowd pleasers. Two standout fish

51

dishes are the expertly steamed salmon fillet presented on a fan of summer squash and accompanied by stewed tomatoes, and sautéed snapper alongside a basil-perfumed mixture of sweet onions, carrots, and celery. All the veal preparations are worth trying. Don't miss the succulent veal chop roasted with whole garlic cloves.

For dessert, all fruit tarts—apricot, kiwi, strawberry, grape, and raspberry—are recommended. The young service staff is competent and nimble, although they sometimes could use reserve troops on busy nights.

AMBASSADOR GRILL

★

1 United Nations Plaza, First Avenue at 44th Street, 355-3400.

Atmosphere: Cool, glassy, and modern urbane setting. Piano nightly.

Service: Can be top-notch if you get a lucky draw; some waiters are a bit green.

Price range: Moderate.

Credit cards: All major cards.

Hours: Breakfast, 7 to 11 A.M., Monday through Saturday; Saturday à la carte brunch, 11 A.M. to 2:30 P.M., Sunday brunch, 11:30 A.M. to 3 P.M.; lunch, noon to 2 P.M., Monday through Friday; dinner, 6 to 10:30 P.M., daily; pretheater $22 prix fixe, 6 to 7 P.M., daily.

Reservations: Requested.

Wheelchair accessibility: All facilities on one level.

The Ambassador Grill is a cool, urbane restaurant in the United Nations Plaza Hotel that offers some compelling French fare at surprisingly modest prices. Moreover, it has become the unofficial gastronomic embassy for Gascony in the southwest of France, the glorious region of ducks, geese, foie gras, confit, and truffles. Several times a year a trio of leading chefs from that region comes to the restaurant to put on Gascon food festivals, and during the year regional specialties are offered on the menu.

Several of the Gascon dishes alone make a trip to the Ambassador Grill worthwhile—and with prix-fixe meals of $21 at lunch and $27 at dinner, you would have to have your own duck supply to find less expensive foie gras. The

52

rest of the menu rolls through peaks and valleys, but by ordering wisely it is possible to have a more than satisfying meal.

The subterranean dining room is striking with its interplay of dark walls, smoky glass panels, and starry lighting. Overhead the illusion of a skylight is created by the angling of many glass trellises that seem to reflect lights out to infinity. In a small open kitchen three white-toqued cooks tend to the sizzling grills. Service is for the most part proper and prompt.

Upon being seated you can begin excavating a ramekin of well-seasoned duck rillettes with toasted croutons. If you are in an experimental mood, try the special Gascon cocktail called a *pousse rapière*—roughly translated as a thrust sword—a French sparkling wine tinted with a regional orange-flavored liqueur. The wine list also carries some moderately priced regional labels, such as the fresh and easy-drinking Colombard, an André Daguin label, a white, and a young faintly tannic Madiran, Domaine Bouscasse, a red (both under $20).

The unqualified best starter is the warm duck foie gras salad, which is on the Gascon side of the menu. It has strips of rare-grilled salmon paired with a meltingly rich slice of the foie gras, seared just enough to form a micro-thin crust, set over a bouquet of mixed greens in a mild wine vinegar dressing ($3 supplement). Soft nuggets of mellow garlic confit add a heady rustic accent.

Recommended appetizers from the other side of the menu are the peppery rockfish chowder, which is actually more like a stew, made with an assertive shellfish stock, tomato, and fillets of rockfish, and a lovely dish of lightly poached shrimp served in a buttery shellfish stock blushed with sweet Sauternes. A cold assorted seafood salad, a special one evening, was also delightful.

Magret, the meaty breast of a fattened moulard duck that is raised to produce foie gras, is competently prepared—sliced, sautéed to rare, and glossed with a red wine sauce ($3 supplement). The restaurant's cassoulet with duck meat may be less rich and complex than it could be, but it is flavorful nonetheless. On Fridays the kitchen turns out a generous and oceanic bouillabaisse spiked with a garlicky aïoli ($4 supplement).

The most interesting seafood selection on the regular menu is called grilled John Dory andouillette with mustard sauce. The fillet of John Dory, also called St. Pierre, having firm, flaky white flesh, is rolled around a stuffing of shrimp-and-scallop mousse, then cooked over a wood fire to impart a strong smoky flavor. The dish, however, needs more of a kick than the pallid mustard sauce provides. An unusual preparation that succeeds is lean Black Angus steak poached to medium rare in beef stock and an emulsion sauce melding egg yolks, mustard, and just a hint of vanilla that comes through moments after you swallow.

High spots of the dessert tray are lush plum tart with a cracker-thin crust, a first-rate crème brûlée, and a fabulous mille-feuille made with sugar-dusted puff pastry disks floating on layers of whipped cream with fresh raspberries.

AMERICA

Poor

9 East 18th Street, between Fifth Avenue and Broadway, 505-2110.

Atmosphere: One enormous room seating 350 with an oversize elevated bar, American scenes painted on the wall, and neon tubes overhead.

Service: Young untrained staff tends to get lost in the shuffle.

Price range: Moderate.

Credit cards: All major cards.

Hours: Daily from 11:30 to 12:30 A.M.

Reservations: Suggested.

Wheelchair accessibility: Several steps at the entrance; all facilities on one level.

🦪 America, New York's largest bar and restaurant, a ten-thousand-square-foot, 350-seat patriotic stadium done in an all-American motif, used to be packed wall-to-wall with yuppies. Its novelty has faded in the past few years, although it manages to lurch along on tourist trade and weekend revelers.

The encyclopedic menu has not improved much; stick with sandwiches, pizzas, and simple grilled items if you want to escape unharmed.

The enormous room has soft murals of all-American scenes on the walls and neon tubes along the towering ceiling. Two sprawling seating areas are separated by a wide central corridor leading to an enormous elevated bar.

More than 160 items are listed covering breakfast through dinner, give or take a dozen or so specials. Not only is the volume of food unrealistic for any restaurant, but the range is astonishing. There is something inherently suspect about a menu that offers sushi, Cajun chicken lips, and three-color fusilli primavera.

Don't expect much help from the green young waiters and waitresses in their open flower shirts. As for the food, which comes in ranch-hand portions, it is dreary at dinner, slightly better at lunch. Prices are remarkably low, which could partly account for the lines at the door.

Many of the appetizers taste as if they had been made in advance and frozen, then thawed in a microwave oven. That would explain freezer burn on the tasteless New Mexican black bean cakes, the stale leftover-tasting barbecued lamb ribs, and the dried-out shrimp cooked in banana leaves with an overly sweet tomato dressing.

Only a handful of dinner entrées sampled can be recommended: grilled chicken with herbs and garlic and an herby soup called New Mexican sopa de fideo, which combines vermicelli with shrimp, red onions, snow peas, carrots, scallions, mushrooms, and coriander.

The list of calamities includes gummy, unseasoned crab cakes; rewarmed barbecued pork with gloppy commercial-tasting dressing; leathery chicken-fried steak in an unctuous batter that slid off onto the plate, and a greasy duck stew with sloppy mixed vegetables, near raw wild rice, and bland pine nut pilaf.

Two of the pizzas sampled at lunch—eggplant, leek, and pepper; and tomato, Cheddar, and chilies on cornmeal crust—at least had been freshly made and had flavor.

The best desserts are the brownies with ice cream and rice pudding with raspberry sauce.

AMERICAN HARVEST

★

3 World Trade Center, in the Vista International Hotel, 938-9100.

Atmosphere: Quiet and spacious dining room decorated in a traditional American theme.

Service: Mannered, callow, and inept.

Price range: Moderately expensive.

Credit cards: All major cards.

Hours: Breakfast, 7 to 10 A.M., Monday through Friday; lunch, 11:30 A.M. to 2:30 P.M., Monday through Friday; dinner, 6 to 10 P.M., Monday through Saturday.

Reservations: Suggested.

Wheelchair accessibility: All facilities on one level.

🍂 American Harvest, the showcase restaurant at the Vista International Hotel in the shadow of the World Trade Center, bills itself as a star-spangled celebration of home-grown provender prepared with allegiance to our culinary heritage. Okay, maybe the Pilgrims didn't garnish salmon steaks with juniper berries and lemon mayonnaise, but why be persnickety and spoil the party? Part of the oversize menu with its colorful photographs of seasonal produce changes from month to month to reflect the progression of the harvest.

The seasonal theme is appealing. The execution, however, is shaky at times. While many straightforward preparations are reliably satisfying—steaks, chops, and grilled seafood in particular—some of the more thematic dishes are fatuous. Take the charcoal-broiled fillet of salmon, for example. It is rosy pink in the center and delicious on its own, so why gussy it up by embedding the flesh with harsh-tasting juniper berries? Moreover, the lemon mayonnaise is bland.

An all-American theme extends to the décor of the three dining rooms, featuring an old-fashioned hanging quilt, glass display cases filled with colorful folkloric wooden carvings, and a giant oil painting of fruits and vegetables. Tables are well separated and the noise level is low, making this a good spot for business entertaining.

The kitchen does not stint on quality of ingredients. Florid slices of lean tenderloin combined with mixed greens and a mustard vinaigrette make a tasty starter, and the bluepoint oysters are icy and fresh. Poached shrimp and sea scallops are impeccable, too, although they could use some herbs to brighten up the cucumber-and-sour-cream dressing. Two of the best starters are the fluffy smoked-salmon mousse over leaves of endive and crisply sautéed sweetbreads atop a bed of chicory. Caesar salad is watery and tasteless.

Among the more satisfying entrées are tender medallions of veal stuffed with julienne of carrots and zucchini, set in a brassy oregano-cream sauce, and the mild pink calf's liver with onions and avocado. Soft-shell crabs, a seasonal delight well worth celebrating, are described as "pan-fried with macadamia nuts." I assumed that they were breaded with crushed nuts, which sounded good; instead, the chef sautés them in butter then opens a jar of macadamia nuts and scatters some around the plate. Roasted duck with rhubarb, moist and full-flavored, is a nice twist on the standard orange sauce, while grilled butterflied shrimp are fine but seemed extravagant at $27. Vegetables are served family style. The California-oriented wine list is reasonably priced and well balanced.

The most noticeable flaw is service. On my first visit two hapless young waiters tried to cover the entire place, with disastrous results. Whenever one of them entered the room, the scene resembled a presidential news conference in which everyone seated wildly gestures in hopes of being acknowledged. Needless to say, the delays were agonizing. What's more, our young server had the irritating habit of referring to customers in the third person, as in, "What would the young lady like today?" and responding to our orders with "Good choice!" and "You've got it!" Service improved considerably on subsequent visits when more staff was on duty.

One expects serious down-home desserts at an all-American restaurant, but except for the lusty thick-crusted apple pie à la mode and a rich, brownielike Derby chocolate pie, most selections are sugary and commercial tasting.

American Harvest displays stadium-size Stars and Stripes on a slightly wobbly flagpole. It needs just a little bolstering before it can stand tall.

AN AMERICAN PLACE

★ ★

969 Lexington Avenue, between 70th and 71st streets, 517-7660.

Atmosphere: Small, slightly cramped dining room in muted colors.

Service: Generally efficient, although on weekend evenings it can be slow.

Price range: Expensive.

Credit cards: All major cards.

Hours: Dinner, 5:45 to 10:45 P.M., Monday through Saturday.

Reservations: Suggested.

Wheelchair accessibility: Two steps down at entrance; dining room on one level; restrooms downstairs.

🦐 Larry Forgione was a pioneer in the renaissance of American cooking when he was chef at the River Café; his highly personal restaurant, An American Place, shows how enticing American cuisine can be, although it is not a uniformly smooth trail.

An American Place has been redecorated recently, adding some color to the formerly drab room. A handsome little wooden bar near the entrance fills up between seatings on busy nights.

The ever changing seasonal menu is small yet well rounded. One of the foremost appetizers is Mr. Forgione's signature dish, a terrine of three smoked fish—salmon, whitefish, and sturgeon—garnished with their respective caviars. The fresh and smooth terrine, stratified with layers of each fish, is nicely seasoned, and the diadem of colorful caviars is as stunning as it is delicious. Less lofty but equally rousing starters are the generous deviled-crab and oyster fritters, animated with black pepper, and a lusty assortment of country hams and sausages.

Southern-fried rabbit with vegetable pasta sounded intriguing, and while the boneless rabbit was moist and well fried, the pasta in creamy garlic sauce needed more zip.

The Stars and Stripes gets a good showing among the entrées, especially in game preparations such as the succulent roast partridge in an apple-cider-and-vinegar sauce with chestnut purée, and rare-roasted slices of tender mallard duck breast. Mr. Forgione likes to surprise diners with unlikely juxtapositions of ingredients, and those surrounding the duck—a slab of ruddy country ham and sweet-edged red-eye gravy—work better than one might think. The most memorable element of the dish is the country samp, nuggets of hominy that have a pastalike texture, enlivened with minced red onions, bell peppers, and coriander.

Grilled free-range chicken, moist, meaty, and flavorful, which comes with wonderful fettuccine loaded down with wild mushrooms, is superb. Barbecued squab with wild rice and apple griddle cakes would have been high on the applause meter as well, had it not been for uneven roasting that left certain sections of the squab too pink inside. If you are in the mood for red meat, go with the lustrous loin of lamb in a bracing dark stock sauce rather than with a light asparagus custard over a bland buffalo steak.

Among seafood entrées, the broiled lobster arrangement looks like something out of a Georgia O'Keeffe painting. The perfectly cooked meat is removed from the shell and reassembled graphically on the plate over a nouvelle version of Newburg sauce, heady with sherry. I was nonplussed by the planked Alaskan king salmon, which had a slightly fishy smell, in a hard-boiled-egg sauce.

Desserts are an adolescent's American dream: velvety and intense chocolate pudding, picture-perfect banana Betty, cinnamon-perfumed apple pandowdy with a buttery crust, and mile-high strawberry shortcake.

AMSTERDAM'S GRAND

★

454 Broadway, at Grand Street, 925-6166.

Atmosphere: High-ceilinged, two-tier restaurant done in black and white. Open rotisserie kitchen and long, comfortable bar. Informal.

Service: Pleasant young staff, generally efficient. Service tends to be better in rear dining room.

Price range: Moderate.

Credit cards: All major cards.

Hours: Daily from 11:30 A.M. to 1 A.M. (kitchen closes around midnight).

Reservations: Suggested.

Wheelchair accessibility: All facilities on one level.

The winning formula that made the original Amsterdam's on the Upper West Side (428 Amsterdam Avenue, 874-1377) a smash hit, which it still is, never quite caught fire downtown. The lower Broadway establishment has been fiddling with its formula for a year now trying to get on track. It still can be recommended for inexpensive rotisserie entrées, salads, a few pastas, good desserts, and affordable wines.

The long, rectangular two-tier restaurant is done in sharp-edged shades of black and white, with a long bar along one side and an open rotisserie grill on the other. No fussy table settings here, and if you want to pick up the fire-blistered and moist roast chicken with your hand and gnaw on the bones, there is no maître d'hôtel around to roll his eyes toward the ceiling. Crisp golden french fries are better than average—and you can eat these with your hands, too.

One of the appealing aspects of Amsterdam's is that you can drop in for a glass of wine and eat just an appetizer or an entrée, and leave without spending $25. If it's a salad you crave, the formidable mound of mixed greens mingled with assorted meats and vegetables is fresh and sprightly.

Ingredients vary slightly from day to day, but foraging usually turns up roasted red and yellow peppers, Black Forest ham, rotisserie-grilled chicken, sirloin strips, sun-dried tomatoes, zucchini, smoked Gouda, duck, and anything else within arm's reach of the chef.

Like the food, the wine list is straightforward and priced for the average financially overextended New Yorker.

You can expect more attentive service in the back dining room than in the front one near the bar. In general the waiters and waitresses are earnest and helpful, although they have yet to be tested under fire.

The short roster of lighter dishes (there is no distinct appetizer list) includes a meatloaf-thick slab of smooth-textured duck-liver mousse that could use a bolstering of seasonings; pretty red-tinted Swedish shrimp—they were pleasantly saline though not as fresh-tasting as those at the uptown restaurant—and delicious, glossy gravlax with a dill-mustard sauce. Pastas have been added to the menu, and most are al dente and well seasoned.

Desserts are intended not to dazzle but to delight, and they succeed, particularly the sharp gooseberry tart and lustrous chocolate velvet mousse cake.

ANABELLE'S

★ ★

1294 Third Avenue, between 74th and 75th streets, 772-8100.

Atmosphere: Comfortable contemporary design in beige and brown. Moderate noise level.

Service: Low-key and knowledgeable.

Price range: Moderately expensive.

Credit cards: All major cards.

Hours: Brunch, 11:30 A.M., Sunday; lunch, noon to 3 P.M., Monday through Saturday; dinner, 6 to 11 P.M., Monday through Thursday, until 11:30 Friday and Saturday; pretheater dinner, 5:30 to 6:30 P.M., Monday through Friday ($29 prix fixe).

Reservations: Suggested.

Wheelchair accessibility: All facilities on one level; restroom for handicapped on same floor.

  With theme restaurants all the rage—from dreamy Provençale to daffy tropical—Anabelle's is distinctive for its lack of a conspicuous label. It is simply a comfortable and welcoming place where the food takes center stage—and what a splendid show it can be.

If one had to define the menu, it might be called French-inspired New American, with a few side trips to Italy along the way.

The restaurant design, by Sam Lopata, is uncharacteristically reserved. Beige walls, a chocolate-brown rug, and brushed copper ceiling set a tranquil stage highlighted by little beveled mirrors all around. Waiters in white shirts and black bow ties are mimicked in little stenciled characters scooting along the tops of the walls.

One starter not to miss is boudin blanc, a brightly seasoned chicken and veal sausage, char-grilled over sautéed leeks and shiitake mushrooms in a light chive cream sauce —the hot dog goes to heaven. Chanterelle mushrooms infuse a husky fricassee filled with pancetta, the Italian smoked pork, and crisply grilled sweetbreads.

Less elaborate but equally compelling appetizers include a butternut-squash soup given extra dimension with crumbled Roquefort and walnuts; excellent grilled quail with sharp mixed greens, lacy french fries, and polenta (it is really too much for an appetizer); fat pillows of ravioli filled with garlicky cod mousse in brown butter sauce; and Malpeque oysters faintly poached in Muscadet and served in a briny cream sauce.

Waiters are well versed in this eclectic menu, and they go through their routine with low-key refinement. The meal's pacing can be noticeably slow, however, with particularly long waits for appetizers.

Grilled red snapper comes with two bright tomato coulis, one red, the other yellow. Swordfish is likewise superb, in a light saline soy butter sauce with grilled baby leeks. Only the seared yellowfin tuna was a letdown—the black-olive tapenade on top and mixed vegetable garnish were wonderful, but someone forgot to pull the fish off the fire until it was gray and dry.

I enjoyed the best veal chop in many months here, swathed with grainy mustard and tarragon along with sautéed endive and gratin potatoes. Soothing loin of lamb comes with brittle sautéed potatoes and a delicious artichoke timbale. Sautéed duck breast is paired with a rich confit of duck leg in a heady red-wine sauce bolstered with black olives—the corn-and-wild-rice fritters on the side, though, were gluey. One of the Italian preparations, angel-hair pasta with shellfish, had freshness going for it but lacked flavor; moreover, the fragile angel hair invariably gets soggy in hot broths.

Desserts are not so consistently stellar as the rest of the menu, but good options run from spicy (really spicy) pears poached in pepper-stoked red wine with caramel ice cream, and lemon meringue tarts to two terrific bread puddings, one with walnuts in cider sauce, the other with chocolate and macadamia nuts.

Anabelle's is a refreshing change of pace. If you want waitresses in cowgirl outfits or little surfers in swizzle sticks, theme restaurants abound. But for compelling food in a cordial setting, Anabelle's is high on my list.

ANATOLIA

★

1422 Third Avenue, between 80th and 81st streets, 517-6262.

Atmosphere: Pastel-and-neon casual dining room; can be loud.

Service: Prompt and congenial.

Price range: Moderate.

Credit cards: American Express, MasterCard, and Visa.

Hours: Lunch, noon to 2:30 P.M., Monday through Friday; dinner, 5:30 to 11:30 P.M., Monday through Saturday, 5 to 10:30 P.M., Sunday.

Reservations: Suggested.

Wheelchair accessibility: Front dining room on main level; ramp to second level; two steps down to restrooms.

🐾 The owners of Anatolia on the Upper East Side had a nifty idea: Take the spirited and salubrious foods of Turkey and the Middle East, serve them with flair in an upbeat setting, and keep prices low. The formula succeeds up to a point, but inconsistency is a lingering problem.

The pastel-washed dining room sets a lighthearted tone with its lavender ceiling, simulated stone walls, faux Doric columns, streaking neon tubes, and spacy saucer-shaped lights. Waiters glide around in their billowing costumes patiently describing the exotic cuisine to customers.

Cold appetizers are presented on a giant tray; many look

more impressive than they taste. A purée of grilled eggplant boosted with garlic and parsley is unpredictable, fresh and deliciously smoky, or bitter with raw garlic. White bean salad flecked with red onions and doused with a lemony vinaigrette is invigorating, as are pan-fried eggplant under a piquant garlic-yogurt sauce, pristine baby octopus salad, and grape leaves stuffed with rice, currants, and pine nuts.

A classic Turkish preparation called Circassian chicken is made by smothering shredded chicken meat with a walnut-and-garlic purée: at one sampling it was peppery and bright, another time drab. One of the recommended beef dishes is called "ladies thigh" kofte, a dill-infused meat patty topped with grated kasseri cheese (a salty sheep's or goat's milk cheese).

Anatolia has an exceptionally well-priced little wine list. Among whites, the William Hill Silver label chardonnay and the J. Phelps sauvignon blanc (both under $20) have enough spunk to match this food; reds to consider in the same price range are the merlots from Acacia and Sterling and the Beringer cabernet sauvignon ($19).

Lamb is a staple in Turkey, and among the renditions offered here are succulent lamb shanks braised in vegetable broth and served with a light lemon sauce (the shank is prepared in tomato sauce occasionally) and sultan's bliss, a tender pan-seared lamb steak in a light tomato sauce accompanied by eggplant purée. The most compelling dish on the menu is boneless quail wrapped in grape leaves and grilled over charcoal, accompanied by rice with currants and pine nuts.

Among seafoods, skewered swordfish is dry and bland. The best is red snapper fillet that had been marinated with Turkish raki (an ouzolike liqueur) and sautéed with onions, olives, peppers, and tomatoes.

If you can get over the psychological hurdle of a dessert pudding that contains shredded chicken, it might be worth trying the kazandibi, which is light, semisweet, and caramelized on top: it tastes nothing like chicken. Other choices are the delicious orange-scented baklava with its brittle pastry crust (walnut and pistachio versions are available, too), fresh chocolate-yogurt tart or, for fiber fans, a honey-drizzled baked disk of shredded wheat.

The Ottoman Empire may not rise again as a culinary force on the strength of Anatolia's cooking; nonetheless this winsome Turkish outpost can be fun, and at benign prices.

AQUAVIT

★ ★

13 West 54th Street, 307-7311.

Atmosphere: Sleek ground-level café and bar; dramatic eight-story atrium dining room.

Service: Informed and professional.

Price range: Expensive (downstairs, lunch prix fixe, $32; dinner prix fixe, $55).

Credit cards: American Express, MasterCard, and Visa.

Hours: Lunch, noon to 2:30 P.M., Monday through Friday (until 3 P.M. upstairs); dinner, 5:30 to 10:30 P.M., Monday through Thursday, 5:30 to 11 P.M., Friday and Saturday (until 10:30 P.M. upstairs).

Reservations: Necessary for dining downstairs.

Wheelchair accessibility: Difficult steps at entrance and to downstairs dining room; special arrangements can be made for patrons who call in advance.

🍴 This dramatic two-level establishment in the former John D. Rockefeller town house on West 54th Street is the first major Scandinavian restaurant to appear in several decades. While some of the ingredients used are exotic—cloudberries, bleak roe, snow grouse—the cooking leans heavily on French technique. It is certainly worth a visit, for some of the food can be as exhilarating as the morning's first ski run on pristine powder.

The upper level is a less formal café with a long bar that serves, among other things, eight varieties of flavored aquavit, the high-octane Scandinavian liquor distilled from potatoes. Light meals and lunches are offered, including smørrebrød, Danish open-faced sandwiches with such combinations as velvety smoked salmon swathed with horseradish cream on rye-pumpernickel bread; liver pâté, bacon, aspic and horseradish; egg and fillet of smoked eel (in the $6 to $9 range). A diverting lunch choice is called "peel and eat" Scandinavian shrimp. These sweet, delicious little critters are attacked with the hands and dipped in a caviar-and-crème-fraîche sauce flavored with dill.

The main event, however, is produced downstairs, a soaring space with birch trees reaching high into the eight-story glass-walled atrium and a sloping gray-tile waterfall. Tables along the gray leather banquettes are packed tighter than a chairlift at Sugarbush, so you might want to request a free-standing table for comfort's sake. Extraneous noise seems to evaporate in this towering place, allowing easy conversation.

Christer Larsson, a Swedish-born chef who trained in restaurants and hotels across Europe, has a masterly touch with North Sea salmon. For appetizers, he makes a salmon tartare blended with minced oysters that is an ethereal briny combination; ditto the sheets of this mildly smoked, silky salmon with horseradish cream. (The only disappointment was gravlax, which lacked distinctive dill flavor, although the mustard sauce had plenty.) An entrée called one-side sautéed salmon is parchment crisp on the bottom, rosy and moist within, set over a glistening chive-butter sauce that allows the pristine fish flavor to shine.

An appetizer to consider is the earthy Arctic venison pâté —it has a distinctive but not overpowering game flavor— adorned with lingonberries and celery root.

The discreet and capable waiters here are well schooled in the differences between a cloudberry and a brambleberry. The wine list is well chosen but frightfully expensive across the board.

Salmon is not the only star of the show here. You can't go wrong with snowy poached turbot with brown butter and horseradish ($6 supplement to $55 prix-fixe dinner)— not so, though, with the sweetbreads (bland and spongy) paired with monkfish in a red-wine combination. Rare-cooked loin of Arctic venison, a tad more assertive than domestic venison, is succulent in its apple-and-juniper-berry sauce. Closer to home, medallions of veal are fork tender in a vibrant herb sauce along with a sweet timbale of beets.

Scandinavians are nuts over berries, and they show up in all sorts of desserts. The Smalandsk cheesecake is delightfully moist and nutty, embellished with tart-sweet lingonberries, cloudberries, and almonds; and terrific brambleberry sorbet is encased in a fragile almond basket surrounded by vanilla sauce. Chocolate cake with a "burned" almond crust is rich and intense; pass on the sugary Swedish meringue cake dessert.

I doubt if haute Lapland cuisine will become the next food fad in New York—for one, the supply of rare Arctic Circle cloudberries would be depleted faster than Louisiana redfish—but for now Aquavit is representing the homeland proudly.

ARCADIA

★ ★

21 East 62nd Street, 223-2900.

Atmosphere: Cozy, attractive dining room with wraparound sylvan murals; bar dining area is loud and cramped.

Service: Forgetful and sloppy in the bar; better in the dining room.

Price range: Expensive.

Credit cards: American Express, MasterCard, and Visa.

Hours: Lunch, noon to 2 P.M., Monday through Friday; dinner, 6 to 10 P.M., Monday through Saturday.

Reservations: Necessary.

Wheelchair accessibility: All facilities on one level.

&❧ When Arcadia was first reviewed in 1985, Anne Rosenzweig was an anonymous young chef who was delighting customers with her eclectic and intelligently assembled American cooking. Before long, as is so often the case, the trend-starved media machine grabbed her and pumped her up larger than a helium-filled character in the Macy's Thanksgiving parade.

The offers started to pour in, for consulting jobs, newspaper and magazine profiles, radio and television interviews, and advertising campaigns. In 1987, she took on a second job as menu mahatma at the rejuvenated "21" Club. At the same time, prices crept up at Arcadia, from $38 for the prix-fixe dinner to $55. All of which raises the question, has Arcadia declined in her absence? Not really.

The food, which Ms. Rosenzweig still oversees, is as alluring as ever. She has shrewdly honed the menu so the kitchen can fly smoothly on autopilot. As for the service, it is as haphazard as ever. If you are relegated to one of the tables in the bar, as my party was one evening without being asked if we had a preference, you can expect to be jostled and jabbed by crowds waiting for tables two inches away and ignored by waiters who need the stamina of a fullback to fight their way to you. The setting and service were slightly better in the cozy dining room, with its wraparound sylvan mural by Paula Davis, soft peripheral lighting, and burgundy banquettes. Just don't get stuck in the two aisle tables unless you want to be intimate with waiters' backs all evening.

Good starters include grilled leeks in golden-brown puff pastry set over beurre blanc with chives, and moist, crumbly corn cakes under a dollop of whipped crème fraîche and two kinds of caviar, golden whitefish and osetra (a $5 supplement, on top of a $55 dinner prix fixe, is excessive for a few dabs of caviar. A pasta special, combining succulent duck confit, shiitake mushrooms, and roasted garlic, was knocked off balance by a surfeit of thyme. A cute concoction called mussels like snails, in which the mussels in their shells were glossed with garlic-and-herb butter, leaves me cold: the result had neither the briny appeal of fresh mussels nor the earthiness of snails. Black bean soup, on the other hand, is an unqualified winner, thick and hammy, zesty with hot pepper, and garnished with a sliver of goat cheese.

Ms. Rosenzweig has a knack for assembling menus that are inventive yet at the same time irresistibly homey. Rarely do I see diners agonize over menu orders as they do at Arcadia. Take, for example, lusciously charred squab with sweet-tart rhubarb sauce accompanied by crisp, beer-battered potato slices and Swiss chard, or molasses-daubed boned quail set over a bed of mâche and dandelion greens along with asparagus and grilled sweet-potato cubes. In both dishes, sweet elements are counterbalanced by pungent ingredients. Salmon steak is delicious, too, on a bed of couscous under an orange-tinted hollandaise sauce that could use a touch of lemon for acidity.

A house specialty is called chimney-smoked lobster. The lobster is smoked and grilled at the same time over a wood-fired grate and served with aromatic tarragon butter. The smoke-tinged meat is precut and served in the shell, accompanied by deliciously crunchy deep-fried celery-root cakes. Equally good are grilled sea scallops over a fricassee of Jerusalem artichokes, scallions, and tomatoes. Buttery sautéed spaetzle adds a soothing touch. At $55 prix fixe, one might hesitate to order chicken, but this is one of the highlights of the menu, the boned chicken incredibly moist, its skin puffed and brittle, paired with terrific zucchini and carrot pancakes and kale.

The wine selection, while relatively limited, is first rate and fairly priced across the board.

Arcadia loyalists will steer you to the ineffably soothing chocolate bread pudding with brandy custard sauce. For an undiluted chocolate fix, try the bittersweet chocolate terrine with whipped cream and almond tuiles. Warm banana dumplings with caramel sauce, however, are achingly sweet. Go instead with the prunes poached in red wine with sharp cinnamon ice cream.

ARIZONA 206

★ ★

206 East 60th Street, 838-0440.

Atmosphere: Rough plaster walls and glowing hearth suggest a Southwestern cave.

Service: Enthusiastic and congenial.

Price range: Moderately expensive.

Credit cards: All major cards.

Hours: Lunch, noon to 3 P.M., Monday through Saturday; dinner, 6 to 11 P.M., Sunday through Thursday, 6 to 11:30 P.M., Friday and Saturday.

Reservations: Required for lunch and dinner.

Wheelchair accessibility: Dining room two steps down; restrooms down flight of stairs.

&. If you want to experience the real flavors of American Southwestern cooking, in all its fiery glory, there is no place like Arizona 206—or its new Arizona 206 Cafe next door (see Diner's Journal section, page 409). The kitchen is run by Brendan Walsh, who has created an exciting and diverse menu that is sure to run your taste buds through Olympic-like trials. He does not, however, assemble unusual dishes merely for shock value. Virtually all his recipes are intelligently conceived and demonstrate just how appealing this style of cooking can be in skilled hands.

As you enter the long, narrow restaurant, the first sensation is the soothing aroma of a crackling fire in the small lounge. The whimsical décor includes undulating molded plaster walls that suggest the Southwest, natural-wood floors and tables, and lovely arrangements of desert flowers —"haute cave," they call it. The banquettes have desert-toned cushions that are more comfortable than the bare straight-backed chairs. Conversations and music ricochet off the hard-edged surfaces, so on busy nights it can be clamorous.

The menu is mercifully limited, so you can get right down to business without having to plow through a hand-scrawled encyclopedia of Western botanical oddities. The bouncy young waiters and waitresses take pride in the food

and are happy to answer questions. Service is casual—
"Who gets the chicken?"—and occasionally forgetful.

Two of the appetizer salads are highly recommended:
grilled lamb salad with fennel, artichoke, green-leaf lettuce,
and chopped tomatoes; and a warm mélange of dark, fibrous mustard greens, hickory-smoked bacon, and exquisite morsels of sautéed sweetbreads coated with corn flour.
In the former, thin slices of lamb are grilled to a lustrous
rare, and the sweet-edged honey-cumin vinaigrette helps
the diverse flavors come together. The sweetbreads, which
are fresh and firm, take on an extra dimension in their
carapace of crunchy corn flour.

One of the better soups is a velvety, sweet purée of assorted squash. It is garnished with a lovely cirrus pattern
of red-pepper cream sauce. The wine list is limited but adequate—and well matched with the food.

Mr. Walsh has a deft touch with game. Don't miss the
rare-grilled barbecued quail nestled in a bed of creamy polenta, or the squab in a cactus-pear sauce accompanied by
peppery spinach and wild rice (a special). One highlight of
the menu is a superb venison chili in which tender morsels
of well-marinated meat are combined with firm-cooked
black beans, corn, red peppers, coriander, garlic cloves,
and tomato. This serendipitous combination is served with
a slab of roasted red-pepper brioche.

Desserts do not fly at the same altitude. Chocolate walnut
cake with espresso ice cream is satisfying, although sweet-
potato pie is run-of-the-mill. A slightly tart cactus-pear
sauce enlivens the passion-fruit sorbet.

ARQUÀ

★ ★

281 Church Street, 334-1888.

**Atmosphere: Large, airy minimalist space with soft
ocher-colored walls. Loud at times.**

Service: Genial and knowledgeable.

Price range: Moderate.

Credit cards: American Express.

**Hours: Lunch, noon to 3 P.M., Monday through Friday;
dinner, 5:30 to 11 P.M., Monday through Thursday, 5:30
to 11:30, Friday and Saturday.**

Reservations: Necessary.

Wheelchair accessibility: Several stairs at entrance; restrooms downstairs.

❧ Arquà is named after a village in northeastern Italy that was the home of the fourteenth-century poet and philosopher Petrarch. Leonardo Pulito, the thirty-year-old Italian-born chef who runs this stylish downtown restaurant with his wife, Antoinette, has a poetic streak himself, as evidenced by his sensitive and lyrical pasta compositions.

The airy and minimalist restaurant is housed in a towering former industrial space that is given warmth by its ocher-toned walls, which evoke ancient sandstone churches aglow at sunset. Large circular Art Deco sconces cast soft light across the tables. All the unbroken hard surfaces, though, intensify noise to a din when the house hits its peak around 9 P.M. The casually stylish service staff is helpful walking you through the all-Italian menu.

The menu reflects Mr. Pulito's highly developed sense of balance when it comes to flavors and textures. The cold antipasto plate, for example, includes slices of rolled veal paired with a sweet-hot mustard aspic, as well as roasted red peppers, onions, and a sprightly bean salad. I could make a lunch of that alone with some of the excellent thick-crusted country-style bread. Another good starter is the pretty arrangement of artichoke leaves slathered with olive purée and crowned with bacon strips and a dusting of Parmesan. Grilled radicchio leaves are enhanced by melted nutty taleggio cheese.

One of the more unusual offerings that many diners might shy away from simply because they can't pronounce it is called sgombretti (scom-BREH-tee), a specialty of Liguria and Veneto. It is a method of preserving fish, usually sardines or small mackerel. Mr. Pulito sometimes uses fresh sardines, filleting them, dredging them in flour, and frying them. When cooled, the briny little fillets are marinated with onions sautéed with oil and vinegar and eaten cold. The combination of tart vinegar and sweet onions is invigorating.

Parties of four or more might nibble on two or three appetizers to leave room for half orders of pasta before the entrée. You might start with pappardelle del dogi, long flat strips of resilient homemade noodles layered with ricotta cheese, and radicchio leaves and Italian sausage—it just needed a few shakes of salt to bring out the subtle flavors. Agnolotti, little spinach-filled pasta curls, are wonderfully light and tasty in their fresh tomato sauce thickened with creamy mascarpone cheese, as are mattonella d'Arquà, thin sheets of pasta layered with artichoke purée and topped with béchamel and grated Parmesan cheese, and fettuccine all'anatra in a gutsy duck sauce.

The Holy Trinity of northern Italian cuisine—gnocchi, risotto, and polenta—is beautifully executed here. I often avoid gnocchi in restaurants because so often they are either rubbery or leaden. The feathery little gnocchi here are the best I have had in ages; the preparation changes daily, usually bathed in some variation of light tomato sauce with sage, basil, rosemary, or other fresh herbs. Risotto, which also comes in various disguises, is outstanding. Polenta was creamy and lusty, blended with sausage and wild mushrooms.

The limited wine list is well chosen, offering some bright and fresh selections

Not all the entrées stand up to the stellar lineup of pastas. Grilled shrimp are visually arresting and cooked to a turn but bland; swordfish and grilled Cornish hen with rosemary suffer the same fate. Better options are the tender calf's liver with onions, flanked by triangles of toasted polenta, and chicken al Prosecco (the sparkling wine from Veneto), in which the breast is combined with a Prosecco-and-cream sauce bound with olive paste and mushrooms.

A standout entrée that is offered as a special most days is salmon steak wrapped in radicchio leaves and braised in white wine and fish stock, then sprinkled with balsamic vinegar to add an invigorating touch before serving.

Desserts are appropriately light—and irresistible. Ricotta cheesecake has a lively lemony touch; cocoa-dusted tiramisù, made with espresso-drenched ladyfingers and sweetened mascarpone cheese, is habit-forming; and the world's lightest napoleon should come under glass to keep the pastry from blowing away.

The migration of ambitious Italian restaurants downtown is a boon to those looking for alternatives to the splashy and expensive uptown scene. Even counting the taxi ride, you'll come out ahead—and smiling.

AUNTIE YUAN

★ ★

1191A First Avenue, near 65th Street, 744-4040.

Atmosphere: Dramatic all-black dining room with pinpoint overhead lighting.

Service: Knowledgeable and efficient.

Price range: Moderately expensive.

Credit cards: American Express and Diners Club.

Hours: Lunch, noon to 4 P.M., daily; dinner, 4 P.M. to midnight, Monday through Saturday, noon to 11 P.M., Sunday.

Reservations: Suggested.

Wheelchair accessibility: All facilities on one level.

𝕒 This stylish Upper East Side establishment owned by David Keh turns out an impressive range of arresting dishes that rival some of Chinatown's finest—albeit at uptown prices.

What the higher tab gets you is a coal-black, sleekly cool dining room with overhead pinpoint lighting illuminating solitary flowers on each table, elegant tableware, an extensive wine list, and captains in black tie. Tables are well separated and conversations are muted. The captains, virtually all non-Oriental, have a good grasp of the food and assure that no dish remains a mystery.

Two giveaway munchies are so good I would return for them alone: one bowl holds shredded Chinese cabbage and ground shrimp in a coriander–sesame-oil vinaigrette, the other has strips of carrots and daikon in a smoldering chili-pepper dressing. Among the appetizers, cold noodles in a peppery sesame sauce flecked with scallion are bright and fresh, while a cold salad mingling shredded duckmeat with strips of crackly skin, scallions, Chinese cabbage, and coriander offers a lovely contrast of flavors.

One arresting hot starter is succulent barbecued quail glazed with a zippy garlic paste. Of the four types of dumplings served, only the shrimp-filled Shanghai-style ones were memorable—seared golden-brown on the outside and so juicy that upon biting into one I nailed a waiter at six paces.

Seafood entrées are fairly reliable. Salmon is prepared in an engaging way—steamed to just pink in the center and garnished with salty fermented black beans and strips of fresh ginger. Steamed flounder is exceptional, set under a snowfall of garlic, fermented black beans, and flecks of hot peppers.

Orange beef is one of those benchmark dishes that can give quick clues about a kitchen. The version here is one of the better ones in town—crisp outside, fibrous and tender within, and not overly sweet.

Peking-duck fanciers should note that Auntie Yuan turns out one of the best—layers of brittle skin with a thin sheen of fat underneath to add flavor, wrapped in a rice pancake, followed by the lustrous meat, which is so rich it needs no sauce. Desserts are few and forgettable.

As diverting as an evening in Chinatown can be, it is nice to know there is a more tranquil alternative when the mood strikes.

AURORA

★ ★ ★

60 East 49th Street, 692-9292.

Atmosphere: Luxurious and quiet with well-spaced tables and supercomfortable chairs and banquettes.

Service: Generally professional; can be imperious.

Price range: Expensive.

Credit cards: All major cards.

Hours: Lunch, noon to 2:30 P.M., Monday through Friday; dinner, 5:30 to 10 P.M., Monday through Thursday, 5:30 to 10:45 P.M., Friday and Saturday. Bar menu available between lunch and dinner.

Reservations: Necessary.

Wheelchair accessibility: All facilities on one level.

Before Joseph Baum went on to renovate the splendid Rainbow Room, the elegant and refined French restaurant, Aurora, was his labor of love. Although it has been overshadowed by the publicity lavished on his new projects, Aurora remains a singular achievement on its own terms. Much of its strength derives from Gérard Pangaud, the chef who once ran a two-star Michelin establishment in France.

You are compelled to take an aesthetic stand immediately upon passing the uniformed doormen and entering the winsomely plush dining room. The interior design, by the graphic artist Milton Glaser and the architect Philip George, precludes neutrality. The room combines a very establishment, corporate ambiance (burnished wood wainscotting, muted colors, cushy leather chairs) with a playful bubble theme more appropriate to a trendy yuppie bar—a blend of martinis and margaritas. The fanciful overhead lights support the theme.

Tables are broad and generously spaced, tableware is weighty and expensive, and best of all, the noise level is muted. The vaguely horseshoe-shaped bar in the middle is a good spot to order lunch from a special grill menu.

As for the food, it can soar as high as Mr. Glaser's bubbles on a windy day. Mr. Pangaud brings with him the new-found Gallic affection for unpretentious "real food": that is, dishes that stress flavor over flair. A good example is the appetizer of crisp-skinned duck confit in a nest of fresh greens, enhanced with strips of cured duck and nuggets of gizzard confit, all in a lively hazelnut dressing. Or the firm, golden-sautéed sweetbreads paired with sliced potatoes, truffles, and a caper-parsley vinaigrette. Other first-rate starters are the luxuriant pheasant terrine layered with buttery foie gras, a glistening mosaic of salmon and leeks, and florid fresh tartare of tuna (a lunch appetizer), jazzed up with lots of pepper and lemon. Globules of golden caviar throughout burst in the mouth, adding a rousing saline accent.

Many of Mr. Pangaud's more refined portraits jump off the canvas as well. A dome of helium-light red-pepper mousse is flanked by shrimps in a zesty basil vinaigrette, while a palette of baby vegetables in puff pastry with a sherry-vinegar sauce also succeeds admirably. Sautéed fresh foie gras is as stunning as it is seductive on a layer of mâche and garnished with sheer slices of black radish. A tangy vinaigrette sauce makes a fine foil.

A few spectacular-sounding dishes fail to live up to their billing. One example is overcooked pasta with scallops and sea-urchin roe in a soupy curry sauce. And doughy Roque-fort-filled ravioli are not rescued by a good walnut sauce.

The service staff, clad in spiffy cream-colored jackets, gets high marks in general for efficiency.

Game fanciers will swoon over Mr. Pangaud's sublime roasted pigeon with aromatic garlic sauce and sautéed po-tatoes, his toothy venison in a poivrade sauce with pearl onions, and the stuffed pheasant breast roasted in a jacket of caul fat until it is golden and succulent. An incredibly tender veal chop, as thick as a Russian novel, comes with cabbage pockets filled with rice and wild mushrooms.

On the seafood side of the menu, salmon steak baked in a mild horseradish crust is always pleasing. So is red snap-per Antiboise, a perfectly cooked fillet on three croutons, slathered respectively with a rustic black-olive tapenade, purée of parsley, and garlic. A potentially stunning dish of lobster meat in a lime and Sauternes sauce has been vi-tiated by slight overcooking on several occasions, while bland tuna steak mounted on a raw-tasting tomato coulis disappointed twice.

What rarely disappoints, though, is desserts. Whoever dreamed up saffron ice cream should be canonized. And the fragile-crusted apple tart with cinnamon ice cream is no slouch, either. The cast is large and ever-changing: lemon-hazelnut torte, chocolate raspberry cake, warm chocolate mousse cake, an intriguing "nirvana of five oranges" featuring various citric delicacies.

AU TROQUET

★ ★

328 West 12th Street, 924-3413.

Atmosphere: Simple, cheerful French ambiance.

Service: Helpful and pleasant but unpolished and at times slow.

Price range: Moderate.

Credit cards: American Express, MasterCard, and Visa.

Hours: Dinner only, 6 to 11 P.M., Monday through Saturday.

Reservations: Necessary.

Wheelchair accessibility: All facilities on one level.

🦞 This alluring little West Village restaurant evokes France in a low-key way—the lettered awning shielding white-framed windows with gauzy curtains, the small bar where handsome young waiters flirt with a pair of neighborhood girls who have stopped in for a drink, the simple and lovingly arranged dining room highlighted with paintings by the owner, and the sincere feeling of hospitality—not a well-rehearsed "Good evening, I'm Reginald your waiter and we will be dining together tonight" type of welcome, but the kind conveyed by a warm smile and a bottle of cool white wine.

Intensely flavorful homemade stocks, the mortar with which all French cooking is built, contribute to some first-rate sauces. One example is the mignonettes de veau à l'estragon. This dish consists of thin medallions of buttery veal cloaked in a meaty veal-stock sauce flavored with aromatic leaves of fresh tarragon. A wedge of crusty potatoes dauphinoise (a casserole of potato slices, cream, nutmeg, salt, and pepper) and a grilled tomato half are typical vegetables. Among the roughly ten daily entrées, others worth singling out are the grilled baby pheasant with raspberry brandy, sautéed shrimp stuffed with celery and bacon, duck with Pommard wine sauce, and chicken breast served with a mustard-cream sauce. The mild-flavored pheasant, charred on the outside, moist and tender within, came with a lustrous semisweet raspberry-brandy sauce. In the shrimp dish, the medium-size shrimp are slit down the middle and stuffed with lightly cooked bacon and celery, then sautéed briefly. It's a simple and tasty combination.

The young waiters can be charming and helpful, although on busy evenings the pace gets bogged down. The wine list is short, but the prices are fair.

The two best appetizers on the menu are the crab in puff pastry set in a pool of mustard sauce, and raw salmon marinated with basil. Other good choices are a salad of endive with Roquefort, avocado, and cucumber; escargots with garlic butter and anise-flavored Ricard, and an assortment of woodsy wild mushrooms tossed in light cream and crowned with a slab of puff pastry. Only the grainy duck-liver mousse is disappointing.

Au Troquet is the sort of homey place where one tends to linger well into the evening sipping espresso or a snifter of Cognac. Try either with a pretty fan of apples marinated in red wine and rum, served with fresh cassis sauce, and garnished with almond slivers.

Overall, Au Troquet is a restaurant I would return to frequently. It offers value for the dining dollar and provides—for Francophiles like myself—the closest experience there is to following one's nose along the Left Bank.

AZZURRO

★ ★

1625 Second Avenue, at 84th Street, 517-7068.

Atmosphere: Cheerful if cramped little dining room. Can be loud.

Service: Friendly and concerned young staff does a first-rate job.

Price range: Moderate.

Credit cards: American Express and Diners Club.

Hours: Dinner, 5:30 to 11 P.M., Monday through Thursday, 5:30 P.M. to midnight, Friday through Sunday.

Reservations: Necessary.

Wheelchair accessibility: All facilities on one level.

≋ Azzurro is a pint-size, family-run Sicilian restaurant that turns out some terrific pastas, salad, and regional seafood. The dining room is a narrow rectangle with brick walls, a white tile floor, and tables along each wall. Overhead a dusk-blue ceiling is freckled with tiny inset lights that resemble stars. The restaurant is run by two personable young men, Marcello and Vittorio Sindoni, and their mother, Maria, who tends the fires in the kitchen.

The food is fresh, pure, and unpretentious. An appetizer of tart, charred fresh endive, tied in little bundles with scallion strips and slickened with olive oil, is a delight. Homemade mozzarella that is so fresh it is still warm is encased in a translucent slice of prosciutto and presented with ripe tomatoes and fresh basil. Caponata is among the best I have had, a chunky mélange of sweet eggplant, garlic, roasted red peppers, and basil.

The cold seafood salad, a special, features a cast of sparkling fresh bay scallops, shrimp, and squid in a mild olive-oil-and-garlic dressing. Minestrone, based on a good chicken stock, is lighter than most versions and explosive with the flavors of fresh vegetables.

Pastas are the highlight of the menu. The portions are so large they are best split between two if ordered as a middle course. Mrs. Sindoni performs magic with lowly cauliflower, blending its florets with pine nuts, raisins, basil, and Parmesan cheese to create a remarkable sauce for al dente rigatoni, an occasional special. Bucatini tossed with shredded sardines, raisins, wild fennel and pine nuts, a Sicilian specialty, is another combination that prompted applause at my table. The combination is saline and faintly sweet at the same time. Other winners include thin noodles in a snowy ricotta cream sauce and penne with delicious roasted eggplant and salty sun-dried tomatoes.

The waiters remain admirably high-spirited and energetic as they weave their way nimbly among the tight tables. The all-Italian wine list is organized by courses, with suggestions for each. Good choices exist for $20 and under.

Entrées are not as uniformly superior as the first two courses. The best are grilled tuna Sicilian style, pan-sautéed and scattered with sweet red onions, basil, roasted peppers, and tomatoes (a special); grilled swordfish glistening under a coating of olive oil; grilled red snapper done the same way; and succulent baby lamb chops. Tagliata, thin slices of sirloin over arugula salad, needs more zip, and boneless chicken in white wine with sausages and mushrooms is on the dry side. Simple grilled chicken with fresh rosemary is a better choice.

There are only two desserts, and they are a must: an espresso-rich tiramisù lathered with whipped mascarpone cheese and dusted with cocoa powder, and an airy napoleon constructed with the most fragile of puff pastry.

THE BALLROOM

★

253 West 28th Street, near Eighth Avenue, 244-3005.

Atmosphere: Countrified and inviting dining rooms in a low-key Spanish motif.

Service: Slow and indifferent.

Price range: Moderately expensive.

Credit cards: All major cards.

Hours: Lunch, noon to 3 P.M., Tuesday through Friday; dinner, 5 P.M. to midnight, Tuesday through Saturday. Closed Sunday and Monday, except for private parties.

Reservations: Suggested.

Wheelchair accessibility: Ramp to dining room level; restrooms down flight of stairs.

❧ The ambiance of The Ballroom exudes the generous spirit and buoyant dining style of the Spanish, even if some of the food is unexciting. The Iberian theme jumps out at you as you enter the elevated back bar, which is festooned with a stunning array of strange and wonderful foods: baby octopus in a sea of red sauce, giant marinated mushrooms, bulbs of baked fennel, stuffed squid, snails with red beans, roasted eggplant, seafood casserole, and more. Dangling overhead like an edible raised curtain are braids of blood-red hot peppers, rosy hams, sheets of powdery dried cod, and plump black sausages. The only problem here is that not everything tastes as good as it looks.

Felipe Rojas-Lombardi, the owner and chef, is a conscientious professional who strives for authenticity. He does things the right way, with no shortcuts. I suspect, though, that the minions who execute his recipes don't always exhibit the same commitment.

How else does one account for a time-consuming pied-de-veau (calf's-foot gelatin) made with a reduction of calf's feet and morels that has no perceptible seasonings? Or resilient baby octopus in paprika sauce that is sharp and invigorating one day, insipid the next?

Tapas can be a meal in themselves or appetizers. If you plan to have a full-course meal in the dining room, it is advisable to reconnoiter at the tapas bar beforehand. Although waiters bring a large tray of these tidbits to your table, often the best ones are missing. Among the most pleasing are the grilled eggplant brushed with a peppery coriander sauce; whole squid stuffed with a herbaceous combination of ground pork, pine nuts, and raisins; spicy cold chicken in tomato sauce; baked fennel; lemony and fresh seviche of scallops with scallions; orejas (thin slices of pig's ears) in balsamic vinegar sauce; and a tasty caponata (eggplant salad). Spanish tortilla, which is akin to a potato omelet, is well seasoned and expertly cooked.

Waiters are generally slow and sloppy, always seeming to disappear just when you need them.

The tapas that fail to excite are the bland mixed vegetables with tarragon (but no salt), grilled calamari marred by sand, and chicken in a lackluster curry sauce. Entrées are limited and change slightly from day to day. Roasted pheasant in a peppery brown sauce with homey braised cabbage is a first-rate autumn dish that is served in cooler months; get a side order of the sweet fried plantains or yucca, a potatolike tropical root sliced to resemble steak fries. The scallops with their coral are perfectly cooked and set in a lemon-butter sauce.

The Ballroom has an adequate wine list of French and Spanish selections, though you could do well with the pleasing house wines, Viña Sol red and white. The cabaret theater in a separate room, where pop singers and other entertainers perform, serves tapas during the show.

The restaurant also offers a colorful buffet lunch composed of tapas and special entrées.

Desserts are not included in the price of the buffet, which is no great loss. The German chocolate cake is gummy, coffee pecan pie has a granitic crust, and tarts are undistinguished. If the rye cake made with rye flour, raspberry purée, and cinnamon cream is available, go for that. The leaden version of Spanish bread pudding, filled with pineapple chunks, is appealing in a macho sort of way. A fittingly Spanish ending to the meal is a glass of sherry and assorted cheeses.

BARBETTA

Satisfactory

321 West 46th Street, 246-9171.

Atmosphere: Plush and baronial dining room; enchanting outdoor café.

Service: Sloppy and forgetful.

Price range: Expensive.

Credit cards: All major cards.

Hours: Lunch, noon to 2 P.M., Monday through Saturday; dinner, 5:30 to 11:30 P.M., Monday through Saturday.

Reservations: Suggested.

Wheelchair accessibility: Three steps at entrance; all facilities on one level.

❧ Barbetta is a sumptuous eighty-two-year-old Italian restaurant on West 46th Street. The setting is palatial, with its pale yellow walls, the rococo sconces and regal chandeliers, and it boasts one of the prettiest outdoor gardens in New York. Lamentably, though, neither the food nor the service does the place justice.

It is possible to have a lovely time at Barbetta, especially if you sit in the garden on a pleasant evening and order the right dishes. Of more than thirty dishes sampled, fewer than a third can be recommended. Here's a winning strategy: start with some roasted peppers or the salad of tomatoes, mozzarella, and basil. The assorted antipasto carries the same peppers but is otherwise unexciting. And the house mixed salad was so drenched in vinegar it was inedible.

Next try one of the risottos, which are skillfully prepared —full flavored and with just the right resilient texture. I had the savory version with wild mushrooms and morsels of chicken liver. If you want to try pasta, go with the tagliatelle, folded flat noodles, in a satiny tomato-cream sauce enlivened with basil. Linguine in pesto sauce was fresh but needed salt to bring out the flavors.

For the main course, the best bet is the simple but compelling pollo al babj, which is a pan-roasted chicken with a blistered golden skin emboldened by pepper. Another satisfying choice is the veal chop al verde, an extra-thick slab rich in flavor and combined with a white-wine-and-parsley sauce.

Broiled Dover sole is a good seafood choice. Cold poached salmon with lemon mayonnaise is exceedingly dry, while the tasteless cold trout has the texture of papier-mâché. String beans, which accompany many entrées, can be old and leathery; other vegetables have steam-table texture and little seasoning.

Barbetta's wine list is substantial, but sloppy and outdated in some areas.

For dessert, look for the fruit tarts of the day, which can be splendid, or the poached peach mired in a dense and concentrated zabaglione.

If you follow those tips, chances are you will come away from Barbetta relaxed and happy, barring any serious service mishaps.

BELLINI BY CIPRIANI

Poor

777 Seventh Avenue, at 51st Street, 265-7770.

Atmosphere: Simple and pleasant café setting upstairs; downstairs is nondescript and overly bright.

Service: Inept.

Price range: Expensive.

Credit cards: All major cards.

Hours: Lunch, 11:45 A.M. to 3:00 P.M., Monday through Saturday; dinner, 5:30 to 11:30 P.M., daily. Closed Sunday July and August.

Reservations: Necessary.

Wheelchair accessibility: Access to street-level dining room; restrooms downstairs.

The pricey café food at this celebrity hangout ranges from dismal to acceptable. Moreover, service is boorish and slapdash, at least in the downstairs room where unknowns are sent (it can be better in the street-level room where Cipriani family members spend their time cosseting the regulars). Downstairs has all the charm of a family restaurant in a shopping mall—nondescript patterned wallpaper, faux marble, wobbly plywood tables—and tortuous lighting that is harsh enough to break the silence of the most resolute double agent.

Waiters are a gregarious lot who seem to enjoy one another's company, for they spend much of their time huddled in the hallway chatting and laughing while customers are left to fend for themselves. Dishes are auctioned at the table, plates are stacked and hauled away diner style, requests for water and bread are forgotten, and getting wine practically requires papal intervention.

You can start off the proceedings with the house drink, a Bellini, which is a pleasing combination of peach juice and sparkling wine. From there, it is mostly downhill. Cold marinated salmon with asparagus and carpaccio of beef are among the best of the changing appetizers. Risottos vary in quality from the colorful yet bland primavera and a cloyingly rich artichoke and shrimp combination to an earthy and aromatic mushroom rendition. Pastas are uniformly disappointing. Tagliolini came in a lifeless pesto sauce; so-called ravioli primavera was nothing more than cheese-filled dough garnished with unseasoned cubes of zucchini and yellow squash. Gnocchi was gluey no matter how it was prepared, and veal cannelloni was a dispiriting mass of melted cheese hiding tasteless noodles and ground veal. One of the house specials, baked green and white noodles, should be served with a television set, for it is a dead ringer for a TV dinner—overcooked noodles in a lavalike gratinéed cheese sauce.

Don't look for bargains on the wine list. Italian whites like Santa Margherita pinot grigio, which costs about $11 retail, go for $30 here; Orvieto Classico, a simple $6 white wine, is an incredible $26. Unaccountably, California wines are among the more reasonable buys.

Underseasoning and overcooking plague the main courses. A veal chop was fat and well cooked but insipid, as were the limp vegetables surrounding it; ditto for the salmon steak and the sea bass with artichokes. Tuna steak supposedly Livornese style was a disaster: the fish was cooked to industrial gray, and black olives were the only hint of its regional affiliation. Rubbery shrimp à la Bellini came with rice that had been reheated so many times it tasted like plastic pellets.

Sorbets, lemon meringue pie, and a fluffy zabaglione-filled layered pastry were the best desserts. Forget the sugary homemade ice cream and achingly sweet chocolate layer cake. All of this comes at a princely price—dinner for four, including cocktails and two bottles of the least expensive wines on the menu, came to $326 before tip.

BICE

★

7 East 54th Street, 688-1999.

Atmosphere: Smart and contemporary café setting. Handsome bar and tiny outdoor café.

Service: Can be curt and indifferent at the door; waiters inside friendly and earnest.

Price range: Moderately expensive.

Credit cards: American Express.

Hours: Lunch, noon to 3 P.M., daily; dinner, 6 to 11:30 P.M., Monday through Saturday, until 10:30 on Sunday.

Reservations: Necessary well in advance.

Wheelchair accessibility: Dining facilities in street-level bar; dining room two steps up, restrooms downstairs.

❧ Bice is the kind of restaurant everyone loves to hate—too chic, too crowded, too self-consciously European—yet everyone wants to visit. When this spinoff of a high-fashion trattoria in Milan opened in June 1987, it was immediately so jammed you would have thought they were giving away Christian Lacroix gift certificates with every carpaccio. It has calmed down in recent months, making it more accessible to mere citizens.

This upscale trattoria has a lot going for it: a strikingly handsome setting, some alluring pastas and salads, terrific people-watching, and a buoyant spirit. Adam Tihany, the designer, has done a masterly job with lighting, which is softly diffused behind brass sconces and the crisscrossed beamed ceilings. The beige-and-wood space is contemporary yet warm, neighborly but not cramped.

Waiters are friendly and unpretentious (although not terribly sharp on the fine points of service). Bice does not purport to be anything more than a splashy café serving simple fare—and that's just what you get, at prices equal to or below other such celebrated hot spots around town. If you accept it on those terms, you can have fun.

Pastas are the kitchen's strength, so I suggest you get right down to business and bypass the mostly run-of-the-mill appetizers. Unaccountably, half portions of the changing pasta selections are not offered, so it will cost you about $16 for an appetizer. Among the best I tried were the rigatoni all'amatriciana in a lusty bacon-flavored tomato sauce sweetened with onions; fettuccine in a light cream sauce with fresh peas and ham; tagliolini in the same cream sauce perfumed with truffles; pappardelle in a beautifully balanced tomato, mozzarella, and basil sauce, and linguine tossed with chunks of fresh lobster, tomato, parsley, and blanched garlic cloves. Pumpkin-filled tortelloni with crushed nuts was a nice idea that needed more seasonings to bring it together. Creamy risotto speckled with chopped fresh clams, parsley, and garlic was a paragon of texture and flavor.

The wine list carries reputable producers at generally fair prices (although some vintages are not listed and others are incorrect). They must store the bottles on Staten Island, for it invariably took our waiters forever to find them.

Among entrées, you can get a tasty rare sliced steak strewn with tart arugula, well-prepared chicken paillard and sugar snap peas (salt and pepper does wonders for the meat), or crisp and firm sautéed sweetbreads with roasted potatoes. Osso buco is dry and uninteresting, while what the menu describes as rack of veal is cafeteria-style pounded veal, as thin as typing paper, heavily battered and deep fried.

A refreshing dessert is the coffee-flavored granita with vanilla ice cream. Tiramisù is rich but lacks the sharp coffee flavor. If you are in an indulgent mood, go for the incredible mud pie, a crenulated mass of superluxuriant chocolate with a bittersweet edge.

BOULEY

★ ★

165 Duane Street, 608-3852.

Atmosphere: Splendid Provençale-style room with well-separated tables and comfortable noise control.

Service: Highly proficient and businesslike.

Price range: Moderately expensive.

Credit cards: All major cards.

Hours: Lunch, noon to 2:30 P.M., Monday through Friday; dinner, 6 to 10:30 P.M., Monday through Saturday.

Reservations: Recommended.

Wheelchair accessibility: Dining room on one level; restrooms downstairs.

🍤 A splendid Provençale flower took root in the craggy industrial terrain of TriBeCa in the summer of 1987. Called Bouley, it is the creation of the French-schooled David Bouley, who made his reputation at nearby Montrachet. In its first year the kitchen and dining room continued to improve, and now it is cruising on a high plateau.

The setting, to be sure, is a jewel. You enter through an immense hand-carved wooden door into a placid country French setting: a vaulted ceiling, romantic lighting reflecting off cream-colored walls, bucolic Impressionist paintings and wildflowers popping out of window boxes. Tables are far enough apart to allow intimacy, and the roomy chairs are covered with soft tapestry.

Mr. Bouley's highly refined and labor-intensive style is risky, and sometimes his kitchen cohorts fail to interpret the chef's whims precisely, rendering some dishes undramatic. Overall, however, the successes outnumber the failures—and some of the former can be inspired.

Among the winning appetizers are a peppy eggplant terrine under a snowy cap of goat cheese, and seductive butternut squash soup lumpy with roasted chestnuts. What's called a panache of salads—beautifully sautéed foie gras of duck along with grilled shrimp and grilled wild mushrooms —is a rousing trio. A lustrous ragout of clams, langoustines, and scallops is enlivened with fennel and some red beets that add a delightful touch of sweetness.

The highly proficient waiters in black tie know all the steps, and every little detail is attended to with great discretion. They are well versed in the wide-ranging, French-leaning wine list, which is particularly strong in Loire selections. Prices are generally fair.

An eight-course tasting menu is available for $65 in addition to the à la carte selections. My favorites were the rack and loin of lamb in a subtle port wine sauce along with an addictive potato purée, and pristine sea scallops seasoned with marjoram in a light butter sauce paired with fettuccine and black olives. You also can't go wrong with the sweet shelled lobster in a concentrated sauce made with red Sancerre wine.

One of Mr. Bouley's golden oldies from Montrachet days, called black bass en barigoule, is a flamboyant orchestration in which all the players belt out different tunes and never combine to form a lyrical unit. The perfectly cooked bass fillet sits over an assembly of sliced artichoke hearts, pencil-thin asparagus, carrots, and tomato in a light stock sauce flavored with garlic cloves—and no salt, which leaves it flat. Lack of salt can also vitiate the roasted pigeon paired with a luscious combination of braised pigeon wrapped inside cabbage leaves with a crown of grilled foie gras. I can't imagine what Mr. Bouley is referring to with his so-called rotisserie duckling with nine spices—on two samplings, I couldn't identify even one spice.

Dessert is the one course at Bouley for which I would ride a pogo stick downtown from Times Square. Two individual soufflés—chocolate pear and hot raspberry—are sublime. An assembly called green apple conversation combines an ethereal apple-filled puff pastry with Calvados sorbet inside a tuile cookie. Bittersweet-chocolate sorbet steals the show when paired with a chocolate ganache terrine and pistachio opera cake.

BRIVE

★ ★

405 East 58th Street, 838-9393.

Atmosphere: Soft and cushioned town-house restaurant that is romantic, relatively quiet, and comfortable.

Service: Gracious and welcoming.

Price range: Expensive.

Credit cards: All major cards.

Hours: Dinner, 6 to 10 P.M., Monday through Saturday.

Reservations: Necessary.

Wheelchair accessibility: One step at entrance.

Brive is a romantic, expensive little East Side restaurant with some highly eccentric food that has found a loyal following since it opened in late 1986. This softly upholstered town house on East 58th Street is the domain of Robert Pritsker, who operated the nouvelle-cuisine Doudin-Bouffant in the same spot between 1979 and 1982. While Mr. Pritsker has moved from the kitchen to the dining room, the food turned out by his crew still reflects his devotion to quality ingredients leavened with a puckish attitude about haute cuisine. If you can get over Brive's relentless case of the cutes on the menu, some arresting food is to be had.

The long, narrow dining area begins in the flower-strewn front room with rust-orange walls and burnished antiques, then tumbles into a slightly more confined back room and finally into a dark and romantic alcove overlooking a small garden. The welcome at Brive is warm and genuine, and the service, while at times overly mannered, could not be more helpful. And you will need help when it comes to this menu, which is cluttered with silly descriptions usually associated with family restaurants designed to resemble pirates' galleons.

If you can muster the courage to order an appetizer described as "calves' brains wrapped and sent from Spain," what you get is delicate poached brains enveloped in almond crêpes ringed by a vibrant gazpacho. Wild? Yes, but the combination works. Salmon terrine flecked with its golden roe that give off a burst of salinity is delightful. A two-course appetizer consists of a warm flan of chicken livers that is silky and mild, followed by a creamy cold chicken-liver mousse flanked by a good homemade aspic and French bread.

Less serendipitous starters are an over-orchestrated dish of mussels that are poached, removed from the shells, swathed in an olive-oil mixture, and huddled in the center of a large plate under bread crumbs. All the manhandling saps the mussels of flavor.

Some of the entrées are stellar. Roasted veal chop with a bright basil sauce is superb, and swordfish over a bed of deep-fried assorted greens an arresting idea. Perfectly grilled squab fanned over orso in a savory stock sauce could not be improved upon, nor could the special of roast tuna steak in a garlic-flecked parsley sauce. Perhaps the most distinctive dish is calf's liver. Dusted with broad crumbs and mustard seeds and black peppercorns, the liver is sautéed and presented next to a clump of tart mustard greens and sweet pears.

Brive has a limited but engaging wine list and splendid desserts. Ultra-rich and smooth chocolate-pistachio praline torte is not to be missed. Another winning combination is poached peaches, canteloupe, and nectarines surrounding an igloo of lustrous mint ice cream; marjolaine cake oozing with hazelnut cream, and blueberry sorbet also leave nothing to the imagination.

B. SMITH'S

Satisfactory

771 Eighth Avenue, at 47th Street, 247-2222.

Atmosphere: Stylish and spacious soft-pastel dining room with Art Deco accents. Loud.

Service: Haphazard and forgetful.

Price range: Moderate.

Credit cards: All major cards.

Hours: Brunch, noon to 4 P.M., Saturday and Sunday; lunch, 11:30 A.M. to 4 P.M., Monday through Friday; dinner, 5 P.M. to midnight, daily.

Reservations: Suggested, especially on weekends.

Wheelchair accessibility: All facilities on one level.

The sleek, futuristic steel-and-glass structure crowned with a pair of truncated pyramidal skylights is an attention grabber along the tawdry strip of Eighth Avenue in the 40s.

It is the home of an aggressively hip new restaurant called B. Smith's, created by Michael Weinstein and company, owners of Ernie's on Upper Broadway and America on East 18th Street. This new venture is named for the co-owner, Barbara Smith, a glamorous former model whose beguilements as a hostess don't quite make up either for the wobbly menu or for service that at times resembles a Three Stooges routine.

In familiar Weinstein style, the décor received first priority, no expense spared, in hopes of creating an immediate sensation. To that end, B. Smith's seems to succeed. The airy postmodern interior sports a gleaming stainless-steel bar up front that attracts a stylish clientele. In the back is a softer-edged dining room dabbed in peach tones and with Art Deco touches. A colorful abstract mosaic covers one wall. One design element not addressed is noise, which can be deafening.

The overly ambitious menu makes for tempting reading, but the execution is something else. The problem here is obvious: the kitchen's wide-angle lens attempts to take in every voguish type of cooking—Cajun, new American, Deep South, Italian—and winds up with very little in focus.

Appetizers and desserts are the most reliable; in fact, it wouldn't be a bad strategy to load up on both ends and leap-frog the middle. Soups are quite good, at least when they arrive hot—the odds are a coin's toss that they will. A thick and garlic-bolstered purée of roasted tomatoes brightened with fresh basil is a fine way to start; at lunch a first-rate peppery lobster bisque, a special, held slivers of sole and shrimp (slightly overcooked).

Among the regular appetizers, shrimp poached in an herby shellfish stock loaded with garlic are light and flavor-packed; by contrast, sparkling fresh bluepoint oysters are bullied by an overly citric beurre blanc and garnish of grapefruit and orange sections. B. Smith's menu also carries a selection of entrée-size salads that could be split if ordered as appetizers, as well as "light plates," sort of in-between portions for the grazing herds. The plain green salads are fine, but steer away from such fatuous creations as duck salad under a syrupy raspberry sauce that belongs on ice cream.

A notable light plate is grilled lean duck sausage infused with fennel along with warm potato salad. In the same category, vermicelli with lobster, onions, tomato butter, and mascarpone was a frumpy and bland mess, while potato-and-leek pancake was sodden and missing the promised caviar garnish.

The asparagus-green waiters and waitresses, ranging from spike-haired to strait-laced, seem perpetually in a fog and tend to disappear for long stretches. The wine selection is adequate but generally overpriced by several dollars a bottle.

Among entrées, overcooking vitiates some otherwise decent preparations; three examples are the chicken paillard, grilled salmon (a special), and grilled shrimp. The last was described enthusiastically by Ms. Smith as shrimp under a mango glaze. On two occasions the thick bright yellow sauce had a cloying flavor that could best be described as melted vanilla ice cream. Even the accompanying banana fritters tasted reheated. The simplest entrées were the most satisfying: grilled lamb chops in a sapid Madeira sauce, steak with french fries, and grilled duck breast flanked by good duck sausage in a heavily reduced red wine sauce.

The scenario brightens with dessert. Except for an overly sugared sweet-potato-pecan pie, other options are worthwhile: dense triple chocolate torte surrounded by a moat of raspberry sauce and crème anglaise, coconut tuiles with white chocolate ice cream, and lavish profiteroles.

BUKHARA

★

148 East 48th Street, 838-1811.

Atmosphere: Handsome and low-key with sandstone-colored walls and soft lighting.

Service: A bit confused but improving.

Price range: Moderate.

Credit cards: All major cards.

Hours: Lunch, noon to 3 P.M., Monday through Sunday; dinner, 6 to 10:45 P.M., daily.

Reservations: Suggested.

Wheelchair accessibility: No.

If you don't mind eating with your hands, Bukhara can be a lot of fun. It is also one of the most handsome and comfortable Indian restaurants to come along in years. Entrées are grilled over charcoal or roasted in the ancient clay oven, the tandoor.

The dining room has rough sandstone-tone walls holding gleaming hammered-brass-and-copper trays and colorful embroidered rugs, soft indirect lighting, and stout teakwood tables set with copper water tumblers and pretty flower-painted plates. Behind a glass partition is a spiffy slate-walled kitchen where chefs tend the tandoor ovens.

The menu is limited to about a dozen entrées, with no appetizers and only three desserts; some of the entrées, however, make good starters when split among two or four. When you are seated, a waiter brings hot hand towels and the menus.

The tandoor ovens turn out a host of terrific breads: nan, a fluffy white-flour disk; roti, a flat, earthy whole-wheat round; and khasta roti, which is a toasted whole-wheat bread sprinkled with cuminseed. The best is mint paratha, the slightly puffed and charred whole-wheat bread that is dusted with dried mint. Bharvan kulcha, an inflated nan stuffed with onions, potatoes, and fresh cheese, is delicious when dipped in a mint-ginger chutney set out on the table.

Bukhara had some service shortcomings in its early days, but revisits have found that to have improved.

This "frontier" style of cooking, said to originate with the Pathan tribes of Peshawar, now part of Pakistan, revolves around marinating primary ingredients in yogurt (or another moistening agent), herbs, and spices, then cooking in the superhot tandoor. This technique reaches a sublime level with chicken Bukhara, in which the whole sectioned bird is infused with yogurt, chili powder, ginger, and garlic, then roasted to falling-off-the-bone succulence. Veal chops, marinated in dark rum and yogurt that is accented with cinnamon, then grilled, also share best-of-show honors. A hint of sweetness from the rum melds with the sharp-edged cinnamon and lingers on the palate. All portions are large enough to share around a table of four.

Another recommended chicken dish, called mellow cream chicken, features bite-size pieces of meat marinated in cream, lime juice, green peppers, and mild cheese, then skewered and nicely charred over the grill.

It is ironic that lamb, for which Indian cooking is justly renowned, is the least appealing of the entrées—it tends to be overcooked and underseasoned. The most expensive item on the menu, duck Bukhara, is to be avoided—it is bland and tastes more like beef than duck.

Two good side dishes are the delicious grilled cubes of fresh cottage cheese flavored with cuminseed and ginger paste, and the exceptionally creamy and rich lentil dish called dal. The dal is best scooped up with one of the flat breads.

The menu writer got fancy when it came to dessert, switching to French to describe "l'orange creme," which is a sprightly orange-perfumed frozen cream served in a carved-out orange peel (spoons are allowed with dessert). The other desserts are humdrum.

Bukhara is a good option for large groups since the serving style lends itself to sharing.

CAFÉ DES ARTISTES

★

1 West 67th Street, 877-3500.

Atmosphere: Gracious café with dark wood walls and splendid murals.

Service: Well-schooled in the food but at times forgetful and slow.

Price range: Moderately expensive.

Credit cards: All major cards.

Hours: Brunch, noon to 3 P.M., Saturday, 10 A.M. to 3 P.M., Sunday; lunch, noon to 3 P.M., Monday through Friday; dinner, 5:30 P.M. to midnight, Monday through Saturday, 5 to 11 P.M., Sunday.

Reservations: Necessary.

Wheelchair accessibility: Front dining room accessible; restrooms two steps up.

🍴 Café des Artistes endures year after year as one of the most gracious and romantic spots in town. Located in a historic turn-of-the century building off Central Park West, its dark, burnished-wood walls, lead-paned windows, sparkling tableware, and famous bucolic murals by Howard Chandler Christy contribute to an ambiance of gentility and anticipation. The food does not always live up to the promise, but there are plenty of beguilements if you choose wisely.

The restaurant is perpetually packed, and it is difficult to get a reservation before 10:30 P.M. on short notice. Even with a booking, chances are you will have to cool your heels at the bar, which is hardly penitential, for it is one of the most fashionable perches in town—and great for celebrity watching. In the downstairs room, tables are jammed together along purple banquettes; the bar level is slightly more private. The service staff is well informed and tirelessly enthusiastic, if sometimes slow and forgetful.

While the menu wanders all over the map, its strength lies in certain ingenuous French bistro dishes. The confit of duck is one of the better renditions around, crisp-skinned, falling-off-the-bone tender, and authoritatively seasoned. It comes with tasty white beans. Another high point is the classic combination of rare-roasted slices of lamb in a zesty pan gravy surrounded by tasty flageolets, the small pale-green French beans. Rack of lamb encrusted with basil and bread crumbs can be recommended. The slide comes among seafood entrées, many of which tend to be overcooked.

Appetizers fare better than entrées. Opt for the creamy and herbaceous squash soup over the pallid seafood gazpacho. Four preparations of salmon presented on a wooden serving board—gravlax, smoked salmon, poached salmon steak, and dill-flavored tartare—are fresh and lively. The cold foie gras terrine rolled in black-pepper crust is silky and delectable along with its duck cracklings and toasted brioche.

Parties of four or more should try the "great dessert plate," a battalion of heavy-duty cakes and pies. Among the best are the tart and airy Key lime pie, moist and nutty sour-cream-apple-walnut pie, zesty orange savarin cake, and velvety chocolate mousse cake. Those of an intrepid spirit might want to attack the "Great Bonaparte," a Himalayan-size napoleon made with puff pastry under an avalanche of whipped cream, lemon curd, and strawberries.

CAFÉ 58

★

232 East 58th Street, 758-5665.

Atmosphere: Subdued, comfortable, informal.

Service: Amiable but slow at times.

Price range: Moderate.

Credit cards: All major cards.

Hours: Lunch, noon to 4 P.M., Tuesday through Saturday; dinner, 4 P.M. to midnight, Tuesday through Saturday, 5 to 11 P.M., Sunday.

Reservations: Suggested.

Wheelchair accessibility: Three steps at entrance; all facilities on one level.

🍴 Café 58 is one of those midtown standbys that is not a destination restaurant but rather a place to drop into when you are in the mood for some undemanding bistro food.

The kitchen could use a jolt of energy, for many of the dishes are tired and forgettable.

I go there primarily for one of my favorite peasant dishes: pied de cochon. This succulent breaded and roasted pair of pig's feet, crisp outside and gelatinous within, is reminiscent of the version in bistros around Les Halles in Paris.

The walls are covered with a dark plaid fabric—the kind one finds on children's bunk beds—and the ceiling is made of eerie crenulated cement that is sprayed to resemble a cave. Wall sconces above the banquettes are mounted on gnarled vine roots.

The appetizers are not nearly as esoteric as the setting. All the familiar tunes are played, and among the better ones are the earthy and lean country pâté, beefy onion soup, scallops in a white sauce with mushrooms, and smoked salmon. Mussels ravigote can be gritty, and the escargots are run-of-the-mill. Most appetizers carry supplementary charges, so the prix fixe is not really valid.

Café 58 usually offers several daily specials in addition to the regular menu. On weekends, it is a creditable bouillabaisse containing pieces of pompano, red snapper, and cod as well as half a lobster, clams, and mussels in a well-seasoned red broth. It is enhanced by a garlic mayonnaise and a peppery rouille (hot mayonnaise with paprika).

Another special is cassoulet, which also is good and garlicky with lots of sausage and duck. Another peasant dish is a winner: tête de veau, or calf's head. You get slices of tongue, meaty cheeks, and brain accompanied by a mild creamy vinaigrette. The onion-flavored boudin, or blood sausage, is simply grilled and served with applesauce and first-rate french fries. We peasants never had it so good. Seafood does not fare as well. Both fish specials sampled—monkfish in a green-peppercorn cream sauce and broiled scrod—are bland. Grilled Dover sole meunière is better.

The limited wine list matches the food well—a few good crus Beaujolais, some Mâcons, a Muscadet, and a Sancerre, many in the $20-and-under range.

Desserts, like the entrées, are meant to satisfy not dazzle. The fruit tarts are good, as is the festive coupe aux marrons (glazed chestnuts buried in vanilla ice cream with whipped cream). Oeufs à la neige, crème caramel, and pears poached in red wine received passing grades.

CAFE 43

Satisfactory

147 West 43rd Street, 869-4200.

Atmosphere: Comfortable, bright and bustling café ambiance.

Service: Can be forgetful and slow at lunch; better at dinner.

Price range: Moderate.

Credit cards: All major cards.

Hours: Lunch, noon to 4:30 P.M., Monday through Friday; dinner, 5 to midnight, Monday through Saturday.

Reservations: Recommended.

Wheelchair accessibility: All facilities on one level.

🍴 Convenient to Broadway theaters, Cafe 43 is a place to keep in mind for a drink and snacks before the show or something more substantial afterward. Its food has plummeted in recent years, though.

The restaurant is a cavernous space with high ceilings, blush walls, arched mirrors, and wide banquettes in a color refrigerator salesmen refer to as harvest gold. The dining room is comfortable and bright, and the high ceilings absorb conversation so even at peak hours you don't have to bellow.

The lunch and dinner menus change often, so the following are typical dishes. Cafe 43 has one of the more extensive wine-by-the-glass menus in town—24 kinds in all, including eight champagnes and sparkling wines. The regular wine list is well represented among California and European selections, all priced fairly.

The most intriguing appetizer on the lunch menu is Japanese-style chicken marinated in rice vinegar that has been stir-fried in a light soy sauce with slivers of carrots, sweet red peppers, and scallions. The chicken is nicely cooked, and the addition of pine nuts before serving adds a crunchy accent. At dinner, fresh salmon slivers marinated in soy sauce and lime, served in a beautiful fan pattern on the plate with cucumbers, are lustrous. They come with a green leaf salad tossed in hazelnut-oil dressing.

Several appetizers are near misses at lunch. A salad of buttery sea scallops served with avocado chunks, broccoli

94

florets, and corn, all swathed in sesame dressing, was marred by a granitic underripe avocado; mozzarella with marinated eggplant was drowned in oil; and acorn squash-leek soup was woefully underseasoned. A better choice at dinner was the shrimp in a light cream sauce dusted with parchmentlike flakes of fried celery.

Some of the simplest dishes are the best bets: medallions of beef under a semisweet caramelized onion purée were delicious. So was the grilled swordfish steak with a pat of tarragon butter. A plump hamburger, cooked rare to order and served with sautéed onions and first-rate french fries, was prepared with obvious care.

Desserts sampled were uniformly good: creamy mango-and-macadamia-nut parfait, fluffy chocolate mousse with candied ginger, an airy eggwhite mousseline resting in a pond of English cream and cranberry sauce (unfortunately the almond slivers on top were stale), moist and chunky chestnut cake, and fruit sorbets.

Service, like the food, rises and falls with the tide of customers. If possible, try the café before or after the lunch crunch, or in the evening.

CAFE GRECO

★ ★

1390 Second Avenue, between 71st and 72nd streets, 737-4300.

Atmosphere: Cool, clean, and informal, with high ceilings, tall windows, and lots of natural wood.

Service: Friendly and competent.

Price range: Moderately expensive.

Credit cards: All major cards.

Hours: Brunch, noon to 4 P.M., Saturday and Sunday; dinner, 6 to 11 P.M., daily.

Reservations: Suggested.

Wheelchair accessibility: Dining facilities in front room; restrooms downstairs.

🍴 Cafe Greco serves a sunny mélange of cuisines under an umbrella called Mediterranean, including dishes from Sicily, the Greek Islands, southern France, and Morocco. The restaurant is a cool and casual spot, with a pretty little bar and café up front that spills out onto Second Avenue; the interior is subdued and restrained by today's aggressive design standards—ocher walls, high ceilings, brass and wood, and tall arching windows that look out on a lighted backyard garden.

The menu is intelligently balanced and wisely limited in size. You can warm up with the sprightly giveaway ratatouille and assortment of intriguing breads, perhaps along with a glass of lovely peach-flavored sparkling wine, a house special. Carpaccio of salmon is a pristine winner, glossed with good olive oil and fresh basil, as is the herb-perfumed little tart holding layers of eggplant, tomato, and zucchini. From Greece comes the excellent phyllo pastry stuffed with spinach and cheese, called spanakopita. The North African contribution, skewered chunks of chicken in tahina—a purée of sesame seeds—is a palate teaser.

An Italian-inspired soup is splendid, combining a clear, richly flavored beef stock with orzo, Swiss chard, and fava beans. A pasta special one day, cappellini with mussels in a fresh tomato and basil sauce, was delicious but marred by grit.

The multinational wine list carries some interesting selections, many under $25. Among whites, the dry and fresh Torres Viña Sol from Spain and the lush Jermann Chardonnay from Italy are recommended; good inexpensive reds include the ripe Sanford Pinot Noir from California and the dry 1982 Sassella from Lombardy in Italy.

Grilled salmon bolstered with a zesty sauce of roasted red peppers, black olives, and fresh tarragon is a dish I would row across the Mediterranean for. The salmon is exquisitely charred outside, ruddy within, and was presented over braised endive with spinach on the side. Two other fish dishes excel: charred halibut steak with a beautifully balanced basil beurre blanc sauce, and expertly sautéed swordfish with a rosemary-scented mayonnaise and buttery baby zucchini.

On the meat side of the menu, you can't go wrong with the rosy medallions of lamb with a light but intense stock sauce, marinated white beans, and Swiss chard, or the simple roasted veal chop with sage leaves and roasted cloves of garlic. Roasted chicken with couscous and grilled leeks is a soothing combination, along with some roasted whole shallots for good measure. The second time I tried it, though, the leg had to be sent back to the oven for further cooking. Grilled rib steak with deep-fried shallots is satisfying but pales next to some other entrées. Finally there is the crisp roasted squab, mild and juicy, in a vermouth-edged stock sauce. The accompanying fried polenta is absolutely addictive.

If all this sun and fun on the Mediterranean coast puts you in the mood for serious desserts, go with the thick and custardy raspberry napoleon, superbly rich chocolate-and-hazelnut sabra cake, anisette-spiked cheesecake, or an assortment of regional pastries. Gelati taste like conventional ice cream.

CAFE LUXEMBOURG

★　★

200 West 70th Street, 873-7411.

Atmosphere: Stylish and lively Art Deco look; can be loud.

Service: Upbeat and energetic.

Price range: Moderately expensive.

Credit cards: American Express, MasterCard, and Visa.

Hours: Brunch, 11 A.M. to 2:30 P.M., Sunday; dinner, 5:30 P.M. to 12:30 A.M., Monday through Thursday, 5:30 P.M. to 1:30 A.M., Friday and Saturday, 6 P.M. to 12:30 A.M., Sunday.

Reservations: Necessary.

Wheelchair accessibility: Small step at entrance; all facilities on one level.

The Lincoln Center area still suffers from a relatively lackluster cast of restaurants, considering the demand for quality dining before and after performances. Several promising places have opened in the neighborhood over the last year, but none so far rivals five-year-old Cafe Luxembourg for its consistently appealing fare and kinetic ambiance.

The Art Deco room has a timeless and indigenous appeal, with its cream-colored tile walls, black and white terrazzo floor, period sconces, and café tables. Patrons cluster at the long zinc-topped bar in the early evening. The dining room, a tightly arranged maze of red banquettes and rattan-style chairs, can be as loud as front row center at the Metropolitan Opera when conversation bounces off the tiles and mirrors. Then, about 9 P.M., a romantic on the staff dims the lights, and suddenly the room becomes soft and seductive.

The seasonal menu—a little French brasserie style, a little contemporary American—is cleverly orchestrated to offer everything from simple salads and steaks to more refined creations, such as a crisply sautéed mahi-mahi in a light, faintly sweet Sauternes sauce offset by piquant strands of ginger. A worthwhile bargain is the daily pre-theater dinner prix fixe at $29, served from 5:30 to 6:30 P.M. Based on my experiences, the young, upbeat staff here is good about getting you out to catch a performance. The scene can become frenzied later in the evening, but in the best brasserie tradition, waiters and waitresses take it all in stride.

Two enticing summer starters are the salad made with chicory, cubes of bacon, garlic croutons, and Roquefort cheese, all in a peppy mustard vinaigrette, and the lemony salad of marinated red snapper brightened with cilantro. The crab cakes have been winners here for years: meaty, golden brown, just peppery enough to enhance the sweet crabmeat, and paired with a rouille, a red-pepper hot sauce.

Aside from the mahi-mahi entrée, another recommended choice is the grilled red snapper in a light champagne vinaigrette. Grilled vegetables served on the side, however, were nearly raw. A pasta special made with shrimp, red and green peppers, and fistfuls of coriander had plenty of flavor, but unfortunately the pasta was gummy.

The most reliable options are the well-aged strip steak, cooked precisely to order, with either sautéed red potatoes or good french fries; thick, tender veal chop with red-pepper-and-tarragon sauce; and delicious calf's liver in a mustard sauce speckled with pink peppercorns and fried leeks. Grilled loin of lamb could not be more flavorful or juicy, with thyme-scented pan juices and a terrific garlic flan; roast veal was equally well done, except for the leathery reheated spatzle on the side. The wine list carries a small but quality selection at fair prices.

Desserts are generally on the light side—to help keep you awake during *La Traviata*—and uplifting. The lemon tart is worth seeking out, as is the formula-perfect crème brûlée.

CAFÉ PIERRE

★

Fifth Avenue at 61st Street, 940-8185, 838-8000.

Atmosphere: Plush, warm, and elegant room. Low noise level.

Service: Professional and attentive, but the kitchen seems laggardly at times.

Price range: Expensive.

Credit cards: All major cards.

Hours: Breakfast, 7 to 11 A.M., daily; lunch, noon to 2:30 P.M., daily; dinner, 6 to 10:30 P.M., daily; supper, 10:30 to 11:30 P.M., daily.

Reservations: Suggested.

Wheelchair accessibility: Several steps down at main entrance; stairless side door can be used on request; restrooms on same floor.

&. Café Pierre is a sanctuary of privilege in the Pierre Hotel, where the ladies appear to have emerged from *Town & Country* magazine and the men wear year-round tans and European suits. For years the café was known as a glorified tearoom, a polite and familiar place to take Aunt Sofie for dinner when she visited from Boston. But as other hotels began to upgrade their restaurants in recent years, the Pierre followed suit.

The old menu has been retired and replaced by one carrying many food fashions of the day, from duck ravioli to lemon mousse. The old-world dining room also got a facelift. But it is still soft and opulent, all done in soothing gray and white, with cloud murals overhead and swags of fabric draping ornate mirrors. Tables are tightly arranged but the noise level is well muted. A cozy piano-bar lounge up front attracts a late-night Cognac-sipping crowd.

The veteran service staff, looking so distinguished and worldly in black tie, is attentive and sophisticated, but the pace of the meal is unaccountably slow—delays seem to originate in the kitchen.

Among the stylish appetizers is a bright, light terrine of scallops, salmon, and spinach with a tart watercress sauce; sautéed fresh foie gras paired with artichoke slivers and a delicate sherry-vinegar glaze, and sautéed shrimp freckled with black pepper in an Oriental-style sweet-and-hot sauce.

Not everything works so well. A potato crêpe filled with smoked salmon and caviar was dusty dry, while the cold foie gras terrine was undercooked in the center.

Entrées are similar at lunch and dinner, supplemented by five daily specials. Simple dishes are the best: grilled fillet of veal in a rich stock sauce flanked by an asparagus flan, a special; tender, thick medallions of veal in the same sauce enlivened with chives; juicy saddle of lamb with braised endive, and noisettes of beef in red-wine sauce with basil.

99

One outstanding offering is a perfectly steamed fillet of sea bass set over a bed of fennel and tomatoes. Baked black bass with baby artichokes, by contrast, was well cooked but lacked seasoning. Duck breast is tender and appealing in a mildly sweet sauce laced with orange confit. The sweet-potato fries with it, however, were limp.

Desserts are uniformly superior, among them pears Hélène under a glazed crème anglaise sauce ringed with warm chocolate; ethereal Amaretto layer cake; buttery apple tart with whipped cream; terrific lemon mousse with raspberry sauce; and potent chocolate terrine. If you really want to splurge, try the profiteroles oozing with mint ice cream, all slathered in chocolate sauce.

Café Pierre has made great strides. This is not the kind of innovative food you rhapsodize about at the office in the morning. It is simply reliable and pleasing, served in the type of refined setting that is nearly extinct today. Aunt Sofie would still be pleased.

CAFÉ UN DEUX TROIS

★

123 West 44th Street, 354-4148.

Atmosphere: Big, bustling brasserie with colorful tongue-in-cheek décor.

Service: Articulate and energetic.

Price range: Moderate.

Credit cards: American Express, MasterCard, and Visa.

Hours: Brunch, 10:30 A.M. to 4 P.M., Saturday, 11 A.M. to 4 P.M., Sunday; lunch, noon to 4 P.M., Monday through Friday; dinner, 4:30 P.M. to midnight, Monday through Friday, 5 P.M. to midnight, Saturday, 5 to 11 P.M., Sunday.

Reservations: Accepted only for parties of five or more.

Wheelchair accessibility: Four steps up at entrance; restrooms down flight of stairs.

🦞 For its reliably animated atmosphere and straightforward bistro fare, Café Un Deux Trois continues to be one of the better bets for Broadway theater-district dining. This cavern of a restaurant can be loud—very loud indeed—at peak hours before and after theater, as the din amplifies off the bare walls and tile floor. This is not the sort of place to hammer out final details on the big new account, but it's a great spot to argue about a play or movie you have just seen —and you can even illustrate your points on the paper tablecloths with crayons set out in a glass.

The vast open dining room is a visual pun of sorts, with its faux marble columns, mustard-colored walls painted to look as if they are peeling, sky murals wrapped in trompel'oeil frames, deliberately chipped moldings, and playful mismatched colors. Waiters and waitresses are extremely well poised and diction-conscious—they even sing "Happy Birthday" in five-part harmony. The service is snappy and efficient under relentlessly fervid conditions.

The short regular menu is supplemented by many daily specials. The most reliable appetizers are the creamy and well-seasoned duck liver mousse that goes well with French bread, and a good grilled boudin blanc (a special)—chicken-and-veal sausage served with sautéed onions and apples. The house pork-based terrine is satisfying if not exceptional, although I didn't appreciate getting a discolored end slice one Sunday evening. At lunch recently the gazpacho was lively and refreshing, garnished with chopped onions and green peppers; so, too, was a special, ricotta-filled ravioli afloat in a summery light tomato-and-herb sauce.

A gutsy grilled steak with french fries is de rigueur at a rollicking brasserie like this—the steak is well cooked and pleasing, but the french fries are woefully limp. The same steak with a green-peppercorn sauce is too timid for my taste, but might be suitable for those who shun hot foods.

Goujonettes of chicken (breaded and deep-fried strips of white meat) are addictively tasty—that is, if you keep them a safe distance from the cloying sweet-hot dipping sauce.

On the entrée list, one old reliable is the simple breaded chicken breast with a mild mustard sauce and julienne of buttery carrots and zucchini. Along with a mixed salad, it makes a satisfying late supper. Steak tartare is competently prepared—studded with saline capers—but paired with the same soggy french fries.

Café Un Deux Trois has the least success with seafood. A special of shrimp in a green-peppercorn cream sauce was bland, while another—sole cooked in a foil pouch with parsley, tomato, zucchini, carrots, and summer squash—was soupy and overcooked.

Desserts are rather predictable. Among the best are crème caramel laced with orange zest, poached pears with chocolate sauce and whipped cream, and a ripe strawberry charlotte. Profiteroles are deflated and taste thawed-out, and chocolate mousse is a faint echo of the real thing.

Café Un Deux Trois is not a place for a gastronomic extravaganza. It is, though, a good spot to savor Broadway nightlife, and a place that, for a relatively moderate price, can turn an evening at the theater into a night on the town.

CAMEOS

★

169 Columbus Avenue, between 67th and 68th streets, 874-2280.

Atmosphere: Pastel and Art Deco second-story dining room with a lively piano bar.

Service: Somewhat lax and confused.

Price range: Moderately expensive.

Credit cards: American Express, MasterCard, Transmedia, and Visa.

Hours: Brunch, noon to 2:30 P.M., Saturday, 11:30 A.M. to 3 P.M., Sunday; lunch, noon to 3 P.M., Monday through Friday; dinner, 5:30 to 11:30 P.M., Monday through Saturday, 5:30 to 10 P.M., Sunday.

Reservations: Necessary at dinner.

Wheelchair accessibility: Long flight of stairs to entrance.

🐾 You climb a long, narrow stairway to this second-floor establishment, then enter a cheerful bar flanked by a white grand piano where a well-groomed fellow plays show tunes. The dining room is long and compact, brightened with sprays of flowers and Art Deco touches. The tight dimensions of the room combined with all the hard surfaces amplify conversation to a distracting level; overlay some Cole Porter tunes, and you wind up conversing nose to nose with your dining partner.

The eclectic menu—a little Italian, a little French, a little American—is characterized by clean, clear flavors, and the chef has fun with his eye-catching presentation. Premium ingredients are used, although occasional underseasoning fails to do them justice.

Top vote getter among appetizers is the superlative fillet of bass in a carapace of golden puff pastry sprinkled with poppy seeds and set over a good sharp beurre blanc. Another winner is the pepper-coated fillet of beef, three thin, ruddy slices enlivened with a caper-mustard sauce. Grilled skewered vegetables escort a pair of sweet freshwater

102

prawns, and a minced salmon and scallop seviche is fresh and nicely presented, although it needed more of its lime-and-sesame dressing. And a warm salad of Brie and goat cheese with tart greens was abused by bitter, overvinegared dressing.

There is something oddly spacy about the service staff. Waiters and waitresses sometimes seem to be floating around the room at random as if they were at a cocktail party; there seems to be little communication among them about who is doing what. Several times a waiter came to our table to take a wine or dessert order, then headed back to the kitchen only to have a colleague come by a minute later and ask the same questions.

Among the entrées, neither of the two pastas sampled was memorable. Primavera sauce one evening tasted like something you would get at a militant health-food restaurant that eschews seasonings; fettuccine weighed down with ungainly boulders of lamb and duck sausage is a near miss—the sausage alone is delicious, but the rest is insipid. A better option is the deftly grilled tuna steak slathered with onions and in a peppery sauce. Swordfish is admirably done, too, in a chive beurre blanc sauce vibrant with lemon; at lunch, it comes in a subtly sweet ginger-and-orange sauce bound with sesame oil. Chicken breast in a balsamic-vinegar sauce with minced herbs is a lively and light lunch entrée, too, ringed with baby vegetables. On the debit side, fresh, firm red snapper cooked in parchment has little flavor other than a few sprigs of thyme.

The chef's grilled Black Angus rib-eye steak is terrific, brushed with a little maple syrup blended with orange rind and soy sauce—the sweet blackened crust imparts an irresistible extra dimension to the lusty beef. Veal chop is excellent, too, sweetened with roasted shallots and perfumed with fresh rosemary; whole medallions of venison are tender and engaging in a sharp green-peppercorn-and-shallot sauce.

Desserts are not up to par here. Soupy vanilla mousse with a core of rum chocolate is achingly sweet, as is the dense chocolate torte. Pecan pie with chocolate sauce is the best of the lot, but lemon tart in a nutty crust had an unpleasant charcoal aftertaste, probably from burned nuts. You might just opt for a glass of dessert wine, lean back, and savor the nostalgic Porter tunes at the piano bar.

THE CAPTAIN'S TABLE

Satisfactory

860 Second Avenue, at 46th Street, 697-9538.

Atmosphere: Kitsch-galore dining room.

Service: Amiable and competent.

Price range: Expensive.

Credit cards: American Express, MasterCard, and Visa.

Hours: Lunch, noon to 3 P.M., Monday through Friday; dinner, 5:30 to 11 P.M., Monday through Friday, 5 P.M. to midnight, Saturday.

Reservations: Suggested.

Wheelchair accessibility: Dining room on ground floor; restrooms two steps down.

❧ I was alarmed to see what has happened to this ten-year-old restaurant, once considered among the better fish houses in town. Not only is its expensive food run-of-the-mill, but also a recent expansion and redecoration have left it appallingly tacky.

The dining rooms feature gaudy hanging lights in the form of grape clusters, multicolored chandeliers, flower-patterned synthetic tablecloths (soiled to boot), ceramic birds dangling overhead, little plaster animals on wall shelves and, in the back, a giant green ceramic peacock.

As you inspect the menu and nibble on the dry, stale bread, a waiter comes by with a large tray holding specimens of the day's seafood selection. He runs through the list, patting his wares like a used-car salesman to emphasize quality. (This unsanitary practice notwithstanding, most waiters and waitresses we met were amiable and attentive.) The seafood at The Captain's Table cannot be faulted for freshness; the kitchen, however, often manages to diminish its appeal by overcooking and underseasoning.

The best appetizers are fresh and saline cherrystones and oysters on the half shell presented over ice. The baked clams, though, are overbreaded. A special one evening, small lobster tails from Australia, was tasty and fresh tasting; jumbo tiger shrimp, on the other hand, were cooked to rubbery stiffness. The kitchen makes a first-class clam chowder, light and generously seasoned. If fresh shiitake mushrooms are available, get them sautéed with garlic.

The large seafood selection is prepared either broiled or sautéed, usually accompanied by unseasoned vegetables on the side. Broiled whole grouper and red snapper were fresh and served with sautéed fennel; fresh lemon was all they needed. Both tuna steak and swordfish were dry, the latter coming with a good garlic sauce. The remaining broiled or sautéed fish had a 50 percent success rate at best.

Red snapper fillet cooked "en papillote" (in aluminum foil, actually) was a sorry sight; its accompanying shrimp were stiff and tasteless, the scallops and mussels just salvageable, all in a light tomato broth. Those who have never tried blowfish might sample it here—the firm, fibrous fillet is slightly browned outside and served with a tasty garlic butter. Sautéed soft-shell crabs are recommended while the season lasts. The wine list is remarkable only for its overpricing. The few desserts are nearly a total loss save for the ice cream and crunchy, semisweet pecan pie.

The Captain's Table, which earned two stars in May 1984, has clearly seen better days. At these prices, it should offer a smoother sail.

CAROLINA

★

355 West 46th Street, 245-0058.

Atmosphere: Pretty main dining room with skylight and mirrors. Low noise level.

Service: Pleasant and informative.

Price range: Moderately expensive.

Credit cards: American Express, MasterCard, and Visa.

Hours: Lunch, noon to 3 P.M., Monday through Friday; dinner, 5:30 to 11:30 P.M., Monday through Sunday; closed Sunday in summer.

Reservations: Suggested.

Wheelchair accessibility: Two small steps at entrance; main dining room and restrooms on same level.

The campfires have dimmed at Carolina, once the hottest restaurant along the West 46th Street Restaurant Row. You can still get an occasional decent grilled fish or soothing regional soup, such as corn chowder, but much of the food has become tired and dull.

The main dining room is still one of the more accommodating on the block, with its arching skylight, gray banquettes, and the wraparound glass walls that multiply the sole palm tree in the middle of the room into an urban grove. The effect is even more enchanting at night. A front room near the bar is lively at lunch, too dark at dinner; an upstairs addition is the least appealing of the three. All three are relatively quiet.

While nibbling on the corn bread—it doesn't seem to taste as good as it used to—consider starting with a bowl of chili. Fresh-tasting, beefy, and stoked with lots of hot peppers, it is one of the few boldly seasoned dishes left. Sweet-tinged corn chowder, made with a milk base and firm kernels of corn, isn't bad either. Both of these are recommended over the dry, sinewy barbecue on lettuce or the smoked salmon with "home-baked" dill bread. At lunch, the bread arrived chilled and soggy-bottomed as if recently thawed. The young waiters at Carolina are sincere and well informed. The wine list is unyieldingly patriotic, offering an adequate and fairly priced selection of American labels.

On the entrée card, one of my favorites from the early days, crab cakes, is as good as ever—two hefty disks generous with crab, slightly peppery, and skillfully deep fried. I wish other seafood entrées were as distinctive. Grilled swordfish steak and grilled salmon are well cooked but lack wood-grilled nuances, skewered shrimp tend to be overcooked and unseasoned.

The restaurant specializes in hot-smoking meats, a technique that involves low-heat cooking with aromatic wood. The meat that profits most from this is the brisket of beef, which can be moist and exceptionally flavorful.

Light and puffy corn pudding and homemade coleslaw were worthwhile side dishes. Another special entrée that satisfied was called Texas tenderloin, marinated strips of grilled steak swathed with sweet onions and served with mashed potatoes.

Most desserts at Carolina are heavy-hitting winners, from the citric lime pie to dense chocolate mud cake and crunchy pecan rolls dipped in chocolate. While the restaurant has slipped a notch from its earlier two-star level, it still has a certain appeal as a theater-district dining option. I just wish Carolina would return to its roots and get back to basics.

CAVALIERE

★

108 West 73rd Street, 799-8282.

Atmosphere: Three dining areas: one in the casual and friendly bar, another more formal, a third in a sunny back room under a skylight.

Service: Generally professional and prompt.

Price range: Moderately expensive.

Credit cards: All major cards.

Hours: Brunch, noon to 4 P.M., Saturday and Sunday; lunch, noon to 4 P.M., Monday through Friday; dinner, 5 P.M. to midnight, Sunday through Thursday, until midnight, Friday and Saturday.

Reservations: Advised.

Wheelchair accessibility: Two steps down into restaurant; main dining room and restrooms on ground floor.

When Cavaliere opened in 1984, it was a neighborly sort of Upper West Side Italian restaurant that was content to serve its steadfast local patrons. Two years later it decided to emerge from the shadows by hiring a big-name consulting chef, Anne Rosenzweig of Arcadia and the "21" Club, to jazz up the menu, and advertisements appeared touting its new image.

The results have been mixed. While the new menu makes for mouth-watering reading, it is far too large and too complicated for the full-time staff to execute smoothly—sort of like putting a couple of teenagers in the cockpit of a 747.

A trim, casual barroom near the entrance holds about ten tables; the main dining room is a dressier affair: mauve-toned walls, chrome sconces, a marble fireplace, and lavish flower arrangements. A breezy skylighted room is in the back.

A good way to start is with a haystack of cleanly fried shoestrings of zucchini sprinkled with sesame seeds and lemon, or with the bright squid-and-potato salad flecked with fresh mint. Mussels steamed with leeks, tomatoes, white wine, and cream also are savory, although a bit gritty. Buckwheat and taleggio fritters over mixed greens is an intriguing concept—however, the little golden-brown torpedoes were doughy and bland; a better choice is the fresh mozzarella flavored with roasted red peppers and olive paste. Premade Caesar salad is watery and tasteless.

A spiffy-looking crew of black-tie captains scurry back and forth keeping waiters on their toes. The captains are well versed in the predominantly Italian wine list, which offers bottles from top producers at fair prices.

If the pastas, which can be split as appetizers, were as good as they sound, Cavaliere would be an Upper West Side landmark. I can recommend only half: the fusilli with pesto and toasty pine nuts, buckwheat pasta with sweet Gorgonzola sauce punctuated with walnuts, and fusilli in a peppery tomato sauce with lots of garlic, basil, calamari, and swordfish. Those that missed the mark included linguine with an anemic garlic-and-anchovy sauce, ribbon pasta in a red-pepper sauce laced with raw garlic, and fettuccine combined with well-cooked salmon and red peppers that lacked last-minute seasonings to pull them together.

Sixteen main courses, not counting the pastas, are supplemented by three or more daily specials. The first order of business for the kitchen should be chopping that list in half. Among those I would retain are the succulent pan-blackened marinated duck breast with wild mushrooms and corn pancakes, golden-sautéed halibut steak—it was not pan-blackened as advertised, but it was probably better this way—paired with a faintly hot Pommery mustard sauce, and chicken calzone, a pocket of pepper-dusted chicken breast pumped up with ricotta cheese, prosciutto, and fresh herbs. Simple grilled veal chop in a viscous red-wine sauce accompanied by sweet roasted shallots and pancetta is satisfying, as is rack of lamb with a spirited tomato-and-zucchini casserole.

For dessert, skip the rich but tasteless tiramisù and go for either the complex Amaretto torte layered with coffee-flavored whipped cream or a lemon tart—and I mean tart—that will have you whistling all the way out the door.

Cavaliere's overstriving menu underscores the potential hazards of advising chefs. If I were giving the advice, it would be: simplify, simplify.

CELLAR IN THE SKY

★ ★

1 World Trade Center, 107th floor, 938-1111.

Atmosphere: Tranquil wine cellar ambiance with classical guitarist.

Service: Attentive and efficient.

Price range: Expensive (dinner prix fixe $77, including wine).

Credit cards: All major cards.

Hours: Dinner, Monday through Saturday, one seating at 7:30 P.M.

Reservations: Required.

Wheelchair accessibility: Restrooms on entrance level; several steps up into dining room.

🐚 Cellar in the Sky is the small, wine-oriented restaurant in the larger complex known as Windows on the World. Cellar seats only 36, and offers a leisurely preset five-course meal built around an aperitif and four wines for $77. If you don't mind surrendering personal choice to fate, Cellar in the Sky can be one of the more enchanting and delectable experiences in town.

The dimly lit, romantic dining room has a cavelike motif sporting wine racks along glass walls. It does not offer the celestial views of the main restaurant, although what you gain in the trade-off is more varied and refined food that is artfully presented and paired with intelligently selected quality wines. A classical guitarist plays nightly. The $77 prix fixe might sound stiff, but considering that no supplements are levied and wine is included, it is really no more expensive than many other first-class establishments in New York City.

The menu changes about twice a month. Typical dinners might begin with such finger foods as silken foie gras mousse on toast, bite-size vegetable tartelets, caviar on buttered brown bread, and buttery smoked sea scallops set over a tangle of julienned leeks. The wines for starters: a zesty Trimbach Riesling on one occasion, a bright and dry Wente Chardonnay another time.

Subsequent courses are gracefully orchestrated to embrace a range of flavors and textures. It might be a terrine of fresh foie gras (not as flavorful as it could be) served with brioche and assorted greens, or a superb dish of fresh and mild calf's liver set over wilted sweet onions with veal stock. The summertime soups are always light and delicate—I preferred the sweet oyster bisque redolent of oyster brine to the cream of sole with chives.

The service staff is attentive and accommodating. Waiters make certain your wine well never goes dry.

Both fish courses excelled: a perfectly cooked, meaty fresh turbot brightened with the lightest of cream sauces, one

109

colored with parsley, the other with carrots. Lobster out of the shell in a truffle beurre blanc was as prettily arranged as it was delicious, surrounded by spokes of asparagus and flecked with black truffles. A luscious Pommard from one of the region's premier vineyards, Rugiens, set the stage for tender squab in a Pinot Noir–based sauce flanked by red and white cabbage; rare roasted strips of duck breast were surrounded by lively fettuccine flecked with fresh sage and nubbins of crisped duck skin.

A small but well-chosen cheese course follows with an appropriate wine. Desserts are satisfying though not memorable—lime tartelet paired with lemon mousse and pale lime sherbet one day, and somewhat dense profiteroles encasing coconut ice cream surrounded by fresh berries another time.

Cellar in the Sky is a celebratory sort of place where decisions are few and the wine flows freely from a regal fountain. For any lofty occasion, it is well worth the ascent.

CENT'ANNI

★

50 Carmine Street, between Avenue of the Americas and Seventh Avenue South, 989-9494.

Atmosphere: Small, minimally adorned dining room with a friendly Greenwich Village ambiance.

Service: Veteran waiters are informed and genial, but not terribly attentive.

Price range: Moderate.

Credit cards: American Express.

Hours: Lunch, noon to 2:30 P.M., Monday through Friday; dinner, 5:30 to 11:15 P.M., Monday through Saturday, 5 to 10:45 P.M., Sunday.

Reservations: Recommended.

Wheelchair accessibility: All facilities on one level.

𝝰 Cent'Anni is a small, clamorous, Florentine-style restaurant in Greenwich Village that has a doggedly loyal following. The kitchen can turn out some lovely dishes when it is in peak form, but often that is not the case.

The ambiance is diverting in a threadbare Greenwich Village sort of way—crowded, bustling, and friendly. White-frocked waiters are enthusiastic and well informed, but not much when it comes to the fine points of service, such as pouring wine and tidying up tables. Even the most diligent of them get lost reciting the unnecessarily long list of specials.

The best starter is still the cold seafood salad, a sparkling assortment of shrimp, lobster, scallops, and squid bathed in a mild olive-oil dressing. There are four pastas on the printed menu and several daily specials, all of which can be split as appetizers. Shells all'amatriciana were on the mark in their fresh tomato sauce bolstered with onions, prosciutto, and olive oil. So was the capellini con aragosta, thread pasta in tomato sauce with chunks of well-cooked lobster and fresh clams. Two disappointments were the rigatoni alla Medici—tube pasta in a buttery but characterless sauce combining chicken, onions, carrots, and cream —and the pappardelle in rabbit sauce, which could have been pork for all the game flavor it had.

One problem with the number of specials is that the kitchen appears overtaxed. Some dishes do not get the attention they deserve. For example, the shellfish special that includes fresh lobster, scallops, and squid can be ruined by sandy and off-tasting mussels and clams. Overcooked roast loin of pork has the texture of a softball, and tripe alla Fiorentina is rubbery from undercooking. Osso buco is restorative and delicious here—the veal shanks are fork-tender and infused with vegetable and herb flavors from long braising. The double-thick veal chop, which is first broiled to impart a nice crust, then sautéed with wine and fresh sage, also is a delight.

Among the notable seafood dishes are the exceptionally fresh broiled whole red snapper basted with garlic and olive oil, and two specials, sea bass fillet in a briny and well-seasoned fish stock, and grilled jumbo Mediterranean shrimp in a sweet-tinged, Cognac-spiked red sauce.

Fruit and cheese are the most suitable desserts. If you're in the mood for something sweet, both the pear tart and the tartufo, chocolate ice cream in a dense chocolate skin, are preferable to the grainy zabaglione. The lavish-looking chocolate mousse cake crowned with chocolate curls is an empty tease.

CHANTERELLE

★ ★ ★ ★

6 Harrison Street, corner of Hudson Street, 966-6960.

Atmosphere: Airy peach-toned room, somewhat austere; well-spaced tables make casual conversation possible.

Service: Excellent and low-key.

Price range: Expensive. (Dinner prix fixe, $65; tasting menu, $85).

Credit cards: All major cards.

Hours: Dinner, 6:30 to 10:30 P.M., Tuesday through Saturday.

Reservations: Necessary, usually several weeks in advance.

Wheelchair accessibility: All facilities on one level.

🦃 Chanterelle is the labor of love of David and Karen Waltuck—he is in the kitchen, she runs the show out front—and it has become one of the most coveted reservations in town.

In the fall of 1988, the restaurant moved from its ten-table SoHo location to slightly more spacious quarters in a landmark TriBeCa building.

Mr. Waltuck's cooking style is difficult to label for it is at once firmly tethered to classic French techniques yet contemporary, inventive, and unfailingly personal—and always conceived with flavor rather than flair in mind.

What you encounter for the $65 prix-fixe dinner ($85 for a more elaborate tasting menu) is a limited but well-balanced selection that changes every two weeks, with only a few dishes appearing regularly. Among them is a plump seafood sausage filled with lobster, shrimp, and scallops, flecked with pine nuts, and set over a pool of luxurious beurre blanc sauce. Two lighter enticements are the cold salad of sweet Louisiana shrimp framed by a vibrant red-pepper purée and cubes of good shellfish aspic, and briefly sautéed shrimp mingled with chunks of refreshing tart bitter melon, a cucumber-shaped vegetable usually found in Chinese soups and stews.

Right alongside these au courant preparations you find such rustic standards as a chicory salad tossed with confit of duck hearts and gizzards, crowned with white truffles and moistened in a warm vinaigrette sauce, and a lustily seasoned country terrine holding a core of foie gras. Soups are outstanding: for example, a fennel-perfumed oyster soup bolstered with bacon bits, and a thick, hammy lentil soup that was so rich with black truffles it should be subject to a federal luxury tax.

From the moment you arrive, the coolly efficient staff tends to every need. A young bespectacled maître d'hôtel who looks as if he could be a prep-school admissions officer comes to your aid if you appear perplexed with the wine list. But don't expect any bargains in this deep but dearly priced document that is top heavy with prestigious high-ticket bottles.

Although there are only six entrées nightly, choosing can be harrowing. Most of the game dishes excel, and you can't go wrong with the succulent little roasted squabs, their pinkish meat faintly gamy, enhanced with an intensely reduced stock sauce along with wild rice and sautéed wild mushrooms; venison steak, also in a bracing stock sauce cut with the meat's marinade and stoked with cracked black peppercorns, was extraordinarily tender and mild-flavored. Those in the mood for something straightforward will be delighted with the fillet of beef in a marrow-enriched red-wine sauce or the picture-perfect rosemary-scented rack of lamb.

An off-menu special one evening, guinea hen braised with leeks, celery, and fennel, explosively aromatic of minced black truffles, was stunning to behold under its lid of puff pastry; while the flavor was superbly complex, the meat was a bit dry from overcooking.

Mr. Waltuck clearly has a passion for seafood for he prepares it with affection and restraint. Salmon steak is sautéed to golden brittleness outside and pale pink within, accompanied by a vernal green sauce sharpened with capers and anchovies; swordfish, too, was memorable in its sheer cream sauce slightly sweetened with beet juice, flanked by sautéed beet greens. And perhaps the most regal liaison of all is perfectly cooked disks of lobster meat sandwiching slices of black truffles, all moistened with lustrous truffle butter.

Portions are just right here so one can approach either the exceptional cheese course or desserts with zeal. A creation dubbed fallen chocolate soufflé will topple the strongest wills, its dry-edged sweetness softened by whipped cream. Another captivating house special is blood oranges under crackling puff pastry resting in a pool of caramelized orange sauce. All the sorbets, especially cassis, were ripe and smooth, and homemade ice creams sampled—ginger, chocolate, coconut, and a blend of prune and Armagnac—are wonderfully potent and velvety.

CHELSEA CENTRAL

★ ★

227 Tenth Avenue, between 23rd and 24th streets, 620-0230.

Atmosphere: Handsome turn-of-the-century tavern.

Service: Amiable and competent.

Price range: Moderate.

Credit cards: American Express and Visa.

Hours: Brunch, 11:30 A.M. to 3 P.M., Sunday; lunch, 11:30 A.M to 3 P.M., Monday through Friday; dinner, 6 to 11 P.M., Sunday to Thursday, 6 P.M. to midnight, Friday and Saturday.

Reservations: Necessary.

Wheelchair accessibility: Two steps up at entrance; all facilities on one level.

&❧ The industrial underbrush of far-west Chelsea, dotted with squat brick warehouses and auto repair shops, is one of the last places you would expect to find dining adventures. That is precisely why Larry McIntyre, an Upper West Side restaurateur, decided to open Chelsea Central there. After a shaky start and a change of chefs, it has become a delightful American-style café.

Mr. McIntyre preserved the turn-of-the-century-tavern feeling of this vintage tavern, with its long mahogany bar, stamped tin ceiling, burnished wainscotting, overhead fans, and tile floor. Café-style tables were loosely arranged in the neighborly back room, where tulip-shaped brass sconces cast comforting light.

The eclectic mix of grilled entrées along with pastas and seafood is intelligently assembled so there is something to fit every taste. Simple preparations are lovingly prepared, from superbly moist wood-grilled chicken sprinkled with cracked pepper to a special of tricolored fettuccine in a zesty, light cream sauce bolstered with smoked salmon, capers, and dill. The wood grill that was installed during renovation is put to good use with the perfectly grilled salmon steak accompanied by al dente spinach pasta in a summery mustard-dill sauce. Another winner is the deliciously seared swordfish with a simple white butter sauce garnished with sweet peppers, coriander, and plum tomatoes. Thyme-scented roast duck could not be better, seductively tender and with thin greaseless skin. Brittle shoestring potatoes are an addictive accompaniment.

Like some other establishments, Chelsea Central, despite constant grumbling by customers and restaurant writers, continues the irksome habit of reciting seemingly endless lists of daily specials. One special to look out for is pecan-coated baked chicken, a delightful combination set over shredded mixed greens along with grapes rolled in Roquefort cheese and toasted pistachios. Another winning Friday special is the heaping bouillabaisse, a deep pool of herby tomato broth with pasta overloaded with mussels, lobster, sea scallops, and swordfish. A sharp, garlic-fueled rouille, intended for blending into the bouillabaisse, comes on the side with croutons.

Chelsea Central's international wine list is impressive more for its shrewd selections and bargain prices than for its depth. The house pours are better than average, too.

Appetizers are not so uniformly appealing as the entrées. Chinese-style dumplings filled with cheese-flecked sausage can be heavy and greasy, and Louisiana shrimp with a spicy red sauce is just a fancy version of shrimp cocktail. Better choices are the grabulous fried oysters served in the shell lined with lemon-pepper mayonnaise along with shoe-string potatoes, and the warm shreds of tender duck over mixed greens with croutons and ricotta. Homemade potato chips the size of rabbit ears are a bit fragile for scooping up the zippy guacamole, but it's worth trying.

Desserts are mostly straightforward American fare. The lemon tart is high on the pucker meter, and cheesecake is unapologetically dense and rich. Chocolate sponge cake and assorted sorbets are satisfactory and no more; those seeking serious sweets might try the exceptional hazelnut tart layered with mocha cream and scattered with chocolate shavings.

CHELSEA TRATTORIA ITALIANA

★ ★

108 Eighth Avenue, between 15th and 16th streets, 924-7786.

Atmosphere: Brick and whitewashed walls, casual and friendly.

Service: Extremely eager to please; efficient.

Price range: Moderate.

Credit cards: All major cards.

Hours: Lunch, noon to 3 P.M., Monday through Friday (the kitchen remains open between lunch and dinner for light meals); dinner, 5 P.M. to midnight, Monday through Saturday.

Reservations: Suggested.

Wheelchair accessibility: Dining facilities on ground floor; restrooms downstairs.

♊ Chelsea Trattoria Italiana is a friendly and easygoing restaurant that serves some top-notch pastas at affordable prices. It is owned by the Bitici brothers (Sergio, Michael, John, and Joseph), who also run Minetta Tavern on Macdougal Street, the Grand Ticino Restaurant on Thompson Street, and Toscana on Third Avenue at 54th Street. Upon walking into this homey Chelsea establishment, your urban stress meter immediately drops to a more healthful level. The brick-and-whitewashed dining room is soothing, tidy, and calm. A cheerful crowd of neighborhood regulars clusters at the bar before dinner, and the tuxedo-clad maître d'hôtel greets you as one of the inner circle, even if it is your first visit.

The menu is not notable for bold innovation but rather for the chef's pure and understated approach. Ingredients are unassailably fresh, and pastas are authoritatively seasoned but not oversauced. You could start off with zesty mussels or clams in an herby tomato broth, or the rather thickly sliced but flavorful carpaccio with pesto sauce (the mixed antipasto is nothing special). Considering the felicitous choice of pastas, however, I recommend starting with half portions of those.

The chef, Charles Sulay, always prepares several daily specials. One evening they included terrific whole-wheat-flour-and-spinach ravioli, called cappelletti, filled with minced mixed vegetables in a cold fresh tomato purée; another is aromatic linguine with pesto sauce and tender young string beans. Fettuccine tossed with wild mushrooms and sun-dried tomatoes is a brassy delight, as is another special, cappellini, glossed with garlic-scented olive oil and al dente broccoli. Tortellini Bolognese misses the mark slightly from oversalting. If you yearn for something to jolt the taste buds, try the tagliolini in a light tomato-based arrabbiata sauce spiked with garlic and hot green peppers.

Risotto, too, is masterfully prepared, especially the one studded with squid, shrimp, clams, crabmeat, scallions, parsley, and just enough hot pepper to keep you on edge.

The service staff combines polite efficiency with refreshing candor. One evening I was in the mood for a steak and ordered the beef Fiorentina. Our captain lowered his notepad, shook his head, and said, "If you want a steak, get a real steak, not one with all that stuff on it." The pan-sautéed fillet that came out was superb, beefy, tender, and juicy. Veal chop with sage would have been better cooked the same way rather than broiled. The veal was top grade and tasty but came out nearly raw in the center and slightly dry outside.

Among seafood dishes, look for the occasional special of sautéed red snapper embellished with black olives, tomatoes, capers, and white wine. Sweetbreads are prepared to the customer's specifications. One of my dining companions asked for them sautéed with white wine, and they were a marvel of subtlety—firm textured, golden, and delicious. Even a lowly chicken breast sautéed with white wine, mushrooms, and sun-dried tomatoes was memorable, for the meat was perfectly cooked and the sauce well balanced.

Desserts are acceptable but nothing to swoon over. I suggest the moist and semisweet orange layer cake and the dense chocolate cake; tiramisù is rich and creamy but lacks the sharp espresso edge it should have, and ricotta cheesecake would be better without the thick, heavy crust.

CHEZ JOSEPHINE

★

414 West 42nd Street, 594-1925.

Atmosphere: Theatrical bistro-cabaret setting festooned with Josephine Baker memorabilia.

Service: Engaging young staff is reasonably efficient and earnest.

Price range: Moderate.

Credit cards: American Express, MasterCard, and Visa.

Hours: Dinner, 5 to midnight, Monday through Saturday.

Reservations: Required.

Wheelchair accessibility: Restrooms up long flight of stairs.

🐌 An exuberant bistro in the Theater Row district, Chez Josephine is the production of Jean-Claude Baker, an engaging Frenchman who runs on a megavolt Duracell. He rushes to greet arriving customers with open-armed warmth, and at the drop of a fork he will regale them with tales of the restaurant's namesake, Josephine Baker, the glamorous chanteuse who was the rage of Paris in the 1920s. Mr. Baker happens to be one of Josephine Baker's

117

celebrated "rainbow tribe," thirteen officially and unofficially adopted children.

The restaurant's delightfully racy décor leitmotif finds the sultry singer in various stages of scanty dress—on the walls, on the menu cover, even on the men's-room door. The long, narrow restaurant has an inviting 1920s feeling, with a zinc-topped bar up front, bistro tables paired with banquettes, and a turn-of-the-century grand piano that has become a magnet for musicians and singers who drift in nightly and spontaneously take turns performing.

The French-American menu is anchored by some alluring peasant dishes: first-rate boudin noir (blood sausage) with red cabbage, onions, sautéed apples, and french fries; fried chicken (called chicken Alvara) flanked by sweet-potato fries and red-pepper corn bread; and seared Black Angus steak in a pink-peppercorn sauce.

Back at the starting line, I can recommend the coarse and flavorful house pâté, the fresh braised leeks in a well-balanced tomato vinaigrette, and the Chinese-style dumplings filled with dill-accented goat cheese and pine nuts in a bright clear broth.

The comely and charming young thespians who tend tables have their hands full trying to keep up with the flamboyant Mr. Baker, who sails around the room like a jittery host at a private party.

Desserts to watch for are the embarrassingly rich chocolate ganache cake from Guy Pascal, called le délice Josephine; lustrous creamy cheesecake, and bulbous tartufo.

Chez Josephine, like its celebrated namesake, exudes irrepressible brio and eccentric charm that makes it instantly likable. Whenever my spirits are deflated, I will return for a plate of soothing boudin noir and a song.

CHEZ LOUIS

★ ★

1016 Second Avenue, between 53rd and 54th streets, 752-1400.

Atmosphere: Comfortable and simply appointed dining room decorated with French posters.

Service: Energetic and capable young staff.

Price range: Moderately expensive.

Credit cards: All major cards.

Hours: Lunch, 11:45 A.M. to 3 P.M., Monday through

Friday; dinner, 6 P.M. to midnight, Monday through Saturday, 5 to 10 P.M., Sunday.

Reservations: Recommended.

Wheelchair accessibility: Steps at entrance and to dining room; flight of stairs down to restrooms.

🍴 You enter the dining room at Chez Louis and pass a long serving station where waiters hack away at sizzling roast chickens and divvy up portions of hulking prime ribs and wildly aromatic suckling pig. A perusal of the premises, where tables fairly sag under the weight of he-man portions, reveals that this place is for serious no-holds-barred eaters. Quantity, though, is not its only distinguishing feature. Most of the food is very good.

Chez Louis, a simply appointed and comfortable bistro, is the creation of David Liederman, the cookie man, who believed strongly that New Yorkers were being overwhelmed by dainty and artsy restaurants where portions hardly sate a kitten. His kitchen specializes in roasting, and the results can be wonderful. The herb-flecked whole chicken for two is a delight in its simplicity: baby chicken, called poussin, is also ineffably moist and delicious, although the onion rings with it are greasy. The favorite at my table one evening was roast suckling pig, which emerged from the oven with brittle dark skin and luxuriant pale meat. It comes with red cabbage and a baked apple.

Among the side dishes are roasted vegetables that arrive on a blazing-hot platter—and don't expect pinky-size carrots or baby zucchini that could double as a lapel pin; these hefty grown-ups, including beets, onions, squash, and whole garlic cloves, are every bit as tasty as their infant cousins. On the other hand, potato pie, a thick and crusty disk, has nothing but bulk going for it.

Another formidable entrée is the double veal rib, a fist-thick cut of lustrously tender meat. Duck confit is generous in flavor but slightly dry, the result of rushing the cooking in excessively hot fat. The confit is better as an ingredient in the heady garlic-haunted cassoulet. Among the better seafood entrées sampled were perfectly grilled giant shrimp served under a sprinkling of black pepper and a douse of lemon. At lunch a slab of salmon steak with a mild mustard-cream sauce was flawless.

The wine list at Chez Louis is worth studying, for occasional off-year bargains turn up among Burgundies and Bordeaux; the California selection is exceptionally well chosen and sensibly priced. The restaurant fills up quickly at lunch and dinner, but the friendly and energetic staff seems to have it all under control.

The size of main courses makes it wise to go lightly on starters. Roasted wild mushrooms and whole garlic cloves are a nice rustic teaser. The combination of grilled leeks and fennel over sheets of prosciutto is superb under a sheen of white butter sauce, while all the soups sampled—black bean purée, French-style onion, and lentil—were packed with flavor.

With portions like these the desserts, thank heaven, are not terribly exciting. A lemon crème brûlée is too dense and thick, and an otherwise good fruit plate held unripe pineapple. Of course, there are plenty of David's cookies and David's ice cream to go around.

And just in case some bantamweight eaters get the bright idea to beat the system at Chez Louis by sharing portions, think again. It says right on the bottom of the menu: Minimum one entrée per person.

CHIKUBU RESTAURANT

★ ★

12 East 44th Street, 818-0715.

Atmosphere: Soft gray and natural-wood dining rooms; low noise level.

Service: Long on politeness, short on performance.

Price range: Moderate.

Credit cards: American Express and Diners Club.

Hours: Lunch, 11:30 A.M. to 2 P.M., Monday through Friday; dinner, 5:30 to 10 P.M., Monday through Saturday.

Reservations: Requested.

Wheelchair accessibility: All facilities on one level.

🍴 Chikubu is a solid and dependable midtown Japanese restaurant, a good bet for lunch or dinner. The cooks specialize in the cuisine of Kyoto, which is known for its cooked dishes. However, exceptionally fresh sashimi is available, while sushi is served only at lunch.

The narrow restaurant is trim and neat, in shades of light gray and blond wood; the noise level is generally low. The service staff is good-natured and exceedingly polite if not always terribly efficient.

It might be a good idea to bring along a Japanese dictionary. Otherwise, since much of the menu is not translated, you'll have to rely on the staff for explanations. One of the best appetizers is dengaku eggplant, a mound of tasty eggplant coated in a sweet soybean paste sprinkled with tiny sesame seeds. Another light primer is called takiawase vegetable, which often changes ingredients. It might feature little squares of acorn squash, turnips, eggplant, and potato, resting in a slightly sweet broth tinged with mirin wine.

Broiled dishes are far superior to fried ones. Shioyaki flounder is best of all—a perfectly cooked whole fish is presented on a stunning blue-and-white ceramic plate in a clear broth under a snowfall of minced Japanese radish. The fried whole flounder is stiff and dry, while both the shrimp tempura and the tatsutaage chicken are greasy.

Try instead the crusty salt-grilled shioyaki salmon or the broiled kabayaki eel. Such familiar standards as chicken teriyaki (glazed skewered chicken) and negimaki (grilled beef rolls with scallions) also make pleasant light lunch entrées. Also notable is yosenabe, an earthenware crock holding a shellfish broth that is set over a burner at your table. A waiter fills it with pieces of flounder, scallions, chicken, cabbage, enoki mushrooms, shrimp, clams, noodles, and more. The broth acquires an intriguing complexity along the way.

Japanese persimmons, engagingly sweet with an acidic edge, are a suitable finale at this unassuming little spot in the heart of the business district.

CHINA GRILL

★ ★

60 West 53rd Street, 333-7788.

Atmosphere: Airy and loud block-long restaurant with an extended bar, open kitchen, and lively crowd.

Service: Eager and well informed; sometimes slow.

Price range: Moderately expensive.

Credit cards: American Express, MasterCard, and Visa.

Hours: Lunch, noon to 2 P.M., Monday through Friday; dinner, 5:45 to 11 P.M., Monday through Thursday, 5:45 to 11:30 P.M., Friday and Saturday, 6 to 10 P.M., Sunday.

Reservations: Necessary, preferably several days in advance.

Wheelchair accessibility: Dining room on ground floor; restrooms downstairs.

❧ The cross-pollination of Eastern and Western cuisines over the last decade has spawned some electrifying food. In September 1987, an offshoot of the restaurant called Chinois on Main in Santa Monica, California, called China Grill, set up shop on the ground level of the CBS building on Avenue of the Americas (at 53rd Street). The Chinese/French fare is light, delightfully presented, and often delicious.

The setting is smashing—a soaring block-long space with jade-colored walls, huge eggshell-colored light shades suspended from the ceiling and an open kitchen behind the extended bar where more than a dozen cooks dash about. The marble floor is inlaid with quotations from the journals of Marco Polo, underscoring the East-West connection. All the hard surfaces ricochet sound back at you like a squash court, so bring earplugs.

An enticing starter is called Chardonnay steamed mussels, a pretty arrangement of plump mussels garnished with fresh coriander and black beans in sake sauce. Tempura sashimi, another winner, is made by wrapping raw slices of tuna in asparagus and seaweed sheets, then flash-frying the assembly until the outside is brittle yet the inside barely warm. The bite-size morsels are delectable in their Champagne butter sauce enlivened with saline sea-urchin roe and wasabi mustard.

When it comes to fresh oysters, my belief is the less done to them the better. The pristine oysters here (the variety changes depending on market conditions) are served raw on the half shell with a compelling sweet-sharp black vinegar sauce laced with shallots. Foie gras comes in unusual guises according to the seasons.

Waiters and waitresses run themselves ragged trying to keep up with the crowds (reservations are required several days in advance unless you can eat at off hours). They are doing a credible job, and with good humor. This is not a place to go if you are on a tight schedule, however, for kitchen delays can occur.

The grilled lamb, a fork-and-knife dish, marinated in jade sauce (a combination of parsley, coriander, mint, and rice vinegar), is tender and pink, set in a peppery garlic sauce. Grilled sea scallops are one of the best choices, set in a zippy red-pepper-and-ginger coulis. Roast duck, on the other hand, is run-of-the-mill, served with a sweet plum sauce.

The dish called sizzling whole fish is not what you might be accustomed to in Chinese restaurants. This one—either catfish or red snapper—is garnished with strips of fresh ginger and quick fried so it is just puffed and golden outside. It comes with a soy-based ponzu sauce, made with lemon, rice vinegar, and mirin wine. Another good seafood option is the grilled redfish presented over a lovely red-onion beurre blanc. A potent curry sauce adds drama to a dish called Shanghai lobster—you can best excavate the meat from the shell with chopsticks. Deep-fried spinach, as light and airy as cotton candy, is a wonderful foil.

Grilled squab is one of those preparations that improved significantly on a second try—the first time it came with reheated fried noodles, but on a revisit the squab was golden-skinned and succulent, and the noodles addictively brittle.

Desserts are just as visually arresting, and, for the most part, beautifully executed. Try any of the luscious home-made sorbets and ice creams in a rainbow of tropical flavors, or, for something more substantial, the warm noodles in honey cream served with sautéed apples and golden raisins. One of my favorites is the quivering coffee-flavored Jell-O—it packs a real caffeine punch—topped with sweet milk and espresso ice cream.

CHIN CHIN

★ ★

216 East 49th Street, 888-4555.

Atmosphere: Handsome and refined front dining room in soft peach and wood tones; back room more whimsical.

Service: Highly professional and friendly.

Price range: Moderately expensive.

Credit cards: All major cards.

Hours: Lunch, 11:30 A.M. to 5 P.M., Monday through Friday; dinner, 5 to 11:30 P.M., daily.

Reservations: Necessary.

Wheelchair accessibility: Two steps at entrance; all facilities on one level.

🍴 Chin Chin is among the most stylish and enticing Chinese restaurants in town. If you have a flash of déjà vu there, chances are you are familiar with Auntie Yuan on First Avenue near 65th Street, where James Chin worked as manager for five years. The other half of the eponymous duo is his brother, Wally.

The Chin brothers, sincere and engaging professionals both, stuffed their backpacks with some choice goodies from Auntie Yuan before blazing their own trail, and many of them have reappeared on the menu at Chin Chin—the terrific cold noodles in fiery sesame sauce, crackling barbecued quail, the pepper-laced orange beef, a host of excellent wines. At the same time, Chin Chin is a highly personal effort, reflecting the brothers' dedication to fulfilling what they call their "lifelong dream."

The two dining rooms are dramatically different. The rectangular front room, with its warm pale peach walls and burnished woodwork, could be mistaken for a tasteful American restaurant were it not for the gallery of charming sepia-toned portraits of the extended Chin family on the walls. Tables along rust-colored banquettes are comfortably sized and conversation is well muffled. The step-down back room could be another restaurant altogether, this one a blizzard of white—walls, ceiling, tablecloths—interrupted only by colorful Oriental pottery perched on wall ledges.

The Chins are keenly attuned to the difference between "uptown" and "downtown" Chinese-food aficionados, and they have cast their lot with the former. Chin Chin's food is scintillating but never startling. (If you have a hankering for braised cod tongue or crunchy duck feet, hop the downtown IRT.) Steamed vegetable dumplings are light and fresh, although my dining crew unanimously preferred the pan-fried pork-filled version brightened with fresh ginger. You can't go wrong with the golden puffed tendrils of fried squid or the succulent shredded duck salad on a bed of crispy rice noodles with tomato and coriander.

A starter called vegetable duck pie is an intriguing deception. A mock duck skin is made by deep frying strips of rice-flour dough embedded with black mushrooms and water chestnuts, which is then served like Peking duck inside a rice pancake along with scallions and hoisin sauce. The combination has the texture of Peking duck, if not the rich flavor. If given the choice, I would go for the real thing, which, by the way, is excellent here—generous with rosy duckmeat. Velvet corn soup, a soothing crab-laced concoction, is just the thing for a frosty fall evening.

The Chin brothers work the dining room like a political advance team, welcoming guests, setting the mood, answering questions, and then standing back to monitor the proceedings. Unlike so many downtown restaurants, which insist upon dumping eight courses on the table at once, meals here are paced to your request. If you like wine with Chinese food—indeed, many sprightly whites go well with it—the impressive and sensibly priced selection here offers a good chance to experiment. Two whites I highly recommend for the price are the Château Ste. Chapelle Johannisberg Riesling from Idaho and the 1986 Tocai Friulano, Ronco del Gnemiz, from northern Italy.

Main courses worth exploring are the crispy whole sea bass, which is impeccably fresh and glazed with a piquant sauce; fleshy prawns prepared Sichuan style with ginger and hot pepper; shredded pork laced with hot and sweet peppers and black mushrooms, and lovely Chinese broccoli swathed in oyster sauce bolstered with garlic. Sautéed mussels in black bean sauce were a good idea, but the mussels were muddy tasting and gritty. I was surprised to see curried lamb stew on the menu, but not surprised to find it starchy and uninteresting.

Chicken with walnuts and leeks is rather tame and nondescript tourist fare. Go instead with the dish called three-glass chicken, in which the meat is braised in an aromatic mélange of white wine, water, and soy sauce, along with garlic, ginger, and coriander. Ten-ingredient rice—packing everything from shrimp to cubes of Smithfield ham—makes a vivid side dish.

Ice cream and fruit are the only desserts.

CHRIST CELLA

Satisfactory

160 East 46th Street, between Lexington and Third avenues, 697-2479.

Atmosphere: Drab and colorless dining rooms with a masculine feeling.

Service: Perfunctory, informal.

Price range: Moderately expensive.

Credit cards: All major cards.

Hours: Lunch and dinner, noon to 10:30 P.M., Monday through Thursday, noon to 10:45 P.M., Friday, 5 to 10:45 P.M., Saturday.

Reservations: Recommended.

Wheelchair accessibility: Elevator between two dining rooms.

🍋 Everything about Christ Cella has a faded, almost sad, patina. Groups of two-fisted ex-linemen still frequent the wood-paneled bar before hunkering down to a meal that likely rekindles memories of the pregame steak dinner. Revisits confirm that the remaining patrons appear to be older New Yorkers who made a habit of going there in its heyday and continue.

The dowdy downstairs dining rooms could probably be described as "homey" if the food were better. The front room upstairs, the largest of all, at least benefits from sunlight and a street view.

Menus are superfluous. Steaks, chops, and several fish entrées were rattled off so quickly in a rote manner by our waiter that we had to ask him to repeat them twice. The veteran service team—our waiter had been there nearly thirty years—has its routine down pat, but don't expect any fine touches.

Lamb chops continue to be among the best bets, char-blackened outside and buttery within. Veal chops are cooked to order and relatively tender but pale tasting. New York strip steak can be rich and beefy, or overcooked and dry depending on luck of the draw. Broiled snapper dusted with paprika has all the flavor of typing paper. It comes with a cereal bowl full of tartar sauce, but even that fails to rescue it.

The anachronistic wine list offers no specific names for Bordeaux châteaux but rather describes them as merely St. Émilion, St. Julian, Medoc, and so on.

The biggest letdown is the famous Christ Cella lobster, which for years has been renowned for its size. Ours was indeed a hefty critter—about three pounds—but its mushy texture hinted that it had passed on to lobster heaven some time before the chef made its acquaintance.

Considering the limited number of side dishes served, one would think the kitchen could do a better job. Not so with the leathery hash brown potatoes, soggy premade Caesar salad, and assorted salad greens with gloppy blue-cheese dressing. The crabmeat salad, which is the best of the lot, comes with the same cliché ketchup cocktail sauce that you find at Peter Luger.

After the meal, a waiter comes to your table lugging a tray holding a giant napoleon the weight of a barbell. Actually, it is pretty good, in a gooey sort of way. Rum cake with chocolate filling is vastly enhanced by a dousing of rum.

CINCO DE MAYO

★

45 Tudor City Place, between 42nd and 43rd streets, 661-5070

Atmosphere: Cheerful pastel dining room with well-spaced tables and a relatively tranquil ambiance.

Service: Congenial but short on the fine points.

Price range: Moderate.

Credit cards: American Express, MasterCard, and Visa.

Hours: Lunch, noon to 3 P.M., Monday through Friday; dinner, 5 to 11 P.M., Monday through Saturday.

Reservations: Suggested, especially for lunch.

Wheelchair accessibility: Bar on street level; lower-level dining area and restrooms accessible through adjacent building lobby.

Cinco de Mayo, or the Fifth of May, is the day in 1862 when Mexico won a famous battle (but ultimately lost the war) against French invaders near the city of Puebla; closer to home, it is the name of a flamboyant SoHo restaurant that in 1983 unleashed the first salvo in the great guacamole invasion of Manhattan. In 1987, the original restaurant opened a second, smaller outpost in Tudor City on the East Side.

The menu is similar at the new spot—a wide-ranging assortment of regional platters supplemented by some inventive daily specials. Overall, the food at the new spot is considerably above that at the SoHo original. While some of the preparations here need more fine tuning, the kitchen turns out some invigoratingly authentic sauces, such as the sharp edged and earthy mole, and a few smoldering chili combinations.

The setting is colorful and convivial yet restrained, befitting this genteel residential enclave overlooking the United Nations. Local residents drop by the long zinc-topped bar in the early evening for margaritas with nachos and peppy fresh guacamole. The lower-level dining room is framed by stripes of yellow neon; walls in soft pastels surround columns ringed in pale serape-style colors. Unlike so many raucous Mexican restaurants in town, the ambiance here is low-key owing to well-separated tables, good acoustics, and a mixed crowd of both neighborhood residents and the tequila-slurping younger set.

A good starter that stands up to the margaritas is called camarones al chipotle, sautéed shrimp in a mildly piquant sauce made with ground smoked chilies—it detonates twice on the palate, leaving a pleasing long aftertaste. Seviche, the assortment of lime-marinated raw fish, on the other hand, was too soupy, making the ingredients soggy.

One of the trendy south-of-the-border snacks around town these days is flautas, lightly toasted corn tortillas stuffed with seasoned chicken, beef, or pork; those served at Cinco de Mayo are of fast-food quality, slightly dry and slathered with sour cream and crumbled white cheese. A gutsy black bean soup comes with do-it-yourself garnishes (chopped onions, tomatoes, hot green peppers, and lemon) that add texture and as much zip as you dare.

The service staff tries to make up in congeniality what it lacks in professionalism.

Entrées rotate daily in a perplexing way. On a Friday evening, for example, one of the two specials was not available, but we were offered another from Thursday, and yet another from Tuesday. Among the dishes generally available daily, one of my table's favorites was the budin de tortilla, which is a Mexican casserole made with alternating layers of soft corn tortillas, shredded chicken, white cheese, and strips of hot chilies. An explosively hot red sauce served on the side can crank up the voltage considerably. Enchiladas verdes, chicken- or cheese-filled corn tortillas painted with a hot chili sauce, are tasty, too, as are the enchiladas with a sharp mole sauce.

You most likely will want something light for the trip back across the Rio Grande, so I suggest the flan sprinkled with almond slivers or, if you have a yearning for something sweeter, the chunky frozen praline soufflé. Pastel de chocolate is a no-nonsense bittersweet cake; guanabana sorbet is unremittingly sweet, as is rice pudding, and a special ladyfinger cake layered with chocolate was as dry as Sonora in August.

In a town occupied by so many spurious Mexican margarita palaces specializing in spiced starch, the stylish new Cinco de Mayo is worth noting as an ambitious and serious spot. It doesn't win every battle, but in the long run it should prevail.

THE COACH HOUSE

★　★

110 Waverly Place, west of Washington Square, 777-0303.

Atmosphere: Early American charm. Red leather banquettes, colorful artwork, brick-and-paneled walls, formally attired staff.

Service: Captains are polite and strive to please.

Price range: Moderately expensive.

Credit cards: All major cards.

Hours: Dinner, 5:30 to 11 P.M., Tuesday through Saturday, 4:30 to 10 P.M., Sunday.

Reservations: Suggested.

Wheelchair accessibility: One step at entrance; restrooms on same level as main dining room.

The Coach House, a Greenwich Village institution under its owner, Leon Lianides, is the kind of place I recommend when someone asks for good old-fashioned American fare in a good old-fashioned American setting.

Any discussion of the Coach House menu must begin with its signature dish, black bean soup, which is back to the level that made it famous. The thick, inky purée is rich with the essence of ham and bolstered with sweet Madeira, giving it an earthy aftertaste. Now they should work on the lackluster gazpacho. Another house special, warm buttery corn sticks, arrive soon after you are seated—they can be a bit dry but the flavor is good.

Appetizers worth trying are the bright and herbaceous eggplant Provençale, which combines cubes of eggplant, capers, raisins, onions, and tomatoes; sautéed shrimp in a mild mustard sauce; and first-rate crab cakes that are replete with sweet meat and contain no bread filler.

The Coach House is one of the few restaurants where captains still refer to women in the third person—"Would the lady care for more sauce?" Such deference seems fitting in this patrician setting. The captains are disarmingly pleasant and efficient. The main dining room is one of the most enchanting in the city. The brick-and-paneled walls adorned with Early American and French art, red leather banquettes, spindly brass chandeliers, lavish flower arrangements, and formally attired staff exude a sense of

129

style and period that is rare today. The upstairs area, used for overflow and parties, has an appeal of its own with a similar color scheme and wine racks lining the walls.

The best black pepper steak in town comes out of this kitchen—a well-aged slab of tender beef embedded with black peppercorns and blanketed in a dark, intensely flavorful veal-stock sauce. Get it with the crusty sautéed potatoes. The all-American chicken potpie, which several years ago slipped to the level of the "two for 99 cents" frozen variety, is now chock-full of moist white meat, fresh peas, carrots, and other vegetables in a light cream sauce.

Prime ribs of beef, a real he-man portion, and rack of lamb are good quality and competently prepared. So are the simple but good sautéed lobster tails atop a heavily reduced and buttery shellfish sauce. Among the disappointments is a dry grilled squab with a sweet-edged sherry sauce, and one preparation that sounded far more tempting than it was: mignonettes of veal with glazed chestnuts. The veal can be slightly dry and the dark brown sauce with mushrooms and chestnuts characterless.

One area in which the Old American Cooking seems as contemporary as ever is desserts, and The Coach House knows how to show them off. The deep-dish apple pie layered with almonds and encased in a thick cinnamon-flavored crust stands alone as an icon of our cooking heritage; the deep-dish peach and plum pie is equally beguiling. Blueberry tart on a brittle sugar crust is ethereal with a crown of unsweetened whipped cream, and the chef's eggy and remarkably light custard set in raspberry sauce would give that cliché crème brûlée a run for its money.

COASTAL

★ ★

300 Amsterdam Avenue, at 74th Street, 769-3988.

Atmosphere: Contemporary glass-fronted dining room with coastal murals covering the walls. Extremely loud.

Service: Polite and eager; sometimes too rushed.

Price range: Moderate.

Credit cards: American Express.

Hours: Brunch, 11:45 A.M. to 3 P.M., Sunday; dinner, 6 to 11:30 P.M. Monday through Thursday, 6 P.M. to midnight, Friday and Saturday, 5:30 to 10 P.M., Sunday.

Reservations: Accepted for four or more.

Wheelchair accessibility: All facilities on one level.

❧ It took about thirty seconds for Upper West Siders to discover the good new fishhouse in their neighborhood called Coastal. The only major drawback here is the crashing noise, which was so loud one evening it nearly knocked me back onto the street when I opened the door. Conversation ricochets off the wraparound windows, stainless-steel bar, wooden floor, and aqua-colored walls covered with a coastline mural.

If you can take the decibels, the rewards are considerable. Somebody in the kitchen knows how to cook fish and season it deftly. Broiled halibut is sublimely moist, with a good lemony hollandaise (the sauce also goes well with the rare-cooked yellowfin tuna). Snowy red snapper is equally pristine under a concassé of plum tomatoes, scallions, and fresh basil. Broiled grouper is elevated by its vibrant Provençale sauce combining olives, capers, and onions.

Several of the seafood pastas need a jolt of seasoning, such as the broiled shrimp over linguine with steamed asparagus, and angel hair entwined with lobster and mussels in light tomato-cream sauce touched with saffron and Parmesan. The kitchen's attempt at Tex-Mexing redfish is a rousing success. Redfish fajitas are made by combining the peppery-coated fillets with grilled onions, warm tortillas, spicy rice, and three ramekins of garnishes: avocado, sour cream, and coriander-tomato salsa. The same formula is a winner with chicken, too.

Cioppino, a fish stew usually associated with San Francisco, tastes as if the overworked kitchen rushes it—the combination was so loaded with tomato that I could hardly find the fish, and garlic slices were almost raw. If you are a lobster fan, the steamed one-and-a-half pounder is a good buy at $16.

The wine list is intriguing and well priced, offering selections from California, the Pacific Northwest, Virginia, New York State, and even Texas. A half dozen are sold by the glass.

In order to keep up with the crowds, the staff sometimes cranks the pace to overdrive. One evening this resulted in our receiving main courses while we were still working on appetizers. In general though, waiters and waitresses are exceedingly pleasant and eager to help.

Among the appetizers worth trying are the trio of vibrant little seviches, each in a large mussel shell: salmon nuggets in tomato concassé, citrus-marinated tuna with red pepper, and red snapper paired with matchsticks of fresh coconut, scallions, and Tabasco. The four-pepper gravlax is alive with fresh dill and moderately hot, while lovely slices of rare-grilled tuna are superb over succotash. Lobster bisque is light in texture but potent with the shellfish flavor, and New England clam chowder is the real thing.

With such care lavished on the fresh fish, I was surprised to find the oysters tasting rinsed and musty. If you like calamari, the deep-fried pinky rings here are terrific, served with a peppery dressing. Crab cakes, on the other hand, were served cold one evening, then were watery and bland the next.

The best desserts are crumbly apple brown Betty, coconut, crème caramel, and thin sugar cookies with vanilla ice cream and fresh strawberries.

CONTRAPUNTO

★

200 East 60th Street, 751-8616.

Atmosphere: Informal; all white; open kitchen.

Service: Confused and haphazard when busy; not very professional.

Price range: Moderate.

Credit cards: All major credit cards.

Hours: Lunch, noon to 5 P.M., Monday through Saturday; dinner, 5 to midnight, Monday through Saturday, 4 to 10 P.M., Sunday.

Reservations: Not accepted.

Wheelchair accessibility: Two flights of stairs to dining room.

🍴 Contrapunto is an upbeat, informal pasta restaurant at 60th Street and Third Avenue that is well worth keeping in mind if you are venturing over to Bloomingdale's territory or one of the movie clusters in the neighborhood.

The menu begins with four appetizers, all good: a mixed green salad with a walnut-oil dressing, grilled mushrooms with garlic, air-dried beef with Parmesan cheese, and a salad of Italian cheeses and roasted peppers. Following those are twenty pastas, both fresh and imported, and a handful of specials.

Almost anything with seafood is a safe bet. Try the cappelli marina piccola, strands of al dente angel-hair pasta flecked with dried tomatoes, shallots, leeks, and basil, all crowned with a diadem of littleneck clams in the shell; or the fettuccine with chunks of sweet fresh lobster in a mild sage-and-butter sauce.

One of the best dishes is brodetto, a souplike mélange of red snapper, half a lobster, sea scallops, squid, clams, garlic, and fresh herbs. The seafood is served atop flaxen strands of angel-hair pasta swathed in a strong fish stock.

The only seafood dish that doesn't make the grade is malfatti aragosta, large pasta squares filled with paltry bits of lobster in a lackluster sauce. Most of the artistically presented vegetable and cheese pastas are bright and flavorful. Among the more intriguing offerings was the fusilli tossed with dandelion leaves, arugula, watercress, fennel, tomato, garlic, and a generous dusting of hot pepper. The heat of the peppers playing off the cool sensation of the fennel is a delight. There are many vegetable variations—some with mushrooms, or leeks, or varied herbs—and most work well.

Another good choice is the giant ravioli stuffed with mascarpone cheese, spinach, watercress, sage, and Parmesan glistening under a sauce of white wine, butter, and olive oil. The fresh pasta is resilient to the bite and the stuffing wonderfully herbaceous.

The wide-open, slightly cramped dining room, all white with spotlit tables, can be deafening at peak hours. Service sometimes resembles a Keystone Kops routine. One white-aproned waiter dashes over breathlessly to take your order, another delivers it ("Who gets the cappelli?"), and yet a third tends to wine and other matters. Keep this in mind if you plan to go to a movie or catch a sale at Bloomingdale's.

Most of the cakes and tarts for dessert taste like decent commercial quality—a bit heavy-handed with sugar. The homemade gelati also were too sweet. A better choice is the homemade sorbet, particularly strawberry or orange.

CUISINE DE SAIGON

★

154 West 13th Street, 255-6003.

Atmosphere: Somewhat faded Oriental ambiance; low-key, harsh lighting.

Service: Halting and slow; occasional language problems.

Price range: Moderate.

Credit cards: All major cards.

Hours: Dinner, 5 to 11 P.M., Sunday through Thursday, 5 to 11:30 P.M., Friday and Saturday.

Reservations: Recommended.

Wheelchair accessibility: Two stairs down at entrance; all facilities on one level.

🍃 Cuisine de Saigon is situated on the ground floor of an old brownstone. The restaurant has been minimally disguised in Southeast Asian attire. As you enter, you pass through a dark bar–waiting room into the dining area with its arched ceiling painted dark red, faded blue-gray walls reminiscent of an old classroom, Oriental paintings, harsh overhead lighting, and simply appointed tables. Waiters are slow and may pretend they understand English better than they do. I recommend going on less crowded weekends if possible.

The four-page menu is tempting to read, but don't be deceived by its size—in many cases you face a Hobson's choice. Two or three of the chef's basic sauces go by several aliases and show up unexpectedly.

For example, the crispy bass features a nicely fried and meaty whole fish sprinkled with shredded ginger and scallions. It is set in a sweet and salty sauce based on nuoc mam, a saline fish condiment, soy sauce, and seasonings. We experienced a flash of déjà vu, however, when the shrimp Saigon style (shrimp blended with bits of pork and scallion) arrived in the same sauce. Chicken Saigon style played nearly the same tune; so did a dish called crispy chicken, which was satisfying but not crispy.

The two barbecued selections—beef and pork—are tasty variations on the same theme, served with lettuce for making little rolls, julienne of vegetables for garnish, and hoisin sauce.

The kitchen's strong suit is broiling; its weakest is frying. Try the shrimp with sugarcane, an engaging combination of shrimp paste molded to a stalk of sugarcane before broiling and served with translucent rice paper, lettuce, coriander sprigs, fresh mint, and pickled onions. The idea is to make cigar-shaped rolls with the ingredients and swab them with sweet hoisin sauce.

The Vietnamese have an insatiable sweet tooth. Only if you have one, too, would I suggest the aromatic duck, cut-up pieces of meat on the bone in a honey-and-hoisin sauce.

Lemongrass, a long, thin herb that resembles scallions, is a staple in Vietnamese cooking. I have a passion for it, so it was disappointing to find barely any in the lemongrass chicken, which was overpowered by a sharp, peanut-laced curry sauce.

Another standard in Vietnamese cooking is the spring roll, which at its best is extraordinarily light, crisp, and exploding with the flavors of fresh mint and vegetables. On a scale of 1 to 10, these are about a 7—the pork-and-shrimp filling is well seasoned and the roll is skillfully fried, but it lacks zip.

For dessert, try the steamed banana cake, a resilient and quivering specimen garnished with coconut milk and peanuts.

DARBAR

★ ★

44 West 56th Street, 432-7227.

Atmosphere: Elegant multilevel restaurant with handsome hammered-brass wall hangings and vivid color scheme.

Service: Adequate and low-key.

Price range: Moderate.

Credit cards: All major cards.

Hours: Lunch, noon to 3 P.M., Monday through Friday; buffet, noon to 3 P.M., Saturday and Sunday; dinner, 5:30 to 11 P.M., Sunday through Thursday, 5:30 to 11:30 P.M., Friday and Saturday.

Reservations: Recommended.

Wheelchair accessibility: Several stairs down to main dining room; restrooms on same level.

≈● Darbar is a dependably rewarding Indian restaurant in midtown that offers the refined Mogul cuisine of northern India. The restaurant is a multilevel affair with a bar downstairs and magnificent hammered-copper hangings on fabric-covered walls. Upstairs the tables often seem too small for the quantities of food that arrive, but aside from that the setting is essentially comfortable and soothingly illuminated.

When a dish calls for hotness, such as gosht vindaloo, the smoldering condiments come at you like an arching curve ball, first making a wide and deceptive approach, then suddenly changing course and zapping into the target. The vindaloo, while delightfully complex and pleasingly hot, is tame compared to murch madras, a south Indian specialty in which chicken pieces are simmered in a rust-colored pepper sauce camouflaged with cinnamon and a touch of lemon. When that detonates on the palate, there is not enough water in Lake Champlain to douse the flames. This, of course, is authenticity in excessive doses.

A more reasonable chicken dish is reshmi kebab, buttery pieces of dark meat rubbed with a mix of Indian spices and roasted on skewers in the tandoor oven. Marinated morsels of lamb aromatic of cardamom and cumin from the tandoor are exceptionally tender, too.

Frying is one of the kitchen's many strengths. This is most graphically seen in the crinkly hot-air balloons of poori, the golden puffs of fried bread. Tandoori roti, a round whole-wheat bread baked in the tandoor, has an earthy and charred flavor. Perhaps the standout, though, is onion kulcha, which is a baked pocket of bread stuffed with sweet onions and fresh coriander. All the breads are wonderful accompaniments to the creamy lentil dish, dal, and the restorative cucumber yogurt mixture called raita.

Vegetarians have a good range of fresh and boldly seasoned dishes from which to choose. My favorites are the grilled eggplant mixture called bayngan bhurta, blended with onions, tomatoes, and spices.

The service staff performs adequately in a low-key fashion, although some waiters can be a bit aggressive trying to sell extra bottles of wine.

Appetizers embrace all the little fritters familiar to fans of Indian cuisine: crisp and fresh vegetable-filled samosas, meltingly tender chicken pakoras, and sour-cream tamarind sauce and a cooling mint sauce. The one unusual starter, crab Bombay, should stay in the subcontinent; the sinewy strips of crab come in a watery coconut-and-tomato sauce. Palak shorba, a spinach soup fragrant of clove, was inedibly salty.

Among the standard Indian desserts, a cardamom-flavored rice pudding called kheer is a refreshingly semisweet punctuation mark, as is nutty kulfi ice cream perfumed with rosewater.

Overall, Darbar is noteworthy not for any unusual fancy footwork, but rather for its steady and reliable performance.

DA SILVANO

★

260 Avenue of the Americas, between Bleecker and Houston streets, 982-0090.

Atmosphere: Rustic Tuscan ambiance but cramped. Outdoor café.

Service: Sloppy and slow.

Price range: Moderately expensive.

Credit cards: American Express.

Hours: Lunch, noon to 3 P.M., Monday through Friday; dinner, 6 to 11:30 P.M., Monday through Thursday, 6 P.M. to midnight, Friday and Saturday, 5 to 11 P.M., Sunday.

Reservations: Suggested.

Wheelchair accessibility: All facilities on one level.

Da Silvano is a casual and rustic Italian restaurant that slipped in quality about two years ago and has not managed to recover fully. It has a pretty sidewalk café that can be delightful on a warm evening.

I suggest you take a tape recorder for the mile-long list of specials recited by waiters. Among the better special appetizers is a salad of fresh and resilient baby octopus in a lemony vinaigrette, and a heaping bowl of meaty steamed mussels in a fresh, oceanic broth. Another seafood salad on the menu, combining calamari rings and mussels in a garlic-and-lemon vinaigrette, was sparkling and invigorating one evening, overcooked and underseasoned another time. Crostini—Italian bread slathered with seasoned chicken liver— is always a good starter. Some tasty cold appetizers were enjoyed at lunch in the restaurant's charming outdoor café, including bread salad with red onions, eggplant Parmigiana, and braised baby artichokes.

Most of the pastas, though, are disappointing: watered-down spaghettini puttanesca, an oily and bland tagliarini with duck liver—both specials—and gummy cannelloni. Nicely seasoned pasta rolls filled with spinach, prosciutto, and ricotta suffer from being served tepid. One intriguing combination is tagliarini crowned with sea-urchin roe and slices of avocado—you mash them into the pasta to form a deliciously saline sauce.

The best dish overall is succulent lamb shanks braised with white wine, carrots, and celery. Of the grilled entrées, salmon with rosemary was done to a turn and breaded jumbo shrimp were simple and tasty. Failures seem to arise from an overtaxed kitchen. One example is the roasted squab, which, while crisp and succulent, lacks the promised cayenne pepper. Fennel-perfumed Italian sausages were partially burned one evening, and lobster stuffed with crabmeat was spoiled.

Flan and good zabaglione with strawberries are recommended over the diner-quality chocolate mousse and the grainy raspberry sorbet. The neglectful service continued to the end—I nearly needed a subpoena to get the check one evening.

DAVID K'S

★ ★

1115 Third Avenue, at 59th Street, 371-9090.

Atmosphere: Spacious, comfortable, and uncluttered setting; flattering lighting and good sound muffling.

Service: Knowledgeable and efficient.

Price range: Moderate.

Credit cards: American Express and Diners Club.

Hours: Brunch, noon to 3:30 P.M., Saturday and Sunday; lunch, noon to 3 P.M., Monday through Friday; dinner, 5 to 11 P.M., Sunday through Thursday, 5 P.M. to midnight, Friday and Saturday.

Reservations: Suggested.

Wheelchair accessibility: Special entrance must be requested to avoid revolving door; three small steps to restroom level.

🍴 David Keh's idea of a fine French dinner, those who know him attest, might be navarin of lamb or a hearty bouillabaisse, with a stop on the way home for some "real food"—a plate of spicy pork dumplings, steamed fish, or crispy orange beef at a Chinese restaurant. Mr. Keh, the indefatigable Manhattan restaurateur, has apparently never felt comfortable with Western food, which is why it came as no surprise when he pulled the plug on his two experiments in Occidental cuisine—the California-style Safari Grill and the Mexican restaurant Café Marimba—and turned them back into Chinese establishments.

In the fall of 1987, he ripped out the leopard-skin banquettes at the old Safari Grill, toned down the spacy pink neon columns, and installed a team of Chinese cooks behind the open kitchen's grills. The revamped establishment is called David K's. The front room, with its glass wall facing busy Third Avenue, is more bustling than the larger back room, with its colorful fabric-covered banquettes, dun-colored rug, and easy lighting. Commodious wicker chairs in both rooms, as well as the Rosenthal china and heavy silverplate table service, are vestiges of Safari Grill.

As Mr. Keh and his wife, Jean, tell first-time customers, the food at this now restaurant has a salubrious bent, with hardly any deep frying, a minimal use of fats and oils, no MSG, and, as the health-food companies like to say, "no artificial anything."

Indeed, the food on the whole is pure and clean tasting, and some dishes excel. One example is the appetizer of airy Chinese noodles tossed with chunks of cool lobster in a bright ginger sauce. Spicy chicken dumplings are engrossing in their warm peanut-butter and sesame-paste sauce, while shredded beef combined with crackling rice noodles and scallions are delicious in their mustard-and-peanut dressing.

David Keh was one of the first Chinese restaurateurs to consider wine seriously, and his list has many fresh dry whites that go particularly well with the food. I usually have the fresh and spicy Hugel Gewürztraminer.

One of the more unusual dishes on the menu is called Peking chicken, which is designed as a leaner and lighter alternative to Peking duck. A chicken is sectioned and deep fried—it is the only fried dish on the menu—until the skin is brittle and golden and the meat is still moist. It is then served with the traditional hoisin sauce, scallion, and pancakes. In this version, the pancakes are made with whole wheat, and, to my taste, they are more flavorful than those made with rice.

Although Mr. Keh is credited with introducing Sichuan cuisine to New York, there are few firecrackers on this menu. About as hot as it gets is a preparation of pork with cashews, leeks, and hot peppers—the meat is extraordinarily tender and the sauce mildly zippy. Another, spicy lamb with scallions, probably could benefit from a bit more spark in the pepper department, for I found it rather flat. Three seafood dishes can be highly recommended: braised sea bass in a garlic-and-ginger sauce garnished with scallions and fresh coriander; sweet prawns cooked simply but lovingly with white wine and garlic, and lobster cooked in a light lemon sauce strewn with lemon rind to impart a nice tart edge.

Finally, there is an homage to Danny Kaye, who was a renowned wokman: an intriguing combination of crunchy shredded vegetables, salty Chinese sausage, and oyster sauce rolled in whole-wheat pancakes. Befitting a healthful menu, desserts are played down, with only ice creams, sherbets, and fresh fruit featured.

DĀWAT

★

210 East 58th Street, 355-7555.

Atmosphere: Streamlined pink-and-pale-green room with flattering lighting, comfortable settings, and low noise level.

Service: Extremely mannered and efficient.

Price range: Moderate.

Credit cards: American Express, Diners Club, MasterCard, and Visa.

Hours: Lunch, 11:30 A.M. to 3 P.M., Monday through Saturday; dinner, 5:30 to 11 P.M., Sunday through Thursday, 5:30 to 11:30 P.M., Friday and Saturday.

Reservations: Suggested.

Wheelchair accessibility: All facilities on one level.

🕮 Dāwat is a stylish East Side establishment whose food has been orchestrated by Madhur Jaffrey, the actress and author of three books on Indian cooking, who is the kitchen consultant. You will find some intriguing and unusual dishes here, although not all of them shine.

The long rectangular dining room, done in subtle pink and pale green with clusters of carved wooden figurines spotlighted on the walls, is comfortable and tranquil. Waiters in chocolate-brown outfits are so polite and solicitous that you spend an inordinate amount of time during the meal nodding and smiling back at them.

The most exciting dish on the menu is an appetizer called bhel poori, an Indian snack that combines crackling puffed rice, wheat chips, fresh coriander, mango powder, and assorted chutneys. The combination is a virtual fireworks display on the palate, detonating with sensations of sweet, hot, and sour. Another arresting tidbit is dahi aloo poori, an eye-watering mix of brittle little wafers tossed with potato cubes and chickpeas in a chili-stoked yogurt-and-tamarind sauce.

It is a never-ending mystery to me how a kitchen can produce stunning and intricate dishes such as these and then turn around and flop with less challenging fare. Consider, for example, the shami kebab, dried-out little hockey pucks of ground lamb with none of the advertised mint flavor, and the doughy and bland vegetable-filled samosas. Deep-fried fritters made with spinach leaves and potato skins, an arresting idea, are so greasy, thick, and flavorless they could be newspaper. Shrimp dabbed with a tangy blend of garlic, mustard seeds, and curry are preferable.

A lovely pea soup, creamy-textured and infused with ginger and cumin, suffered from being served tepid—barely warmed food is a recurring problem on busy evenings. One outstanding poultry dish is called chicken jal frazie, a relatively simple combination of marinated chicken and delicious sweet red peppers. Tandoori-cooked specialties are nicely done. Red-coated chicken, moistened in a yogurt marinade, is succulent and piquant; so too are lamb cubes that are marinated in yogurt, garlic, and ginger and roasted on skewers in the clay oven. Seekh kebab, minced herbed lamb molded around a skewer, is assertive and moist.

Two seafood dishes from Madhur Jaffrey's repertory are exceptionally good. One has shrimp adrift in a refined coconut-milk sauce freckled with mustard seeds and hints of curry and tamarind; another features salmon fillet swathed in a tingling sharp coriander chutney and steamed in a banana leaf—the fish is perfectly cooked and the sauce invigoratingly complex. Such a dish proves the kitchen knows how to use hot spices, so why is lamb vindaloo, that most fundamental of Indian hot dishes, a toothless tiger? Moreover, many of the Indian breads are disappointments. A house special bread studded with nuts and dried fruits is gummy in the center, and mint-flavored paratha is oily and leaden. Get the puffed poori or the whole-wheat tandoori roti.

Aside from pleasing renditions of standard Indian desserts—mango ice cream, creamy rice pudding sprinkled with pistachios, and cottage-cheese dumplings flavored with cardamom and rosewater—an uncommonly good carrot halva is worth trying. It is made by cooking grated carrots in butter and sugar until almost caramelized and serving them with pistachios and whipped cream.

DEVON HOUSE LTD.

★ ★

1316 Madison Avenue, at 93rd Street, 860-8294.

Atmosphere: Formal and understated with two cozy and romantic dining rooms.

Service: Well informed if slightly mannered; generally efficient.

Price range: Expensive.

Credit cards: All major cards.

Hours: Dinner, 6 to 11 P.M., Monday through Saturday.

Reservations: Suggested.

Wheelchair accessibility: Three small steps down, dining room on one level; restrooms downstairs.

❧ Devon House Ltd. is one of New York's most proper and patrician restaurants. The hushed ambiance here is as far removed from those cacophonous new California-style grilleries as Tower Records is from the Pierpont Morgan Library's manuscript room. The food is essentially Continental, with a dash of West Indian salsa sprinkled in by the Jamaican-born owner and chef, Yvonne Scherrer. Those looking for a romantic, serene setting and food that usually satisfies—and occasionally excites—would do well to visit Devon House.

Daily specials are numerous, and among the best are the coarse-textured and deftly seasoned rabbit pâté glazed with flambéed port, and a bowl of huge and meaty fresh mussels steamed in an exquisite broth containing fennel, saffron, tomato, and scallions. Escargots are prepared in an unusual way that is exceptionally tasty. They are served without their shells, in a satiny garlic-tinged cream sauce colored with little bits of tomatoes and scallions.

Some of the soups sampled were standouts. One evening it was a thick, stewlike blend of puréed leeks, lettuce, and spinach in a flavorful chicken stock.

The earnest if slightly mannered service staff is well versed in the food—occasional lags seem to originate in the kitchen. The well-heeled and soft-speaking patrons don't seem to mind, as Devon House's courtly pace casts a pleasing sedative spell on all who enter.

Some of the classic French and Italian dishes fall short of the mark: veal chop with a lackluster imitation of osso buco sauce, and tough medallions of veal with foie gras and a morel cream sauce. The more engaging entrées are those with Jamaican accents. Fresh salmon takes on an entirely new personality when prepared in the Caribbean style. The fillet is lightly marinated in oil and seasonings, then briefly braised in salmon stock, white wine, and Jamaican peppers. As a finishing touch, it is popped under a broiler just to sear the top, leaving the bottom nearly raw.

Game fanciers might enjoy the nicely roasted half pheasant, crisp-skinned and moist, presented with a red-wine sauce aromatic of fresh sage. Equally pleasing is the roasted Cornish hen with an exotic-tasting sauce combining pineapple, green peppercorns, and lime. Rack of lamb comes in a tasty green-peppercorn sauce, but when I had it the meat tasted halfway to muttonhood. A better choice would be the well-aged, tender fillet of beef cooked to order in a zippy Pickapepper sauce (a condiment bottled in Jamaica) with capers.

For those who enjoy cheese before dessert, or in lieu of it, there is a cart with a limited but good selection; cheeses are served with a glass of port.

Desserts can be heavenly. Try the airy and intensely fruity raspberry mousse cake or the invigorating lemon custard tart.

DIECI X

★ ★

1568 First Avenue, near 81st Street, 628-6565.

Atmosphere: Cozy, low-key, and relatively tranquil.

Service: Prompt and earnest if occasionally careless.

Price range: Moderate.

Credit cards: American Express, MasterCard, and Visa.

Hours: Dinner, 5:30 to 11:30 P.M., daily. Closed Sundays in July and August.

Reservations: Required.

Wheelchair accessibility: All facilities on one level.

🐄 While I cringe at the thought of a $17 bowl of pasta—even one spiked with vodka and sprinkled with caviar—I must admit this specialty at Dieci X is delightful, in a decadent sort of way. As one might guess, Dieci X is one of those swanky East Side Italian restaurants that cater to a polished, meticulously groomed clientele that rarely cringes at dinner tabs. What makes it stand out among this gilded circuit of restaurants is some zesty and intelligently conceived food.

In fairness it should be added that, aside from this extravagant pasta, prices at Dieci X are comparable to those at similar establishments in the area. Al dente penne with its rich, assertive tomato sauce, faintly briny with the caviar, is indeed the best in a strong lineup of pastas. Don't expect to detect nuances of an extra dry vodka martini in this dish—the alcohol all but evaporates in the cooking and what remains is a hint of hot peppers that are marinated in it to impart flavor. Another superior option is the angel-hair pasta with mussels and scallops in a sprightly red sauce. One of the more original dishes is called pizzoccheri ortolana, robust buckwheat fettuccine tossed with mushrooms, assorted vegetables, and thin slices of tender veal.

Dieci X offers all the creature comforts associated with this genre of restaurant—a cozy, low-decibel dining room with softly illuminated tables and urbane Italian ambiance. The waiters in black tie can be careless at times, especially when it comes to getting orders straight and explaining dishes. The pace of the meal, though, is leisurely but not laggard.

Seafood is fresh and prepared with care, whether it is an appetizer of sautéed jumbo shrimp with mushrooms, garlic, white wine, and cherry tomatoes or the entrée of fresh, meaty red snapper baked in a balloon of parchment paper along with summer vegetables julienne and a dabble of fresh tomato sauce. The single soup offered, called summertime minestrone, was a surprise. It turned out to be full-bodied and dark, replete with mushrooms, assorted vegetables, black truffles, and tomatoes—ideal for après-ski parties, perhaps, but not steamy city nights. Mushroom fanciers may want to try an occasional special if they have it, giant cultivated mushrooms from Italy that are nearly the size of Frisbees. They are sautéed in olive oil and garlic until crisp. Their firm meaty texture and surprisingly mild flavor are not unlike veal.

Speaking of veal, that comes in several forms. A good summer version is called veal giardino, in which a veal chop is dipped in eggs and bread crumbs then sautéed and presented under a mound of arugula, endive, radicchio, onions, and tomato. A veal-chop special one evening, purportedly sautéed with cognac, was nondescript with little detectable seasoning. Calf's liver, by contrast, was exceptional: pink, delicate, and paired with wilted sweet onions and a heady wine sauce cut with vinegar, which added a vibrant edge.

Dieci X is one of the few places in town where roasted baby goat is on the regular menu. The tender and mild-flavored meat is cut into bite-size chunks and marinated with rosemary and sage.

Desserts are a fifty-fifty proposition. It would be difficult to find a better tiramisù—this one is an espresso-soaked vanilla cake that is pumped up with satiny custard and mascarpone cheese, all dusted with bittersweet chocolate. Fresh apricot tart and tartufo, the Italian chocolate-covered ice-cream ball, are pleasing as well. Skip the gelatinous raspberry mousse, gummy crusted apple tart, and flossy and pallid zabaglione bloated with egg whites.

Judged solely on the basis of food and service, Dieci X merits two stars. A bargain it is not, but for a splurge it is worth keeping in mind.

DOCKS OYSTER BAR AND SEAFOOD GRILL

★

2427 Broadway, near 89th Street, 724-5588.

Atmosphere: Clean, bright, black-and-white tile oyster bar with an elevated informal dining room.

Service: Expect to wait for your table on busy nights; the staff is well informed about seafood and effective under pressure.

Price range: Moderate.

Credit cards: American Express, Diners Club, and Visa.

Hours: Brunch, 10:30 A.M. to 3 P.M., Sunday; lunch, 11:30 A.M. to 3 P.M., Monday through Saturday; dinner, 5 P.M. to midnight, Monday through Saturday.

Reservations: Required.

Wheelchair accessibility: One small step at entrance to lower level of dining room; restrooms downstairs.

&. This black-and-white tiled fishhouse on upper Broadway is a good sleeves-up, oyster-slurping, lemon-squirting spot with a lively scene every night. It offers an ever-changing assortment of fish—everything from fresh tuna and mako shark to jackfish and Mediterranean rouget—as well a broad sampling of clams and oysters.

Frying is one of the kitchen's strong points. Those who harbor fond memories of crunchy fried clams and oysters at the boardwalk will be delighted with the light and greaseless renditions here. If Docks has one area that needs fine tuning, it is grilling—about half of the fish I sampled were overcooked by a minute or so, which drained them of flavor and texture.

The long tile bar with its glass-enclosed shellfish display is a diverting place to have a glass of white wine and an assortment of oysters that may include assertive and saline Belons, tender Wellfleets, mild Apalachicolas, bluepoints, and Chincoteagues. Clams, either on the half shell or "steamers," are delightful, too. Because of the crowds at Docks, you may have to spend fifteen minutes or so at the bar waiting for a table, even with a reservation.

An assortment of daily specials is listed on a blackboard over the open kitchen. An exuberant fellow who served us one evening was impressively knowledgeable about every kind of fish and shellfish, and he was not abashed about peppering his commentary with "Now this is a really great choice" and "These just came in this afternoon."

Aside from all of the good fried seafood, which might be shared by a group as an appetizer, and the raw clams, other superior choices are the light and crisp calamari rings served with a smoky cumin-laced hot sauce, and steamed giant New Zealand mussels, a special, in a splendid saffron-perfumed cream broth. Two occasional specials that do not make the grade are a seafood boudin that is bready, dry, and tasteless, and "tuna fingers," which are battered and deep-fried strips of tuna that come out tasting like generic fish substance.

Docks has a fine wine list with generally budget-conscious prices. Service has been a chronic problem at Docks. I have received a fair number of letters from readers complaining about abrupt treatment—although when I have gone, unrecognized, waiters and waitresses have been pleasant.

Lobster fans will be happy with the freshness of the steamed monsters here, ranging in size from two pounds up (prices vary). Entrées come with crunchy fresh coleslaw and a choice of potatoes (french-fried yams are terrific) or dill-flavored rice. Swordfish, thick tuna steak, and mako shark all were dry to my taste, and fried catfish was undistinguished. When special bouillabaisse-type dishes are featured, I suggest you try them. A rouget casserole one evening holding lobster, clams, scallops, and whole rouget was heady with oceanic aromas and deftly assembled so each ingredient was properly cooked.

Desserts are surprisingly good, especially the peerless chocolate mud pie that is creamy, unremittingly rich, and exquisitely lumpy with nubbins of semisweet chocolate. Apple crumb cake, Key lime pie, and chocolate-chip ice cream are exceptional, too, while only a cloying raspberry pie should go back to the galley for reworking.

Docks has a terrific Sunday brunch. Try the scrambled eggs with Nova and sweet onions.

THE DOLPHIN

★ ★

227 Lexington Avenue, between 33rd and 34th streets, 689-3010.

Atmosphere: Pleasant, simple brick and blond wood; insufficient lighting at lunch.

Service: Earnest and enthusiastic, but sometimes slow.

Price range: Moderately expensive.

Credit cards: All major cards.

Hours: Lunch, noon to 3 P.M., Monday through Friday; dinner, 5 to 10:30 P.M., Monday through Friday, 5 to 11 P.M., Saturday, 5 to 10 P.M., Sunday.

Reservations: Recommended.

Wheelchair accessibility: All facilities on one level.

🐾 The Dolphin, in an inconspicuous nook in Murray Hill, is a hidden gem for those who covet fresh, minimally fussed over seafood. The owner and chef, Elio Rugova, used to run the kitchen at The Captain's Table on Second Avenue and 46th Street, where his skillful handling of the daily catch attracted an enthusiastic following.

The Dolphin dining room is trim and neat, with a long brick wall on one side, blond wood paneling on the other, bent-cane chairs, simply appointed tables, and a large mural of a frolicking dolphin. At lunchtime, the lights are so dim it takes five minutes to accustom yourself; afterward, when you head into the bright sunlight, the optic blast can bring you to your knees.

An impressive variety of domestic and imported fish is served, either broiled with a coating of oil and mixed herbs, or poached with hollandaise sauce. The fish of the day are presented on a large platter, wide-eyed and glistening fresh. The platter might hold red snapper, sea bass, Dover sole, flounder, trout, striped bass, and a seafood brochette, as well as filleted fish that are too large to serve whole, such as salmon and turbot.

Virtually every broiled and poached fish is first-rate.

Broiled sea bass, for example, has a crackling skin and moist, glossy white meat. The light coating of oil and a dusting of mixed herbs impart an aromatic Provençale accent. The fish come on a large oval plate with a supporting cast of boiled potatoes and garlicky sautéed spinach.

The chef has a delicate touch with soft-shell crabs when they are in season. They are sprinkled with seasoned bread crumbs and quickly sautéed, which is all they call for. The only loser is the seafood brochette—a mixture of lobster tail, shrimp, onions, and green pepper—which can be quite dry.

One of the few more elaborate dishes is red snapper baked in parchment paper, garnished with mussels, bay scallops, tomatoes, and herbs, I have had it twice—once it was heady with herbs and delicious, but another time it was overcooked. The menu carries some token meat dishes; however, going to The Dolphin for steak is like going to Palm Springs to ski.

Several appetizers are worth mentioning. Oysters on the half shell—usually bluepoints or Belons—are sparkling and delicious, served with a tart mignonette sauce; cherry-stone clams, nearly the size of quahogs, are remarkably tender. Calamari salad here is usually excellent.

Service is adequate, although busy evenings can be a bit hectic.

Dessert is not a priority here. Your sweet tooth may be sated with a goblet of strawberries under an avalanche of heady zabaglione; if not, walk down to Second Avenue where there are ice cream parlors galore.

EAST

★

1420 Third Avenue, between 80th and 81st streets, 472-3975.

Atmosphere: Handsome Japanese country setting. Low tables where guests sit on the floor. Deep pits allow legs to dangle below.

Service: Confused and inattentive.

Price range: Moderate.

Credit cards: American Express, MasterCard, and Visa.

Hours: Lunch, noon to 2:30 P.M., Monday through Friday, noon to 3 P.M., Saturday; dinner, 5 to 11 P.M.,

Sunday through Thursday, 5 to 11:30 P.M., Friday and Saturday.

Reservations: Recommended.

Wheelchair accessibility: Several stairs lead to dining room; low tables unsuitable for handicapped.

🍴 Upon entering East, the handsome, countrified Japanese restaurant on the Upper East Side, you are stopped at an alcove of little wooden lockers and asked to remove your shoes. You are then ushered into the dining room, which has two sections of low-slung tables separated by a center aisle that is as shiny as a new bowling lane from constant sock buffing. Under each communal table is a knee-deep pit for those who consider sitting in a lotus position for two hours about as relaxing as doing one-arm pushups.

East, which has two other branches in Manhattan—on Third Avenue near 26th Street and on East 44th Street—may not serve the most exciting Japanese food in town, but it is an entertaining setting with more than enough good dishes to please the crowd. It is a popular spot among the young and limber East Side set—so much so that the man who takes reservations warned me that tables are held only fifteen minutes beyond the appointed hour.

A few suggestions to get the proceedings off on a high note include the broiled halved eggplant swathed with sweet miso sauce, cold spinach dusted with fish meal in a sesame-accented soy sauce, and cold bean curd with chopped scallions and ginger. The kitchen is not very adroit at frying, as evidenced by the leathery deep-fried tofu and the heavy, inelegant vegetable tempura (also available as an entrée). And negima, that benchmark dish of grilled scallions rolled in sliced beef that is found in nearly all Japanese restaurants, is thick and chewy.

An alternative way to start is with an assortment of sushi or other raw-fish specialties. The sushi deluxe plate features a nicely balanced variety of sushi and sashimi: tuna, salmon, crab, surimi, fluke, yellowtail, and mackerel. All were pleasingly fresh and well presented; some were spiked with hot wasabi mustard that shot straight to the nasal cavity. The standout sushi was yellowtail, a thickly sliced, flapping fresh fillet that was extraordinarily buttery and oceanic. The maki rolls wrapped in seaweed sheets, while fresh, were not as crisp as they should have been. Your luck should be better at the sushi bar, where they are prepared in front of you and served immediately.

Waiters and waitresses at East skid along the polished floors wearing elfin red socks. However, during my three visits, they often seemed to be skidding past our table to

149

someone else's. When things get busy in the dining room, busboys sometimes resort to the unsightly practice of scraping leftovers onto a platter right at your table, cafeteria style, instead of carrying them one by one into the kitchen.

Main courses comprise some lovely grilled seafood items. Salmon teriyaki, a beautifully grilled plank of fillet, is arresting with its pickled ginger garnish—just go lightly on the exceedingly sweet sauce. Ditto for the otherwise good chicken teriyaki. The careful grilling here makes any of the daily grilled fish specials worth trying.

East may not be the place for assiduous sushi mavens who scrutinize fish textures the way numismatists study coins, but for a lighthearted evening in a convivial setting, it can fit the bill.

ENCORE ENCORE

★

318 West 45th Street, 489-6100.

Atmosphere: Dark room with black walls and pinpoint lighting, reminiscent of a late-night music club.

Service: Bumbling and naïve.

Price range: Moderate.

Credit cards: American Express, MasterCard, and Visa.

Hours: Lunch, noon to 2:30 P.M., Wednesday and Saturday; dinner, 5:30 P.M. to midnight, daily; supper, midnight to 2 A.M., daily.

Reservations: Suggested.

Wheelchair accessibility: Small steps at entrance; all facilities on one level.

🍷 The ingenuous American food at this theater district newcomer is compelling, even if the ambiance is rather dark and eerie. The menu is tightly organized and reasonably priced, offering such arresting fare as garlic-accented roasted chicken with shiitake mushrooms and sweet-potato chips, savory rack of lamb with eggplant, couscous and roasted red peppers, and grill-charred New York sirloin with clean, crunchy french fries.

Service, however, is the one drawback. Even at the slowest of times in the dining room waiters and waitresses have a hard time getting everything straight. Aside from being slow and forgetful, they are barely familiar with the chef's creations. "What's in the shrimp salad?" I asked at lunch, trying to get some idea of its preparation.

"I don't really know," the ·waiter replied. "Shrimp, I guess." About a dozen letters from exasperated readers recount similar experiences.

I continue to go, however, because I like the homey and flavorful food. Live music is also featured several nights a week. Among other satisfying entrées are the lovely fricassee of lobster brightened with Sauternes and ginger, and the peppery grilled duck breast counterbalanced with a semisweet plum chutney and wild rice. The rack of lamb is sublimely juicy, and the couscous is particularly good when it soaks up the excess. At lunch, the changing grilled fish specials are reliable—tuna with string beans and sautéed endive was a nice recent choice. The kitchen has a nice touch with pastas, too. Fettuccine with fresh salmon and sugar snap peas was beautifully balanced, and so was the same pasta tossed in a lusty, multidimensional blend of bacon, onions, arugula, and cream.

For starters, there is a briny plate of steamed mussels in a saffron broth with basil, fat pillows of woody wild-mushroom ravioli garnished with grilled shiitake, and a remarkably light scallop flan perfumed with truffle juice. Chicory salad with savory duck confit was sabotaged by too much dressing.

Desserts are reliably satisfying, including the sharp lemon tart, warm and rich crème brûlée, and intense mocha chocolate cake. Puff pastry with fruit would have been enjoyable had the strawberries been riper.

ERMINIA

★

250 East 83rd Street, 879-4284, 517-3410.

Atmosphere: Small romantic room; rustic décor, candlelight, soft music.

Service: Professional and low-key.

Price range: Moderately expensive.

Credit cards: American Express.

Hours: Dinner, 5 to 11 P.M., daily.

Reservations: Required.

Wheelchair accessibility: One small step at entrance.

🍂 Erminia is an enchantingly romantic little spot, a snug Upper East Side hideaway of barn board and brick, dried flowers, rustic bric-a-brac, candlelight, and soft music. It attracts an urbane and self-possessed clientele, the type of diners who eschew the fervid fishbowl scene in favor of soft intimacy. Some couples even hold hands there.

The traditional Italian food, like the setting, is safe and familiar. On a gastronomic bar graph, neither the highs nor the lows are dramatic. If everything clicks, however, you can enjoy a tranquil evening with straightforward food and discreet service and return home without a ringing in your ears from the clamor.

Two suggested starters are the crisply sautéed baby artichokes flecked with garlic and glazed with good olive oil, and terrific fresh mozzarella, silken and faintly nutty, alongside roasted red peppers and billowy leaves of vibrant basil. The carpaccio of smoked filet mignon is rather thick and chewy, although flavorful. Steamed clams and mussels are presented in a zesty tomato sauce.

With a bowl of pasta costing $16 or more, one might resent being charged an extra dollar for sharing a portion as an appetizer. We paid up to try as many as possible. My favorites are the least elaborate: briny pasta with white clam sauce that is redolent of garlic and fresh basil, and pappardelle tossed in a lovely ricotta cheese sauce. Vermicelli pizzaiola, described as having a sauce built with garlic, tomato, olives, and julienne of veal, is overly sweet to my taste; to find the alleged veal requires sharp vision at tight focus. A special one evening, angel-hair pasta with shellfish, was remarkable for its tastelessness.

Wood-fire grilling is a specialty, and it is generally executed with care. If you prefer meat on the rare side, though, make sure to speak up or it will come out the far side of medium. Baby lamb chops, veal chop, and a mixed grill including beef, lamb, chicken, and fennel-perfumed sausage all benefit from the open-fire cooking. Each comes with little mounds of tasty polenta strewn with strips of prosciutto. Among the nongrilled items, both chicken dishes—one sautéed with lemon and wine, the other with sausage in a vibrant vinegar-edged sauce—are pleasing.

On the seafood side, zuppa di pesce, served inside a large halved lobster shell, is 80 percent squid and can have an acrid burned-garlic sensation; thick rings of squid in a rugged tomato-herb sauce are better.

Desserts are limited to a respectable chocolate mousse, rich tartufo, over-sugary napoleon, and berries with pallid zabaglione.

While Erminia has some rough spots, it still holds appeal

to those seeking a special ambiance and undemanding fare.

FELIDIA

★

243 East 58th Street, 758-1479.

Atmosphere: Upscale rustic setting; cramped and overcrowded in the evening, more pleasant at lunch.

Service: Professional, but overtaxed at dinner, therefore slow and rushed.

Price range: Expensive.

Credit cards: All major cards.

Hours: Lunch, noon to 3 P.M., Monday through Friday; dinner, 5 P.M. to midnight, Monday through Saturday.

Reservations: Suggested.

Wheelchair accessibility: Dining room on one level; restrooms downstairs.

Felidia, the most handsome and popular restaurant on East 58th Street, draws a well-heeled East Side clientele. The handsome bar is a bibulous holding pen of impatience and famine, where patrons wait a half hour or more for reserved tables. When Felidia is at its best, few Italian restaurants can match it. Problem is, it's not always at its best.

The two-level restaurant with its brick walls, lush foliage, and barreled skylight would be more enjoyable if several tables were removed from each level. As it is, customers are literally back to back and waiters have to suck in their stomachs to get through the mob.

The vast menu—four pages and as many as three dozen daily specials—focuses on northern Italian cooking, especially the cuisine of Trieste. But freshness problems plague the kitchen, no doubt because of the overly ambitious offerings. Highly touted specials such as Adriatic scampi can be over the hill and mushy.

At the same time, though, if you hit it right some fish specials can be terrific. A special one evening of fusi, little folds of pasta, came in a terrific sauce of broccoli di rape and sausage; another winner was ravioli filled with ricotta and spinach glossed with a beautiful sage-and-butter sauce. Not all pastas are as successful. The trenette primavera can be a clumsy combination of large zucchini chunks, broccoli florets, green beans, and peas in an underseasoned cream sauce. Fusilli puttanesca comes with a sauce featuring black and green olives, capers, tomatoes, peppers, and garlic. It flops because the competing ingredients are not integrated into a sauce, but rather taste as if they have been thrown together at the last minute.

Among seafood offerings, there might be a lovely sautéed snapper in a white-wine-and-thyme sauce; branzino (a delicately textured Italian sea bass) prepared similarly; deep-fried calamari, resilient to the bite and fried to a crisp golden color; or grilled Dover sole meunière.

When game is offered it is worth trying. Pheasant is expertly prepared, roasted until crisp and served with a heady wine-and-stock sauce that is flambéed at tableside. Osso buco was superb the last time I tried it, richly flavored, moist, and tender. While lamb chops in a brown sauce with chives cannot be faulted, the last time I was there overcooking ruined the roasted baby lamb, a special. Roast suckling pig, another special, was succulent and moist inside, but the skin, which our waiter had described enthusiastically as "crisp and dry," was flaccid and greasy.

The service staff is well meaning and generally knowledgeable, but overextended. Be prepared for exasperating delays.

The wine list is exceptionally rich in Italian labels. If you are in the mood to splurge, there are plenty of opportunities to sample some rare old Barolos.

Appetizers offer some of the tastier choices: mussels in wine and garlic, asparagus au gratin, tangy broccoli di rape —sautéed in olive oil and garlic—and a soothing soup from Trieste called yota, combining sauerkraut, white beans, and pork. A buffet table near the bar also offers a colorful assortment of cold appetizers, ranging from assorted cheeses to smoked fish and roasted peppers.

Desserts are rich and spirited. Among the best: vanilla semifreddo filled with almonds and garnished with raspberry sauce, and zuccotto Fiorentino, a dome-shaped genoise lined with crushed hazelnuts and holding a mass of dense whipped cream.

THE FOUR SEASONS

★ ★ ★

99 East 52nd Street, between Park and Lexington avenues, 754-9494.

Atmosphere: Palatial scale that affords the luxury of privacy at well-spaced tables. The rosewood-paneled Grill Room is masculine and trim, while the glittering Pool Room is romantic and plush.

Service: The huge platoon of captains, waiters, and busboys works as a crack team.

Price range: Expensive.

Credit cards: All major cards.

Hours: Pool Room, lunch, noon to 2:30 P.M., Monday through Friday; dinner, 5 to 11:30 P.M., Monday through Saturday. Grill Room, lunch, noon to 1:45 P.M., Monday through Saturday, dinner, 5 to 11:30 P.M., Monday through Friday.

Reservations: Required; two weeks in advance for weekend evenings.

Wheelchair accessibility: Elevators available for handicapped.

🦐 The Four Seasons has been getting a lot of competition in the power-dining scene in recent years, yet it remains the main lair of powers-that-be in the publishing and financial worlds. The palatial scale of the place, which fairly exudes power and money, is one reason. Then, too, there is the food, under the Swiss-born chef, Seppi Renggli. His eclectic style melds Oriental accents with regional American and modern French cooking to forge a cuisine of his own. And long before American chefs began clucking about "New American cooking," Mr. Renggli was turning out stunning dishes using native provender.

Dining at The Four Seasons differs dramatically according to when you go and where you sit. The legendary Grill Room, with its Astrodome ceiling, rippling copper chain curtains and dark, masculine rosewood walls, is the ultimate power lunch spot, an unrivaled arena of high-rolling executives.

The menu in the Grill Room has been updated to emphasize lighter and more healthful fare, dubbed spa cuisine. Typical of the chef's approach is moist baked swordfish enhanced with olives and scallions, or escalope of veal in a faintly hot soy-and-wasabi-mustard sauce. Mr. Renggli is fond of curries, and he makes the shrimp and beef versions fiery, the chicken one less so. A house favorite is the pair of lightly breaded and golden crab cakes, which are excellent. The accompanying curried mustard sauce flecked with crunchy deep-fried capers is terrific.

In contrast to the importunate Grill Room, where almost

no one eats dessert, the lavish Pool Room with its graciously appointed tables, lofty palm trees, and gurgling illuminated marble pool is for romance and extravagance. A laundry list of all the dishes tasted could run on forever, so the following is a representative sampling.

Terrines are consistently superior, especially the one combining pheasant, quail, and mallard duck served with cranberry relish. Cold breast of pigeon with tart red currants is another winner.

The hot appetizers are unqualified successes. The mildly spicy and generous crab gumbo is loaded with shards of sweet white meat, okra, celery, and green and red peppers; another good choice is the oversize ravioli stuffed with minced lobster spiked with jalapeño peppers and root vegetables mired in a bracing lobster cream sauce. It is ringed by speckled pieces of lobster meat sautéed in black butter. Game fanciers will not be disappointed with the pappardelle swathed in a winy venison ragout sauce.

If I had to pick a favorite entrée from Mr. Renggli's repertory, it would be his duck au poivre. He serves two perfectly cooked legs and a breast. Atop the breast is a potato-chip-crisp layer of skin. The brassy cracked-pepper sauce is piquant enough to warm the soul without searing the lips. Wild rice dotted with pine nuts complements it beautifully. It is ironic that the chef can make such a peppery duck yet turn out an anemic imitation of Paul Prudhomme's blackened redfish. The fish's skin tasted acrid, and the sauce of sweet peppers and onions didn't rescue it.

Those pitfalls aside, the roster of superior dishes is extensive: from snapper baked in a crust of sea salt and pepper with two sauces—a rich tarragon or a lighter blend of lemon, olive oil, and parsley—to scallops of veal with ginger, and breast of pheasant with golden Gorgonzola polenta. Desserts are justly renowned. The Gilbraltar-like "fancy cake" soaked with Curaçao is a must. Hazelnut layer cake is outstanding, too, as are all of the homemade sorbets and soufflés.

The Four Seasons is extravagantly expensive for non-expense-account types (count on $70 to $80 per person at dinner, about $60 at lunch), but prices are more reasonable at pre- and post-theater hours, with prix-fixe dinners at $41.50.

FU'S

★ ★

1395 Second Avenue, between 72nd and 73rd streets, 517-9670.

Atmosphere: Modern, comfortable, semiformal.

Service: Friendly and helpful, although the kitchen can be slow.

Price range: Moderate.

Credit cards: All major cards.

Hours: Lunch, noon to 3 P.M., daily; dinner, 3 P.M. to midnight, daily; dim sum brunch, noon to 4 P.M., Saturday and Sunday.

Reservations: Recommended.

Wheelchair accessibility: Multilevel, crowded dining room.

In just a few years Fu's has become an institution of sorts among Chinese food aficionados on the East Side. It wears no regional badge; selections include dishes from Peking, Sichuan, Hunan, Shanghai, and Canton. The food is seasoned with authority and sauces are light and pure—the chef doesn't believe in heavy cornstarch thickeners. Moreover, many preparations are as pretty to look at as they are delicious.

Fu's has a sporty little black-lacquer bar near the entrance facing Second Avenue. The two-tier dining area is covered by the obligatory gray felt wallpaper of upscale Chinese restaurants, with comfortable cranberry banquettes around the perimeter, inset lighting, fresh flowers, and crisp linen (set with knives and forks, which you can exchange for chopsticks).

Everything in the restaurant is orchestrated by Gloria Chu, an ebullient, welcoming host who overflows with more energy than the Hoover Dam. She is a walking encyclopedia of Chinese food and customs and will happily walk you through (sprint is more like it) the menu, recommending dishes to match individual tastes. The service staff also is cordial and helpful, if occasionally hampered by a slow kitchen.

Ask Mrs. Chu about the daily specials, particularly the exquisite blanched and seared calamari. The fresh, resilient rings are swathed in a black bean sauce bolstered with

157

hot red peppers, scallions, green peppers, and onions. The seasonings create a sensation on the palate that is just this side of burning and slightly salty.

Appetizers represent mostly familiar fare. Start with the various dumplings, such as the combination of two pork and two shrimp steamed dumplings that are gracefully seasoned with fresh coriander and ginger and enveloped in delicate fluted skins, and the crescent-shaped fried dumpling featuring the same fillings and a slightly crunchy scored exterior.

Spareribs can be the most prosaic appetizers in a Chinese restaurant, but the two versions at Fu's are irresistible. The regular barbecued pork ribs are meaty, well trimmed of fat and perfectly charred so that they are still moist and succulent. The honey baby spareribs consist of pork ribs hacked into bite-size nuggets that have been glazed with honey before grilling. It is the kind of dish children go wild over, that is if adults don't beat them to it.

One of the few disappointments among the appetizers is the doughy and greasy spring roll.

There is a baker's dozen of special entrées on the menu, among them first-rate Peking duck (it is available every day so there is no need to call ahead). A female chef with a little girl's smile and a big man's cleaver performs the surgery at tableside. Rice pancakes are filled with crackly golden skin moistened with a thin layer of fat, rosy duckmeat, scallions, hoisin sauce, and translucent slices of cucumbers.

Orange beef garnished with hot and sweet preserved strips of orange rind is as good as you will encounter anywhere; another superior selection is pan-fried whole flounder under a shower of ginger, scallions, and parsley. Delicious duckmeat comes with an earthy black bean sauce, and eggplant family style is made from sweet purple eggplants that are mashed and laced with red pepper strips.

Fu's offers some special steamed dishes for customers who are limiting cholesterol, sodium, or carbohydrate in their diets. Those sampled were fresh and satisfying, if at times a bit underseasoned to the nondieting palate. Among them were steamed shrimp with ginger and scallion sauce, steamed flounder with the same sauce, steamed chicken with black mushrooms, and steamed shrimp dumplings.

You may want to end the meal with a glass of the surprisingly pleasant house cocktail, plum wine cut with brandy —it is undietetic, uncompromisingly Oriental, and utterly bone warming on a frigid winter evening.

GALLAGHER'S

Satisfactory

228 West 52nd Street, 245-5336.

Atmosphere: Vintage steakhouse with wood-paneled walls, sports photographs galore, and exposed wood-burning grills.

Service: Routine and reasonably efficient.

Price range: Moderately expensive.

Credit cards: All major cards.

Hours: Noon to midnight, daily.

Reservations: Recommended, especially weekends.

Wheelchair accessibility: All facilities on one level.

🕭 A natty, flush-faced old Irish gent is sitting at the bar at Gallagher's, clutching a Scotch on the rocks and a tumbler full of memories. "I've been coming here since 1921," he volunteers to the first-timer sitting next to him. "I saw every big-shot Wall Street tycoon here in the old days—hoodlums, every one of them. But they sure liked a good time."

Sounds like the opening scene of a James Cagney movie, and except for the style of dress among customers on this bustling weekday evening, the setting could well be the 1920s. Sixty-year-old Gallagher's is a remarkably well-preserved time capsule in the heart of the Broadway theater district, a virile steakhouse devoted to hearty American food and heated sports badinage. Lamentably, the conversation is more alluring than the food.

Gallagher's is the sort of restaurant I wanted to love, for it has a wonderful unvarnished charm and nostalgia as thick as a double lamb chop. There is the grand old mahogany bar presided over by a wise-cracking chap with an endless repository of anecdotes on any given topic, the smoke-tinted pine walls covered with photographs depicting sports legends of the two- and four-legged variety (the owner breeds horses upstate), and the glowing open kitchen where steaks sizzle over wood fires.

The old-time waiters sometimes seem to be on autopilot as they go through their nightly paces, but the job gets done. The best strategy at Gallagher's is to begin with something as simple as the cherrystone clams or bluepoint oysters on the half shell, which were well iced and fresh (our waiter steered us away from the broiled oysters, which he candidly described as "terrible"), or the winter elixir of oxtail soup, a beefy broth replete with winter vegetables and beef.

Vichyssoise was insufficiently chilled and had a sour taste; gazpacho was pallid, too. The major problem with entrées is overcooking, which ruined a perfectly good pork chop one evening, a veal chop one out of two times, and most of the seafood—particularly salmon steak and swordfish. Moreover, some food comes to the table tepid. The only seafood I recommend is the two-and-a-half-pound steamed lobster.

Of course, most patrons come here for steak, and the broiled sirloin is nicely charred over hickory fires and reasonably tasty. Get a side order of Lyonnaise potatoes, or hash browns; baked potatoes were tired and appeared to have been reheated, perhaps more than once. Broiled mushroom caps glazed with butter were fresh and flavorful, while creamed spinach needed a good jolt of salt and pepper to bring it to life. Other meat suggestions are the prime ribs of beef, a juicy monster, and the succulent double rib lamb chops.

Cheesecake, if you can handle it after all this, is the preferred macho dessert—and it is the real thing here. Deep, cinnamon-spiked apple pie is a winner, too. A brick of frozen chocolate mousse comes under a glacier of whipped cream and chocolate sauce—not bad, and the kind of dessert a twelve-year-old would love. Other offerings were humdrum, and coffee was watery and lukewarm.

GAYLORD

★

87 First Avenue, near 5th Street, 529-7990.

Atmosphere: Cheerful pastel-colored dining room illuminated by multicolor ceiling lights.

Service: Scattered on weekends, considerably more attentive on weeknights.

Price range: Inexpensive.

Credit cards: All major cards.

Hours: Lunch, noon to 3:30 P.M., daily; dinner, 4 P.M. to midnight, daily.

Reservations: Recommended on weekends.

Wheelchair accessibility: All facilities on one level.

❧ When you see a silk-garbed doorman posted outside an extravagantly designed restaurant amid nitty-gritty Little India in the East Village, can Benetton be far behind? Gaylord, a splashy pastel-and-neon newcomer to this neighborhood in transition, at first seems as out of place as a sommelier in a luncheonette. A closer look, however, reveals that prices say downtown, even if the décor says Columbus Avenue.

The 100-seat restaurant has a little bar up front flanked by a platform where a trio of musicians sit cross-legged and play traditional Indian music on weekends. Inside, the arched ceiling is lined with lights that cast a rainbow of purple, pink, yellow, blue, and aqua. Faux windows along one wall open toward an illusory subcontinental sun, while along the back wall two large portholes offer views of the chefs at work.

The staff is generally attentive and helpful, except when the place fills up on weekends, and things get confused. Two tasty starters are the small dishes of shrimp swathed in a piquant sauce made with onions, hot peppers, bell peppers, and coriander, or the less fiery dish of lump crabmeat sautéed with mixed spices and tomato. Both come with puffed and golden-blistered poori bread. Keema nan, the carbon-speckled tandoori bread, is delicious stuffed with spicy minced lamb. Skip the assorted hors d'oeuvres, which include some doughy and leaden fritters, and choose instead either the sprightly fried chickpeas spiked with chili powder and coriander, or the chicken chat, a hot-cool dish combining shredded meat with cucumber in a tamarind sauce.

I have had little success with tandoori chicken, which can be chokingly dry. Fish tandoori, though, is terrific. Cubes of mako shark are marinated in hot-edged mixed spices and roasted in the tandoor oven. The firm-fleshed fish emerges unbelievably succulent. A good accompaniment is the saffron-perfumed rice with nuts and dried fruit, called kacchi biryani.

Indian desserts are typically quite sweet, but some of these—galub jamon (honey-dipped fried cheese balls) and kheer (cardamom-scented rice pudding)—exceed even normal sucrose levels. Less cloying are the frothy Indian ice creams, called kulfi; gajar halwa, shredded carrots cooked in milk and honey, and firni, a semisweet milk pudding brightened with rosewater.

THE GIBBON

★

24 East 80th Street, 861-4001.

Atmosphere: Cozy downstairs bar, waiting room, and dining area in an Oriental motif; the formal grand parlor upstairs is more comfortable and elegant.

Service: Generally sharp and efficient, with occasional lapses.

Price range: Moderately expensive.

Credit cards: All major cards.

Hours: Lunch, noon to 2 P.M., Monday through Friday; dinner, 6 to 10 P.M., Monday through Saturday.

Reservations: Necessary.

Wheelchair accessibility: Three steps down from sidewalk to enter ground-level dining area; restrooms on same floor.

The Gibbon was one of the first restaurants in New York to apply the aesthetics of Japanese cuisine to the canvas of French gastronomy. The result was a visually arresting tableau, one that held appeal to those seeking lighter fare that eschewed butter and cream in favor of an Oriental approach based on soy sauce and fresh herbs. The formula still yields some delightful meals, although the kitchen's timorous approach to seasoning leaves some otherwise meritable dishes flat.

The Gibbon is patronized by a well-to-do, conservatively dressed clientele. The ground level has a small bar and a snug waiting room with a brick fireplace, all done in an Oriental motif. In the back is a compact dining room holding a handful of tables separated by bamboo dividers. Upstairs is more formal, a grand brownstone parlor dominated by tall Japanese silkscreens. Tables are rather tightly packed along the tufted banquettes, but conversation is muffled adequately by the plush upholstery.

Some of the starters are unalloyed Japanese fare, such as the cleanly fried, brittle tempura of crunchy lotus root and shrimp, and the artsy assortment of glistening sashimi—fluke, tuna, yellowtail, and shrimp. Ikuo Kamata, the Japanese-born chef and part owner who has been with the restaurant from the beginning, has a masterly eye for presentation. All of his creations are attractively sculpted and displayed on differently colored ceramic dishes that highlight his handiwork.

One example is cucumber sliced into florets stuffed with nubbins of fresh lobster in a cooling lemony mayonnaise; another, a special, is fresh artichoke hearts garnished with curled lemon slices holding butterflied shrimp that are delicious when dabbed with a subtle mustard vinaigrette. It took courage to order a dish described as shrimp and marinated lotus root served with strawberry vinaigrette. The Gibbon's combination was not as bizarre as it sounded, although the sugary sauce would be best left off.

The restaurant's wine list is well stocked with first-rate California and French selections at affordable prices. Waiters are attentive, generally efficient, and more than willing to explain the polymorphic cuisine.

Entrées are just as graceful looking as the appetizers, but some lack flavor. Veal paillard purportedly comes with a watercress sauce. Instead, however, you receive a pale-tasting soy-and-butter sauce with a clump of watercress on the side. Tasteless brown rice and bland green beans add little. Pompano is steamed nicely, but its garnish of wild mushrooms, seaweed, and snow peas, all in a clear light broth, also suffered from the blands on two occasions. You would be better off with the chef's superior rendition of negima, strips of charred lean beef rolled around asparagus and scallions, or the juicy rack of baby lamb. Simple but vibrantly seasoned sautéed sea scallops with garlic and lemon butter also can be recommended. Sushi—more or less the same cast seen in the appetizer sashimi—is beautifully presented and as fresh as a Pacific breeze. Top-quality salmon is prepared in an unusual and engaging manner, too—rolled around green soba noodles and presented with a zesty ginger-and-scallion sauce on the side.

The light and pristine food here may leave you with a hankering for something sweet. The best bets are the frothy and tart lemon mousse and the homemade banana ice cream. The so-called bittersweet chocolate cake is terribly sugary and has an airy commercial texture, and chocolate mousse is pallid. If the pineapple is ripe, it benefits from a dousing of Cointreau.

The Gibbon deserves credit for its stamina and imagination, and a full house daily attests to its enduring appeal. In sum, however, the menu has too many potholes to merit higher than a one-star rating—the regulars, clearly, know how to steer around them.

GOTHAM BAR AND GRILL

★ ★ ★

12 East 12th Street, 620-4020.

Atmosphere: Spacious and comfortable multitiered dining room with postmodern décor including a pink-marble bar, tall columns, high ceiling, and parachute shades.

Service: Attentive and professional.

Price range: Moderately expensive.

Credit cards: All major cards.

Hours: Lunch, noon to 2:30 P.M., Monday through Friday; dinner, 6 to 10:45 P.M., Monday through Thursday, 6 to 11:30 P.M., Friday and Saturday, 5:30 to 9:45 P.M., Sunday.

Reservations: Suggested.

Wheelchair accessibility: Multilevel dining room.

❦ The stunning postmodern Gotham remains a trend-setter under the direction of its inventive and intelligent chef, Alfred Portale. His cooking is contemporary and personal, but not freewheeling; his dishes are visually dazzling but rarely incongruent.

The roster of appetizers is so alluring you will be hard-pressed to choose. Ultra-thin sheets of veal carpaccio alternate with beef carpaccio to form an arresting mosaic with mixed greens—it is as delicious as it is attractive. Even something as straightforward as borscht is superb, made with an excellent stock and heady with fresh dill. A succulent roasted quail, crisp-skinned and pink inside, comes with celery root, sliced potatoes, and a nest of marinated shiitake mushrooms and curly endive swathed in a walnut-oil vinaigrette.

Gotham's seafood salad is the best I have had in town. Arranged in a teepeelike shape that defies gravity, it combines lovely greens with exquisitely fresh squid rings, lobster, scallops, octopus slices, and mussels. Tiny red beads of flying-fish roe add a lovely saline edge. The entire combination is tossed in a lively olive-oil-and-lemon vinaigrette.

Among the dozen regular entrées, remarkably, there is hardly a clunker. Every one of Mr. Portale's seafood dishes is uncompromisingly fresh and exceptionally well presented. Typical of his style are meaty grilled Santa Barbara shrimp in an herb-infused tomato-based sauce along with a galette-shaped potato salad stippled with capers and tinged with hot mustard; equally alluring are the fillets of sautéed Norwegian salmon set atop a mound of spinach and accompanied by grilled fennel and a superb shallot-and-saffron custard.

On the meat side of the menu, one of the best selections is a dish of rosy slices of roasted squab with pan juices over a bed of wild mushrooms and Swiss chard. It comes with delicious spaetzle in mustard butter. Rolled veal tenderloin stuffed with spinach and pine nuts in a port-wine sauce makes a harmonious marriage. Grilled loin of lamb with sweet roasted shallots and thin golden slices of potatoes surrounding an artichoke heart could not have been improved.

The wine list is full of good choices at fair prices.

The kitchen's impressive pace does not flag near the finish line. Desserts are sublime, from the lustrous warm raspberry gratin with Grand Marnier butter and the heady bourbon soufflé to the old-fashioned apple-and-apricot charlotte made with slices of French bread. It is served with a ball of seductive honey-vanilla ice cream atop a brittle tuile cookie and garnished with tiny lavender flowers.

GREAT SHANGHAI RESTAURANT

★

27 Division Street, at Catherine Street, 966-7663.

Atmosphere: Clean and trim room in gray and white; well-spaced tables.

Service: Businesslike and low-key but lacking personality.

Price range: Moderate.

Credit cards: American Express.

Hours: Lunch and dinner, 11:30 A.M. to 10 P.M., Sunday through Thursday, until 11 P.M., Friday and Saturday.

Reservations: Necessary.

Wheelchair accessibility: Dining facilities on ground floor, restrooms downstairs.

❧ Great Shanghai Restaurant is a bustling Chinatown spot that specializes in the maritime cuisine of the south called Soo-Hang. The extensive menu carries a little of everything, however, from the familiar to the exotic—and the overall quality is impressive.

The dining room, recently redecorated, is clean and contemporary, all light gray and white with a tile floor, saucer-shaped sconces, and tables that are relatively well spaced (at least for Chinatown). A handsome, glass-enclosed private room in the back can be requested for special parties.

Among the best appetizers are the ginger-packed pork dumplings, fried to golden brown on one side; bright and fresh steamed vegetable dumplings; and squiggly home-made noodles coated with sprightly sesame paste. An unusual preparation worth trying is called assorted meat with mung bean sheet. These translucent and slightly gelatinous sheets provide a neutral base for the lively mélange of shredded vegetables, chicken, beef, and pork in a light, tasty wine sauce.

Many Chinese restaurants have adopted the pretentious practice of calling old-fashioned egg rolls "spring rolls," which in fact bear little resemblance to the Chinese counterpart. The "spring rolls" at Great Shanghai are simply decent egg rolls—seasoned pork and minced vegetables in a thick hide of fried dough. One of the cold starters, called pigeon with wine sauce, had an odd chemical aftertaste, perhaps from the marinade.

The waitresses at Great Shanghai are taciturn and businesslike. Once your food is delivered, you are on your own. If you want extra rice or water, you have to flag them down. And at 10 P.M., whether you are finished or not, the waitresses sit down to dinner.

Seafood entrées are, on the whole, the strongest choices. The fried whole sea bass is one of the better versions in Chinatown, crisp and meaty in a sweet-edged sauce studded with garlic cloves. Sautéed prawns in ginger sauce, one of the Soo-Hang specials, is extraordinarily delicate, garnished with julienne of carrots and scallions. Shrimp in garlic sauce and snow peas is a scorcher but good if you can take the heat. A dish called scallops, shrimp, and seafood stick is a tame but pleasing Cantonese-style casserole loaded with firm-cooked vegetables—seafood stick is a euphemism for surimi, the sweetened processed fish.

On the meat side, double sautéed pork with chili sauce is not so fiery as it sounds; it is combined with tofu and black mushrooms. Sliced beef with orange sauce, however, is tough and dry, while chicken with cashew nuts is tender and mildly seasoned. Get a side order of the excellent sautéed green beans with nubbins of pork and fistfuls of garlic scattered throughout.

Great Shanghai's owners, the Wu brothers, also have six ...ng Duck Restaurants in Manhattan, so one would expect a good rendition of this specialty. It's not the best I've had in town—the skin is not so crisp as it could be—but the meat is moist and the garnishes fresh and attractively presented.

Great Shanghai has always been a dependable spot in Chinatown, and now, with its spiffed-up dining room, it is more appealing than ever.

GREENE STREET RESTAURANT

★ ★

101 Greene Street, 925-2415.

Atmosphere: Theatrical multitiered SoHo loft with a bandstand.

Service: Pleasant and competent.

Price range: Moderately expensive.

Credit cards: All major cards.

Hours: Brunch, 12 to 4 P.M., Sunday; dinner, 6 to 11:30 P.M., Tuesday through Thursday, 6 P.M. to 12:30 A.M., Friday and Saturday, 4 to 8 P.M., Sunday.

Reservations: Suggested, especially on weekends.

Wheelchair accessibility: Dining area is multitiered and the restrooms are up a long flight of stairs.

⌘ As a rule, the food at nightclub and discothèque restaurants is about as titillating as a Mantovani festival. No matter, you go to these nightspots primarily for the music, the scene, or the dancing and feel satisfied if you manage to slice your steak without breaking into a sweat. Greene Street Restaurant is a serendipitous exception.

The dramatic breakthrough loft, with its brick walls, shadowy theatrical lighting, and sixty-foot-high mural, has a bandstand in the center where jazz is featured nightly. Waiters and waitresses in black tie put in a lot of mileage crisscrossing the vast space, and they do a creditable job with good humor. The Chinese-born chef, Shao Kwoan Pang, offers a well-rehearsed medley of American, French, and Italian dishes at fair prices.

Safe and familiar starters include the goat cheese and mixed greens, and sautéed sea scallops in a bright lemon-butter sauce with spinach. The Oriental influence can be seen in the pretty tableau of smoked salmon rolls set over a fan of sliced cucumbers with a crème-fraîche-and-cucumber salad alongside. And even if lobster ravioli has the ring of a cliché these days, this rendition is still worth trying. The pasta is exceptionally light and the filling redolent of fresh tarragon. Two dishes that need more rehearsal are the rich lobster sausage paired with an inappropriately rich herb mayonnaise and the underseasoned fettuccine with asparagus and salmon.

The music at Greene Street—either piano or light jazz—adds a soothing backdrop during the week; on weekends, however, it can be rattling.

The entrée selection is wisely orchestrated to offer adequate options but not overextend the kitchen on busy evenings. Reliable choices include the beefy grilled sirloin steak with a mild green-peppercorn sauce, roasted potatoes, and carrots, and the lovely rack of lamb in a rosemary-perfumed red-wine reduction along with slices of roasted eggplant and herbed tomatoes. Another straightforward winner is the moist chicken breast surrounded by roasted garlic cloves and baby vegetables (the baby carrots and zucchini were nearly raw, however).

Dover sole, a special, was filleted at the table and served with a good caper-and-butter sauce. It's a shame the staff took so much care to serve a fine fish, them plopped down unseasoned vegetables on the side. Other specials were veal chop, tender and well cooked, in a lusty wild-mushroom sauce with roasted potatoes and spinach; firm, rich sweetbreads in a Madeira-and-wild-mushroom sauce, and pink slices of duck breast in a brandy sauce flavored with lingonberries, along with wild rice and sautéed apples. Red snapper fillet, cooked to a turn, came in a parsley-and-white-wine sauce that could have used a pinch of herbs but was pleasing nonetheless.

Greene Street has an exceptionally deep wine list with a wide range of prices and a changing selection available by the glass. Among desserts, the crème brûlée and white-chocolate mousse will hardly inspire you to break into song: both are pale and boring. Chocolate mousse cake and the cappuccino mousse with raspberries, however, are uplifting. Fruit tarts are as pretty as they are delicious, and sorbets are pure and ripe.

The overmiked singing notwithstanding, Greene Street offers a harmonious blend of good food and genial service in a rakish SoHo setting.

HARLEQUIN

★

569 Hudson Street, at West 11th Street, 255-4950.

Atmosphere: Sophisticated and distinctive all-gray décor.

Service: Professional and efficient.

Price range: Moderate.

Credit cards. All major cards.

Hours: Lunch, noon to 3 P.M., Monday through Saturday; dinner, 5:30 to 11 P.M., Monday through Saturday, 5:30 to 10:30 P.M., Sunday.

Reservations: Suggested.

Wheelchair accessibility: Four steps up at entrance; dining room on one level; restrooms down a flight of stairs.

When Harlequin opened in Greenwich Village in 1985, it showed great promise of offering New Yorkers a non-clichéd version of Spanish cuisine, particularly the little-known foods from the northern coastal areas of Galicia and Asturias. While the restaurant offers some intriguing regional specials from time to time, the promise has not been entirely fulfilled.

The owners, Ileana and José Barcena, remain as gracious and enthusiastic as ever; they seem genuinely grateful that you have chosen their restaurant, which is rare today. The well-trained service staff reflects their attitude, endearing Harlequin to its cadre of regulars. Throughout the year, the Barcenas put on ambitious Spanish wine and food events.

The dining room hardly looks Spanish, all cool gray with well-separated tables and dishware that carries the frolicking Harlequin logo. On one side of the dining room is a sparkling little bar and on the other a glass display case filled with Lladró porcelain statuettes.

One of the best appetizers is still the shrimp in cream of garlic, a half-dozen grilled shrimp arranged atop two sauces: one an aggressive blend of garlic, cayenne, white wine, lemon, and brown stock, the other a thick and heady combination of garlic, white wine, fish stock, and cream. Brandada de bacalao—what the French call brandade de morue—is terrific here, a garlic-powered purée of dried, salted cod and potatoes that is eaten with toasted black bread. The snowy purée is passed under the broiler before serving to give it a golden-brown crisp surface.

Eggplant terrine, on the other hand, is flaccid and bland, while the crown of crab and avocado tastes like something served at a wedding reception. White gazpacho was thin but pleasantly tart on a first try, inedibly sour a second time. Spanish food aficionados may want to watch for occasional specials of angulas, the bean-sprout-size white eels that are prepared in the traditional manner: placed in a little earthenware crock and cooked in sizzling olive oil flavored with shards of fresh garlic.

Harlequin has one of the strongest Spanish wine lists in the city, and prices are reasonable. The paella for two here is still unrivaled in New York. In Spain, there are as many recipes for this national dish as there are provinces: some with meat, some with shellfish, some with neither. Mr. Barcena does not take sides. He throws in everything—chunks of lobster, shrimp, sausage, clams, mussels, scallops, and sometimes pork and chicken—all fresh and well cooked. The yellow rice is moist and complex, with a blend of saffron, garlic, crushed tomatoes, and chicken stock. Another good choice is a special of merluza (hake), a fairly meaty and mild white fish, presented in a garlicky wine broth with tender clams and herbs. A dish called pixin al eneldo (Asturian monkfish with dill sauce) was well cooked and enhanced by a bright, slightly tart sauce; it was much better than the dolphin fish (sometimes called mahi-mahi) surrounded by a bitter red-pepper purée.

Among the meat dishes, honey-glazed rack of lamb for two is always satisfying, as are the firm and rich lamb sweetbreads paired with medallions of veal and wild mushrooms. A homespun preparation called aguja de res—Spanish pot roast, really—came off lame from lack of seasoning.

For dessert, fruit tarts are anything but light and delicate, but I liked them nonetheless; flan, or crème caramel, is on the mark, but frozen raspberry soufflé is just adequate. On a sweltering summer evening fruit sorbets are a good choice.

Overall, Harlequin is still one of those engaging, family-run restaurants that you naturally want to like, despite the occasional lapses. With a few refinements in the kitchen, Harlequin could become an object of high passion.

HATSUHANA

★ ★ ★

17 East 48th Street, 355-3345.

Atmosphere: Bright, clean, and trim dining rooms on two levels, each with long sushi bars.

Service: Better at sushi bars than tables; can be slow at busy times. Staff is congenial and earnest.

Price range: Moderately expensive.

Credit cards: All major cards.

Hours: Lunch, 11:45 A.M. to 2:30 P.M., Monday through Friday; dinner, 5:30 to 9:30 P.M., Monday through Friday, 5 to 9:45 P.M., Saturday and Sunday.

Reservations: Required for dinner.

Wheelchair accessibility: Small steps at entrance; dining room on two levels with stairs.

🍤 Hatsuhana is arguably the best Japanese restaurant in New York. You will not find more pristine sushi and sashimi, although the unusual specialties that used to make a visit here so exciting are now rarely available.

The cheerful dining rooms on two levels, each with elongated sushi bars flanked by rows of simple wooden tables, provide a suitable stage for the colorful production put on by the personable sushi chefs. I have found that the best place to enjoy the show is front-row center at the sushi bar, where a dialogue can be established with one of the masters. If you leave your fate in their hands, some strange and wonderful surprises may be in store.

The extensive menu is not without its charms, either, especially among the unusual appetizers. With fish as fresh as this, some of the least elaborate presentations are the most appealing: negihamachi, chopped, mild-flavored yellowtail flecked with scallions; negitoro, chopped belly of tuna, which is more assertive and rich, prepared the same way; and sabagari-maki, slices of silver-skinned mackerel blended with pickled ginger and wrapped in Japanese white radish. Two soy-based sauces are set out for dipping. Another delicious if unfelicitously translated dish is broiled squid feet (geso-yaki). The resilient little tentacles, broiled to a turn, are available in a butter sauce, miso, or just plain salt.

A few of the cooked appetizers, however, are forgettable.

171

Hatsuhana dumplings, bite-size packets enclosed in gossamer sheets made of pressed vegetables, are filled with dry, tasteless ground beef. The familiar dish of scallions wrapped in beef strips, called negimayaki, can be superb when made with first-rate meat. At Hatsuhana the beef is thick and tough.

If you want a cooked appetizer, try chawanmushi, an ethereal steamed egg custard enhanced with bits of shrimp, white fish, and minced vegetables; the broiled strips of duck breast with scallions, or the fantastic meat-stuffed broiled eggplant with soybean paste. A personal favorite is torame, or "tiger's eye," which is rings of squid stuffed with salmon, then broiled. The saline and faintly smoky salmon marries beautifully with the tender charred squid.

The highlights of Hatsuhana's menu, though, are sushi and sashimi, which come in many varieties. A good way to get acquainted with the chefs' style is with the Hatsuhana special, which includes both of the raw-fish specialties as well as tempura and grilled skewered fish. The sashimi features sparkling strips of roseate tuna, white fluke, and mackerel, each over a mound of white radish and two kinds of seaweed. The sushi arrangement, served with hot wasabi mustard, soy sauce, and pickled ginger, is equally colorful and fresh—tuna, yellowtail, avocado, and briny giant clam over hand-packed rice. On two occasions, though, the sushi rice had none of the traditional vinegar flavor, which left it flat.

Also included in the Hatsuhana special is the expertly fried tempura of shrimp, fish, broccoli, and sliced sweet potato—it can also be ordered as an entrée by itself. The grilled skewered tuna with shrimp and vegetables is also succulent. In fact all grilled teriyaki-style fish are highly recommended.

When the dining room is full, which is almost always, service can get bogged down. The sushi bar is a better bet if you are on a tight schedule. It is advisable to make dinner reservations no later than 8 P.M. since the kitchen closes down at 9:30.

HUBERTS

★ ★ ★

575 Park Avenue (entrance on 63rd Street), 826-5911.

Atmosphere: Elegant, vaguely Japanese dining room with soft filtered light and plenty of elbow room.

Service: Competent and discreet.

Price range: Expensive (lunch prix fixe, $34 and $44; dinner prix fixe, $60, plus 18 percent service charge).

Credit cards: All major cards.

Hours: Lunch, noon to 2 P.M., Monday through Friday; dinner, 6 to 10 P.M., Monday through Saturday.

Reservations: Necessary.

Wheelchair accessibility: One step at entrance to main dining room; restrooms on ground level.

❧ Like upwardly mobile immigrants, Huberts restaurant has followed each surge of its success with a move to a better neighborhood. Karen Hubert and her chef and husband, Len Allison, started in 1976 with a Victorian-style nook in Boerum Hill in Brooklyn. In 1981, they crossed the East River and settled on East 22nd Street, near Gramercy Park, where their ingenuous charm and ecumenical cooking continued to win followers. In early 1988 they reached the residential summit: a Park Avenue address.

Their new residence is as different from their cozy, subterranean 22nd Street home as champagne is from 7-Up. You are greeted at the handsome Australian-ash bar, which flanks the main dining room, a serene and soft-edged space that evokes a Japanese mood. Artificial light is filtered through amber window panels, tables are well spaced, and the acoustics are kind to conversationalists. A second dining room at the other end of a long hallway reflects the same mood. The discreet service staff has its hands full at the moment, as the place is filled nightly with an urbane East Side crowd, but so far it is holding up well.

The Oriental accent is no accident, for the owners are enamored of Japanese aesthetics and cuisine (in fact, two of the chefs are Japanese), which is evident in such intriguing appetizers as soft-shell crab marinated in a cool combination of ponzu (a Japanese citrus vinegar), soy sauce, sake, and lime juice, as well as a bright shrimp salad embellished with threads of daikon (a Japanese radish), cucumbers, black seaweed, and a piquant rice-vinegar dressing.

Mr. Allison's Cook's tour then moves on to the American bayou with grilled shrimp in an invigorating beer-based sauce stoked with Cajun spices. Another zippy starter, a Huberts standard, is lean, well-seasoned rabbit sausage with a smoky Mexican mole sauce. Less assertive but equally enticing are the gravlax terrine stratified with a combination of mild horseradish, crème fraîche, and cream cheese, and fettuccine with crisped nuggets of sweetbreads and oysters.

Huberts has always boasted one of the more intelligent wine lists in town, not showy and encyclopedic but in harmony with the food and full of surprises. Prices are reasonable, too.

While many entrées excel, several are diminished by oversmoking. On two occasions, an otherwise well-prepared grilled lobster with a chili poblano sauce had an acrid aftertaste; grilled tuna with a lovely endive ragout was so smoky I kept a wary eye on the room's sprinkler system in case a hasty exit was required.

That aside, some of the more compelling dishes include pink-roasted duck with haricots verts, poached pear, and a crunchy vegetable strudel bulging with shredded leeks, cabbage, celery root, carrots, and ginger. Pan-blackened salmon—which in lesser places translates as burned—is the real thing here: peppery and crisp outside, blush pink within, served with cornmeal-dusted okra and roasted potatoes. Rack of lamb comes with a soothing goat-cheese lasagna, and country captain chicken is an exuberant orchestration of spices, curry being dominant, with couscous on the side. Wild boar, however, was a bore, chewy and bland in its apricot-based sauce.

A fine selection of cheeses rolls your way before dessert, although some people may resent paying $10 for it on top of a $60 prix-fixe dinner (the surcharge is not added if you skip dessert).

The sweets are winners all, especially the frozen espresso mousse with pear sorbet, blood orange tartlets with ginger–cherry blossom ice cream, peach sorbet in the shape of a rose, and blueberry tartlets with kirsch-and-cinnamon ice cream.

IL CANTINORI

★

32 East 10th Street, 673-6044.

Atmosphere: Charming Tuscan ambiance with stucco walls, dark woodwork, and appetizer-filled sideboards. Front room can be loud.

Service: Professional and considerate, well-informed about the food and wine.

Price range: Moderately expensive.

Credit cards: American Express, Carte Blanche, and Diners Club.

Hours: Lunch, noon to 2:45 P.M., Monday through Friday; dinner, 6 to 11:15 P.M., Monday through Thursday, 6 to 11:45 P.M., Friday and Saturday, 5 to 11 P.M., Sunday.

Reservations: Required.

Wheelchair accessibility: One step at entrance; all facilities on one level.

🍴 Il Cantinori specializes in the foods of Tuscany, and when the kitchen is on a roll you are in for a sublime experience. If this charming Greenwich Village spot has a fault it is over-ambitiousness—the menu and specials are too copious for the kitchen to handle.

The dining rooms blend rusticity with sophistication—stucco walls, handsome sideboards filled with regional appetizers, and soft lighting.

One of the charms of Tuscan restaurants in Italy is the colorful array of cold antipasti always on display that one can nibble for starters. The selection here is visually alluring and tasty—zucchini with capers, sliced eggplant, marinated artichokes, slabs of snowy mozzarella, marinated mushrooms, silvery sardines, and more. One evening a waiter suggested we try some deep-fried baby artichokes that had just come out of the kitchen, and they were a delight: seductive fresh florets with crisp golden petals.

One of the best appetizers, though, is a special assortment of grilled vegetables—endive, white chicory, and asparagus—teamed with wild mushrooms, fresh mozzarella, and basil, all under a dousing of balsamic vinegar and olive oil. Dry veal carpaccio, on the other hand, tasted as if it had been sliced in advance.

The service staff is exceedingly professional and considerate. The regular menu carries a half-dozen pastas that are usually supplemented by three or four specials. Odds for success are fifty-fifty in either camp. The best among the standards are a classic spaghettini alla puttanesca, a zesty mélange of olives, tomato, capers, and anchovies, and the al dente tagliolini swathed in a buttery tomato-accented sauce bolstered with ground hot and sweet sausage and fresh peas. One superior special includes spaghetti and a garlic-tomato sauce studded with delicious fingernail-size squid.

Other pastas I would pass up are the gummy penne in a ground veal sauce and a special, fettuccine in game sauce that tasted oddly like strong chicken livers. We had the

175

same seesaw experience with risotto: the so-called seafood version was dry and appeared to contain nothing but squid; the one flavored with fresh spinach and mint was sprightly and well textured.

The kitchen seems more confident with entrées, whether it is a succulent homespun osso buco with carrots and mashed potatoes, or juicy roasted quail with polenta cubes in a tomato-herb sauce (both specials).

Two game-dish specials got thumbs down from my table: papery dry pheasant, and venison overpowered with grappa.

The traditional sweet wine called vin santo, into which Italians dunk hard almond biscuits, is a fitting dessert. If you are in a more expansive mood, the tiramisù is one of the better renditions around, espresso-drenched ladyfingers with mascarpone cheese. Zabaglione with strawberries and zuppa inglese are oversugared and commercial tasting, while profiteroles are old and dry.

IL MULINO

★

86 West 3rd Street, between Sullivan and Thompson streets, 673-3783.

Atmosphere: Lively bar where customers wait for tables in the crowded, dim dining room.

Service: Perfunctory and somewhat careless.

Price range: Expensive.

Credit cards: American Express.

Hours: Lunch, noon to 2:30 P.M., Monday through Friday; dinner, 5 to 11 P.M., Monday through Saturday.

Reservations: Necessary.

Wheelchair accessibility: Can accommodate if notified in advance.

&❧ There is something disarmingly maternal about a place that starts piling food in front of you before the menu is presented. Il Mulino makes one feel like a scrawny G.I. on a weekend furlough at Mom's. First comes a plate of peppery fried zucchini, followed by delicious slabs of toasted Italian bread under a pile of minced garlic, chopped basil, and tomatoes; then slices of richly marbled salami.

As if that were not enough, the waiter lugs over a wheel

of Parmesan the size of a Fiat's tire and gouges out a big chunk. "Too many people leave restaurants hungry these days," volunteers the proprietor, rubbing his midsection.

It doesn't take long to realize that this largesse is part of a larger sales pitch—the equivalent of getting free white-wall tires with your $32,000 BMW. When we got down to business at lunch, an appetizer of sautéed porcini mush-rooms set us back $18; mozzarella cheese with tomato and olive oil was $12, as was a marinated orange for dessert.

Il Mulino has a sizable and nearly evangelical following that lines up three deep at the small front bar every night waiting for an open pew. Management must have a policy of not honoring reservations at night. I waited half an hour on three occasions.

You don't go to Il Mulino for the atmosphere. The drab little dining area, pressed between the kitchen and bar, seems to be illuminated by a few near-dead flashlights. The menu is just a formality. A captain comes by and runs off an impossibly long list of specials, by which time you are so mellow from your extended happy hour and sated from all the tidbits on the table that you would just as soon order espresso and call it a night.

If you stick it out, a few dishes are worth trying. Skip such run-of-the-mill starters as clams Casino and go for one of the better pastas. Half orders are not allowed—You don't want to go home hungry, do you?—so the $12 por-tion of angel hair tossed with a peppery sauce replete with fresh clams, mussels, and squid should be shared. The tre-nette with pesto is tasty, as is the rich and meaty spaghetti Bolognese, although it's mired in enough sauce for three portions.

Oversaucing is the rule rather than the exception here. Two particularly unfortunate examples were a special of pappardelle in a champagne cream sauce with truffles, a swampy, oversalted mess (and hardly grazed by truffles), and fillet of red snapper, which came under such a deep sea of garlicky tomato sauce that it never surfaced. A $40 rub-bery lobster was beyond rescue from its potent garlic sauce. The menu carries no fewer than a dozen veal preparations. The juicy, softball-size veal chop garnished with brittle leaves of sage had to be sent back because it was raw in the center—but it was good on the rebound. Chicken dishes range from satisfying—morsels sautéed with garlic and wine—to dreadful, such as the special of chicken with sau-sage and peppers in a gelatinous sauce reminiscent of Chinese fast food. Both mammoth steaks on the menu are winners, one simply broiled, another aromatic of shallots, sage, and wine.

While Il Mulino partisans speak lovingly of the warm personal service, my three dinners (lunch was much better) found waiters who brokered food at the table, or, if not, often served it to the wrong person.

After such a food assault, fruit is the most appropriate dessert. You can get a terrific zabaglione with fresh strawberries or raspberries here, a lovely poached pear or that $12 orange marinated in Grand Marnier—the waiter makes quite a show sectioning it at the table.

IL NIDO

★ ★

251 East 53rd Street, 753-8450.

Atmosphere: Tuscan ambiance, comfortable and elegant.

Service: Professional and congenial.

Price range: Expensive.

Credit cards: All major cards.

Hours: Lunch, noon to 2:15 P.M., Monday through Saturday; dinner, 5:30 to 10:15 P.M., Monday through Saturday.

Reservations: Necessary.

Wheelchair accessibility: Two steps down at entrance; all facilities on one level.

🐚 The well-heeled faithful still line up nightly at Il Nido, a luxury midtown Italian restaurant. Among the appeals are the handsome Tuscan décor with its rough plaster walls crisscrossed by timber beams, the inviting cordovan banquettes and gentle lighting, and the engaging owner, Adi Giovannetti.

Some of the food, particularly daily specials, can excel, but many of the menu workhorses are run-of-the-mill, especially considering the prices.

Superior choices among the seafood dishes are red snapper with clams and zuppa di pesce, a heaping bowl of shrimp, mussels, clams, squid, and red snapper fillet in a well-seasoned tomato broth. Pastas are uneven. Two better selections are linguine all'amatriciana, sporting a sauce of tomatoes, prosciutto, and onions, deftly balanced between salty ham and sweet onions; and tortellini with four cheeses—taleggio, fontina, Gorgonzola, and Bel Paese—is surprisingly subtle and complex.

One of the best dishes under the pasta category actually

178

has no pasta at all: ravioli malfatti. The name means "badly made ravioli" because it is essentially the filling for ravioli —spinach, eggs, and cheese—without the pasta envelope. One gets three tasty green igloos of filling seasoned with nutmeg on top of a tomato sauce with Parmesan sprinkled over them. A special one evening, agnolotti filled with pumpkin purée, was superb, served in a creamy tomato sauce.

Appetizers are the highlights of the meal. Both the bresaola, air-dried beef, and the carpaccio, gossamer slices of raw beef, are as delicious as they are attractively presented. The former has just enough moisture so it is not leathery to the bite, while the latter is lustrous and fresh, drizzled with olive oil, minced onions, and herbs. Spiedino alla Romana, deep-fried skewered layers of bread, ham, and cheese, is golden-crisp and enhanced with a pleasantly salty anchovy sauce. Mr. Giovannetti goes to great lengths to import seasonal specialties, such as truffles and wild mushrooms, and if you happen to drop in when they are available a treat is in store.

Meat entrées offer little excitement. Probably the most interesting dish is boneless chicken with chicken livers and eggplant smothered in melted cheese—a homey if heavy combination. Chicken with prosciutto and cheese, and chicken with garlic cannot really be faulted—but they are nothing one couldn't find at a neighborhood pasta house. The same goes for breaded veal chops and breaded lamb chops.

For dessert, there are always plenty of ripe fruits and berries, which are sublime when mired in the excellent zabaglione—ask for the version made with Cointreau and champagne. If you are up to it, try the button-popping zuppa inglese, which looks like a giant napoleon that has tumbled off the back of a bicycle. This asymmetrical concoction has multiple layers of rum-soaked puff pastry sandwiching whipped cream and fresh raspberries, all crowned with a dollop of zabaglione. Afterward, the staff is very accommodating about carrying you off the banquette.

INAGIKU

★

111 East 49th Street, 355-0440.

Atmosphere: Opulent Japanese ambiance with pagoda-theme tempura bar.

Service: Friendly and eager although sometimes slow.

Price range: Moderately expensive.

Credit cards: All major cards.

Hours: Lunch, noon to 2:30 P.M., Monday through Friday; dinner, 5:30 to 10 P.M., daily.

Reservations: Necessary.

Wheelchair accessibility: Dining room has several levels separated by small steps; restrooms on ground floor.

☞ Inagiku, the opulent Japanese restaurant in the Waldorf-Astoria Hotel, has always been my favorite spot for tempura. A large circular wooden bar under a pagoda-like roof surrounds the white-frocked chefs who make all sorts of sizzling and crisp tempura—shrimp, lobster, beef, vegetable, and more that is served just seconds out of the deep fryer along with a dipping sauce. It took me a long time to sample the rest of the menu—and while some of it is fine, I think I'll stick to the tempura bar from now on.

The dining area behind the bar at Inagiku is richly appointed in gold-patterned wallpaper and deep red rugs. Tables are well separated, and the noise level is low. The restaurant attracts an army of dark-suited Japanese businessmen at lunch and a well-heeled mixed clientele at dinner. Those seeking even more privacy can reserve the handsome tatami rooms in advance.

The menu is relatively unadventurous. Sushi, either as an appetizer or an entrée, features slices of tuna, fluke, salmon, and shrimp—all unquestionably fresh, although the rice lacks vinegar flavor. Ikura (salmon roe) and uni (sea urchin) are good, too. Sashimi features more or less the same cast.

When it comes to cooked items, the kitchen frequently overdoes it. Dinner appetizers of grilled shrimp on bamboo skewers were tough and so was the chicken yakitori prepared the same way. Stick with appetizer tempura, which was as fresh and light as ever.

The Inagiku seafood special, for $28, is rather paltry for the price. It combines small pieces of broiled lobster that, though well cooked, arrived nearly cold, and salmon stuffed with lobster meat in a light creamy sauce along with a soy-based dipping sauce. One evening I tried a special called seafood cooked on a stone. It rated high marks for theatrics but made little sense from a culinary standpoint. The roaring-hot rock came out covered with scallops on skewers, salmon steak, Alaskan crab claws, clams, and lobster in the shell. No matter how fast you wolf down your meal, the items that sit on the stone longest overcook. All came with a soy-and-seaweed sauce.

At lunch one day I tried the beef cooked over stone, which can be superb if the meat is top quality—which this wasn't. A better choice was the shikino obento, or special lunch box. One of the pretty black lacquer boxes contained sashimi of fluke and tuna, pickled vegetables, and something that could best be described as chicken meatballs (they were mildly seasoned and moist). The second box held a dried-out piece of cooked salmon and pickled lotus root, and the third a big rice ball, tamago (the sweet, egg-based sushilike dish), and pineapple. The assorted hot platter on the lunch menu, an appetizer, was the best part of the meal: tender negimayaki (broiled strips of beef and scallions), grilled shrimp and scallops on skewers, and chicken teriyaki with sweet sauce. Miso soup is superior, too, filled with little white mushrooms.

The traditionally garbed waitresses are extremely gracious and warm-hearted, although sometimes service is slow.

Inagiku is one of those narrowly focused restaurants that do one thing very well. For tempura, its lively bar can't be beat.

INDIAN BRASSERIE

Satisfactory

327 West 57th Street, 581-1745.

Atmosphere: Clean and minimalist décor with large banquet room in the back.

Service: Pleasant but inattentive.

Price range: Inexpensive.

Credit cards: American Express.

Hours: Lunch, noon to 3 P.M., daily; dinner, 5 to 11 P.M., daily.

Reservations: Requested.

Wheelchair accessibility: All facilities on one level.

🍴 The term Indian Brasserie seems like an oxymoron, for the freewheeling, gregarious nature of a typical French brasserie has little in common with the usually subdued Indian dining room.

181

If Indian Brasserie wants to live up to its name, its first task is to speed up the service staff from 33 rpm to at least 45 rpm—the lethargic pace can be especially aggravating if you are trying to catch a show or movie. Some of the food here is sassy and complex, although the kitchen has a tendency to overcook meats and shellfish.

The long, white-walled dining room has a long bar, rust-colored banquettes, and white bent-cane furniture. The décor is minimalist as Indian restaurants go, with a sitar mounted on one wall, a bronze ship model on the other.

Mulligatawny soup, which approximates an Indian national dish and comes in a dozen regional variations, is exceptionally good here, made with an aromatic chicken stock enlivened with garlic, coriander, cream, and a touch of lemon. It is a delectable starter with some puffed and blistered onion-stuffed kulcha bread from the tandoor oven. Paratha, though, the layered buttery bread, is soggy and limp, and the balloon bread called poori suffers from the greasies.

Appetizers need help. The assorted hors d'oeuvres plate is about as exciting as a documentary on American toll-booth architecture. Many of the items taste premade and reheated. Pakoras, the mixed vegetable fritters, are leaden little fried dough balls that could double for stun-gun ammunition; minced lamb fritters, called shami kabab, have the consistency of baby food but are at least well seasoned.

The scene brightens with main courses. Chicken rubbed with spices and lemon and cooked in the tandoor comes out sizzling on a metal plate along with sliced onions. The meat is succulent within and slightly tangy outside. Unaccountably, the same chicken is dry in the mixed tandoori grill, which includes lamb, chicken, and shrimp. Overcooking also vitiated jhinga shahi, a platter of spicy jumbo shrimp cooked in the tandoor.

Three side dishes to try are paneer palak, cubes of resilient cottage cheese cooked with mildly seasoned spinach; bengan bharta, a piquant eggplant-and-onion combination aromatic of turmeric, and lamb biryani, a tasty combination of rice, yogurt-marinated lamb cubes, onions, and almond slivers. The couple who had saffron rice at lunch probably enjoyed it, but by the time I got an order at 9 P.M., the reheated grains had turned to pebbles. The standard Indian desserts are agreeable.

The West Side needs a good, affordable Indian restaurant. To fill that need, Indian Brasserie needs a jolt of energy on the service floor and some extra spark in the kitchen.

INDIAN OVEN 2

★

913 Broadway, at 21st Street, 460-5744, 460-8310.

Atmosphere: Minimalist white-and-gray rooms with a cathedral ceiling.

Service: Friendly but amateurish.

Price range: Moderate.

Credit cards: All major cards.

Hours: Lunch, noon to 3 P.M., Monday through Saturday; dinner, 5 to 11 P.M., Monday through Thursday, 5 P.M. to midnight, Friday and Saturday, noon to 11 P.M., Sunday.

Reservations: Suggested.

Wheelchair accessibility: Several steps up at the entrance; restrooms downstairs.

🍴 What can you say about an Indian restaurant that advertises "cuisines indigenous to the mother country" and at the same time offers summer beverages with such names as Silk Panties, Fuzzy Navel, and Stealth Bomber? Indian Oven 2, the downtown branch of Indian Oven on Columbus Avenue, has some other surprises in store, including an untraditional décor that could pass for a California yuppie grill and live Spanish guitar music alternating with traditional Indian sitar.

As for the food, it is relatively inexpensive and can be pleasing if you order the right dishes, but nothing compels one to cancel a weekend in the Hamptons to return. Hot dishes are indeed hot, but few have the depth or complexity that distinguishes Indian cooking at its best—they taste as if pepper has been heaped on at the last minute. Service could use a shake-up, too. Waiters and waitresses are friendly and exceedingly deferential, but they easily get overwhelmed and tend to drop out of sight when you need them.

The dining room is uncharacteristically austere, with a cathedral ceiling, white walls trimmed with gray wooden beams, snazzy high-backed bentwood chairs, and diffused lighting. Housekeeping could be improved—the black banquettes were loaded with crumbs one evening.

I am addicted to Indian breads of all sorts, so it is a letdown to get a sodden deep-fried poori, which should be light and puffed; a better choice is the tandoor roti, the unleavened whole-wheat bread that comes out of the tandoor oven charred and smoky. Kheema paratha, whole-wheat bread stuffed with piquant ground lamb, is invigorating, while nan, the tandoor-baked white bread, can be delicious when soaked in various sauces.

One of the better sauces comes with a tikka makhani, boneless chicken in a blend of tomato and butter touched with pepper; but murg tandoori, the whole sectioned chicken, marinated in yogurt and spices, then roasted in the tandoor, resembles run-of-the mill barbecue chicken. Fans of fiery Indian food usually order a vindaloo gosht, the traditional simmered lamb. This version has plenty of heat, but most of it assaults the lips and tip of the tongue rather than arising in the aftertaste, as a vindaloo's heat should. Chicken vindaloo has the same one-dimensional flavor. Hyderabadi biryani, a lamb-and-rice casserole seasoned with saffron and garnished with sliced eggs and nuts, is recommended for those who shun hot peppers.

One house specialty is called raan of mutton, a marinated leg of lamb roasted in the tandoor oven. The meat is seductive, aromatic of cumin, cardamom, and ginger—it is a shame that they sometimes overcook it. The best seafood dish is called patra ni machi, a Parsi specialty from Bombay in which a whole pompano is seasoned, then baked inside banana leaves. The leaves infused the fish with an exotic dry-edged taste, and the coriander-flavored coating added to its appeal.

Vegetarian dishes are done particularly well, especially the peppery mélange of peas, corn, cauliflower, green beans, and fresh cheese baked in the tandoor. Desserts are forgettable.

INDOCHINE

★ ★

430 Lafayette Street, 505-5111.

Atmosphere: Large and airy dining room; can be clamorous when busy.

Service: Enthusiastic, but uneven and occasionally slow.

Price range: Moderate.

Credit cards: American Express.

Hours: 6 P.M. to 12:30 A.M., daily; closed Christmas Day.

Reservations: Necessary.

Wheelchair accessibility: Several steps at entrance; all facilities on one level.

❧ Since opening in late 1984, Indochine has been serving a consistently enticing mélange of Vietnamese and Cambodian food. It still lures a late-night polyglot crowd that provides a diverting sideshow.

The dining room is hollow and airy with a neocolonial feeling. Large green palm leaves decorate the walls, complementing green banquettes and yellow tablecloths. Despite the departure of the original Asiatic chef last year, Indochine's food quality has remained fairly consistent. One of the biggest hits on the menu is sweet-and-sour shrimp soup. The orange broth, generous with perfectly cooked shrimp, gets its sweetness from slices of pineapple and its tartness from chunks of tomato and a generous amount of tamarind seasoning. This combination attacks the tip of the tongue first with sweetness, then with a slightly sour sensation, and finishes with the smooth, lingering aftertaste of a good fish stock.

Another exceptional soup is the sliced beef with rice noodles, onions, Chinese cabbage, and bean sprouts—all cooked to a turn. The sweetened beef broth, cut with aromatic fresh coriander, added an extra dimension.

The young and eager service staff at Indochine sometimes gets overwhelmed when the place fills up.

Appetizers shine more brightly than entrées. Steamed shrimp with a supporting cast of fresh mint, basil, red peppers, shallots, and lemon juice in a slightly sweetened vinaigrette are a sparkling success. The same steaming treatment was given to mottled strips of fresh squid, with equally tantalizing results. Rouleau de printemps (spring rolls), a staple of Vietnamese cuisine, is a bright and fresh mixture of chopped chicken and shrimp, mint, scallions, vermicelli, and lettuce wrapped in a large rice pancake. It is dipped in a sweetened sauce based on nuoc cham, a condiment made with salted anchovies and spices. Pâté imperiaux, golden deep-fried tubes of rice pancakes stuffed with seasoned pork, carrots, and Oriental vegetables, was a crunchy delight—it was also good with the dipping sauce.

Steamed Vietnamese ravioli, served in a bamboo box, can be bland; better choices are the puffy scampi beignets and the salad of thin, carpacciolike beef in a stimulating hot sauce with shallots, Chinese cabbage, red peppers, and mint.

The best entrée is boneless, deep-fried chicken wings stuffed with vermicelli, bean sprouts, lemongrass, galangal (in the ginger family), and diced chicken. This labor-intensive enterprise, when bolstered with the dipping sauce, is a real palate teaser. Fish is prepared in interesting ways, such as a fillet of sole wrapped in a banana leaf and infused with the haunting tropical flowers of banana and coconut.

Brochettes of beef fillet garnished with lemongrass and red pepper and resting on angel-hair noodles were under-seasoned. So were roast chicken chunks with lemongrass.

Indochine is always a good place to take out-of-town visitors who want to brush shoulders with the downtown artsy scene, yet eat good food, too.

JANE STREET SEAFOOD CAFE

★

31 Eighth Avenue, corner of Jane Street, 243-9237.

Atmosphere: Friendly neighborhood spot in a rustic, tavernlike setting.

Service: Congenial but often too rushed to tend all the tables effectively.

Price range: Moderate.

Credit cards: American Express, MasterCard, and Visa.

Hours: Dinner, 5:30 to 11 P.M., Monday through Thursday, 5:30 P.M. to midnight, Friday and Saturday, 4 to 10 P.M., Sunday.

Reservations: Not accepted.

Wheelchair accessibility: One step at entrance; all facilities on one level.

🦐 It's easy to sail right by the Jane Street Seafood Cafe on lower Eighth Avenue without ever noticing it, as I have done dozens of times. The weathered-wood façade clings to the bow of a big brick apartment house, and the lack of a conspicuous sign leaves the impression it is just a neighborhood watering hole with New England pretensions. Inside, however, is a neighborly, sleeves-up fishhouse that prepares a staggering variety of fish and shellfish.

Despite its effective camouflage, the restaurant is usually packed and reservations are not accepted. The lack of a sit-down bar or waiting area forces patrons to line up in the cramped foyer. Tables are tightly arranged in the tavernlike setting with its brick-and-natural-wood walls, low lighting, and blackboard menus. The casually dressed service staff is sometimes hard to distinguish from the casually dressed patrons; once, in fact, while I was cooling my heels at the entrance, another customer asked me for a bottle of wine, a request I duly conveyed to the bartender.

The kitchen prepares fish in a light and salubrious manner, with few cream sauces or elaborate garnishes. Sometimes the result is too timidly seasoned for my taste, or in some cases not seasoned at all.

Bowls of good creamy coleslaw are set out on the table for starters. Some of the better appetizers are the brittle fried zucchini sticks, succulent sweet littleneck clams, and cleanly fried bluepoint oysters with tartar sauce. Mussels steamed in wine and sherry with shallots and garlic had good flavor but were sandy; baked clams oreganato were run-of-the-mill and chewy. The Manhattan clam chowder scored high marks for flavor—the tomato-based broth was rich and faintly spicy—but the clams were rubbery from overcooking.

You will need the help of the staff to decipher some of the dishes, such as squid Rudolfo and monkfish mahnken. Waiters and waitresses are chatty and cooperative, although the fervid pace of the dining room keeps them on the run, perpetually lunging from one table to another. The extensive wine list is well matched to the food, and the prices are fair. Plenty of good whites that complement the fish are available for less than $15—for example, the Mâcon-Blanc Villages from Jadot and the Torre di Giano white from Lungarotti. Chalkboard wine-by-the-glass specials are available daily

Frying is performed well here, so you can usually rely on the crispy golden-brown fried fillet of sole or, when they are available, the fried soft-shell clams. Other winning options are the poached fillet of ruddy king salmon enhanced with a mild dill sauce and the oversize portion of red snapper under a profusion of sautéed onions, tomato, and basil—tasty, if hardly dainty. Most of the entrées come with the same supporting cast, insipid brown rice and a vegetable of the day, such as baked acorn squash.

One of the frequent specials is called sole Portuguese, a fresh, firm fillet riding a garlic-loaded crest of tomatoes and mushrooms. Another house special is dubbed Jane Street sole, seasoned with mixed herbs, dusted with Parmesan cheese, and crowned with a slice of broiled tomato. The mysterious monkfish mahnken turned out to be a pleasant surprise, the meaty medallions sautéed in butter with florets of broccoli and onions, then combined with a sherry sauce spiked with Tabasco.

Among the dishes to skip are the boring sautéed shrimp

with mushrooms and the underseasoned fillet of bluefish cooked in wine and garlic, both the sort of seafood preparations you expect to find at the Sandpiper Room of a highway motel chain. Whole rainbow trout is engaging on the plate and perfectly cooked, but looks are not everything. It cries out for seasoning. A better choice is the moist grilled swordfish aromatic of oregano.

Some of the desserts have sweetness going for them but little else, such as the dryish chocolate truffle cake and the achingly sweet chocolate pie. The zesty and fresh apple-raisin pie, made without sugar, is a refreshing way to end the meal, as are the good assorted sorbets. If your taste runs to more serious sweets, go with the intense chocolate mud cake or the frozen mocha pie.

JEZEBEL

★ ★

630 Ninth Avenue, corner of 45th Street, 582-1045.

Atmosphere: A vast room filled with antiques and bric-a-brac. Stylish crowd.

Service: Congenial, but slow and confused.

Price range: Moderate.

Credit cards: American Express.

Hours: Dinner, 6 and 9 P.M. seatings, Monday through Saturday.

Reservations: Required until 9:30 P.M.

Wheelchair accessibility: All facilities on one level.

🍴 The darkened windows along a shabby stretch of Ninth Avenue belie the fantasy world that awaits within. You enter the dining room at Jezebel and find yourself in a vast and marvelously cluttered expanse, a cross between a leafy nightclub and a vintage clothing boutique.

Palms and assorted foilage sway under the breeze of big room fans; lacy, multicolored shawls hang from ceiling pipes; eccentric old lamps flicker in every corner; antique furniture mixes with white wicker chairs and porch swings suspended from the ceiling. Add to this potpourri Oriental rugs, vintage posters, lace-covered tables, and crystal chandeliers and you have one of the most intriguing settings in New York—just a short walk from the Broadway theater district. Jezebel, a black-owned soul-food restaurant, is noteworthy not only for its authentic food but also for its ultra-stylish mixed crowd.

The restaurant is the creation of Alberta Wright, a former antiques dealer who swapped sideboards for Southern-fried chicken. When she decided to open the restaurant and had to choose a décor, it seemed only natural to bring her treasures with her.

Even the waitresses have a period look about them—although sometimes it's difficult to figure out what period—decked out in everything from slinky cocktail dresses to flowing peasant skirts. Too bad they are not as efficient as they are attractive. Service is absentminded and exasperatingly slow, especially when the place fills up, which is usually twice nightly, at the 6 and 9 P.M. seatings. (If you have theater tickets, though, they make a point of getting you out on time.) I have never seen so many birthday parties in a restaurant—one evening I counted seven—and the staff spends an inordinate amount of time serenading revelers at their tables. Perhaps they should allow the piano player to sing "Happy Birthday" and let the waitresses tend to more pressing business.

The soul-food menu is as unalloyed as anything you will find uptown, and much of it is inviting. Start with the superior corn bread, which is moist and crumbly and minimally sugared, and the fresh baking-powder biscuits. Smothered garlic shrimp is one of the better appetizers, the shrimp cooked to a turn and the zesty red sauce crackling with hot pepper. Rib bits, little hacked-up morsels of sweetly coated pork ribs, are habit-forming.

Among the soups sampled, my favorite was the Pinesville (peasant) cow pea made with small beans resembling lentils and a richly flavored stock. Charleston she-crab soup was unusual but appealing, a frothy broth packing lots of fresh crab flavor and lightened with cream.

Main courses are portioned for field hands, so go lightly on appetizers and bread. You can get fine fried chicken here, crisply fried outside, succulent and mildly peppery, flanked by deliciously fresh collard greens and run-of-the-mill potato salad—I preferred that to the spiced honey chicken, which, while competently cooked, was a little too sweet for my taste. Yet a third poultry preparation is chicken with waffles, a late-night Harlem tradition harking to the Jazz Age. Late-night revelers would stop at such all-night haunts as Wells on 133rd Street for a plate of this sobering combination. At Jezebel, it is smashing: a portion of good roast chicken under pan-dripping gravy alongside fluffy, golden waffles with butter. I held back on the maple syrup, however.

Curried goat is not something you will find in the postmodern yuppie palaces around town. The falling-off-the-bone braised meat comes in a brassy sauce generous with cayenne pepper, along with rice, beans, and collard greens. Smothered pork chops tasted as if they had been cooked a bit too long, for the meat had a flabby, bready texture under its thick gravy; the accompanying okra was good but the grits were mushy, as if they had been reconstituted. Two shrimp dishes are worth trying: one an aggressively spicy Creole recipe, the other featuring a fiery garlic sauce with rice, cauliflower, and zucchini.

Jezebel has a small, standard wine list. Beer and bourbon go well with this type of food.

One would expect first-class sweet-potato pie here, but what came out was a loosely bound and soggy-crusted wedge under whipped cream. Bread pudding was the unequivocal dessert winner—crusty, studded with raisins, and sweetened with Grand Marnier. Light and creamy chocolate cheesecake is satisfying, and strawberry shortcake, made with those light fresh biscuits, is the real thing.

JOHN CLANCY'S

★ ★

181 West 10th Street, 242-7350.

Atmosphere: Graceful and stylish Greenwich Village ambiance; upstairs quieter than downstairs.

Service: Highly professional and congenial.

Price range: Moderately expensive.

Credit cards: All major cards.

Hours: Dinner, 6 to 11:30 P.M., Monday through Saturday, 5 to 10 P.M., Sunday.

Reservations: Necessary.

Wheelchair accessibility: Four steps down to dining room; women's room on same level, men's room downstairs.

John Clancy, the cooking teacher and author, no longer owns John Clancy's restaurant. His former chef, Sam Rubin, does—although Mr. Rubin is no longer chef. He now oversees the dining rooms. These changes, however, have not affected the quality at this handsome all-seafood restaurant in Greenwich Village.

Mr. Rubin has preserved the upbeat feeling of the place.

The step-down main dining room and bar is done in white-washed brick walls and pearl gray, with pastel garden prints on the walls; the upstairs, done in similar colors, is more intimate.

The kitchen still excels at mesquite grilling. Among the eight or so daily entrée specials that can be recommended are a perfectly grilled whole red snapper, the skin seared and crisp and the ivory-white flesh moist and mildly smoky, swathed with a Mexican-inspired sauce made with stewed tomatoes, olives, and shallots; similarly cooked whole pompano with a bright combination of saffron and ginger; and plump whole sea bass enlivened with a zesty cilantro salsa. It is refreshing to see fish served whole on the bone, for the flavor and texture are undeniably better this way; however, since many Americans are not in the habit of filleting fish at the table, waiters should offer to help.

Two letdowns were a less-than-fresh-tasting grilled tuna steak flavored with a Moroccan mélange of spices, and overcooked swordfish. If the jumbo Ecuadorean shrimp are available, they are worth trying, for the thick, meaty monsters are sweet, heady with the aroma of the wood grill, and enlivened with a peppery red barbecue sauce.

Lobster américaine is a classic (and time-consuming) preparation that many restaurants try to simulate using shortcuts. The rendition here, however, is more authentic tasting than most, a bracing red sauce redolent of lobster essences with hints of garlic, cayenne pepper, cognac, and lots of tarragon. The lobster meat is partly cooked out of the shell, then returned to it before serving.

Another unqualified winner was the halibut steak in a sesame sauce garnished with delicious roasted baby eggplant. Most dishes come with the same undercooked broccoli and carrots. The well-trained service staff is particularly vigilant and agreeable, always willing to accommodate special requests. The wine list is substantial, split evenly between French and American, and reasonably priced.

Portions are large here, so you may want to opt for a light starter, such as oysters on the half shell, which vary from day to day but are always icy and fresh, or the subtle, delicately flavored gravlax under a dollop of caviar-freckled crème fraîche. Lobster bisque is the real thing, fired up with a belt of sherry; a special of corn chowder one day, though, was floury and bland.

John Clancy's is one of the few restaurants in town that serve the dessert English trifle, a wide-mouth goblet layered with sherry-soaked genoise, raspberry purée, crème anglaise, and whipped cream—deadly but good. Crème brûlée is too dense and thickly encrusted with sugar; try instead the chocolate roll oozing with whipped cream and drizzled with warm chocolate, or the seductive caramelized black walnut pie. The diet smasher's award goes to the embarrassingly large portion of Grand Marnier chocolate mousse cake wrapped in genoise and smothered in whipped cream.

The demand for quality seafood houses is greater than ever, so it is no surprise that John Clancy's is filled most nights while many other restaurants in the neighborhood languish.

KEEN'S

★

72 West 36th Street, between Fifth Avenue and Avenue of the Americas, 947-3636.

Atmosphere: Clubby and masculine, replete with mementos from the turn of the century.

Service: Amateurish and slow.

Price range: Moderately expensive.

Credit cards: All major cards.

Hours: Lunch, 11:45 A.M. to 3 P.M., Monday through Friday; dinner, 5:30 to 11 P.M., Monday through Friday, 5 to 11 P.M., Saturday. Pub menu of lighter fare—including oysters, mussels, and chowder—in the barroom from lunchtime to 9:30 P.M., Monday through Friday.

Reservations: Recommended.

Wheelchair accessibility: Four steps at entrance; restrooms on same level as main dining room.

🍴 This landmark steakhouse, dating to 1885, is a bustling lunch spot among the garment district crowd, and a popular spot for private parties in the evening. It can be relied upon for good steak, chops, and shellfish.

The four main dining rooms and the gleaming old bar still have the look and aroma of a creaky old men's haunt (in 1905, the actress Lillie Langtry broke the sex barrier by successfully suing Keen's for discrimination). Thousands of numbered clay pipes hang from the ceiling. One could spend a day perusing the vintage photographs, newspaper clippings, and posters covering the walls. While the food has improved significantly under the current chef, service remains amateurish and slow.

Appetizers include many old standards—shrimp cocktail, smoked salmon, and escargots—as well as some more alluring selections. Oysters—plump and tasty Chincoteagues while they're in season—are prepared differently every night. Sometimes they are dredged in flour and briefly sautéed, then napped with a subtle red-wine-and-butter reduction laced with julienne of leeks and tiny cubes of baby yellow beets. A similar preparation pairs oysters with a light Riesling sauce studded with scallops.

Ragout of wild mushrooms with cabbage and parsley in a buttery red-wine sauce is a good starter, as is scallop-carrot-and-potato chowder. Grilled rabbit sausages, though, are skinny and dry, and cold poached salmon with horseradish sauce (an appetizer for two or an entree) is served too cold and on the dry side.

The cynosure of the menu is still mutton chop, a massive section of double-cut loin that is thoroughly charred outside and succulently pink in the center as requested. The flavor is surprisingly tame for mutton.

Broiled filet mignon, rack of lamb, and a thick, crusty veal chop smothered in wild mushrooms are all skillfully grilled.

Ordinarily, I steer away from seafood in a chophouse, but the chef here makes a concerted effort. Whole spicy sizzling fish is prepared by rolling a black bass in chestnut flour and spices, then sautéeing it. While I could not detect any spices, the fish was moist and flavorful nonetheless. It was presented over wild rice with a bizarre blend of applesauce and wasabi, which tasted as strange as it sounded.

On Saturday evening, which is the slowest night of the week in this part of town, diners are invited to have coffee and dessert in front of a crackling fire in the Bull Moose Room. Warm gingerbread with whipped cream and an unrepentedly rich hazelnut meringue cake with layers of chocolate ganache and buttercream are the recommended choices. Sitting in snug leather chairs under the watchful eye of a massive bull moose mounted above the hearth, one feels like old J. P. himself wheeling and dealing with his cronies. All that's missing is the pipe, so bring your own.

KING FUNG

★

20 Elizabeth Street, just south of Canal, 964-5256.

Atmosphere: Enormous dining room with well-spaced circular tables and harsh lighting. Family atmosphere.

Service: Good-natured and energetic.

Price range: Inexpensive.

Credit cards: American Express, MasterCard, and Visa.

Hours: 8 A.M. to 10 P.M., daily.

Reservations: Accepted.

Wheelchair accessibility: One step up at entrance; all facilities on one level.

🐚 Sunday night at King Fung, a sprawling, harshly lighted establishment in Chinatown, is about as close as you get to the feeling of a boisterous and colorful family restaurant in Hong Kong. Large circular tables are occupied by three or four generations; adults belt down water glasses of Johnnie Walker Red with their prawns and spicy pork (alcoholic beverages are not served, but customers may bring their own) while spring-loaded children with kidneys the size of lentils race back and forth to the restrooms, dodging nimble waiters carrying oversize platters.

King Fung can be an amusing place if you are in the right mood. Moreover, some of the dishes on the budget-priced menu are first-rate. You would have a hard time finding a better Peking duck in town. The version here is presented whole at the table, its honey-gold skin brittle and delicious with just enough fat to moisten the succulent meat. The accompanying pancakes are fresh and almost translucent, making for a light and elegant combination. By contrast, the plain roasted duck is fatty and tastes steamed.

Starting with the appetizers, steamed pork dumplings are light and well seasoned, while fried dumplings tend to be gummy inside. Dry scallop soup, thick with black mushrooms and shredded vegetables, also is intensely flavorful. Sliced chicken with bamboo shoots, which sounds prosaic, is in fact a paragon of subtle Cantonese-style cooking. Each vegetable—scallions, carrots, and bamboo shoots—is cooked to a turn, and the faintly salty seasoning brings out the best in the chicken.

Most of the seafood dishes are superior. Baked lobster Chinese style is delivered sectioned in the shell and glossed with a combination of light soy sauce, egg, scallion, and black beans.

King Fung is foremost a Chinese restaurant for Chinese customers, as evidenced by the host of strange and intimidating dishes that I politely passed up: duck webs, fish lips, sea cucumber, and preserved egg. I do have a weakness for tripe, but the preparation here was too austere for my taste:

194

bright and fresh but plain and unsauced, with only scallion and shards of ginger to help it.

The good-natured and forever hustling service staff does a good job, and most waiters can explain the food relatively well. The restaurant offers a dim sum menu for breakfast and lunch as well, starting at 7:30 A.M.

For Peking duck and lobster I would return eagerly—and if you go on Sunday the sideshow is included.

KITCHO

★ ★

22 West 46th Street, 575-8880.

Atmosphere: Plain and simple; back room slightly more atmospheric; private rooms upstairs.

Service: Friendly, helpful, and efficient.

Price range: Moderate.

Credit cards: American Express and Diners Club.

Hours: Lunch, noon to 2:30 P.M., Monday through Friday; dinner, 6 to 10:30 P.M., Monday through Friday, 5 to 10:30 P.M. Sunday.

Reservations: Suggested.

Wheelchair accessibility: No steps; elevators connect all dining rooms.

This twenty-year-old midtown Japanese restaurant is about as chic as a Honda Civic, notable more for its longevity than its luster. Its formula for graceful aging is unglamorous and straightforward: a warm and efficient staff combined with dependably fresh and attractive Japanese food.

The two downstairs dining rooms are trim and functional, nothing more; I prefer the back room for its more benevolent lighting. The private tatami rooms on the upper two floors, where diners can shed their shoes and formality and sit on the floor, are snapped up quickly by the Japanese clientele, so reserve them well in advance.

The written menu is deceptively short. I strongly advise that you flatter one of the delightfully maternal waitresses into looking after your welfare, for through their lenses the horizon widens considerably. On two occasions our guide was a perceptive woman who suggested tasting dinners that included most of the regular menu offerings as well as a sampling of some arresting specials.

Many bright tidbits get you off on a high note. A little ceramic bowl of boiled spinach in a cooling sesame-sprinkled sauce, called shitashi, is a refreshing primer, as is sunomono, a salad mingling shreds of crabmeat with sheer slices of cucumber in a faintly saline sauce. In contrast, warm bean-curd cake anchored in a pool of scallion-laced soy sauce is forgettable. Broiled baby clams topped with scallions and bacon are sweet but rubbery from overcooking.

The sashimi assortment sparkles: pristine fluke and yellowtail flounder, ruby-red tuna, buttery rich toro, or tuna belly, and, most notably, exquisite raw fresh shrimp that hardly require chewing. The sushi plate features a similar cast, in addition to tuna rolled in rice and encrusted with sesame seeds.

The showstopper at Kitcho is stone cooking, a do-it-yourself technique performed at the table with your own searing-hot rock. Dip some of the top-quality cubed steak into soy sauce and let it sizzle on the stone until it becomes salt-encrusted and juicy rare; the shrimp-and-squid combination is delicious this way, too. Other recommended cooked entrées are the light and clean shrimp-and-vegetable tempura; deep-fried slices of breaded pork, which are crisp and addictive with some hot mustard (an off-menu item), and the impeccably grilled salmon fillet (another off-menu dish). Only skewered pork served over bland cabbage, onions, and vegetables survived undevoured. Our waitress suggested a special soup as a last course, Japanese style, and it was splendid: a clear mushroom broth served in a pretty little teapot and replete with shrimp, seafood, and gingko nuts. Brighten it with a squeeze of fresh lime juice.

Fresh fruit and good ice creams—ginger, green tea, vanilla—are offered as a light and cleansing finale. That is, if you clean your plate.

KURUMA ZUSHI

Satisfactory

18 West 56th Street, 541-9030, 541-9039.

Atmosphere: Simply appointed sushi bar and dining room with a private tatami room.

Service: Perfunctory.

Price range: Moderate.

Credit cards: All major cards.

Hours: Brunch, noon to 2:30 P.M., Saturday; lunch, noon to 2:30 P.M., Monday through Friday; dinner, 5:30 to 10 P.M., Monday through Saturday.

Reservations: Recommended.

Wheelchair accessibility: One step between bar and dining room.

❧ What can you say about a Japanese restaurant that serves commercial-tasting beef Wellington and something misidentified as "poulet a la Kive"? For one, it can be surmised that Kuruma Zushi, which garnered three stars in its old Madison Avenue location under different ownership, lost more than a few fragile dishes in the move to West 56th Street in 1983. For while many of the raw-fish preparations are still laudable, the kitchen seems to have developed an identity crisis, weaving in and out of Continental cuisine for no apparent reason.

The restaurant also has a simple Oriental décor with a sushi bar up front, a small dining room in the back, and a large private tatami room.

Don't tempt logic by ordering the beef Wellington, which is sodden, as if it has been defrosted poorly, and comes with bland canned foie gras. One hot Oriental entrée, chicken teriyaki with peach, was even more bizarre—the meat was soaked in shallots and soy sauce, crowned with a wizened pear, not a peach, and garnished with wilted watercress and iceberg lettuce.

The irony of all this is that much of the sushi and sashimi is quite good. One of the better appetizers is usuzukuri, composed of pearly sheets of mild-tasting yellowtail flounder arranged in a fan pattern around a dollop of seaweed. Also enjoyable is the bright and wonderfully briny sea urchin nested on seaweed.

One of the more exotic dishes is grated fresh Japanese yam potato with fresh tuna. This Oriental oddity takes some time to appreciate, sort of like sumo wrestling. The neutral-tasting white potato has a slimy texture, similar to okra, but somehow it works well with the rich tuna and some dipping sauce. Broiled squid legs are a misnomer— they are actually dry and rubbery slices of squid body— while a preparation called nuta turned out to be morsels of lovely fresh tuna steak over boiled scallions. The achingly sweet sauce, though, spoiled it for me.

Several options are available for complete Japanese-style dinners that combine sushi and starters and a special entrée. The one we chose featured sort of an Oriental surf-

and-turf for the main course: a tasty fried fillet of yellowtail flounder paired with slices of bland steak. We always seemed to do better à la carte, beginning with some of the first-rate sushi—either tuna, yellowtail flounder, squid, crab roe, or fluke—followed by some seaweed rolls called tekka maki.

The seaweed rolls at Kuruma Zushi are some of the best I've had in a long time. The seaweed sheets are lightly toasted so they are crisp, the rice is well seasoned with vinegar and sugar, and the ingredients, whether fish or vegetables, are always fresh and vibrant.

Lunch is a better option than dinner since the sushi bar is going full tilt and the options seem more varied and fresh. If Kuruma Zushi would drop its silly European affectations on the menu—if I want chicken à la Kiev I'll go to the Russian Tea Room—and focus on what it does best, it could soon restore the cachet enjoyed in its old location.

LA BOÎTE EN BOIS

★

75 West 68th Street, 874-2705.

Atmosphere: Attractive country French setting in tiny, slightly cramped room.

Service: Competent but not overly helpful in describing the menu.

Price range: Moderate.

Credit cards: None.

Hours: Dinner, 5:30 to 11:30 P.M., Monday through Saturday, 5 to 10 P.M., Sunday.

Reservations: Necessary.

Wheelchair accessibility: All facilities on one level.

🍴 The dining scene near Lincoln Center has improved precious little in the past two years, which makes this alluring French bistro such a find.

La Boîte en Bois (The Wooden Box) is the creation of Alain Brossard and Jean-Claude Coutable, who toiled side by side in the kitchens of Régine's, Vienna Park, and Chez Pascal before setting out on their own. Mr. Coutable tends the fires in the back while Mr. Brossard works the dining room. They offer straightforward and for the most part well-prepared bistro-type food at reasonable prices.

When the owners chose the name Wooden Box, they must have had a matchbox in mind, for the tiny step-down dining room, while cheerful and tastefully done, is exceedingly cramped on busy nights. The French-speaking waiters, who are competent in a laconic sort of way, have mastered the task of shuffling sideways across the room with their elbows high, resembling old vaudeville teams.

Mr. Coutable is not trying to make any statements with his cooking, thank heavens—we get plenty of that elsewhere. If anything, he is just saying, "Eat, it's good for you." His strength seems to be seafood, including such winning preparations as salmon baked in parchment paper with a mustard-cream sauce, and monkfish in saffron sauce. The pink and moist salmon fillet arrives in an inflated parchment balloon accompanied by boiled potatoes and julienne of well-seasoned carrots and zucchini. The thick and firm fillets of lotte, or monkfish, rest in a pool of heady saffron sauce. The other fish on the regular menu, fillet of snapper in a lustrous herb-butter sauce lightened with champagne, was marred by slight overcooking on my last visit.

Among the better meat dishes are succulent lamb chops garnished with fresh rosemary; veal cutlet with three types of wild mushrooms (chanterelles, shiitake, and white) in an earthy veal stock sauce; and the firm, fresh veal kidneys in a flavorful Bordelaise sauce. Chicken fricassee, in which a cut-up chicken was braised with mushrooms and thick country bacon, can be timidly seasoned; filet mignon under a sward of shallots is all pomp and little substance.

The best appetizer is Marseilles-style fish soup, an intensely flavored homemade fish stock perfumed with saffron and thickened with flecks of fish. The only improvement needed is more zip in the garlic mayonnaise that comes with it.

The kitchen turns out some nice fruit tarts, a good oeufs à la neige with hazelnuts, and a surprisingly pleasing orange salad confit of orange rind floating on a good orange sorbet. Frozen bitter-chocolate mousse is a big letdown because of the inferior chocolate used.

La Boîte en Bois tends to fill up early before showtime at Lincoln Center so it is wise to reserve well in advance.

LA CARAVELLE

★ ★

33 West 55th Street, 586-4252.

Atmosphere: Old-world charm with good noise control.

Service: Highly skilled and amiable but slow.

Price range: Expensive.

Credit cards: All major cards.

Hours: Lunch, noon to 2:30 P.M., Monday through Friday; dinner, 5:30 to 10:30 P.M., Monday through Saturday.

Reservations: Recommended.

Wheelchair accessibility: All facilities on one level.

The venerable La Caravelle, now run by André Jammet (Roger Fessaguet, the co-owner, left in the summer of 1988) is sometimes overlooked by those in search of a pampering Gallic experience with all the flourishes. It should not be.

The gifted American chef, Michael Romano, a disciple of Michel Guérard, does an admirable job walking the tightrope of classic cuisine, as expected from many longtime patrons, and keeping the restaurant in step with today's lighter style.

One enters a long corridor flanked by bright red banquettes that are populated by privileged old-time customers. The main room, wrapped in murals of vernal Parisian street scenes, has a soft, genteel glow. Well-distanced tables and acoustical tiles allow for discreet conversation.

Mr. Romano has many strengths, and among the first you encounter are his ethereal terrines. The best is an airy hot mousse of sole, snow white on the bottom, basil green on top, set in a lovely tomato-cream sauce. At lunch a cold buffet cart holds a silky scallop terrine studded with tender sea scallops, a florid salmon terrine embellished with a coil of spinach in the center, and an earthy textured terrine of trout layered with carrots and zucchini. Of the meat terrines, one made with duck liver was good and peppery while the quail terrine blended with foie gras and truffles was oddly characterless.

Fresh foie gras is now available in a score of New York restaurants, but rarely have I had it prepared as well as at La Caravelle. One evening the delicate liver was flash-sautéed to leave it seared outside yet pink within and paired with a mild vinegar-edged stock sauce and fresh chervil.

One vestige from the old La Caravelle is the French style of service, in which captains prepare plates at tableside. The service team is highly skilled and engagingly fussy.

Entrées at dinner seem to hold up better than those at lunch. In the evening perfectly cooked sea scallops atop braised lettuce in a vibrant chervil cream sauce are far better than the lunch offering of overcooked scallops mired in a bland cream sauce with endive. Grilled red snapper at lunch was dried out, while at dinner sautéed Dover sole was delicious amid cubes of potatoes, artichoke hearts, and tomatoes. The only fish that disappointed at dinner was blandly poached turbot that came with a creamy mustard sauce.

Desserts trundle by on a three-tier cart, and there are plenty of winning options. A towering chocolate charlotte is terrific, intense, moist, and set in a pool of crème anglaise. Sugar-dusted lemon custard cake is tart and refreshing, as is a luscious plum tart loaded with ripe fruit that bursts in the mouth. Crème brûlée is more like a flan than a rich custard. Chocolate mint soufflé is not to be missed—the aroma of fresh mint bursts from the crust like a geyser.

The updated La Caravelle is seaworthy again, reflected in its rise from one- to two-star status. While it may not be a culinary Columbus, its voyages can be enchanting nonetheless.

LA CÔTE BASQUE

★ ★ ★

5 East 55th Street, 688-6525.

Atmosphere: Old-world charm and glamour in a glowing and comfortable dining room.

Service: Proper and attentive, although not always congenial with newcomers.

Price range: Expensive.

Credit cards: All major cards.

Hours: Lunch, noon to 2:30 P.M., Monday through Saturday; dinner, 6 to 10:30 P.M., Monday through Friday, 6 to 11 P.M., Saturday.

Reservations: Necessary.

Wheelchair accessibility: One small step up at entrance; all facilities on one level.

🐌 Habitués of this fortress of classic French cuisine look for comfort, cosseting, and food they can really get their teeth into. And that, for sure, is what they get from the chef-proprietor, Jean-Jacques Rachou. La Côte Basque is to the pastel tableaux of new American cuisine as Rubens is to Georgia O'Keeffe. The wraparound dining room, which was much expanded several years ago, still exudes a time-less glamour with its murals of coastal France, red leather banquettes, splendid flower clusters, and a well-turned-out crowd.

Some longtime customers grouse that service has lost its personal touch since the expansion. Still, familiar customers get a gushing welcome, although hoi polloi are lucky to get a second glance. Because I was known to the manage-ment, I sent two dining companions in advance one eve-ning to claim our table under their name. They were coolly dispatched to a bench in the foyer until my arrival, at which point we were whooshed into the dining room. The service staff in general, though, is attentive and professional.

Mr. Rachou's cooking style is as deeply rooted as a Bor-deaux vine. It is characterized by intensely reduced sauces, lavish presentation, and prodigious portions. Certain ap-petizers, such as the couronne de fruits de mer, a spectac-ular-looking seafood salad, are larger than entrées in some other restaurants. The salad features sweet, fresh cold lob-ster, crab, and shrimp encircled by summer vegetables with a tarragon mayonnaise. A lobster terrine, more modestly proportioned, is built upon a foundation of lobster mousse alternating with layers of green beans, tomato, and carrots —all bright and lively.

Another hefty, though superb, starter is le vol au vent de St. Jacques, a beehive of puff pastry holding buttery bay scallops in a rich fish-stock-and-cream sauce brightened with Sauternes. The addition of chives and a touch of vin-egar give it a sprightly edge. The seafood casserole changes daily, and it is worth trying. Served in a silver terrine, my version combined a rich, creamy fish stock replete with per-fectly cooked morsels of lobster and scallops. This is a bet-ter option than the salty fish soup.

Fresh foie gras is treated with dignity. Quickly seared and pink in the middle, it is nestled among shiitake mush-rooms and a first-rate veal-stock sauce. Lighter appetizers are available—sparkling cold salads, rosy cold poached salmon, vegetable combinations, and the like—and the attentive staff is reasonable about preparing various combinations.

La Côte Basque has one of the most impressive (and expensive) wine cellars in town. The list is top-heavy with $30-and-up bottles and heavily biased toward reds.

Entrées religiously follow the bible of classic French cooking, and most dishes are paragons of the genre. It might be as rudimentary as homey roast chicken with pan juices and tarragon sauce, lusty steak au poivre, or a more intricate creation such as succulent stuffed quail in pastry crust with truffle sauce. All reflect the Rachou style—brassy, indulgent, and comforting. Roast duck is similarly memorable, with puffed crisp skin, savory meat, and a well-balanced pepper sauce. Pasta with shiitake mushrooms makes a good earthy sidekick.

If elephants had edible sweetbreads, they would probably be about the same size as those served here. Once you get over their staggering size, you will find them to be fresh, firm, and delicious, in an engaging veal-stock sauce tinged with Madeira and garnished with pearl onions. Simple grilled seafood—sole, salmon, and red snapper—is always good. What is described as salmon with sorrel, though, turned out to be rather heavily battered fillets in a thick red-wine sauce that suffocated the delicate fish.

Polite protestations will not keep the pastry cart from your door. Assuming your will is broken, let me suggest the airy vanilla bavarois with raspberry sauce, the excellent hazelnut dacquoise, a ripe white peach tart, and the silky, concentrated chocolate mousse. Frozen raspberry soufflé is as stunning to behold as it is delicious, luxuriant with vanilla and fresh fruit.

La Côte Basque's traditional style, like a button down oxford shirt, may not suit everyone in this lean and restless era. But for those who yearn for unabashed luxury and uncompromising classic fare, it is still the place to go.

LAFAYETTE

★ ★ ★ ★

65 East 56th Street, 832-1565.

Atmosphere: Plush and civilized. Well-spaced tables, quiet.

Service: Low-key and excellent.

Price range: Expensive.

Credit cards: All major cards.

Hours: Lunch, noon to 2:30 P.M., Monday through Friday; dinner, 6:30 to 10:30 P.M., Monday through Friday, 6 to 10:30 P.M., Saturday.

Reservations: Required at least a week in advance.

Wheelchair accessibility: All facilities on one level.

❧ The Drake Hotel opened its sumptuous restaurant, Lafayette, in July 1986, with the reserve and discretion of a Swiss banker—actually, the hotel is owned by two Swiss companies, Swissair and Nestlé S.A. Within two years it became one of the city's most exhilarating dining rooms under the direction of two French chefs: Louis Outhier, the consultant, who had a Michelin three-star restaurant on the French Riviera, and his startlingly gifted protégé, Jean-Georges Vongerichten, who is the full-time chef.

Mr. Outhier closed his own restaurant, L'Oasis in the town of La Napoule, to consult at a half-dozen establishments around the world. He certainly need not lose sleep over his New York operation when on the road. Mr. Vongerichten, a thirty-one-year-old native of Alsace, brilliantly executes the sunny, herb-infused cuisine of Mediterranean France for which his mentor is renowned. Cream is virtually absent in the kitchen; instead, fresh vegetable juices or olive oil are the foundations for many sauces. The young chef's repertory is exquisitely refined yet never fussy, and the galaxy of flavors found on the menu reflects Mr. Vongerichten's cosmopolitan background.

After training for three and a half years at Auberge de l'Ill in Alsace, Mr. Vongerichten joined Mr. Outhier's flying chef squadron, where he has been ever since, with the exception of stints with Paul Bocuse and another apprenticeship in West Germany. Mr. Vongerichten's assignments have taken him to restaurants in Bangkok, Singapore, London, and Boston before coming to New York.

Lafayette's dining room is plush and spacious, done in soothing shades of beige and cream. Tables are widely spaced, and extraneous sound is muffled. The crepuscular lighting sometimes makes it difficult to read the menu. When a waiter saw us straining, he came by and gave us tiny flashlights, the kind children twirl at the circus. In addition to the $55 prix-fixe dinner menu ($37.50 at lunch) one can order from two tasting menus, at $65 and $75.

You can begin with such light offerings as slices of turnip wrapped around goat cheese to form little ravioli, in a richly flavored duck broth along with strips of rare duck breast. Another is a carpaccio of tuna and black sea bass molded together to create a marbled effect, ringed with minced sweet pepper, eggplant, zucchini, and olives glossed with saffron-and-basil vinaigrette. Sea urchin is given a new dimension here. The saline roe is the base for a terrific cold soufflé ringed by fresh periwinkles, Belon oysters, and clams in a shellfish stock enhanced with lemongrass.

A provocative starter that borrows from Asian cooking is called crab and Swiss chard cannelloni. Fresh crabmeat and Swiss chard are enveloped in sheets of fresh pasta and set over a pale yellow sauce made with reduced vegetable bouillon and carrot juice, then seasoned with cardamom and bound with a little butter—an extraordinary fusion, just faintly sweet from the carrots. Another Eastern-influenced creation is perfectly cooked shrimp with pearl onions, fresh peas, and bacon in a complex yet incredibly subtle broth blending carrot juice, lime juice, nutmeg, and cinnamon. Typical of the Provençale style is fresh crayfish arranged over a fan of zucchini and ripe tomatoes in an aromatic basil-and-olive-oil dressing. In cooler months, foie gras is prepared masterfully, in more than a dozen ways.

The service staff at Lafayette is as refined as the food. They never hover, never fawn, yet when you need something, they magically appear. The international wine list has fine selections in every price range. Temperature-controlled rooms assure that the reds are always cellar temperature.

Mr. Vongerichten's light touch with seafood makes for some dynamic entrées. Fillet of salmon is hidden under a brittle lid of potatoes Maxim and ringed with a sweetly perfumed sauce of sherry vinegar, leeks, and caviar; halibut is equally arresting as a special, set in a vegetable-enriched fish-stock sauce bound with beurre blanc, accompanied by a "spaghetti" of blanched cucumbers. For showmanship, nothing matches the whole sea bass in a meticulously sculptured pastry crust with a tarragon-tomato sauce.

Roasted guinea hen, more meaty and flavorful than chicken, comes in an assertive olive oil sauce bolstered with herbs and lemon rind along with an airy timbale of parsley. Roasted rabbit with crisply fried leeks is flavorful but sometimes dry. Spit-roasted baby goat, its meat ruddy and mild, is compelling in its reduced marinade with fresh peas and carrots. The list of superlatives goes on.

The pastry chef, Jean-Marc Burillier, has vastly improved the desserts in the past year. Among those to watch for are the exceptionally light meringue and Bavarian cream pie, the two-layered cake of passion fruit mousse and chocolate over a bright citric sauce, gratin of wild raspberries, and hazelnut anisette layer cake. Only a chocolate truffle and Grand Marnier cake came up short by chocoholic standards. A puff pastry and rhubarb tart ringed with straw-berry purée is a serendipitous way to celebrate the season of renewal—and one of New York's newest four-star chefs.

LA GAULOISE

★ ★

502 Avenue of the Americas, between 12th and 13th streets, 691-1363.

Atmosphere: Comfortable and unpretentious bistro setting.

Service: Generally professional.

Price range: Moderate.

Credit cards: American Express, MasterCard, and Visa.

Hours: Brunch, noon to 3 P.M., Saturday and Sunday; lunch, noon to 3 P.M., Tuesday through Sunday; dinner, 5:30 to 11:30 P.M., Tuesday through Sunday.

Reservations: Suggested.

Wheelchair accessibility: One step at entrance; all facilities are on one level.

&. For more than a decade, long before French bistros became the rage in Manhattan, La Gauloise has been quietly and competently serving up such homespun fare as mussels marinière, pepper steak and french fries, roasted rabbit, roast chicken, and crème brûlée. This handsome and genial spot on the northern rim of Greenwich Village is still doing so today and at prices that make it worth a detour for those seeking a civilized business lunch or a pretheater dinner.

Speaking of pepper steak, of which I am an ardent fan, the version prepared here is among the best I have found in town—assertive, piquant, and in a sheer cream-based sauce that masks the harshness of the peppers without snuffing out the flame. Buttery, crisp-skinned rösti potatoes, carrot purée, and assorted vegetables round out this most satisfying repast. Roast chicken, the other touchstone of bistro fare, is prepared with motherly love as well.

In this era of unremittingly chic restaurant design, La Gauloise is as comforting as a down pillow. Polished dark-wood trim and mirrored panels combine with etched-glass room dividers and benevolent lighting to provide an authentic French setting. Jacques Alliman, one of the original partners—the other, Camille Dulac, left several years ago to run Le Chantilly in midtown—is a likable fellow and vigilant host.

Appetizers are the weakest players in the lineup. Rillettes of salmon are dry and uninteresting; confit of duck, in a pretty green-bean salad, is properly rich textured but needs more seasonings, and smoked trout, a special, was mealy and paired with a thin, pale raifort sauce. Tasty and fresh pâté de campagne is a reliable starter.

The wine selection is thoughtfully attuned to the menu, although you will be hard-pressed to find many bargains.

The chef's major strength is sauces, which are concentrated and harmoniously seasoned. The delicately seared sheet of salmon paillard, for example, is paired with a refined tarragon sauce that lets the luxurious fish shine through. That would have been the case with grilled tuna steak, under a vinegar-edged white-wine-and-horseradish sauce, had the fish not been dry from overcooking. The accompaniments were better: couscous, carrot purée, and a vibrant ratatouille.

Sweetbreads are given a brittle carapace when sautéed in butter, and the richness is cut by a piquant green-peppercorn sauce. Lamb steak, something you don't find often in restaurants, is a restorative winner with its pan drippings sweetened with roasted shallots. If you like rabbit, try the beguiling preparation of tender white medallions bolstered with a mild tarragon-mustard sauce. While soft-shell crabs are in season they are worth getting, simply sautéed in butter until crackling and golden outside.

The dessert cart carries familiar bistro regulars. The best bets are the excellent crème brûlée with a lid of translucent burnt sugar, pears poached in red wine, custardy bread pudding with coffee sauce, and classic oeuf à la neige. Don't risk the guilt for puny and oversauced profiteroles or the grainy and overly sweet charlotte of pears.

There is something reassuring and warm about La Gauloise that goes beyond a laundry list of dishes. It may be the unpretentious setting, the neighborly crowd it attracts, or the genial pampering by Mr. Alliman. A real French bistro is a place that puts one at ease. On that account, La Gauloise continues to succeed.

LA GRENOUILLE

★

3 East 52nd Street, 752-1495.

Atmosphere: Plush and soft-edged dining room resplendent with flowers.

Service: Generally efficient, if colorless and routine.

Price range: Expensive.

Credit cards: All major cards.

Hours: Lunch, noon to 2:30 P.M., Tuesday through Saturday; dinner, 6 to 11:30 P.M., Tuesday through Saturday.

Reservations: Necessary.

Wheelchair accessibility: All facilities on one level; management requests advance notice to reserve the most accommodating tables.

❧ La Grenouille, still run by the Masson family that started it, has been on a regrettable slide for the past few years, partly the result of staff defections and inconsistency in the kitchen. The current chef, Gérard Chotard, joined the team in late summer of 1987, but so far he has not enlivened the sometimes stodgy, high-priced food.

The capacious, richly upholstered dining room is partitioned in two—the front reserved for celebrities and regulars, the equally accommodating back, ringed by soft crimson banquettes, for the rest. Prodigious clusters of seasonal flowers tower in the corners. Unfamiliar patrons run the risk of being sentenced to a Gallic purgatory along the back wall, hard against the kitchen door, where the clatter and chatter can be unnerving.

Seasoned French waiters, with a few notable exceptions, are efficient but lack the vitality and spirit one expects at this level of restaurant. Among the appetizer specials, a lobster terrine was attractively arranged on the plate, fresh and brightly seasoned—our waiter arrived with the accompanying toast just as I was taking a last bite ("I guess it's too late for this," he said). For a $16 supplement, you can get a slab of rosy duck foie gras along with a thin, commercial-tasting gelatin purportedly made with Sauternes. The same foie gras shows up in a nice green salad sprinkled with black truffles that, too, have lost their punch.

Crab cakes are plump and deliciously sinewy; another

special, lobster mousse, sweet and light, was set in a compelling sweet-edged port sauce. Such menu standards as baked littleneck clams are rubbery, and the purée of pea soup called St. Germain is anemic. Lobster bisque, though, is the real thing, velvety and intense. I don't know where La Grenouille gets its dense whole-wheat raisin rolls, but they are more suited to a delicatessen than an haute French establishment.

The wine list has a few reasonable buys in the $20-to-$35 range but prices shoot up quickly to the $70-and-higher range.

The best entrées include a snappy steak au poivre with a delicious celery purée, rack of lamb with a tarragon-perfumed stock sauce, and grilled sole with a mild mustard sauce (and limp haricots verts). Braised sweetbreads were lusty in their morel sauce on the first visit, yet on a second try the morels were pale-tasting and the sauce watery. Chicken in a champagne cream sauce had more richness than flavor. A better option is the pot-au-feu, an occasional special, a savory combination of oxtail, duck confit, and winter vegetables.

The lunch menu offers something called jardinière of seasonal vegetables. The season must be winter, for everything tastes frozen: soggy broccoli and turnips, pale plum tomatoes, waterlogged baby corn—all heaped unceremoniously on the plate without seasoning. Another special, described by our waiter as "braised veal in brown sauce," was so dry it tasted like overcooked turkey breast. Lobster is delicately prepared, however, served out of the shell in a herbaceous clear sauce along with chives, tomato, and potatoes.

As for desserts, the soufflé for two—we opted for raspberry with raspberry sauce—was so sugary we could not finish it. Another night, chocolate soufflé was excellent. Bread-and-butter pudding was less impressive looking but a winner, all crusty and moist. Chocolate mousse was sublime.

La Grenouille still carries the prices and trappings of a first-class French restaurant, yet in recent years the food quality has dropped from four stars to one. You can't eat the flowers.

LA MÉTAIRIE

★

189 West 10th Street, 989-0343.

Atmosphere: Small, dark, romantic dining room.

Service: Informal but efficient and friendly.

Price range: Moderately expensive.

Credit cards: American Express, MasterCard, and Visa.

Hours: Dinner, 6 to 11 P.M., Monday through Thursday, 6 to 11:30 P.M., Friday and Saturday, 5 to 11 P.M., Sunday. Closed Sundays in summer.

Reservations: Required.

Wheelchair accessibility: One small step at entrance; all facilities on one level.

  La Métairie, a warm and welcoming French bistro in the West Village, is such a pint-size place it gives the resident of a Manhattan studio apartment the impression of returning home to Gracie Mansion after dinner. Some might call it intimate, others romantic. Whatever, it is a charming neighborhood spot that favors solid bistro food that is as honest as a country prior.

The dining room, which can squeeze in about two dozen with a crowbar, has a dark, lodgelike feeling with several tables in the center and banquettes around the walls. Two doves in a cage hanging from the ceiling oversee the proceedings.

A new chef arrived recently so the menu is undergoing significant revisions. For starters, there is a pleasantly gamy and well-seasoned duck pâté. It comes with a small terrine of airy duck-liver mousse tinted with port wine. Puff pastry filled with lobster is well made but marred by a stodgy brown sauce. Roseate gravlax is sparkling, firm, and redolent of dill, while the lamb's-lettuce salad with a warm bacon dressing tends to be too much of a good thing—the dainty greens sometimes are inundated in dressing.

Grilled fish are prepared with care, whether Dover sole with mustard butter or salmon with dill sauce.

The last time I had the sautéed boneless lamb with mint sauce it was on the tough side and lacked mint flavor. Better was the boned duck in a Calvados-accented sauce with raisins and apples. The duck was tasty, relatively lean, and greaseless.

The kitchen turns out some fine French desserts, such as tarte Tatin, a multilayered upside-down apple tart with a caramelized glaze, and a good bombe glacée with praline ice cream. My favorite, however, is the richly smooth and tropical papaya ice cream served in a frozen papaya shell.

LA MÉTAIRIE (East)

★

1442 Third Avenue, at 82nd Street, 988-1800.

Atmosphere: Enchanting farmhouse setting.

Service: Generally professional but can get overwhelmed.

Price range: Moderately expensive.

Credit cards: American Express, MasterCard, and Visa.

Hours: Brunch, 12 to 3 P.M., Saturday and Sunday; lunch, noon to 3 P.M., Monday through Friday; dinner, 6 P.M. to midnight, Monday through Saturday, 5 to 11 P.M., Sunday.

Reservations: Necessary.

Wheelchair accessibility: One step up at the entrance; all facilities on one level.

La Métairie is the uptown branch (in name, not style) of the minuscule French bistro on West 10th Street owned by Sylvain Fareri, a Tunisian-born Frenchman. The setting is so enchanting—a tasteful stucco farmhouse motif complete with a stone hearth, gleaming copper sconces, brass lanterns, clumps of dried wildflowers—that one expects wonderful earthy French food to emerge from the kitchen. That was not the case in the restaurant's early days. However, in July 1988 a first-rate French chef, Patrice Boely, formerly of the Polo in the Westbury Hotel, joined the staff. As this book went to press changes for the better were being made.

When dishes succeed here, they can be memorable. Garlic mousse is a knockout, a quivering light custard bursting with flavor and flanked by sautéed shiitake mushrooms. Another recommended starter is the oversize ravioli filled with a fricassee of scallops and lobster in a frothy champagne-butter sauce. On the lighter side are a sprightly salad of endive, beets, and cool fresh oysters sprinkled with lime, and buttery Scottish salmon glossed with a lovely walnut-oil-and-vinegar dressing.

On the other hand, the appetizer of artichoke terrine with lobster sauce is a disappointment. The light and creamy terrine has intense artichoke flavor but not a fleck of perceptible seasoning. The lobster sauce is luxuriant, but the combination is unbalanced. Sweetbread-and-foie-gras terrine rates an A+ for texture and freshness but, once again, is bland.

Take your time with the appetizers because the next course may not be ready for a long time. Service is well schooled but exceedingly slow when under pressure. La Métairie's wine list salutes all the big-name producers, but it is hardly a bargain-hunter's paradise—Mâcon-Lugny, which sells for about $6 retail, is an insult at $21.

The kitchen specializes in wood-fire grilling, and to underscore that point the kitchen door is opened from time to time, allowing scintillating campfire aromas to fill the dining room. I was befuddled by the grilled dishes sampled, however, for few had any wood-grilled flavor. Two seafood entrées—Hawaiian tuna steak and swordfish—tasted as if they had been oven-broiled then cosmetically cross-hatched with a red-hot iron, an age-old steakhouse trick.

Some of the best entrées are on the nongrill side of the menu. Rack of lamb Provençale style was superbly tender and vividly seasoned with garlic, rosemary, and thyme, accompanied by sautéed potatoes—better than the grilled lamb chop with mint butter. Sautéed veal chops savoyarde, encased in Gruyère cheese, ham, and tomato flavored with Madeira, was succulent and arresting, too. On Thursdays during the cold months the kitchen prepares a terrific bollito misto, the Italian boiled dinner—a bargain at $15 (lunch) and $22 (dinner).

The dessert highlight is called honey crisp, layers of brittle ultra-thin pancakes sandwiching fluffy whipped cream and mixed berries, all in a moat of patterned crème anglaise. Homemade ice creams and fruit sorbets are intense and summery; blueberry dacquoise is a winner, too.

LA MIRABELLE

★

333 West 86th Street, between Riverside Drive and West End Avenue, 496-0458.

Atmosphere: Quaint and simple little dining room off the lobby of a residential hotel. Moderate noise level.

Service: Amiable and efficient.

Price range: Moderate.

Credit cards: All major cards.

Hours: Dinner, 6 to 10 P.M., Monday through Thursday, 6 to 10:30 P.M., Friday and Saturday.

Reservations: Suggested.

Wheelchair accessibility: Two steps at entrance; all facilities on one level.

🐌 La Mirabelle, a little pearl of a French restaurant ensconced in a thread-worn aristocratic hotel residence on West 86th Street, is a far cry from the splashy pastel grilleries that are ubiquitous on the Upper West Side.

The restaurant belongs to Annick Le Douaron and Denise Vienot, two welcoming and delightful entrepreneurs who once worked together at La Bonne Bouffe in midtown. They handle everything up front, while the chef, Joel Gaidon, and his nephew, Frank Rozet, run the kitchen. The three tiny dining rooms are charming and tranquil in their own anachronistic way: pink-and-white wall panels with ornate moldings, icicle chandeliers, a little service bar on one side, and simply appointed tables. You are greeted warmly by the owners and offered a cocktail or a selection from the limited wine list while perusing the short, classically oriented menu.

This is nostalgia food, the kind of straightforward, flavorful repasts that the owners no doubt served to their families back home. There are no surprises here, but plenty of delights—and at affordable prices. Start with the vernal soupe au pistou, a restorative mélange of fresh spring vegetables in a flavor-packed broth, and creamy coquilles St. Jacques with its thin lid of molten cheese. Glossy sautéed chicken livers with bacon and raspberry vinegar is another invigorating starter. So is the subtly exceptional vichyssoise. The only disappointments are the house pâté and three-fish mousse, both of which are oversalted.

Eight regular entrées are supplemented by two or three daily specials. Almost all are French standards performed to the letter of the old book. Some of the sauces may be a bit thick for modern tastes, but they do not lack flavor, as is so common in today's lighter style of cooking. Dover sole with lemon and butter, sautéed soft-shell crabs with chopped fresh tomatoes (a special), monkfish in a sauce of tomatoes, white wine, and tarragon—all are nicely cooked, and served with al dente buttered carrots and creamed green beans. No cuisine minceur disciple, this chef. All desserts are homemade. Among the best are the fragile-crusted and delicious tarte Tatin, a rich strawberry-and-whipped-cream cake, and an embarrassingly intense chocolate mousse cake made with good-quality chocolate. Ideally, that is how it should be—every neighborhood should have

213

a modest restaurant serving wholesome, lovingly prepared food for a fair price. Unfortunately, though, that is the ideal. La Mirabelle is a special little place, and its "neighborhood" is lucky to have it.

LA PETITE FERME

★

973 Lexington Avenue, between 70th and 71st streets, 249-3272.

Atmosphere: Cozy and romantic Provençale setting.

Service: Casual and easygoing.

Price range: Moderately expensive.

Credit cards: All major cards.

Hours: Lunch, noon to 2:30 P.M., Monday through Saturday; dinner, 6 to 10:30 P.M., Monday through Saturday.

Reservations: Suggested.

Wheelchair accessibility: Five steps at entrance; restrooms down steep flight of stairs.

🐚 Few Manhattan restaurants are as casually enchanting as La Petite Ferme. This little nook resembles a dollhouse, with its stucco walls, farmhouse shutters, rough-hewn beams, stenciled wallpaper, and glazed earthenware plates. The once-spirited country food, however, has wilted a little.

It is not that the provender is of inferior quality, but rather that too often seasonings are in short supply, resulting in dishes that are fresh but flat. This is all the more frustrating because expectations are higher when the restaurant's daily chalkboard menu carries only four changing entrées and a handful of appetizers.

As you peruse the wine selection, a plate of golden homemade potato chips is placed on the table along with dense-crusted French bread. If game terrines are available, I suggest you try one. The rabbit-and-duck terrine is richly flavored and faintly peppery, served with hot mustard and cornichons. Steamed asparagus glossed with butter is soothing if hardly provocative; a more distinctive starter is creamy and aromatic mushroom soup. Mussels are a house special, big meaty monsters in a snappy mustard vinaigrette—one evening they tasted old and limp, another night resilient and fresh.

The casual waiters and waitresses have an easygoing attitude about service that might be nettlesome elsewhere but seems appropriate in this tranquil setting—except when our waiter inadvertently served two of our entrées to an adjacent table.

A French restaurant does not come to mind when one yearns for a good poached lobster, but the sweet and meaty two-pounder here, slickened with a shallot-flecked, red-wine-vinegar sauce, equaled that served at most of the better fishhouses in town. Fillets of sole rolled around an underseasoned salmon mousse with beurre blanc, however, were bland.

Meat entrées suffer less from the blands: entrecôte with maître d'hôtel herb butter stands well on its own, full flavored and tender; chicken in a classic chasseur sauce, combining mushrooms and shallots, is ruggedly enjoyable, while a moist chicken breast in a pallid wine-and-herb sauce falls flat.

La Petite Ferme is one of those soothing spots where you tend to linger longer than usual before facing the shrill of the real world. The uniformly good desserts make it even more tempting to dally. Fruit tarts are winners all, especially the brittle-crusted, glistening raspberry; the dense fudgelike chocolate terrine benefits from its pool of crème anglaise, and fruit sorbets—passion fruit, papaya, kiwi, and raspberry—are smooth-textured and vibrant.

LA RESERVE

★ ★ ★

4 West 49th Street, 247-2993.

Atmosphere: Elegant cafélike dining rooms with comfortable fabric banquettes, oversize paintings, and soft lighting.

Service: Snappy; mostly European veterans, thoroughly professional and congenial.

Price range: Expensive.

Credit cards: All major cards.

Hours: Lunch, noon to 3 P.M., Monday through Saturday; pretheater dinner, 5:30 to 7 P.M., Monday through Saturday; dinner, 7 to 10:30 P.M., Monday through Thursday, 7 to 11:30 P.M., Friday and Saturday.

Reservations: Suggested.

Wheelchair accessibility: All facilities on one level.

&❦ André Gaillard, the young Burgundian chef at this splendid midtown setting, continues to improve the menu here and win a wide circle of followers. His cooking orientation is strongly classical, his touch is light. This is evident in some of his appetizers, such as the warm lobster-and-asparagus flan, which is an ethereal delight infused with shellfish flavor and garnished with a diadem of lobster morsels. It is presented in a pool of tangy watercress sauce with asparagus spears. Watercress was well chosen, for its slight sharpness cuts through the rich lobster flavor like a razor, yielding a vivid taste sensation.

His most dazzling creation, a special, was the seafood charlotte. It consisted of a silky sole mousse cooked in a charlotte mold and filled with pieces of scallops, shrimp, tomato, and mushroom, seasoned with flecks of fresh tarragon. Clinging to the surface were strips of carrots and turnips. The sauce, a beurre blanc garnished with laces of pousse-pied, a seaweed from Brittany, formed a tableau that was as arresting as it was delicious.

Less elaborate starters included slices of fresh salmon and calico scallops marinated with dill, and a delectable slab of fresh foie gras sautéed with hydromel (a fermented-honey mixture), garnished with baby vegetables, and served with a crunchy potato basket filled brim-high with woodsy wild mushrooms. In the near-miss department were a chewy lobster salad and a pâté of duck liver that left an acrid aftertaste.

One of the soups sampled—jellied lobster tail flavored with chili peppers—was outstanding, ideal for a warm summer day. The cold aspic soup, intensely flavored with lobster essence, was as briny and refreshing as an ocean spray, and the pinch of chili added a rousing extra dimension.

A crew of mostly veteran European waiters provides sharp and attentive service. The captains are familiar with the wine list, which is a bit pricey on the lower end of the scale but offers a good range.

Mr. Gaillard happily does not belong to what might be called the "kitchen sink" school of cooking—a little of this and a little of that and a little more of this until the dish is so cluttered one's palate goes tilt like a pinball machine. His fish preparations, for example, are well focused and straightforward. A crisp-skinned grilled fillet of red mullet was memorable, with the judicious addition of clove giving a subtle zip to the sauce. A sprinkling of fresh coriander did the same with a buerre-blanc-coated poached salmon. But turbot with lemongrass and caviar fell flat because the fish was overcooked and the lemongrass imperceptible.

If you try only one fish, though, get the regal poached Dover sole: two firm and fresh fillets sandwiched around a well-seasoned layer of creamy artichoke mousse. The fillets, embellished with threads of various root vegetables and slivers of truffles, were served in a glossy pool of beurre blanc dotted with tiny lobster-filled ravioli.

In the meat category, you can enjoy a good roasted duck with a gingered cranberry sauce, tender fillets of lamb in an aromatic saffron-and-mint sauce, equally good veal in a sherry-vinegar sauce, and a wonderfully earthy fricassee of veal kidneys and sweetbreads with red cabbage in a mild curry sauce.

Desserts are copious and ever-changing. Tops among them was a mango mousse cake oozing with the flavor of that tropical fruit under an unsweetened soft meringue lid. Equally good was the warm, ripe pear enclosed in phyllo sheets that folded open at the top like a budding flower, surrounded by a semisweet chocolate sauce. Other winners include the plum tart with fresh raspberry sauce, an intensely fruity bavaroise of raspberries, and moist carrot-and-pistachio layer cake veined with whipped cream. Exceptions were a dark and textureless version of crème brûlée, a sodden-crusted apple tart, and a run-of-the-mill chocolate cake topped with a dry cream puff. La Réserve's two dining rooms are as enchanting as ever, with their beige and peach banquettes, high ceilings, giant printings of birds in marshlands, and soft lighting. With the marked improvement in food, it is a formula for success.

LA TULIPE

★ ★ ★

104 West 13th Street, between Avenue of the Americas and Seventh Avenue, 691-8860.

Atmosphere: Intimate and formal.

Service: Cool and inattentive; waits for entrées can be extremely long.

Price range: Expensive.

Credit cards: All major cards.

Hours: Dinner, 6:30 to 10 P.M., Tuesday through Sunday.

Reservations: Necessary.

Wheelchair accessibility: Two steps at entrance; all facilities on one level.

🐝 La Tulipe remains one of the most popular luxury restaurants in Greenwich Village, largely on the strength of the pampering French fare turned out by Sally Darr, the chef and co-owner. Recent visits have found it to be less intimate and charming than before—in fact it can be rattlingly loud when full. Moreover, the indifferent service staff has not improved. Wine is left unpoured, water glasses remain empty, and every little request seems to require wild gesticulating to get the attention of the urbane-looking maître d'hôtel, who manages to be everywhere yet nowhere. At nearly $60 prix fixe, one expects much better. The food, however, is as good as ever.

You enter the restaurant's little Parisian-style bar then pass down a hallway into a dining room with chocolate-colored walls, corduroy banquettes, and graceful tulip sconces. The seasonal regular menu carries about five appetizers. Shrimp is prepared with a delightful Oriental touch in a salad with ginger and scallions and a warm sesame sauce, and lovely leek terrine comes with a sharp mustard sauce. Fresh foie gras may be sautéed lightly and placed over a slice of garlic toast with raisins, pearl onions, and a sweet duck-stock sauce.

Even tomato soup can be memorable. You receive a bowl with leaves of fresh mint and basil on the bottom as well as julienne strips of tomato and a dab of crème fraîche. The steaming soup, thick and unseasonally flavorful, is poured over the condiments, then stirred.

Mrs. Darr's entrées are always well conceived; she stresses flavor over flashiness. A magnificent game dish is blush-red slices of grilled squab laid over a hillock of sautéed spinach, onions, and pine nuts, all surrounded by a parapet of couscous. Another inspired country preparation is confit of duck legs with lentils. A lustrous special one evening was boned baby chicken stuffed with foie gras and served with a sauce rich with morels and cèpes. Lamb is always arresting, whether with couscous and spinach flecked with pine nuts and raisins, or grilled with mustard butter and potato galettes.

The restaurant excels at seafood dishes: typical of the preparations are red snapper cooked in parchment paper with herbs and vegetables; remarkably sweet sautéed bay scallops presented over sautéed spinach and doused with sizzling brown butter and an oceanic ragout of seafood—scallops, whitefish, lobster, mussels, shrimp—in an excellent red shellfish stock.

La Tulipe has some stellar desserts. Apple tart is brittle and delicious, two-layer ganache-and-bittersweet-chocolate cake is smooth and intense. A tall wedge of temptation called bombe Javanaise comprises coffee ice cream and chocolate mousse in a cloud of whipped cream, all surrounded with pecans and caramel sauce. The other choices are crumbly tulip-shaped tuiles filled with vanilla ice cream, toasted almonds, and hot chocolate sauce, and l'île flottante with praline sauce.

LAVIN'S

★

23 West 39th Street, 921-1288.

Atmosphere: Classy café ambiance; excellent wine bar.

Service: Competent and congenial.

Price range: Moderately expensive.

Credit cards: All major cards.

Hours: Lunch, noon to 2:30 P.M., Monday through Friday; dinner, 5:30 to 9 P.M., Monday through Friday; bar open until midnight.

Reservations: Necessary, especially for lunch.

Wheelchair accessibility: Three steps up at entrance; all facilities on one level.

🍷 Lavin's, a comely American restaurant in the heart of the busy garment district on West 39th Street, is a lively spot at lunchtime, but subdued at night. The large rectangular dining room has a classy café feeling with carved oak-paneled walls and symmetrical rows of neighborly tables. In the front of the house is Mr. Lavin's pride and joy, a comfortable wine bar offering an ever-changing selection of by-the-glass offerings. Mr. Lavin, the owner (his son now oversees the restaurant as father tends to Sofi on Fifth Avenue), an oenophile with a particular fondness for California, always has delightful surprises on his wide and fairly priced list.

The lunch menu is not only bigger but also better than that at dinner. The cooking here is particularly well suited to working people because of its light and salubrious approach, minimizing cream, butter, and salt. Sometimes the kitchen goes a bit too far, especially in omitting salt, which can result in healthful but flat-tasting food.

Winning appetizers at lunch and dinner include a lustrous mesquite-perfumed carpaccio of beef, wonderfully smoky and moist, and a vivid carpaccio of tuna with capers. Oysters on the half shell are unassailably fresh and flavorful—all the more reason not to gussy them up with a confetti of vegetables that only muddle their flavor and texture. The only soup sampled, a rough-textured gazpacho, was refreshing and delicious with a zippy undercurrent.

Pastas, which can be split as appetizers, have their ups and downs. The best sampled were spaghetti Provençale-style colored with green beans, carrots, broccoli, and red peppers, all glossed with a light butter-and-chicken-stock sauce and dusted with Parmesan cheese; a more hearty rendition blended mild and lean veal sausage, asparagus, and tomato. One pasta appetizer to sidestep is ravioli filled with sinewy scallops and shrimp in a jarring lemon sauce.

The service team at Lavin's, mostly well-scrubbed collegiate types, manages to keep a fairly steady pace at lunch, which is no minor feat.

As for entreés, simple grilled items fare best, such as the terrific swordfish steak, cooked to just pink in the center and jazzed up with a spirited tomatillo sauce spiked with cilantro. Grilled veal chop is done with equal skill, and paired with deliciously crunchy straw potatoes. One flop among the grilled items is calf's liver, which was overcooked and had to be returned; the reprise was better but sorely needed salt.

All notions of health food are tossed overboard when it comes to the uniformly excellent desserts: chunky bread pudding moistened with a heady bourbon sauce, profiteroles with luxuriant mint ice cream and chocolate sauce, silky crème brûlée, and a flourless chocolate cake that is so rich it should be subject to a windfall-profits tax.

While it is likely you will have a two-star lunch at Lavin's, the less favorable odds at dinner preclude a two-star overall rating. One is more appropriate.

LE BERNARDIN

★ ★ ★ ★

155 West 51st Street, 489-1515.

Atmosphere: Luxurious and clubby room with well-spaced tables.

Service: Knowledgeable and efficient.

Price range: Expensive (lunch prix fixe, $40; dinner prix fixe, $65).

Credit cards: All major cards.

Hours: Lunch, noon to 2:15 P.M., Monday through Saturday; dinner, 6 to 10:15 P.M., Monday through Saturday.

Reservations: Necessary.

Wheelchair accessibility: All facilities on one level.

꙳ Le Bernardin is nothing short of a revolutionary seafood restaurant that has forged new frontiers in fish cookery in this country. Gilbert Le Coze, the chef, and his sister, Maguy, the alluring hostess, originally had hoped to run their original Le Bernardin, in Paris, simultaneously with the New York branch. The overwhelming success on this side of the Atlantic forced them to make a decision in 1987; fortunately for fish lovers, they chose New York.

The dining room, which is in the $16.5-million restaurant complex at the Equitable Assurance Tower (Palio and Sam's Restaurant share the ground floor), was designed by Miss Le Coze with the architect Philip George (and bankrolled by Equitable, which has a lease arrangement with the owners). It exudes a lavishly clubby and corporate feeling: a soaring teak ceiling, gray-blue walls, generously spaced tables, and larger-than-life paintings of fishermen and their catch.

Mr. Le Coze, who grew up on the Brittany coast, where his family has a hotel and restaurant, is fanatical when it comes to freshness. Such dedication can be seen in a glistening array of oysters (Belons, Cotuits, bluepoints) and addictive littlenecks on the half shell, and in the lagniappe of periwinkles that you pick out of their shells with pins. The flavor is akin to being gently washed by an ocean wave.

Under the category of raw appetizers, don't miss the pearly sheets of black bass flecked with coriander and basil and lacquered with extra-virgin olive oil, a sensational combination, or the sparkling salad of marinated fish. Deepfried squid can be delicious.

The rest of the starters are terrific and, like all dishes here, are minimally cooked to allow the freshness of the sea to shine through. Among my favorites are sea scallops in various guises. In one preparation, attributed to the French chef Georges Blanc, three giant scallops on the half shell are served in an exquisite sauce combining the scallops' brine, some butter, and a dash of saffron. They are garnished with asparagus, thin strips of fresh tomato, and fennel sprigs. Two sheets of fresh salmon are pressed over basil leaves and mixed herbs and presented atop strips of fennel and diced ripe tomatoes, all drizzled with olive oil and lemon—a startlingly simple yet sublime combination.

If you have never tried a sea urchin, those saline little porcupines of the sea, let Mr. Le Coze make the introduction. He scoops out the orange roe and blends it with butter, then returns it to the shell, where it is mixed with the urchin's warm briny nectar.

From time to time patrons, especially first-timers, write to me about abrupt or indifferent service at Le Bernardin. This may reflect occasional overbooking and a harried staff. Some contend they get the bum's rush when a table is booked for a second seating. It is difficult to gauge how often these unforgivable lapses occur, for most of the time the staff is crisply professional. Le Bernardin's wine list is well attuned to the food, but pricey.

As for entrées, thin strips of blush-pink salmon are presented on a red-hot platter in a bubbling sorrel-and-white-wine sauce. Mr. Le Coze times the presentation so perfectly that the fish actually finishes cooking at the table on the hot plate. A thick slab of salmon, just this side of sushi in the center, comes in a small casserole atop an ethereal tomato-cream sauce, and garnished with fresh mint. There was some quibbling at my table about whether the poached halibut in a warm herb vinaigrette was a tad too acidic, but all agreed they had never tasted halibut so moist and fresh.

Other memorable selections include flash-sautéed shrimp emboldened with cracked pepper paired with eggplant caviar, superb turbot with lobster sauce, and lightly browned codfish in red-wine sauce.

When it's time for dessert, you can either remain afloat with a palette of intense, fresh fruit sorbets or sink to the ocean floor with the meltingly rich chocolate cake, a buttery thin apple tart, or a dazzling sampler of caramel sweets: caramel ice cream, flan, oeuf à la neige, and caramel mousse. My favorite is the trio of pears, which combines a cinnamon-tinged poached pear along with a warm tiny pear tart and pear sorbet.

LE CHANTILLY

★ ★

106 East 57th Street, 751-2931.

Atmosphere: Plush and comfortable old-world dining room with generously separated tables.

Service: Professional and vigilant.

Price range: Moderately expensive.

Credit cards: All major cards.

Hours: Lunch, noon to 3 P.M., Monday through Saturday; dinner, 5:30 to 11 P.M., Monday through Saturday. Closed Saturday for lunch in summer.

Reservations: Suggested.

Wheelchair accessibility: All facilities on one level.

🍃 Since 1986 Le Chantilly has had a new manager-partner, Camille Dulac, formerly of La Gauloise, who teamed up with the chef, Roland Chenus, to update the veteran French establishment's image.

They brightened up the premises, reupholstered the banquettes, and added a few more dreamy murals of the famous French château that is the restaurant's namesake. The result is one of the more serene and civilized settings in town, with amply separated tables that allow for privacy.

Those with an archaeological bent will be able to unearth a few artifacts from the old menu, although most of Mr. Chenus's offerings are new or at least old jewels in new settings. Instead of serving snails the traditional way, in a ramekin with garlic butter, he now gift wraps them in thin ravioli along with wild mushrooms and tomatoes and sets them adrift on a satiny cream sauce. The success of this dish rests in the restrained garnishes that allow the snails' flavor to come through. A similar approach using crayfish just misses the mark because of oversalting.

One of the more compelling menu innovations is called beignet of wild salmon, which involves coating the fillet on one side in a crêpelike batter and sautéing it. It is presented over wilted spinach with a beurre blanc sauce tinged with blackberry vinegar. Not every success is so laboriously crafted. Sweet freshwater prawns from Hawaii, a special, are simply grilled and garnished with ginger-and-herb butter; a light and spirited alternative is excellent gravlax paired with anise-infused tuna and black bass marinated with (insufficient) dill—all displayed over julienne of leeks in a vinaigrette sauce.

Service has seen a dramatic turnaround at Le Chantilly; it is much more animated and attentive than before. The wine list, too, has been bolstered, especially among Bordeaux, but prices are on the high end all around.

As for main courses, the performance is considerably stronger among meat dishes than seafood. You can get a good broiled Dover sole here at lunch, and one of the dinner highlights is a tableau of sea scallops and shrimp over a glistening ginger cream sauce flecked with tomato—just don't chomp down on one of the big anise seeds. However, disappointments include a naked slab of poached halibut in a pallid tomato sauce, and a special grilled tuna steak that is so dry a bucket of ginger vinaigrette could not revive it. Grilled lobster would please most aficionados, although I find little evidence of the promised Thai herbs in the butter sauce.

The winner at my table one evening was the superb roasted squab—the pink-cooked breast meltingly tender and flavorful and the crisp-skinned leg meat dark and rich. It came with warm chicory salad tossed in a light sesame oil. Roast Muscovy duck likewise was falling-off-the-bone tender, and its pleasingly pungent sauce, combining lime and bitter oranges, was a rousing surprise.

The classic French desserts are as uncompromisingly delicious as ever, especially the airy charlotte anchored with passion-fruit mousse, pear tart with a sublime buttery crust, and a light and semisweet pear clafoutis. Only mocha layer cake is too sweet and a bit dry. Soufflés in every color float across the dining room all evening long. Of those sampled, chocolate with crème anglaise surpasses the grainy lemon with raspberry sauce.

LE CIRQUE

★ ★ ★ ★

58 East 65th Street, 794-9292.

Atmosphere: Plush, densely packed room done in a rococo style, good acoustics despite large crowds.

Service: Unflappably seasoned European staff, highly professional and cordial.

Price range: Expensive.

Credit cards: American Express, Carte Blanche, and Diners Club.

Hours: Lunch, noon to 3 P.M., Monday through Saturday; dinner, 6 to 10:30 P.M., Monday through Saturday.

Reservations: Necessary well in advance.

Wheelchair accessibility: Dining room on one level; restrooms four steps down into an adjacent hotel lobby.

🐌 Le Cirque is one of those rare institutions that have it all: consistently titillating food, expert service, superb wines, and world-class people-watching. Le Cirque's unparalleled spirit springs from the staff and customers who fill it. On any evening the celebrity scorecard overflows, and overseeing it all is the ineffable charming workaholic owner, Sirio Maccioni.

Daniel Boulud, the young Burgundian who has been in charge of the kitchen since late 1986, is awesomely versatile—with the help of the city's largest kitchen brigade.

One starter that has become one of Mr. Boulud's signature preparations is called sea scallops fantasy in black tie, an individual silver casserole dish of exquisite sliced sea scallops layered with black truffles, moistened with buttery vermouth and truffle juice. Next to that you can find something as unabashedly earthy as a cold terrine of beef shanks with leeks in a faintly piquant raifort sauce speckled with diced vegetables, or tissue-thin carpaccio of red snapper glossed with truffle oil and under a cover of arugula and fresh chervil. Foie gras comes in no fewer than two dozen costumes, depending on Mr. Boulud's whim (sautéed with Concord grapes and cranberries was inspired).

Since I am known to the staff and can't objectively judge the service, I resorted to sending first-timers there three times and asked them to report their impressions. The unknowns said they were always greeted politely, although twice they had to wait fifteen minutes for a table. Once seated they were always treated courteously.

Trying to describe Mr. Boulud's vast lunch and dinner entrée repertory in this space would be like itemizing the holdings of the Metropolitan Museum of Art on a postcard. We'll have to browse. One world-class dish, if one can be so effusive about a fish, is the roasted black sea bass wrapped in diaphanous sheets of sliced potatoes, all golden crackling, set in a concentrated Barolo wine sauce brightened with shallots and fresh thyme. Simpler but also sublime was the grilled salmon atop a sward of fennel studded with walnuts and bathed in a walnut-oil vinaigrette. Mr. Boulud, who stalks the markets of Brooklyn's Atlantic Avenue to sate his passion for the best spices, has flushed more than a few highly powdered cheeks in the dining room with his brassy lobster in curry sauce. However, a special of rouget, the delicate Mediterranean fish, was lost under its rich lobster-and-wild-asparagus sauce. Much better was the fat fillet of grouper over sautéed cabbage and shiitake mushrooms in a sublime white-wine sauce infused with rosemary.

The new selection of roasts and game is stellar, and the distinctive sauces with each, passed through Mr. Boulud's alembic, emphasize purity and accessibility over elaborateness. Take, for example, his navarin of lamb. It may be lighter and daintier than a thick-sauced home version, but the verdant flavors come rolling through.

A frequent special is five-hour braised lamb, a wondrous twist on the navarin redolent of garlic, fresh tomato, and cardamom and coriander, served with cinnamon-perfumed couscous and raisins. On Thursdays you may find the best pot-au-feu (or the Italian version, bollito misto) on this side of the Atlantic (elevated from peasant status with slabs of foie gras). Pasta primavera was introduced to this country at Le Cirque, so you should try this lustrous version if for nothing other than historical purposes.

Magret of duck is cooked to a perfect blush, touched with plum-sweetened stock; fork-tender venison has a diadem of autumnal purées (chestnut, spinach blended with pear, and pumpkin) and a juniper-honey sauce.

Equal to the menu in breadth and quality is Mr. Maccioni's international wine list, one of New York's greatest— over five hundred bottles on the regular list, and at fair prices for a luxury establishment.

Some of the leading pastry chefs in the country have waved their wands at Le Cirque, and the newly assembled team under the Austrian-born Farbinger Markus is more than carrying on the tradition: three-tiered raspberry napoleon that is so light it should come with fishing weights to hold it down, mango curls paired with ripe mango ice cream and mixed berries, a brittle web of spun sugar holding luscious fresh figs and vanilla ice cream, splendid chocolate sorbet served in a porcelain egg, and the signature crème brûlée—much mimicked but still the paragon.

LE CYGNE

★ ★ ★

55 East 54th Street, 759-5941.

Atmosphere: Elegant and colorful two-level town house. Moderate noise level.

Service: Excellent.

Price range: Expensive (lunch prix fixe, $32; dinner prix fixe, $56).

Credit cards: All major cards.

Hours: Lunch, noon to 2 P.M., Monday through Friday; dinner, 6 to 10 P.M., Monday through Friday, 6 to 11 P.M., Saturday.

Reservations: Required.

Wheelchair accessibility: Two steps at entrance; dining rooms on several levels that are difficult to negotiate.

Le Cygne is a demure haven of comfort and civility in bustling midtown, a place that rarely gets mentioned in the media tally of power spots, glamour roosts, or celebrity hangouts. That is one reason it is so appealing.

Opened in 1969 by the partners Gérard Gillian and Michel Crouzillat, the restaurant later moved into a two-story town house. The small dining rooms on both levels sport distinctive charms. Muted lighting and cool peach-and-gray tones lend a bright and cheerful mood; misty murals of wildflowers brighten the gloomiest Manhattan day, as do vibrant fresh bouquets on the tables that appear to have been snipped from the painted countryside. The upper level, reached by dual winding staircases, has an airy and contemporary feeling with its arched ceilings and back-lighted opaque glass panels.

Pierre Baran, former sous-chef at Le Cirque, took charge of the kitchen in 1986, and he has been holding up the restaurant's tradition of straddling the middle of the French highway. Mr. Baran has a fine touch with seasonings and a graceful, but not faddish, eye for presentation.

Appetizers are uniformly wonderful. Try the glistening tableau of salmon and sea bass in a coating of aspic, or succulent little scallops from Maine in a bright lime-accented fish stock with julienne of endive. Both meat terrines are paragons of the art: a rough-textured and mildly livery country pork terrine and, my favorite, a luxurious

227

duck rendition, speckled with nutty black truffles, and molded around a pink core of silky fois gras.

Oyster fanciers will not be disappointed by the icy Belons when they are in season, or, even a rarer treat when in season, the remarkably oceanic thumbnail-size Olympias from Washington State. A more substantial starter would be the firm, thin medallions of sweetbreads—simply sautéed and set over a glossy vinegar-edged veal-stock sauce. The only loser was fricassee of baby shrimp—the Provençale-style broth was fresh and herbaceous, but the shrimp were tasteless.

A subcategory among the entrées offers house specialties, and all those sampled are worth seeking out. Beautifully sautéed fresh foie gras, silken and delicate, may come in a pool of port wine and cognac sauce ringed by tiny tart gooseberries; If they have the smoked magret, don't miss it: a florid slice of moist duck breast with haunting woody nuances, served with a buttery foie gras mousse.

From the moment you enter the cool gray portals of Le Cygne, the staff keeps a distanced eye on you to fill every need or whim—but never in an ingratiating or overfamiliar way. First-time customers seem to get the same cosseting as regulars. The wine list seems to have more low-end selections than it once did, although prices are generally high.

Among the entrées, one of the more unusual offerings is highly recommended: a deftly sautéed fillet of baby silver salmon prepared like a pepper steak. The salmon is coated with crushed black pepper, sautéed, and served with a sauce combining fish stock, tomato, and cognac—the interplay of hot and sweet is a delight. Lobster ragout also comes in a heady shellfish-and-tomato broth, although the lobster meat is a bit overcooked; the same flaw marred grilled Dover sole on two occasions. If you like frogs' legs, the version here, simply prepared in garlic and butter, is the best I have had in New York.

Other highlights include the rosy roasted squab—just gamy enough to let you know what you are eating—in an earthy mélange of cloves, cèpes, and artichokes; another engaging preparation is the duck breast in a yin-yang sort of sauce balancing tart vinegar and sweet honey.

When the pastry cart rounds the bend, it is worth taking a ride. Crème brûlée is excellent, glassy crusted and embarrassingly rich, as is an orange-and-Grand Marnier mousse and a chocolate layer cake with bittersweet chocolate curls on the roof and intense chocolate mousse on alternating levels. Most tarts sampled—apricot and raspberry in particular—are stellar. Only a white-and-dark chocolate charlotte disappoints because of dryness.

LE PÉRIGORD

★ ★

405 East 52nd Street, 755-6244.

Atmosphere: Soothing old-world charm with well-spaced tables, low noise level, and low-key colors.

Service: Proper and knowledgeable but slow at times.

Price range: Moderately expensive (lunch prix fixe, $24; dinner prix fixe, $48).

Credit cards: All major cards.

Hours: Lunch, noon to 3 P.M., Monday through Friday; dinner, 5:30 to 10:30 P.M., Monday through Saturday.

Reservations: Necessary.

Wheelchair accessibility: One step down at entrance; restrooms downstairs.

🍴 Le Périgord, a cozy spot with an old-world ambiance on the eastern reaches of 52nd Street, is far from the business executives' midtown lunch circuit, so if you are trying to steal a client from the competition it is a relatively safe place to do it.

Le Périgord caters to a regular and well-heeled clientele, mostly older, mostly conservative, who enjoy being cosseted by the seasoned team of captains. The dining room is attractive in the genteel way—no jarring murals or theatrical lighting here. The swirled peach-and-pale-blue fabric-covered walls are soothing and warm; extravagant flower arrangements and well-spaced tables add to a sense of luxury.

The food harmonizes with the atmosphere. The young French-trained chef, Antoine Bouterin, is skilled at mixing up his pitches to offer something for everyone. His menu pays obeisance to classic cuisine yet at the same time keeps in step with the latest trends. You will find dishes as home-spun as Cornish hen Périgourdine and braised beef with carrots or as au courant as sliced duck breast with essence of passion fruit or gratin of shrimp coated with sesame seeds in lobster-and-shrimp sauce.

The appetizer list is somewhat daunting at first—nearly two dozen choices including soups. One can minimize guesswork by picking from a cold buffet table that holds cold poached bass with green sauce, shimmering Scottish smoked salmon, and fresh vegetables. One of the best items, which is not on display, is the cold vegetable pâté filled with little cubes of firm-cooked carrots and zucchini bound in a cooling, full-flavored aspic. It is served with a sour-cream-based herb sauce.

A standout appetizer, sometimes offered as a special, is salmon tartare blended with Worcestershire sauce, capers, and a touch of curry that gives it a piquant edge.

Among the hot starters, try the vegetable tart with truffles. It is really more like an airy quiche made with puréed leeks, celery, carrots, zucchini, and tomato; the subtle lemon-butter sauce around it is laced with truffle slices. This one is beautifully displayed on the plate, as are most of Mr. Bouterin's preparations.

Service is professional in the best French tradition, yet there are often inexplicably long lags between courses. The captains are exceptionally well informed about the entrées and wines, which is a blessing since there are wide selections of both.

The chef has an innovative touch with seafood. One stellar dish is rolled fillets of sole, crowned with truffle slices and set in a mild garlic purée garnished with carmelized garlic cloves and baby carrots; another typical of his style is deftly roasted turbot fillets resting in a nest of homemade noodles swathed in a light curry sauce.

If you are in the mood for more familiar fare, such as rack of lamb or sliced veal au jus with tarragon (a special), you can't do better than here. Kidneys Bordelaise also are paradigmatic—the firm, dark kidneys are served with a burnished stock sauce studded with sweet roasted shallots. Get them with a side order of sarladaise potatoes, a thick disk of sautéed sliced potatoes layered with truffles ($6 supplement at dinner).

The overloaded dessert cart carries something for everyone, from ripe and luscious fresh fruit sorbets and seasonal berries with sabayon sauce to towering chocolate layer cakes with bittersweet-chocolate shavings clinging precariously to the sides, to first-rate fruit tarts and citric lemon meringue pie.

LE RÉGENCE

★ ★ ★

Hôtel Plaza Athénée, 37 East 64th Street, 606-4647.

Atmosphere: Plush, hushed, and ultra-French.

Service: Professional and congenial.

Price range: Expensive (lunch prix fixe, $28.50; dinner prix fixe, $57.50; five-course tasting menu, $65).

Credit cards: All major cards.

Hours: Breakfast, 7 to 10 A.M., daily; lunch, noon to 2:30 P.M., daily; dinner, 6 to 10 P.M., daily.

Reservations: Necessary, especially at dinner.

Wheelchair accessibility: Ramp access to dining room and restrooms.

🦐 Le Régence, the opulent, old-world French restaurant in the Hôtel Plaza Athénée, got a new lease on life in 1987 when a new team of French restaurateurs took over the kitchen after the defection of Daniel Boulud and several of his lieutenants to Le Cirque.

The hotel hired as consultants the estimable Rostang clan from France, the Flying Wallendas of French cuisine— father Jo and son Philippe, who own La Bonne Auberge in Antibes, a Michelin two-star restaurant, and another son, Michel, whose namesake restaurant in Paris also has two stars. One or more of the Rostangs visit Le Régence monthly to oversee the menu. So far the strategy is paying off, for the food has been restored to its former high level.

Of course, that means diners have to pay for all the consulting fees and airline fares, so this is not a budget restaurant: dinner prix fixe at $57.50 (count on $80 or more with wine, tax, and tip), lunch at $28.50. The setting is indeed regal, a soft and stately den done in turquoise and white trim, with velvet banquettes, soft leather armchairs, ornate mirrors, and benign lighting. The gentle art of conversation can be pursued here without a megaphone, and the European-style staff is meticulous and proper without being stuffy.

The Rostang style of cooking is generally contemporary and light, emphasizing flavor over flair, and is sometimes unpredictable—soy butter may show up with grilled fish, or vinegar and honey in a scallop preparation. Among the starters, two arresting dishes are the corn pancake studded with bits of smoked salmon, set over a lustrous curry sauce —the sweet kernels of corn play off the salty salmon, while the zesty sauce adds just the right fillip to bring it all together; less complex but equally compelling is the luscious onion tart over mixed greens.

If you haven't had your fill of baby ravioli by now, the lobster-stuffed little pouches here are as light and fresh as can be, glossed with an olive-oil-and-lobster-coral sauce; more original is the sublime salmon-and-scallop tart. Sheets of raw salmon envelop sweet sea scallops, onions, and cream sauce aromatic of dill, all framed in a crust that is so thin it resembles matzoh. If you are feeling particularly flush, you might want to spring for the galette (a flat round tart) of buttery, crisped vermicelli swathed with beluga caviar in a shallot-butter sauce—extraordinarily good, but worth a $30 supplement?

Le Régence takes its wine seriously, but some of the prices on the impressively stocked list are, at over three times the retail prices, unconscionable.

Several seafood entrées excel. Thin slices of black bass were presented over a crêpe and enhanced with a caviar-freckled sauce, beautifully grilled red snapper came with charred scallions and a lovely soy-butter sauce, and skate was paired with braised cabbage leaves in a subtle sweet-and-sour sauce.

Mustard is put to good use to enliven the sauce with slices of rosy beef fillet. Lemon adds a diverting sharpness to the sauce for duck breasts, which come with good corn pancakes. Veal chop was plump and succulent at dinner, while paillard of veal at lunch was equally flavorful, although the sorrel sauce was a bit timid to my taste.

Not all desserts are worth the guilt—particularly a flossy and tasteless pear soufflé and a bizarre almond-and-pineapple tart with coconut sauce, the kind of cloying dessert you expect at a pseudo-Polynesian establishment. The sorbet assortment is stunning, presented under a web of spun sugar. Cold chestnut soufflé is splendid, as is the ultralight and ripe mango mousse. A Rostang specialty is the pear poached in red Burgundy with black currants, under a dome of pastry—the only way to improve it would be with a scoop of vanilla ice cream.

Le Régence has bounced back with style. For a civilized business lunch or a self-indulgent special-occasion dinner, it is a place to be pampered in the loftiest French style.

LE ZINC

★

139 Duane Street, 732-1226.

Atmosphere: Authentic and lively bistro feeling in a room that resembles a Victorian-era parlor car.

Service: Occasionally rushed, but competent.

Price range: Moderate.

Credit cards: American Express, MasterCard, and Visa.

Hours: Lunch, noon to 3 P.M., Monday through Friday; dinner, 6 P.M. to midnight, Monday through Thursday, 6 P.M. TO 12:30 A.M., Friday and Saturday, 6 to 11 P.M., Sunday.

Reservations: Suggested.

Wheelchair accessibility: One step up from street; restrooms downstairs.

❧ When Le Zinc opened in 1983 on Duane Street in TriBeCa, the notion of a hip French bistro so far off the beaten track was still a novelty, and soon it overflowed with a trend-chasing polyglot crowd. The scene, however, was more alluring than the food in those days. Eventually, as new hot spots took root in this once barren terrain, competition turned fierce, and Le Zinc had to fight back. In the past three years, improvements have been made in the kitchen.

The dining room is reminiscent of a cavernous Victorian-era railroad car, with its barreled ceiling, dark wood trim, brass chandeliers, zinc-topped bar, and red banquettes. The slow and easy ambiance accelerates as the evening wears on and the music amplifies. Service, however, remains at 33 rpm, which leads to some noticeably long waits between courses.

Unalloyed bistro food is the current fare. While commitment to quality is evident here, your experiences can vary depending on the day of the week. Weeknights are superior to weekends, especially Saturday night, when food and service are most erratic.

If you want to get off to a lofty start, try the buttery cold duck foie gras paired with a good homemade aspic. The hot foie gras, though, can be disappointing—seared outside yet raw inside and slightly greasy, served over mixed greens with sautéed apples. Tender, thin asparagus nestled next to a dome of puff pastry benefits from a light beurre blanc, while escargots are prepared in an unusual and appealing way: swathed with a tarragon-and-mint beurre blanc–style sauce. Both shellfish starters are winners, the clear and icy Virginia oysters on the half shell with a tart mignonnette sauce and meaty fresh steamed mussels in a terrific oceanic broth.

One reliably good choice is the Provençale fish soup, fortified with an intense homemade stock, along with a potent garlic rouille. Although pastas are often offered, my advice is to leave that to the Italians. Le Zinc's version of frisée aux lardons, the salad usually made with chicory, croutons, cubes of bacon (and sometimes a poached egg) in a warm vinaigrette, is weighed down with so much bacon that the salad wilts into a sodden heap.

The small wine selection starts with a decent house wine, Beaujolais Villages, although for a few dollars extra you can get the superior crus Beaujolais called Brouilly. Among whites, the Muscadet for around $15 is a solid choice, especially with seafood.

Among the fish main courses that harmonize with the Muscadet are the thick fillets of roasted monkfish in an assertive fresh dill sauce, and delicate sea bass over a vivid fennel coulis ringed with carved vegetables, both specials. A winning seasonal lunch entrée is the cold poached coho salmon in a spirited basil sauce. A thin plank of overcooked tuna steak, though, is not resuscitated by its glossy butter sauce.

Such soul-warming dishes as confit of duck are normally associated with cold-weather dining, but the succulent portion here is worth tossing aside the rules for—especially if the air conditioning is cranked up. Kidneys are given a nice twist in a semisweet orange-and-Calvados sauce, garnished with orange rind and apples. Steak tartare, another bistro standard, contains more mustard than a Yankee Stadium hot dog, consequently you can't taste the beef. Have instead the tender, fist-size pavé, or the butt steak in a mildly piquant green-peppercorn sauce along with good thin french fries. Lamb steak—more flavorful than the beef to my taste —is nicely seared, juicy, and served with crisp sautéed potatoes and green beans.

Aside from a pallid chocolate mousse, desserts are uplifting, especially the ice-cream-filled profiteroles with chocolate sauce, the hazelnut-and-chocolate marjolaine, ripe fruit sorbets, and the thick-crusted tarte Tatin.

Le Zinc is holding its own among the fervid downtown competition. With a little more consistency in the kitchen, it could be a pacesetter.

LOLA

★

30 West 22nd Street, 675-6700.

Atmosphere: Elegant café ambiance with pastel-colored walls adorned with attractive prints and drawings and soft lighting. Annoyingly loud when full.

Service: The comely young staff is outgoing and helpful but occasionally awkward.

Price range: Moderately expensive.

Credit cards: American Express.

Hours: Brunch, noon to 4 P.M., Sunday; lunch, noon to 3 P.M., Monday through Friday; dinner, 6 to 11 P.M., Monday, 6 P.M. to midnight, Tuesday through Saturday, 6 to 10 P.M., Sunday.

Reservations: Suggested.

Wheelchair accessibility: All facilities on one level.

🍲 Lola is a stylish restaurant with a Caribbean accent in the blossoming Madison Square neighborhood. On paper, at least, the menu lineup is enticing. In reality, though, some dishes fail to excite. Moreover, the noise level can be numbing. There is barely a soft surface in the house, so when conviviality peaks, usually about 10 P.M., the dining room becomes a huge echo chamber.

While perusing the menu, you can be priming your palate with sharp little cayenne-spiked shortbread cookies made with cheese and pecans. And when choosing, keep in mind that on the whole, the appetizers are better than the entrées. Bermuda seafood chowder is consistently pleasing, a rich sweetish broth chock-full of fresh tuna and vegetables; sweet-potato vichyssoise, which is served hot, is another winner. West Indian potato-and-shrimp fritters sound intriguing, but upon first sampling they were a letdown, undercooked and 90 percent potato; several nights later, they were a pleasant surprise—crisp, well seasoned, and amply filled with shrimp. Even the accompanying chopped-tomato-and-basil garnish came to life.

The outstanding appetizer is grilled calf sweetbreads, which are firm, fresh, and infused with a faint smoky flavor. They come with a tart salsa of parsley, garlic, capers, and olive oil. Skip the watery and tasteless grilled polenta and try instead the mountain of ultra-thin cayenne-laced onion rings.

The service team is long on personality though occasionally short on finesse. (The ebullient "Lola" Bell has an on-and-off relationship with the restaurant.) No useful help is offered regarding the wine list, which is fairly priced but includes several clunkers. Play it safe with well-known producers and you'll do fine.

If you'd like to try something with a West Indian accent, you might choose the sharp shrimp-and-chicken curry served with rough-textured wild-rice waffles.

As for the so-called 100-spice Caribbean fried chicken, it sounds more ominous than it is. What you get is perfectly acceptable fried chicken coated with mildly hot dried spices and a Chinese-inspired three-cabbage salad.

Even the most humble West Indian restaurant should be able to turn out a creditable shellfish gumbo; the rendition here, though—with shrimp, clams, mussels, ham, and rice—is lackluster. So are the ersatz osso buco, the dried-out veal paillard, and the colorless tenderloin of pork roasted in milk and garlic. Simple grilled dishes fare better, such as the lovely lamb chops with golden-fried shoestring potatoes, and the swordfish steak enhanced with a caper-dill crème fraîche sauce.

The ricotta-flavored gelato, while not exactly a staple of Jamaican cuisine, is still worth trying. So, too, is the light and creamy Frangelico pumpkin cheesecake.

Keep Lola in mind for Sunday brunch, when gospel singers shake the house.

LUSARDI'S

Satisfactory

1494 Second Avenue, at 78th Street, 249-2020.

Atmosphere: Clubby and inviting room with a well-attired clientele.

Service: Sometimes forgetful and inattentive.

Price range: Moderately expensive.

Credit cards: All major cards.

Hours: Lunch, noon to 3 P.M., Monday through Friday; dinner, 5 P.M. to midnight, Monday through Saturday, 4 to 11 P.M., Sunday.

Reservations: Necessary.

Wheelchair accessibility: All facilities on one level.

My suspicion is that Lusardi's overtaxed its limited talent pool by opening a sister restaurant recently, called Due, in early 1988. How else can one account for the lifeless pastas, clumsy appetizers, and nondescript entrées that are the rule more than the exception?

The setting is indeed beguiling: creamy yellow walls, brass lamps, wood-framed windows behind gossamer white curtains, and a wall rack loaded with wines. As for the service, waiters have a professional mien but are lazy about refilling glasses and removing dirty plates; and they never seem to know who ordered what dishes—at $18 for a bowl of risotto with vegetables, it's the least one can expect.

Among appetizers, the assorted grilled vegetables are a safe option—radicchio, endive, zucchini, and red peppers. Tuna carpaccio, however, was a sodden mess, tasting as if it had been recently defrosted (and lacking any of the promised truffle oil); bruschetta was nothing more than pale out-of-season chopped tomatoes and onions heaped on toasted bread. Two starters that can be recommended are the sheets of lean air-cured beef over arugula with olive oil and lemon that were pleasantly salty, and the firm and fresh sliced mushrooms and artichokes under olive oil and shavings of Parmesan cheese. Cold seafood salad—calamari and scallops with olives—is fresh and lively.

None of the pastas sampled left a deposit in my memory bank. Penne in tomato sauce with basil and black olives was fine if ordinary, as was tortelloni in a four-cheese sauce. Ravioli filled with ricotta and spinach, a special, barely rose above pizzeria fare, and paglia e fieno, the thin two-toned pasta tossed in a cream sauce with peas and prosciutto, was bland.

The quality of veal here is excellent, especially the thick, juicy chop garnished with fresh sage; the medallions of veal under melted fontina cheese are tender and flavorful, too. Not much can be said for seafood. Swordfish was over the hill and flaccid; salmon purportedly cooked in cognac, white wine, and lemon was fresh and well cooked but devoid of those flavors. The only plate that went back to the kitchen empty was the fried seafood platter (calamari, scallops, and shrimp). Several chicken dishes sampled were well cooked—pollo Abruzzese (tomato, rosemary, white-wine sauce), pollo Valsugana (shallots, pepper, tomato, cream)—yet one-dimensional.

We were in the mood for some wonderfully corrupting desserts when the waiter came by and ran off eight choices. After we ordered, he returned from the kitchen with a chagrined expression to say, "We only have two left, tartufo and strawberries with zabaglione." The former was ordinary, the latter insipid, the sauce lacking Marsala flavor. Another evening, we had a good, coffee-infused tiramisù served in a wine goblet, and sufficiently corrupting flourless chocolate cake.

Lusardi's may have fallen into the entrepreneurial trap of believing that if one successful restaurant is good, two are better. In this case, the growing pains may be too severe.

LUTÈCE

★ ★ ★ ★

249 East 50th Street, 752-2225.

Atmosphere: A town house with an airy and cheerful garden dining room, an intimate anteroom, and a pair of formal, old-fashioned rooms upstairs.

Service: Highly professional staff, knowledgeable and correct.

Price range: Expensive (lunch prix fixe, $35; dinner prix fixe, $58, with some supplements).

Credit cards: All major cards.

Hours: Lunch, noon to 2 P.M., Tuesday through Friday; dinner, 6 to 10 P.M., Monday through Saturday, except from Memorial Day to Labor Day, when the restaurant is closed Saturday. The restaurant also usually closes in August.

Reservations: Necessary well in advance.

Wheelchair accessibility: Two steps down at entrance; restrooms upstairs.

Is Lutèce over the hill? In the past few years some food mavens have grumbled about the performance of this twenty-eight-year-old legend, speculating that André Soltner, the chef and owner, had lost his spark.

Indeed, there was cause for concern. Mr. Soltner's chef de cuisine for eleven years, Christian Bertrand, left the restaurant in 1987 to open his own establishment in Greenwich, Connecticut. His replacement, Jean-Michel Bergougnoux, chef at Le Régence, was not in place until that fall (and he departed a year later). The interregnum was rocky, thus the murmurings. Repeated visits reaffirm, however, that Lutèce, while hardly a gastronomic trailblazer, is still among the city's most beguiling restaurants —and, with prix-fixe meals at $35 for lunch and $58 for dinner, equally or less costly that other luxury establishments in Manhattan.

Much of that appeal centers on Mr. Soltner himself, the affable, self-effacing host who wouldn't leave his cherished restaurant unless under subpoena.

First-timers at Lutèce are invariably surprised by its unassuming setting. Lutèce is not a "designed" or "conceptualized" environment; it is simply a comfortable place, enhanced by the intangible ornamentation of countless memorable times.

You enter the charming pint-size barroom with its zinc-topped bar, marble café tables, and framed posters of Paris. Down a narrow hallway, past the partly exposed kitchen, you enter a cozy anteroom, then beyond it the cheerful main garden room with its green slate floor, white wood trim, and a high Quonset-hut-like ceiling. Light filters through the translucent ceiling during the day, casting a soft glow. Upstairs are two small, more formal rooms with crystal chandeliers, oil paintings, and subdued lighting.

The classic French menu is merely a formality, for Mr. Soltner and his staff conjure up a host of daily specials that should be considered carefully. In spring and summer you might start with a light and vibrantly seasoned vegetable terrine, layers of spinach and carrot, ringed by sliced scallops in a lovely vinaigrette. A slice of fresh salmon, lightly smoked in the kitchen, is seared until its skin side is crisp, the flesh still deep pink, and is presented over a shallot-infused vinaigrette; the smoky fish and sweet shallots play off each other beautifully.

In cooler weather you might sample the superb Alsatian onion tart, sautéed foie gras with apples and vinegar, or the chausson, a golden turnover stuffed with crabmeat, scallops, and minced vegetables with a tarragon-loaded sauce choron. If Mr. Soltner comes to your table and sizes you up as an adventuresome eater, he may offer some of his more rustic offerings: a cold terrine of eel bound with an excellent gelatin made with bones and herbs, or onglet, a sinewy yet full-flavored cut of beef favored by the French but rarely served in this country. (It was indeed exceedingly chewy to American tastes.)

The wine list at Lutèce is dog-eared and rather stodgy for a restaurant of this caliber. Prestigious old bottles can be found, but pickings are relatively lean and predictable at the lower end. Some of the best bargains, especially among whites, continue to be from Alsace. Several captains can be relied upon for sound advice.

The highly professional French service staff at Lutèce has a reputation for sometimes being haughty with unknown customers. I receive letters occasionally from diners who complain about indifferent treatment. In my experience—at first incognito, although later known to the staff—this is not the case. Whether these are isolated incidents or a pattern of behavior is difficult to assess.

The food at Lutèce is classic but not static, intensely flavorful yet not weighty. My idea of a transcendent Lutèce meal is something like baby lamb—real baby lamb, succulent and buttery—roasted to perfection with fresh herbs and paired with sautéed potatoes, mellow duck confit over mixed greens, or flawless golden sweetbreads with morels, lots of them. Roasted rabbit, which is so often dry and bland in restaurants, is incredibly tender here, the slowly simmered sauce robust with a vegetable-and-stock reduction.

At lunch a baby chicken is served split and partly boned, with cubes of buttery polenta and a splendid asparagus sauce. One of the few failures was a dry roulade of veal stuffed with Gruyère in a banal brown sauce. I'm also not wild about Alsace-style escargots in brioche—sort of a snail submarine sandwich—in which the nubbins of escargots are lost in their garlicky log of brioche. Sautéed John Dory fillets, firm and mild, are extraordinarily good in a cream red-pepper purée, as were all fish preparations sampled.

For dessert, tarte Tatin is wondrously light and delicious. Pineapple in puff pastry with crème anglaise sounds suspicious but actually works, crème caramel with orange rind is simple and good, and the chocolate mousse terrine is downright dangerous. I could have passed up the eggy, undercooked Grand Marnier soufflé, and gratin of grapefruit was overly acidic—although the same dessert with pears was good.

You dine at Lutèce not to ride the latest wave in French cuisine, but rather to stroll leisurely through familiar terrain, sniffing the flowers along the way. And how sweet they can be.

MAMMA LEONE'S

Poor

261 West 44th Street, 586-5151.

Atmosphere: Touristy Neapolitan-grotto look. Enormous open room upstairs.

Service: Abysmal.

Price range: Moderately expensive.

Credit cards: All major cards.

Hours: Lunch, 11:30 A.M. to 2:30 P.M., Monday through Saturday; dinner, 4 to 11 P.M., Monday through Friday (a late dinner menu is available from 9:30 P.M. to midnight), 4 P.M. to midnight, Saturday, 2 to 9 P.M., Sunday.

Reservations: Suggested.

Wheelchair accessibility: All facilities on one level.

🍷 Mamma Leone's reopened to much fanfare in early 1988 on 44th Street at Eighth Avenue, four blocks from its former home, which is to become a residential tower. For years this six-hundred-seat Neapolitan tourist haunt has been considered little more than a garish sideshow in the Broadway theater district, hardly worth serious scrutiny. Yet all the hoopla over its new place piqued my curiosity, so I decided to give it a try.

The *Playbill*-toting customers who wander into this eighty-two-year-old institution are met by a host and escorted past white plaster nymphs, leafy grottoes, brick arches, and Chianti-filled wine racks into one of the downstairs dining rooms or upstairs to a sprawling open room overlooking West 44th Street.

Upon being seated you are presented with a platter of Italian breads strewn with cottony cubes of pale tomato and garlic, which they call bruschetta; a rubbery brick of tasteless mozzarella the color of old soap; a dish of olives; slices of pepperoni; and a basket of breadsticks.

As for the service staff, I have had warmer encounters with people serving me traffic summonses. The weary veterans I encountered, all wearing gold badges with their tours of duty—"Mamma Leone's Since 1954"—trudge around their defined stations with the apparent goal of exerting the least possible energy on an eight-hour shift. When I made the unpardonable mistake of asking a waiter assigned to the adjacent territory for a clean fork—mine was smudged and encrusted—he grunted and pointed to another waiter at the far end of the room.

We waited fifteen minutes for a bottle of wine from the arrogantly overpriced list, only to have our waiter plop it down unopened, then disappear—not to fetch a corkscrew, however, but to take a dessert order from another table. Ten minutes later he returned, desserts and corkscrew on his platter. Why make two trips when one will do?

As for the food, it is scarier than anything conjured up in *The Phantom of the Opera* at the Majestic Theatre next door. When I asked our waiter what was in the appetizer called stuffed tomato and zucchini, he muttered something incomprehensible, flashed an exasperated look, then finally said, "Bread crumbs, you know, bread crumbs." Bread crumbs they were, over a fibrous halved tomato and a woody, hollowed-out zucchini. Stuffed clams had even more bread crumbs, sodden and sticky ones, with barely a hint of clams. Minestrone Leone put canned soup in a favorable light, and sheets of prosciutto did little for a hard, overchilled, unripe melon.

Forget any of the pastas that come with industrial-grade tomato sauce. One mildly satisfying addition to the updated menu is fettuccine with salsa aurora (tomato, cream, and porcini). Fusilli puttanesca, on the other hand, is a bland and soupy mess. Roasted leg of veal with grilled polenta, for $29.95, features two anemic slices of dry meat lying in a puddle of watery juice, along with a pale yellow slab that tastes like day-old Cream of Wheat. Roast chicken, for $24.95, arrived looking like one of those shriveled delicatessen birds after about nine hours on the rotisserie— and it tasted even drier. One dish that survived the kitchen relatively undamaged was osso buco, a tender braised veal shank with an inoffensive vegetable sauce. Seafood? Don't even ask.

For dessert, you can attack a wedge of the Sahara called cheesecake or get a sugar rush from an awful rendition of tiramisù. As a final insult, they try to trick tourists into tipping on the tax as well as the food by combining the two on credit-card receipts.

Mamma Leone's is to Italian cuisine what break-dancing is to classical ballet—but not half as amusing.

MANHATTAN ISLAND

★

482 West 43rd Street, 967-0533.

Atmosphere: Casual glass-fronted dining rooms in a tropical theme overlooking the health-club swimming pool. Outdoor café near the pool.

Service: Friendly and eager if lacking finesse.

Price range: Moderate.

Credit cards: American Express, MasterCard, and Visa.

Hours: Noon to 11 P.M., Tuesday through Saturday, noon to 9 P.M., Sunday and Monday.

Reservations: Required for pretheater dinner, 6 to 8 P.M.; suggested at other times.

Wheelchair accessibility: Elevator at 484 West 43rd Street to the third-floor dining room, where all facilities are accessible.

242

🐟 My experiences in most health-club restaurants lead me to suspect that their chefs are quietly in cahoots with the asparagus-thin aerobics instructors, whose job it is to inflict pain and help patrons shed weight. It was with such limited expectations that I first jogged over to the new dining spot called Manhattan Island on the third floor of the Manhattan Plaza Health Club on West 43rd Street, a short walk from both Broadway and Off Broadway theaters.

The sinus-clearing aroma of chlorine leads the way up the stairs to the restaurant, where two sunny, glass-enclosed dining rooms face the rooftop swimming pool. On clement days, meals are served on an outdoor terrace. The indoor spaces are done in a leafy tropical theme with lots of wicker and colorful fabrics.

The affordably priced, contemporary American menu is limited but well honed. A half dozen or so specials supplement the daily menu. One of the best sampled recently was cold tube-shaped pasta tossed with a brightly seasoned sauce combining dice-size cubes of fresh mozzarella, fresh basil, and tomato; cappellini, another special, came in a yellow tomato sauce with shredded basil that needed a boost of seasonings, if only salt and pepper. Linguine paired with a salty-edged sun-dried tomato sauce was nicely balanced. One of my favorite light lunch entrées is the rousing sesame-flavored noodles with morsels of chicken and crunchy pecans.

Salads and soups make for engaging light lunches, too. Tuna Niçoise-style is made with fresh grilled tuna, red potatoes, tomatoes, hard-cooked eggs, asparagus, and black olives; gravlax is lean and cool, perfumed with fresh dill; and vegetable chowder is a terrific creamy mélange of corn, bacon, hot peppers, zucchini, and squash. Cold cucumber soup was a fresh and summery winner as well. Only the cold seafood salad was humdrum.

Everything about Manhattan Island is casual and relaxed, including the genial if green service staff. The restaurant's wine selection is well attuned to the food and sensibly priced. One of the better deals among whites is the 1986 Aligote (about $11), a full ripe Burgundian white with a perky touch of acid.

Entrées are for the most part familiar American dishes. Crab cakes are fat and crusty, loaded with fresh-tasting crab, and served with coleslaw. Paillard of chicken sandwich with basil mayonnaise, and sliced steak set over arugula and toasted country bread make fine lunches. Both come with a side of potato salad given extra voltage with minced jalapeño pepper. Manhattan Island gets my vote in the chicken-hash competition: the bubbling casserole, blistered and crispy on top, holds chunks of well-seasoned chicken in a luxurious cream sauce.

From the grill, you can get succulent lamb chops with a bland portion of orzo and vegetables on the side, fiery cayenne-dusted shrimp on skewers, and rare-cooked salmon steak in a tame mustard-and-caper sauce. Lime-basted swordfish was dry and uninteresting, served with the same bland orzo. Grilled baby chicken needed some help in the herb department, too.

The pride of the dessert card, to my taste, is the knockout peanut-butter pie, easily worth a week of aerobic penance. Under a thick hide of chocolate is a velvety peanut-butter cream filling over a crumbly crust. Less weighty is the refreshingly sharp lemon tart. Lemon tea cake is a dried-out little rectangle; go instead with the no-nonsense brownies under a scoop of vanilla ice cream and steaming chocolate sauce.

Manhattan Island is the kind of unpretentious and affordable place this neighborhood needs. Who knows, walking past those red-faced exercisers on the way out may even rekindle your desire to get in shape. Think about it over lunch tomorrow.

THE MANHATTAN OCEAN CLUB

★

57 West 58th Street, 371-7777.

Atmosphere: Handsome and soothing dining rooms with hand-painted ceramics on display.

Service: Competent and genial.

Price range: Moderately expensive.

Credit cards: All major cards.

Hours: Noon to midnight, Monday through Friday, 5 P.M. to midnight, Saturday and Sunday.

Reservations: Recommended.

Wheelchair accessibility: Six steps up at entrance; steps up from bar to dining area; restrooms downstairs.

🥢 The name Manhattan Ocean Club summons images of an exclusive wood-paneled enclave festooned with navigational charts and nautical art, where Montauk Magellans repair to sip Scotch and swap sea yarns of high adventure on Long Island Sound. In fact, it is neither a club nor does it look particularly maritime; rather, it is a handsome and sophisticated midtown seafood house where the food, which for years was one notch above galley grub, has improved noticeably.

The main dining room, two flights below street level, is done in unaggressive creams and pastels. Pretty hand-painted reproductions of Picasso ceramics are mounted on the walls behind glass. This clean, tasteful setting is muddled only by the pretentious Doric finials on the building's rectangular support columns—sort of like putting a Rolls-Royce hood on a Volkswagen Beetle. A twisting stairway leads to an upstairs room adorned with Picasso prints.

The four-and-a-half-year-old Manhattan Ocean Club is owned by Alan Stillman, a restaurateur and wine aficionado who also runs two of the city's most popular steakhouses: the Post House and Smith & Wollensky. It is no surprise that the wine list is intelligently assembled and fairly priced, especially among domestic selections. The service staff is competent and amicable, although someone should be on hand to offer help with wines.

As for the food, serious piscivores will be pleased with a good deal of the daily catch. A fine way to start is with a creation dubbed tonno con vitello (tuna with veal sauce), a tongue-in-cheek twist on the Italian classic vitello tonnato (veal with tuna sauce). Surprisingly, it works beautifully: a thick rectangle of tuna steak is coated with ground black pepper and seared until blackened outside and sushi-cool in the center. It is garnished with a light veal mousseline seasoned with capers. Clams baked with crushed filberts and pesto are a bore; go instead with the selection of five oysters baked five ways: one with anise-flavored Pernod, others with a sharp curry, a sweet compote of peppers, bright pesto (minus nuts), and oregano.

If you have a yearning for crab cakes, these two hefty patties are better than average and nice and peppery; clam chowder gets off to a promising start: it smells like the real thing, is nicely seasoned and chunky with potatoes, but, alas, there is little evidence that any clams dropped in for a visit. A special one evening of fettuccine with smoked shrimp and tomatoes sorely needed a boost of salt to bring out the flavors.

Daily fish offerings are highlighted by fish drawings on the menu. You might check the mahi-mahi, a Pacific dolphin with a meaty mild flavor, delicious with a glaze of citrus butter and crispy spaetzle. Tuna steak is charred outside and rare within, brightened with a tomato-and-mint vinaigrette, and farm-raised striped bass is enhanced by a basting of soy sauce, ginger, and garlic. Halibut is cooked to a turn, too, ringed with an excellent beurre blanc sauce enriched with fish stock and garnished with crushed tomatoes. The shoestring potatoes could become addictive; unseasoned sautéed spinach, on the other hand, should be eaten only because it's good for you.

On the negative side are a flaccid sautéed Dover sole that had been out of the English Channel a day or so too long, dried-out swordfish au poivre, and heavy, overly breaded soft-shell crabs with Brazil-nut butter. Most vegetables come à la carte.

Desserts, like everything else here, are copious. A condominium of puff pastry is mortared by light chocolate mousse and banana slices, all in a pool of dry-edged chocolate sauce. Plum cake tasted rancid one evening—I couldn't force myself to try it again. I can recommend the nutty crusted raspberry-and-peach torte as well as the house-special chocolate basket, a little shopping bag of molded chocolate filled with white-chocolate mousse and surrounded with strawberry sauce. A triple-header dessert combines beguiling pot de crème, grainy crème brûlée, and ripe raspberry mousse.

MAN RAY

★ ★

169 Eighth Avenue, between 18th and 19th streets, 627-4220.

Atmosphere: Lively Art Deco bistro.

Service: Overwhelmed on busy nights, resulting in delays.

Price range: Moderate.

Credit cards: American Express.

Hours: Brunch, 11:30 A.M. to 3:30 P.M., Sunday; lunch, noon to 3:30 P.M., daily; dinner, 5:30 P.M. to midnight, daily.

Reservations: Suggested.

Wheelchair accessibility: One step up at entrance; bar and small dining area on one level, main dining area four steps down; restrooms downstairs.

🦞 An enigmatic portrait of a 1930s starlet by Man Ray, the Surrealist photographer, keeps you slightly on edge as you sit at the bar and sip an aperitif at this leading Chelsea bistro. Art Deco light fixtures and spindly wooden bar stools from vintage Paris Métro cars contribute to the period setting, where the focus is on ingenuous French bistro fare that is as warming as a thick pair of wool socks.

The menu blends many homey French standards—cassoulet, pot-au-feu, calf's liver and steak—with a few contemporary flourishes. The service staff can fall behind on busy evenings, but the performance seems to have improved in the past year.

On a brutally cold evening, purée of fennel soup is just what's needed to kick-start your failing engine—the light cream-based blend is subtle and restorative. Manhattan clam chowder is exemplary, too, flavorful of clam brine, cubed vegetables, and bacon. The house terrine is fine-textured and faintly livery, but it cries out for pepper to give it zip. It is rare to find spicy North African sausage, merguez, in local restaurants; the elongated little firecrackers served here are lean and snappy, accompanied by delicious chickpeas in cumin dressing and cooling cucumber salad.

The only forgettable appetizer is a smoked-fish plate combining nondescript salmon, mackerel, and trout. Better options are the charcuterie plate of smoked meats, and a winter green salad flecked with crisp bacon and duck cracklings, bathed in a well-balanced warm vinaigrette.

The wine list at Man Ray, while limited, is intelligently chosen to complement this type of food, and it is fairly priced.

If you are looking for a robust, belt-stretching cassoulet, this is the place. A deep ramekin overflows with buttery confit of duck legs, garlic sausage, pork confit, and beans. The choucroute garnie is first-rate, too—only larger. I challenge any two people to take on this Matterhorn of assorted sausages and meats in vibrant sauerkraut aromatic of juniper berries. On the lighter side are a lovingly grilled coho salmon in a red butter sauce with grilled leeks, carrot purée, and spinach; sliced duck breast painted with lime butter; tender and mild calf's liver with mustard sauce, and grilled chicken given a sharp edge with a coating of herby black-olive purée.

Grilled loin of lamb can be on the tough side but tasty in its garlic-butter sauce, and rare-cooked sirloin steak with a good béarnaise sauce is satisfying.

I don't usually expect to beat the drum over desserts at a bistro like this, but Man Ray's selection has a few superlatives. Paris-Brest is one of them: a dome of sugar-dusted puff pastry pumped up with layers of whipped cream and chocolate cream. Crème caramel is not just any old egg custard—this one has a faintly burned caramel that gives it a wonderful lingering aftertaste. Even a simple chocolate roll is seductively moist and rich, as is vanilla ice cream under

the same superb caramel sauce, garnished with caramelized walnuts.

MARCELLO

★ ★

1354 First Avenue, near 73rd Street, 744-4400.

**Atmosphere: Contemporary, understated setting in
shades of beige and rose. Large photo mural of Florence
on back wall.**

Service: Professional and well informed about the food.

Price range: Moderately expensive.

Credit cards: All major cards.

Hours: Dinner, 5 P.M. to midnight, daily.

Reservations: Necessary.

**Wheelchair accessibility: One step up at entrance; dining
room on one level.**

🐄 Situated on the Upper East Side, where high-priced
pasta houses are commonplace, Marcello is noteworthy on
two accounts. While not exactly cheap, it is a notch below
much of the competition in price; more important, though,
is the spirited cooking of the chef, Gianvito Fanizza.

The contemporary dining room is done in shades of beige
and rose, with plants here and there to soften the hard
edges. The addition of sound tile in the ceiling has muffled
somewhat the once-distracting clatter on crowded evenings. The rear wall, near the kitchen, is covered with a
striking floor-to-ceiling black-and-white photograph of
Florence. As waiters scurry back and forth with orders, it
seems as though they are making fleet-footed tours of the
Uffizi museum. Overall, the professional and well-informed
service staff is holding up well.

Pastas, which can be ordered in half portions for appetizers, are more compelling than most of the starters. One of
the best is al dente fresh fedelini (thin spaghetti) with firm-
cooked shrimp and tart radicchio with a touch of tomato
for color. Equally memorable is the fusilli in a luxurious
blend of creamy mascarpone cheese with a dash of brandy.
A mixed-seafood pasta, offered as a special one evening,
was outstanding: flossy egg noodles glossed with an herby
white wine replete with mussels, clams, shrimp, and bay
scallops, each perfectly cooked. A diverting dish to share

among several diners is the trio of fresh pastas on one plate —shells in a vibrant pesto sauce, tortellini stuffed with porcini mushrooms and ricotta in a light tomato sauce, and thin pasta with a smoky blend of pancetta, porcini, and fresh peas.

Gnocchi fans no doubt will be pleased with the firm, fresh version here, swathed in fontina cheese and butter. Spaghetti with clam sauce is a paragon as well.

If you want to begin with a lighter antipasto, try the salad of orange sections, shrimp, and black olives. A special of sautéed porcini with garlic curiously lacked flavor.

Among entrées, seafood blue-ribbon winners include the sparkling fresh red snapper sautéed in wine, tomatoes, and herbs and the meaty Dover sole paired with a faintly sharp blend of mustard, green peppercorns, and brandy. A mound of brittle fried zucchini is a side dish not to be missed. Zuppa di pesce, a ubiquitous dish that is a swampy bore in many restaurants, is exceptional in the hands of Mr. Fanizza. A shallow pool of thyme-scented shellfish stock overflows with shrimp, salmon, monkfish, mussels, and clams. Only the baby squid with olives and artichokes is disappointing. The dark sauce is viscous and cloying.

The chef respects good-quality veal, allowing the meat to shine through when prepared Milanese-style with a sprightly garnish of marinated tomatoes, onions, and peppers. Other winners are scallops of veal prepared with a sauce of wild mushrooms, and with an earthy combination of chestnuts and wine.

Don't miss the ethereal tiramisù, a fortress of espresso-soaked ladyfingers, mascarpone, and whipped cream. This dish has become somewhat of a cliché in Italian restaurants around town, but few surpass Marcello's. The combination of fresh raspberries with balsamic vinegar is rousing, too.

MARIE-MICHELLE

★ ★

57 West 56th Street, 315-2444.

Atmosphere: Contemporary and comfortable, with Art Deco touches.

Service: Pleasant and efficient.

Price range: Moderately expensive.

Credit cards: All major cards.

Hours: Lunch, noon to 3:30 P.M., Monday through Friday; dinner, 5:30 to 11 P.M., daily. (Note: free parking after 5:30 P.M.)

Reservations: Suggested.

Wheelchair accessibility: Two steps down at entrance; all facilities on one level.

❧ Marie-Michelle Rey is a kinetic, sophisticated hostess who in 1987 took over a compact Continental restaurant on West 56th Street, stenciled her name on the front door, and began charming the midtown business crowd with her magnetic personality and seductive French food. Ms. Rey is no stranger to the restaurant business. A French-born former model, she learned the trade while working with her former husband, Georges Rey, who had a namesake restaurant for eighteen years just around the corner.

Marie-Michelle is an urbane and comfortable spot, done in shades of rust and beige with a smoky mirrored wall on one side and gentle lighting. Villeroy & Boch china in a spiffy Art Deco pattern and pretty flower clusters around the room contribute to the polished scene. The chef, twenty-five-year-old Edward Brown, put in time with Alain Senderens in Paris and later with Christian Delouvrier at New York's estimable Maurice before opening the new restaurant. You can see the influence of his mentors in such cerebral preparations as lobster fricassee infused with fresh ginger and garnished with red peppers, chives, and zucchini—an invigorating combination. At the same time, he can turn out a succulent roast chicken in pan juices with dauphinoise potatoes or wonderfully simple lamb chops accented with a whiff of thyme.

Several fish dishes are worth noting, especially the panaché de poissons with basil sauce—a stellar trio of perfectly sautéed salmon and red snapper along with lobster meat enhanced with a basil-perfumed beurre blanc speckled with caviar, which adds a lovely saline touch. It comes with a German-style potato salad of red potatoes, onions, and vinegar. Less elaborate but pleasing preparations include the sautéed Dover sole with a subtle coriander sauce; feuilles, or leaves, of Norwegian salmon in a clean, light Beaujolais sauce, and, at lunch, baby salmon with a lemony beurre blanc sauce cut with capers. Ms. Rey, who orbits the room fielding questions and making suggestions, some of which have already been made by her well-trained service staff, creates a lively and sociable scene. Her wine list lacks the muscle to support the diverse menu, although a cadre of French standards are available at fair prices.

250

Whether or not Ms. Rey suggests the appetizer called plateau du pêcheur, or seafood plate, I suggest you try it: it's a tasting plate of excellent icy Belons oysters, cherrystone clams on the half shell, marinated sea scallops, and lustrous gravlax with anise sauce. Lean, tasty duck terrine is cushioned on rich-flavored aspic. I have always felt that such prissy preparations as asparagus in a dome of puff pastry with lemon-butter sauce were gilding the lily; the ingredients here are good, although I would prefer more asparagus and less fluff.

Desserts hold their own in this impressive lineup. Crème brûlée is thicker than most versions but delicious under a burnished sugar crust, fruit tarts are beautifully presented and delicate, and sorbets (especially cassis and passion fruit) are refreshing and ripe. Don't miss the apple napoleon, a caramel-varnished lid of brittle pastry over apple slices and pastry cream garnished by puffs of whipped cream holding mint leaves. Only chocolate mousse was unpleasantly sweet.

MAURICE

★ ★ ★

Hotel Parker Meridien, 118 West 57th Street, 245-7788.

Atmosphere: Luxurious and spacious with relatively moderate sound level.

Service: Sharp and professional.

Price range: Expensive.

Credit cards: All major cards.

Hours: Breakfast, 7:30 to 9:45 A.M., Monday through Friday; lunch, noon to 2:15 P.M., Monday through Friday; dinner, 5:30 to 10:30 P.M., daily.

Reservations: Necessary.

Wheelchair accessibility: Nine steps up at entrance.

🍴 The Hotel Parker Meridien was one of the first New York City hotels to take dining seriously when it hired the celebrated French chef Alain Senderens as a consultant in the early 1980s. Mr. Senderens severed his ties with the hotel in 1985, but his studious protégé, Christian Delouvrier, has blossomed on his own and helped turn Maurice into one of the most elegant and arresting luxury dining rooms in town.

The dining room is sumptuous and comfortable: it has a soaring ceiling, mirrored wall panels alternating with flowered murals, a resplendent cluster of illuminated white birch branches in the center, and generously spaced tables. Oriental-style rugs and upholstered banquettes help keep background noise to a minimum.

Mr. Delouvrier's dishes are as visually arresting as they are well honed. Distinctive flavors are distilled from robust stocks and the prodigious use of fresh herbs, and cream is usually eschewed for a lighter approach based on olive oil.

A paragon of Mr. Delouvrier's style is his garbure: a purée soup of cabbage, assorted vegetables, and fresh foie gras, it is a silken liaison, imbued with the sweet richness of duck liver and the nuttiness of truffles. Another soup sampled, a seafood broth with scallops, oysters, and mussels, is outstanding as well for its freshness and concentration of shellfish essences. Or how about glistening plump oysters wrapped in poached lettuce leaves under a truffle-perfumed beurre blanc?

One winning starter that remains from the early Senderens days is translucent ravioli filled with scallops, zucchini, and fresh thyme; a light glaze of beurre blanc is all it needs. Smoked salmon served warm over a fan of cucumbers with caviar-dotted crème fraîche was too salty one evening, better on a second visit, and a vegetable soup, called pea stew, was underseasoned.

The uniformed staff at Maurice is highly disciplined, attending to all the fine points of service. After dining in so many slapdash and trendy "Who gets the chicken?" dining rooms it is a pleasure to be pampered a bit. The wine list is manageable in size and offers a smattering of good buys in the $20-to-$30 category.

If I were forced at forkpoint to choose a best dish among the entrées, it would be a toss-up between the succulent and mild-flavored roast squab over a bed of earthy lentils enhanced with cubes of country bacon and minced carrots, and the special duck "Apicius," a signature dish of Mr. Senderens. This elaborate preparation is made by degreasing the duck in warm water then roasting it with a basting glaze of honey, coriander seeds, cuminseed, saffron, and white pepper. The meat is served with caramelized strips of the basting sauce on top and a sauce made from the duck drippings cut with red vinegar. The combination of sweet, spicy, hot, and tart is sublime.

If you are a game fan, venison steak, an occasional special, is lovely combined with sautéed cabbage enlivened with sweet-hot red peppercorns. Other sure bets are calf's liver in wine-vinegar sauce, and saddle of lamb with a red-pepper mousse and slices of a thin-crusted vegetable tart. The only letdown among meat entrées is the dry veal matched with heady truffle-flecked pasta.

On the seafood side of the menu, a thick and meaty fillet of John Dory roasted in a crust of rock salt is superb with its confit of tomatoes, as is red snapper over a purée of bell peppers and olive oil.

You may opt for the well-tended cheese platter instead of dessert, but then you will miss such terrific temptations as the tower of brittle pastry built upon layers of whipped cream and fresh raspberries, a superbly intense yet light chocolate mousse, a sharp lemon tart, and the gratin of fruits in a frothy champagne sabayon. Only the béchamel-and-chocolate cake, smothered in cream, is excessively rich and heavy.

MELROSE

★　★

48 Barrow Street, 691-6800.

Atmosphere: Dim, tightly packed front room; larger back room has a makeshift, low-budget look.

Service: Casual but competent.

Price range: Moderately expensive.

Credit cards: All major cards.

Hours: Dinner, 6 P.M. to midnight, Monday through Saturday, 5 to 10 P.M., Sunday.

Reservations: Necessary.

Wheelchair accessibility: Two steps down to dining room level; restrooms on ground floor.

🦐 Richard Krause, a tall, reedy Californian, looks more like a bass player for the Grateful Dead circa 1970 than a leading New York chef. An alumnus of Spago in Los Angeles, he made his mark here at Batons, which closed in late 1987, before opening his own place, called Melrose, a few months later.

Melrose is not your typical breezy, bright California-style restaurant. Housed in the dim basement of a West Village row house, it has a low-ceilinged rectangular front room with silver-gray walls that are symmetrically smudged with black, as if someone had rubbed charcoal against them.

Tightly packed tables line two rows of banquettes. You walk through the kitchen to reach the back room, which looks like a suburban garage converted into a party room on a tight budget. Green mosquito netting covers the ceiling, which flickers with strands of Christmas lights. Support poles are camouflaged with burlap. Perched on a rim along the walls are pine branches and stout metal garden lanterns that cast weak light across the room. It's not the sort of place I would care to see in broad daylight.

This makeshift setting has not deterred fans of Mr. Krause's cooking, who fill both rooms nightly. In frigid weather they come to thaw out with bowls of his recuperative winter vegetable soup, lumpy and delicious with lentils, leeks, corn kernels, and parsnips. Big meaty oysters are cloaked in a mild curry sauce and garnished with salty salmon caviar, a lovely combination; and shiitake mushrooms are nicely charred over a wood-fired grill and paired with yellow tomatoes in a basil-infused vinaigrette.

One of Mr. Krause's much-imitated signature dishes from Batons is potato pancakes topped with crème fraîche and three caviars (sturgeon, salmon, and whitefish). He has fiddled with the formula, replacing bite-size potato pancakes with deep-fried clusters of shoestring potatoes, which, besides being impossible to pop in your mouth, tend to mask the caviar flavor. A Japanese-inspired starter called stir-fried chicken salad rolled in cabbage leaves is a good idea botched by overcooked chicken. Another cross-cultural experiment works better: thin pasta tossed with tender strips of stir-fried duck along with snow peas, cabbage, and red peppers.

The casually correct waiters here are well trained and go through their ministrations with low-key efficiency. The wine list—half American, half French—is well chosen and priced fairly.

Mr. Krause's grill cooks do a masterly job, whether it is with the pepper-coated shell steak ringed with a compelling sauce of sweet sake, soy, and chopped fresh oysters; the buttery medallions of veal in a port-wine cream sauce strewn with shiitake mushrooms along with gratin potatoes, or the crackling roast chicken with ratatouille and roasted garlic cloves. Pepper-flecked salmon steak is cooked to barely pink within and is accompanied by black-and-white pasta (squid ink and saffron) in a pleasingly salty Japanese miso-based sauce.

One fussy creation that does not quite work was the whole lobster with mussels, set over rice with a black-bean sauce that overpowers everything, leaving a strong salty aftertaste. Two superior seafood options are grilled whole Florida red snapper in a lustrous red-wine sauce enriched with bone marrow, and rare-grilled tuna steak in a vinaigrette sauce jazzed up with mango, tomato, and scallions. Finally there is a simple but exquisite roast duck, its skin lacquered and crisp, the meat buttery and rich—sweet plum sauce and ginger-scallion pancakes add the crowning touch.

Melrose's pastry chef, Heidi Bein, is so good she should be put on retainer by top New York health clubs. One winsome concoction worth trying is the toasted angel food cake sandwiching dry-edged coffee ice cream—the plate is given a Jackson Pollock look with a spattering of melted chocolate. Speaking of chocolate, the terrific semisweet soufflé cake packs a wallop of it. Raspberry tart with a thick and moist brown butter crust is a winner, as is the flaky homemade apple strudel, sharp with cinnamon and floating on a pool of caramel sauce, and the cognac-glazed spice cake.

Melrose may not have a sunny California setting, but much of the food shines brightly, casting a warm glow on all who dine there.

MÉNAGE À TROIS

★

134 East 48th Street, 593-8242.

Atmosphere: Subdued, tasteful dining room in beige and wood; good noise control.

Service: Amateurish and slow.

Price range: Moderately expensive.

Credit cards: All major cards.

Hours: Lunch, noon to 2:30 P.M., Monday through Friday; dinner, 6 to 10 P.M., Monday through Saturday.

Reservations: Suggested.

Wheelchair accessibility: Most of dining room on one level; restrooms on same level.

❧ Antony Worrall-Thompson, the jet-propelled chef-owner who presides over this and sister establishments in London, Bombay, Stockholm, and Melbourne, has built a reputation as a proponent of grazing foods—that is, many small dishes in lieu of a traditional three-course meal. While his sculpted food presentation harks back to earlier days, his recipes are forward-looking and, for the most part, solidly grounded.

255

Since most portions fall between traditional appetizer and entrée size, one can assemble a meal any which way. Moreover, if you are in the mood for just one dish, or dessert only, the manager will not roll his eyes in exasperation.

The dining room was carved out of a former coffee shop in the Lexington Hotel. It is done in soothing beiges with wood trim, comfortable banquettes, and well-distanced tables. As good as the food is at times, service can be bumbling and forgetful. The eight-page menu is daunting in size. Under the heading "Cold taste teasers" is "Josephine's delight," comprising three creamed eggs in ramekins—one crowned with sevruga caviar, another with smoked salmon mousse and bits of smoked salmon, and a third with scallop mousse studded with diced scallops. They all were pleasing, although the caviar was my favorite.

Another example of the chef's unbridled imagination is called Hanbury yolk. The foundation of these two towers is quail eggs on artichoke hearts, topped with good smoked salmon, oysters, minced scallops, lobster meat, and caviar. They sit in a moat of vibrant dill-accented red-pepper mousse. Pastas are generous enough to be entrées. The best I sampled combined fresh green-and-white pasta with nubbins of nicely charred salmon, salty-edged sun-dried tomatoes, roasted red peppers, and diced bacon. Another winner melded wild mushrooms, foie gras, and truffles in a luxurious sauce that exuded a lovely autumnal essence.

One hot creation not to be missed is the trio of crunchy deep-fried pastry packages, one filled with lobster and snow peas, the others with turbot and leek, and crab and cucumber. These light, greaseless parcels, made with Chinese dumpling skins, are arranged in a lovely champagne sauce.

Among the seafood preparations, one visually arresting dish combines a light and flavorful scallop timbale with a band of spinach mousse in the center, surrounded by succulent grilled morsels of lobster, turbot, and halibut in a sweet-tinged tomato-dill sauce. A felicitous twist on the seafood pastries combines three steamed packets—crabmeat wrapped in leeks, scallops in cabbage leaves, and lobster in spinach—in a luxurious oyster-and-caviar sauce. Lobster and scallop tempura, though, is doughy and nearly burned.

A recommended meat threesome is called ménage of baby fillets, featuring rare-roasted lamb over a tomato concasse spiked with raspberry vinegar, beef on curried eggplant, and veal mingled with wild mushrooms. It is an inspired triple play. Ballottine of baby chicken is stuffed with a cloyingly rich mass of crabmeat and diced artichoke. The list of trios goes on with a success rate of about 70 percent.

Desserts are some of the most titillating offerings: sugar-dusted strawberry fritters with an orange-and-Grand Marnier dip, a terrific assortment of chocolate goodies—an intense terrine, a velvety mousse, a white-chocolate mousse, a chocolate truffle and ice cream—as well as three irresistible crème brûlées, flavored with orange, mint, or chocolate.

METRO

★ ★

23 East 74th Street, 249-3030.

Atmosphere: Formal, subdued, and clubby.

Service: Overtaxed staff struggles to keep up, with limited success.

Price range: Moderately expensive.

Credit cards: All major cards.

Hours: Brunch, noon to 3:30 P.M., Sunday; lunch, noon to 2:30 P.M., Monday through Friday; dinner, 6 to 11:30 P.M., Monday through Saturday.

Reservations: Necessary.

Wheelchair accessibility: All facilities on one level.

🍴 Patrick Clark, who for nearly ten years was part of a trend-setting team that created the Odeon (TriBeCa's seminal American bistro) and Cafe Luxembourg (still among the best restaurants near Lincoln Center), has set out on his own. This time, though, rather than setting trends, his new Metro seems to be defying them. As New York diners seek informality, he has opened a place that could be the executive dining room of a blue-blood Wall Street law firm. What's more, in these parlous economic times when many restaurants are scaling down to survive, he rustles up $14.50 caviar crêpes and $27 grilled tuna. Does Patrick Clark know something the rest of us don't?

While the setting is princely, the food still has populist appeal. Mr. Clark, a home-grown product of the cooking program at New York City Technical College and of a subsequent stint with Michel Guérard in France, built his reputation feeding the white-socks-and-fork-size-earring set in TriBeCa. You can't get too froufrou with them. Thus, what you find are generally well conceived, accessible treats like roasted squab with risotto, loin of lamb with fried onions, and Black Angus steak with red-wine sauce.

The setting, in the former Adam's Rib, was designed by Adam Tihany (as were Bice, Remi, and the new Huberts). You enter a warm, subdued bar where a half dozen or so couples are twiddling swizzle sticks while waiting for their tables—and waiting and waiting. "We're so sorry for the delay," a captain apologized after a half hour, offering a bottle of wine on the house. You finally proceed down a long, solemn tunnel, past a small dining alcove—smokers' purgatory, near the kitchen door—then into the main arena.

Mr. Tihany's familiar trademarks work their charms: the backlighted faux windows, rich mahogany paneling, and banquettes that don't force you to sit like a marine. Waiters in natty red ties and red-striped shirts with little Metro logos on the pockets think they are still at the wham-bam Odeon. The preliminaries go well, but once your order is taken and the wine is poured (once), don't expect much more.

Beguilements on the menu included a summery sugar-snap-pea soup, velvety and slightly sweet; richly flavored lobster bisque holding sweet nubbins of meat (and a shard of shell); beautifully browned nuggets of sweetbreads in a nest of mixed greens and hazelnut-oil vinaigrette, and lustrous, rich foie gras (albeit a paltry thin serving for $18) tamed by a good sherry-vinegar sauce.

The main event features everything from the simple and restorative—grilled swordfish paired with a pleasingly salty Provençale-style black-olive butter and a well-seasoned vegetable medley—to more involved creations, such as lobster out of the shell in a seductive whiskey-and-saffron cream sauce with shiitake mushrooms.

Sheets of rare duck breast fanned around the plate were succulent, although the mango sauce was oddly cloying; clay-pot-roasted chicken should have been liberated from its pot sooner—the breast meat was dry—although the potato pancakes and whole garlic cloves around it were irresistible. The roasted squab with porcini risotto could not have been better, and roasted lamb with fried onions was stellar one evening. The best seafood dish sampled was a special of buttery halibut perched over a plateau of couscous flecked with minced vegetables. Grilled "sushi-quality yellowfin tuna," garnished with sweet sautéed onions, was a tad overcooked to my taste.

If you want to exit on a light note, try any of the excellent fruit sorbets and fragile tuile cookies. Crêpes filled with cherries and encircled with zabaglione are forgettable. Crème brûlée is on the mark, as is a hazelnut-rum marjolaine with bittersweet chocolate sauce and a parapet of crushed nuts.

MEZZOGIORNO

★ ★

195 Spring Street, 334-2112.

Atmosphere: Playful trattoria with long marble-topped bar and café tables.

Service: Excellent and genial young staff.

Price range: Moderate.

Credit cards: None.

Hours: Lunch, noon to 3 P.M., Monday through Friday; dinner, 6 P.M. to 1 A.M., Monday through Friday; open noon to 1 A.M., Saturday and Sunday. Pizza served noon to 4 P.M. and 10 P.M. to 1 A.M.

Reservations: Necessary, especially Friday and Saturday.

Wheelchair accessibility: All facilities on one level.

🐌 If you are a fan of the buoyant northern Italian fare at Mezzaluna on the Upper East Side but rarely find a free table in its dollhouse-size dining room, an alternative is the SoHo branch that opened in 1988, called Mezzogiorno. The menu at this casually sophisticated trattoria is similar to that of the original: sprightly carpaccios and salads, vivid pastas, and excellent brick-oven pizzas.

You encounter a long marble-topped bar at the entrance flanked by café tables along the white-paned windows (for smokers); the playful back room has a long tan banquette along one wall and tables surrounding a faux marble column. Nearby, behind the bar, is a giant ceramic mask whose mouth is the opening for the pizza oven. The walls are full of glass-covered boxes holding bizarre three-dimensional collages. Music and conversation ricochet off all the hard surfaces; when the place fills up, it can be clamorous.

The food, fortunately, is more disciplined than the art. All eleven meat carpaccios can be highly recommended. Among my favorites are the cold beef version scattered with crunchy shards of raw artichoke hearts and slivers of sharp Parmesan cheese, all speckled with good olive oil and black pepper. The one seafood carpaccio offered on the regular menu, made with swordfish, had a mealy texture.

Arresting appetizers include a light and crumbly flan made with ricotta cheese set in a shredded-lettuce sauce brightened with lemon, and bresaola, diaphanous slices of dry salted beef, layered over lamb's-lettuce salad and morsels of creamy goat cheese. Risotto is unusual but delicious. The rice is cooked with a potent dose of saffron, cooled, then molded into pancakes and sautéed until lightly charred on the bottom.

Salads can be ordered as starters or main courses. They are excellent, whether the curly endive with pancetta and a poached egg (a nice Sunday brunch) to shrimp with slivers of zucchini sautéed in olive oil.

The young Italian waiters in their jaunty yellow-striped shirts and blue aprons are the type of easygoing professionals you rarely find on this side of the Atlantic. They exude a passion for the food and pride in their métier that is contagious. The wines are well matched to the food, starting with refreshing northern Italian whites in the $20-to-$30 range.

Beguiling pastas include orecchiette, "little ears" in Italian, with sausage and batons of fennel in a light tomato sauce; fazzoletti (folded thin sheets) with wild mushrooms, and tagliolini with shrimp, arugula, and tomato. The only letdown was gummy black linguine, made with squid's ink, in a hot-pepper-and-tomato sauce.

Four or five specials are offered daily. Pink-tinted gnocchi, made with potato and tomato, is supple and light, bathed in fresh tomato sauce and garnished with shredded basil. Lasagna is compelling, too, sheets of al dente pasta holding cubed eggplant and tomatoes, bound with a cheesy white sauce.

The pizza chef tends the wood oven at lunch and after 10 P.M. The thin crusts are nicely charred, with toppings ranging from potato and sun-dried tomato to pancetta and onion, mixed vegetables, and wild mushrooms.

Dozens of Italian restaurants make the ladyfingers-and-sweetened-mascarpone-cheese dessert called tiramisù, but Mezzogiorno's is one of the best. Other happy endings are the faintly chewy hazelnut-and-chocolate torte with intense vanilla ice cream, and assorted fruit under a foamy avalanche of zabaglione that has been passed under the broiler until browned and bubbling. A fine selection of Italian dessert wines and grappas are offered by the glass.

MITSUKOSHI

★ ★ ★

461 Park Avenue, at 57th Street, 935-6444.

Atmosphere: Comfortable, though overly lit; clean and colorful sushi bar; tatami rooms Westernized for comfort.

Service: Charming and well meaning if occasionally hampered by overburdened kitchen.

Price range: Moderately expensive.

Credit cards: All major cards.

Hours: Lunch, noon to 2 P.M., Monday through Saturday; dinner, 6 to 10 P.M., Monday through Saturday.

Reservations: Recommended.

Wheelchair accessibility: Elevator to basement-level dining room; all facilities on one level.

🍴 Mitsukoshi ranks at the top of the list of sushi mavens in Manhattan—including a lot of Japanese clientele who help fill it at lunch and dinner.

This polished restaurant below a porcelain and pottery shop of the same name at Park Avenue and 57th Street has three seating areas: the rather garish, overilluminated main dining room with faded yellow-gold wallpaper, the sushi bar, and the private tatami rooms. Don't worry, these tatami rooms are Westernized with a sunken well under the table so you can dangle your feet below. In the main dining room, traditionally garbed waitresses with permanently etched smiles do their best to please, although understaffing seems to be a problem that causes delays.

Salmon caviar wrapped in a seaweed sheet with rice and grated white Oriental radish (ikura oroshi) is particularly good; the large golden eggs are bright and firm so that they pop when chewed. Slices of resilient fish cake with marinated cucumbers (itawasa) are delightfully evocative of the sea. They are complemented nicely by a wasabi-stoked soy sauce.

For those who seek a really fresh oceanic sensation, the squid or whitefish sashimi swathed with sea-green urchin roe is worth trying. One of my dining companions remarked, "It's like lying in the surf face down."

Several appetizers fall short of the mark. Deep-fried tofu cubes with a scallion-and-ginger soy sauce (agedashi tofu) are soggy and bland. Yamakake, a crock holding grated Japanese potato over cubes of tuna sashimi, is a peculiar preparation. The potato tastes like warm egg whites, and all it does is blunt the flavor of the tuna.

Many of the entrées are expanded versions of appetizers. Among the better ones is a light and brittle tempura featuring vegetables, shrimp, whitefish, and a tangy ginger dipping sauce. Grilled fish of the day—usually red snapper or salmon—is perfectly charred and moist. Grilled filet mignon (filet kuwa yaki) is top-quality and cooked to order. Shabu shabu, a caldron of simmering broth in which diners cook their own food that is heated at the table, is as diverting as it is delicious. The colorful selection includes lustrous thin slices of lean beef, Chinese cabbage, mushrooms, tofu, scallions, carrots, and rice pasta.

Excellent sushi and sashimi are available in the dining room and tatami rooms, but it is more fun to have them at the sushi bar. Places should be reserved in advance. The cozy, aseptic bar has ten seats facing two or three chefs.

MONTRACHET

★ ★ ★

239 West Broadway, at White Street, 219-2777.

Atmosphere: Casually elegant dining room with soft lighting and rust-pink banquettes.

Service: Friendly and generally efficient.

Price range: Moderately expensive. (Prix-fixe dinners at $25, $29, and $45, as well as à la carte.)

Credit cards: American Express.

Hours: Lunch, noon to 3 P.M., Friday; dinner, 6 to 11 P.M., Monday through Saturday.

Reservations: Suggested.

Wheelchair accessibility: Small step at entrance; all facilities on one level.

&❧ Montrachet is disarmingly casual, with few of the flourishes of a typical New York three-star restaurant. It is a low-key place housed in one of those high-ceilinged former downtown industrial spaces, which has been tastefully redone with a polished mahogany-and-onyx bar, pale green-blue walls, pinkish-rust banquettes, and soothing lighting. While the setting is relatively austere, the food is sumptuous—and very reasonably priced considering the effort that goes into it. Dinners are prix fixe at $25, $29, and $45, depending on how elaborate you want to get.

The current chef, Debra Ponzek, ably follows the tradition established by her two predecessors, David Bouley (now at his own restaurant, Bouley) and Brian Whittmer. Her cooking is generally light, pure, and bursting with flavor—no foppish presentation or gimmicks are necessary.

Among the superb starters is a salad of roasted squab with wild mushrooms (or the same squab over a bed of garlic-boosted lentils); the chef makes a vibrant terrine encased in strips of pasta, layered with red peppers, goat cheese, and spinach, all surrounded by a warm tomato-and-dill sauce. Foie gras comes with a lovely sweet-tart shallot glaze.

At 90 percent of the restaurants I visit, bread is not worth writing about; most of it comes from the same three or four commercial sources. Montrachet's bread, which also comes from the outside, is exceptional—thick-crusted, earthy, and with a little crunchy "lid," giving it the appearance of a tiny soup terrine.

Drew Nieporent, the owner, is a tireless and cheerful host who doesn't miss a thing. His waiters scurry around the room in black shirts, pants, and ties looking like a team of cat burglars. Montrachet has an excellent and fairly priced wine list, featuring some uncommon regional wines from France and California. The wines-by-the-glass are always interesting, too.

Among entrées, two winners are the roasted pheasant with orzo and a Provençale-style black-olive sauce, or lovely rack of lamb with vegetable-flecked couscous. Black sea bass is superb in a light saffron-perfumed vinaigrette sauce, and roast kidneys come in a wonderfully intense Chiroubles sauce. If you want something more homey, try the roast chicken with garlic and potato purée.

Desserts maintain the kitchen's high standards. The most extravagant is the combination of two hot soufflés—raspberry, and pear with chocolate—inflated disks bursting with fruit essence, dusted with sugar, and draped in fresh strawberry sauce. As if that is not enough, you are given a ball of superb vanilla sorbet as a cooler. Crème brûlée is the real thing, with a glassy caramelized crust enclosing a dense, eggy custard. A slice of layered hazelnut ice cream topped with Grand Marnier truffles and a coffee sauce is beyond resistance. A tarte Tatin of pear and apple, with a thin, buttery crust and caramel sauce, melts in the mouth. If you are too impatient to let it cool, Calvados sorbet comes to the rescue.

THE NICE FULTON

Satisfactory

64 Fulton Street, second floor, 732-8787.

Atmosphere: Clean and contemporary dining room with a spacious bar.

Service: Adequate.

Price range: Moderate.

Credit cards: All major cards.

Hours: 11:30 A.M. to 9:30 P.M., Monday through Friday, 3:30 to 9:30 P.M., Saturday.

Reservations: Suggested for lunch.

Wheelchair accessibility: Elevator available to dining room on second floor; restrooms on same level.

&❦ The original Nice Restaurant in Chinatown has been one of my favorites for years, so when it opened a branch on Fulton Street in Manhattan's financial district in 1987, hopes were raised for serious Chinese food amid the canyons of fast food and delicatessens. Unfortunately, that is not the case, for the Nice Fulton is a sanitized clone of the raucous original, fine for a quick lunch if you work in the neighborhood, but hardly worth a long trek after sundown.

The new Nice, on the second story of a renovated building, is decorated in calming tones of gray and rose, with a spacious bar on one side and uncharacteristically well-spaced tables.

The Chinatown restaurant has some terrific specialties that I couldn't wait to try—roast suckling pig with salty soybeans, a minced squab in lettuce, and whole squab braised in wine—but alas, they are absent here. Our waiter told us that any such requests, even for Peking duck, had to be made a day in advance.

That left us with a rather tame roster of essentially Cantonese preparations. Some of them are quite good, however, like the starters of pan-fried dumplings—moist, fresh, and bursting with ginger flavor—and light, golden shrimp rolls. Spareribs are sweetish and undistinguished. Two vegetable dishes that can be appealing starters are cubes of cleanly fried tofu filled with shrimp, and shredded eggplant and sweet peppers with an assertive garlic sauce.

Entrées are generally well cooked but many of the sauces are pallid or overly sweet. I can recommend the tender morsels of orange beef, slightly caramelized and offset with pungent orange rind, tender chicken with black beans and hot chili, and chicken and assorted vegetables with a bold garlic sauce. Shredded pork with garlic sauce was moist and generously seasoned, too.

Anything that says sweet on the menu can be dangerous unless you are the type who empties four sugar packets into your coffee. Sweet-and-sour pork and sweet-and-sour prawns are two to avoid. Even some of the supposedly hot dishes have so much sugar they are overpowered: jumbo shrimp in spicy hot sauce was neon red and inedibly sweet.

Service is adequate although the taciturn waiters do not exactly overburden you with suggestions or descriptions of dishes.

The check arrives before you have time to ask about desserts. No matter. There aren't any, except for fortune cookies. If I were writing the fortunes, they would say: Take subway to The Nice in Chinatown. Better Food.

THE NICE RESTAURANT

★ ★

35 East Broadway, 406-9776, 406-9510.

Atmosphere: Expansive, bright, and festive. Large circular tables and comfortable bent-cane chairs. Noise level moderate.

Service: Good-natured and generally efficient waiters. Some have difficulty speaking English.

Price range: Moderate.

Credit cards: American Express.

Hours: 8 A.M. to 11 P.M., daily.

Reservations: Suggested.

Wheelchair accessibility: Ground-floor dining room and restrooms on one level.

🍷 If you are looking for fresh and well-seasoned Hong Kong–style Chinese food, The Nice Restaurant should be your destination. This is one of those airy, animated, and overly adorned places that seem to serve more people than is humanly possible, and with impressive results and good cheer.

The expansive upstairs dining room exudes a festive air with its shiny gold columns, bright lighting and tables full of voracious families. The downstairs is used for overflow and parties. The waiters, a small army of them, are a good-natured and efficient lot, though some have real difficulty with English. The Nice serves only beer and soft drinks but patrons are allowed to bring their own wine. Through trial and error I have arrived at a list of recommendations that would constitute a memorable feast.

A good way to start is with the shrimp-paste rolls. They are not on the printed menu but in a little photo album that comes with it. The dishes are not identified, so you have to go on faith. On the bottom of page four is a picture of white egg-roll-size cylinders of shrimp paste that have been wrapped in translucent rice paper and lightly deep-fried. The crackling wrapper and mild-flavored shrimp are wonderful when dipped in one of the several sauces provided—sweet, hot, and hotter. A soup pictured on the first page filled with shredded crab and dried scallops is rich with shellfish flavor but far too gelatinous for my taste.

Another shellfish recommendation from the photos is deep-fried prawns. Like all fried dishes sampled, these tasty little balls are skillfully prepared in clean oil, leaving them puffed and light. Both the shrimp-paste rolls and the prawns are engagingly presented with carved turnip flowers and cucumber fans.

The roast suckling pig is one of the best in town. Its lacquered skin is lined with a thin layer of fat and rests upon slices of succulent and moist pork. The sweet and salty meat lies upon a base of sweet-cooked soybeans that are so good you can eat them like candy. Roasted duck prepared in a similar manner is equally delicious. Bypass the insipid steamed fish and another humdrum dish called filet mignon on skewers.

I have saved the best three exhibits for last. First is the traditional Cantonese dish of minced squab in lettuce. This rendition is more complex in flavor than most, combining moist cubes of squab, diced salty Chinese bacon, and sour preserved vegetables. Diners wrap the ingredients in lettuce, choose from several sauces, and eat it like a taco. One of the most intriguing preparations is called soyed squab in pot, in which a whole squab, head and all, is cut up and placed in a small ceramic crock and baked in a blend of soy sauce, wine, vinegar, sugar, and spices. When the lid is removed at the table, puffs of perfumed steam rise to reveal the exquisite meat, which is imbued with the heady marinade.

266

Finally, there is salt-baked chicken, an incredibly moist and velvety preparation that will disappear instantly at your table because of its universal appeal.

Don't miss the dessert of coconut-tapioca-melon soup (last photo in the album), a cool and refreshing finale to such a varied meal. If you want the soup served in an elaborately carved melon as presented in the photograph, it is necessary to make a request a day in advance. It is a fitting punctuation mark to a meal that strays from the familiar path followed in New York.

OCEAN REEF GRILLE

Satisfactory

11 Fulton Street, in South Street Seaport, 608-7400.

Atmosphere: Dramatic glass-enclosed dining room with period boats suspended from the ceiling.

Service: Lazy and forgetful.

Price range: Moderate.

Credit cards: All major cards.

Hours: Lunch, 11:30 A.M. to 3 P.M., Monday through Friday; dinner, 5:30 P.M. to midnight, Monday through Friday; 11:30 a.m. to 11:30 P.M., Saturday and Sunday.

Reservations: Suggested.

Wheelchair accessibility: Elevators and restrooms for handicapped available.

🦪 Urban mariners who drift into the South Street Seaport searching for nourishment encounter a plethora of rollicking watering holes, a few jaunty shellfish bars, and a treasure chest of snack stands. Beyond that, the full-service restaurants have a reputation for serving the sort of monotonous galley chow that could spark a mutiny on the Love Boat.

The striking Ocean Reef Grille atop the Fulton Market got off to a leaky start in 1987: not only is the name misspelled, but the service was hopeless and the food wildly uneven as well. In March of 1988, the restaurant hired a kitchen consultant, Karen Lee, a Chinese cooking teacher and the author of three cookbooks. Ms. Lee added some Oriental touches to the menu with such dishes as scallops with jade sauce and charred shrimp with red ginger barbecue sauce.

While most of the contributions are well conceived, they are often botched in the execution, mostly from over-cooking.

The setting is stunningly designed, a wide-open, glass-enclosed expanse that simulates a multitiered ship deck. Suspended from the ceiling are thirteen life-size boats, from a nineteenth-century Norwegian sailboat to a four-teen-foot New England Banks dory. At night, the craft are dramatically illuminated against a sky-blue backdrop. In warmer months, drinks and meals are served on a wrap-around terrace overlooking the seaport.

Ocean Reef Grille bustles at lunchtime with the down-town business crowd; at dinner, though, the quarterdeck is nearly deserted. The service team seemed in a fog, from the bartenders gazing at MTV on overhead monitors to the waiters, who, when not engaged in idle chatter in a corner, tended to shuffle around aimlessly. They also had an un-canny knack for serving dishes the customers did not order.

One of the better starters is crab cakes, moist and gener-ous, paired with a soy-based dipping sauce and "Napa cab-bage slaw"; we called it coleslaw when I was growing up. Warm sesame-seed-coated goat cheese was tasty atop its raft of olive-oil-brushed toast, surrounded by toasted red and yellow peppers; the accompanying green beans, how-ever, were overrefrigerated. The kitchen's version of tuna Niçoise was particularly dispiriting: a woefully overcooked slab of tuna was ringed by cold, unseasoned green beans, red onions, hard-cooked eggs, and soggy olives. A better bet is the roasted oysters under a mild saffron-curry butter.

The Ocean Reef Grille has some appealing wines on its moderate-size list; unfortunately, four of the first five I or-dered were out of stock.

Among entrées, the wok-charred salmon was nicely blackened outside and rosy within, although I did not de-tect any of the cilantro listed on the menu, and the stir-fried watercress needed salt. You can get a good steamed or grilled lobster here, or, if you want the lobster shelled, try it with the saffron-scented pasta and grilled fennel in a beguiling lobster-stock sauce.

Another of Ms. Lee's creations, wok-charred shrimp, was spoiled by a powerful smell of iodine, and the sauce tasted like bottled barbecue dressing. Six charcoal-grilled fish are served daily, but the only one I had that survived the in-ferno was Canadian salmon, its meat ruddy and rich, ac-companied by tasty al dente julienne of vegetables. Desserts are copious and rich but cloying, typified by the brownie-like pie with strawberries and strawberry sauce.

THE ODEON

★

145 West Broadway, at Thomas Street, 233-0507.

Atmosphere: Art Deco cafeteria with close tables, and rattling noise level in the evening.

Service: Young and congenial staff tried hard to keep up with the fervid pace at night; lunch service better.

Price range: Moderate.

Credit cards: All major cards.

Hours: Brunch, noon to 3:30 P.M., Sunday; lunch, noon to 3 P.M., Monday through Friday; dinner, 7 P.M. to 12:30 A.M., daily; light supper, 1 to 2:30 A.M., Sunday through Thursday, 1 to 3 A.M., Friday and Saturday.

Reservations: Recommended.

Wheelchair accessibility: Dining room on one level; restrooms downstairs.

&❧ The Odeon's casual and stylish ambiance, satisfying food, and congenial service continue to draw an enthusiastic crowd from the downtown community, despite heavy competition in the neighborhood in recent years.

The Art Deco former cafeteria has a long bar against one wall, a tile floor, and bistro tables crammed in tighter than cars in a midtown parking lot. On busy evenings, which is to say all the time, the din is loud enough to wilt your salad. One soon notices, though, that some of the crackling artistic energy that once made this scene so diverting is fading as the clientele metamorphoses from brash bohemian cool to corporate gray.

The food has lost some of its vibrancy. Overcooking and underseasoning drag down a number of potentially appealing dishes, which may indicate an overworked kitchen. Consider the pan-roasted loin of lamb in a walnut-butter sauce, with spinach and golden Maxime's potatoes. Everything was tasty except the medallions of lamb, which were tough and dry. The same fault marred the chicken breast with fresh ginger and summer vegetables. And at lunch a gray paillard of veal resembled the steam-table meat substance served at my college cafeteria.

Such strikeouts aside, The Odeon still turns out a host of appealing preparations that make it worth recommending. Two of the best entrées are homemade fettuccine with Gulf shrimp and a baked red snapper in saffron broth with artichoke hearts. The pasta sauce is assertive with shellfish flavor and laced with sweet red, green, and yellow peppers; the moist, meaty snapper is delicious in its bright herby broth. Rare-grilled tuna bolstered with a zippy red-pepper-and-jalapeño vinaigrette is vivid and fresh; poached salmon in a green-pepper sauce garnished with salmon caviar is a winner also—the combination of hot and salty played off one another nicely. New York strip steak, well seared and flavorful, is the best meat entrée, but the french fries, which were once first-rate, are now limp.

The affable young waiters and waitresses wearing floor-length bistro aprons do as well as they can under the clamorous circumstances. (Service at lunch is better.) The Odeon has a limited but intelligently chosen wine list that complements the food.

Appetizers have a higher percentage of winners than entrées. Crab cakes are excellent—brittle outside, meaty and faintly peppery inside. Another good choice is chilled Gulf shrimp framed in salsa mayonnaise exploding with fresh coriander.

The meal can end on a high note if you opt for the terrific chocolate terrine with a hint of orange, the poached white peach in Sauternes sabayon, or the puckering lemon tart.

OMEN

★ ★

113 Thompson Street, between Prince and Spring streets, 925-8923, 925-8208.

Atmosphere: Comfortable brick and wood multilevel dining rooms suggesting a Japanese country inn.

Service: Gracious and sincere if occasionally slow on busy evenings.

Price range: Moderate.

Credit cards: American Express and Diners Club.

Hours: Dinner, 5:30 to 11:30 P.M., Tuesday through Sunday.

Reservations: Suggested.

Wheelchair accessibility: Steps at entrance; all facilities on one level.

ॐ This charming SoHo Japanese restaurant specializes in soothing and salubrious fare. Oriental lanterns hang from a timbered ceiling, spacy electronic music pulses from above, and striking calligraphy adorns the walls.

The restaurant's signature dish, called Omen, is a beguiling soup made by steeping seaweed in chicken stock and spiking it with soy sauce, sake, and mirin, a sweet and syrupy rice wine. It is accompanied by a pretty ceramic plate holding a colorful array of partially cooked vegetables including white radish (also known as daikon), lotus root, broccoli, carrots, and burdock root, as well as raw spinach and scallions. All of the vegetables are plunged into the broth followed by the long, white wheat-flour noodles, called udon. The crowning touch is a sprinkling of crunchy sesame seeds.

You can order from among five-course prix-fixe menus or choose à la carte. Although the obliging young waiters and waitresses are a little shaky in the English department, they make a valiant effort to explain unusual dishes. It is always prudent to ask questions in Japanese restaurants, for they are known to offer innocent-sounding dishes that turn out to resemble the sort of creatures that wash up at the seashore, causing children to squeal. The staff is generally efficient, however on crowded evenings the pace slows down considerably.

Surprisingly, sushi is not served at Omen, yet a wide range of uncompromisingly fresh sashimi is available. A good sampling is the assorted sashimi plate, which holds pieces of florid and smooth tuna and cool thin slices of octopus, as well as squid, giant clam, and fluke. One of the more intriguing preparations is raw tuna with Japanese yam. Deep-red tuna cubes rest in a pool of soy sauce and are covered with matchstick strips of Japanese yam and crowned with a quail egg. The neutral-tasting yam has a texture that suggests egg whites. The combination is a singular sensation that took me two samplings to begin to appreciate.

Two other uncommon preparations worth trying are the avocado and shrimp with miso sauce, and the spinach and scallops with peanut cream. The former consists of a ripe avocado half stuffed with marinated cucumber slices and topped with whole shrimp. The savory sauce combines egg yolks, rice vinegar, salt, and sugar. The second dish, one of my favorites, features scallops and blanched spinach swathed in a peanut-cream sauce tinged with mirin, sake, and soy sauce.

Other winning choices are the blanched spinach with meaty shiitake mushrooms and sesame seeds (goma-ae), which has a delightful contrast of textures; spinach salad sprinkled with briny flaked bonito (oshitashi); crunchy Chinese bok choy cooked in a strong fish broth flavored with sake (nappa-ni); and scallops tossed in a blend of lemon juice, sake, soy sauce, and sugar, garnished with snow peas. The tempura dishes—shrimp and vegetable, vegetable only, and tofu—are unremarkable.

The three chicken dishes on the menu are superior—all are variations of boned roasted meat marinated in a sweetish soy sauce cut with sake and mirin. The sansho chicken is extraordinarily buttery and moist, with what tastes like hints of orange (I was told later that it was the effect of sake). It comes with hair-thin strands of carrot and white radish. The others are chicken with grated radish (tori-mizore), and cold chicken with cucumber (tori-tosazu).

Japanese beer is the best accompaniment to these salty flavors. A nice way to clear the palate at the end is with some ice cream: the dry-edged green tea or the creamy red bean.

While Omen's unconventional dishes contribute to its appeal, so, too, does the staff's easygoing, unreverential approach to Japanese dining. It's worth the trip.

107 WEST

Satisfactory

2787 Broadway, at 107th Street, 864-1555.

Atmosphere: Friendly and casual setting with glass-enclosed café.

Service: Eager if haphazard.

Price range: Moderate.

Credit cards: American Express.

Hours: Brunch, 11:30 A.M. to 3 P.M., Sunday; dinner, 6 to 11:30 P.M., Monday through Thursday, 6 P.M. to midnight, Friday and Saturday, 5:30 to 10 P.M., Sunday.

Reservations: Accepted only for groups of six or more.

Wheelchair accessibility: All facilities on one level.

🍴 Expeditions into the swampy terrain of Cajun restaurants, New York–style, reveal that what started as a distinctive and well-defined regional cuisine has gradually been taken over by glorified fast-food entrepreneurs who have homogenized it into a barely familiar hodgepodge that originates in a deep fryer and terminates in indigestion—greasy greasy with hot hot.

This affliction taints part of the menu at 107 West, on Broadway at 107th Street, a breezy and moderately priced restaurant that is popular with the young uptown set. The menu winds through the lands of Cajun, Creole, Tex-Mex, Southwest, and the Deep South, with a few detours for pasta. Not all of the Cajun and Creole dishes disappoint—in fact, the gumbo and jambalaya are quite good—but the surfeit of heavy, deep-fried foods combined with some inept grilling diminishes what could be a welcome high spot in the gastronomic marshlands south of Columbia University.

A glass-enclosed sidewalk café is a pretty urban setting, and the trim, casual back room with overhead fans and a neighborly bar is appealing as well. Waiters and waitresses, student-age all, are disarmingly friendly, often confused, and never bashful about describing dishes as "really fantastic" and "my all-time personal favorite."

Among the appetizers, my all-time personal favorite is the chicken-and-andouille gumbo. It is a thick and lusty combination of smoked chicken, spicy smoked sausage, and Cajun rice. A special soup one day, black bean and okra, was bold and satisfying, too, and just mildly piquant. Except for fresh oysters on the half shell and tasty deep-fried chicken wings, the remaining appetizers resembled the kind of food normally served on trays clipped onto car windows. Deep-fried Cajun crab fingers could have been battered napkin for all their flavor; ditto the fried shrimp called Cajun popcorn. I've rarely met a grilled eggplant I didn't like —until now. Undercooking on two occasions left it dense and waxy.

Several entrées are satisfying. Fajitas made with grilled chicken and garnished with guacamole, grilled onions, sweet peppers, black-eyed peas, and Cajun rice made a lively combination; hickory-smoked ribs seemed to have been grilled in advance and reheated, but the flavor was agreeable and the coleslaw was good (skip the sweet sauce). Probably the best entrée was jambalaya. A deep Dutch oven held a mountain of peppery shrimp, sausage, smoked chicken, red peppers, onions, and rice.

Beyond that, the river is rough going. Grilled chicken is dry and served with fried bananas that are dead ringers for commercial baby food, fried chicken is undercooked, seafood fricassee is tasteless. For dessert, pecan pie is fresh and minimally sweet, and apple pie homey and good. The rest are supermarket sweets.

ORIENTAL TOWN SEAFOOD RESTAURANT

Satisfactory

14 Elizabeth Street, south of Canal Street, 619-0085.

Atmosphere: Crowded, bright, and loud.

Service: Routine and rapid.

Price range: Inexpensive.

Credit cards: None.

Hours: Breakfast, 9 A.M. to noon, daily; lunch, noon to 3 P.M., daily; dinner, 3 to 11 P.M., daily.

Reservations: Suggested.

Wheelchair accessibility: All facilities on one floor.

🍴 This bright and bustling Cantonese restaurant is always jammed with large tables of Chinese families, which, according to conventional wisdom, is an encouraging sign. Three excursions into the vast and sometimes forbidding menu left me less than overwhelmed. A handful of dishes rise above the mediocre, but few compel one to race back downtown.

The dining room is one of those compact megawatt affairs with rows of bare light bulbs along a reflective gold ceiling. Big round tables are as tightly packed as a midtown parking garage. If you arrive around 7 P.M., chances are you will have to line up at the door, next to the fish tank and tall cellophane bags of carryout shark fins.

The menu goes on forever, although variety is not so great as it seems. Seven or eight standard sauces mate with chicken, beef, pork, seafood, and vegetables, so a little tasting goes a long way. Beer is the only alcoholic beverage. Waiters are a harried lot, ricocheting from one table to the other, so don't get fancy and start asking lots of questions. One evening I asked if it would be possible to have dishes served several at a time rather than all at once. "No," our waiter replied emphatically, ending the discussion.

A good light way to warm up is with the golden bean-curd cubes holding morsels of shrimp in the middle. They are delicious with some of the coriander-flecked soy sauce. Every Chinese family in the house seemed to be eating a special: giant steamed oysters smothered in black-bean-and-ginger sauce. This creation might not be for oyster purists—the boldly salty sauce masked all the briny oyster flavor—but the combination had appeal in its own right.

274

Another dish on the specials list was better than average, too: shrimp braised with black pepper over sautéed Chinese broccoli. Although the pepper level could have been cranked up a few notches for my taste, the sauce was appealing, redolent of fresh ginger, and the shrimp well cooked. Shrimp Sichuan, on the regular menu, was not so compelling. The medium-size shrimp are just this side of raw, and the sauce was timid.

I have had some exceptional squab at Chinese restaurants over the years, although this was not one of them. Roast squab with salt and garlic sauce was tough and bland.

When the waiter drops a plate of quartered oranges on your table, don't be silly and ask for a dessert list. Suck on an orange and go home.

ORSINI'S

★ ★

26 East 63rd Street, 644-3700.

Atmosphere: Opulent and spacious décor; good noise control.

Service: Generally attentive and improving.

Price range: Moderately expensive.

Credit cards: All major cards.

Hours: Lunch, noon to 2 P.M., Monday through Friday; dinner, 6 to 10:45 P.M., Monday through Saturday.

Reservations: Necessary.

Wheelchair accessibility: Several large steps at the entrance; all facilities on one level.

After others failed at two attempts to revive the former Quo Vadis restaurant on East 63rd Street, two seasoned professionals, Armando and Elio Orsini, took over the establishment in late 1987. The brothers had operated the fashionable Orsini's on West 56th Street for thirty-one years until its closing in 1984. At their new venture, they have taken the hard edges off the soaring premises by covering the banquettes with patterned fabric, changing the art, and reserving one of the cavernous rooms for private parties. Pale yellow walls and a magnificent carved wood ceiling decorated with cloud murals contribute to an aura of opulence.

The bronzed, impeccably dressed Armando Orsini is an urbane and sharp-eyed host who discreetly circulates around the room, sensing precisely when to intercede to fill a customer's needs, no matter how small, and when to keep a distance. His service staff, which was a little careless and confused in my early visits, seems to be improving.

Don't come to Orsini's looking for so-called nuova cucina. The menu is classic and conservative, just like the well-heeled, dressy clientele. Stimulating starters include a nicely executed veal tonnato, slivers of veal cloaked in a cold tuna-fish sauce with capers; baby clams in a savory garlic broth; and bresaola, salty sheets of dried beef over a sward of greens, glossed with lemon and olive oil. Cold poached salmon with fennel mayonnaise, however, was dry.

Half portions of pasta are a good way to begin, and a few excel. Fettuccine in a light cream sauce with shards of fresh salmon and piquant green peppercorns is an absorbing combination; equally good is malfatti (random-cut pasta), which is tossed in a first-rate pesto sauce with crunchy roasted pine nuts and ultra-thin string beans—light and resilient gnocchi can be had in the same sauce. A dish called farfalle Michelangelo '65—it sounds more like an Italian sports car than a pasta—is one of the chef's signature creations, a symphonic mélange of bow-tie pasta with slivers of chicken, salty prosciutto, earthy porcini mushrooms, and artichokes, all in a light cream sauce. And if you are a mushroom fan, the pappardelle in a heady porcini mushroom sauce is a must. The only pasta that missed the target, and not by much, was the linguine with clam sauce, which was skimpily sauced.

The kitchen turns out a fine risotto, one aromatic of porcini mushrooms, another with seafood (mostly squid) redolent of shellfish broth. For such a well-honed and sophisticated restaurant, it is surprising to find such a sorry wine list. The small, predominantly Italian selection is not only mundane but also wildly overpriced.

Entrées are for the most part familiar Italian fare but done with uncommon flair. You can opt for something as light and satisfying as succulent grilled baby chicken seasoned with rosemary and paired with a potato basket holding sweet pearl onions, or a firm, fresh Dover sole with pesto sauce. Grilled salmon was perfectly cooked and arrived flanked by two sauces, both good but incompatible—a mildly sharp mustard sauce and a smoky roasted red-pepper purée.

Veal is sublimely tender here, whether sliced and sautéed with porcini mushrooms, butter, and lemon, or "Orsini style," with artichokes and peas in a clear white-wine sauce touched with vinegar. One indication of the vigilance and professionalism of the owners is that they noticed that we did not finish the calf's liver, which came in a bland white-wine-and-vinegar sauce, and they did not charge us.

For dessert, there is a terrific timbale of warm chocolate laced with ginger in a pool of crème anglaise, a light ricotta-cheese tart with orange sauce, and excellent homemade sorbets (gelato is not nearly so good). It seems that no Italian restaurant can resist serving tiramisù. This stratified version is exquisitely airy and rich, but it lacks the required sharp edge of espresso.

ORSO

★ ★

322 West 46th Street, 489-7212.

Atmosphere: Bright, sunny, and casual setting with open kitchen and skylight.

Service: Good-natured and generally efficient.

Price range: Moderately expensive.

Credit cards: MasterCard and Visa.

Hours: All-day menu, lunch, dinner, and late supper, noon to 11:45 P.M., Monday, Tuesday, Thursday, and Friday, 11:30 A.M. to 11:45 P.M., Wednesday and Saturday.

Reservations: Necessary.

Wheelchair accessibility: Several steps down to dining room; restrooms downstairs.

🐾 Orso has become the in place for actors, actresses, and sundry Broadway theater moguls. Its formula is simple: a stylish setting, snappy service, and satisfying, simple food at moderate prices. The Italian trattoria fare seems less consistent in the past year than previously, but overall there are some dependable standards that make this one of the best after-theater spots in the neighborhood.

Orso is owned by Joe Allen, whose namesake restaurant is next door, and is managed by family members. The front room has a small bar flanked by several tables and followed by a step-down main dining room under an arching sky-light that makes for a cheerful setting at lunch. The restaurant is done in clean tans and oak, sporting celebrity photos on the walls and an open tile-and-steel kitchen in the rear. In recent years Orso has become something of a youthful Sardi's as theater people mingle with agents and journalists over salads and thin-crusted pizzas. Even the comely and generally efficient young service staff exudes a certain dramatic flair, although not in an overbearing way.

Orso's menu is wisely limited in size and emphasizes freshness over elaborate preparation. Consider, for example, the individual-size pizzas. They have thin, yeasty crusts and vibrant toppings: fennel-perfumed sausage, mozzarella, garlic, and tomato; red peppers, onion, garlic, and tomato; and basil, Parmesan, mozzarella, and tomato. My favorite is the pizza bread, shards of thin, brittle pizza dough infused with garlic and olive oil. It is absolutely addictive.

One of the better appetizers is delicious salt-crusted grilled shrimp served in the shell—the sweet meat is heady with smoky nuances. Other good options are bresaola, the air-dried beef, paired with radicchio salad and asiago cheese; and a tender slab of cold veal with a caper-speckled purée of tuna sauce. On the debit side are undercooked grilled eggplant and overmarinated raw salmon with green-peppercorn sauce.

A well-chosen all-Italian wine list has some good bottles in the $13-to-$18 range that marry well with this style of food.

The chef makes sprightly à la minute sauces for pastas, and most are satisfying. Among the best are spaghetti with mussels and clams; fusilli with broccoli di rape, chopped tomatoes, and pecorino cheese; and taglierini alla puttanesca that is lusty with anchovies and black olives.

Meat entrées fare better than seafood. Succulent little grilled quail with a brandy-laced stock sauce were stellar; so, too, was a lovely rolled veal tenderloin stuffed with spinach and mildly tart goat cheese. The only real flop among meat dishes is the desiccated and tasteless roasted pork chop with leeks and currants.

Desserts range from a first-rate tortoni to a ripe blueberry tart and the traditional almond biscuits with sweet dessert wine. A pear ice was pallid; far superior was an unusual dessert combining sweetened cream of ricotta with fresh whole cherries.

OYSTER BAR AND RESTAURANT
IN GRAND CENTRAL STATION

★ ★

Grand Central Station, lower level, 42nd Street and Vanderbilt Avenue, 490-6650.

Atmosphere: The sprawling main dining room with its vaulted ceiling has a grandeur reminiscent of the heyday of rail travel. The wood-paneled tavern room is more sedate. Dress is informal.

Service: Variable. Overall efficient if not terribly professional. Off-peak dining times are better and more relaxed.

Price range: Moderate.

Credit cards: All major cards.

Hours: 11:30 A.M. to 9:30 P.M., Monday through Friday.

Reservations: Recommended, especially for lunch.

Wheelchair accessibility: All facilities on one level.

This may not be the best seafood restaurant in town, but it certainly is the best train-station dining around. The grand vaulted ceilings and snaking counters seem timeless in this New York landmark building, and if you order smartly you can have some first-rate fish and excellent wine.

The main dining room, which has both counter service and tables, is a dish-clattering, cacophonous, and fast-paced dining arena that exudes a sense of urgency. If you seek a more soothing setting, try the handsome tavern with its wood-paneled walls, old ship prints, softer lighting, and diminished noise level.

Trying to describe the enormous menu in a short review is like reducing a whale to a fish stick. As a rule, stay with simple preparations and savor the seafood's freshness; sauces are not the kitchen's métier.

Oyster fans invariably begin with a sampling from the dozen exquisitely fresh varieties posted. All those listed are not always on hand, although I have sampled as many as nine types on one plate. Every one is as fresh as an ocean mist and distinctly flavorful. When the kitchen tries to gussy up oysters with cream sauces and the like, the results can be dispiriting.

Of the two clam chowders, the milky and chunky New England version has more shellfish character than the timidly seasoned red-broth Manhattan. Smoked salmon, which is flavored over fruitwood on the premises, is too intense for my taste.

One of the famous old preparations at the Oyster Bar is pan-roasted shellfish; either oysters, sea scallops, shrimp, lobster, clams, mussels, or the works. Every one is terrific. If you sit at the counter near the white-frocked cooks, you can watch these remarkable stewlike dishes being prepared.

The Oyster Bar wine list is renowned for its selection of California whites—more than 100, at reasonable prices (though many seem to be out of stock). Eight token reds are available. The service staff is enormous, and your treatment varies greatly, depending on the luck of the draw.

Of the house specialties, bouillabaisse is a standout. Its herby tomato-based broth, generous with saffron, is filled above tide level with mussels, shrimp, lobster, clams, and whitefish. Also recommended are the meaty golden-fried crab cakes accompanied by good thin french fries. The long list of mostly broiled fish fillets changes daily according to availability, and they are consistently fresh and well prepared.

Desserts are surprisingly good. The hefty deep-dish apple pie with an earthy whole-wheat crust is homey and satisfying. Strawberry galette in season features a layer of brittle puff pastry garnished with almonds and sandwiching fresh whipped cream and ripe strawberries. The only losers are a gelatinous blueberry pie and commercial-tasting raspberry cheesecake.

OZEKI

★

158 West 23rd Street, 620-9152, 620-9131.

Atmosphere: Low-key Japanese ambiance with a medium-size sushi bar, small yakitori bar, and two small dining rooms with colorful Japanese prints on the walls. The ventilation needs improvement.

Service: Language can be a problem at times, especially at the sushi bar. Service is occasionally slow.

Price range: Moderate.

Credit cards: All major cards.

Hours: Lunch, noon to 2:30 P.M., Monday through Friday; dinner, 5:30 to 10:30 P.M., Monday through Thursday, 5:30 to 11 P.M., Friday and Saturday, 5 to 10:30 P.M., Sunday.

Reservations: Necessary for more than four people.

Wheelchair accessibility: All facilities on one level.

🕭 A yakitori bar, where portions of seafood and meat are brushed with special sauces and seared over charcoal, is the main attraction at Ozeki, a handsome little restaurant on West 23rd Street.

Near the entrance to the restaurant is a sushi bar refulgent with glistening fresh fish ranging from blood-red tuna to silvery mackerel. Next to it is a smaller yakitori bar, where a chef tends little hibachi grills. A wooden partition holding potted plants separates the larger back area into two dining rooms. Colorful Oriental prints add to the pleasing, understated environment. One area where improvement could be made is ventilation; cooking fumes sometimes fill the restaurant.

Ozeki is a good spot for a light lunch—that is, if you are not on a tight schedule. Service in the back room runs hot and cold. It is much better in the evening; at lunch the sushi bar, with sometimes only one chef on duty, can be exasperatingly slow.

Try several tidbits from the yakitori menu for starters: ikanosugatayaki, which is an eight-syllable way to say grilled squid, and chicken yakitori, bite-size pieces of chicken coated with teriyaki sauce and grilled on skewers with onions. The chalk-white fresh squid, about four inches long, is perfectly cooked, sliced into a half dozen rings, and reassembled on the plate with the blackened tentacles set on the side as garnish. The delicious, resilient rings come with a zesty soy-ginger sauce. The less exotic chicken nuggets, glazed in a reddish-orange sauce, are tender, moist, and sweet.

Two other noteworthy selections from the yakitori grill are the smoky peeled eggplant, set in a light broth perfumed with fresh ginger, and the "surprise" grilled item, described on the menu as "For Your Stamina." This, of course, could not be passed up, even at the risk of being served some bizarre-looking creature from the murky waters under docks. It turns out to be grilled chicken gizzards, chicken livers, chicken hearts, mushrooms, and green peppers, all coated in a light, semisweet glaze. The hearts and livers are the most tender and enjoyable; the gizzards I find bland and cartilaginous.

Among the more conventional fare, beef negimaki—thin

slices of grilled beef rolled around scallions—is recommended over the mushy pork loin in ginger sauce. Many of the soups are richly flavored and complex. Only the tempura soba, a vegetable broth filled with tempura shrimp and vegetables, is ill-conceived—the crackling tempura crust inevitably gets soggy and slides off. We moved on to sample the shrimp tempura, a generous lineup that is billowy, golden, and well drained.

The dinner menu is a slightly expanded version of the lunch card. A good way to begin is with the succulent little pan-fried pork dumplings that are so moist they pop when you bite into them. Airy, golden-fried tofu squares with a soy-based tempura sauce also are good starters, preferable to the soggy cold tofu cubes on ice. One of the better raw-fish appetizers is sunomono, which includes shrimp and strips of assorted fish in a shallow pool of vinegar-and-sesame-oil sauce garnished with lettuce and crunchy sesame seeds. The assorted sashimi and sushi plate is fresh and oceanic if prosaically presented.

Language barriers prevent a give-and-take between customer and chef, which is so important at sushi bars.

No one goes to Japanese restaurants expecting a fantasyland of desserts. Ginger ice cream is as whimsical as they get. Skip the green-tea and red-bean ice cream, which were crystallized on three occasions.

PALIO

★ ★

151 West 51st Street, 245-4850.

Atmosphere: Awe-inspiring décor, from the elegant bar with a wraparound wall mural to the plush, high-ceilinged dining room. Spacious and comfortable.

Service: Well informed and professional.

Price range: Expensive (lunch prix fixe, $32.50; pretheater prix fixe, $35.00).

Credit cards: All major cards.

Hours: Lunch, noon to 2:30 P.M., Monday through Friday; dinner, 5:30 to 11 P.M., Monday through Saturday.

Reservations: Necessary.

Wheelchair accessibility: All facilities on one level; accessible by elevator.

≥● Palio is one of the more enigmatic restaurants in New York, a perpetual challenge to figure out. One day it can be inspired, the next just better than average, a third dispiriting. The restaurant is run by Tony May, the owner of three other Italian restaurants in the city, La Camelia, Sandro's, and San Domenico; he imported as chef Andrea da Merano, who has a considerable following in his native Italy. The restaurant is named after the Palio of Siena, a centuries-old festival that culminates in a reckless horse race around the city's piazza. This leitmotif is most stunningly evoked in the ground-level bar, which you pass through en route to the second-story restaurant. The bar is dominated by a bold and bawdy 124-foot-high wraparound mural of the Palio by one of the country's hottest contemporary artists, Sandro Chia.

A reverential gentleman in a dark suit escorts you on an elevator to the main dining room with its soaring coffered ceiling, colorful Palio theme banners on the walls, trellised woodwork, and plush, well-spaced tables. No expense has been spared; the shimmering brass service plates have pretty hand-painted tile insets, the cutlery and glasses are exquisite, and baby roses sprout from handsome silver boxes. The lengthy, leather-bound menu looks like a diploma.

Service has deteriorated, based on several revisits—wine is left unpoured, appetizers linger too long on the table, and no one seems in charge. Lunch seems better than dinner.

Appetizers are divided into cold and hot preparations, soups and pastas (the pastas can be had in half portions). In the first category, one of the best was fresh baby octopus, remarkably tender and faintly sweet, bathed in a blend of strong olive oil, tomatoes, capers, and celery. Two other heady starters were marinated salmon swathed with a woody truffle paste, and tender rings of calamari in bright herb-flecked tomato sauce and a disk of good polenta.

You would be hard-pressed to find a more buttery carpaccio anywhere. The sheets of florid red beef were so good I didn't even mind that the advertised balsamic vinegar was missing and that the smattering of fresh foie gras over it added little. Bypass the delicatessen-quality turkey in a light tuna sauce.

The best hot starter is beautiful fresh mussels in an aromatic saffron broth. Baby squid in a vivid olive-oil-and-parsley-based sauce would have excelled had it not been for undercooking, which left the squid crunchy. A good strategy is to have one of the pastas as a warm appetizer, or risotto, which is among the best I have had in some time. The rice is barely resilient, as it should be, and the cooking broth is deep and richly seasoned—one risotto is made with rare-roasted pieces of quail, another with tiny sweet peas. Two pastas can be highly recommended: fettuccine in a lustily seasoned Bolognese sauce and fusilli carbonara, with postage stamps of pancetta in a mildly tart pecorino sauce.

Seafood fanciers can't go wrong with the lustrous steamed bass fillets festooned with asparagus and zucchini in a vernal herb-flecked broth; another spirited creation is rolled salmon fillets, rare pink in the center, brushed with a blend of black olives, spinach, and pink peppercorns—a nice contrast of flavors. Shrimp coated with dill and parsley arrived dry and overpowered by herbs.

Finally, among meat entrées the best bets were sage-perfumed roast squab, and poached breast of capon stuffed with prosciutto and set over a vernal green sauce. A veal chop was tasteless and medallions of lamb were dry. Tender, plump breast of pheasant with a juniper-berry sauce and shiitake mushrooms was cooked to a turn, as were lamb chops with braised celery.

It is rare these days to find a first-class assortment of cheeses, and at Palio not only is the selection diverse but also in peak condition. If you crave something sweet, try the fabulous homemade fruit sorbetti or the intriguing black polenta pudding, light and bittersweet, in a velvety white-chocolate sauce. In fact, most of the desserts are smashing, with the possible exception of a flossy "nuova cucina" rice pudding.

PALM

★

837 Second Avenue, near 45th Street, 687-2953, 599-9192.

Atmosphere: Sawdust-covered floors, wooden chairs, caricature-covered walls; loud and bustling.

Service: No-nonsense veteran waiters are affable and generally efficient.

Price range: Expensive.

Credit cards: All major cards.

Hours: Lunch, noon to 5 P.M., Monday through Friday; dinner, 5 to 11:30 P.M., Monday through Saturday.

Reservations: Necessary for lunch; accepted at dinner only for six or more.

Wheelchair accessibility: Two steps at entrance; restrooms downstairs.

❧ To love Palm one has to be the type who revels in a Pamplona-like atmosphere with sawdust-strewn floors, smoke-smudged walls festooned with celebrity caricatures, wham-bam service, and lumberjack-size portions. I get a kick out of steakhouses like this—that is, assuming the food is equally engaging. At Palm, unfortunately, that is no longer the case. You can still get a first-rate sirloin here, and if luck is on your side, good brittle cottage fries. The rest, however, is as unpredictable as the stock market.

One vexing affectation at Palm is the lack of a menu. A waiter comes to your table and runs on several varieties of steaks, chops, lobster, broiled fish, and two or three appetizers. If pressed he will concede a veal dish or two. To get more out of him (and there is more) requires the persistence of a district attorney. In fairness, though, the waiters, mostly affable, wisecracking veterans who do their jobs well, are simply trying to steer customers toward the best dishes.

The seventeen-ounce sirloin steak that made Palm famous is still a winner—seared under a super-hot broiler to impart a blackened crust while remaining juicy and succulent within. The thin disks of cottage fries and tangle of deep-fried onion can be fresh and crunchy one night, but on another, tepid and leathery from sitting in the kitchen too long. Other vegetables range from acceptable to cafeteria-style. The wine list is thin and undistinguished.

Another of Palm's erstwhile favorites is called steak à la stone, featuring sliced strips of sirloin steak over a mound of sautéed onions and pimientos. Once again, the meat can languish in the kitchen too long and begin to turn steam-table gray from the heat and moisture of the onions. Veal chops and double-cut lamb chops are generally reliable and tasty. Filet mignon, on the other hand, would be hard to identify if eaten blindfolded, so lacking it is in flavor.

As for the four-pound lobsters that come to the table split, broiled, and with melted butter, they are less succulent than steamed lobsters but delicious in their own right with a nice smoky tinge. In my experience broiled fish is usually overcooked and underseasoned. Except for a garlicky plate of sautéed shrimp with herbs, other appetizers are forgettable: bready and chewy baked clams, tasteless crab salad, and papery shrimp with cocktail sauce.

If there is room for dessert, try either the top-notch creamy cheesecake or the awesomely rich chocolate mousse cake.

The similar if more subdued Palm Too across the street serves more or less the same fare. Although the original

Palm has lost its edge as an all-around restaurant, I can still recommend it for a stiff drink and a slab of sirloin—which, after all, is what the place is really all about.

PAMIR

★ ★

1437 Second Avenue, between 74th and 75th streets, 734-3791, 650-1095.

Atmosphere: Dim nightclub feeling with candlelit tables and Oriental rugs on the walls.

Service: Eager—sometimes too eager—and helpful.

Price range: Inexpensive.

Credit cards: MasterCard and Visa.

Hours: Dinner, 5:30 to 11 P.M., Tuesday through Sunday.

Reservations: Necessary.

Wheelchair accessibility: Front dining room on one level; restrooms downstairs.

🍲 Afghan food may not be high on the beautiful people's list of chic cuisines, but to my taste this dynamic, budget-priced spot deserves wider attention.

Pamir is a long, dimly lighted place with a Middle Eastern nightclub feeling to it. Oriental rugs, sundry wall hangings, and soft music contribute to its mysterious charm. The candlelit tables are closely arranged to accommodate an avid clientele nightly. Polite waiters in white shirts and black vests are eager to please and happy to order tasting meals for those who want to experience a wide range of dishes. Because the dining room is so busy, they are sometimes overzealous when it comes to clearing plates, so it is advisable not to leave the table for any reason until you are finished; you might come back to find another party enjoying appetizers.

Afghan food is a blend of Middle Eastern cuisine with spicy Indian accents, emphasizing lamb, chicken, and vegetables. This can be seen in such appetizers as sambosa goushti, puffed triangles of light and well-fried pastry stuffed with a mixture of ground beef and chickpeas redolent of cumin and cinnamon; bulanee gandana, thin turnovers filled with scallions and herbs that are eaten with a yogurt sauce; bulanee kachalou, another turnover, somewhat dry though, stuffed with mashed potatoes, ground beef, and spices; and aushak, flat scallion-filled ravioli sauced with a combination of seasoned yogurt and ground meat.

Afghan soup, called aush, is a tasty combination of noodles, mixed vegetables, and spiced ground beef in a mint-laced meat broth. House salads, which come with the dinner, must be an affectation meant for Americans—iceberg lettuce and anemic winter tomatoes. Beer goes well with this earthy food, which is just as well, because the wine list is mundane.

Entrées include various marinated lamb kebabs, which are grilled nicely just to medium rare, as well as highly seasoned kofta kebabs, balls of ground beef or lamb. The most intriguing main courses, though, are the rice-based dishes, norange palaw and quabilli palaw. The former is a circular mound of saffron rice laced with almonds, pistachios, and thin strips of orange zest. Underneath the rice is an aromatic lamb stew that when mixed with the rice yields a complex and subtle mélange of flavors and textures. Quabilli palaw is made with brown rice and has for garnish almonds, pistachios, carrot strips, and raisins that give it extra sweetness.

The only dessert worth going out of the way for is firnee, a semifirm custard brightened with rosewater. While Pamir is limited in what it does, it does it well, and at remarkably low prices.

PARIOLI, ROMANISSIMO

★ ★

24 East 81st Street, 288-2391.

Atmosphere: Luxurious town-house setting.

Service: Generally professional and formal.

Price range: Expensive.

Credit cards: American Express and Diners Club.

Hours: Dinner, 6 to 11 P.M., Tuesday through Saturday.

Reservations: Necessary.

Wheelchair accessibility: Five steps at entrance; all facilities on one level.

Strand for strand, Parioli, Romanissimo is New York's most expensive Italian restaurant. A three-course meal with the most humble wine easily tops $80 a person before tax and tip, and if your blood runs hot for appetizers like risotto with wild mushrooms ($26) and such entrées as rack of veal ($64 for two), tack another digit onto the total. And what do you get for these prices? An urbane setting, pampering service, and Italian fare that is generally pleasing but hardly provocative.

Parioli, Romanissimo moved in 1984 from First Avenue to an airy town house on East 81st Street. You enter through a hushed little bar and proceed down a corridor to the main dining room, a stately parlor with a fireplace and a high, ornately molded ceiling. The mottled ocher walls are warm and soothing—but not the clownish paintings all about, made even more obtrusive by their harsh illumination. Beyond a leafy atrium is a smaller back room.

The menu carries five regular appetizers and a half dozen pastas. The pastas are not served in half portions, our captain informed us, "but the portions are not large." Among the pastas is the remarkably light homemade ravioli stuffed with wild mushrooms in a frothy cream sauce. The aforementioned mushroom risotto was a paragon of this northern Italian staple—light, creamy, and boldly flavored. Another subtly good starter is the carpaccio of lamb. Little petals of lamb are seared outside, raw in the middle, and served with a mild red-pepper-and-cream sauce.

The captains and waiters here go through their ministrations with cool solemnity. They know how to pamper their well-heeled patrons, many of whom are regulars. The only irksome flaw is that often dishes arrive at different times, so that one diner sits awkwardly while others at the table politely watch their food get cold. The wine list boasts some of Italy's best producers; whites are more reasonably priced than reds.

The entrée roster is like a rushed bus tour of Rome: you are exposed to a plethora of images but remember few details. Nine veal dishes are offered, including a thick, tender veal chop stuffed with fontina cheese with an oversalted stock sauce with truffles; and bland veal Milanese, in which the same cut is pounded, breaded, and sautéed. The best of the lot is the roasted rack of veal in a lovely reduced sauce of pan drippings. Garlic-encrusted rack of lamb is succulent and delicious, too.

As for the roasted branzino, a type of sea bass from the Mediterranean, it must have made the journey here on the Concorde. The portion for two carried no price on the menu, and none was offered by the waiter. The whole silvery fish is ceremoniously presented, then filleted at tableside and served under a tarragon-and-fennel sauce, which the rather pale-tasting fish sorely needs. The tab: $76. You get a clump of watercress on the side. Broccoli purée is $9 extra.

The most impressive aspect of Parioli, Romanissimo is the cheese cart, an incredible selection of French, Italian, and American cheeses in excellent condition. They are wonderful with a glass of port—even though $16.75 for a glass of 1977 Graham is extortionate. Fruit tarts are uniformly pleasing, raspberries come with a frothy zabaglione, and chocolate cake is intense.

PERIYALI

★ ★

35 West 20th Street, 463-7890.

Atmosphere: Trim and clean whitewashed walls and wooden floors.

Service: Amiable and efficient.

Price range: Moderate.

Credit cards: American Express, MasterCard, and Visa.

Hours: Lunch, noon to 3 P.M., Monday through Friday; dinner, 6 to 11 P.M., Monday through Thursday, 6 to 11:30 P.M., Friday and Saturday.

Reservations: Necessary, especially at dinner.

Wheelchair accessibility: Four short steps at entrance; all facilities on one level.

☙ Think of Greek food, as represented in the archipelago of New York, and the clichés abound: twirling gyros of gray lamb and foil-wrapped pita bread at sidewalk stalls; clattering coffee shops where taciturn waiters wear too-tight red vests and perpetual five o'clock shadows; stucco-and-plastic-flowered dining rooms specializing in skewered lamb, moussaka, and mountains of iceberg lettuce with feta. Then there is that nonstop bouzouki music.

The clichés are shattered at Periyali. This trim and tasteful spot in Chelsea demonstrates that Greek restaurants can have more than proximity to the office and blinding speed going for them. The owners, Steve Tzolis and Nicola Kotsonik, came to this novel concept after years of experience. Mr. Tzolis owned a cluster of coffee shops around town before opening the French bistro La Gauloise and later, with Ms. Kotsonik, Il Cantinori, a handsome Tuscan restaurant in Greenwich Village.

Periyali came into focus when these entrepreneurs lured Victor and Irene Gourias, a husband-and-wife cooking duo who have a restaurant called Patmian House on the island Patmos, to New York.

Periyali is a long, clean, whitewashed spot with cushioned wooden banquettes along one wall, a Mediterranean cornucopia and photographs of Greece on the walls, and a long polished wood bar in front. Billowy fabric between the overhead rafters adds a soft edge to the room—without doing much for the noise, though, which can be rattling. Two smaller back rooms are more tranquil.

While the setting is upscale, the food is down-to-earth. A standout appetizer is the red-wine-marinated octopus grilled over charcoal. The slightly blackened tendrils are delightfully chewy and full of the herby marinade flavors. White beans tossed in a garlic-infused vinaigrette are simple and tasty, as is the tossed salad with cleanly fried calamari and, an occasional special, golden deep-fried smelts with lemon wedges.

Waiters are amiable and efficient. The wine list carries some uncommon and pleasing Greek wines, most under $20. Among the entrées, lamb, naturally, is a highlight. I much prefer an occasional special, succulent oregano-dusted leg of lamb with roasted potatoes, over the skimpily seasoned and slightly overcooked chops. Another special at lunch was terrific: buttery braised lamb shank in a garlic-powered tomato sauce with orzo on the side. Rabbit stew sounded promising, but the meat was on the dry side and the tomato-based sauce, while flavorful, had a floury texture. Moussaka, the casserole of eggplant and ground lamb, is seductive under its blistered lid of béchamel.

Seafood entrées change daily. Grilled porgies swathed with olive oil are fresh and delicious along with couscous flecked with sweet red peppers, as is the baked red snapper in a tomato-onion-garlic sauce. Swordfish was highly recommended by our waiter, but the thick plank of fish was dry.

Desserts at Periyali reveal that not all Greek pastries ooze honey. Baklava is relatively light, made with toasted almonds instead of walnuts. Moist and minimally sweet lemon semolina cake is worth trying, too, as is galaktobouriko, a semolina custard pie wrapped in phyllo pastry. The house Greek coffee is so thick with sediment you could plant a flag in it.

PESCA

★

23 East 22nd Street, 533-2293.

Atmosphere: Coolly refined and stylish café dining room.

Service: Likable and earnest.

Price range: Moderately expensive.

Credit cards: American Express.

Hours: Lunch, noon to 3 P.M., Monday through Friday; dinner, 6 to 11 P.M., Monday through Saturday, 6 to 10 P.M., Sunday. Closed Sunday in summer.

Reservations: Suggested.

Wheelchair accessibility: One step at entrance; all facilities on one level.

❧ Pesca is one of the prettiest seafood restaurants in New York—but that's where the superlatives end. It has been plagued by changes in management and in the kitchen for years and thus has never really found itself. Lunch is still popular among a well-heeled executive crowd.

This coolly elegant café is wrapped in shades of salmon-pink, with handsome nautical artwork.

When the kitchen is at its best you can get a good risotto, gumbo, lobster, or San Francisco–style cioppino, fish stew. However, when it comes to the touchstone of all good fish-houses—unembellished fresh fish expertly broiled or sautéed, which most seafood fans crave—it can be a letdown.

Service can be exasperatingly slow at peak times. Unassailably fresh and well-iced Wellfleet oysters make a bright starter, as does the light and nicely seasoned seafood chowder holding chunks of salmon, celery, and carrots.

At dinner an appetizer called mussels cataplana is outstanding: a mound of meaty steamed mussels awash in a tide of herb-scented broth with tomatoes, onions, garlic, and spicy chorizo sausage. The kitchen has a real flair with risotto, a dish that I savor but often encounter in restaurants either undercooked and pebbly or overdone and gluey. The two sampled here, one with shrimp and aromatic wild mushrooms, the other a special made with shrimp, fennel, onions, and artichoke, were heady, smooth textured, and delicious.

The pace of the congenial service staff is better at night

than at lunch. While the kitchen excels at risotto, it flops at pasta—or at least the flaccid and tasteless heap called seafood lasagna. The best main courses are cioppino, the saffron-tinted stew afloat with half a lobster, shrimp, clams, mussels, and sea scallops, and the roast lobster sprinkled with corn kernels.

Broiled sea bass at lunch looked like something you would get on a hospital tray—an unseasoned and unappetizing white fillet served on a white plate flanked by unseasoned carrots and green beans. Tuna steak was hardly better. Broiled red snapper was satisfying with a tomato coulis and red-onion marmalade.

For dessert, get the ultra-rich flourless chocolate-mousse cake if you dare, or the lighter pear poached in Gewürztraminer. Tropical sorbets such as mango and coconut are satisfying, too.

PETALUMA

★

1356 First Avenue, at 73rd Street, 772-8800.

Atmosphere: Expansive, open café with convivial bar and exposed kitchen.

Service: Composed and pleasant young staff, although amateur.

Price range: Moderate.

Credit cards: All major cards.

Hours: Lunch, 11:30 A.M. to 5 P.M., daily; dinner, 5:30 P.M. to midnight, Monday through Saturday; noon to 11 P.M., Sunday.

Reservations: Suggested.

Wheelchair accessibility: Two steps up at entrance; all facilities on one level.

🍴 Petaluma, the striking Italian bar and restaurant, has undergone several major changes in recent years, flip-flopping from a California-style grazing field for yuppies to a more serious Italian dining spot. Its latest approach is more appealing than ever.

Petaluma's menu carries about a dozen regular appetizers, an equal number of entrées, and as many daily specials. A good way for two or more people to start is to nibble on a pizza, then get an appetizer and an entrée. Thin-crusted pizzas have the burnished edges and smokiness expected from wood-burning ovens, and the toppings are fresh and tasty. They come in many guises, from simple—tomato and fresh basil—to overloaded with leeks, ham, arugula, tomato, and mozzarella.

Another good appetizer is the moist and mild slices of smoked tuna with marinated artichokes, or mussels steamed in white wine and garlic.

Service has improved markedly over the past year or so. The short wine list is well chosen and priced fairly.

Pasta specials are the strong suit of the kitchen. Typical of the repertoire is fusilli alla puttanesca, a sauce of ripe tomatoes, capers, black olives, and garlic; another winner is bucatini amatriciana (tomato, onions, and pancetta).

In contrast to the pasta crew, which toils out of sight of the public, the grill chefs could benefit from a few cooking lessons. While simple preparations such as butterflied baby chicken with mustard sauce are competently prepared, more delicate items, such as fish, sometimes can be over-cooked. One notable exception was a lovely pompano in a white-wine sauce presented over nicely seasoned spinach.

Among the desserts, the puckery lemon tart with a thin, buttery crust is a standout. Authentic strawberry short-cake, with baking powder biscuits, fresh whipped cream, and ripe berries, is a runner-up, while chocolate-mousse cake is merely sugary icing on chocolate cake.

PETER LUGER

★

178 Broadway, Brooklyn, (718) 387-7400.

Atmosphere: Old New York charm in a century-old landmark. A neighborly old barroom fills up nightly with a gregarious crowd, and the wood-trimmed dining rooms are austere and Germanic, appropriate for a no-frills steakhouse.

Service: Lighthearted and chatty veteran waiters who perform their duties in a casually efficient manner. Don't expect them to lay a napkin on your lap.

Price range: Moderately expensive.

Credit cards: Peter Luger charge cards.

Hours: 11:45 A.M. to 10 P.M., Monday through Thursday,

11:45 A.M. to 11 P.M., Friday, 11:45 A.M. to 11:30 P.M., Saturday, 1 to 10 P.M., Sunday.

Reservations: Recommended.

Wheelchair accessibility: One step at entrance; all facilities on one level.

✿ For more than a century this landmark in the Williamsburg section of Brooklyn, in the shadow of the Williamsburg Bridge, has been a crowded, no-frills, elbows-on-the-table steakhouse. The river has isolated it from the ebb and flow of food fads in Manhattan that have compelled similar establishments to water down their menus with such "fancy food" as escargots, veal piccata, and shrimp scampi.

Menus are strictly for the tourist trade, offered to those who insist upon seeing one. The first time I requested a menu, the waiter replied with the same quip that has been drawing chuckles there since the McKinley administration: "Sure you can see a menu, but first I'll ask you how you want your steak done."

Your choices are juicy slabs of broiled porterhouse steaks in portions serving one to four, and fist-thick double lamb chops. Both are nicely encrusted from high-fire broiling and succulent (roast prime rib is an occasional special, but I never had the opportunity to sample it).

Leaning on the long, elbow-worn oak bar at Peter Luger while waiting for a table, you feel as if you are a thousand miles from Manhattan. At one corner of the room, four white-haired neighborhood cronies chew on thick stogies and debate politics in Brooklyn accents as thick as Luger's lamb chops. Local couples in sports clothes banter with the bartender and sip Bloody Marys while businessmen in pinstripes from "the City" belt down martinis and swap jokes.

The main dining room is vaguely Teutonic, with its exposed wooden beams, burnished oak wainscotting, brass chandeliers, and scrubbed beer-hall tables. The veteran waiters are a jocular bunch if you get them going and are casually efficient. On our first visit we ordered a porterhouse for three and lamb chops for one. The formidable cut of singed steak had been sliced in the kitchen and placed on a hot platter. Our waiter set a small dish under one end of the platter to let juice run into a corner while commenting, probably for the hundredth time that week, "If you don't like this steak, you don't like steak!" He then portioned out enough beef to sate a tugboat crew. The beef was cooked rare as ordered and had a good meaty flavor and plenty of juice for bread dipping.

The lamb chops were equally flavorful and profited from

the same skilled broiling. The perennial salad of sliced onions and tomatoes is only worth ordering during peak tomato season; the dreary horseradish-tomato sauce slathered over it could be done without. Shrimp cocktail is available, but chances are the waiter won't tell you about it unless you are a regular.

Among the side dishes, German fried potatoes were burned around the edges and underseasoned on two occasions. They also showed signs of having been prepared in advance and reheated before serving. The bland creamed spinach would prompt a groan in a prep-school dining hall, though the steak fries were better than average.

If you finish all this and still want dessert, there is sweet pecan pie that is brought to the table with a bowl filled with enough fresh whipped cream to paint a stripe across the Williamsburg Bridge, as well as a lightweight chocolate mousse and good dense creamy cheesecake.

PETROSSIAN

★

182 West 58th Street, 245-2214.

Atmosphere: Plush Art Deco theme.

Service: Uneven, from friendly to pretentious.

Price range: Expensive (pretheater prix fixe $35, $42, and à la carte; after-theater prix fixe, $29, $42, and à la carte; caviar menu: $110).

Credit cards: All major cards.

Hours: Brunch, 11 A.M. to 4:30 P.M., Sunday; lunch, 11:30 A.M. to 3:30 P.M., Monday through Saturday; dinner, 5:30 P.M. to midnight, Monday through Saturday, 5:30 to 11 P.M., Sunday; caviar bar, midnight to 1 A.M., daily. Closed Sunday in summer.

Reservations: Absolutely necessary.

Wheelchair accessibility: Six steps at entrance; dining room on one level; restrooms down flight of stairs.

This sumptuous spot in the Alwyn Court on West 58th Street strives to feed the soul as well as the body with regal silver platters of foie gras, caviar, smoked salmon, and champagne. For Armen and Christian Petrossian, who own the famous Parisian caviar shop, believe there are enough

New Yorkers in need of periodic pampering as well as visitors who want to put on the dog to keep this fantasy alive.

The dining room is a splendiferous work of art or an ostentatious conceit, depending on whom you consult. The theme is Art Deco, with magnificent rose-colored Italian granite floors and bar, snappy designer stools, etched glass mirrors, crystal chandeliers, and a banquette upholstered in gray kid leather with mink trim.

The cynosure of the menu is caviar—$69 for 50 grams of beluga, $42 for osetra, $34 for sevruga, and $29 for pressed. You can taste 30 grams of each, plus smoked salmon and dessert, for $110. The caviar is excellent, and it is stunningly presented on silver-lined black lacquer plates complete with a golden spoon. The foie gras, too, is rich and smooth. Try it with an aromatic hot truffle in its juice accompanied by a glass of Sauternes. Also memorable is the extravagant foie-gras-and-fresh-vegetable salad studded with truffle slivers.

Foie gras cognoscenti will note that the version sold here is mi-cuis, that is, partly cooked before exportation from France. It is firmer and drier but similar in flavor to the fresh domestic product now available in New York. Truffle fans must try the truffle consommé, which is so earthy and luscious you will want to lick the bowl. Petrossian's smoked salmon at best is firm, lean, and buttery.

Petrossian entrées change periodically. Best bets are the simple sautéed salmon or tuna, lamb, and steak.

If you're still in the mood for dessert after all this, mocha layer cake with a buttery mocha-cream filling is suggested. Fruit tarts are light and delicious, too.

PHOENIX GARDEN RESTAURANT

★ ★

46 Bowery, inside the arcade just north of Elizabeth Street, 962-8934, 233-6017.

Atmosphere: Two compact rooms, rough-edged and simple, loud and friendly.

Service: Friendly and quick—sometimes too quick.

Price range: Inexpensive.

Credit cards: None.

Hours: 11:30 A.M. to 11 P.M., Sunday through Thursday, 11:30 A.M. to 11:30 P.M., Friday and Saturday.

Reservations: Accepted only for parties of eight or more.

Wheelchair accessibility: Dining room on one level; restrooms one flight up.

❧ The grimy and cheerless arcade running just off the Bowery north of Elizabeth Street has seen better days. Those who venture within, however, will find a compact and cacophonous little restaurant, Phoenix Garden, that runs perpetually on overdrive, spinning out some splendid Cantonese dishes.

"How many, how many are you?" barks the no-nonsense hostess before you have both feet in the door. If a table happens to be empty, you will find yourself coatless, hatless, perched at a table and holding a menu faster than you can open a fortune cookie. Twenty seconds later a good-natured waiter appears, pad poised for action: "Ready?" he asks. If you are not, just point out that you are in no particular rush and he will cheerfully slow the pace—no offense, he insists, just a local habit.

One does not go to Phoenix Garden to soak up the décor, unless you are an aficionado of ersatz-brick wallpaper and fluorescent lighting. What one does go for is some of the best roasted squab and duck around, as well as a host of exceptionally spirited Cantonese specialties. The meaty little squabs are roasted to a caramelized sheen, then sectioned and served three ways—plain, with lemon sauce, or with apricot sauce. Aside from the excellent plain squab, I sampled it, skeptically, with the lemon sauce, and found that the combination worked remarkably well—the tart-sweetness brought out the best in the distinctive-tasting meat. The roast duck, done with equal skill, can be dabbed with some sweet plum sauce or, if the mood strikes, a smoldering-hot chili-pepper sauce that is placed on every table. (Braised duck served with mustard greens, oddly enough, was tough and chewy.)

The technique of cooking chicken in a salt crust or some variation of it exists in many cuisines; the salty baked chicken at Phoenix Garden rivals the best of them. The meat, even the breast sections, is seductively moist, and just enough salty sensation remains from the cooking to season it gently. Another house specialty is called pepper and salty shrimp, and it is not to be missed. The hefty whole shrimp are aggressively seasoned with salt and pepper and deep-fried to a brittle and greaseless perfection. They are absolutely addicting.

The Cantonese style of serving lobster cut up in the shell makes for a long evening's work, but it is worth it. The sweet meat is suffused with the flavors of ginger and scallions or, in another rendition, with salty black-bean sauce.

Beer is served, but if you want to sate your thirst with wine, you may bring your own.

Do you really want desserts after all this? No? Good. There's nothing worth mentioning. Phoenix Garden is one of those steady and enduring spots that Chinatown regulars have coveted for nearly two decades. A garden spot it's not, but the harvest is impressive.

PIERRE AU TUNNEL

★

250 West 47th Street, 582-2166, 575-1220.

Atmosphere: Homey French-bistro feeling with well-spaced tables and good noise control.

Service: Professional.

Price range: Moderate.

Credit cards: American Express, MasterCard, and Visa.

Hours: Lunch, noon to 3 P.M., Monday through Saturday; dinner, 5:30 to 11:30 P.M., Monday, Tuesday, Thursday, and Friday, 4:30 to 11:30 P.M., Wednesday and Saturday.

Reservations: Necessary, particularly for pretheater.

Wheelchair accessibility: Three steps down at entrance; restrooms down long flight of stairs.

🍷 Nearly forty years on the scene, Pierre au Tunnel is recommended as a homey theater-district French bistro that can easily become habit forming—that is, if you know your way around the menu. Mellow peasant-style dishes and Gallic classics are the specialties here, so stick with those and you will be happy.

The setting is warm and familiar, with a cozy little bar up front and a rustic French feeling in the dining room. Tables are well spaced and noise is muted, making this a fine spot for business lunches. French waitresses in black-and-white outfits can be either matter-of-fact or endearing, but they are nearly always efficient.

The most dependable appetizers are the moist and rich pork terrine, robust onion soup and pâté de tête (a well-seasoned gelatin-bound head cheese). Salads are prepared with care, especially such occasional specials as the combination of rare-sautéed salmon with green leaf lettuce in a mild vinaigrette, and the mixed green salad crowned with broiled disks of goat cheese.

Leek tart was flavorful and fresh but the crust was under-cooked, while carrot soup was pale and mussels ravigote lacked the aromatic herb flavor they should have. The dinner menu carries an exceptionally light and vivid scallop mousse glossed with chive butter.

The wine list sensibly matches the food, and at relatively modest prices.

If you are an aficionado of the classic French country dish tête de veau, this is one of the best places in New York to have it—a mélange of brain, tongue, cheek, boiled potatoes, and carrots with a zippy mustard vinaigrette bolstered with capers and eggs. Less intrepid diners would be happy with the juicy lamb chops with sautéed potatoes or the lusty beef à la Bordelaise. Seafood is not always so successful. The two best dishes sampled were poached grouper in a lovely beurre blanc sauce and swordfish steak in a rosemary-perfumed broth; simple sole à la meunière, on the other hand, was leathery from overcooking, and what the menu calls scampi Escoffier was nothing more than chewy little shrimp in a thick brown sauce. The Friday bouillabaisse was generous with cod, mussels, clams, and eel, but the broth was watery and the flavors were not integrated.

Desserts are generally attractive and pleasing— raspberry tart with an airy puff-pastry crust, peach tart layered with coconut cream, and crème caramel among them. Pierre au Tunnel is a survivor in a dwindling genre of family-owned French restaurants in the theater district. For a pretheater meal or a sedate business lunch, it's worth keeping in mind.

PIG HEAVEN

★ ★

1540 Second Avenue, corner of 80th Street, 744-4887.

Atmosphere: Barnyard motif. Usually clamorous and crowded.

Service: Competent, amiable, and well informed.

Price range: Moderate.

Credit cards: American Express and Diners Club.

Hours: Noon to midnight, Sunday through Thursday, noon to 1 A.M., Friday and Saturday.

Reservations: Suggested.

Wheelchair accessibility: All facilities on one level.

🐷 The silliness at Pig Heaven, part of the David Keh restaurant empire, belies some of the most serious and authentically delicious Chinese food around. (Those who do not eat pork have a choice of many other dishes.)

As you enter the restaurant, past the giant wooden piglet holding a menu card at the front door, into the pink barnboard-lined dining room with a frieze of illuminated pigs all around, past tables of voracious customers chowing down like farmhands at sunset and sipping tea from mugs sculptured like pigs' snouts, oinking and giggling, you begin to question the wisdom of coming to a place called Pig Heaven for a serious Chinese meal.

Start with the excellent dumplings—fried, boiled, or steamed. The tubular fried version, brashly seasoned with ginger and black pepper, is crisp and golden brown on the bottom, soft on top. Equally tasty are the hand-crimped steamed and boiled dumplings that spurt juice when bitten —often all over your tie.

Other appetizers worth trying are the cold hacked chicken, shards of white meat swathed in a zesty combination of sesame paste and hot oil, and the sesame-flavored scallion pancakes. Impeccably fresh kidneys, blanched and sliced in florets, are served with a Hunanese black-peppercorn sauce that has a slightly bitter and numbing edge— appealing in a painful sort of way.

Appetizers that do not hold up as well are the thin crusty vegetable pie served with pancakes, which is a leaden and redundant concoction; dried out white-cooked pork, and undistinguished spring rolls.

There are nineteen pork specials. The Cantonese-style suckling pig at Pig Heaven is truly heavenly, the skin is potato-chip brittle, and underneath are a layer of fat and a strip of juicy meat. It will never make the American Heart Association's menu suggestions, but you are certain to leave the restaurant with a smile. Another good selection is minced pork sautéed with corn, bell peppers, and pine nuts.

Fish is prepared with equal skill, especially the whole braised carp with Sichuan hot bean sauce and the braised red snapper with whole garlic cloves.

Three-glass chicken, a house specialty, is worth trying. The cut-up chicken is placed in a crock, mixed with ginger and assorted vegetables, and doused with a glass each of Chinese rice wine, soy sauce, and water. It is covered and cooked until the sauce reduces to intensely flavorful brown drippings.

The largely non-Oriental waiters are amiable and well informed about the menu. They manage to keep their cool when nights are hectic, which is often.

Desserts are a far cry from the usual litchi nuts and fortune cookies. The crusty and custardy bread pudding with orange sauce is irresistible. Frozen praline mousse, studded with pecans, is far better than the grainy apple-caramel sundae. A whimsical way to end the meal is with a Peking snowball, an igloo of whipped cream encasing a deadly rich chocolate core. Garnished with some silly cookies, it looks like something that would be served at an eight-year-old's birthday, which seems fitting here. Pig Heaven brings out the kid in all of us.

POSITANO

★ ★

250 Park Avenue South, at 20th Street, 777-6211.

Atmosphere: Airy and bustling, chic and informal.

Service: Young staff, friendly but sometimes slow.

Price range: Moderate.

Credit cards: All major cards.

Hours: Lunch, noon to 3 P.M., Monday through Friday; dinner, 5:30 to 11:30 P.M., Monday through Thursday, 5:30 P.M. to 12:30 A.M., Friday and Saturday.

Reservations: Necessary.

Wheelchair accessibility: All facilities on one level.

While typical in many ways of the theatrical new genre of Italian restaurants, Positano rises above the pack in one crucial respect—the food can be very good. The restaurant is co-owned by Bob Giraldi, the music-video and television-commercial director. Housed in a pre–World War II building with neo-Gothic accents on Park Avenue South, Positano has dining areas on three tiers—a large dining platform on top, a bar in the middle, and tables around the perimeter of the ground floor. The room is painted pink and white, including the massive columns and overhead heating pipes. Everything from the green marble tables to the pink-rimmed wineglasses and sleek oil-and-vinegar cruets says high-toned Italian design.

Since Positano opened in late 1984 it has been filled with a mixed group, ranging from the neighborhood after-work business crowd to the artsy aviator-jacket types who stroll in after 9 P.M. The food is based on the Campania region of Italy's Amalfi coast, but there is really a bit of everything on the menu. One of the most alluring appetizers is batter-fried artichoke hearts with mozzarella—fresh artichokes are covered with a light egg batter and cheese, then fried until golden and served in a zesty tomato sauce.

Crostino is simple and good: slabs of Italian bread layered with tomatoes and slices of fresh mozzarella, all drizzled with olive oil. If your mussels steamed in wine, garlic, and herbs are overcooked, as mine were, all is not lost: the broth makes for great bread dipping. Sundry salad plates are colorful and refreshing with well-balanced vinaigrettes.

In restaurants like this, I like to order a half portion of pasta before the entrée; that is not possible here, unless you order a whole portion and split it with someone, at a $1 surcharge. This annoying policy notwithstanding, most of the pastas are superior. If they have it, try the rigatoni with the tomato-cream sauce spiked with pimiento and hot pepper flakes, or farfalle, bow-tie-shaped noodles, tossed with broccoli and zucchini in a satiny and herbaceous cream sauce. The list goes on: penne with a tomato, parsley, and tuna sauce (a special one day), paglia e fieno with bits of ham and firm peas in a tomato-cream sauce, and penne with sautéed eggplant.

The young and casual service staff, donning oversize bowling shirts and pastel ties, does a reasonably good job until the place fills up late at night, at which time waiters and waitresses start doing confused pirouettes as requests assault them from all sides. Pay attention to such daily specials as the superb osso buco. The veal shank, nearly the size of a man's fist, is so tender that *buttery* seems the only word that can describe it.

Freshness and simplicity are the hallmarks of fish cookery here. Sautéed baby squid with garlic, olive oil, and parsley is the kind of dish you rarely find in New York—usually the squid are big and tough. Here the five tiny squid, served with the tentacles, are charred on the outside, resilient but not chewy. Garlic oil is all they need. Another dish that is delicious in its simplicity is broiled red snapper with a shower of vinegar and mint garnish.

The kitchen turns out an intoxicating custard cream cake soaked with cherry liqueur, a crunchy chocolate-almond torte, and excellent gelati.

PRIMAVERA

★

1578 First Avenue, corner 82nd Street, 861-8608.

Atmosphere: Formal and urbane.

Service: Uneven, depending on whether you are known.

Price range: Expensive.

Credit cards: All major cards.

Hours. Dinner, 5:30 P.M. to midnight, Monday through Saturday, 5 P.M. to midnight, Sunday.

Reservations: Necessary.

Wheelchair accessibility: All facilities on one level.

Primavera, a clubby, expensive Italian restaurant on First Avenue, has a loyal Upper East Side following. With its burnished mahogany walls, soothing paintings, tulip-shaped lamps, women in subdued silk dresses, and men in somber suits, it has the feeling of an Ivy League club. Indeed, sometimes it can be harder to get into than Yale because regulars book tables well in advance.

Primavera's allure cannot be just the food and warm ambiance, however, for with a few exceptions it offers a fairly predictable curriculum. If you start with the seafood appetizer, you get a generous amount of baby squid along with tiny chunks of octopus in an oregano-scented vinaigrette. In my experience the seafood was a bit overcooked but otherwise flavorful and fresh; baked clams are rubbery, and stuffed mushrooms are a stodgy concoction of bread crumbs and a tasteless brown sauce.

Better choices are the hearty minestrone soup, blushing fresh carpaccio with a basil-lemon mayonnaise, and any appetizer featuring the creamy-textured and slightly nutty buffalo mozzarella from Italy.

Half portions of pasta can be obtained as a second course. Here again, chances of success are fifty-fifty. The best pasta I have sampled at Primavera is the tortellini with peas and prosciutto. The tortellini were resilient and tasty, while the cream sauce had a delightful smoky tinge. The penne in a fresh and lively tomato sauce with bits of bacon can be good, too.

Service can be as crisp and attentive as you'll find anywhere—that is, if you are a regular. Otherwise it is a roll of the dice.

Sautéed veal with prosciutto and spinach was flaccid when I tried it, and paillard of beef was thick and without flavor. Simple grilled meats, such as veal or lamb chops, are the best options.

Primavera's wine list is a pretentious document unsuited to the cuisine. There are many expensive and prestigious Bordeaux and Burgundies running into the hundreds of dollars but scant choice for those looking for a pleasant drinking wine under $20.

One nice touch is the huge and varied assortment of fresh fruit that is presented at the end of the meal. That and the winy tiramisù, made with ladyfingers, mascarpone cheese, and heavy cream, are the best desserts.

PRIMOLA

★ ★

1226 Second Avenue, between 64th and 65th streets, 758-1775.

Atmosphere: Spare and pleasant with a lively and genial crowd.

Service: Effective under pressure, and the staff is well informed about the food.

Price range: Moderately expensive.

Credit cards: American Express.

Hours: Lunch, noon to 2:30 P.M., Monday through Friday; dinner, 5 P.M. to midnight, daily.

Reservations: Strongly recommended.

Wheelchair accessibility: One small step down at entrance; restrooms downstairs.

&⬥ Primola is one of the more spirited and alluring Italian restaurants on the East Side. While the setting is somewhat spare, the animated and polyglot crowd that settles in nightly adds a patina of elegance and élan. As for the food, it is for the most part fresh, skillfully prepared, and vividly seasoned.

Juliano Zuliani, a co-owner, is one of those hosts who can work a crowd like a veteran pol, greeting customers warmly, often by name. Waiters seem to thrive on the relentless pressure here, and they do an impressive job, all things considered.

The dining area sports pale yellow walls holding a hodge-podge of watercolors and Italian poster art, wood wainscot-ting, well-separated tables, and pretty flower clusters. The extensive menu, orchestrated by Mr. Zuliani's partner, Franco Iacoviello, is merely a launching pad, for specials abound. Half orders of pasta can be had as starters. Two occasional specials that excel are lithe homemade ravioli filled with seasoned ricotta, spinach, and herbs under a bright tomato-and-basil sauce, and fettuccine in a rustic blend of assorted wild mushrooms and tomato. On the printed menu, the spinach gnocchi are resilient and light under a gratinéed mozzarella-and-tomato sauce, and fede-lini, vermicellilike pasta, comes tossed in an herby white wine sauce with broccoli florets, zucchini, mushrooms, and tomatoes.

One of the more rarefied pastas, fedelini swathed in a garlic-butter sauce flecked with salmon roe, was bold and briny but slightly dry from too little sauce; likewise, the shellfish sauce over tagliolini, while generous with lobster and crab, was oddly sweet.

Among the regular appetizers, you can't go wrong with the fresh and simple littleneck clams and mussels in a white-wine broth, good lean carpaccio of beef with well-aged Parmesan, faintly crunchy sautéed sliced artichokes, and splendid salmon marinated with fresh fennel, red on-ions, and capers. Only the cold seafood salad is bland.

Wine aficionados will not be terribly challenged by the run-of-the-mill and overpriced list at Primola—reds are slightly more interesting than whites.

Entrées boast a high winning percentage. The most im-pressive special is roasted whole sea bass for two, an exqui-sitely fresh creature that needs nothing more than its sprinkling of balsamic vinegar and olive oil. An order of grilled fennel, endive, and asparagus on the side is a perfect mate. Other first-rate selections are the grilled giant shrimp seasoned with lemon, garlic, and oregano, and grilled baby snapper, a special, with a subtle balsamic-vin-egar sauce.

Grilled quail, a special, were moist and flavorful over slabs of polenta bolstered with Parmesan cheese, and baby lamb chops seared over coals were bone-gnawingly succu-lent. Chicken is best ordered in a stew-type preparation, such as a special combining boned meat with sweet sau-sage and green peppers.

The generous portions here may leave scant room for des-sert, but if you pace it well you might try the moist and crumb-encrusted ricotta cheesecake, the glassy crème brû-lée, lush raspberry-and-strawberry tart, or flavor-packed homemade ice creams.

PROVENCE

★ ★

38 Macdougal Street, at Prince, 475-7500.

Atmosphere: Casual, stylish country bistro with romantic backyard garden.

Service: Overburdened and rushed at times. Often mobbed.

Price range: Moderately expensive.

Credit cards: American Express.

Hours: Lunch, noon to 2:30 P.M., Tuesday through Sunday; dinner, 6 to 10:30 P.M., Tuesday through Thursday, 6 to 11 P.M., Friday and Saturday, 5:30 to 10:30 P.M., Sunday.

Reservations: Necessary.

Wheelchair accessibility: Dining area on one level; restrooms downstairs.

⟋ Michel Jean is a native of the Provence region in southern France, and his roots run deep in that sun-baked soil. In 1986, with his wife, Patricia, he opened the restaurant Provence with the goal of celebrating the area's foods and wines. It has been a hit from opening day, largely because of its reasonably priced, fresh, and spirited foods that include such specialties as salt cod sautéed with garlic and mixed vegetables, anchovy-and-onion tart, herb-perfumed fish soup, rabbit with basil sauce, oceanic bouillabaisse, and more.

The ambiance is pleasing and unpretentious. Pale yellow walls hold scallop-shaped sconces, dried flowers add a countrified accent, and tables are neighborly but not cramped. In the back is a romantic little garden with a stone fountain.

Little surprises abound on the menu that add an authentic touch, whether it is an intriguing giveaway called poutargue, croutons coated with the roe of gray mullet; crunchy little salad greens called purslane; or the Jeans' terrific homemade peach wine.

A wonderful introduction to Provençale fare is the morue St. Tropez, a fillet of salt cod sautéed with a lusty combination of tomato, anchovies, bay leaves, black olives, and garlic. It is superb along with some of the chewy country bread. Eggplant purée, fortified with fistfuls of garlic, is a tantalizing choice too, accompanied by three rounds of toast, one slathered with tapenade of black olives, the others with prosciutto and diced tomato, and puréed egg yolks blended with mustard and chickpeas. Other surefire starters are the sweet and buttery sea scallops nested on mixed greens in a delicate vinaigrette, and a well-seasoned terrine of rabbit in aspic.

Pissaladière is sort of a Provençale pizza topped with onions, anchovy, and tomato. It can be deliciously light and herbaceous, although the version here is doughy and dry. Raw tuna marinated in lime, basil, and minced peppers is an invigorating way to start the meal, as is the excellent cold cauliflower soup, a special.

Mr. Jean's authentic approach extends to the well-priced wine list, which offers a sampling of Provence labels. The crisp white Cassis is delightful (about $25); among reds, the Bandol is a ripe and pleasing bargain for about $20.

Dezso Szonntagh, the Hungarian-born chef who came over from Le Cirque, is not diffident with seasonings, as can be seen in the tarragon-bolstered veal medallions in lemon sauce, a serendipitous combination; tender strips of lamb alongside a thyme-and-garlic-haunted ratatouille; and the gutsy bouillabaisse, replete with mussels, clams, eel, and snapper in a rich tomato-tinged fish stock.

A heady specialty from the Mediterranean coast that is rarely found in restaurants here is called bourride, which is a fish stew bound with garlic mayonnaise. This rendition ranks right up there with those I have had in France—a garlic-fueled combination of lotte, squid, and cod.

After all this garlic, your staggering taste buds will yearn for something sweet and reviving. Homemade fruit sorbets doused with eau de vie will do the trick; light and semi-sweet orange terrine with white-chocolate sauce is a winning combination, too. Those who believe that Le Cirque serves the best crème brûlée in the galaxy will be amazed by the perfect clone here, which Mr. Jean obviously has studied meticulously. If you really want to be Provençale, have some of that peach wine, sit back, and peel a fresh peach.

PRUNELLE

★ ★

18 East 54th Street, 759-6410.

Atmosphere: Handsome, understated room with burled-maple walls, gentle lighting, and lavish flower displays.

Service: Staff is professional and pleasant although sometimes there are long lags between courses.

Price range: Expensive.

Credit cards: All major cards.

Hours: Lunch, noon to 3 P.M., Monday through Friday; dinner, 5:30 to 11 P.M., Monday through Sunday.

Reservations: Necessary.

Wheelchair accessibility: All facilities on one level.

🐌 Prunelle, owned by Jacky Ruette and Pascal Dirringer, is an opulent and generally reliable luxury French restaurant. It is also one of the few such midtown spots that are open on Sunday evening, which is good to keep in mind.

The entire dining room is done in gleaming burled maple, with Art Deco etched-glass partitions, luxuriant flower arrangements, and gentle indirect lighting adding to its low-key allure.

When the restaurant first appeared in 1983 the food was as ambitious and as pretty as the setting, but uneven. Based on recent visits, however, that is no longer the case —the food is consistently satisfying, and sometimes extraordinary, at both lunch and dinner. Mr. Dirringer, the chef, has forged a taut menu that straddles the fence between classic French cuisine and nouvelle-style touches. Without exception his sauces are intensely flavorful while light, and presentations are appealing without being contrived. He has a penchant for baby vegetables—carrots, turnips, squash. After eating here several times, you may begin to crave foods bigger than your thumb.

Good starters abound. One of my favorites was a special one evening of steamed shrimp wrapped in spinach and set in a lustrous velouté sauce; another winner is the sweet smoked shrimp alongside slices of translucent smoked sable paired with a tart watercress sauce. Fanciers of fresh foie gras should try the version here, seared outside, silky within, and garnished with orange sections, wild rice, and a rich Madeira sauce.

Lighter options at lunch include a bright tarragon-flavored crab salad nestled in an artichoke heart surrounded by spokes of firm-steamed asparagus, and a golden puff pastry atop white and green asparagus in a thyme-accented champagne-vinegar sauce. Mussel soup, faintly briny and heady with saffron, is always a good option.

The service team at Prunelle is highly professional and congenial; unaccountably, though, there can be undue lags between courses. I suspect this is the fault of the kitchen, not the waiters.

Among the entrées, seafood is executed especially well. Salmon, in particular, is terrific, sautéed to just the other side of sushi in the center and glossed with a red-wine butter sauce. Lobster comes in a tasty and unusual guise —shelled, steamed with shredded romaine lettuce, and served over the lettuce with fennel and baby vegetables. If you go while soft-shell crabs are in season, try the crackly browned ones here surrounded by a fresh and pulpy tomato-basil sauce. Another special, coho salmon, was delicious in its sweet-edged sauce of wild leeks.

One of the special meat dishes sounded as if it might be cloying but turned out to be among the better entrées I sampled. It combined medallions of first-rate veal paired with a seductive lobster sauce and a disk of beef tenderloin in a refined stock sauce. Confit of duck was the real thing, crisp and buttery, escorted by florid slices of duck breast speckled with ginger. Crunchy disks of roasted potatoes were the perfect accompaniment. Finally, there are firm and well-browned sweetbreads over a sward of wild mushrooms and flanked by all those baby vegetables.

Portions are copious at Prunelle, so when the well-maintained assortment of cheeses and fruits rolls your way on its marble-topped trolley it may be necessary to choose between that or dessert. If you opt for the sweets, recommended choices are the changing varieties of splendid fruit tarts topped with everything from blackberries to kiwi, strawberries, and mango. Praline layer cake is moist but undistinguished. Mimosa sherbet made with champagne and orange is so good I wouldn't mind letting it thaw and sipping it with a straw.

QUATORZE

★ ★

240 West 14th Street, 206-7006.

Atmosphere: Casual and comfortable bistro; can be loud when full.

Service: Capable and efficient.

Price range: Moderate.

Credit cards: American Express.

Hours: Lunch, noon to 2:30 P.M., Monday through

Friday; dinner, 6 to 11:30 P.M., Monday through Saturday, 5:30 to 11:30 P.M., Sunday.

Reservations: Necessary, especially for dinner.

Wheelchair accessibility: Two steps down at entrance; all facilities on one level.

&♣ When the French bistro Quatorze opened in late 1985 along West 14th Street, a Latin-flavored commercial strip of bodegas, cut-rate clothing emporiums, and bilingual driving schools, it seemed as incongruous as Yves Montand in a salsa band. Yet the restaurant was an immediate hit, for both its ingenuous, reasonably priced food and its casual, convivial setting. It remains so today—deservedly.

Quatorze is the sort of place you go to for sustenance, not surprises. On a slushy winter evening when your bone marrow feels like sorbet, a lusty bowl of cabbage-and-white-bean soup is so restorative it should be delivered around the neck of a Saint Bernard. Follow that with a grilled sirloin steak with an herby béarnaise sauce, a woodpile of brittle french fries, and a glass of robust red wine, and spring seems just around the corner.

Quatorze's modest setting is as guileless as the food—a long, pale-yellow-toned room with maroon wood trim, Art Deco sconces that cast even light, French posters, and neighborly banquettes. Waiters minimize banal chatter and get right down to business in a genial, professional manner. On busy evenings, the gregarious crowd can be distractingly loud; lunch is a much more tranquil affair.

The menu is concise, supplemented by several daily specials. Among the reliable starters are pristine oysters on the half shell (varieties depend on the season), mildly livery terrine enlivened with green peppercorns, and sweet marinated herring with onions. The classic French salad called frisée aux lardons (chicory with bacon and croutons in a warm bacon vinaigrette) is nicely turned out here, almost a meal in itself. The regular house green salad, though, was harsh with too much vinegar. An inviting special one evening was bay scallops wedged between sheets of airy puff pastry ringed with a red-pepper purée; beef barley soup rich with a good stock was bracing, too.

The wine selection at Quatorze is a paragon of what a bistro wine list should be—it complements the food perfectly and is priced right.

When I want something homey and straightforward, I get the grilled half chicken with french fries, knowing the herb-seasoned meat will be crisp-skinned and cooked to a turn. Green beans and carrots come on the side. Grilled fillet of salmon comes with a fine choron sauce (a béarnaise sauce blended with puréed tomatoes). Quatorze makes much ado about its choucroute garnie, the Alsace specialty of sauerkraut with pork and assorted sausages, but I could never warm to it. On more than one occasion, the sauerkraut was limp and tasted as if it had been reheated repeatedly; except for the snappy garlic sausage, the rest of the meats were humdrum.

A special of pork chops stuffed with prunes sounded compelling, but was dried out. Duck is prepared in an interesting way. The breast is grilled rare—that's French rare, which means it makes a touch-and-go landing on the pan—and the sinewy leg is braised to succulent tenderness, served with pan juices and roast potatoes.

The dessert of choice is still the thin, buttery apple tart the size of a Volkswagen hubcap, followed by an excellent crème caramel and a deadly rich flourless chocolate cake.

When Quatorze opened, it was the forerunner of what has become a bistro blitz in New York. In many ways, it remains in the forefront.

THE QUILTED GIRAFFE

★ ★ ★ ★

15 East 55th Street, in the AT&T arcade, 593-1221.

Atmosphere: Futuristic mini-amphitheater with stainless-steel walls, speckled granite floors, and gray leather banquettes.

Service: Highly professional.

Price range: Expensive (lunch prix fixe, $40, and $60 tasting menu; dinner prix fixe, $75, and $100 tasting menu; service charge of 18 percent is added to the bill).

Credit cards: American Express.

Hours: Lunch, noon to 2:15 P.M., Tuesday through Friday; dinner, 5:30 to 10:30 P.M., Monday through Saturday.

Reservations: Necessary well in advance.

Wheelchair accessibility: Main dining room and restrooms on one level.

🍴 Susan and Barry Wine took a big gamble in 1987 when they moved their highly personalized restaurant, The Quilted Giraffe, from its cozy town house on Second Avenue to a high-tech extravaganza in the AT&T arcade on

Madison Avenue between 55th and 56th streets. Some patrons likened eating in the new gleaming stainless-steel-and-marble room to spending a few hours in a walk-in cooler, while others found the design bold and exciting. It is anything but neutral. The same can be said about the eclectic and exquisitely presented food, which has survived the move exceedingly well.

The dining room is a two-tier, mini-amphitheater arrangement with gray leather banquettes around the perimeter, black granite tables, Buck Rogers–style steel lighting columns, perforated stainless-steel walls, and handsome tableware. Copious flower arrangements and soothing lighting soften the hard edges.

The Wines fuss over every minute detail of the operation, and their vigilance shows—the food is as provocative to behold as it is delicious, and the service staff is highly professional.

Two menus are available: a four-course à la carte for $75, and the six-course tasting menu for $100. The Wines have traveled extensively in Japan, and the Oriental influence in design and food presentation is evident in their restaurant. For example, one of my favorite starters is their individual pizzas combining sashimi tuna, ricotta cheese, and Japanese wasabi mustard—the crust is yeasty and puffed and the snowy ricotta carries a faintly hot undercurrent from the mustard. On the entrée list, a superbly fresh grilled salmon comes with a sweetened Japanese hot mustard.

Another stellar selection is golden sautéed morsels of sweetbreads set in a sublime caramel soy sauce—just faintly sweet—enhanced with sesame oil. Translucent homemade potato chips on the side are irresistible.

Mr. Wine's much imitated beggar's purses—ultra-light crêpes filled with beluga caviar and a touch of crème fraîche secured with scallion strips—are the type of treat one should consume while supine on a couch with a bottle of champagne. A portion of five carries a $30 supplement. The computerized wine list, which is printed daily, is steeply priced but well chosen.

Among the entrées, confit of duck is superb, cooked to the point of buttery tenderness with thin blistered skin. It comes with lovely homemade creamy garlic potatoes. Two other earthy winners are tender calf's liver in a crunchy carapace of crushed nuts, and rare-roasted rack of lamb swabbed with Chinese mustard along with brittle homemade potato chips and sugar snap peas.

You don't see many interesting cheese platters in this abstemious age—dieters usually forgo those calories and zero in on dessert—but this one should not be dismissed.

About a dozen varieties of American and imported cheeses are offered, all in peak condition.

The all-American desserts are an adolescent's dream—and not bad for older kids either. Hazelnut waffles under an igloo of unstintingly rich vanilla ice cream and maple sauce may be a bit excessive after a full meal, but it is suitable for sharing. In the same category is apple-and-pear crumple, a pleated disk of fragile dough holding diced fruit and crowned with sharp cinnamon ice cream. Pecan squares—they are fresh and not overly sweet—are another good option, or the embarrassingly rich chocolate soufflé whose crater oozes espresso ice cream that is so intense it could be served alone in demitasse cups. For a $10 supplement, you can have your table loaded down with a bit of everything.

THE RAINBOW ROOM

★ ★

30 Rockefeller Plaza, 65th floor, 632-5000.

Atmosphere: Sumptuous Art Moderne dining room with panoramic views and revolving dance floor.

Service: Waiters professional and pleasant, but the pacing of the meal is slow.

Price range: Expensive.

Credit cards: American Express.

Hours: Pretheater dinner, 5 to 6:15 P.M., Tuesday through Saturday; dinner, 6:30 to 10:15 P.M., Tuesday through Saturday; supper, 10:30 to 11:30 P.M., Tuesday through Saturday.

Reservations: Required well in advance.

Wheelchair accessibility: Gradual terraced dining room that could be negotiated with help; restrooms down a long corridor with several steps.

The two-year, $25-million face-lift of this two-story complex, whose cynosure is the Art Moderne ballroom called The Rainbow Room, is a success in more ways than one. The gracefully terraced room wonderfully evokes another era in New York: wraparound views of the city and beyond, aubergine silk walls, cast-glass balusters, a tiered bandstand, period outfits on the service staff, and a giant crystal chandelier poised over the revolving dance floor. The renovation, overseen by Joseph Baum, the restaurant consultant, does not make The Rainbow Room feel like a new or, heaven forbid, trendy place. It's as if ghosts of the pre-war years have been jitterbugging up there all along—and they just recently invited us to join in.

The food soothes but never distracts, just like the mollified pop and show music performed by a tag team of bands (one a twelve-piece brass-and-keyboard ensemble, the other a bloodless salsa group). André René, the chef whom Mr. Baum recruited when he created Windows on the World in the late 1970s, turns out a fine Black Angus sirloin with an herby béarnaise sauce, juicy rack of lamb for two, and rosy venison steak in a grand veneur sauce touched with red currants—the meat entrées come with festive pommes soufflées. Or you can nibble down memory lane with lightened renditions of such culinary artifacts as lobster thermidor or tournedos Rossini, a rare-cooked (and rather bland) filet mignon under a slab of foie gras and set in a truffle-enriched stock sauce.

Pigeon en cocotte is a solid winner: succulent braised squab in a lustrous stock sauce flanked by fresh green peas and pearl onions. Dried-out grilled swordfish cannot be rescued by its pretty diadem of baby carrots and marrow-enriched red-wine sauce, and roulade of red snapper and salmon is tasteless unless you dredge it in lots of the roasted red-pepper purée—a timbale of eggplant and tomato alongside is bright and tasty, though.

Out on the wooden turntable, couples who for years have been looking for a place like this where they could dance are spinning in blissful unison. Women weighted down with jewelry parade their most showy lamé and sequined gowns; many men dress up in tuxedos just for fun. An evening at The Rainbow Room runs on for at least three hours. You can't really fault the enthusiastic and well-trained waiters; one suspects that either the kitchen is slow or the meal is paced that way for dancers. (An $8-a-person music charge is imposed on weeknights, $12 on weekends.)

Appetizers are almost uniformly good. The shellfish extravaganza is a diverting way to start, an ice platter heaped with mussels, oysters, clams, lobster, crab, and more (depending on the season). Two starters that seem appropriate in this setting are the excellent steak tartare crowned with iced sevruga caviar, and oysters Rockefeller, the shells lined with blanched spinach and slivers of fennel, all under a light glaze. The Rainbow Room's international wine list offers something for every taste and budget, with decent selections starting under $20.

For dessert, an intensely nutty frozen praline soufflé is

scooped out in the center and lubricated with hot chocolate sauce; chocolate sorbet is sharp and refreshing as part of a trio that also includes mango and lemon. Skip the boring pear charlotte for the crumbly crusted fruit tarts. If you are in a particularly nostalgic or silly mood, order the baked alaska and marvel at the flaming volcano of meringue-covered sponge cake and ice cream.

The Rainbow Room is a musical time machine that blasts off nightly with a crew of insouciant mirthmakers (at about $100 a person). The food happens to be agreeable, although I suspect most people come here for the spectacle, the dancing, the view—and a sweet sip of nostalgia.

RAINTREES

Satisfactory

142 Prospect Park West, at 9th Street, Park Slope, Brooklyn, (718) 768-3723.

Atmosphere: Pleasant, casual former cigar shop with tile floor and café tables.

Service: Slow and amateurish.

Price range: Moderate.

Credit cards: All major cards.

Hours: Brunch, 11:30 A.M. to 3:30 P.M., Sunday; dinner, 5 to 10:30 P.M., Monday through Thursday, 5 to 11:30 P.M., Friday and Saturday, 5 to 10:30 P.M., Sunday.

Reservations: Suggested.

Wheelchair accessibility: All facilities on one level.

The increasingly affluent Park Slope section of Brooklyn is long overdue for a first-class restaurant. Eight-year-old Raintrees, housed in a charming turn of-the-century tobacco shop where a former marble-topped soda fountain now serves as a wine bar, is making efforts in that direction. It has a long way to go, however.

Raintrees reflects an all-too-common story of a kitchen attempting too much with too little—like trying to pull a freight train with a moped. The result is an oversize menu on which more than half the dishes are mediocre.

The scene is casual and congenial with its well-trod tile floor, soft salmon-colored walls, café tables covered with paper, and on the back wall a large Georgia O'Keeffe–style painting of a flower. The greenhorn waiters and waitresses are earnest but amateurish, and the kitchen can be so slow —one Saturday night we waited one hour for appetizers— that you would be well advised to pack a snack at home to tide you over.

Recommended appetizers include the thick and flavorful carrot soup, grilled fennel sausage on a nest of sautéed spinach and escarole, and artichoke leaves combined with baby shrimp, bay scallops, and capers in a vinegar-edged tomato sauce.

The chef has an affinity for vinegar, for it shows up often —in the case of the wild mushroom salad, the inedibly acidic dressing could be used to clean copper pots and pans. Gravlax is nothing more than smoked salmon, and curried oysters could be curried napkins for all the flavor they have. And when the kitchen is done with the snails— first sautéing them with garlic and shallots, flaming them with vermouth and cognac, then mixing in some Roquefort cheese and encasing the whole concoction in puff pastry— you almost need a degree in archaeology to excavate them.

Pastas range from pleasing—cioppino, a fresh and peppery combination of shellfish and pasta over linguine—to insipid, such as the boring and watery cannelloni filled with spinach and ricotta. Among meat entrées, if you stick with the sirloin steak with tarragon butter and french fries, or the Raintrees burger (under sharp melted Monterey Jack cheese and smoked bacon), the odds are in your favor. Paillard of chicken—not really a pounded paillard but a broiled double chicken breast—with a light, peppy mustard sauce is another good option. Baked catfish was nicely enhanced with black beans, shrimp, and red peppers. Game hen was papery dry, as was salmon in herb sauce. A fatty duck was hardly helped by its sticky sweet black-currant sauce, raw broccoli, and granitic wild rice.

Raintrees offers an exemplary wine list with some good bargains, especially among American producers.

Desserts are the best course. Try the terrific mud pie, dense, rich, and evil, or the snappy pumpkin ice cream laced with cinnamon. Cranberry tart and a relatively light pumpkin cheesecake were exceptionally good, too.

On the whole, though, Raintrees has much paring and refining to do before it becomes more than a comfortable neighborhood hangout.

RAKEL

★ ★

231 Varick Street, at Clarkson Street, 929-1630.

Atmosphere: Soaring postmodern SoHo loft space; stylish and refined.

Service: Generally professional with occasional lapses.

Price range: Moderately expensive.

Credit cards: All major cards.

Hours: Lunch, noon to 2:15 P.M., Monday through Friday; dinner, 6:30 to 11 P.M., Monday through Thursday, 6:30 to 11:30 P.M., Friday and Saturday.

Reservations: Recommended.

Wheelchair accessibility: All facilities on one level.

While French bistros—and their newly cultivated hybrid, the American bistro—are budding all over town, Serge Raoul, owner of the neighborly Raoul's in SoHo, has defied the trend and aimed his sights higher with Rakel. Along with his chef and partner, Thomas Keller, he has created one of the handsomest and most provocative restaurants in the SoHo area, featuring an inventive menu full of surprises.

The cavernous postmodern setting with its cloud mural covering the ceiling, brawny white columns, and oversize tables can give you a Lilliputian complex at first. But as the eyes gradually adjust to the scale and absorb all the fine details lavished on the room, it begins to wear comfortably.

Mr. Keller has the sensitivity of a sculptor when it comes to textures, for his dishes are often animated with crunches here and crackles there that catch the palate off guard. This can best be seen in the terrific appetizer of calf sweetbreads. Firm, fresh, and sautéed to golden perfection, the sweetbreads are drizzled with a bright sesame vinaigrette and set over a tangle of hair-thin deep-fried leeks. Another winning combination is the light and greaselessly fried oysters paired with leeks steeped in cream and dabbed with a sharp wasabi-mustard butter. A lustrous foie gras terrine bolstered with Armagnac is veined with nutty black truffles, while slices of ivory-colored sea scallops are cushioned on a bed of faintly tart lamb's lettuce under a flurry of minced black truffles, all moistened with a truffle vinaigrette brightened with orange zest.

317

Crab-cake fans will not be bowled over by the generous but minimally spiced version here bound with scallops and cream.

Rakel's service team has matured over time and now runs a fairly tight ship. The wine list merits special mention. While the selection is relatively modest, it harmonizes well with the food and is exceptionally well priced. Parties of four or more would do well with the bargain-priced magnums on the list.

Assertive wines are needed to go the distance with Mr. Keller's entrées. One stellar selection among the seafood is a golden disk of roasted monkfish (lotte in French) garnished with brittle garlic chips and set over a pulpy red-pepper vinaigrette; on the same plateau is poached lobster nested on wilted arugula and paired with crisp-edged sautéed vermicelli. Its cream sauce is tinged with saline lobster coral.

Meat dishes are uniformly good, and a few are superb. Among the best are exquisitely tender duck breast with green lentils and bacon, extraordinarily tender roasted veal chop circled by roasted shallots and garlic cloves, and pan-cooked shell steak in a classic Bordelaise sauce accompanied by a mellow marrow custard.

Rakel has a fine list of cognacs, Armagnacs, sherries, and assorted liqueurs, many of which could regally punctuate the meal along with an assortment of handmade chocolates. More substantial desserts include an irresistibly light and luxuriant bittersweet chocolate tart with a pear coulis, and a mocha cheesecake that has a texture bordering on a mousse. Other offerings are less exciting, such as the overly sweet homemade ice creams and a shallow pond of crème brûlée that is half sugar glaze.

REMI

★ ★

323 East 79th Street, 744-4272.

Atmosphere: Sophisticated yet casual setting.

Service: Warm and competent.

Price range: Moderately expensive.

Credit cards: All major cards.

Hours: Brunch, noon to 3 P.M., Sunday; lunch, noon to 3 P.M., Tuesday through Saturday; dinner, 6 to 11:30 P.M., daily.

Reservations: Necessary.

Wheelchair accessibility: One step at entrance, all facilities on one level.

❧ Remi is one of those rare places that combine a striking setting, attentive service, and distinctive food. The name in Italian means oars, and both the menu and the design theme reflect maritime Venice.

The restaurant is owned by its designer, Adam Tihany, who also designed (but does not own) Bice on 54th Street, and the chef, Francesco Antonucci (formerly of Alo Alo). Peach-toned walls take on a soft glow under indirect lighting that flares from ceiling beams. Long gondola oars crisscross overhead, and on the walls hang sketches of 18th-century Venetian glass. Inside the entrance is an engaging little bar where you can sample, if you dare, eighteen brands of grappa. In a display case nearby are a half dozen other flavored grappas made by the Venetian-born chef.

Some excellent pastas can be found on the changing menu. Among the specials I enjoyed were maccheroni, or macaroni, with tender morsels of duck breast, tomato, and rosemary; farfalle (butterfly shapes) tossed with mixed vegetables and shiitake mushrooms; conchiglie (small shells) in a sauce fragrant with fresh fennel along with sweet sausage, and fusilli (corkscrews) tossed with cubes of smoked bacon and grilled radicchio in a light tomato sauce.

Mr. Antonucci never oversauces his pastas, as so many other restaurant chefs do, and he has a deft touch with seasonings. Risotto is another good option, whether with delightfully chewy porcini mushrooms or fresh spinach (both specials). Gnocchi, which so often are gummy and heavy, are light little pillows here, barely resilient, and swathed in a pink tomato-cream sauce. Only one of the pastas failed to stir me, whole-wheat linguine with onions, anchovies, and olive oil—the anchovy flavor didn't come through.

Pastas can be ordered in half portions as starters. For something lighter, you could go with the tangy endive salad with sardine dressing or the bite-size spinach crêpes filled with faintly tart goat cheese and mild ricotta. Grilled vegetables were overcooked and underseasoned.

Remi's wine list is well matched with the food and priced fairly across the board. The comely young service staff is congenial with its urbane clientele, but not overly familiar, and is always attentive.

Many of the entrées are simple trattoria fare, satisfying but not memorable. One that compels me to return, though, is the terrific sautéed red snapper presented over a sward of sweet onions soaked in vinegar—the yin-yang effect of sweet and sour is inspired. Grilled salmon ringed by colorful baby vegetables and scalloped potatoes is excellent, as is herb-dusted baked monkfish with peppers, tomato, and eggplant.

Both veal dishes sampled—one pounded and battered, the other a fat chop—were unremarkable; good sliced sirloin came with a mustard sauce that could have used more pizzazz. Try instead the meltingly tender lamb chops surrounded by roasted garlic cloves and gratin potatoes, or mild calf's liver with onions and crusty grilled polenta.

The special house dessert is broiled zabaglione, which resembles an igloo in late June, only this thawing concoction is laced with Marsala and has a core of ice cream. Flourless chocolate cake is sublime; peach sorbet and Prosecco wine served in a pretty tulip-shaped glass is a refreshing punctuation mark.

Remi succeeds admirably in evoking the spirit and flavor of Venice. Put your gondola in overdrive and head right over.

RENÉ PUJOL

★

321 West 51st Street, 246-3023.

Atmosphere: Old-world French background with timbered walls, stucco, and fireplace.

Service: Can be haphazard and slow at lunch; better at dinner.

Price range: Moderately expensive.

Credit cards: All major cards.

Hours: Lunch, noon to 3 P.M., Monday through Friday; dinner, 5 to 11:30 P.M., Monday through Saturday.

Reservations: Suggested during theater hours.

Wheelchair accessibility: Three steps at entrance; all facilities on one level.

🍷 René Pujol is among the few survivors on the endangered-species list of family-run French restaurants in the Broadway theater district. As so many in this aging fraternity succumb to old age or indifference, René Pujol has remained relatively vigorous. The menu is built upon the culinary crossbeams of classic bourgeois fare, with just a few nods to contemporary tastes.

The dining rooms have period stucco-and-timber walls holding copper knickknacks and an oversize mural of the home country, a fireplace, and red plaid rugs. At lunchtime the place is jumping, while at night it languishes.

Upon being seated you are served a ramekin of pork rillettes, a lusty blend of shredded and aggressively seasoned meat moistened with—dare I say it?—pure fat. It is delicious smeared over French bread. Lunch and dinner menus are essentially the same except for specials. Onion soup, steaks, simple sautéed seafood, stews, and such are the path to satisfaction. Sauces, especially those made with cream and eggs, are mighty rich for contemporary tastes.

The appetizer list offers no surprises. Duck terrine is rustic and tasty, generously spiked with cognac. Lean fresh salmon perfumed with dill and served with a dill mayonnaise is more interesting than plain smoked salmon. An example of the chef's heavy hand with cream is the cloyingly rich fish mousse, an outer ring of scallop-and-pike mousse surrounding a core of lobster dotted with pistachio shards. As the cold weather comes on you can't go wrong with the intense and soothing old-fashioned onion soup.

Service at lunch can drag when the pace gets frenetic; on slow evenings the operation is smoother. The wine list has much of historic interest, with many fine old vintages in the three-digit category; at the same time, you can find a few pleasing lesser Bordeaux and Burgundies in the $20 range.

Square meals, not adventurous ones, are what you should seek among the entrées. Rack of lamb for two with pan juices and assorted tiny vegetables cannot be faulted. A special, steak with four kinds of peppers—black, white red, and green—sets off an intriguing volley of sensations (but the regular streak au poivre with black pepper that's on the menu is muted under a stodgy thick sauce). Pink-sautéed veal kidneys are fresh and assertive in their red-wine sauce.

A lunch special, roast chicken in tarragon sauce, was more compelling than a similar dish in a pale Calvados cream sauce garnished with apple slices. For fish, go with the Dover sole meunière, which is undramatic but fresh, or the poached salmon with a good lemony hollandaise sauce. Grilled tuna prepared Provençale-style with sun-dried tomatoes and peas, a lunch special, was lively but overcooked by about two minutes; on a second sampling it was better.

Several desserts are arresting: a coal-black slab of chocolate marquise set in a pool of crème anglaise, pear charlotte in a multicolored fresh fruit sauce, and bright fruit sorbets.

Orange cake is gelatinous and overly sweet; a sugary glaze also mars the apricot fruit tart.

René Pujol holds the torch of classic French food in this once solidly Gallic neighborhood. While there are ample good dishes to satisfy theatergoers, some updating in the kitchen would make the torch burn brighter.

RESTAURANT NIPPON

★ ★

155 East 52nd Street, 758-0226, 688-5941.

Atmosphere: Low-key and relatively quiet traditional Japanese setting.

Service: Friendly and efficient.

Price range: Moderate.

Credit cards: All major cards.

Hours: Lunch, noon to 2:30 P.M., Monday through Friday; dinner, 5:30 to 10 P.M., Monday through Thursday, 5:30 to 10:30 P.M., Friday and Saturday.

Reservations: Recommended.

Wheelchair accessibility: Dining room on ground floor; restrooms four steps up.

🍂 Twenty-five-year-old Nippon is the granddaddy of Manhattan Japanese restaurants, dating from an era when all but the most adventurous Americans would sooner swim to Japan than bite into a chunk of raw fish. Today, of course, sushi has become the fast food of the executive set, and the competition is intense.

Over the years, Nippon has managed to remain as fresh and high-spirited as its food, making it a favorite among Japanese businessmen at lunch and a more diverse clientele at dinner.

The two-tiered dining room, with a wide, comfortable sushi bar on the upper level—a good place to spread out a newspaper or magazine if dining alone—is pretty and low-key, done in blond wood and shades of beige and tan. Tables are rather tightly arranged, although the noise level is well muffled. Private tatami rooms should be reserved several days in advance.

Waitresses in traditional garb range from the seasoned no-nonsense veterans who happily order for you if you display the slightest hesitation ("Get the tuna, you will like it") to diffident young women with inexhaustible patience.

The menu seems endless, but closer inspection reveals that many dishes show up in various preset banquets. Tempura is offered as a starter. The deep-fried morsels of shrimp, broccoli, and eggplant were a bit greasy one evening at dinner, much better several days later at lunch. Yamakake, cubes of glistening fresh tuna along with scallions in a sweetish mustard sauce, was invigorating, as was a house special, aigamo-hasamiyaki, slices of rare-cooked duck coated with a sweet glaze. A rousing Japanese ponzu sauce (vinegar, hot peppers, and grated radish) failed to revive the rinsed cherrystone clams, and an artful arrangement of raw beef in a flower was fresh and tasty, although icy cold from the refrigerator.

Sushi and sashimi are available in all sorts of combinations. One good way to sample the day's bounty is with the special assortment dish, a moderate-size portion of tuna, fluke, shrimp, squid, salmon eggs, and sea urchin. The seafood was uniformly fresh and attractive; just as important for sushi is the rice, which was adhesive without being gummy and was nicely flavored with vinegar and sugar. Japanese beer or sake enhance both. The wine selection is spotty and overpriced.

Grilled entrées, particularly the salmon and porgy, are skillfully cooked but unseasoned. I dabbed them with some mustard-stoked soy sauce and did just fine. On the meat side of the menu, grilled chicken teriyaki is delicious in its sweet-edged glaze, served with broccoli and bean sprouts. Negimayaki, the scallion-stuffed beef rolls, are soggy and oversauced, lacking the crisp grilled texture they should have.

Often I find the Japanese seafood casseroles that are prepared at the table more entertaining than flavorful, but the yosenabe here is subtle and wonderfully saline. It combines clams, shrimp, lobster, tuna, and salmon with cabbage and translucent rice pasta.

If you are in a serious fish-eating mood for lunch, try the colorful combination special called makunouchi-bento, served in a compartmentalized platter. Aside from sashimi and assorted sushi, there is a refreshing little watercress-and-sesame salad, glazed yams, assorted tempura, sweet omelet, and more. There appears to be a logical progression in eating this mini-buffet of contrasting flavors, moving gradually from hot to sweet. Judging from the bemused look of the tempura chef as he watched me leapfrog through the courses haphazardly, I didn't even come close. It sure was good, though.

RESTAURANT RAPHAEL

★ ★

33 West 54th Street, 582-8993.

Atmosphere: Refined and rustically elegant. Relatively quiet. Pretty backyard garden café.

Service: Professional and knowledgeable; slow at lunch.

Price range: Expensive.

Credit cards: All major cards.

Hours: Lunch, noon to 2:30 P.M., Monday through Friday; dinner, 6 to 10 P.M., Monday through Friday, 6 to 11 P.M., Saturday. Closed Saturday from Memorial Day to Labor Day.

Reservations: Suggested.

Wheelchair accessibility: Three steps down at entrance; all facilities on one level.

❧ Raphael is a demure and proper establishment that attracts a starched and wing-tipped masculine clientele at lunch and prosperous couples at dinner. The contemporary French fare has improved dramatically in recent years, making this a special little spot in bustling midtown.

The food is just contemporary enough to keep adventuresome diners aroused without scaring away the traditionalists. The menu is virtually identical at lunch and dinner except for a few specials. A soothing starter is the salad of duck confit, the meat rich and pleasantly salty, combined with mixed greens and crunchy deep-fried celery chips. Another earthy winner is the well-seasoned terrine of rabbit bound with a flavorful aspic. You may encounter two trendy ravioli dishes, one featuring a lustrous filling of foie gras and wild mushrooms in a sparkling duck consommé, the other filled with red snapper and celery in a buttery shellfish stock perfumed with oceanic sea urchin.

The veteran French service staff is most accommodating and genteel. At dinner, when the room is quieter, service is highly personal and leisurely; at busy lunchtime, it can be exceedingly slow, which may actually be the fault of the kitchen.

Entrées follow the same steady course as appetizers, with

rare-roasted lamb moistened in its own juices and fanned on the plate with slices of tomato and zucchini, top-notch veal chop under a luxuriant morel-cream sauce, and lovely golden sweetbreads embellished with a sherry-vinegar sauce laced with confit of leeks. The kitchen is equally deft with seafood. A firm and fresh grouper fillet is presented over a purée of eggplant and garnished with julienne of sweet red and green peppers; at lunch I enjoyed perfectly cooked morsels of golden monkfish set atop a diaphanous butter sauce. Those with a slight sweet tooth would enjoy the pasta with lobster meat in a curry sauce cut with apples and raisins.

If you have some wine left in your goblet after the main course, you might consider the fresh and mildly tart disk of goat cheese sprinkled with crushed walnuts and set over mixed greens. The thin-crusted hot apple tart is terrific; so, too, is the warm passion-fruit mousse with raspberries.

The tariff for a three-course meal here is steep, particularly at lunch, where a couple could easily spend $85 exclusive of tip and tax.

RISTORANTE DA UMBERTO

Satisfactory

107 West 17th Street, 989-0303.

Atmosphere: High-ceilinged, tri-partitioned space done in sponged ocher walls; very loud.

Service: Frazzled and confused.

Price range: Moderately expensive.

Credit cards: American Express.

Hours: Lunch, noon to 3 P.M., Monday through Friday; dinner, 5:30 to 11 P.M., Monday through Thursday, 5:30 to 11:30 P.M., Friday and Saturday.

Reservations: Necessary.

Wheelchair accessibility: Dining room on ground level; restrooms downstairs.

🍸 A Florentine-style restaurant called Ristorante da Umberto appeared on a drab block in the eastern reaches of Chelsea in early 1988, and before you could say tiramisù, it was mobbed. Early raves brought even more pastaphiles, making the towering echo chamber called a dining room so loud it could wilt your radicchio.

I don't doubt that da Umberto was an interesting, perhaps even special, spot when it opened. But its apparent decline from sheer exhaustion or incompetence underscores the danger of rushing out too soon to review a new place. Many well-intentioned restaurateurs are naïve about pacing. They burn out early, like those marathon runners who sprint to the head of the pack at the outset, then collapse before the midway mark. Three recent visits reveal that da Umberto, while capable of turning out a few good gutsy North Italian dishes, has already become inconsistent and fatigued.

The first warning of a breakdown was the greeting, or lack of one. We stood in the shatteringly loud foyer, huddled with other diners next to the long marble-topped bar, waiting for a nod of recognition. The entire place is done in sponged ocher walls with wine racks serving as room dividers and with exposed heating ducts. Finally a wilted-looking host shuffled over and led us through two semipartitioned dining rooms into a third room adjacent to the glass-enclosed kitchen.

Some of the best food can be found on the cold buffet table: chunky and boldly seasoned caponata, smoky roasted peppers, refreshing slices of fennel, white-bean salad, grilled artichokes, snowy fresh mozzarella, and more. If you order white wine, it will come refrigerator-cold and be poured into frosted glasses, the way fancy pubs like to serve beer.

Half orders of pasta were not available, our waiter told us on a frenetic Saturday night, "because the chef will start throwing pots and pans at me if I ask for that now." At least he's honest. The Italian waiters here have frazzled looks and, most likely, significant hearing loss from the constant din. It's self-service when it comes to pouring wine, and not much else gets done without a lot of wild gesticulating by the diner.

Of the pastas we sampled, fusilli with mixed seafood was pleasing, made with cubes of good smoked tuna, black olives, and garlic; fettuccine with salmon in a light cream sauce was a winner, as was the farfalle with pesto. It was difficult to warm up to the pasta with lobster sauce because shell shards had me worried about some expensive recent dental work. Gnocchi all'arrabbiata was forgettable, too: gummy little pellets in a standard red sauce stoked with hot pepper flakes.

The best entrées are the homiest ones: a special of roast pork infused with garlic, or moist roasted quail stuffed with zesty sausage (although the accompanying polenta had solidified into dry sponges). The veal chop is simple and excellent, and if your taste runs to tripe, the tomato-and-olive-based stew here does it justice. Unaccountably, the kitchen makes a mess of veal paillard: it is bland and soggy from its soupy rosemary-and-wine sauce. A special of veal with artichoke hearts and tomato was utterly tasteless, too.

Among seafood options, salmon with mustard sauce was satisfying on two occasions, and a special of grouper was a mixed bag; the garlicky tomato sauce was good, but mussels and clams ringing the plate were rubbery. Soft-shell clams suffer the same fate as veal paillard, arriving in a lake of broth.

Except for a good moist cheesecake, desserts are dreary: a cloying and rubbery concoction misidentified as profiteroles (actually a white-chocolate-mousse cake of sorts), inedibly sweet raspberry cake, oversugared poached pears, and gluey napoleon.

THE RITZ CAFE

Satisfactory

2 Park Avenue (entrance on 32nd Street), 684-2122.

Atmosphere: Sprawling Art Deco café with two long mahogany bars and an informal open dining room.

Service: Rushed and workmanlike at lunch; calmer at dinner.

Price range: Moderate.

Credit cards: All major cards.

Hours: Same menu from 11:30 A.M. to 11 P.M., Monday through Friday, 4:30 to 11 P.M., Saturday.

Reservations: Recommended for lunch.

Wheelchair accessibility: All facilities on one level.

℮ Since The Ritz Cafe opened in early 1986 in a largely commercial district on 32nd Street off Park Avenue, it has been struggling with an identity crisis. It took over a cavernous, classy brasserielike setting originally occupied by the short-lived La Coupole, but its Cajun-Creole theme failed to attract the crowds necessary to keep such a large vessel afloat. In midcourse, it jettisoned the hot sauce and billed itself as a seafood restaurant.

Repeat visits reveal that the new tack is hardly more successful than the first. The Ritz Cafe attracts a large lunch crowd, but most nights you could practice fly casting in the dining room with little fear of snagging a customer.

The dining room is a partitioned arena with a high ceiling, Art Deco chandeliers, etched-glass room dividers, pale yellow walls, period wall moldings, and full-length glass panels. Two handsome mahogany bars flank the front of the room; one is converted to a shellfish station where you can drop in for a frosty beer and some fresh oysters. In fact, shellfish and appetizers at the bar are the best things this place has to offer.

Littleneck and cherrystone clams on ice are clear and fresh-tasting, and you might follow them up with a sampling of applewood-smoked shrimp with a zippy Creole remoulade sauce (one of the few bayou specialties remaining from the old menu, along with a peppy seafood gumbo thick with shrimp and bits of salty ham). Cornmeal-battered fried oysters are good, too, along with their mildly peppery salsa. When the kitchen tries to get fancy with oysters by warming them and dousing them with citrus beurre blanc, the result is unappetizing to behold—the oysters are an anemic gray—and tasteless.

Better options are the cleanly fried tendrils of calamari with a spicy red sauce, and Gulf shrimp steeped in a garlic-infused broth brightened with fresh herbs.

Service is rushed and sporadic at lunch, leisurely and friendly at dinner. A major problem with entrées is overcooking. It ruined an otherwise good salmon steak served with a tomatillo salsa (on two occasions), as well as grilled swordfish with herb butter. Yellowfin tuna was in trouble from the start. The menu described it appetizingly as "flash-grilled over charcoal with lemongrass and an Oriental dipping sauce." Instead, it was dried out over charcoal and devoid of any lemongrass, a lovely herb often used in Vietnamese cooking. The dipping sauce tasted like soy sauce with some sesame seeds sprinkled over it.

One of the better entrées is nicely cooked sea scallops with a bright assortment of green and red peppers, carrots, onions, and broccoli. Linguine with clam sauce, though, is a real dud—devoid of seasoning and overcooked.

Two desserts are worth considering: Jack Daniels–chocolate ice cream (if you close your eyes and concentrate, the whiskey can be detected in the aftertaste) and fresh, chunky apple pie.

THE RIVER CAFÉ

★ ★ ★

1 Water Street, Brooklyn, (718) 522-5200.

Atmosphere: Romantic dining room on a barge with stunning views of Manhattan and the East River.

Service: Professional if sometimes mannered.

Price range: Expensive (dinner prix fixe, $52).

Credit cards: All major cards.

Hours: Brunch, noon to 2 P.M., Saturday, 11:30 A.M. to 2 P.M., Sunday; lunch, noon to 2 P.M., Monday through Friday; dinner, 6:30 to 11 P.M., Sunday through Thursday, 7 to 11:30 P.M., Friday and Saturday.

Reservations: Necessary two weeks in advance.

Wheelchair accessibility: Ramps into dining room; all facilities on one level.

🦪 The River Café, on a barge on the Brooklyn shore of the East River under the Brooklyn Bridge, remains one of the most spellbinding settings in New York. The vista of lower Manhattan across the busy waterway is stirring any time of day but especially at dusk, when the sky deepens to silvery indigo and the lights begin flickering in the glass towers. The dining room—with a piano bar on one side and rows of well-spaced tables, all with good views —attracts a blend of special-occasion revelers, out-of-town visitors, and well-heeled New Yorkers. Despite the festive nature of the place, noise is rarely bothersome.

The River Café has seen three chefs in the past six years: first Larry Forgione, who established it as one of the premier all-American restaurants in the country; then Charles Palmer, who added his own distinctive touch until quietly moving on last December to open his own place. Since early 1988, the chef has been twenty-six-year-old David Burke, an inventive former sous-chef at the café who spent most of 1987 training in France with such luminaries as Gaston Lenôtre, Georges Blanc, and Marc Meneau.

Mr. Burke obviously has fun with food presentation, and many of his winsome creations leave diners loath to disassemble them. The pristine carpaccio of yellowfin tuna comes with a dome of salmon tartare on top pierced with two corrugated potatoes and a ruffle of crème fraîche speckled with black olives. Bright green snow peas ring the dish.

Quail legs are stuffed with foie gras, enveloped in pasta, and served so the bones form little handles; the legs and sautéed quail breasts are set in a clear, heady mushroom broth flecked with pistachios.

A starter called warm pastrami-cured salmon belly was too provocative to pass up. This eccentric twist on the New York deli staple is cured in coriander, salt, pepper, and sugar overnight, then brushed with a mélange of peppery spices and smoked. The ruddy strips of salmon are pleasingly salty and leave a piquant echo on the palate. They are served with creamy mashed potatoes and artichoke sections rubbed with mustard oil.

The café's service staff is well informed and highly proficient. The recently updated wine list, which includes a special selection of older California vintages, reflects considerable care.

Mr. Burke is a flashier chef than his predecessor, sometimes a bit too flashy. Some of the best entrées are the least cerebral: superb aged Black Angus sirloin, grilled over fruitwood and served with a lusty red-wine sauce and rösti potatoes, or the perfectly sautéed salmon steak embedded with cracked pepper and ginger, over an invigorating red-wine-and-butter sauce perfumed with ginger. Tuna steak also is masterly prepared, under a thin golden roof of sautéed potatoes. A sweet, buttery sea scallop is set in the center of the plate and everything is ringed with a vegetable-bouillon-based sauce scattered with minced black olives, carrots, white beans, and broccoli florets.

One effort that failed to excite my intrepid crew of tasters was the overproduced grilled chicken breast that came with a staggering supporting cast: mushroom sausage, morels, black-olive pasta, and tomato sauce, all of which muddled the plot.

Several desserts are worth rowing across the East River for: the incredibly light timbale-shaped banana-and-chocolate parfait with light and dark chocolate sauces; a raucous assortment of sublime chocolate pastries, ice creams, and cookies, and sharp, moist cinnamon pudding with crème anglaise. Plum tart is a distant runner-up, although the lemon cream accompanying it is great, and crème brûlée is a winner.

ROSA MEXICANO

★ ★

1063 First Avenue, at 58th Street, 753-7407.

Atmosphere: Elegant grill restaurant with soothing Mexican décor and lively ambiance.

Service: Knowledgeable about the food and accommodating. The back room moves at a better pace than the front.

Price range: Moderate.

Credit cards: All major cards.

Hours: Lunch, noon to 3:30 P.M., Monday through Saturday; Sunday buffet, noon to 3 P.M.; dinner, 5 P.M. to midnight, daily.

Reservations: Necessary.

Wheelchair accessibility: One step at entrance; all facilities on one level.

🍴 Rosa Mexicano is among the most elegant and best Mexican restaurants in town. It has a stylish ambiance, gregarious clientele, a good-time bar, and a diverse range of bracing foods. It eschews the leaden and starchy clichés of most Mexican restaurants in New York and attempts to serve what Mexicans really eat. It's also one of the few such places where you will not wish for a stretcher to carry you home after dinner.

The menu, orchestrated by Josephina Howard, who helped open Cinco de Mayo in SoHo several years ago, is notable for its clean and bright seasonings and relatively light touch. Moreover, the fare is well balanced, offering moderate portions of stimulating appetizers followed by a host of grilled meats and fish, stews and soups.

The front room has a long, often crowded bar where exceptionally good margaritas flow like the Colorado River in March. The more elegant back room is done in rose-colored stucco with pink banquettes and a magnificent cluster of flowers in the center.

The house special margarita, made with pomegranate, is more accessible to the novice than the slightly more aggressive traditional rendition made with tequila, Triple Sec, lime juice, salt, and crushed ice. A few of these on an empty stomach will put you in such a mañana mood that anything the waiter suggests will seem just dandy. It's worthwhile to go over the menu carefully, though, because some arresting selections are available for all tastes.

Rosa Mexicano does not belong to the fire-thrower school of Mexican restaurants. Hot peppers and spices are added for seasoning, not scorching—although some dishes come with condiments on the side that you can add to taste. Two authentic and zesty appetizers are taquitos de tinga poblana and taquitos de moronga. The first combines tasty shreds of roast pork, chili chipotle (actually smoked jalapeño chilies), diced onions, and tomato rolled in soft flour tortillas like thick cigars; the other taquitos hold morsels of earthy blood pudding, sliced onions, and fresh coriander.

The guacamole is justly famous. A waiter brings a ripe avocado to the table and prepares it to the preferred degree of hotness. The avocado is cubed, not mashed, and blended with tomato, coriander, assorted minced peppers, and fresh lime juice. Another engaging starter is briefly sautéed oysters served chilled and in the shell with the natural brine and lemon juice—a rousing summer dish.

Starters that don't make the grade are fishy-tasting steamed clams in a chili-laced broth and bland jalapeño peppers studded with dry sardines.

Service in the back room is better than in the front, where understaffing can lead to delays. Waiters are well versed in the menu and are usually happy to accommodate special requests.

Grilled entrées are particularly well executed, whether it is the crusty seared shell steak under strips of sautéed chilies poblanos and onions, mildly piquant chicken, or fist-thick beef ribs basted with lemon juice and beer and accompanied by four garnishes (tomatillo, spicy tomato, coriander-onion salsa, and beans). Grilled marinated red snapper is fresh and well cooked but oddly lacks flavor at times. Try the coriander-flecked baked snapper instead.

Unfortunately the roasted duck breast and leg consistently suffer from overcooking, for the sauce of puréed green tomatoes, green chilies, and pumpkin seeds is terrific. Fanciers of chilies rellenos will find the version here more refined than most: a single large poblano chili is stuffed with mild white cheese, lightly battered and fried, then presented in a sparkling tomato broth.

The consistently best entrée to my taste is carnitas, a simple but delicious combination of succulent cubed pork paired with soft flour tortillas and four sauces that you add to taste, at your own risk: fiery mole sauce, coriander-onion vinaigrette, red tomato, and green tomatillo.

A few tropical desserts are worth considering. Flan with coffee sauce is a good combination, and mango fruitcake—

sort of a bread pudding with frothy mango sauce—is a nice twist on the north-of-the-border version. While I found the crêpes smothered with caramelized sauce of goat's milk and sherry too sweet, several diners at my table liked it. Mango ice cream is a ripe and refreshing alternative, although papaya is pale and icy—maybe dropping it into a margarita would help.

ROUMELI TAVERNA

★

33-04 Broadway, Astoria, Queens, (718) 278-7533.

Atmosphere: Festive and informal dining room with illuminated vines on the walls and ceilings and a buoyant Greek clientele.

Service: Glum and workmanlike.

Price range: Moderate.

Credit cards: American Express.

Hours: 11:30 A.M. to 1:30 A.M., daily.

Reservations: Suggested.

Wheelchair accessibility: Dining room on one level; restrooms in the basement.

🍴 Distinctive Greek cuisine is difficult to come by in New York City, even in Astoria, Queens, our own little Peloponnisus just across the East River. The restaurant scene there is just as volatile as in Manhattan, with reputations rising and falling like the river tide. One of the more reliable and diverting spots in the neighborhood is Roumeli Taverna along bustling Broadway (just two blocks from the N subway stop).

It's always Christmastime inside the Roumeli Taverna, where the stucco walls are hidden behind a jungle of leafy vines ablaze with hundreds of tiny bulbs. At the entrance, a glass counter displays the evening's provender, everything from glistening whole porgies to ruddy lamb livers, calf brains, and huge coiled octopus. The dining room is convivial and casual, packed nightly with Greek couples and families stabbing mounds of lamb and polishing off bottles of retsina wine to the background of bouzouki music.

Waitresses here, pen in mouth and notepad in apron, are, shall we say, somewhat lacking in the fine art of hospitality. Sullen and uncommunicative, their conversational skills are confined to "Ready yet?" "Anything else?" and "Don't have it."

The menu carries the familiar Greek standards—fat and flaky spinach pie, tasty stuffed grape leaves, crisply fried eggplant, a rather heavy and grainy taramasalata (red-caviar-and-potato-dip purée), and vibrant hummus (chick-pea-and-garlic-purée)—as well as more exotic fare. Octopus marinated in lemon, olive oil, and oregano is delicious, as are deep-fried tiny Mediterranean fish similar to smelts (they are misidentified as smelts on the menu). Deep-fried calamari hacked into the size of napkin rings are tasty with a drizzling of lemon. The appetizer of broiled kasseri, a salty hard cheese, was burned. If you are not a fan of retsina wine, two dry whites that go well with this food are Demestica ($12) and St. Helena by Chaia ($12).

The best entrées are simple grilled fish, either porgies (a real bargain at $12), snapper (prices vary with size), or mullets ($12), which are served whole, on the bone, with lemon halves (and a festive maraschino cherry). Lamb is prepared in myriad ways. The best is a frequent special of roast baby leg of lamb with potatoes, which is a slab the size of a sneaker, moist and rich, served room temperature, and sitting in a pool of oil—Greeks cook everything with oil, so you have to roll with it. Barbecued lamb, however, was oddly flavorless, and the house special, mezeli à la Greek, was a muddled mess—overcooked gray meat suffocating under a layer of salty melted cheese and broiled tomatoes.

Beef sweetbreads, more assertive than those from veal, are nicely deep fried. I never had the chance to sample barbecued goat, suckling pig, or something called "the secret of Platon" (I assume he is the cook).

"Don't have it," our waitress grumbled.

When the time came for dessert I asked, diffidently, what was available.

"Nothin'," she said matter-of-factly.

"Nothing at all?" I replied, thinking perhaps she misunderstood.

"Nothin'," she repeated.

In a weird way, I really love this place.

RUSSIAN SAMOVAR

★

256 West 52nd Street, 757-0168.

Atmosphere: Soft and comfortable room with well-spaced tables, soft lighting, and good noise control.

Service: Friendly and well informed about the food.

Price range: Moderate.

Credit cards: American Express, MasterCard, and Visa.

Hours: Lunch, noon to 3 P.M., daily; dinner, 5 P.M. to midnight, daily.

Reservations: Suggested.

Wheelchair accessibility: Two small steps down from street entrance; restrooms downstairs.

🦡 Russian Samovar is an understated and moderately priced theater-district restaurant offering a standard repertory of Russian dishes. If you are in the mood for a jolt of good vodka and perhaps a simple plate of grilled lamb or seafood, this is a good place to go; more involved presentations, though, can be dim from underseasoning.

The dining room is conspicuously conservative in the traditional scarlet-felt department. Except for several gold samovars on display and a stocky bearded manager who looks as if he stepped out of a Dostoyevsky novel, one might mistake this place for a French bistro. Straw-colored fabric covers the walls, well-spaced tables and long banquettes provide more than adequate comfort, and lighting is softly diffused. A polyglot pianist-singer provides a soothing backdrop nightly.

Two nice starters are the eggplant Samovar, thin sheets of grilled eggplant sprinkled with coriander and ground walnuts, and spicy Georgian dried beef, comprising thinly sliced strips of reddish-brown beef rubbed with hot paprika. Cucumber-and-onion salad swathed in yogurt comes to the rescue.

Satsivi, the Georgian specialty made with boneless chunks of chicken in a walnut-and-garlic sauce, is disappointingly watery and bland; kholodetz, veal chunks in aspic, also lacks seasoning. The biggest letdown, though, is the borscht. Everything is there—cabbage, beef, beets, sour cream—except flavor. A better choice is the assertive chicken-liver terrine bolstered with cognac, or, if you are feeling flush, an ounce of caviar—salmon, sevruga, or osetra—with toast or blinis.

It is difficult to assess service because every time I dined there fewer than six tables were occupied—I am told it is busier just before Broadway curtain time. Our waitresses were familiar with all the dishes and had plenty of time to linger and answer arcane questions. There were few questions about the wine list, though, for it is one of those colorless, mass-produced documents assembled gratis by wine companies.

Grilling is the kitchen's strength at the moment. Try the karsky shashlik—marinated lamb chops slightly charred outside and juicy within—with cabbage salad (and some zippy sauce made with plums, coriander, garlic, and hot spices); salmon shashlik—cubes of delicately cooked salmon in a light white-wine sauce flanked by dill-seasoned potatoes and onions—is equally good. Partly boned and grilled Cornish hen may not seem terribly ethnic, but no matter; it is deftly done, crisp and succulent. The hen is far better than what is dubbed Russian village steak—a leathery slab with soggy onion rings.

No visit to a New York Russian restaurant would be complete without a chicken Kiev or some dumplings. The former is certainly satisfying; when pricked with a fork, it scored 8 out of 10 on the butter-spurt meter. The meat-filled dumplings, called pelmeni, are nicely seasoned and come either in a sour-cream-and-mustard sauce or in the "royale" version, in which the sauce is freckled with some saline osetra caviar.

The two best desserts are those bought from the company Les Délices Guy Pascal, a French pastry wholesaler, and given Russian-sounding names: cake Kiev, a crunchy baked meringue-and-walnut confection, and cake Anna Pavlova, an embarrassingly rich triple-decker of chocolate mousse, mocha cream, and toasted almonds known as a délice cake in French.

Russian Samovar does not forge any new frontiers in this hearty traditional cuisine, but if you are looking for an undemanding meal in accommodating surroundings before or after theater, it is a place to note.

THE RUSSIAN TEA ROOM

★

150 West 57th Street, 265-0947.

Atmosphere: Exuberant holiday feeling with tinsel-draped chandeliers, bright colors, and celebrity crowd.

Service: Generally cordial but sometimes slow.

Price range: Expensive.

Credit cards: All major cards.

Hours: Lunch and dinner, 11:30 A.M. to midnight, Monday through Friday, 11 A.M. to midnight, Saturday and Sunday.

Reservations: Necessary.

Wheelchair accessibility: Main dining room on street level; restrooms upstairs.

𝕫𝕬 The Russian Tea Room remains a special place, if not necessarily a special restaurant. Where else can you have Christmas in July: pine-green walls, bright red banquettes, tinsel-draped chandeliers decorated with gleaming Christmas-tree balls; "Russian" waiters named Salvador and Bob decked out in festive red tunics, and stargazing and Stolichnaya in abundance?

The food, at least in recent years, has been secondary to the ambiance. Regulars who know the menu stick to a few well-executed dishes—chicken à la Kiev, lamb chops, blinis with caviar—and sit back and enjoy the show. Deeper expeditions into the menu can be risky and expensive.

The Tea Room still sizzles at lunch in the main downstairs room; the after-theater crowd enlivens the place about 10:30 P.M. A large upstairs room, dubbed Siberia by regulars and celebrity spotters, is less kinetic than downstairs, but it is commodious. Service is generally cordial but can be slow, so make it clear if you must leave at a certain time for a concert or play.

The cold borscht is delightful, a creamy pink broth chunky with sweet beets and cucumber and amply seasoned with fresh dill; the warm borscht is built on a good beef stock and garnished with a cloud of sour cream. A special soup of leeks, watercress, and potatoes, though, is saltier than the Black Sea.

Follow-up visits in the past year have found the zakuska, a Russian appetizer plate, falling in quality: commercial-tasting smoked salmon and capers, dry chicken livers, overly sweet marinated herring, good salmon caviar and sour cream, scallop seviche that is also too sweet. If you are feeling extravagant, blinis and caviar are always a treat (à la carte prices start at $20.50 for two ounces of red salmon caviar and reach $47 for one ounce of beluga—blinis are $6.75 extra). The buckwheat blinis are light-textured and delicious with a coating of melted butter, a dollop of sour cream, and some caviar.

Reliable entrées include the chicken à la Kiev, which seems lighter than it used to be, a rolled, breaded chicken breast that spurts herb butter when the waiter cuts into it. Grilled chicken breast, an occasional lunch special, is moist and flavorful, too, set over semolinalike grain enhanced with currants, saffron, and almonds. Another light lunch option is fresh salmon swathed in a mayonnaise dressing over radicchio.

Lamb dishes are a mixed bag: the simple lamb chops can be good, as can the karsky shashlik supreme, a fillet paired with a piece of kidney; on the other hand, luli kebab, a traditional ground lamb dish from the Caucasus, tastes like a bad version of diner meat loaf. Duck is well roasted, although its unappetizingly sweet sauce is studded with hard, unripe cherries.

The best dessert is still cranberry kisel, which is essentially a purée of cranberries, cream, and sugar. It is refreshing and both tart and sweet. Kasha à la Gourieff was described accurately by our waiter: "It's kind of like Cream of Wheat, with some apricots and almonds in it." It was nostalgic, all right, and not bad.

The Russian Tea Room has made some changes for the better, although it is still recommended as much for its fanciful mood as its food.

SABOR

★

20 Cornelia Street, 243-9579.

Atmosphere: Small, cramped dining room with a casual Latin atmosphere.

Service: Capable and matter-of-fact.

Price range: Moderate.

Credit cards: American Express, MasterCard, and Visa.

Hours: Dinner, 6 to 11 P.M., Sunday through Thursday, 6 P.M. to midnight, Friday and Saturday.

Reservations: Recommended.

Wheelchair accessibility: All facilities on one level.

🍲 The pint-size Cuban restaurant Sabor in Greenwich Village, which most nights is packed, seems to have mellowed over the years. Recent revisits found the menu is essentially the same, and prices are certainly right, but some dishes have lost their punch. Nonetheless, it is still a good bet for budget dining in Greenwich Village.

The setting has not changed. The narrow room with cream-colored brick walls brightened with woven baskets is designed for limber ectomorphs. You reach your seat by inhaling deeply, standing on tiptoe, and wedging yourself sideways into the allotted slot. A fresh lime margarita makes it all seem a bit more comfortable—and three of them make the place seem absolutely palatial.

It has always seemed curious that Sabor, which is widely regarded as one of the better Cuban restaurants in New York, is owned by two non-Cuban women, Gail Stratton and Ronnie Ginnever, who split cooking duties.

A good introduction to this zesty Caribbean fare is the frituras de malanga, deep-fried balls of a neutral-tasting Caribbean root vegetable that are enlivened with generous amounts of garlic and parsley. Tamales were engrossing, too, the packed mass of cornmeal and spices cooked inside a corn husk that keeps the mixture moist and lends it a smoky sweet aftertaste. Crescent-shaped empanadas were filled with lean, spicy chorizo, but the pastry was burned. Bite-size conch fritters, a special one evening, nearly suffered the same fate. Only the edges were blackened, which added an addictive appeal to these chewy disks seasoned with sweet and hot peppers and lime.

When it comes to entrées, don't expect the matter-of-fact service personnel, either of them, to offer a long exegesis of Cuban cuisine. "Good," replied our waiter when one of my companions asked how a shrimp sauce tasted. "And what about the pineapple-and-sherry sauce with the loin of pork?" he was asked. "Very good," he offered.

Armed with that illuminating information, we opted for a special called shrimp in a piquant green sauce made with parsley, garlic, and capers (the shrimp were rubbery from overcooking). A whole baked snapper comes out cooked to a turn and blanketed with a similar sauce, brightened with a touch of lime juice. The zarzuela de mariscos is a rather tame choice, although fresh and nicely presented; it is a combination of mussels, clams, and scallops in a pulpy red sauce touched with saffron. A more distinctive preparation is shrimp cooked in a sweet-sharp sauce made with coconut milk, curry, and onions, an occasional special. It comes with delicious and exotic-tasting rice flecked with mustard seed, turmeric, coriander, and lime.

Several earthy meat dishes are appealing, including braised oxtail in a garlicky tomato sauce and the ropa vieja, or old clothes, shreds of well-braised flank steak in a red sauce aromatic of cloves and cinnamon. I must have received the last leftover slice of carne estofada, described as pot roast stuffed with chorizo, olives, capers, raisins, and prunes, for it tasted like dried-out cafeteria grub. Good black beans come with entrées. Two other side dishes worth ordering are the cleanly fried sweet plantains or the potatolike yucca (another root vegetable) dabbed with lime-sharpened olive oil and garlic.

Sabor will prepare a complete feast around a roast suckling pig for groups of eight or more for $40 a person.

Sabor's Key lime pie does not have the tart citric edge I remember, but it is still pleasing. Another winner is the coco quemado, a thick, hot coconut custard with a blistered coconut crust. It's flavored with sherry and cinnamon and is served under a melting glacier of fresh whipped cream. Sharp, semisweet chocolate ice cream is a fine palate cleanser.

While Sabor has lost some of its sassy Latin flair, it still offers some sunny Cuban fare at serendipitous prices.

SAL ANTHONY'S

★

55 Irving Place, between 17th and 18th streets, 982-9030.

Atmosphere: Convivial main dining room with well-spaced tables.

Service: Congenial and competent.

Price range: Moderate.

Credit cards: All major cards.

Hours: Brunch, noon to 3 P.M., Sunday; lunch, noon to 3 P.M., daily; dinner, 4:30 to 10 P.M., Monday through Thursday, 4:30 to 11 P.M., Friday and Saturday, 3 to 10 P.M., Sunday.

Reservations: Suggested.

Wheelchair accessibility: Special elevator entrance available for those who request it in advance.

𝒢 Sal Anthony's is one of those durable neighborhood institutions that have survived by cosseting a core of regulars, the type of customers who dismiss the menu with a wave and ask for "the usual." Watching all the cheek-pecking and bear-hugging there one evening, I felt like a first-time visitor to an exclusive private club. Although the food and service merit one star, it is clear that inner-circle members enjoy a little something extra in the ambiance that keeps them coming back.

Housed in a brick row house on tranquil Irving Place, the restaurant has a safe and neighborly feel to it. The main room is not particularly distinguished—a mix of brick walls and faint flowered wallpaper, bright lighting, well-spaced tables—but it assumes a festive air when filled with bonhomous customers. A small anteroom is rather frumpy by comparison.

Although the ample menu is littered with the sort of humdrum Italian fare you find at glorified pizzerias, a few outstanding dishes make a visit worthwhile. Many of the regulars go straight for the prime steak and cipollini, a terrifically juicy and assertive steak strewn with sautéed onions. The fist-thick broiled veal chop could not be better, either.

Other veal dishes are competently prepared, if not memorably, such as the saltimbocca, rolled around mozzarella and presented over wilted escarole, and the veal piccante, which is tender and lemony. Both come with tough-skinned reheated potatoes. Sautéed escarole flecked with garlic is a good à la carte side dish.

Seafood is not Sal Anthony's métier, so stick with unfussy preparations like shrimp marinara avellino, plump tender shrimp in a brassy red sauce aromatic of oregano and garlic.

The large service staff does a competent if not meticulous job. No one seems well versed in the superior wine list, which is especially strong among Italian and French labels, and fairly priced.

Pastas can be ordered as appetizers or entrées. By far the best is the outstanding linguine tossed with freshly shucked sweet clams and whole garlic cloves. Many others pale by comparison, like the linguine à la Sal Anthony's, combining peas, porcini mushrooms, and garlic in a flat-tasting tomato-cream sauce, and the listless fusilli filetto di pomodoro, in an undistinguished red sauce.

A good way to start is with the boldly seasoned Caesar salad for two or the sparkling seafood salad, combining squid, octopus, conch, and black olives in a lemony basil vinaigrette. Strips of eggplant sandwiching ricotta cheese under a molten layer of mozzarella and tomato sauce is soothing and filling. Braciole, rolled beef stuffed with pine nuts, Parmesan cheese, and garlic, is papery dry, and the dreary risotto tastes like leftover rice combined with leftover peas, prosciutto, peppers, and mushrooms.

If the prodigious portions here leave room for dessert, try the strawberries with whipped cream, the moist and relatively light cheesecake or tartufo. Zuppa inglese is all richness and little flavor, and chocolate cake is cloyingly sweet.

SAM'S CAFÉ

★

1406 Third Avenue, at 80th Street, 988-5300.

Atmosphere: Cheerful if loud American-style bistro popular with young professional types.

Service: Young, green staff that does its earnest best.

Price range: Moderate.

Credit cards: All major cards.

Hours: Dinner, 6 to 11:30 P.M., Monday through Saturday; open at 5 P.M. for cocktails.

Reservations: Recommended.

Wheelchair accessibility: All facilities on one level.

&❧ Sam's Café, on Third Avenue at 80th Street, owned by Mariel (Sam) Hemingway, her husband, Stephen Crisman, and Mr. Crisman's brother, Eric, turns out easygoing and generally tasty American fare in a lively setting.

The glass-enclosed front room, which is the more clamorous of the two, has a long bar on one side and about a dozen tables on the other. The back dining room sports an arched ceiling with skylights that creates an illusion of spaciousness. The artwork is, well, funky. Good-looking young waiters and waitresses make up in earnest charm what they lack in finesse.

There are few peaks and valleys on the menu, just a pleasant breezy plateau. Salads are good: one combining a disk of goat cheese on a garlic crouton embedded in shredded radicchio, arugula, and assorted other greens tossed in a walnut vinaigrette; another with sweet charred endive surrounded by sautéed wild mushrooms, and the herbivore's special, called Sam's Salad, a hillock of sugar snap peas, fennel, carrots, beets, and Bibb lettuce in a well-balanced vinaigrette.

The polenta, which changes daily, is generally a good bet, especially the version enhanced with mild fontina cheese and semifirm asparagus tips. Fanciers of steak tartare will enjoy the freshly ground patty of beef that is deftly seasoned with capers, onions, Worcestershire sauce, and eggs.

The restaurant's wine list is sensibly priced with a good selection of reputable American and French selections in the $12-to-$25 range.

Skillfully roasted free-range chicken, meaty and crisp-skinned, as well as chicken paillard with sage butter are two reliable entrées. Fish selections change daily. Rare-grilled tuna steak garnished with fresh ginger and surrounded by snow peas and grilled scallions is an unmitigated success. Another pleasing preparation is lotte, or monkfish, fillet, nicely sautéed and draped in a fresh roasted red-pepper purée. A baked salmon-steak special was a hit at my table, too. The sauce combined faintly tart crème fraîche, Pommery mustard, and enoki and shiitake mushrooms.

What could be a more fitting dessert for an all-American-style bistro than chocolate cake? This one is intense and lingering. Strawberry shortcake suffers from the drys; go instead with the fresh fruit or caramel custard.

SAM'S RESTAURANT

★

152 West 52nd Street, 582-8700.

Atmosphere: Expansive and elegant space with a Western theme.

Service: Congenial and earnest.

Price range: Moderately expensive.

Credit cards: All major cards.

Hours: Lunch, noon to 2:45 P.M., Monday through Friday; dinner, 5:30 to 11:30 P.M., Monday through Saturday; pretheater seating from 5:30 to 6 P.M.

Reservations: Suggested.

Wheelchair accessibility: All facilities on one level.

In late 1987 the third gastronomic cornerstone was wedged into place at the Equitable Center on Seventh Avenue at 52nd Street, this one an all-American grill backed by that all-American girl of the big screen, Mariel Hemingway. Called Sam's (Ms. Hemingway's moniker among friends), it is the sport-shirt alternative to its very proper neighbors, Le Bernardin and Palio.

That's not to say this is just another yuppie watering hole. The setting is awesome in its dimensions—a Grand Central Terminal with Western accents, all earth tones and burnished wood, a vivid mural of nasturtiums by James Rosenquist, brass-and-clay-colored chandeliers suspended from a twenty-eight-foot-high ceiling, a bronze bison grazing on top of the circular bar, and plenty of elbow room for weary urban cowboys to stretch out after a hard day on the corporate range. The high ceiling and the rugs dissipate conversation and background music on all but the most crowded evenings, when things get loud. The moderately priced menu was described by our waiter as American nouvelle, "which is two bites more than French nouvelle."

Some of this food will be familiar if you have been to the Hemingway-Crisman clan's other restaurant, the bistro-size Sam's Café on Third Avenue at 80th Street (owned by Ms. Hemingway, her husband, Stephen Crisman, and his brother, Eric). If I had to recommend only two entrées, they would be the New York shell steak, a ranch-hand portion that is well aged, beefy, and deliciously seared (along with a sweet-potato gratin), and the hefty hamburger, perhaps the best in town, made of ground beef grilled succulently rare, paired with excellent shoestring potatoes. One preparation I have always liked at the original Sam's, the rare grilled tuna, is disappointing here. The first time I tried it, the tuna was cooked until gray and dry; the second time it was medium rare but served nearly cold and lacking seasonings.

The best seafood dish is called tournedos of salmon, set over a faintly sharp watercress-butter sauce with a pretty supporting cast of pearl onions, green beans, and potatoes. Grilled black bass is competently cooked and fresh but the sauce is lackluster. If you really want to roll up the flannel sleeves and dig into some hearty food, try the braised chicken (although it looked roasted to me) in a flour-thickened gravy embellished with oysters with chive-flecked biscuits on the side—satisfying in a down-home way and filling to be sure. I have also enjoyed the grilled lamb with roasted eggplant slices, and grilled duck breast in a good stock sauce enriched with duck liver (I barely detected the liver, though) flanked by zestily seasoned black beans.

The young, neighborly waiters and waitresses are earnest

and strive to please in their own casual way. The short wine list offers a half dozen creditable choices for less than $20.

The obligatory pastas and pizzas are offered as starters. If you like heavy-hitting blue cheese, try that version, scattered with onions and with a toasty thin crust; leeks, apple-smoked ham, and mild goat cheese is a harmonious combination, too. I didn't have much luck with the pastas, though, which were either overcooked or underseasoned. Better options are the deliciously peppery crab cakes, the grilled shiitake mushrooms with a roasted red-pepper salad, and the moist, assertively seasoned duck terrine. Eggplant and anchovy mousse is insipid baby food, and red-onion tart is overwhelmed by nutmeg flavor.

For dessert, my top choices are the crunchy and moderately sweet pecan pie or the cinnamon-edged yam custard. The stratified chocolate rum cake was intense and boozy the first time, dry the next, while sugar-dusted apple cheesecake with raisins and frozen praline terrine are respectable and mercifully not overly sweet.

The midtown theater district needed a place like Sam's, a casually elegant and diverting spot where it is possible to dine for less than the price of a blockbuster Broadway musical. It should enjoy a long run.

SAN DOMENICO

★ ★ ★

240 Central Park South, 265-5959.

Atmosphere: Luxuriant, spacious room; low noise level.

Service: Vigilant and professional.

Price range: Expensive. (Lunch prix fixe, $29.50; tasting dinner, $55)

Credit cards: All major cards.

Hours: Lunch, 11:45 A.M. to 2:30 P.M., Monday through Saturday; dinner, 5:45 to 11 P.M., Monday through Saturday, 5:45 to 10 P.M., Sunday.

Reservations: Necessary.

Wheelchair accessibility: Several steps down to dining room; restrooms on same level.

ॐ This luxurious restaurant on Central Park South by Tony May (of Palio, Sandro's, and La Camelia) is modeled after the original San Domenico in Imola, a small town in Emilia-Romagna. The chef, Valentino Marcattilii, who garnered two stars from the Michelin Guide in 1979, came to New York in mid-1988 to start the branch and now spends most of his time in New York, with occasional trips to Italy.

Most of the northern regional cuisine here is faithful to tradition yet at the same time exquisitely refined and beautifully presented. It is expensive—count on $70 and up per person with wine, tax, and tip—but unlike so many places in this price range, San Domenico delivers food that is as original as it is delightful.

When you enter the extravagant 130-seat dining room (the former Alfredo's restaurant), the price tag is understandable: terra cotta floors imported from Florence, ochertinted stucco walls applied by artisans sent from Rome, scalloped glass sconces on marble columns, rich leather chairs, orange tablecloths, and matching doilies on silver plates. Waiters in screeching-red blazers are urbane and vigilant; waitresses in prim black dresses with white bonnets look as if they just emerged from an Amish prayer meeting.

Among the more titillating antipasto selections are perfectly steamed sea scallops and potatoes sliced into translucent disks and garnished with scallop roe and a chive-flecked olive-oil dressing. Pan-roasted sweetbreads came in a sublime garlic-enhanced tomato sauce enriched with smoked bacon (unfortunately, they were slightly overcooked).

Pastas elevate San Domenico above the pack. You would have to go to Genoa to find a dish as authentic as the potato-filled spinach ravioli swathed in a sunny pesto sauce with lacy young string beans. Seafood ravioli is sublime, too, in a sauce of garlicky broccoli, olive oil, and white wine. Even the most homespun dish can be an epiphany here, such as the pasta from Abruzzi called spaghetti alla chitarra—fresh pasta dough rolled by hand over a guitarlike device—in an explosively fresh basil and tomato sauce. A similar contraption is used to form the tiny curls of pasta called garganelli, a specialty of Imola. They are served in a whimsical butter-based sauce stippled with beluga caviar and chives. And if you are tired of restaurant gnocchi that is better suited to slingshots than to sauce, try the lovely rendition here with melted fontina cheese and sage leaves. San Domenico has a nine-hundred-label wine list, primarily Italian and American, but don't expect any bargains. As for entrées, overcooking diminished the lamb chops in a rousing rosemary-and-balsamic-vinegar sauce and on one occasion the squab with braised radicchio and excellent polenta (the second sampling was superb). Guinea hen braised with savoy cabbage and mushrooms was a good, gutsy choice, as were roasted rabbit in a rosemary-infused rabbit-stock sauce and succulent Muscovy duck with black olives.

The kitchen respects fresh seafood, never obscuring its flavor by oversaucing. Good examples are the light and herby lobster fricassee with sliced artichoke hearts and the fillet of red snapper with tomatoes and arugula. Roasted porgy in an orange-scented sauce, however, was hopelessly overcooked. A refreshing punctuation to this cuisine is any of the velvety sorbets, brandy-soaked prunes with chilled lemon cream, or orange-soaked baba brightened with fresh mint. If you have a weak spot for tiramisù, the mascarpone al caffè is virtually the same thing with a different name and is terrific.

SAN GIUSTO

Satisfactory

935 Second Avenue, between 49th and 50th streets, 319-0900.

Atmosphere: Soft and minimalist dining room, slightly cramped when full.

Service: Confused and inattentive when busy.

Price range: Moderately expensive.

Credit cards: All major cards.

Hours: Lunch, noon to 3 P.M., Monday through Friday; dinner, 5 to 11 P.M., Monday through Saturday.

Reservations: Suggested.

Wheelchair accessibility: One small step into dining room; restrooms on one level.

る The Mediterranean-style marble-and-wood bar at the entrance is an inviting spot, with its gleaming copper pans adorning whitewashed walls. The main dining room, in shades of beige with just a few plates and decorative utensils to break up the expanse, is tightly packed and a bit too neighborly when full—the sort of place where you often hear, "I'll have what that gentleman at the next table is eating."

Don't expect any surprises on the menu, which could be swapped with any of a dozen upscale northern Italian res-

347

taurants on the East Side. Clams Casino are competently prepared as part of a shellfish-assortment appetizer; mussels done the same way, however, are tasteless. Succulent breaded scallops are meltingly good, and shrimp dusted with bread crumbs are fresh and tasty.

Some of the pastas can be pleasing, so you might consider starting with half portions as appetizers, then moving on to main courses. The chef has a nice touch with the rigatoni amatriciana, delicately balancing the smoky bacon, sweet onions, and slightly acidic tomatoes. Paglia e fieno, the combination of green and white noodles, also is a savory mélange in its light tomato sauce flavored with prosciutto and sweet fresh peas. Another good choice is the homespun and herb-bolstered Bolognese sauce with spaghetti.

On the debit side are a doughy and stale-tasting special of seafood-stuffed tortellini and angel hair tossed with dry little shrimp in a boring tomato-based sauce; rigatoni in a tomato-and-prosciutto sauce was raw and hardly touched by the ham, while white clam sauce on angel hair can be unbearably salty. Better alternatives are the intensely flavored risottos, especially if they have the one with the clams, shrimp, and lobster.

None of the main courses is memorable, although some are satisfying. A whole grilled red snapper is moist and fresh, glossed with olive oil and minced garlic; hefty grilled shrimp in a potent sherry sauce is good, too. A breaded swordfish special at lunch put frozen fish sticks in a favorable light. Overcooking mars several dishes, including the papery rolled beef stuffed with radicchio in a brown sauce and dried-out roast quail. If you are a fan of veal chops, the sage-perfumed version here is a winner.

Service has improved slightly here, but it can be slow and inattentive when the place is busy.

The best dessert is the light Yugoslav crêpes, called palatschiken, oozing with chocolate sauce. Fruit tarts are ripe and fresh with buttery, brittle crusts. The house mutation of tiramisù is a swampy, overly sweet concoction served in a goblet. And for all the showmanship that comes with the zabaglione preparation, the result is anemic.

SARABETH'S KITCHEN

Satisfactory

423 Amsterdam Avenue, between 80th and 81st streets, 496-6280.

Atmosphere: Stylish and handsome restaurant cum bakery; back dining room comfortable and casually elegant.

Service: Enthusiastic but sometimes forgetful and hampered by a slow kitchen.

Price range: Moderate.

Credit cards: All major cards.

Hours: Breakfast, 8 to 11:30 A.M., Tuesday through Friday; brunch, 9 A.M. to 4 P.M., Saturday and Sunday; lunch, 11:30 A.M. to 3:30 P.M., Tuesday through Friday, tea and pastry until 5 P.M., dinner, 6 to 10:00 P.M., Tuesday through Friday, desserts until 11:30 P.M., dinner, 6:30 to 11 P.M., Saturday, desserts until midnight, dinner, 6 to 10 P.M., Sunday, desserts until 11 P.M.

Reservations: Suggested for dinner.

Wheelchair accessibility: Front dining area accessible; restrooms downstairs.

❧ Sarabeth's Kitchen is standing room only at Sunday brunch. That and breakfast are the restaurant's best efforts and include many first-rate baked goods. Lunch features some satisfying salads and simple chicken and fish dishes, while dinner for the most part is clumsy and wildly uneven. Service at all three is good-natured but haphazard and slow.

Homemade soups are a soothing way to begin lunch or dinner. I can recommend either creamy tomato soup or the oregano-flecked yellow squash soup. A surfeit of cream rendered the zucchini version unbearably rich. At lunch one of the best salads is called autumn sonata, a medley of poached chicken breast strips over two cabbage salads— one red, the other green—julienne of carrots, pink peppercorns, and toasted pumpkin seeds. A hot vegetable salad, on the other hand, was colorful and fresh but utterly bland with little evidence of the promised orange-butter sauce.

Sautéed chicken breast with mustard sauce and a garnish of sliced almonds is preferable to the warm smoked-chicken salad in which the meat had a powerful and acrid flavor, which is often the result of dipping the chicken in a smoke-flavored brine rather than smoking it the traditional way. Fresh sautéed tuna is abetted by a mélange of olives, string beans, sun-dried tomatoes, and a rosemary vinaigrette.

On the dinner menu, one of the least elaborate preparations is the best—nicely grilled leg of lamb flanked by cloves of roasted garlic, haricots verts, and carrots. When the kitchen leaves familiar ground, though, it starts to stumble. Grilled spiedini or pork stuffed with Parmesan cheese, mozzarella, and prosciutto had the texture of a catcher's mitt; a perfectly good roast chicken was spoiled by a dessert-sweet honey-and-pecan sauce. Among seafood main courses, grilled jumbo shrimp were sweet and delicious in a rum-laced pepper sauce; cold poached salmon, on the other hand, was an icy, unappetizing slab of bland fillet surrounded by grapefruit sections and a thin basil sauce that failed to rescue it.

Not surprisingly, desserts are the most consistent course. Pies and cakes are top-notch, especially the cinnamon-tinged pumpkin pie and the potent chocolate mousse wrapped in génoise with crème anglaise.

SAY ENG LOOK

Satisfactory

5 East Broadway, 732-0796.

Atmosphere: Red-felt-and-dragon theme.

Service: Indifferent management, inattentive service.

Price range: Inexpensive.

Credit cards: American Express, MasterCard, and Visa.

Hours: 11 A.M. to 10 P.M., Sunday through Thursday, 11 A.M. to 11 P.M., Friday and Saturday.

Reservations: Suggested.

Wheelchair accessibility: Dining room on street level; restrooms down flight of stairs.

👋 Part of the adventure in going to Chinatown is that you can never be sure if the place you so enjoyed the last time will bear any resemblance in décor or food to what you find today—or if it will even exist. Say Eng Look, which received three stars in 1982, has undergone dramatic, and lamentable, changes.

Not only has the Shanghai-style food sunk to a mediocre level, but to make matters worse, management seems indifferent about the whole operation. When I arrived at the half-empty restaurant one evening at 8:30 in a group of four, we were greeted with the warmth usually accorded Internal Revenue Service auditors. At 9:30 P.M. on two occasions, in the middle of our meal, we were asked if we wanted anything else because the kitchen was about to close. "What do you have for dessert?" I asked. "We don't emphasize that," the manager said, which hardly seemed a vote of confidence for the Italian spumoni and tortoni listed on the menu. Meanwhile, the staff was sitting at a round table off in a corner wolfing down dinner.

The red-felt dining room is done up in gold dragons, ornate mirrors, and other Chinese ornamentation; I never saw the upstairs. The menu carries 122 dishes, plus about 40 specials. When faced with such a staggering array, I believe the prudent course is to rely on the specials or solicit the help of a waiter. Since our waiter was rather sullen and uncommunicative on the first visit, we rolled the dice and went with an assortment of specials.

Fried wontons were dusty and insipid little doughballs that needed more help than the sweet plum sauce could provide them; shrimp toast was much better, puffed to golden-brown and tasty, while cold noodles in sesame sauce were totally bland. From that inauspicious start we moved on to one of the best specials encountered, paper-thin sheets of bean curd wrapped around fish fillets and cleanly deep-fried. You dip the rolls in salt as you eat them. Beef with scallops and snow peas, which was recommended by a waiter one evening, could have come from a can for all the flavor it had.

Few of the regular entrées received more than lukewarm response from my table, including the sweet-and-sour fish (more sweet than sour), so-called crisp aromatic duck (it was crisp but virtually unseasoned) with gummy steamed dumplings, and nondescript beef with scallions. The only dishes sampled that had any zip were the combination of peppery shredded pork and pleasantly salty chicken accompanied by sautéed watercress, and the tai chi chicken fortified with stir-fried black mushrooms. The kitchen does a creditable job with roasted whole carp presented in a pool of richly flavored fish broth along with scallions and assorted Chinese vegetables.

THE SEA GRILL

★ ★

19 West 49th Street, in Rockefeller Center, 246-9201.

Atmosphere: Handsome and roomy space facing the ice-skating rink and outdoor garden.

Service: Efficient and knowledgeable about the wine and food.

Price range: Expensive.

Credit cards: All major cards.

Hours: Brunch, noon to 2:45 P.M., Saturday and Sunday; lunch, noon to 2:45 P.M., Monday through Friday; dinner, 5 to 10:45 P.M., Monday through Saturday, 5 to 7:45 P.M., Sunday. Closed Sunday in summer.

Reservations: Recommended, especially for lunch.

Wheelchair accessibility: Elevator access to the restaurant; all facilities on one level.

&❧ There are a handful of restaurants in town that, because of their view or viewpoint, capture the unflagging vitality of this metropolis—Windows on the World, the "21" Club, The Four Seasons, and The River Café among them. To this list must be added The Sea Grill at Rockefeller Center, a sophisticated, subterranean setting facing the ice-skating rink (in warm months the area becomes a graceful outdoor café).

The Sea Grill is the most ambitious operation in a three-restaurant complex that includes the humdrum American Festival Cafe and an annex called the Bar Carvery, and until recently it was more alluring for its fancy address than its fish.

In 1988, a new chef came aboard, and the improvement was dramatic. Twenty-seven-year-old Stefano Battistini earned his stripes at two of Switzerland's finest restaurants, Chez Max in Zurich and Giradet in Crissier. Mr. Battistini has a light and clean style with fresh fish and a witty approach to presentation. He favors olive oil, vegetable purées, and fresh herbs in his sauces, which always highlight the natural texture and flavor of the particular fish, never obscuring them.

You descend to the restaurant from street level in a little glass capsule and enter a long, wood-paneled dining room with gurgling illuminated pools, pretty flower displays, and floor-to-ceiling wine racks along one wall. Outside, the gushing fountains surrounding the gold sculpture of Prometheus seem to have gone psychedelic—every minute or so the water changes from after-shave blue to lollipop red to an eerie green.

At lunch The Sea Grill is a masculine lair of expense-account business types; at dinner, when a pianist is in residence, a well-dressed mix of local people and out-of-towners fills the room.

352

Mr. Battistini's style is reflected in a sparkling appetizer called medallions of lobster tartare. The barely steamed lobster meat is coarsely chopped and arranged over spokes of endive and garnished with strips of sun-dried tomatoes and fresh tarragon, then drizzled with extra-virgin olive oil and lemon. Another visual and textural delight is the trio of sea scallops gift-wrapped in strips of zucchini and set over a crayon-yellow bell-pepper coulis flecked with fresh chervil.

Among hot starters, crab cakes are plump and vibrantly seasoned, with two assertive sauces (one made with lobster essences, the other chives); al dente fettuccine is particularly good tossed with sweet little fresh shrimp from Maine and a faintly smoky roasted-red-pepper sauce.

The Sea Grill boasts an excellent all-American wine list at relatively modest markups. Waiters have a good working knowledge of the wines and can guide you in the right direction. In fact, the service is thorough and professional in all respects. One astute fellow even waited until I had tasted my food before asking the compulsory "Some freshly ground pepper?"

Nearly all the seafood entries can be recommended. Tops on my list are the rare-grilled tuna steaks in a light ginger-butter sauce paired with curls of brittle deep-fried ginger, and the salmon steak poached in sparkling wine and court bouillon. The blush-pink salmon is surrounded by little balls of carrots and zucchini afloat in the chervil-scented sauce. Grilled swordfish is superior, too, escorted by plum tomatoes, capers, and scallions in a light parsley-butter sauce. Soft-shell crabs were cooked to a turn but nearly drowned in their soupy fish-stock sauce cut with a mustard vinaigrette.

On the meat side of the menu, sautéed fillets of veal come with terrific galettes of cheesy polenta and a rosemary-accented brown-butter sauce; guinea hen, on the other hand, is dry and not helped by its undistinguished foie-gras-and-wine sauce. One would expect good rösti potatoes from a Swiss-trained chef, and these thick golden brown pancakes are wonderful.

For dessert, go with the bright Key lime pie, velvety Prometheus chocolate cake, or the assortment of ripe tropical fruit mousses. What's billed as bittersweet orange custard is neither bitter nor custardy but rather soupy, and cappuccino flan is a dud, although the mocha sauce with it is good.

SEVILLA RESTAURANT AND BAR

★

62 Charles Street, 929-3189, 243-9513.

Atmosphere: Tavernlike setting with a lively, informal crowd.

Service: Efficient and pleasant.

Price range: Moderate.

Credit cards: All major cards.

Hours: Lunch, noon to 3 P.M., Monday through Saturday; dinner, 3 P.M. to midnight, Monday through Thursday, 3 P.M. to 1 A.M., Friday and Saturday, 1 P.M. to midnight, Sunday.

Reservations: Not accepted.

Wheelchair accessibility: All facilities on one level.

🍴 Sevilla is notable not only for its satisfying and budget-priced food but also for the warm, neighborly feeling of this Greenwich Village hangout.

The dining room has a long, well-worn bar, red vinyl booths, ersatz Tiffany lamps, red-and-white tablecloths, bullfight posters, and, watching over the proceedings, a giant bull's head. The place is packed nightly with everyone from corporate types out for a quick, cheap meal to the Village flannel-shirt set.

You can settle in with a pitcher of sangria, which is delightfully fruity yet not too sweet, or a bottle of Spanish wine—the Marques de Caceres and Federico Paternina are good dry whites under $12; Marques de Riscal, about the same price, makes a harmonious red that stands up to this lusty food.

The menu appears enormous at first, but a lot of it involves basic dishes with minor twists. Grilled shrimp are dressed up in a half dozen ways, and if they don't overcook them—the odds are slightly in your favor—most are pleasing. The version with hot garlic sauce makes a zippy starter. Actually, no matter how you order shrimp (with white-wine sauce, green sauce, or simply grilled), they come with garlic, and lots of it. Another good starter is the steamed mussels, which float in on a high tide of garlic-infused broth.

A touchstone of Spanish restaurants is the tortilla. Not the gloppy tortillas filled with iceberg lettuce found in so many second-rate Mexican restaurants, but rather a densely layered potato and egg omelet. Sevilla turns out the real thing, lightly browned and encrusted, studded with sweet peas and onions. The tortilla is listed as an entrée, but I like it as an appetizer shared among four or more diners. On frigid evenings when even macho matadors don long johns, try the caldo Gallego, the Iberian answer to Mom's chicken soup. A real blood warmer, it is so thick as to mimic a stew, combining white beans, pork, ham, potatoes, and greens.

Hearty fills, not Spanish thrills, are what you can expect from the entrées. Chicken dishes are the most reliable meat courses—and at less than $10, don't dare ask if they are the free range variety. Chicken Riojana comes in a big metal crock, the meat succulent and tender in its thickened red-wine sauce. It is served with heaps of mildly seasoned yellow rice. The simple chicken with hot garlic sauce will assure a wide berth on the bus ride home. Shrimp with green sauce (olive oil, parsley, garlic, and onions) arrives in the same well-used container, the sauce not as robust as I would like, but that didn't stop my table companions from polishing the metal crock with garlic bread.

The three versions of paella—one with just seafood; another with seafood, sausage, and chicken; the third with lobster added—vary in quality depending on when you order them. In my experience, the rice is moister earlier in the evening, and the ingredients fresher tasting.

Late at night, the chicken can be tired and dry. More consistently satisfying is the mariscada, or mixed shellfish with green sauce, a garlic-blasted assembly of mussels, clams, shrimp, and scallops. A good steamed lobster in the same herby green sauce is one of the most expensive items on the menu at $20.25. Pounded, breaded veal with almond sauce is a bit sweet for my taste; barbecued pork comes with the same sauce.

Predictably, flan (caramel custard) is the dessert of choice here, and it is one of the best renditions in New York—firm and rich yet not too eggy, glazed with caramel sauce. Cheesecake, from Miss Grimble, has a nice tart edge, too. Vanilla custard comes in a distant third.

SHUN LEE

★

43 West 65th Street, 595-8895.

Atmosphere: Dramatic black-and-white design scheme; comfortable banquettes, and acceptable noise level.

Service: Congenial, friendly, and helpful.

Price range: Moderate.

Credit cards: All major cards.

Hours: Noon to midnight, daily.

Reservations: Required for dinner, must be made the preceding day.

Wheelchair accessibility: Two small steps lead into the dining room; restrooms on main level.

Shun Lee is a perplexing place. One day you go there and have an inspired Chinese meal, the next time it is lackluster at best. To be sure, it is one of the more stylish and comfortable uptown Chinese restaurants, and service is top-notch. By ordering selectively you can assemble some engaging meals; random experimentation, however, can be risky business.

Patrons enter a dark tunnel-like corridor where playful papier-mâché monkeys frolic overhead. The open main room, with a sunken center, is also done in haunting black. Encircling it on a high ledge are red-eyed, tongue-thrashing dragons made of netted papier-mâché.

To start off on a high note, order the Peking pan-fried dumplings, which are nicely seared outside and filled with well-seasoned pork; Shanghai-style steamed dumplings, however, are doughy and bland. Crispy shrimp balls, resilient and golden-fried, are fresh and tasty when smudged with sweet sauce or hot mustard.

Among the cold appetizers, hacked chicken, a simple standard dish that is usually reliable in the humblest of Chinese restaurants, is humdrum here—strips of chicken breast in a lackluster sesame sauce devoid of the essential hot pepper. Far better are the moist thin slices of duck accompanied by a saucer of Oriental-style nitroglycerin that goes by the generic name "spicy Hunan sauce." A moistened chopstick of this is all you need, or dare. I am not a fan of kidneys in general, except at Shun Lee, where they are extraordinarily subtle and delicious. Sliced into little florets, the pale pink meat is swabbed in a zesty sauce combining ginger, hot peppers, and soy.

The entrée list is sizable and ecumenical, offering dishes from most of the regional Chinese cuisines. A sampling of more than twenty entrées and side dishes reveals that while several house specialties excel, a substantial number of dishes are just plain boring, slathered with nondescript vegetable sauces.

Among the happy exceptions are firm fresh-water prawns sautéed with rice wine, ginger, scallions, and oyster sauce, and savory red-cooked duck, in which the meat is marinated in soy sauce and sugar, then briefly fried to crisp the skin. The duck is presented over a bed of sautéed spinach. Another delicious dish is humble pig's knuckles, which are stewed in soy sauce and red wine for hours until the meat and gelatin fairly melt off the bone.

Given these successes, how can the kitchen botch something as straightforward as orange beef? The rendition here is an indigestible heap of meat cubes in a starchy and tasteless sauce. If you want citrus flavor, get instead the light and clean lemon chicken brightened with minced lemon rind. "Sizzling" scallops, coated with lotus flour and panfried, fizzles; the mushroom-loaded sauce lacks spark. Shun Lee's version of Peking duck, prepared at tableside with much fanfare, is flavorful although rather inelegant— the waiter stuffs the pancakes to capacity with awkwardly large chunks of meat.

It is unusual to find bread offered in lieu of rice at a Chinese restaurant. Of the three sampled, though, only sesame-sprinkled fried bread was notable; the others were starchy and bland.

Recommended side dishes include bright sesame noodles, pan-fried Singapore-style noodles with curry, vibrant Sichuan-style eggplant and fresh broccoli in garlic sauce. Desserts for the most part are satisfying if unexciting. Coconut custard with melba sauce, an occasional special, and sweet glutinous rice pudding are enjoyable, as is fresh fruit.

SIAM INN

★

916 Eighth Avenue, between 54th and 55th streets, 489-5237.

Atmosphere: Informal, dimly lit dining room with Thai artwork on the walls.

Service: Friendly and competent.

Price range: Moderate.

Credit cards: American Express and Diners Club.

Hours: Lunch, noon to 3 P.M., Monday through Friday; dinner, 5 to 11:30 P.M., Monday through Saturday, 5 to 11 P.M., Sunday.

Reservations: Suggested for pretheater.

Wheelchair accessibility: All facilities on one level.

❧ Siam Inn, a dimly lit, pleasantly appointed restaurant, is fairly typical of the genre of Thai restaurants in town, perhaps a notch better than average. It turns out several bright dishes that reflect the exotic allure of this cuisine.

Start with an appetizer called curry puffs, inflated crescents of light pastry stuffed with a sweetish combination of curried ground chicken, potatoes, and onions. It comes with a vinegar-based cucumber sauce that foils the sweetness nicely. Another good preliminary is spicy fish cakes made with ground kingfish, which are crusty and browned outside yet moist within.

The best entrée is the steamed seafood combination. It comes to the table enclosed in aluminum foil that is molded into the shape of a swan. Inside are mussels, shrimp, squid, cubes of salmon, fermented black beans, and ginger in a pool of aromatic fish broth enlivened with fresh lemon. You could round out this meal with a platter of Bangkok duck—the meat is rich and succulent, the skin crisp, and the mildly sweet sauce tinged with tamarind and curry. So much for the menu's A-team; now for a tour of the dugout.

If the kitchen has one overriding flaw that debases some otherwise good preparations, it is a relentless sweet tooth. The cold spring-roll appetizer, for instance, is a combination of bean sprouts, Thai sausage, bean curd, and minced vegetables wrapped in rice paper—but a lollipop-sweet sauce overwhelms it. Thai salads—lettuce, cucumber, bean sprouts, and bean cake—suffer the same fate under a shower of sweet coconut-milk and peanut dressing.

Even the most famous Thai dish of all, pla lad prig, is marred by a sucrose attack. The deep-fried red snapper set over a bed of spinach is mired in a thick sauce that is both aggressively sweet and aggressively hot at the same time—the ensuing battle on the palate leaves the fish all but lost. Another familiar preparation, beef saté, was disappointing. The strips of meat had been overmarinated before grilling, leaving them unpleasantly mealy. You would be better off with the shrimp in mild curry sauce cut with coconut milk and red peppers.

Two satisfying entrées are the broiled salmon with a garlic-and-scallion sauce and frogs' legs in a straightforward garlic sauce. At lunch the sautéed shrimp in garlic sauce was drenched in oil. The best side dish is pad thai, a tasty mélange of minced shrimps, egg, dried bean cake, and bean sprouts.

Probably the most suitable beverage with this assertive cuisine is beer; wine fanciers will find a tiny but relatively decent selection. The staff at Siam Inn is accommodating and efficient in a laconic sort of way, and the setting is usually tranquil enough for easy conversation. Don't bother with the commercial-tasting desserts—carrot cake, assorted pies, and the like. Siam Inn, which earned two stars in 1981, has slipped a notch to one-star status.

THE SIGN OF THE DOVE

★ ★ ★

1110 Third Avenue, at 65th Street, 861-8080.

Atmosphere: Romantic grand grotto effect with brick arches, soft lighting, and generously spaced tables.

Service: Staff polite and professional, but exceedingly long delays occur between courses.

Price range: Expensive.

Credit cards: All major cards.

Hours: Brunch, 11:30 A.M. to 3 P.M., Sunday; lunch, noon to 2:30 P.M., Tuesday through Saturday; dinner, 5:30 to 10 P.M., Monday through Saturday, 6 to 10 P.M., Sunday; caviar menu, 10 P.M. to midnight, daily.

Reservations: Recommended.

Wheelchair accessibility: A separate ground-floor entrance on 65th Street accommodates the handicapped; restrooms, however, are up five steps.

🍂 Once just a frilly restaurant for out-of-towners, The Sign of the Dove has seen a dramatic turnaround under the chef, Andrew D'Amico. Combined with an elegant and romantic setting, it is now a favorite among discriminating New Yorkers.

A piano bar near the entrance, done in brick and marble and rose-tinted wood, is a soothing place to pass the time if your companion is fashionably late. The main dining rooms, separated by brick arches with wrought-iron fili gree, are enchanting with eruptions of spring flowers, skylights, soft indirect lighting, and well-separated tables.

Virtually every appetizer sampled can be recommended. Aside from the superb oyster casserole, another superior dish is the gossamer oversize ravioli stuffed with mellow slices of duck confit and shiitake mushrooms flanked by a lusty fricassee of wild mushrooms; another is roasted sections of tender quail on a cushion of sautéed spinach with artichoke hearts, chanterelle mushrooms, and a poached quail egg.

In a beguiling setting such as this, I am usually content to linger between courses, but exasperating delays here could try the patience of even the most starry-eyed paramours. This affords one ample time, perhaps too much, to investigate the superior and affordably priced wine list.

Something for every taste can be found among the entrées. Winning seafood dishes include a deftly grilled salmon fillet over a zesty ragout of winter greens, and goujons (finger-size strips) of impeccable red snapper and bass that form spokes around a core of rosemary-flecked pasta, all ringed by a subtle zinfandel-wine sauce bound with veal stock. Mr. D'Amico's twist on the garlicky Provençale seafood stew called bourride, however, lacks the gutsy rusticity of the original. Scallops, prawns, and medallions of lobster ride a tide of ultra-light chervil-and-tomato sauce thickened with a timid aïoli.

Meat and game preparations are more straightforward. Sections of roast baby pheasant, golden and succulent, are ineffably good over braised lentils sweetened with caramelized onions; another stellar choice is medallions of fork-tender veal matched with wild mushrooms and a helium-light garlic custard. It takes pluck to serve boiled beef in such a luxury restaurant, yet a ruddy chunk of tenderloin achieves aristocratic stature in the company of firm-braised carrots, onions, artichokes, snow peas, and leeks, especially when dabbed with some horseradish-cream sauce. The broth is rather bland, but a pinch of the coarse salt that comes on the side does the trick.

An after-dinner cheese plate deserves plaudits for its all-American emphasis, but, truth be told, the domestic Brie is a pale cousin to its French counterparts. The sweets are not quite up to the standard of the rest of the menu: a rich layered bittersweet (more sweet than bitter, really) terrine in a lovely orange-cream sauce, buttery apple and pear tarts, exceedingly sweet raspberry mousse cake, and terrific

360

homemade ice creams—prune Armagnac, vanilla, and toasted almond.

SISTINA

★ ★

1555 Second Avenue, between 80th and 81st streets, 861-7660, 861-7661.

Atmosphere: Spare, bright, cheerful

Service: Patient and attentive when waiters aren't overburdened by crowds.

Price range: Moderately expensive.

Credit cards: American Express.

Hours: Lunch, noon to 2:30 P.M., Monday through Saturday; dinner, 5 P.M. to midnight, daily.

Reservations: Necessary.

Wheelchair accessibility: Two steps up at entrance; restrooms downstairs.

🍷 Sistina is a smart and contemporary Sicilian-owned restaurant that draws an insouciant gang of regulars who revel in its unpretentious charm and generally pleasing fare.

The rectangular dining room is trim and cheerful—unstained oak walls, bent-cane chairs, rows of tables with starched white napery. Trim Italian waiters make everything sound irresistible as they describe the food with finger-kissing gesticulations.

Among the better starters are the two types of crostini. The crostini supremi features two thick slices of Italian bread coated with intense olive oil and layered with roasted peppers, mozzarella cheese and anchovies; the polenta crostini is made by topping crisp slabs of cornmeal toast with white beans in tomato sauce, fresh parsley, and Parmesan cheese.

Delizia di mare, or seafood salad, is sparkling: a briny assortment of squid, octopus, shrimp, black olives, and tomato in a mild oregano-scented vinaigrette. One exasperating feature of this restaurant is the untranslated Italian menu. Some of the dishes' esoteric names leave even Italians scratching their heads: pollo Vesuviano (exploding chicken?), filetti di sogliola gran successo, and so on. As a result, waiters spend all evening lunging from one perplexed table to the next.

One item that doesn't need translation is fresh white truffles, served in the fall, which a waiter waved under our noses, making his easiest sale of the night. They are shaved over tonnarelli (thin spaghetti) with a light cream sauce. Nearly all the pastas are superior, including the penne ai sette re, tubular noodles swathed in fresh tomato, basil, argula, and garlic; the same noodles all'amatriciana, a lusty sauce made with tomato, garlic, basil, and chunks of smoky pancetta bacon; and lustrous, fresh linguine ai frutti di mare overflowing with shrimp, squid, scallops, mussels, and clams.

When they have fresh giant Spanish shrimp, ask for them grilled and with lemon wedges. The grilled bay scallops, on the other hand, tasted poached and were mired in a watery, tasteless sauce. Better are the crisp and golden fried calamari and the striped bass cooked in parchment paper. By far the best side dish is deep-fried zucchini sliced into threads so thin they crackle and break when you touch them.

Top-quality veal is served here, and among the better preparations are costoletta Val d'Aosta, a thick, tender chop stuffed with prosciutto, mozzarella, and mushrooms that is roasted and served with a white-wine sauce, and veal scaloppine sorpresa, breaded medallions sautéed with artichoke hearts and fresh peas, lemon, and wine. The sauce has a stimulating citric edge.

Desserts are satisfying if unexciting—crème caramel, ice cream, chocolate mousse cake. Strawberries with winy zabaglione are better. The most intriguing dessert, however, is fresh raspberries with a dousing of balsamic vinegar. The unlikely combination, both sweet and tart, is absolutely ethereal.

SMITH & WOLLENSKY

Satisfactory

201 East 49th Street, 753-1530.

Atmosphere: Bustling, masculine, and loud.

Service: Steakhouse hit-and-run.

Price range: Expensive.

Credit cards: All major cards.

Hours: Lunch and dinner, noon to midnight, Monday through Friday, 5 P.M. to midnight, Saturday and Sunday.

Reservations: Suggested.

Wheelchair accessibility: All facilities on one level.

❧ Just getting in the door at Smith & Wollensky, one of Manhattan's most fervid steakhouses, can be like trying to run a goal-line quarterback sneak against the Chicago Bears. And once you hit pay dirt, chances are you will be dispatched for a short time to the bar, where backslapping businessmen revel in the kind of uninhibited camaraderie usually seen in locker rooms and restaurants that serve Brobdingnagian slabs of meat. And yes, an arm-wrestling match did transpire at a corner table one evening.

As for the food, it's about what one would expect at a sprawling barn that serves about seven hundred meals a day—a few good broiled steaks and chops escorted by a host of wham-bam premade appetizers and side dishes ranging from better than average to insipid. The wine list, however, has been upgraded vastly in recent years, and it now boasts one of the finest collections of classic (and expensive) older vintages from France and California.

Smith & Wollensky has a masculine brass-and-dark-wood steakhouse atmosphere. The two enormous dining rooms, one upstairs, have their own kitchens. Tan-jacketed waiters lunge about auctioning food at each table ("Who gets the sirloin!") and somehow manage to keep a fairly good pace feeding so many people.

Before running down the menu, I will suggest some combinations that embrace the best of the kitchen's efforts. Start with the house special, a hammy pea soup, or the fresh and tasty split lobster. For the main course, go with either lamb chops, fist-size monsters broiled rare as ordered and nicely encrusted, or the imposing slab of first-rate prime ribs in their own lustrous juices. Black-seared and buttery hash browns and crackling fried zucchini sticks are far superior to the leaden and undercooked steak fries; sautéed spinach is fresh and nicely seasoned, too. For dessert, pecan-walnut pie, moderately sweet and fresh, is a winner; so, too, is the excellent creamy cheesecake.

Now back to earth. Most of the remaining appetizers barely rise above tavern fare: thick and old-tasting asparagus, utterly bland and overpriced stone crabs, and tasteless lump crabmeat salad.

The remaining meat entrées can be disappointing, especially the monstrous and bland filet mignon and the chewy, unremarkable New York sirloin. A better choice is the steak au poivre, in which an oversize fillet is rescued by a zippy sauce. The restaurant's macho image is best reflected in the lobster selection, which begins with four-pounders and goes up. We managed to find an aberrant runt weighing in at 3½ pounds. It was perfectly cooked, sweet, and filled with bright red roe. The only other seafood sampled, tuna steak, was cooked to the texture of the canned variety.

An unconventional but satisfying apple brown Betty, doused with cream at the table, is recommended. Skip the supermarket-quality chocolate mousse cake.

At big-deal expensive steakhouses such as Smith & Wollensky, I expect to find consistently good steaks, potatoes, and ungussied vegetables. The sheer size of this frenetic feeding institution makes that a fifty-fifty gamble at best.

SOFI

★ ★

102 Fifth Avenue, near 15th Street, 463-8888.

Atmosphere: Soaring loft space warmed by paintings, rugs, and soft light.

Service: Sincere and efficient.

Price range: Moderately expensive.

Credit cards: All major cards.

Hours: Lunch, noon to 2:30 P.M., Monday through Friday; dinner, 6 to 11 P.M., Monday through Saturday.

Reservations: Suggested.

Wheelchair accessibility: All facilities on one level.

🍴 Sofi was opened in early 1987 by Richard Lavin, who also owns Lavin's restaurant on West 39th Street. His new venture occupies a soaring loft space that has been transformed into a warm and graceful spot. The food is just as harmonious.

Just inside the entrance is a homey little alcove of couches and upholstered chairs where you can sip an aperitif and monitor the human tide floating down the avenue. Overhead is an exuberant oversize painting of fruits and vegetables, a visual harbinger of things to come. As many as twenty wines are offered by the glass from the handsome vintage bar. Speaking of wines, the list of bottles is imaginatively assembled to match the food and remarkably inexpensive.

The long, cavernous dining room, with a rim of tables in a second-story loft, has stout columns painted to resemble marble, pretty little sconces that shoot light up along the mottled burnt-sienna walls, brightly woven rugs, and exquisitely appointed tables.

The cross-cultural menu, orchestrated by Dennis Mac-Neil, a Lavin's alumnus who put in time with Alain Senderens in Paris, is sunny and salubrious, with scant cream and butter in evidence. Aggressively seasoned stocks and vegetable purées are the crossbeams of Mr. MacNeil's creations.

Mr. Lavin has always been popular among herbivores, and his gardener's salad shows why: a sparkling composition of arugula, chicory, and other greens is the nesting for marinated mushrooms, lumps of eggplant caviar, and terrific thin curls of deep-fried artichoke hearts. Addictive threads of deep-fried leeks and deep-fried zucchini add extra texture.

Pastas can be ordered in half portions for starters. The best is earthy spinach linguine in a rustic all'amatriciana sauce. Rotelle primavera tossed with cubes of fresh salmon is one of those cleaning-out-the-refrigerator creations that are too cluttered to form a coherent whole.

While my four visits to Sofi were unannounced, I am known to Mr. Lavin and his staff, so naturally, service was at its earnest best. In such cases, I try to get around this by asking friends who have been there how they were treated, and the reports were unanimously positive, notwithstanding occasional waits for reserved tables.

Main courses follow the same breezy high road. Dover sole is grilled to a turn and enhanced with a light red-wine sauce touched with salmon fumé. It comes with haricots verts, pearl onions, and undercooked baby carrots. Plump, butter-browned sea scallops are given an unusual twist, cushioned by "Denver crêpes," a thin mosaic of diced ham and sweet peppers along with spinach and julienne of leeks. Monkfish larded with prosciutto was undercooked, even for this sushiphile age, while pearly lobster meat adrift in a sharp-toned ginger sauce sweetened with shallots and brightly colored with julienne of vegetables is a delight.

Tender scallops of veal get a rousing boost from pungent pecorino cheese, and slices of rosy lamb in a lusty stock sauce ring a mellow eggplant-tomato-zucchini timbale.

The clean, pure food at Sofi's never leaves you bloated, so dessert is your chance to make up for all that good behavior. Start with my nominee to the ice-cream hall of fame, chunky homemade hazelnut praline, with chocolate sauce for good measure. Parchment-thin tuiles sandwiching poached pineapple and whipped cream are difficult to eat gracefully, but delicious; and the granités of tangerine, lemon-lime, and strawberry are as refreshing as spray from a burst fire hydrant on an August afternoon. The hazelnut torte is so intensely nutty—too much for me—that it should carry a warning.

SPARKS STEAKHOUSE

★ ★

210 East 46th Street, 687-4855.

Atmosphere: Bustling and masculine steakhouse ambiance in large, wood-lined dining rooms.

Service: Efficient in a brisk manner.

Price range: Expensive.

Credit cards: All major cards.

Hours: Lunch, noon to 3 P.M., Monday through Friday; dinner, 5 to 11 P.M., Monday through Thursday, 5 to 11:30 P.M., Friday and Saturday.

Reservations: Required.

Wheelchair accessibility: All facilities on one level.

❧ Sparks is a paragon of that much imitated institution known as the New York steakhouse.

It sports dark burnished woodwork that glows under amber lighting, starched white tables that are well separated, and a bonhomous bar where whiskey still appears to edge out white wine and Perrier. Moreover, the rosy, dry-aged steaks with charred, salt-edged crusts are among the best in town.

Sparks is not the kind of place where you go for a romantic evening or for people-watching. A sizable percentage of the nightly crowd consists of ex-college-linebackers-turned-pin-striped-businessmen who congregate at large tables to tackle thick steaks and swap tall tales. Service is efficient in a brisk sort of way. The place spins at 78 rpm in order to keep up with the huge volume, and consequently dishes sometimes appear a bit too quickly for comfort. If you are in a leisurely mood, make it known.

Typical steakhouse appetizers are offered, and on the whole they are superior to those in similar establishments. The lump-crabmeat-and-scallop starter is fresh-tasting, buttery, and not overcooked (the scallops, however, look and taste like ocean calicos, not bay scallops as described on the menu). The combination of sautéed shrimp and breaded baked clams is also well prepared. Icy bluepoint oysters on the half shell and oceanic little cherrystones are first-rate.

The menu carries an adequate selection of fish. However, going to Sparks for grilled tuna is like spending a winter weekend in Aspen playing tennis. My favorite steak is the unadorned prime sirloin—broiled exactly to order, incredibly tender, and intensely beefy. Close runner-ups are the thick and buttery rib lamb chops and the juicy charred veal chop. Filet mignon, which so often is textureless and bland, is anything but that here—juicy, firm yet tender. Side dishes include hash brown potatoes—golden and moist once, a bit dry another time—baked potatoes (same inconsistency), and nicely cooked spinach and broccoli.

Only when the kitchen tries to get a little fancy with beef does it get into trouble, so in general avoid sauces.

Of the seafood entrées sampled, swordfish steak, tuna steak, and rainbow trout usually cannot be faulted. Enormous lobsters, split and broiled, are available in three sizes: small, medium, and something resembling a Japanese subcompact. Our nearly 3½-pounder was fresh and well cooked, with lots of briny roe. I just wish waiters would reveal prices as they describe the selections—in this case $45.

The Sparks wine list is legendary. I find it curious, though, for a restaurant that takes such pride in the depth of its cellar to lack a sommelier who could help guide customers through it. For dessert the highlights are a good creamy cheesecake and a baseball-size chocolate-covered tartufo with whipped cream.

Sparks is a well-focused restaurant that knows exactly what its clientele wants and how to provide it with impressive consistency. For first-rate steak, it is my prime choice.

SUKHOTHAI

★

149 Second Avenue, at 10th Street, 460-5557.

Atmosphere: Pub atmosphere with brick walls, brass rails, long bar, and high ceiling. Noise level moderate.

Service: Slow and confused when the restaurant is more than half full.

Price range: Inexpensive.

Credit cards: American Express, MasterCard, and Visa.

Hours: Dinner, 5 to 11 P.M., Sunday through Thursday, 5 P.M. to midnight, Friday and Saturday.

Reservations: Suggested on weekdays, required on weekends.

Wheelchair accessibility: Flight of stairs up to entrance.

❧ Sukhothai is on the second story of an aging building in a former English-style bar and grill. The Thai family that took over did not try to Orientalize it. Instead, they left intact its long wooden bar, brick walls, brass railings, and garish multicolored glass ceiling panel. The air-conditioning system leaves much to be desired at times, so dress lightly on warm days.

Most of the wooden tables are a bit wobbly—and so is the service. The small staff, besides having difficulties with English, becomes easily overtaxed.

These inconveniences aside, there are several good reasons to visit Sukhothai. It offers some zesty hot and spicy dishes as well as a few nicely fried tidbits at budget prices. Foremost among them is the appetizer of deep-fried minced shrimp with Thai spices wrapped in bean curd. The cooks are deft at frying, and these flavorful little dough pockets are light, mildly seasoned, and strong with the flavor of shrimp. They come with an invigorating sweet-and-sour sauce. Exotic and equally tasty starters are the kingfish dumplings perfumed with curry. They are served with sliced cucumbers soaked in a tart fermented fish sauce that has just a hint of sweetness. The kingfish has a chewy texture and a flavor not unlike pork.

Both of the satés—char-broiled morsels of marinated chicken or beef swabbed with peanut sauce—are moist and delicious. Another pleasing offering is a deep bowl of plump mussels steamed in peppery broth flavored with scallions, green peppers, bay leaf, lemon, and lime. The fried bean cakes are greaseless and crisp but devoid of flavor, and Thai salad is a lackluster mound of pale greens and sprouts.

Thai food embraces diverse taste sensations—hot, spicy, citric, sweet, herbaceous—so when you order, remember to choose dishes that span the flavor range to get the full effect. This is easier said than done at Sukhothai because some of the asterisks printed on the menu, which supposedly indicate dishes that are hot and spicy, seem to be tossed around at random.

Soups are accurately labeled, and some are exceptional.

368

The hot-and-sour shrimp soup, redolent of fragrant lemon-grass, combines fish sauce with Oriental mushrooms, chili, and lime to achieve just the right balance between hot and sour, pushing you right to the threshold of peppery pain, then backing off and soothing the palate with fresh lime. Another multidimensional taste sensation is set off by the exotic chicken soup that combines coconut milk, lime juice, chili paste, and loads of fresh coriander. The coriander imparted a dry edge that foiled the sweet coconut.

The entrée list looks impressively large at first, but upon closer inspection one realizes that many of the preparations are the same, only the main ingredient is different. Seafood seems to be the best bet. Aside from the aforementioned grilled shrimp, deep-fried whole sea bass under a blizzard of garlic is a good rendition of this standard Thai dish. Another good selection is the seafood combination with Thai spices. The food came out in an inflated foil bag the size of a football. When pierced, it releases a cloud of saline steam. When the air clears, it reveals the familiar Thai cast of characters—shrimp, squid, mussels, and scallions tossed with rice noodles and stoked with whole red chili pods. The combination is fresh, evenly cooked, and resting in a pool of broth that is dotted with explosive mines of hot chili pods. Navigate around them at all cost. While Sukhothai has limited ambitions, it does enough things well to give you a taste of Thailand's intriguing cuisine at budget prices.

TANDOOR

★

40 East 49th Street, 752-3334.

Atmosphere: Roomy and comfortable with dim lighting and low noise level.

Service: Indifferent and slow.

Price range: Moderate.

Credit cards: All major cards.

Hours: Lunch, noon to 3 P.M., daily; dinner, 5:30 to 11 P.M., daily.

Reservations: Recommended.

Wheelchair accessibility: Main dining room and restrooms on one level.

❧ Delicious Indian breads, good tandoor-roasted special-ties, and authentically hot and spicy stews are what you get at Tandoor, the spacious, low-key midtown restaurant.

The main dining room is accommodating with its tufted red banquettes, ornate wall moldings, and Indian paint-ings. Unfortunately, the phlegmatic waiters do not contrib-ute to a welcoming atmosphere—they tend to be distant and slow—but if you are willing to endure that inconve-nience, there is some pleasing food to be had.

As the restaurant's name implies, the ancient art of bak-ing foods in the clay tandoor oven is a specialty. Tandoori chicken, in which the meat is marinated in yogurt and spices and tinted bright orange with a natural dye, is right on target—succulent, complexly seasoned, and faintly smoky. A similar dish in which the chicken is boned before baking, called tikka, is the best of all, buttery tender and suffused with complex spices.

I rarely like fish cooked in the super-hot tandoor oven because it tends to dry out quickly, but the chefs here could teach their counterparts at other restaurants a thing or two. Both the tandoori fish tikka, made with tilefish, and the tandoori shrimp are delicious—spiced just enough to add a sharp edge without masking their delicate flavors.

To serious Indian food enthusiasts, vindaloo, the smol-dering dish from Goa on the southwestern Indian coast, is the real test of a chef's mettle. Both the lamb and the fish vindaloos at Tandoor are among the better ones in town. The slow-burning tomato-based sauce, kindled with hot peppers, ginger, and garlic, is as warming as a potbellied stove in January.

I suggest you bypass most of the appetizers and go right to the entrées. Traditional starters such as chicken chaat, for example—cold slices of tender white meat in a mint sauce—had an old and acrid flavor; on another occasion the alu chaat, a coriander-spiced potato salad with the same sauce, was much fresher. Mulligatawny soup is good, a soothing and subtle blend of chicken stock, lentils, com-plex spices, and cream. It is especially good with any of the wonderful homemade breads: puffed and charred tandoor-baked nan; exquisite onion kulcha, a nan stuffed with sweet spiced onions and coriander; earthy whole-wheat chapati; and the buttery multilayered paratha. The daily lunch buffet is a bargain at $10.95.

In addition to the handful of dessert items on the menu, there is a small pastry cart carrying lovely sweet honey buns soaked in syrup called gulab jamun, as well as ras malai, the sweetened cheese dumpling flavored with rosewater and nuts (which was dry), and a bland coconut cake. The standouts, however, are the two fresh and intensely flavored ice creams—mango and fig.

TATANY

★　★

388 Third Avenue, near 28th Street, 686-1871.

Atmosphere: Trim and informal restaurant with a pleasant sushi bar and two dining rooms.

Service: Relatively fast-paced and efficient despite the crowds.

Price range: Moderately expensive.

Credit cards: All major cards.

Hours: Lunch, noon to 2:30 P.M., Monday through Friday; dinner, 5:30 to 10:30 P.M., Monday through Thursday, 5:30 to 11:30 P.M., Friday, 5:30 to 11:30 P.M., Saturday, 5:30 to 10:30 P.M., Sunday.

Reservations: Not accepted.

Wheelchair accessibility: One step at entrance; all facilities on one level.

🐟 Tatany is a relentlessly popular Japanese restaurant on Third Avenue near 28th Street—and for good reason. The fish is among the freshest around. Every evening a legion of seafood aficionados invades this animated, moderate-size restaurant with its simply appointed sushi bar and dining area in front and a more densely populated room in back.

Waiters are impressively vigilant about removing used dishes and glasses even at the busiest times. Overflow customers pass the time with warm sake or cold Kirin at a tiny bar near the entrance. An unflappable host in a Tatany T-shirt does his best to direct the flow smoothly. Reservations are not accepted, and you may wait up to forty minutes for a table at peak hours. For the most part, though, the wait is worth it.

For instance, five Japanese pasta dishes are offered. My favorite, called shrimp and wakame, combines fettuccine-shaped noodles, nuggets of shrimp, and resilient seaweed in a deliciously concentrated fish broth. The portion is large enough for four diners. Another pasta, called yaki-udon, is not so successful. Its noodles are mired in a viscous and excessively sweet sauce holding mixed vegetables and beef. Yosenabe, described on the menu as a Japanese bouillabaisse, is an evocative creation based on a flavorful and crystalline fish broth embellished with fresh clams, chicken, shrimp, assorted fillets of fish, and crinkly saline seaweed.

Purists contend that the touchstone of a Japanese restaurant is its raw fish. The trio of seafood samurai behind this sushi bar turns out an exemplary array of sashimi, sushi, and assorted maki (seaweed rolls). The mixed sushi platter includes tuna, salmon, fluke, shrimp, and maki, usually made with tuna. With the exception of one sinewy piece of salmon, the rest of the fish sampled was uncompromisingly firm and fresh. Yellowtail flounder in particular was astoundingly pristine and buttery. An important element sometimes overlooked in sushi bars is the rice, which is critical. At Tatany, it is just right, moderately sticky and neither too sweet nor too vinegary.

An exceptional maki worth trying is the toasted salmon skin, which is brittle and oceanic, packed in rice with minced green onions and rolled in a lightly toasted seaweed sheet, all crowned with a sprinkling of tiny red lumpfish caviar. It makes an arresting composition of texture and flavor. Frying is done well, too, as evidenced in the puffed and golden tempura of shrimp with vegetables, fried eggplant with sweet miso paste, and golden cubes of bean curd. A staple in New York Japanese restaurants, negimaki, the scallion-stuffed beef rolls, is relatively inelegant and bland.

The ginger-flecked ice cream is a sprightly palate cleanser; vanilla with red-bean sauce is sweeter but equally good. A special one evening was tempura ice cream, which is an intriguing dish, essentially a ball of vanilla ice cream coated in tempura batter and quickly deep-fried to the point at which the crust becomes hot and crisp yet the ice cream remains intact.

TAVERN ON THE GREEN

★

Central Park West at 67th Street, 873-3200.

Atmosphere: Festive, lavish setting featuring two main dining rooms with views of illuminated trees and outdoor patios.

Service: Generally professional, if brisk and businesslike.

Price range: Moderately expensive.

Credit cards: All major cards.

Hours: Brunch, 10 A.M. to 3 P.M., Saturday and Sunday; lunch, 11:30 A.M. to 3:30 P.M., Monday through Friday; pretheater dinner, 5:30 to 6:15 P.M., Monday through Friday; dinner, 5:30 P.M. to midnight, Monday through Friday, 5 P.M. to midnight, Saturday, 5:30 P.M. to midnight, Sunday.

Reservations: Necessary.

Wheelchair accessibility: All facilities on one level.

❧ The sheer size of the place, which has five hundred seats and churns out fifteen hundred meals a day, reflects the formidable scale and feverish pace of New York. The glass-enclosed, often loud Crystal Room is a circus of lavish chandeliers, balloon clusters (given to birthday parties), and snugly arranged tables. The smaller Chestnut Room is more subdued. A leafy outdoor courtyard is a delight in the warm months.

The food, which had been mostly forgettable tourist fare, had markedly improved under Georges Masraff, former chef and owner of Quai des Ormes, a stylish little establishment along the Seine River in Paris. Leaving a relatively small, highly personal restaurant to tackle Tavern on the Green must be like swapping a Boston whaler for the *Queen Elizabeth 2.* He has risen to the challenge, though.

The new chef has trimmed the menu and added a contemporary French touch. Typical of his successes is the appetizer of buttery sautéed sea scallops presented over faintly tart Chinese cabbage in a vinegar-edged sauce, a clever contrast of textures and flavors. Seafood sausage (made with fish and shellfish) was fresh and delicious, too, along with basil-perfumed potato salad. Crab cakes enriched with chunks of fresh lobster were moist and well seasoned, and lobster bisque was a pure oceanic winner.

Certain pitfalls can be expected in a restaurant of this size. For instance, pheasant terrine anchored with foie gras was dry and served too cold. Tuna carpaccio was fresh and pretty with its garnish of scallions, red onions, and lime, but it needed a dressing. And the saffron-tinted shrimp risotto was undercooked.

Don't expect to get too chummy with the service staff, for the workload here requires a hit-and-run strategy; for the most part, though, the waiters and waitresses are professional and accommodating. The formerly pretentious and haphazard wine list was significantly improved in 1988, and now good selections can be found in all price ranges, as well as by-the-glass offerings.

Mr. Masraff has added some alluring seafood entrées to the new menu. Among my favorites is the perfectly sautéed salmon steak in a white peppercorn-stoked sauce, along with taglierini cooked with fresh peas and bacon in a rich red-wine sauce. Ginger-perfumed shrimp in a light, clean shellfish sauce with scallions, carrots, and artichokes was a felicitous combination, as was a simple sautéed sea bass accompanied by translucent slices of barely cooked fresh fennel and a peppy black-bean-and-sweet-pepper relish. Only tuna steak one evening was dry from overcooking. Other good choices are the thick, juicy veal chop served with braised endive and roasted potatoes set in a lovely veal broth, rack of lamb bolstered with garlic, and tender venison in a concentrated red-wine sauce freckled with piquant pink peppercorns and truffles. Sweetbreads were flaccid from insufficient draining before cooking. In a shortcut version of cassoulet, tender cubes of lamb and confit of duck came in undercooked beans.

Desserts have always been exuberant here, and they still are. Crème brûlée, with a brittle sugar glaze, is exceptionally light; assertive hazelnut mousse is drizzled with warm chocolate and set in a pool of coffee sauce.

One bizarre-sounding dessert we ordered only for comic relief: called Scotch old-fashioned, it is described as a Chivas Regal frozen soufflé with Drambuie sauce, pineapple, oranges, and cherries—one could get a hangover just contemplating it. Amazingly, it was the hit of the evening. The Scotch added a complex and dry edge to the soufflé, while the sauce was only minimally sweet. In a way, that bibulous dessert could be a metaphor for Tavern on the Green—lighthearted, unpredictable, and just a wee bit zany.

TERRACE

★ ★

400 West 119th Street, corner of Morningside Drive, 666-9490.

Atmosphere: Romantic, low-lit dining rooms with panoramic views of Manhattan.

Service: Straightforward and professional.

Price range: Moderately expensive.

Credit cards: All major cards.

Hours: Lunch, noon to 2:30 P.M., Tuesday through Friday; dinner, 6 to 10 P.M., Tuesday through Saturday.

Reservations: Necessary.

Wheelchair accessibility: Several steps at entrance but ramp available (call in advance); all facilities on one level.

The Terrace has many enticements, foremost among them the sensational view from its glass-enclosed perch on the 14th floor of a Columbia University residence hall. Off to the northwest one sees the illuminated bracelet of the George Washington Bridge, and to the south, the brilliant spires of midtown Manhattan. The two spacious dining rooms are romantic in an old-world manner, with low lighting, tall candles, harp or piano music, and a solitary rose on each table.

As for the food, it continues to lean heavily on classic French preparations that are carried out with a light touch. Superior appetizers include the fresh and vivid poached oysters served on the half shell—the shells are lined with minced mushrooms and shallots, and the oysters are glazed with a champagne sauce. The house pork terrine is well seasoned and bolstered with just a touch of liver, while the sautéed foie gras with raspberry vinegar and truffles—something of a cliché these days—gets high marks for flavor and texture. A near miss was a crayfish terrine that, while bright and fresh, failed to convey the flavor or texture of those delicate little critters, and rather dull marinated raw salmon.

The tuxedoed captains know their jobs and perform them congenially and efficiently. The wine selection runs deep, especially through Bordeaux, and prices are more or less in line.

The entrées may not dazzle with bold juxtapositions of exotic ingredients, but that's not the intention here. The Terrace offers reliability over rakishness: a Mercedes versus a Ferrari. Florid and tender rack of lamb with fresh mint purée, sweetbreads in a port-and-truffle sauce, lobster cloaked in a Pernod beurre blanc, beef tenderloin in a tarragon-and-green-peppercorn sauce—all are straightforwardly pleasing.

Other winners are two specials: a deftly grilled red snapper accented with garlic and herbs, and blush-pink poached salmon ringed with scallop mousse and spinach. Two dishes that fail to deliver on their promises are flaccid veal with morels and sweet-onion mousse, and bland quail with shallots, ginger, and herbs.

It is only fitting that such a traditional restaurant will

roll out the old multitiered, silver dessert chariot. In this case, though, showmanship superseded logic, for several nicely made cream-based desserts—rum-spiked chocolate cake with mocha filling, and hazelnut meringue cake with strawberries and buttercream—got too warm sitting out all evening. The kitchen excels at puff pastries and tart crusts. Try the exceptional raspberry napoleon, orange-chantilly pie, and a bulbous caramelized apple tart (mislabeled tarte Tatin). And the crème brûlée here is one of the best in town—with a burnished glassy sugar lid over a silky custard.

TEXARKANA

Satisfactory

64 West 10th Street, 254-5800.

Atmosphere: Handsome Southwest ambiance, yet often crowded and noisy.

Service: Pleasant and functional, but don't expect fine touches.

Price range: Moderately expensive.

Credit cards: All major cards.

Hours: Dinner, 6 P.M. to midnight, Sunday through Thursday, until 2 A.M. Friday and Saturday.

Reservations: Recommended, especially on weekends.

Wheelchair accessibility: Several steps to dining area; men's room on same level, women's room upstairs.

🍤 The watered-down food at this Greenwich Village restaurant is even more disappointing against such a handsome and sophisticated backdrop. You enter an inviting handcrafted bar where urbane couples mingle in the early evening, and then you pass into the softly glowing dining room dominated by a brass-rimmed fireplace where suckling pig spins over white-hot coals. The crenulated walls mirror soft orange-yellow desert tones; tables in the middle of the room, however, are a bit too shadowy to read the menu. Most nights the corral is packed with a high-spirited, youthful crowd, so if you seek privacy, ask for a table in the overhead balcony.

The first hint that Texarkana's roots are shallow is the gumbo, which any Southwesterner worth his jalapeño should be able to make well. This lip-searing rendition has no depth; the heat is superficial, as if sprinkled in at the last minute rather than integrated into the ingredients. It's like a campfire made of newspapers—all flames and no embers. Cajun popcorn—deep-fried nuggets of batter-dipped crayfish tails—likewise had no spunk. The batter was tasteless and doughy. On the other hand, charred raw beef —well-marbled slices of crisp-seared tenderloin paired with a high-voltage green chili sauce—was a winner.

Other starters sound intriguing but turn out to be all hype, like the unpleasantly sugary barbecued pork and the utterly tasteless Southern-style pickled shrimp with an overrefrigerated horseradish sauce. Salads are nicely prepared, especially the cool mélange of jícama, that crunchy white-fleshed root, with Boston lettuce and a zippy Cajun-style dressing.

The list of main courses is supplemented nightly by about a dozen specials, many of which run out by 8:30. To sample the roast suckling pig, it is usually necessary to order it when you call for reservations—although I was never told this on three recent occasions. The smoky slabs of tender pork can be worth the effort, though, if they don't overcook it as they sometimes do. The meat comes under a burnished layer of pigskin that has succulent shreds of fatty meat clinging to the underside, and on the side is enough moist, peppery corn-bread dressing to feed a tugboat crew. Blackened sea trout has a tingling peppery coating that pleases, too. Get it with a side order of fried okra.

Other satisfying choices are the tender barbecued veal chop with green chili sauce, and pearly Gulf shrimp, quickly sautéed with lemon, lots of garlic, and scallions. The landscape gets rather desolate on the farther reaches of the menu. Étouffée, that traditional crayfish stew, tastes like tomato sauce spiked with Tabasco; leathery barbecued tenderloin must have been left on the campfire overnight, and duck breast is equally desiccated.

The service staff is good-natured under sometimes hectic conditions, but don't expect to have your wine poured during the meal or see used glasses and plates whisked away.

Several desserts may provide succor if the preceding courses leave you unsatisfied. Jeremy cake is an addicting cube of steamed chocolate under a cloud of whipped cream; lemon cheesecake is tart and moist, and chocolate-pecan pie is stellar.

TOMMY TANG'S

★　★

323 Greenwich Street, between Duane and Reade streets, 334-9190.

Atmosphere: Breezy and informal if occasionally overspirited with pop music.

Service: Pleasant and knowledgeable about the unusual food.

Price range: Moderate.

Credit cards: All major cards.

Hours: Lunch, 11:30 A.M. to 3 P.M., Monday through Friday; dinner, 6 P.M. to midnight, Monday through Saturday.

Reservations: Suggested.

Wheelchair accessibility: Two small steps at entrance; restrooms downstairs.

🦐 Along sun-streaked Melrose Avenue in Hollywood, that buoyant runway of West Coast with-it-ness, Tommy Tang has been nurturing the dressed-to-thrill set for six years with his pop renditions of Thai cuisine.

Mr. Tang, who has become a full-time celebrity and entrepreneur in recent years while leaving the cooking to his family and staff, brought his winsome production to New York in 1986, and it has turned out to be arguably the best Thai restaurant we have.

Tommy Tang's occupies a moderate-size Art Deco space near burgeoning Battery Park City. No brass icons or embroidered red-and-gold fabrics here. The only clue that this is not just another TriBeCa grill-and-grin yuppie playroom is black lacquered chopsticks on the tables. The breezy two-level room is done in eggshell-colored walls with color-splashed fabrics clinging haphazardly to the ceiling. Tables are well spaced, but the piped-in music at times shatters easy conversation.

As for the food, I would trek to TriBeCa in a flash if only for the terrific saté of chicken, an appetizer. The bite-size squiggles of meat are marinated overnight in coconut cream laced with curry, garlic, and coriander, then skewered, barbecued, and served with two zesty dips, one made with crushed peanuts, the other with cucumber. Curiously, this same technique leaves strips of beef exceedingly salty. The foldout menu, which lists sixty-seven items, not including desserts, is filled with invigorating and boldly seasoned dishes, some traditional, some innovative.

Another vibrant appetizer is the mee krob, which combines brittle sweet noodles with nubbins of shrimp, pork, and eggs garnished with bean sprouts, scallions, and coriander. The frail noodles literally melt in your mouth, leaving a sweet echo.

Two familiar starters are better than average: Thai toast, crispy little disks made with shrimp, pork, and mild spices, and crisp vegetable-filled egg rolls. A spicy chicken soup (tom kha kai) is wonderfully complex with nuances of lime, coconut, hot chili, and scallion. Least memorable are the bland fried wontons stuffed with chicken and vegetables. The one salad sampled, called yum yai, is a refreshing sweet-and-hot assembly of shrimp and chicken with greens in a lemon-based dressing.

The best of Tommy Tang's dishes are intended to ambush your taste buds at several twists in the road. For example, the spicy mint noodles with beef (they can also be ordered with chicken or pork) first assault the tip of the tongue with the freshness of mint and faint sweetness from shrimp; next comes a volley of sundry spices and textures on the palate, followed by the afterglow of heat. This triple whammy is plainly evident in the blackened chili fish. A fillet of red snapper is seasoned with a mélange of red and black pepper, garlic powder, and Thai red peppercorns. It is then panfried and served under an intricately spiced— and hot!—sauce combining serrano chilies, fresh ginger, and garlic.

One of the house specialties, Thai pasta, is an unqualified success: cold spinach noodles are swathed in a restrained hot and spicy garlic-and-black-bean sauce along with shards of chicken. Duck fanciers should try the highly touted Tommy duck, a crackly skinned and succulent creation in which the meat is marinated in ginger and soy, then steamed. As a final touch, the duck is flash-deep-fried and glazed with a sweet plum-and-ginger sauce. It is available Thursday through Saturday.

The young American staff is well versed in the menu, so don't be shy about asking questions. Dishes come out of the kitchen at a fairly brisk clip and are intended for sharing. The wine selection is well attuned to the food, both in price and style.

The commercial-quality French desserts are a letdown after such an exotic culinary tour. In New York, where most Thai restaurants are hushed and polite family affairs,

Tommy Tang's is a brash change of pace. For pungent food and a sassy social scene, it's worth the trip.

TOSCANA

★ ★

200 East 54th Street, 371-8144.

Atmosphere: Ultra-stylish modern décor reminiscent of a luxury liner.

Service: Generally competent and well intentioned.

Price range: Moderately expensive.

Credit cards: All major cards.

Hours: Lunch, noon to 3 P.M., Monday through Friday; dinner, 5:30 to 10:30 P.M., Monday through Saturday.

Reservations: Suggested.

Wheelchair accessibility: All facilities on one level.

ℰ Toscana, the Tuscan-style Italian veteran that moved into striking new quarters on the 54th Street side of the oval-shaped "lipstick" building on Third Avenue in 1987, is a dynamic new spot worth visiting, both for its evocative design and for the food, some of which is outstanding.

The restaurant is owned by the Bitici brothers—Sergio, Michael, John, and Joseph—who also operate Minetta Tavern (113 Macdougal Street), Chelsea Trattoria Italiana (Eighth Avenue near 16th Street), and the Grand Ticino Restaurant (228 Thompson Street). The new Toscana is by far the largest and most ambitious, not to mention the most pricey.

You enter through a classy café, all marble and pearwood and copper, where light meals are served all day. The main dining room is a sweeping curvilinear affair reminiscent of a great luxury liner, almost Scandinavian-looking in its spareness and use of light wood. Rippled waves of blue glass hang from an overhead faux skylight, reinforcing the oceanic theme. The asymmetrical molded wooden armchairs are befuddling at first—one armrest extends farther than the other—but once you get the hang of it, they are fine. My one gripe with the room is the uneven lighting. Tables at center stage are under the spotlights, but those around the rim are lost in the shadows and a miner's helmet is needed to read the menu.

While the kitchen has its peaks and valleys, all in all the

odds are well in your favor at Toscana. Two dependable appetizers are the exceptional vitello tonnato, thin sheets of cold veal under a refined tuna-and-anchovy sauce, and pristine carpaccio of beef garnished with sharp slivers of Parmesan cheese and white mushrooms. On the disappointing second visit, we sampled overly salted smoked swordfish and a clashing creation called warm shrimp and artichokes in two sauces, one fresh tomato and the other lemon-and-pepper—the sauces were rivals, not partners.

Another evening our capable and congenial captain, a James Caan look-alike, suggested a special of shrimp paired with Tuscan white beans, called borlotti, and mixed greens in an olive-oil vinaigrette, it was a splendid match. Two soups tried were sublime, too, the turbid and flavor-packed shellfish broth holding perfectly cooked scallops, shrimp, oysters, and clams, and a fresh vegetable soup enhanced before serving with herb-flavored extra-virgin olive oil that contributed a haunting woody flavor.

The service staff tries hard to please and, for the most part, succeeds. When I asked our captain if we could taste a sliver of cured goose along with our appetizers, he came back with four beautifully garnished mini-servings—and didn't charge us (it was buttery and delicious, by the way).

Several of the pastas, which can be had in half portions as starters, excel. If it's available, try the occasional special of taglierini smothered in a voluptuous lamb ragù, the next best thing to renting an Italian grandmother. One of the most luxuriant dishes is the thin cheese-filled ravioli arranged around zucchini flowers, baby zucchini, and diced vegetables in a clear aromatic broth.

Fettuccine with shrimp and radicchio in a smoky tomato sauce was a bright winner, as were two specials: angel-hair pasta tossed with eggplant, tomato, fresh basil, and resilient little cubes of mozzarella, and green fettuccine with scallops and spinach. Sail past the dry and tasteless fish ravioli in an elusive saffron sauce and the gummy gnocchi (an occasional special); opt instead for the boldly seasoned risotto blended with smoked provola Tuscan cheese and escarole.

Few of the entrées were as memorable as the best pastas. My favorites were the firm and well-crisped sweetbreads under a subtle asparagus sauce along with roasted potatoes and haricots verts. The assorted mixed grill was simple yet compelling, an assortment of shrimp, snapper, and sea scallops brightened with fresh herbs. Red snapper with diced tomatoes and thyme was fresh and skillfully cooked, although the herby tomato-and-olive sauce seemed to overpower the delicate fillet.

When desserts come rolling around the bend, you might

punctuate the meal with the good cheese and fruit selection, a lush peach tart, nutty Linzer torte, or the exemplary crème caramel. The rest is not very exciting, including the soupy and too sweet rendition of tiramisù.

TRASTEVERE

★　★

309 East 83rd Street, 734-6343.

Atmosphere: Tiny candlelit room with brick walls and oil paintings. Romantic though cramped.

Service: Good. Leisurely pace.

Price range: Moderately expensive.

Credit cards: American Express.

Hours: Dinner, 5 to 11 P.M., daily.

Reservations: Necessary.

Wheelchair accessibility: One step at entrance; all facilities on one level.

Trastevere is a romantic little Roman-style restaurant on the Upper East Side owned by the indefatigable Lattanzi family—they also have Trastevere 84 a block away, as well as Erminia on East 83rd Street and Lattanzi on West 46th Street. The candlelit dining room, slightly larger than a bus shelter, is adorned with old prints and oil paintings.

The menu carries pasta with such traditional sauces as amatriciana, white sauce with clams, and primavera, in addition to such familiar dishes as chicken with Marsala wine and mushrooms, veal scaloppine, and shrimp with garlic and wine.

You would do well to start with one of the better appetizers, such as the lightly fried and tasty spiedino alla Romana made with prosciutto, mozzarella, and anchovy sauce, or the bright vegetable salad for two combining green beans, artichoke, zucchini, roasted potatoes, broiled tomato wedges, and red peppers.

Many patrons split a portion of pasta as a first course. Linguine with white clam sauce is a model of how the dish should be done. It is made with aromatic basil leaves, lots of garlic, and good olive oil. The sparkling little clams are cooked to tender perfection and arranged, still in the shells, over the pasta. Trastevere's version of capellini primavera is a welcome change from the run-of-the-mill preparation, which is so often filled with woody hunks of underseasoned vegetables; this one blends al dente capellini with firm, steamed morsels of broccoli florets, zucchini, and fresh peas in a vibrant tomato-and-basil sauce.

One expects a much better wine list in a restaurant of this caliber and price range. Some of the commonplace Italian whites and reds are significantly overpriced.

Among meat entrées a nod goes to the vitello Trastevere, a pummeled piece of top-quality veal that is breaded and nicely fried, then served under a knoll of tomatoes and lettuce in a subtle vinaigrette—it makes a fine warm-weather dish. That old Italian workhorse veal piccante benefited from the same tender breaded veal in a lemony wine-and-butter sauce. Of the chicken dishes sampled, pollo alla Romana—moist chicken nuggets in a tomato-wine sauce bolstered with green peppers, onions, and rosemary—packs plenty of flavor; not so the pollo alla Gaetanto, which features the same chicken—this time dried out—in a nondescript garlic-and-mushroom sauce.

Shrimp are exceptionally well prepared, whether in the scampi Angela (sautéed with garlic and wine), or as part of the excellent zuppa di pesce replete with white fish, clams, mussels, lobster, and squid in a lively tomato-based broth.

And for dessert? Just what you might expect—a baseball-size tartufo with a dark chocolate "hide" enclosing chocolate ice cream. The surprisingly light and flaky napoleon is a winner, while the leaden, fudgelike chocolate mousse is guaranteed to energize you for the evening.

TRUMPET'S

★

Park Avenue at 42nd Street, 850-5999, 883-1234, ext. 66.

Atmosphere: Softly lighted, warm and comfortable, if institutional, ambiance. Generously spaced tables.

Service: Highly professional and courteous.

Price range: Expensive.

Credit cards: All major cards.

Hours: Lunch, noon to 2:30 P.M., Monday through Friday; dinner, 5:30 to 10:30 P.M., daily.

Reservations: Suggested.

Wheelchair accessibility: Special elevator and ramp at entrance; restrooms on same level as dining room.

🕭 Trumpet's, the showcase dining room at the Grand Hyatt on East 42nd Street, near Grand Central Terminal, has been trying diligently to establish an identity as a first-class dining room, and some of the efforts are paying off.

It's an adventure getting to the dining room as you wander wide-eyed through the soaring marble lobby with its waterfalls, palm trees, sundry cocktail lounges, and crowded piano bar where backslapping conventioneers frolic in the evening. Trumpet's is warm and softly illuminated, if institutional-looking, all burnished wood and mirrors and cushy banquettes. One appealing aspect of this and many other hotel restaurants is the extravagant space between tables.

The hotel's executive chef, the German-born Helmut Leuck, and Trumpet's day-to-day chef, Larry Sather, execute a highly inventive international menu—perhaps too ambitious to be consistently successful. But when they score, it's a real crowd pleaser. Take, for example, the appetizer in which sea scallops are coated with ground black pepper, flash-sautéed, and served in a lustrous chive-butter sauce along with miniature powder biscuits—the butter tames the pepper to a pleasingly piquant level. Or the lean smoked salmon garnished with a fried quail egg surrounded by fresh spinach cooked with anise, which gives the fish a cool and sassy edge. A daily special was inviting as well, lamb meatballs studded with pine nuts and served along with saffron noodles tossed in olive oil and Parmesan cheese.

Sometimes, however, this culinary tag team gets carried away. One example is the rubbery wonton skins filled with marinated foie gras (the liver was all runny and murky-tasting) flanked by snow peas and shiitake mushrooms. Galantine of duck flavored with almonds was tasty; I could have done without the chunky applesauce-and-tomato marmalade along with it, though. And terrine of turbot anchored by a fresh-water prawn was too gelatinous and lacked seasonings.

The service team at Trumpet's is unfailingly courteous and low-key, which, combined with the low noise level, makes this a fine spot for discreet business dining. The wine list reaches for the stars—in Bordeaux and Burgundy in particular—leaving scant options for mere earthlings.

Overcooking vitiates a few entrées, but overall they are solid. Among my favorites was a special of perfectly cooked salmon fillet set over slices of roasted eggplant, all swathed with a zesty parsley-pesto sauce, and red snapper rubbed with mixed herbs and ground peppercorns (black and green) along with a fresh tomato coulis.

Another recommendation is the pan-fried Dover sole embellished with black olives and diced along with a garlic tuilier, sort of an unsweetened dessert tuile cookie with garlic in the batter.

If the kitchen can produce triumphs such as those, how does it manage to trip up on such straightforward preparations as tournedos of beef with tarragon (gray and dry), swordfish (overcooked), and duck (tough and dry) with sweet-and-sour plum compote? The biggest seller in the house, and deservedly so, is a crunchy pecan-breaded chicken breast paired with apple fritters and cider sauce.

Port and assorted cheeses are offered after the entrées, but we headed straight to the fanciful-looking sweets. One memorable selection is called a chocolate envelope. It looks like half a tissue box dipped in chocolate, then filled with strawberries and a light-textured sabayon-type sauce. Less dramatic but equally good are the chocolate-macadamia cake, warm pear tart crowned with glazed pecans, and a trio of tropical sorbets with different fruit sauces. Raspberry soufflé was primarily hot air, and mocha mousse was too sugary.

20 MOTT STREET RESTAURANT

★

20 Mott Street, 964-0380.

Atmosphere: Bright, bustling, three-tier restaurant.

Service: Waiters can be helpful when you get their attention; however, they are easily distracted.

Price range: Moderate.

Credit cards: American Express, MasterCard, and Visa.

Hours: 8 A.M. to midnight, daily.

Reservations: Suggested.

Wheelchair accessibility: Steps at entrance and to restrooms.

🍃 If you are a fan of Chinese-style roast duck, hop in a cab and scoot down to 20 Mott Street Restaurant, a Cantonese restaurant in Chinatown. The duck is one of the best in town—remarkably succulent and flavorful meat, lustrous burnished skin, and a base of earthy black-bean sauce.

Not everything is so memorable; nevertheless, there are other reasons for trying this bright, airy three-story restaurant. Start with the unusual spring rolls, dark golden thick cylinders stuffed with Chinese mushrooms, pork, and tofu, or the fried dumplings made with rice-flour dough around an aromatic blend of tender spiced pork. Pass over the salty spareribs; instead, get the plump golden-fried crab claws.

The menu at 20 Mott Street is typically encyclopedic. But if you can get the undivided attention of one of the waiters, who seem to enjoy hobnobbing with Oriental customers to the exclusion of befuddled Caucasians, ask about off-menu specials. With a little luck, you'll discover the delicious deep-fried squid and buttery scallops served on lettuce leaves with a sweetish sauce.

One evening, we spotted a waiter darting out of the kitchen with an overflowing platter of steaming hard crabs in a glistening sauce. We quickly ordered the dish by pointing furiously, only to discover it is called crabs with black bean sauce on the menu. Excavating crab with chopsticks is no picnic, but the effort was worth it, especially with that spicy bean sauce. The restaurant serves beer and plum wine to quell the fires, but nothing else. Among the soups tried, a tart and fresh watercress and sliced pork in tasty broth was better than the pallid sliced-fish soup (the latter was an off-menu special).

The entrée list is so large I can offer only a cross section based on more than two dozen dishes sampled. While the plain roast duck is superb, the more elaborate Peking duck is disappointing. It comes out in two courses: the first featuring small overly thick pancakes sandwiching fatty duck skin, scallions, and hoisin sauce; the second is a platter of the duckmeat mixed with julienne vegetables, which was better.

The salt-cooking technique, an ancient one in which foods are submerged in salt and either baked in a very hot oven or deep-fried, works exceptionally well with delicious little shrimp in the shell as well as lightly battered fried oysters. One of the more exotic dishes is a Malayan specialty called Singapore Mai Fun, a platter of al dente rice noodles laced with scallions, shrimp, and pieces of ham in a light and zesty curry sauce.

Some of the Chinese mixed vegetables are flat-tasting; pan-fried noodles with seafood and vegetables also are humdrum. If you want greenery, get Chinese broccoli with oyster sauce, or watercress with a tart bean-cake sauce.

Chinese desserts are always a dubious proposition to the

uninitiated. Nonetheless, curiosity compelled me to inquire about the Chinese red-bean drink.

"It is a warm soup," our waiter explained, adding with a sheepish grin, "It is a little, uh, strange." "All the better, bring it on," I replied in a silly show of gastronomic bravado. In a word, the sweet, milky dessert is, uh, strange.

"21" CLUB

★ ★

21 West 52nd Street, 582-7200.

Atmosphere: Formal upstairs dining room is clubby and comfortable; famous wood-paneled barroom downstairs noisy and masculine.

Service: Generally professional although sometimes slow when the restaurant is crowded.

Price range: Expensive.

Credit cards: All major cards.

Hours: Lunch, noon to 3 P.M., Monday through Friday; dinner upstairs, 6 to 10:30 P.M., downstairs, until 11 P.M., Monday through Saturday; supper downstairs, 11 P.M. to 12:30 A.M., Monday through Saturday. Closed Saturday in July and August.

Reservations: Necessary.

Wheelchair accessibility: Ramp at entrance; barroom and restrooms on ground floor; elevator to upstairs dining room.

❧ The refurbishing of the legendary "21" Club in early 1987 sparked frissons of alarm and apprehension among its legions of devotees unlike anything in memory—as if the Department of the Interior had decided to jazz up the Lincoln Memorial to put Honest Abe more in sync with the 1980s.

Much of that silly, extravagantly expensive experiment has been dismantled—the executive chef, Alain Sailhac, formerly of Le Cirque, lasted only fourteen months before walking. Anne Rosenzweig, the celebrated American chef brought over from Arcadia, has a lofty title but is rarely seen in the kitchen. Thus, "21" is once again in transition.

The tumult began in January 1985, when the Berns and Kriendler families, who had been associated with the onetime speakeasy since its founding at another site in 1921, sold their interests to Marshall S. Cogan, a "21" habitué and business executive, for an estimated $21 million.

Two things remain immutable at "21": the legendary bar, which has been polished up but essentially unaltered; and prices: lunch runs about $40 to $50 a person, dinner is $65 and up, up, up depending on the wine.

The bar, with its long, arching wooden bar, banquettes under the toy-festooned ceiling, and vintage cartoons and newspaper clippings on the walls, is as virile and vibrant as ever. The more formal upstairs dining room has the warm and welcoming feeling of a country cabin after a day of skiing. The thick carpet with its "21" insignias, fabric panels above the glowing wood wainscotting (the wood is painted to look more textured than it is), and floor-to-ceiling curtains muffle noise well. Brass chandeliers, leather banquettes, and tables with plenty of elbow room add to the pampering ambiance.

Some beguiling food can be found on the revised menu, or what's left of it. Black Angus steak in a hot mustard crust is one dependable winner. Sweetbreads are excellent, sautéed to golden-brown perfection along with delicious roasted tomatoes and the heady truffle-freckled potatoes; exquisite fresh turbot fillet is likewise superb.

Butterflied pan-fried shrimp in herb butter are bright and tasty, as are gossamer slices of marinated sea scallops nested over mixed greens in a good vinaigrette.

Among the other entrées, red snapper fillet atop lustrous creamy risotto is an extraordinary match; so, too, is roasted monkfish crowned with beef marrow and set in light red-wine fumé with spinach. Wild duck stew is deliciously assertive, garnished with pearl onions and string beans.

The dandified version of chicken hash, which is really a deliciously seasoned creamed chicken ringed by a rampart of wild rice, is soothing; and the oversize and overpriced hamburger ($21) can be lean and beautifully charred one day, inedibly dry the next.

Desserts are worth exploring. Pecan maple pie is not as gooey sweet as you get down South, but I prefer it the "21" way. The chestnut dacquoise is terrific with its chewy crust, as are the assorted soufflés. Only the dainty rice pudding is disappointing, not even close to a good lumpy diner version.

The renowned wine list has ample selections in the $20-to-$30 range, although it really gets impressive a few notches above.

UNION SQUARE CAFE

★ ★

21 East 16th Street, 243-4020, 243-4129.

Atmosphere: Low-key, comfortable dining rooms with a neighborhood feeling; good oyster bar.

Service: Young, enthusiastic, and well informed about the food; sudden rushes of customers can lead to a slow pace.

Price range: Moderately expensive.

Credit cards: American Express, MasterCard, and Visa.

Hours: Lunch, noon to 3 P.M., Monday through Saturday; dinner, 6 to 10:45 P.M., Monday through Thursday, 6 to 11:45 P.M., Friday and Saturday; oyster bar open noon to 10:45 P.M., Monday through Thursday, 6 to 11:30 P.M., Friday and Saturday.

Reservations: Suggested.

Wheelchair accessibility: Dining room on ground level; restrooms downstairs.

This tasteful and unpretentious northern Italian restaurant has garnered a national reputation in just a few years, and deservedly so. The rustic food is ingenuous and inventive, and the wine list is excellent. Danny Meyer, the engaging young owner, plays host to a fast-paced publishing-world crowd at lunch and a diverse clientele at dinner.

The restaurant is designed on a human scale, which allows for that rarest of commodities nowadays—civilized conversation. On entering, you pass a long, handsome bar where a changing roster of sparkling fresh oysters is served atop iced seaweed with black bread and butter. In the back is a cozy room with a double-height ceiling and winsome murals painted on the wall; the main dining room is characterized by simple rustic touches, kind lighting, and well-spaced tables.

The food, like the décor, is genuine and eclectic. The chef, Ali Barker, straddles the border between France and Italy in his cooking. This leads to some unlikely juxtapositions. It's possible to begin with veal tonnato or risotto with escargots, roasted peppers, and garlic, then move on to a homey French offering like grilled rabbit loin in a roasted-garlic beurre blanc with tomatoes and a garlic confit.

A lighter way to begin is with one of the house favorites, pappardelle of zucchini, thin flat strips of zucchini in a fresh tomato sauce flecked with garlic and shallots. The kitchen is not timid in the seasonings department. When a dish advertises garlic, brace yourself. This is wholesome, rustic cooking, not dainty big-city fare. On wintry days the black-bean soup with lemon and a shot of Australian sherry is a superb antifreeze.

Mr. Meyer is passionate about his wines, and his highly personalized list offers many good selections in the $15-to-$25 range. Union Square Cafe is one of the few restaurants in town that offer a good selection of dessert wines by the glass. The young service staff is earnest and well informed.

The most unusual dish on the menu is the marinated "fillet mignon of tuna." Recommended for fish lovers only, this whale-size slab of florid tuna is seared on the outside and progressively rare toward the center; the core is virtually warm sushi. A confetti of ginger shavings adds a vibrant dimension. A deliciously whimsical club sandwich is made with this tuna on sourdough bread with Niçoise olives.

Union Square Cafe is a delightful place for lunch. You can get anything from a freshly ground hamburger and good french fries along with zippy black-bean soup—made with duck and veal stock—to a rosy salmon steak in a red-wine sauce colored with saffron potatoes and carrots.

For dessert, go with the thin-crusted apple tart, Italian pear torte in a cornmeal crust, or the fudgelike ganache cake with hazelnuts. My favorite finale to a meal there, though, is a glass of sweet vin santo with almond biscuits. Dunking is not only allowed, but expected.

VICTOR'S CAFÉ 52

★

236 West 52nd Street, 586-7714.

Atmosphere: Festive nightclub ambiance. Skylight in the back room creates a sunny, cheerful setting at lunch.

Service: Amicable. Capable at lunch and on weeknights, slow and harried on busy weekends.

Price range: Moderate.

Credit cards: All major cards.

Hours: Noon to midnight, Sunday through Thursday, noon to 1 A.M., Friday and Saturday.

Reservations: Suggested.

Wheelchair accessibility: Dining area on ground floor; restrooms several steps down.

❧ The granddaddy of Cuban cuisine in New York is Victor del Corral, who opened the original Victor's Café twenty-five years ago on Columbus Avenue. I have fond memories of that steamy and colorful spot in its heyday, before yuppification washed over the neighborhood, when exuberant Latin couples packed the place late at night sharing pitchers of fruity sangria and excavating earthenware crocks overloaded with arroz con pollo. Mr. del Corral sold the café in 1982, although it retains his name, and he now concentrates on his second, larger establishment opened seven years ago in the Broadway theater district, called Victor's Café 52.

The dramatic new Victor's looks like the kind of palmy nightclub you would find in Miami, a glittering expanse of mirrors, greenery, tile, and celebrity photos. The back room is crowned by an expansive skylight, which makes for a cheerful, sunny setting at lunch. Many of Victor's original Cuban customers, now older and more rakishly attired, fill the tables and the dance floor on weekends. A pianist is always on hand, sometimes supported by strolling tuxedoed violinists.

How about the food? A revamping of the menu in the last year has led to marked improvements, with some lusty Latin specialties added. Start off with some tamal Cubano, seasoned cornmeal flecked with red peppers steamed in a corn husk. Hacked chunks of tender chicken in a spirited sauce of garlic and red peppers prime the palate, as do three superior soups: a hammy chickpea-and-cabbage combination, earthy black bean, and restorative garlic soup with a poached egg floating in the middle.

The fried chorizo, or Spanish-style sausage, is rather mundane, reheated not fried; clams in green sauce are on the chewy side and the sauce is overthickened. If you have never eaten fried yucca, a root vegetable with a potatolike texture also known as cassava and manioc, try it here. The tuber is sliced into finger-size strips and golden-fried, then served with a bright coriander-vinaigrette dip.

Waiters are for the most part cheerful and eager; service is adequate on weeknights, frenzied and slow on weekends. The limited international wine list fails to mention vintages, which makes it more difficult to select bottles, but prices are fair. You can't go wrong with the simple and appealing Marques de Caceres, red or white, for about $16.

Many patrons in Cuban restaurants go immediately for the paella. Victor's is acceptable—a heaping portion of lobster, clams, sausage, rice, and vegetables—but nothing to bang the congas over. More distinctive options include the sopon de pollo, a savory chicken-and-rice stew bolstered with green olives, red peppers, and fresh peas. Grilled pork chops strewn with garlic slivers and paired with sweet fried plantains is a delight, too. The Argentine-style marinated flank steak, called churrasco, is exceedingly tender and delicious when drenched in chimichurri sauce, the garlicky vinaigrette. Fried chicken sounded exotic—described on the menu as marinated in garlic and bitter orange juice—but what came out, while crisp and moist, had neither of those flavors. Fresh ham described in a similar way was a bore, too—and as dry as parched palm leaves.

A typical peasant dish, ropa vieja, which combines shredded flank steak with garlic, tomato, onions, and green peppers, was tasty but tepid. The best seafood entrées sampled were a meaty red snapper baked over a bed of sweet peppers and sliced potatoes, and shrimp in a mildly seasoned Creole-style sauce.

Desserts include a flan, which was light and semisweet, and a sugary mound of rum-sprinkled bread pudding. If you don't know how to rumba, learn a few steps before you go—you'll need the exercise after all this.

THE VILLAGE GREEN

★ ★

531 Hudson Street, between Charles and 10th streets, 255-1650.

Atmosphere: Romantic little brick-and-wood dining room downstairs; jazz featured at upstairs bar nightly except Sunday.

Service: Professional and eager to please.

Price range: Moderately expensive.

Credit cards: All major cards.

Hours: Brunch, noon to 3 P.M., Sunday; lunch, noon to 3 P.M., Monday through Friday; dinner, 6 to 10:45 P.M., Monday through Thursday, 6 to 11 P.M., Friday and Saturday, 7 to 11 P.M., Sunday.

Reservations: Suggested.

Wheelchair accessibility: Steps up to bar and restrooms; steps down to dining room.

જ If you have been searching for that culinary grail known as the romantic little neighborhood restaurant that serves lovingly prepared food in a civilized setting, look no further. The Village Green has been rejuvenated under new ownership and has vastly improved.

The 1827 row house retains all of its warm, venerable charm, with a handsome old bar upstairs where jazz is featured and the enchanting thirty-seat dining room below with its brick walls, wood trim, period sconces, and twinkling candlelight. What's more, the food, under the Louisiana-born chef, Tony Najiola (formerly of The River Café and La Reserve), is as serendipitous as the setting. Mr. Najiola's contemporary American creations crackle with energy and imagination, while at the same time they are intelligently defined by his keen sense of flavor affinities.

The menu is manageable in size—about seven appetizers and entrées supplemented by a few daily specials—which does not necessarily make choosing any easier, since everything sounds so arresting. I flip-flopped several times one evening trying to decide between two entrées, the pepper-encrusted tuna steak with a lemon mignonette sauce, and the grilled baby chicken with a sweet garlic sauce and grilled radicchio. After leaning on a companion to order the chicken so I could taste it, I tried the tuna. It was cooked to a turn, just pink inside, and vibrant with lemon. A black-olive purée over croutons lent a salty edge that brought it all together. As for the chicken, it, too, was deftly cooked, scattered with roasted garlic cloves, tart radicchio leaves, and a garlic-infused chicken-stock sauce.

Mr. Najiola's Dixie heritage can be seen in his fondness for pepper. He puts it to savory use on the pan-roasted duck breast, in which the meat slices are rimmed with a mélange of peppers and spices and matched with ripe plums poached in a peppered veal stock and sharp sautéed Swiss chard. One of the few near misses over the course of three visits was a slightly overcooked roulade of chicken breast stuffed with foie gras, pine nuts, and mixed herbs.

The chef's delights included roast loin of mustard-rubbed lamb stuffed with spinach along with eggplant and roasted shallots, lobster out of the shell glossed with a glistening rosemary-orange-butter sauce offset by tart Swiss chard, and a special one evening of garlic-and-thyme-encrusted halibut accompanied by roasted potatoes and braised rhubarb stems.

The restaurant's wine list is filled with uncommon surprises from California, the Pacific Northwest, and New York State.

Several appetizers change seasonally, but among those that won unanimous high marks at my table were the crisply sautéed strips of foie gras presented over a tangle of curly endive flavored with a sherry vinaigrette with shallots, garnished with crescents of mango.

Special pastas of the day can be ordered in half portions. Fettuccine topped with crumbled goat cheese, black olives, and tomatoes was a light and invigorating starter, while the same pasta with scallops, pecans, and capers was way too salty.

Desserts include a gutsy hazelnut-mocha mousse over pecan shortbread with cinnamon whipped cream, a high-voltage, high-density chocolate mousse, exceptionally light ricotta cheesecake with sliced peaches, and sliced white peaches served in a stem glass and drenched with Sauternes. A glass of cognac at the bar, where jazz is featured, is a fitting way to punctuate the experience—Greenwich Village as one always imagined it could be.

VIOLETTA

★ ★

1590 First Avenue, between 82nd and 83rd streets, 517-7090.

Atmosphere: Two narrow salmon-colored dining rooms are short on elbow room but long on charm.

Service: Concerned and efficient.

Price range: Moderately expensive.

Credit cards: All major cards.

Hours: Dinner, 5 P.M. to midnight, Monday through Saturday, 4 to 11 P.M. Sunday.

Reservations: Suggested.

Wheelchair accessibility: One step at entrance; restrooms downstairs.

🍲 Violetta is owned by John Angelis, a Roman, and Peter Peros, from a section of northern Italy that is now Yugoslavia; the chef, Luigi Cuzo, is from Lake Como, north of Milan, and the menu reflects the cuisine of all three heritages.

The restaurant has a rather confining layout, two long narrow rooms anchored by a bar at one end. Mirrors on the salmon-toned walls, strategically aimed spotlights, and expansive flower displays give the illusion of a bit more space. The entire staff is warm and concerned, without being fawning or overly familiar. Indeed, when the owners describe daily specials, you get the impression they want to pull up a chair and join you.

Speaking of those specials, two off-menu specials are terrific: one is fusilli in a delicate cream sauce counterbalancing salty pancetta and sweet fresh peas; the other was angel-hair pasta in a zesty blend of tomatoes, onions, and minced jalapeño peppers. In fact, all of the pastas are distinctively seasoned and fresh-tasting. Spaghetti with white clam sauce is sparkling and pristine, its sweet, barely cooked clams presented in their shells; penne combined with sautéed arugula and radicchio is bracingly tart, while farfalle comes with a summery broccoli, zucchini, and garlic combination. The chef's earthy amatriciana sauce is satisfying although not memorable, and the ziti paired with it can be so al dente it poses hazards to dental work.

Other good appetizers include a special of cold mussels under a vibrant pesto sauce (grit marred a few of them), and sautéed shrimp glossed with a caper-and-white-wine sauce. One of the few boring dishes is a special, veal tonnato—chilled slices of good veal slathered with a feeble tuna sauce that tastes mostly of commercial mayonnaise.

Among entrées, a double-thick monster veal chop yielded to a knife like custard and had a succulent flavor brought out by its mild mustard coating. The mixed grill, called pollo a modo mio, is simple and tasty, too—moist chicken, herb-flecked sausage, and cubes of tender beef in a lusty garlic sauce. If veal in orange sauce sounds like some scary alien from the land of California cuisine, take heart: the sauce is not as sweet as one might suspect, but rather is cut with orange rind and some of the white pith to add refreshing tartness.

Back on familiar terrain, two seafood preparations, both specials, are outstanding: red snapper fillet alla Livornese, combining black olives, capers, tomato, and herbs, and a whole roasted orata, or basslike Mediterranean fish, brushed lightly with olive oil, garlic, and parsley, which were all it needed.

Desserts are something of a letdown, except for a good espresso-drenched version of tiramisù, the ladyfinger-and-sweetened-mascarpone confection.

VOULEZ-VOUS

★ ★

1462 First Avenue, at 76th Street, 249-1776.

Atmosphere: Glass-fronted, contemporary design; comfortable and relatively quiet.

Service: Friendly and capable.

Price range: Moderate.

Credit cards: All major cards.

Hours: Brunch, 11:30 A.M. to 4 P.M., Sunday; lunch, 11:30 A.M. to 4 P.M., Monday through Friday; dinner, 5:15 P.M. to midnight, daily.

Reservations: Strongly suggested.

Wheelchair accessibility: All facilities on one level.

When the windchill hammers the thermometer into single digits, one of the most effective human antifreezes is a bracing stew along with a slab of rough country bread and a glass of husky red wine. To the French, that translates as pot-au-feu, and one of the best around is ladled out at Voulez-Vous.

Pot-au-feu is just one of the enticements at this moderately priced French bistro on the Upper East Side. The glass-fronted contemporary dining room gives scant hint of the rustic fare within. It is comfortable and mercifully muted by sound tile and has tinted-mirror walls, stout cushioned chairs, and a sleek bar in the back. Jacques Rameckers, the genial owner, is a no-nonsense host who keeps tabs on his young, earnest staff.

As for that pot-au-feu, a Tuesday special, it arrives in a capacious bowl steaming like a manhole cover in February. Contents include a meaty beef shank, with a dollop of custardy marrow oozing from the bone, submerged in a clear, full-flavored broth strewn with carrots, potatoes, and leeks.

Wednesday is couscous day at Voulez-Vous, but the version here needs some beefing up before it can be recommended. A stingy portion of the nubbly semolina grain cushions an assortment of spicy merguez sausage, stewed chicken, meat patties combining lamb and beef, and chickpeas—but no other vegetables—all moistened with a broth stoked to your specifications with fiery harissa sauce. If you show up on Thursday, navarin of lamb with orange zest is available; Friday is bouillabaisse, and Saturday rack of veal with truffle sauce. You can also get a garlic-bolstered cassoulet brimming with moist duck, country sausage, and lamb.

The Alsatian staple, choucroute garnie, is prepared daily and is a mellow assembly of smoked sausages, pork chops, smoked chicken, sauerkraut, and potatoes, enlivened by sharp juniper berries. Have it with a glass of crisp Sancerre ($19 a bottle). Another daily feature is called matelote of swordfish, a lusty red-wine-based stew studded with pearl onions, bacon, and mushrooms—the braising technique keeps the fillet moist and imbues it with flavor.

When the chef strays from the home fires and makes a stab at cosmopolitan cooking, things can go downhill. Trenette with crabmeat in a vermouth cream sauce was limp and lifeless; a daily special, pasta with artichokes, was barely a notch better. And two attempts at grilling swordfish over mesquite left the charred fillet papery dry. The wood-fire cooking worked better, though, with chicken, which was brightened with a piquant ginger glaze and accompanied by a sweet-hot orange mustard. Eggplant caviar and al dente carrots rounded out this beguiling bargain ($11.50).

Three other notable dishes are the aggressively seasoned filet mignon au poivre and french fries, the first-rate steak tartare, and a lovely seafood special, red snapper layered with tomatoes and zucchini in a light, lemony butter sauce.

Befitting the prodigious main courses, appetizers are lightweight primers. Billi bi, a velvety cream-of-mussel soup tinged with saffron, is a lustrous starter here; equally good is the mussel salad, which is not really a salad but rather wine-steamed mussels in a terrific broth laced with julienne of red and yellow peppers. Caesar salad was too timid for my taste, and three-layered vegetable terrine needed a jolt of seasonings.

For dessert, go with profiteroles—ice-cream-filled puff pastry under an avalanche of whipped cream and chocolate sauce—the excellent crème brûlée, sharp-edged frozen cappuccino soufflé, or the light yet intense chocolate mousse cake.

THE WATER CLUB

★

On the East River at 30th Street, 683-3333.

Atmosphere: Glass-enclosed barge on the East River with a panoramic view of Queens and parts of Manhattan. On deck is an alfresco bar.

Service: Amiable and efficient.

Price range: Moderately expensive.

Credit cards: All major cards.

Hours: Brunch, noon to 2:15 P.M., Saturday, 11:30 A.M. to 2:45 P.M., Sunday; lunch, noon to 2 P.M., Monday through Friday; dinner, 5:30 to 11 P.M., Monday through Thursday, 5:45 to 11 P.M., Friday and Saturday, 5:45 to 10 P.M., Sunday.

Reservations: Suggested.

Wheelchair accessibility: All facilities on one level.

🍶 The Water Club was designed in 1982 as a middle-class alternative to the splashy River Café. Its ambiance is a bit less starchy, the food more familiar, and prices closer to sea level. Even the view—oil tanks and factories of Queens as opposed to the glass-and-steel redwoods of Wall Street—reflects this distinction. Nonetheless, if you order wisely at The Water Club you can have an enjoyable meal in one of the more inspiring settings the city has to offer.

The entrance to the restaurant resembles a pricey yacht club, with a long, burnished bar along one side and, along the other, an iced display of various fish and shellfish. Before entering the main dining room, which is in a barge tied to the pier, you might want to walk updeck to the open-air bar. It is a delightful spot to enjoy an aperitif while watching barges and pleasure boats ply the river.

The three-tier main dining room is wrapped in glass offering views from every table. Little nautical flags hanging from the ceiling add to the clubby feeling.

The menu is expansive, and there are always a half dozen or more specials. They are worth considering because some of the better dishes sampled were among them. For example, it could be creamy fresh salmon rillettes accompanied by a slice of light scallop mousse garnished with two buttery whole sea scallops (the delicate roe was attached). The combination comes in an aromatic tarragon sauce. Another delicacy is the foie-gras terrine, two slices of silky foie gras veined with truffle-laced gelatin. Fresh oysters of different varieties—Belons from Maine, Malpeques from Cape Cod among the best—are icy and glistening fresh. The chef knows how to fry shellfish without destroying it. His oysters and clams are lightly breaded and minimally fried in good oil, letting their flavors shine through.

The Water Club's setting naturally puts one in the mood for seafood entrées, however one must exercise caution. Poached halibut, a special one evening, had been submerged a little too long and then dressed up in a bland champagne-hollandaise sauce. Grilled swordfish may be well cooked but in my experience lacks flavor.

The Water Club turns out some of the best crab cakes in town—plump little golden-brown disks loaded with well-seasoned crabmeat. A hillock of crunchy deep-fried parsley in the center of the plate is a pleasing mate. Tuna steak, a heavyweight delicacy of the deep that has been roughed up more than a Saturday night wrestler by careless cooks, also is remarkably good. It was crosshatched on the surface and blush-pink in the middle, set in a soy-based sauce and garnished with juliennes of leek and carrot.

On the other side of the menu, slices of duck breast with a semisweet fresh cherry sauce and wild rice suffer from overcooking. Another dry combination is pork chops stuffed with corn bread and bacon. Better selections are the prime ribs of beef and broiled lamb chops with a fresh mint sauce.

Some inventive side dishes enliven the meals. Try potatoes colcannon, which are good old-fashioned buttery mashed potatoes topped with scallions and lots of fresh pepper; potatoes O'Brien don't look anything like what you'd find on the old sod, but they are engaging nonetheless—crunchy little cubes of fried potatoes tossed with bits of sweet bell peppers. Lumpy corn fritters are as down-home as a Kentucky farm breakfast.

The blue ribbon for dessert goes to the warm apple tart with its thin and buttery puff-pastry crust, followed by the towering frozen Amaretto soufflé. Cheesecake tastes as though it had a surfeit of gelatin, and a cloying concoction called chocolate raspberry barquette is more suitable for a Little League banquet. Both fresh berries with sabayon and coupe aux marrons (ice cream sundae with glazed chestnuts) could prompt a smile at the end of the meal.

WATER'S EDGE AT THE
EAST RIVER YACHT CLUB

★

East River Yacht Club, 44th Drive at the East River, Long Island City, Queens, (718) 482-0033.

Atmosphere: Great views; stodgy, mismatched décor. Well-spaced tables. Romantic.

Service: Polite and eager but green and lacking professionalism at times.

Price range: Moderately expensive.

Credit cards: American Express and Diners Club.

Hours: Brunch, noon to 3 P.M., Sunday; lunch, noon to 3 P.M., Monday through Friday; dinner, 6 to 11 P.M. Monday through Saturday, 5 to 10 P.M., Sunday.

Reservations: Suggested.

Wheelchair accessibility: One step up to entrance and restrooms; one step down to dining room.

&. A yacht club on the industrial waterfront of Queens may seem as improbable as a polo field on Wall Street, but there it sits, all cool-white and glassy, offering a stunning panorama of midtown Manhattan across the East River. What's more, the club's recently revamped public restaurant, called Water's Edge, can be surprisingly good.

The menu carries an ambitious range of seafood, game, and meat entrées. The service is wobbly, and prices are hardly provincial (count on about $50 a person with wine), but if you seek generally pleasing fare in a romantic waterside setting, Water's Edge is worth adding to your ports of call. And in the summer, you can get there by the ferry that the restaurant runs to and from Manhattan.

The gentrified main room is a curious mix of sleek marine white and somber men's club oak that was imported to lend an air of seriousness to the space. The result, though, is a jarring hodgepodge. Severe, high-backed, Victorian-style chairs add to the dignified discomfort. Tables are generously spaced to allow privacy. An upstairs banquet room seats six hundred.

By sticking to the most straightforward preparations and avoiding whimsical sauces and pastas, you should do fine. One could start with potent dill-infused gravlax or superior smoked tuna accompanied by lemon, capers, and a mild horseradish-cream sauce. My favorite appetizer is called Cape Cod chili. It is an unlikely combination of beans, lobster, shrimp, and scallops in a rousing hot sauce foiled with a touch of sweetness from the onions. Grilled peppered salmon sounded tempting but was overcooked.

The chef is conscientious about the quality of his seafood, and it is best when garnished least. Among the recommended dishes are a thick plank of grilled yellowfin tuna painted with sweetish hoisin sauce, sautéed Dover sole garnished with rings of sweet red peppers, and an exceptionally zesty rendition of blackened snapper—it was zippy with pepper but not burned, as it so often is elsewhere. Poached salmon was cooked to a turn, but its lobster sauce, speckled with black truffles, was utterly bland.

The wine list is scattered and uneven, but there are enough reasonably priced bottles to meet most needs. One vexing service practice is that after pouring the wine, waiters place the bottle in a storage bucket far from your table. Invariably, when you want some wine, no one is around to retrieve it.

Simple steaks and chops are reliably good; two exceptional entrées are the rack of lamb over well-seasoned hot lentils, and a special, venison steak in a faintly sweet stock sauce replete with meaty shiitake mushrooms.

For dessert, you can't go wrong with the splendid tarte Tatin featuring caramelized apples and almond slivers, excellent pecan pie built on a layer of bittersweet chocolate, or rich and intense chocolate mousse cake.

WILKINSON'S SEAFOOD CAFÉ

★　★

1573 York Avenue, between 83rd and 84th streets, 535-5454.

Atmosphere: Brick and aged wood, soft lighting and handsome bar make for a relaxing café setting.

Service: Congenial and well informed.

Price range: Moderately expensive.

Credit cards: All major cards.

Hours: Dinner, 6 to 10:30 P.M., Monday through Friday, 6 to 11 P.M., Saturday, 5:30 to 9 P.M., Sunday.

Reservations: Strongly suggested after 6:30.

Wheelchair accessibility: Dining room on ground floor; restrooms downstairs.

🍸 A mostly young, well-turned-out Yorkville crowd frequents this informal, inviting dining room with its exposed-brick and aged-wood walls, friendly bar, overhead blade fans, soft frosted lights, and etched glass. Cool piped-in jazz strikes a laid-back tempo.

Start off with one of the house signature appetizers, either tempura-light fried calamari rings in a pulpy tarragon-tomato sauce or the lustrous warm oysters glossed with orange butter—the success of this preparation is the invigorating blend of briny oyster juices with the tart-sweet butter. Shimmering gravlax paired with a mild horseradish-and-caper sauce is another winner. Less appealing is the underseasoned seafood sausage.

Carnivores would enjoy the scarlet sheets of first-rate carpaccio brushed with a zippy combination of capers, onions, and mustard.

Even when entrées fall short, it is not for lack of freshness but rather misjudgment with herbs and seasonings. Poached gray sole in a sloppy coriander-and-red-onion vinaigrette that separated at the table was one example; watery and bland mako shark was another. Aside from these, however, every other fish selection I sampled was a winner. One of my favorites was broiled marinated swordfish, something I rarely order because so often it is cooked to the consistency of newspaper. This succulent steak had been broiled to barely pink inside and coated with its pungent soy-based marinade. The leathery string beans, woody carrots, and unseasoned broccoli added little. Two other recommended fish that share an Oriental touch are the grilled salmon steak in a bright lime-teriyaki butter, and flaky red snapper set over a terrific sauce made with sake and fermented Chinese black beans.

Closer to home you can enjoy the big pearly sea scallops nestled in spinach leaves with a lovely lemon-saffron sauce or a golden strudel filled with dill-accented crabmeat and surrounded by a sweet leek purée and sugar snap peas. Passable steak and chicken are available if you lose your sea legs.

Portions are generous but not overwhelming, so chances are you will have room for the deceptively light and semi-sweet white-chocolate mousse, the cleansing lemon tart, or the caramelized baked apple tart.

If Wilkinson's were closer to midtown it would probably be mobbed every night. I'm glad it's not, for it's always nice to know there is a welcoming port of call over the horizon.

WINDOWS ON THE WORLD

★

1 World Trade Center, 107th floor, 938-1111.

Atmosphere: Wide, glass-enclosed wraparound restaurant with stunning views of New York City and the harbor.

Service: Professional and reasonably prompt.

Price range: Moderately expensive

Credit cards: All major cards.

Hours: At lunch the restaurant is a private club; brunch, noon to 7:30 P.M., Sunday; dinner, 5 to 10 P.M., Monday through Saturday; bar, noon to 1 A.M., Monday through Saturday.

Reservations: Required.

Wheelchair accessibility: Several steps down to dining room; restrooms on same level.

🦐 Windows on the World, on the 107th floor of the World Trade Tower, is one of the most dramatic settings in New York. While the food may not be as stimulating as the view, it is certainly respectable.

The Continental-style menu is nicely balanced and contemporary without lapsing into trendiness. Stocks are homemade, the quality of provender is top-notch, and seasonings are generally employed with skill. When the kitchen stumbles, it is usually a consequence of trying to feed the estimated four thousand customers who pass through weekly—similar sauces show up in a variety of dishes, and a few items must be prepared in enormous quantities a bit too long in advance.

Windows offers good value for the dollar, with a four-course dinner as well as à la carte options. The prix-fixe menu has considerable appeal. It might begin with a platter of sparkling Cotuit oysters on the half shell paired with a tart mignonette sauce, or the lovely chilled pea soup suffused with fresh mint. A double beef consommé is clear and intense, garnished at the last minute with strips of scallion-laced pancakes—an unlikely but winning combination. Only the salmon-and-leek terrine fell short because of dryness.

The expanded à la carte offerings include sheets of bright

mint-marinated fresh salmon with an Indian-style yogurt-and-cucumber sauce.

Two pleasing entrées on the prix-fixe menu are succulent roast baby chicken with an intensely reduced veal-stock sauce garnished with miniature vegetables, and pale slices of buttery veal in the same stock sauce bolstered with white mushrooms—this veal stock, albeit good, is the fuel that propels most of the kitchen's meat dishes.

Best bets on the regular menu include most steaks and chops, such as the pink-roasted rack of lamb for two, the double-thick lamb chops with savory gratin potatoes, and a crusty and beefy sirloin steak for two in a heady red-wine-and-stock sauce sweetened with shallots and beef marrow.

Soft-shell crabs do not fare so well; the dizzying ascent to the 107th floor left them pale and lifeless. A fricassee of lobster and crayfish is better.

The army of service personnel somehow manages to keep this three-ring circus moving right along, and with relatively good cheer. The complexion of the multitiered dining room changes dramatically on weekends, when it is inundated by tourists who are forever jumping out of their seats to press their faces against the windows while trying to illuminate the entire island of Manhattan with flash cameras. At such times the noise level can be jarring.

The wine list at Windows is justly famous, not only for its wide selection of French and American labels, but also for its prices, which are among the lowest I have encountered anywhere in town—in some cases only 25 percent above retail.

The best desserts are the luxurious frozen raspberry soufflé, a rich and creamy hazelnut dacquoise, and a classic New York–style cheesecake that is so weighty you may not need the elevator to sink to ground level. Floating islands must react badly to heights, for they are more like flaccid islands, and the white-chocolate mousse is gelatinous and pallid.

ZARELA

★ ★

953 Second Avenue, between 50th and 51st streets, 644-6740.

Atmosphere: Pleasant brick-and-wood-paneled former wine bar with Mexican touches.

Service: Pleasant and knowledgeable, but there can be long waits between courses.

Price range: Moderate.

Credit cards: All major cards.

Hours: Lunch, noon to 3 P.M., Monday through Friday; dinner, 5 to 11:30 P.M., Monday through Thursday, 5 P.M. to midnight, Friday and Saturday.

Reservations: Necessary.

Wheelchair accessibility: Bar and small dining area on street level; main dining room and restrooms upstairs.

After three years at the former Café Marimba, Zarela Martinez opened her own place in late 1987, called Zarela, in the former Tastings on Two on Second Avenue. What the new location lacks in dramatic décor (Café Marimba was indeed striking; Zarela so far has a makeshift look), it makes up for in the scintillating and sassy food—a case of substance over style (and at lower prices). Zarela's cooking is aggressive yet refined without lapsing into cuteness, and varied enough for all tastes, from the macho asbestos-palates to those who prefer low-voltage spiciness.

The long tiled bar up front serves peppy margaritas that you tend to drink faster than you should while dipping nacho chips into a pepper-stoked salsa. Ms. Martinez has added Mexican touches here and there to the brick-walled, publike downstairs dining room, including a trio of mariachis. The wood-paneled upstairs room is less raucous and more comfortable.

Virtually all the appetizers are recommended, including the moist and soothing tamales, which are little cigar-shaped rolls of corn masa and chicken steamed in corn husks and brightened with sharp-edged mole sauce, and chilaquiles, which are fried tortilla strips overlaid with shredded chicken, tart sour cream, and white Cheddar cheese baked until molten and bubbly—they come with either hot ranchero sauce or bright green tomatillo sauce. Those with sensitive palates can feel safe with the flautas, chicken-filled tacos served with fresh guacamole; lightly puffed fried calamari rings that you dip in a mild tomato sauce, and the enchiladas de mole in a sweet and pungent mole sauce.

When Zarela cranks up the BTUs, look out. Twice I tried the poblano relleno, believing from experience that the poblano chili is among the least explosive of its family. The bulbous pepper is stuffed with diced chicken and dried fruits and set over a roasted tomato sauce. The first sensations in the mouth are of the sweet fruit and the smoky sauce, then a hint of cinnamon, followed by a gradual attack of heat that, within ten seconds, breaks out into a battle of the Alamo on the palate. Another fiery but far more benign preparation is snapper hash, one of Zarela's signature dishes from Café Marimba, seasoned with diced tomato, scallion, jalapeños, coriander, and clove.

Most entrées are winners. Two of the best are the fajitas, slices of sinewy but fork-tender barbecued skirt steak served with guacamole, hot tomato salsa, and soft tortillas; and the grilled pork tenderloin under strips of smoky and sweet ancho chilies and poblano chilies in a roasted-tomato-and-garlic sauce. It is delicious with a side of frijoles charros, a crock of pinto beans cooked with tomatoes, onions, pickled jalapeños, and beer.

Dinner entrées do not come with vegetables (lunch entrées do), so you have to choose them à la carte. Fried cauliflower had an acrid old-oil flavor; better choices are calabacitas con queso, a splendid mélange of zucchini, corn, and poblano chilies in a tomatillo cream sauce; and the arroz con crema, a sharp and mildly hot combination of rice, white Cheddar cheese, sour cream, corn, and poblano chili.

Two seafood entrées were superior: lovely seared tuna, rare in the middle, dabbed with mole sauce, and shrimp sautéed with garlic and two kinds of chilies.

One does not normally think of exciting desserts south of the border, but the praline-hazelnut flan is worth dropping a few pesos, as is the terrific bread pudding studded with dried fruit and doused with applejack brandy–butter sauce. Cinnamon-spiked apple pie has a wonderfully brittle crust (it comes with ice cream or melted Cheddar cheese); only the white almond cajeta torte went unfinished—a fluffy and sugary creation not worth the calories.

DINER'S
JOURNAL

The Diner's Journal column in *The New York Times* is a vehicle of ferreting out special dishes, offbeat restaurants, great bars, breakfast nooks, little-known bargains, and scores of other colorful dining spots that might otherwise be overshadowed by the restaurants that get the star treatment in the weekly dining column. It is a casual, chatty, and highly personal forum. I have more fun investigating the city for these little gems than with anything else. The material in this section consists of a set of specific restaurant reviews, followed (beginning on page 442) by restaurants listed thematically. Both listings are alphabetical and the categories can be found in the table of contents on page ix. Prices mentioned in this section are subject to change

ABYSSINIA

🍴 You sit on squat wooden stools and pick from a communal plate with your hands at this spare but pleasant Ethiopian restaurant at 35 Grand Street, at Thompson Street. Ethiopian food, at least as represented here, is serious hot stuff. Doro wot, chicken and hard-cooked eggs in a smoldering red sauce, tops the list, followed by azefa wot, which combines lentils, red onions, garlic, ginger, and hot peppers in a lemon-tinted hot sauce. These can be tempered with yekik wot, a refreshing dish of split peas in a relatively light lemon sauce ($6.50).

One of the best dishes is kitfo, Ethiopia's version of steak tartare; the beef is pulverized to a paste and mixed with spiced butter and chili powder, giving it a rich, elegant flavor. Diners scoop up food by hand, using flat, spongy sheets of Ethiopian bread, called injera. Service tends to be lackadaisical, so go when you have plenty of time. Entrées are in the $10-to-$15 range. Abyssinia is open for dinner from 6 P.M. to midnight daily; and for lunch from noon to 4 P.M., Saturday and Sunday. Telephone: 226-5959.

ARIZONA 206 CAFE

🍴 Fans of blazing Southwestern cooking may want to stop by Arizona 206 Cafe, a smart and neighborly annex to the Arizona 206 restaurant at 206 East 60th Street. Done in clean desert tones of stucco and unfinished wood, this casual spot sports firm, fabric-covered banquettes, little tables scattered about, and an exposed kitchen behind a tile service counter. Brendan Walsh, the resourceful young chef, has created an all-day tasting menu that features appetizer-size portions for $6 to $12.

Titillating options might include a tender sheet of cold beef marinated in dried chilies, cumin, and coriander with roasted red peppers; grilled sweet onions in a smoldering mole sauce; deliciously smoky grilled vegetables accompanied by a snowy goat-cheese croquette; corn-dusted fried oysters and tortillas with hot sauce; and hacked smoked duck enkindled with jalapeño peppers and sweetened with tangerine glaze. Wines by the glass are served, as are some serious desserts.

Arizona 206 Cafe is open noon to midnight, Monday through Saturday, 4 to 11 P.M., Sunday. Telephone: 838-0440.

AU GRENIER CAFÉ

🐌 Upper Broadway in the Columbia University neighborhood abounds with little ethnic storefront restaurants catering to student tastes and budgets. One that is worth investigating even if your diploma is getting yellow around the edges is Au Grenier Café, a sunny walk-up French bistrolike place at Broadway near 111th Street, where lunch fare includes some tasty soups, salads, and pâtés—and at bargain prices.

The clean and simply appointed dining area with its brick walls, lacquered wooden tables, and tall windows overlooking the avenue attracts a casual crowd of students and area businesspeople. A chalkboard lists a dozen wine specials by the glass. Lunch might begin with a beefy and sweet-edged onion soup gratinée and chewy rye bread. Various pâtés, which come from the reputable Les Petites Cochons, are reliably fresh and well seasoned—a country blend flecked with green peppercorns, rabbit with Armagnac, duck with port wine, and more.

The changing selection of salads makes for an engaging light lunch (prices range from about $3 to $5 for a chunky chicken version). The hands-down best is firm and sprightly lentil salad in a vinaigrette blended with red pepper, scallions, red onions, and parsley. The others are invariably fresh, although a few needed an extra shot of seasonings. The dinner menu, which has not been sampled, offers the same salad selection as well as steaks, chops, fowl, and other straightforward fare in the $10-to-$16 range.

Au Grenier Café, one flight up at 2867 Broadway, between 111th and 112th streets, is open for brunch on Sunday, 11 A.M. to 3:30 P.M.; lunch, Monday through Friday, 11 A.M. to 3:30 P.M.; and dinner, daily 6 to 10 P.M. Telephone: 666-3052.

BACI

𝒵𝒶 Some of the best pasta on the Upper West Side is dished out at this spiffy little café owned by the Sindoni family, who also own Azzurro on 84th Street and Second Avenue. The selections change daily, but among those I have enjoyed are the penne with eggplant, garlic, and tomato sauce (€11.50), spaghetti tossed with a light Sicilian-style sauce of marinated black olives and tomato ($15 as part of a three-course weekend brunch), and linguine in a tuna-and-tomato sauce ($10.50 at lunch, $11.50 at dinner). It can be shatteringly loud at night; lunch is much more peaceful. Appetizers are pure and simple, and desserts are purely fattening, especially the terrific tiramisù that oozes with mascarpone cheese. Baci, at 412 Amsterdam Avenue, between 79th and 80th streets, serves lunch from noon to 3 P.M., Monday through Friday; brunch, noon to 3 P.M., Saturday and Sunday; dinner, 5:30 to 11 P.M., Monday through Thursday, until midnight Friday and Saturday, and 5:30 to 10:30 P.M., Sunday. Telephone: 496-1550.

BELLEVUES

𝒵𝒶 You would be hard-pressed to find a less likely place for a French bistro in midtown than the seedy, depressing stretch of Ninth Avenue near 37th Street, but this one is no usual French bistro. Bellevues—it seems to be a tongue-in-cheek reference to the setting—is owned by partners who include Florent Morellet, who owns the popular all-night French diner called Restaurant Florent at 69 Gansevoort Street.

Bellevues has a similar stripped-down 1950s look, with a long gleaming counter and aqua banquettes as well as the same solid French fare for a good price. You can start with a moist and mildly livery country terrine with lentils ($4.25 at dinner, $3.50 at lunch), gutsy boudin noir with apples and onions ($5.75 as an appetizer, $10.50 as a dinner entrée) or escargots in an intense winy sauce ($5.50 dinner, $4.75 lunch). Pleasing entrées include a peppery lamb curry with raisins and carrots ($11.75), nicely cooked calf's liver with bacon and onions ($11.50 dinner, $8.75 lunch) and exceptionally tasty skate with a coriander garnish ($12). Tuna steak with basil butter ($13) was overly charred and a tad dry.

For dessert there are such French standards as a deep crock of rich, custardy crème brûlée and tarte Tatin with a dollop of crème fraîche.

Bellevues, 496 Ninth Avenue, at 38th Street, serves lunch 11:30 A.M. to 3 P.M. Monday through Friday and dinner from 6 P.M. to midnight, Monday through Saturday, until 11:30 P.M. Sunday. Telephone: 967-7855.

BISTRO d'ADRIENNE

&. Some of the most authentic French bistro food in New York is served in a most unbistrolike setting. Bistro d'Adrienne is the homespun, inexpensive counterpart to the luxurious restaurant called Adrienne, both in the new Hotel Maxim's de Paris on Fifth Avenue at 55th Street.

The bistro is plush and urbane, with soft oversize chairs, thick rugs, pink marble tables, and long, burnished bar. If such rustic specialties as tripe, boudin noir (blood sausage), and duck stew make your pulse quicken, then this place is strictly high-impact aerobics. The tripes à la nissarte are the real thing, tender yet resilient, coddled in a bold garlic-boosted tomato-and-vegetable sauce ($15). Fresh cod, a greatly underappreciated species, is perfectly poached and paired with a heady garlic mayonnaise ($16); cut-up sections of duck come in a bacon-enhanced braising liquid made with red wine, fresh baby turnips, and mushrooms ($17).

For starters, there is a terrific cold terrine of shredded oxtail on a tangle of poached leeks in vinaigrette ($6), and marinated fresh mackerel with cucumber salad ($5.50).

The bistro has an excellent little wine list with uncommon regional selections in the $20-and-under range. For dessert, try any of the fruit tarts or the crusty crème brûlée, and a high-octane espresso.

Bistro d'Adrienne, 700 Fifth Avenue is open for lunch from noon to 3:30 P.M., Monday through Saturday; dinner, 6 to 11:30 P.M., daily. Telephone: 903-3918.

BRASSERIE

&. It's not easy to find comfortable places to dine after midnight in New York aside from clattering delicatessens or oppressively illuminated pizza parlors. Brasserie, in the

Seagram's Building on East 53rd Street, is a spot to keep in mind for its clean, casual ambiance and agreeable food served around the clock. The fare hardly rivals La Coupole in Paris, but the kitchen turns out a creditable steak with good french fries ($15.95) and a decent chicken paillard (if they don't overcook it) with herb butter ($11.75). Start off with the cheesey onion soup ($3.95 small, $4.95 large) and top it all off with a fruit tart or crème caramel ($3.95). The espresso packs a Mike Tyson punch. Sunday brunch is a particular bargain at $14.95, including a glass of sparkling wine. Brasserie, 100 East 53rd Street, is open 24 hours daily. Telephone: 751-4840.

CABANA CARIOCA

🐾 If you are the type who measures food bargains by the pound, this has to be the heavyweight champ of Manhattan, a gutsy Brazilian dining room where hulking portions keep happy patrons coming back for more. Cabana Carioca is an amiable two-story establishment; the upstairs offers the more tropical atmosphere. It has colorful folk murals and a crowded little bar where excitable Brazilian men, some with mustaches so thick and bristly they could be sold as shoe brushes, watch soccer games from Rio and drink beer.

The rows of tables in the small dining room are so close you can't help but sniff the aroma of your neighbors' food —and given the friendliness of most Brazilians, don't be surprised if you're offered a taste.

If you're looking for a more intimate setting, try the pleasant, wood-paneled downstairs, which is less crowded (and less funky) than upstairs.

Every Wednesday and Saturday Cabana Carioca (123 West 45th Street, Telephone: 581-8088) and its less cluttered sister restaurant, Cabana Carioca No. II, just down the block (133 West 45th Street, Telephone: 730-8375), haul out batches of the Brazilian national dish, feijoada. For $8.95, you get an individual Dutch oven heaped with black beans, ham hocks, smoky sausage, and shoulder of beef—a rich and boldly seasoned combination. Other lusty stews, seafood casseroles, and simple chops and steaks are in the $9-to-$14 range. A buffet lunch is now offered downstairs—eight cold dishes, twelve hot dishes plus dessert— for $8.95. Upstairs the same buffet costs only $5. "You have paper placemats so we charge less," the owner explained. Cabana Carioca serves lunch noon to 4 P.M., Monday through Friday; dinner, 5 P.M. to midnight, Monday through Saturday. Cabana Carioca No. II serves lunch noon to 4 P.M. Monday through Friday; dinner 5 to 10 P.M., Monday and Tuesday, 5 to midnight, Wednesday through Saturday.

CAFE NICHOLSON

&. Cafe Nicholson may not be the most chic or ambitious restaurant in town, but if a prize were awarded for eccentricity, it would win spatulas down. John Nicholson has been in the food business since the early 1950s, first as a partner in an American café with Edna Lewis, the author of several books on southern cooking, and for more than a decade on his own at a fanciful little spot tucked under the entrance to the 59th Street Bridge.

The bespectacled, chatty Mr. Nicholson is literally a one-man show: cook, dishwasher, floor washer, maître d'hôtel, and waiter (although he brings in service help when the place is busy). Don't expect to just walk into Cafe Nicholson —the restaurant, which seats about 35, opens according to Mr. Nicholson's personal schedule. If things are slow or he has something better to do, he just locks up and takes off. In the winter he may decide to take an extended trip through Costa Rica or Mexico.

If you can catch him in residence, you are in for a singular experience. The romantic main dining room, covered with ornate nineteenth-century hand-painted tiles, looks as if it belongs in a Spanish nobleman's villa. Handsome antique furniture, artwork, and pottery have been collected by Mr. Nicholson on his jaunts around the globe. Mr. Nicholson's cooking repertory is limited but satisfying: cheese soufflé, roast chicken with herbs, filet mignon, pork chops, fillet of sole, and chocolate soufflé. Dinner is prix fixe at $40, including a mundane house wine.

An equally ornate private room is available for parties.

Cafe Nicholson, at 323 East 58th Street, between First and Second avenues, is open for dinner from 6 to 9 P.M., Tuesday through Saturday. Telephone: 355-6769.

CALI VIEJO

&. Along busy Roosevelt Avenue in Queens, the sights and aromas of South America belie the street's very North American name. Deep-green plantains, strings of garlic, clumps of fresh coriander, and odd-shaped tropical melons are bargained for in machine-gun Spanish. Storefront restaurants, most of them owned by Colombians, display their menus, handwritten in Spanish.

One of the tastiest introductions to Colombian food can be found at Cali Viejo, a cheerful little nook in the shadow of the elevated train tracks, and the even smaller Cali Viejo II a few blocks away.

The owner, Jose Bastidas, seems to know everybody in the neighborhood. The eat-and-run patrons, virtually all of whom are South American, stop by to gobble up the earthy envueltos de maíz (crisp, honey-sweetened fritters) and tamales filled with spicy chunks of pork and peas. You can sit at one of the rickety Formica-topped tables and order the works, which is Cali Viejo's version of a dégustation menu. It is guaranteed to have you speaking Spanish in no time.

Cali Viejo, 84-24 Roosevelt Avenue, between 84th and 85th streets, Jackson Heights, Queens, is open from 11 A.M. to 10 P.M., daily. Telephone: (718) 424-2755. Cali Viejo II, 73-10 Roosevelt Avenue, between 73rd and 74th streets, is open from 8 A.M. to 10 P.M., daily. Telephone: (718) 446-2625.

CARIBE

😋 Caribe, a funky, moderately priced tropical restaurant in the West Village, looks more like a florist's shop than a restaurant, with its jungle of palms thriving in both dining rooms, one with flamingo-pink walls and wicker furniture.

Among the more satisfying dishes here is a huge portion of braised fork-tender oxtail in a brassy broth that is delicious when soaked up with bread. Along with the chewy golden disk of fried plantain, the dish features sautéed bananas, yams, and rice with beans. Most dinners here are under $10.

You can start with a gutsy black bean soup aromatic with onions and bay leaf along with a giveaway starter of innocent-looking steamed green cabbage that detonates on the tongue with hot pepper.

Other menu regulars are Jamaican-style curried goat, churrasco (the steak in batter from Little Havana in Miami), and jerked chicken. Caribe, at 117 Perry Street (at Greenwich Street), serves dinner only, from 5 P.M. to 11 P.M., Monday through Thursday, until midnight Friday and Saturday. Telephone: 255-9191.

CARNEGIE DELI

New York City is synonymous with the clattering and chattering institution known as the delicatessen. To devotées of corned beef, pastrami, chicken dumpling soup, and "a bagel with a schmeeer!" there is no place like the Carnegie Delicatessen, at 854 Seventh Avenue, at 55th Street.

The atmosphere is something right out of a Woody Allen parody of New York Jewish culture—in fact, the Carnegie played a large role in *Broadway Danny Rose.*

The reason Carnegie's corned beef is so superior—remarkably tender and lean yet intensely flavorful—is that big slabs of brisket are cured in house and hand trimmed. The Carnegie also prepares its own peppery pastrami in a slow smoker that was especially made for it in Canada. A sandwich of either is served on the best-quality rye bread, weighs in at a pound and three-quarters, and stands five inches high on the plate, fairly daring you to finish it. Perpetual lines outside the door at lunchtime attest to the Carnegie's reputation as New York's best.

The Carnegie Deli is open from 6 A.M. to 4 A.M., daily. Telephone: 757-2245.

CHANTAL CAFÉ

If the price of Broadway theater tickets burns a big hole in your pocket, you can at least have an enjoyable and affordable meal at Chantal, an amiable little French restaurant on the edge of the theater district—lunch is from $10 to $15, dinner is prix fixe at $16.95 (with several supplements). Start off with a richly flavored onion soup, warm garlic sausage, or a pork terrine. Reliable entrées include beef braised in a red-wine sauce, sautéed shrimp with garlic and tomatoes, and sautéed chicken with raspberry-vinegar sauce. Daily specials include coq au vin (Monday), boeuf bourguignon (Tuesday), cassoulet (Wednesday), navarin of lamb (Thursday), bouillabaisse with lobster (Friday), and blanquette de veau (Saturday). Supplements range from $2 to $6.

The setting is crisp and casual, with a pretty, skylighted back room, and the staff couldn't be nicer. Chantal, 257 West 55th Street, serves lunch from 11:30 A.M. to 3 P.M., Monday through Friday; dinner, 5:30 to 10:30 P.M., Monday through Saturday. Telephone: 246-7076.

CHEZ JACQUELINE

🐌 Run by Jacqueline Zini and her Italian-born husband, Giovanni, this trim little bistro offers a solid range of country fare such as the garlicky codfish-and-potato purée called brandade de morue, escargots in a pastis-perfumed tomato sauce, and meaty fresh mussels in a zestily seasoned tomato-and-white-wine broth. A special entrée to watch for is tender tripe in a soothing tomato sauce. Herb-encrusted rack of lamb is delicious, as is stuffed quail in potato baskets. With a good bottle of wine and lovely homemade desserts, dinner for two runs about $55, before tip. Chez Jacqueline, 72 Macdougal Street, is open from 6 to 11 P.M., Sunday through Thursday, and 6 to 11:30 P.M., Friday and Saturday. Telephone: 505-0727.

CHITA

🐌 Chita is a playfully designed restaurant on theater row on West 42nd Street, named for Chita Rivera, the rubber-limbed singer and dancer of Broadway fame. The 175-seat dining area is a winsome hodgepodge of colors: black-and-white tile floor, fuschia walls, leopard-skin banquettes, fake palm trees, and framed photos of Miss Rivera in various high-stepping poses.

The menu carries the predictable blend of pastas, pizzas, salads, and grilled entrées, along with a sampling of Puerto Rican–style dishes—Miss Rivera and her sister, Lola del Rivero, the restaurant manager, are of Puerto Rican heritage.

The cooking is uneven. At lunch, grilled marinated shrimp are nicely seasoned, although the watery polenta with them needs help ($7.50). A fricassee of scallops is tasty and copious, presented over toasty kernels of corn, leeks, and diced tomatoes ($6.50). The one pasta tried, fusilli with shreds of tender duck, roasted peppers, and scallions, was tasty but soupy ($9.50).

At dinner, you can start with a seductively charred quail presented over black-eyed peas and spinach ($5.50). An entrée of pepper-dusted tuna steak is oddly bland, although the blend of vegetables under it livens things up ($16.50).

Chita, 444 West 42nd Street, serves lunch from noon to 3:30 P.M., daily; dinner, 4 to 10:30 P.M., daily; late supper, 10:30 P.M. to midnight, daily; and Sunday brunch, noon to 3:30 P.M. (prix fixe $12.95). Telephone: 695-4747.

CORNER BISTRO

❧ If Greenwich Village leaves you weary and hungry, an inviting little spot to recuperate with a bowl of chili or a fist-size hamburger is Corner Bistro, 331 West 4th Street. Slide into one of the high-backed wooden booths across from the long mahogany bar where neighborhood regulars hang out and watch sports events on the overhead television. The brick-walled back room is snug and romantic in a bohemian sort of way.

The juicy "bistro burger" ($4.75) should come with dry-cleaning instructions, for if you try to take a bite out of this monster—wrapped with bacon and topped with tomato and lettuce—it will fight back to the death, squirting and sliding all over the place. It comes with a woodpile of excellent rust-colored french fries. The preferred beverage with this all-American duo is McSorley's ale on tap ($1.50). The chili is fresh but meekly seasoned for my taste, but you get lots of it for $3.25. Corner Bistro is open from 11:30 A.M. to 4 A.M., Monday through Saturday, and noon to 4 A.M., Sunday. Telephone: 242-9502.

DAVID K'S CAFE

❧ A variety of intriguing Chinese pasta dishes can be sampled at David K's Cafe, a casual, comfortable spot that is one of the better bargains on the East Side. Situated in the former Mexican restaurant Cafe Marimba, the new café retains some of the haunting charm of its predecessor, including the cool indirect lighting that casts shadows on the off-white walls, sleek black tables, and handsome earth-toned tiles. Spacey background music by Kitaro has replaced peppy mariachi music, and Oriental porcelain and bronze are displayed where sun-bleached logs once evoked desert scenes.

From the appetizer selection, winners include a richly flavored cold terrinelike combination of shredded lamb bound in gelatin ($4.50), meaty honey-glazed pork ribs ($5.95), sparkling homemade noodles tossed with shredded beef and thin strips of cucumber ($6.95), and fettuccinelike pasta (called northern family noodles) under a sauce combining minced pork, dried bean curd, scallions, fresh coriander, and hoisin ($6.95). Pan-sticker dumplings are superb, too, filled with beef and scallions ($7.50 for six) or with shrimp (the house special version, $7.95 for six).

David K's Cafe, 1115 Third Avenue (entrance on 65th Street between Second and Third avenues), is open from 5

P.M. to midnight, Monday through Thursday, to 1 A.M., Friday, noon to 1 A.M., Saturday, and noon to midnight, Sunday. Telephone: 935-1161.

DIVA

At first glance Diva looks like any number of popular East Side neighborhood bistros: a snug bar up front, whitewashed brick walls, soft lighting, closely clustered tables, hustling waiters and waitresses. The menu, a mingling of mostly seafood, salads, and pastas, is au courant as well. The only hints that something different is going on here are the unusual number of men wearing yarmulkes, and the wine list, which carries labels like the 1987 Baron Herzog sauvignon blanc.

Diva is a dairy kosher restaurant and, to paraphrase the old rye bread commercial, you don't have to be Jewish to like it. The cooking is straightforward, fresh, and well seasoned with light, herb-infused sauces.

A meal may start with a tasty steamed artichoke in a parsley broth ($5.95); zucchini stuffed with mushrooms, tomatoes, and Parmesan cheese ($5.95); and al dente penne (an entrée portion split by two as an appetizer, $16) in a ripe, pulpy tomato sauce with arugula and ricotta cheese. Entrées include a deftly poached salmon steak vigorously seasoned with fresh dill, along with firm-poached carrots and new potatoes ($19.75); excellent whole brook trout poached in a combination of lemon juice, capers, and white wine ($16.95); and a lusty linguine putanesca with tomato, anchovies, capers, and black olives ($16).

There is nothing in the Talmud that says kosher desserts can't be decadent; hence, the white and black chocolate mousse under curls of semisweet chocolate.

Diva, 306 East 81st Street, is open from 5 to 10 P.M., Monday through Thursday; after sundown, Saturday (closed Saturday in summer); 4 to 10 P.M., Sunday. Telephone: 650-1928.

DOMINICK'S

Dominick's, the pint-size, wildly popular Italian institution on Arthur Avenue in the Bronx, has expanded by about a third, but that doesn't seem to alleviate the lines outside this thirty-four-year-old Bronx institution. About a half dozen more communal tables have been added by moving the kitchen farther into the back of the building.

At 3 P.M. on a typical Sunday, customers are lined up in the foyer, while inside, packed tighter than a jar of Italian peppers, gleeful diners dig into oval platters of homemade lasagna, stuffed shells, ziti in red sauce, bresaola, pork chops, and more.

Affable waiters in kitchen whites still approach your table and ask, "Whadda' you guys want?" There are no menus, no reservations, no credit cards, no wine lists, no desserts, and no checks (they just tell you the price at the end of the meal, which can vary from visit to visit depending on the waiter's math and mood).

The food is still as homespun and copious as ever. A dainty Sunday repast for two began with a large mixed salad, slabs of terrific home-baked bread, a bottle of Corvo (a dry Italian white wine from Sicily), and a platter combining shells stuffed with ricotta cheese in red sauce and splendid ravioli. Next came a softball-size portion of bresaola (the dried salt beef in a tomato-and-parsley sauce). It seems that everyone punctuates the Dominick's experience with an espresso and Sambuca—they plop the bottle on the table so you can help yourself. Dinner for two costs from $35 to $45.

Dominick's, 2335 Arthur Avenue, between East 186th Street and Crescent Avenue, serves from noon to 10 P.M., Monday, Wednesday, Thursday, and Saturday, noon to 11 P.M., Friday, and 1 to 9 P.M., Sunday. Telephone: 733-2807.

THE "11" CAFE

🍴 The "11" Cafe is a tidy and welcoming little Venezuelan restaurant in the East Village that offers some lusty national specialties at budget prices. Its compact dining room and bar with a dozen colorful tables sports a buoyant tropical décor; a tape deck near the coffee machine pours out big band Ricky Ricardo Latin tunes, which prompt an occasional South American customer to break into a few samba passes.

The phone-booth-size kitchen in back produces a wide range of tasty arepas, which refers to thick cornmeal tortillas that are filled with a variety of fillings and eaten as snacks or appetizers ($3.50). I can highly recommend the smoky and succulent roast pork, which is terrific with a sprinkling of the liquid fire they call hot sauce. The shredded beef is delicious, too. The same pork is served as part of an entrée, called pabellon de pernil, flanked by white rice, brassy black beans, and sautéed sweet plantains ($8.50). Another good choice is called la hallaca, which is essentially a Venezuelan tamale made with cornmeal-encased bits of pork, beef, and chicken steamed in banana leaves ($9). Beer, sangria, and Spanish wines are available, unless you are in a political frame of mind and opt for the house Cuba libre (rum, Coke, and bitters).

The "11" Cafe, 170 Second Avenue, at 11th Street, is open Monday through Friday from 4 P.M. to midnight, Saturday and Sunday from noon to midnight. Telephone: 982-4924.

ERNIE'S

🍴 Ernie's, 2150 Broadway, between 75th and 76th streets, is a cavernous warehouse frequented by a late-carousing young crowd. It is as much a place to experience as a place to eat. Pizzas are probably the most reliable offering, and they come in a dozen guises, like fresh sage, onion, smoked mozzarella, and sun-dried tomatoes; eggplant, leeks, and roasted garlic cloves; or duck sausage, leeks, and fresh sage ($6.50 to $8.50). Pastas ($8.95 to $12.95) and grilled entrées ($10.50 to $14) are a little more risky.

Ernie's serves lunch from noon to 4 P.M., Monday through Friday, 11:30 A.M. to 4 P.M., Saturday and Sunday; dinner, 5:30 P.M. to midnight, Monday through Saturday, 5 P.M. to midnight, Sunday. The bar buzzes until well after 11 P.M. Telephone: 496-1588.

EXTERMINATOR CHILI

🍴 Looking for an amusing place to have a good cheap lunch or to sate the postmovie munchies? Try Exterminator Chili, a wacky dinerlike eatery at 305 Church Street (at Walker) in the lower Broadway section of Manhattan. The name of this is quite apt. Chili comes in three gradations on the gastronomic Richter scale: residential (mild), commercial (medium), and industrial (Is there a gardening hose in the house?). For about $5 at lunch, you get a hefty bowl of chili served with slaw or potato salad and, if desired, a topping of sour cream, onions, and Cheddar cheese. A mild vegetarian chili also is available for the same price. At dinner, portions are larger and prices slightly higher. The types of chili sampled—I drew the line at commercial grade—were fresh and tasty.

Exterminator Chili, which is run by a team of pot-wielding Marx Brothers characters, is a wonderfully campy throwback to the 1950s. You sit in worn vintage booths surrounded by pop icons from the Howdy Doody era—color-by-numbers art adorns pink stucco walls with fake hewed-timber crossbeams, a wagon-wheel chandelier hangs from the turquoise ceiling, and all sorts of memorabilia clutter every horizontal space.

The menu also carries burgers, sandwiches, salad plates, and a dense sweet-potato pie right out of the Crisco Homemakers Cookbook. If you are nice, the counterman may let you pet one of his rubber monkey heads, the ones advertised in comic books that "amazingly grow hair!" when you set them in water.

Exterminator Chili is open for breakfast and lunch from 8 A.M. to 4 P.M., Monday through Friday; dinner, 6 to 11 P.M., Monday through Thursday, 6 P.M. to midnight, Friday, and on weekends from 11 A.M. to midnight, Saturday, and 11 A.M. to 11 P.M., Sunday. Telephone: 219-3070.

FRANK'S

 è In an era when many restaurateurs value décor and service over good cooking, it is reassuring to dine in a homey, unpretentious place like Frank's, at 431 West 14th Street, in the heart of Manhattan's wholesale-meat district. This seventy-year-old steakhouse, with its pressed-tin ceiling, languid overhead fan, sawdust-strewn tile floor and long, elbow-worn mahogany bar, is as comfortable as an old flannel shirt. It has been known to generations of butchers and truck drivers as a place to start the day with coffee and rolls at 2 A.M. and, after the cooks come in at 4 A.M., virile breakfasts of everything from steak and eggs to kidneys, liver pancakes, and bacon.

Frank's has a sizable seafood selection and pasta. The steaks are better than average quality and cooked to order, but it is a pasta appetizer that shines on this menu. Tagliarini puttanesca, thin, homemade egg noodles with a sauce blending tomatoes, capers, black olives, garlic, and anchovies, is delightfully executed. *Puttanesca* translates as "prostitute-style," named after the prostitutes of Rome, said to favor this dish. The pasta is cooked al dente, and the sauce is brassy and beautifully balanced. It is served as a daily special about three nights a week; always call ahead and ask if they have it. Frank's is open for breakfast, lunch, and dinner from 4 A.M. to 10 P.M., Monday through Friday; and for dinner only, 5 to 11 P.M., Saturday. Telephone: 243-1349.

FUKUDA

❦ Amid the clamorous backdrop of the West Village, Fukuda is a serene nook where you can enjoy bright fresh sushi and sashimi along with an array of Oriental tidbits at moderate prices. Run by a solitary chef who whirls at 78 rpm behind the sushi bar and a service team of two, this unassuming little spot—about thirty seats including eight at the bar—has a family feeling to it, which perhaps explains its possessive and cliquish following.

A broad sampling of the menu recently revealed that the unassailably fresh raw fish is the major draw. The assorted sushi plate is a visual and textural delight combining tuna, salmon, shrimp, flounder, squid, and mackerel; sashimi is equally good. All of the assorted handrolls are made with crackling fresh seaweed sheets and tasty garnishes.

Several special appetizers are worth sampling. Hasu hakata features two slivers of crunchy lotus root sandwiching ground shrimp and set in a zesty vinegar-based sauce; broiled rounds of eggplant swabbed with a combination of sweet miso sauce and ground chicken is intriguing as well.

Sake drinkers might want to try the house brand, which is milky white and served cold—it's especially effective as an antidote to wasabi overdoses.

Fukuda, 61 Grove Street, is open for dinner Tuesday through Sunday, from 5 P.M. to midnight. Telephone: 242-3699.

GAGE & TOLLNER

❦ In 1879, when Charles M. Gage opened his seafood restaurant, Brooklyn was a separate city. A decade later Mr. Gage and his partner, Eugene Tollner, moved to a stately period building near Brooklyn's City Hall. Nearly a century later, its burnished wood walls, faded tin ceiling, and gas-lighted chandeliers (recently converted to electric) have acquired a ghostly patina that evokes images of stogie-chomping pols and well-heeled burghers of the day slurping fresh oysters and hoisting frosted beer steins. The food has not aged as well as the setting, however, for much of the fish and chops sampled recently were overcooked and underseasoned.

A few dishes are worth sampling, however: oysters rolled in cracker meal and sautéed in butter until they acquire smoky charred edges, pristine crabmeat salad, and fried eggplant. Clam bellies, alas, were unavailable when I last visited. Drinks are deep and robust, and the uniformed waiters are caring in their own laconic way.

Gage & Tollner, 372 Fulton Street, at Jay Street, serves lunch and dinner, noon to 9:30 P.M., Monday through Friday, 4 to 10:30 P.M., Saturday, 2 to 9:30 P.M., Sunday. Closed Sunday in July and August. Telephone: (718) 875-5181.

GELATERIA SIRACUSA

૨૯ The gelati wave that washed over New York in recent years has given New Yorkers a kaleidoscopic selection of this Italian ice cream. Some of the best gelati I have tasted are served at a sparkling little spot called Gelateria Siracusa, 65 Fourth Avenue, between 9th and 10th streets. It makes a half dozen or so flavors in $4, $3, and $2 sizes. My favorites are the nutty hazelnut and ricotta. Open 5 P.M. to 11 P.M., Sunday through Thursday, and 4:30 P.M. to 12:30 A.M., Friday and Saturday. Telephone: 254-1940.

GIORDANO

૨૯ This is the Mamma Leone's of the far West Side—a sprawling Neapolitan grotto that is big on theatrics but lacking in the kitchen. A little courtyard in the center of the complex is a delightful place for lunch. Too bad the food is barely cafeteria quality—soggy pasta with clam sauce that has an odd chemical aftertaste, desiccated veal paillard, soggy premade Caesar salad, over-the-hill shrimp. It's a shame, for the ambiance deserves better. Giordano, 409 West 39th Street, is open from noon to 11 P.M., Monday through Thursday, noon to midnight, Friday and Saturday, and 5 to 11 P.M., Sunday. Dinner about $25 per person before wine, tax, and tip. Telephone: 947-3883, 947-3884, 947-9811.

GRAMERCY PARK BISTRO

૨૯ Hidden in a narrow arcade of antique-jewelry shops in the Gramercy Park Hotel, this spare and tranquil little spot turns out some soothing Polish specialties at remarkably low prices. "Krystyna & Mom," the business card reads, meaning the soft-spoken, welcoming daughter who tends to the cream-colored dining room that currently doubles as an art gallery for a Polish painter, while Mom tends to the pierogi in a kitchen down the hall. If your red-blood count needs a boost, get some of Mom's scarlet borscht for $3.50 —"All beets, Polish style," Krystyna Jurewicz explains. "Not like the Russian type with cabbage."

As for those pierogi, they are light and well-seasoned little pillows, stuffed with minced mushrooms and sauerkraut or creamy farmer's cheese ($4.95). I haven't tried everything on the menu, but the roasted veal with caper sauce was satisfying ($11.75), along with the chewy dense brown bread; roast duck with sliced apples was moist and tasty, even though the skin was nearly blackened ($13.95). Mom's kielbasa is top-notch as part of the combination platter with sauerkraut and stuffed cabbage ($11.95). Get the sweet little squares of poppyseed cake for dessert ($2.50). Wine is BYO, so you save even further. Gramercy Park Bistro, 4 Lexington Avenue, at 22nd Street, serves lunch from noon to 3 P.M., Monday through Saturday; dinner, 6 to 10 P.M., Monday through Saturday. Telephone: 473-9004.

GULF COAST

ᏪᎢ This cacophonous Cajun/Tex-Mex spot on West Street along the Hudson River serves generally fresh and satisfying fare, including soft-shell crabs in season, steamed shrimp with hot sauce, tamales, and the like. The attire runs from rolled-up workshirts to Wall Street pinstripes. The average tab for a complete dinner with several drinks is about $25. While the downstairs dining room does not have a view of the river (the front bar has a partial view), a second-floor addition offers a panorama of the harbor.

Gulf Coast, 489 West Street, near West 12th Street, serves lunch and snacks from noon to 5 P.M., Wednesday through Saturday; brunch, noon to 3 P.M., Sunday; dinner, 5 to midnight, Monday through Thursday, 5 P.M. to 1 A.M., Friday and Saturday, 4:30 to 11:30 P.M., Sunday. Telephone: 206-8790.

HAMBURGER HARRY'S

ᏪᎢ This sleek grillery has two locations: 157 Chambers Street downtown (Telephone: 267-4446), and near Times Square, at 145 West 45th Street (Telephone: 840-2756). They sport violet walls, neon highlights, blond wood tables, and an open charcoal-mesquite grill. Their thick hamburgers are made with good-quality semilean ground beef and are served on sesame-seed buns. Prices range from $4.50 for the "naked burger" (served without a roll) to $6.50 for both the caviar-and-sour-cream burger and the "ha ha burger" (chili, Cheddar cheese, chopped onion, guacamole, and pico de gallo hot sauce). Coleslaw is freshly made and tasty, although french fries are sometimes soggy. Both Hamburger Harry's locations are open from 11:30 A.M. to midnight, daily.

HAYATO

❧ It is said that the food at a good Japanese restaurant evokes sensations of the sea. At Hayato, a sushi bar and restaurant at 571 Third Avenue, between 37th and 38th streets, the illusion is taken one step further. Patrons at the sushi bar and tables in the front dining room are treated to an audio-visual display projected on two walls that shows rolling ocean surf to the soothing background music of Kitaro, the composer of futuristic-sounding "new age" works.

I wouldn't say that food necessarily tastes better with celluloid ocean spray bathing your face, but it certainly creates a relaxing atmosphere. Fresh and attractively displayed options include the sushi combination, chirashi, and an assortment of vegetables and fish in seaweed rolls.

Occasionally, the video switches to dramatic scenes of surfers gliding across monstrous waves or to wind-surfing competitions. The highlight of the show, however, is when videotape cameras aim at the sushi chefs behind the bar. This allows diners who are sitting at the other end of the room to watch their food being prepared. If you happen to be sitting at the sushi bar, the camera may catch you in the unflattering pose of trying to daintily bite a tuna roll in half, only to have the rice fall on the counter and the fillet dangle from your mouth like a piece of bait. No matter, it's all part of the show. Hayato is open for lunch from noon to 2:30 P.M., Monday through Friday; dinner, 5 to 10:30 P.M., daily. Telephone: 883-0453.

THE HEALTH PUB

❧ Considering the sizable demand for vegetarian fare in New York, there are few places around that make an effort to be distinctive in either ambiance or food. A happy exception is The Health Pub, a cheerful vegetarian café at 371

Second Avenue, at 21st Street. The two large dining rooms are crisp and tidy, done in soft beige with butcher-block tables.

The menu sounds so appealing that even hard-core junk-food addicts might be tempted. Cold soba, the Japanese buckwheat noodles, with snow peas is an attractively arranged appetizer laced with julienne strips of carrots, cucumber, and Chinese radish, all in a dynamic sesame sauce fired with a touch of hot pepper oil ($4.50). Salads are giant and delicious, including one made with watercress, pears, avocado, and lime ($5.75).

An entrée of whole-grain polenta is crispy outside and delicious, paired with a pulpy sun-dried-tomato sauce, chickpea salad, and well-seasoned broccoli di rape ($8.50). I had a little difficulty getting a handle on a Thai-inspired dish made with braised tempeh (a culture of soybeans, grains, and legumes) cooked in coconut milk ($9.25). A good guiltless dessert is the autumn squash pie with a toasted-oat crust, just faintly sweetened with maple syrup, vanilla, and rum ($3.50). No alcohol is served, but all sorts of freshly made fruit and vegetable drinks are available.

The Health Pub is open from 11 A.M. to 11 P.M., daily. Telephone: 529-9200.

HSF

&. The little dim sum carts roll by endlessly, and a couple can eat until they fall over on the simulated leather banquettes without spending $50—individual plates from the carts generally range from $2 to $2.75. The steamed shrimp dumplings and fried pork dumplings are nicely seasoned and fresh; other highlights are the hacked-up steamed spareribs; sesame-sprinkled chicken patties; stuffed green peppers, and stuffed eggplant. Wine by the glass and Chinese beer are available. The room is trim and comfortable, with beige tablecloths and soft lighting. Most of the waiters' and waitresses' English is incomprehensible to Americans, but just point to things that look good and you'll do fine. HSF, 578 Second Avenue, between 31st and 32nd streets, serves lunch from 11:30 A.M. to 3 P.M., daily; dinner, 3 to 11 P.M., daily. Telephone: 689-6969.

HSF (CHINATOWN)

&. HSF's original and larger site, at 46 Bowery, south of Canal Street, offers a similar range of food. The setting is louder and brighter, filled with many Chinese families. The show starts rolling at breakfast and continues to midnight. Continuous service 7:30 A.M. to 2 A.M., daily. Telephone: 374-1319.

KODAMA

♨ This trim and friendly little Japanese restaurant offers a dozen appetizers as well as a wide variety of fresh and reasonably priced sushi ($1.50 to $3.00) that you can order à la carte. Try the cleanly fried and crunchy tempura of shrimp and vegetables; the superior negimaki, grilled beef rolls holding scallions; light and tasty shrimp dumplings; or broiled chicken on skewers with a sweet-edged sauce. Lunch runs $15 to $20 per person, dinner about $20 to $25. Kodama, 301 West 45th Street, is open for lunch from noon to 2:30 P.M., Monday through Saturday; dinner, 5 to 11:30 P.M., Monday through Saturday, 5 to 10:30 P.M., Sunday. Telephone: 582-8065.

LA BONNE SOUPE

♨ Customers line up outside the door of this rustically humble French bistro in midtown, attesting to the singular bargains within; lunch is a real crush, dinner less so. As the name promises, the soups are indeed good—particularly mushroom barley with lamb ($6.50), and lusty cheese-encrusted onion ($6.50), both of which come with good French bread, a green salad, and dessert. Watch for other specials, such as the brandade de morue ($8.75) daily during the cool months, a garlicky purée of codfish and potatoes that you can scoop up with toasted French bread ($8.75), or the little crock of fragrant bouillabaisse ($14.95). The downstairs dining room is lined with neighborly banquettes; two dining rooms upstairs are festooned with a fabulous collection of colorful Haitian primitive-style paintings. Keep this spot in mind for late dining. La Bonne Soupe, 48 West 55th Street, serves from 11:30 A.M. to midnight, daily. Telephone: 586-7650.

LA FUSTA

€ *Parrillada* is the Spanish term for mixed grill, which in the Argentine tradition usually means a mini-charcoal barbecue presented at a heaped table featuring T-bone steak, marinated skirt steak, morcilla (blood sausage), sweetbreads, kidneys, calf's liver, and sausage. At La Fusta, a popular neighborhood Argentine restaurant in the Elmhurst section of Queens, the lusty and well-cooked parrillada (sans kidneys and liver) comes with a jar of chimichurri, a piquant sauce made with garlic, parsley, and olive oil. The parrillada is $12.50 per person.

For starters, try the thick-crusted empanadas de carne, redolent of garlic and minced olives ($1.60), or the typically Argentine salad of shrimp, fresh watercress with onions ($2.50). La Fusta is a casual and congenial spot with stucco and timber walls festooned with horse-racing memorabilia —*la fusta* means rider's crop—red checkered tablecloths, a friendly staff.

I was pleasantly surprised by the Argentine wines sampled, including the clean, crisp Navarro Correas white and the easy-drinking red from the same house (both $18). For dessert, flan with dulce de leche, the sweetened caramelized milk, is a must if you want to be truly Argentine; another good choice is the thin apple pancake flambéed with rum ($2.80). La Fusta, 80-32 Baxter Avenue, Elmhurst, Queens, serves dinner from 4 to 11:30 P.M., daily. Telephone: (718) 429-8222.

LA KASBAH

€ Couscous, tagine, spicy lamb kebabs, and other Middle Eastern specialties are featured at La Kasbah, an engaging glatt kosher restaurant on West 71st Street off Columbus Avenue. This moderately priced spot has two simply appointed peach-and-white dining rooms serving authentically prepared dishes. La Kasbah is owned by David Dery, who was born in Morocco and reared in Israel.

Three varieties of couscous—chicken, lamb, and vegetarian (all under $20 per person)—are prepared in the traditional way, letting the ingredients cook slowly over a double steamer to meld their flavors. Portions are enormous. Tagine, a lamb stew made with prunes, celery, pine nuts, raisins, and rice, is also full-flavored and thoroughly satisfying. From the grill come highly seasoned lamb and chicken kebabs. For starters, there is a deliciously smoky

429

baba ghannoush, the Middle Eastern eggplant dip, as well as hummus, tahina, and falafel. Several simple kosher table wines are available.

La Kasbah, 70 West 71st Street, is open for dinner from 5 to 11 P.M., Monday through Thursday, 1 to 11 P.M., Sunday. Telephone: 769-1690.

LA MEDITERRANÉE

❧ It will never make anybody's list of Manhattan's ten most chic restaurants, nor will you see it mentioned in the society columns accompanied by photographs of insouciant celebrities clinking glasses and pecking cheeks. La Mediterranée, on Second Avenue at 50th Street, is about as voguish as spats—but considerably more comfortable. Quite simply, it is a wonderfully homey and neighborly spot that gives you a warm feeling upon entering, with its timber-and-stucco façade, faux wooden shutters, colorful murals of France, and cozy banquettes.

The moderately priced menu is just as familiar and soothing, running from hot sausage and potato salad, calf's liver with raisins, lamb chops, and assorted daily stews and roasts, such as a poached stuffed chicken and winter vegetables.

Prix-fixe lunch is $19.75. Prix-fixe dinners are $19.75 from 5:30 to 6:45 P.M. and $22.50 afterward. The food is generally wholesome and satisfying (specials are the best bets). On Sunday evenings, a beaming Frenchwoman strolls through the dining room singing "La Vie en Rose" and other nostalgic hits, occasionally joined by the owner, Robert Chamou.

La Mediterranée, 947 Second Avenue, is open for lunch from noon to 3 P.M., Monday through Friday; dinner, 5:30 to 10 P.M., Monday through Sunday. Closed Sunday in summer. Telephone: 755-4155.

LANDMARK TAVERN

❧ Dating to 1868, Landmark Tavern, 626 Eleventh Avenue, corner of 46th Street, has a splendid Old New York feeling with its burnished wood bar, huge brass wood-burning stove, uneven floors, and smoke-smudged ceiling. This is a great place for a drink, although don't expect much from the food. Strip steak with pommes soufflés is pleasing, and simple burgers and grilled items are reliable if not exciting. The kitchen has an aversion to seasoning of any kind, so vegetables, stews, and shepherd's pie come out utterly bland. The bar stocks a fine old selection of single-malt Scotches and cognacs. Brunch is served from noon to 4:15 P.M., Saturday; 11:30 A.M. to 4:15 P.M., Sunday; lunch, noon to 4:30 P.M., Monday through Friday; dinner, 5 P.M. to midnight, Sunday through Thursday, 5 P.M. to 1 A.M., Friday and Saturday. Dinner about $25 before wine, tax, and tip are counted. Telephone: 757-8595.

LE MADELEINE

🦆 Le Madeleine, an engaging little French bistro on West 43rd Street near Ninth Avenue, is often overlooked as a moderately priced dining option in the theater district, although it shouldn't be. It is a lively spot at night, where theater people gather at a long bar to leaf through issues of *Variety* and talk shop. The dining room is low-key and charming, with brick walls, wooden banquettes, and butcher-paper-covered tables. During the warm months, a backyard garden is open for dining.

The menu is straightforward bistro fare with more than a few appealing dishes. Mussels marinière are plump and well cooked in their flavorful white-wine-and-herb sauce— they make a good light lunch along with a salad and some French bread for dipping in the broth. Soupe au pistou, while thicker than the traditional version, is tasty and well seasoned. Simple grilled fish are usually nicely done as well.

Not everything is so successful, but you should do well by sticking to homey soups, stews, and salads. Dinner entrées range from $9.95 to $18. Le Madeleine, 403 West 43rd Street, is open daily from noon to midnight; brunch Saturday and Sunday from noon to 3:30 P.M. Telephone: 246-2993.

LES DÉLICES GUY PASCAL

🦆 One of the most civilized ways to lift the spirits on a dreary winter afternoon is to slip into a pastry shop and thaw out with a cup of steaming cappuccino and something sweet. If you find yourself trudging around the Upper East Side, one welcoming spot is Les Délices Guy Pascal, 1231 Madison Avenue, at 89th Street. Mr. Pascal, former pastry chef at La Côte Basque, opened this shop, one of three in Manhattan (the others are at Zabar's, Broadway and 80th Street, and in the Place des Antiquaires, 125 East 57th Street).

This cheerful little shop, with a dozen tables, serves Mr. Pascal's pastries, as well as a small menu for light lunches or dinners. Of the entrées sampled, pâté de campagne and ratatouille quiche were among the best choices. Most of Mr. Pascal's cakes, tarts, mousses, and breads, however, are superior. The shop is open 8 A.M. to 10 P.M., Monday through Saturday, and 9 A.M. to 8 P.M. on Sunday. Telephone: 289-5300.

MANHATTAN BISTRO

𝕖𝕝 Patrons come to this bustling bistro amid the SoHo art galleries wearing everything from business suits to Bruce Springsteen T-shirts. It's a big, stark, smoky spot with a lively bar and some decent food. Try the tasty and well-seasoned rillettes of pork ($4), grilled Black Angus steak with sauce choron ($19), or boudin noir (blood sausage) with good french fries ($8). The short wine list has some uncommon selections in the $20-and-under range. Service is uneven but well meaning.

Manhattan Bistro, at 129 Spring Street, serves lunch from noon to 4 P.M., daily; dinner, 6 P.M. to midnight, Monday through Saturday, 6 to 11:30 P.M., Sunday. Telephone: 966-3459.

MEZZALUNA

𝕖𝕝 This exquisite little fifty-seat trattoria is still one of my favorite casual restaurants in town—problem is, I can rarely find a table it is so crowded. Recently I have gotten around the problem by stopping by at off hours, say 2:30 to 3 P.M. for a late lunch.

Mezzaluna—Italian for half moon, or in this case for a semicircular chopping blade with a handle at each end—is designed with whimsical good taste, from colorful drawings and collages that cover one wall to a painted-sky ceiling, designer plates and chairs, marble tables, and hand-painted ashtrays.

The menu specializes in pastas and pizzas, which are cooked in a wood-fired brick oven. For starters, there are eight variations on carpaccio, all superbly fresh. One favorite is tissue-thin slices of beef resting on a bed of glistening arugula with slices of Parmesan cheese as garnish. Drizzled with olive oil and dusted with fresh pepper, it is a tasty and invigorating appetizer. The carpaccios also come with radicchio and Romano cheese, with avocado, with fontina cheese, and with herbs.

Among pastas sampled, you find everything from meat-filled pumpkin tortellini in a light pink sauce of cream, chopped tomato, and herbs to homemade ravioli stuffed with fresh mushrooms in a cream sauce. The pizzas, which can serve as an entrée for one or be split in a multicourse meal, are bright and fresh, with a thin, slightly puffed crust. Among the toppings are tomato and fresh basil; eggplant and black olives; basil pesto; and a combination of zucchini, carrots, tomato, peppers, and leeks. Lunch runs about $25 to $30, dinner a bit more (not including wine). Mezzaluna is at 1295 Third Avenue, between 74th and 75th streets. Mezzaluna is open for lunch from noon to 3 P.M., Monday through Friday, noon to 3:30 P.M., Saturday and Sunday; dinner, 6 P.M. to 1 A.M., Monday through Friday, 6:30 P.M. to 1 A.M., Saturday and Sunday. Telephone: 535-9600.

MICKEY MANTLE'S

🐾 Old No. 7, the booming Bronx Bomber himself, Mickey Mantle, has come a long way—from the batter's box to battered chicken, so to speak, with his sports bar and restaurant on Central Park South. If you are lucky you might just spot him there—he drops in under contractual obligation from time to time.

Mickey Mantle's is as much a baseball shrine as a dining spot. The contemporary blond-wood-and-beige space is loaded with sports memorabilia, including the uniforms of Mantle, Babe Ruth, and Joe DiMaggio, autographed photos, paintings, posters—even nonstop videos replaying old World Series footage interspersed with worshipful interviews with the Mick. The service staff, wearing floppy baseball shirts, is as eager and enthusiastic as a bat boy on opening day.

The predominantly male hero worshipers who fill the place can choose from appetizers that include a nicely seasoned veal-and-chicken sausage with red cabbage ($6), garlicky sautéed shiitake mushrooms ($8), or a rather cloying chicken salad drenched in smoky barbecue sauce ($12), and a juicy rare-grilled hamburger with soggy french fries ($10 at lunch, $13 at dinner). A "Spring Training Special" changes daily. One example might be a deftly grilled chicken breast paired with a tame tomato salsa ($12). Dinner entrées—chicken-fried steak with cream gravy, lamb chops, pecan-breaded chicken—run in the $14-to-$25 range. The wine list has a good selection in all prices. Mickey Mantle's, 42 Central Park South, is open from noon to 2 A.M., daily. Telephone: 688-7777.

MIKE'S AMERICAN BAR & GRILL

꿈 Tenth Avenue and 46th Street is not the sort of neighborhood frequented by window shoppers pondering a cute spot for lunch. If David Ludtke has his way, however, his eccentric little restaurant, called Mike's American Bar & Grill, might be reason enough to venture into Manhattan's western frontier. How about grilled game hen with moist and crumbly corn-bread dressing and vegetable salad? Or nicely charred fresh vegetables on a skewer with a red-pepper cream sauce? Or grilled bluefish with red-tomato salsa? Prices are generally under $15.

The restaurant is the reincarnation of a former shots-and-beer bar by the same name. From the outside, with its smudged aluminum and a grimy sign that looks as if firemen used it for hatchet practice, it is hardly the kind of place you would be attracted to. The inside, however, is all spruced up, in a funky kind of way.

An enormous wooden bar takes up most of one side of the room. The yellow-checked tile floor has been scrubbed down, the walls painted bold yellow, and wooden tables are covered with last year's Christmas wrapping paper. Great golden oldies filter in through a good sound system. The various soups and salads sampled were homey and flavorful; the dinner menu offers a wider selection, with items such as grilled smoked duck and marinated leg of lamb.

Mike's, 650 Tenth Avenue, between 45th and 46th streets, is open for lunch from noon to 4 P.M., Monday through Friday; dinner, 5:30 to 11:30 P.M., Monday through Thursday, 5:30 to midnight, Friday and Saturday, 5 to 10 P.M., Sunday. Telephone: 246-4115.

MONTE'S VENETIAN ROOM

꿈 It takes a capacious imagination to liken the Gowanus Canal to the waterways of Venice, but try to imagine it in better days, say 1906, when Monte's Venetian Room opened near this busy Brooklyn waterway. Run by Nick Monte, who was born in the same building, this old-world Neapolitan restaurant is adorned with evocative murals of Venice and period memorabilia. The kitchen serves familiar and generally well-prepared fare at prices that haven't been seen in Manhattan since the Eisenhower administration.

A mound of addictive deep-fried zucchini sticks arrives as you are seated. Among the better selections are melanzane Romana (ricotta-stuffed eggplant), pasta with white clam sauce, zuppa di mussels, and assorted shrimp dishes, such as the garlicky house favorite, "shrimp à la Monte." Baked clams are 80 percent bread crumbs. Count on about $20 per person with a glass of wine.

Monte's Venetian Room, 451 Carroll Street, serves lunch noon to 3 P.M., Monday through Friday; dinner, 3 to 11 P.M., Monday through Friday. Telephone: (718) 624-7860, (718) 624-8984.

MOROCCAN STAR

&. Some of the best dining bargains in New York can be found along Brooklyn's Atlantic Avenue, home of about a dozen Middle Eastern and North African restaurants. One of these is Moroccan Star, 205 Atlantic Avenue, a simple, tidy restaurant that serves a mélange of Arabic and European dishes for prices so low you can't help suspecting they are a mirage.

The kitchen of this family-run restaurant is presided over by Ahmed Almontazer, formerly of Luchow's, the Four Seasons, and the Brasserie in Manhattan, which explains the Continental accent on the menu. However, forget the beef stroganoff and crêpes, and head right for the lamb steak, a juicy, intensely flavorful slab of meat that makes you wonder why this dish is not generally served in Manhattan steakhouses. The best side dish is al dente baby okra.

Other good choices on the menu are pastilla (sometimes spelled pastila or bastila), traditionally a semisweet pigeon pie in paper-thin pastry, and tajine. The pastilla is made with chicken, raisins, garlic, and spices, and is served in a large wedge, like a thick slab of pizza.

The tagine, while different from the version served in Morocco, is nonetheless satisfying. It is a savory lamb stew with carrots, prunes, and dried almonds, and it is meant to be eaten in large pockets of pita bread. Beer and wine are not served, but you may provide your own. Moroccan Star is open from noon to 10 P.M., Sunday through Thursday, noon to 11 P.M., Friday and Saturday. Telephone: (718) 643-0800.

NEW PROSPECT CAFE

❧ Standing-room crowds nightly attest to the good food at bargain prices offered by this neighborly little restaurant on bustling Flatbush Avenue. The small gray-and-white dining room with its chalkboard specials and budget-priced wine list attracts a gregarious flannel-shirt-and-corduroy clientele. The food is imaginative and consistently good—not to mention remarkably inexpensive by Manhattan standards. Among the winning starters: sesame-coated chicken wings in a soy-based sauce, a tasty zucchini timbale with roasted red-pepper sauce, Parmesan-laced polenta accompanied by roasted whole garlic. Entrées range from a fresh and bright bouillabaisselike concoction to crisp-skinned and succulent game hen with apples and green peppercorns to eggplant rollatini with polenta and roasted peppers.

New Prospect Cafe, 393 Flatbush Avenue, at Eighth Avenue, serves brunch from 10:30 A.M. to 3:45 P.M., Sunday; lunch, 11:30 A.M. to 4:30 P.M., Tuesday through Saturday; dinner, 4:30 to 10 P.M., Sunday through Thursday, 4:30 to 11 P.M., Friday and Saturday. Telephone: (718) 638-2148.

NICOLE'S CAPRI

❧ Nicole's Capri, 442 Tenth Avenue, between 34th and 35th streets, is a pretty little oasis in the industrial tundra of Tenth Avenue. The pine-wood dining room with its gold-tinted mirrors on the ceiling and hip saucer-shaped sconces is an inviting spot. The food, however, is not as bright. Antipasto is a sloppy assortment of cold cuts and underseasoned vegetables; ravioli tastes as if it had been frozen then blasted in the oven for a quick thaw (the kitchen has a one-sauce-fits-all approach to most pastas). Of the half-dozen entrées sampled, only the lamb-and-sausage mixed grill was satisfying. Dinner is about $25 before wine, tax, and tip are counted. Nicole's is open from noon to 10 P.M., Monday through Thursday, noon to 11 P.M., Friday, 5 P.M. to midnight, Saturday. Closed Saturday during July and August. Telephone: 947-0769.

PASTA & DREAMS

ॐ Pasta & Dreams, 1068 First Avenue, between 58th and 59th streets, a clone of the popular Mezzaluna, is a cheerful little spot, about the dimensions of the pint-size Mezzaluna, done in bright yellow and pink with yellow cane chairs and a clay-colored tile floor.

The lunch menu carries a number of prix-fixe meals, mostly under $15. You will find combinations such as a sparkling salad of arugula, green leaf lettuce, and radicchio; spaghetti with fresh tomato sauce and basil; a glass of wine, beer, or mineral water; and coffee

A la carte choices include summary dishes such as tagliatelle with asparagus, farfalline with salmon and spinach, and penne with zucchini and mozzarella. The inexpensive wine list offers some reliable Italian labels by the glass and the bottle. Pasta & Dreams has opened a second, much larger outlet, at 2161 Broadway, and is planning yet a third on East 94th (due to open in late 1988).

Pasta & Dreams on First Avenue is open for brunch from noon to 4 P.M., Saturday and Sunday; lunch, noon to 3 P.M., Monday through Friday; dinner, 6 to 11 P.M., Monday through Thursday. Telephone: 752-1436. The Broadway location is open for lunch from noon to 3:30 P.M., Monday through Friday; dinner, 5 P.M. to midnight, Monday through Friday, noon to midnight, Saturday and Sunday. Telephone: 724-4324.

PASTA PRESTO

ॐ You don't go to Pasta Presto for gastronomic enlightenment, but you do go for satisfying bargain-priced fare in an upbeat setting. Pastas are in the $6-to-$12 range.

The two dining rooms, with white brick walls, café tables, and bent-cane chairs, are filled nightly with a mixed informal crowd. Among the fresh and appealing appetizers are eggplant-and-zucchini salad in a light, creamy vinaigrette sauce and fresh-green-beans-and-tomato salad; the cottony winter tomatoes, though, could have been left out.

The menu carries about sixteen pastas and one or two daily specials. Penne with prosciutto, firm-cooked broccoli, and garlic is vibrant and light; spaghetti with chunks of chicken and eggplant in marinara sauce is nicely seasoned and al dente, and daily specials, such as farfalle with a dill-accented cream sauce, shrimp, and crab, hit the spot. Not all pastas are unqualified successes, but at these prices you can afford to experiment and get to know the best offerings. Simple Italian wines run $12 or so.

Pasta Presto, 613 Second Avenue, serves lunch from noon to 5 P.M. daily; dinner, daily, 5 to 11 P.M. (Another branch of Pasta Presto is at 93 Macdougal Street, at Bleecker Street). Telephone: 889-4131.

RESTAURANT FLORENT

It's an Edward Hopper painting come to life, this World War II coffee shop turned French bistro in the heart of the gritty West Side meat-market area. Formerly the R & L Restaurant, a stainless-steel-and-Formica hash house that catered to butchers and truck drivers in the market's heyday, it was taken over by a genial young Frenchman, Florent Morellet. The new owner changed the name to Restaurant Florent while leaving the period décor largely intact.

The menu has abandoned "Adam and Eve on a raft" (poached eggs on toast) for French onion soup gratinée, duck mousse, couscous, sweetbreads, grilled calf's liver, and other homey Gallic fare. Not only is much of the food surprisingly well prepared, it's also a bargain—a three-course meal runs about $25, or a bit more with wine.

Duck liver mousse is freshly made, creamy, and well seasoned, and rillettes of pork are appropriately rough-textured and peppery. Although I had heard good reports about the tripe, my waitress steered me instead to the fresh, golden sautéed sweetbreads with thin, crunchy french fries. Two dining companions enjoyed the inky and oniony boudin noir and a nicely poached monkfish swathed with onions and leeks. Florent is a good spot for a leisurely weekend breakfast.

Restaurant Florent, 69 Gansevoort Street, half a block west of Greenwich Street, is open 24 hours daily. Telephone: 989-5779.

RIO MAR

From the outside, Rio Mar looks like a frayed Latin shots-and-beer bar catering to butchers in the old West Side wholesale meat district. "It's a great place," a usually sensible friend assured me. "Nobody knows about it." With more than a little skepticism, I gave it a try.

The downstairs bar of this family-run establishment is hardly encouraging, with its spooky ice-blue lighting and hunched men lounging at tables in the shadows. Upstairs, however, is altogether different. The small L-shaped room is clean and functional, with yellow walls holding a haphazard gallery of bullfight paintings and assorted posters. The waiters are warm and friendly, although their English can be spotty. As for the food, it is fresh, pure, authentically Iberian, and remarkably cheap.

Caldo gallego, a foggy bowl of kale, white beans, potatoes, and assorted meats, rivals the best I have had in Spain ($2.50). Homemade chicken soup is the real item, made with chicken carcasses, gizzards, and vegetables ($2.50). The more adventurous might sample the pristine octopus salad with sliced onions in a zippy red sauce ($4.75). A limited wine list carries some of Spain's better-known labels.

Shellfish is lovingly prepared, too, whether in the aromatic paella loaded with shrimp, chicken, sausage, and mussels ($11.25) or the terrific mariscada Rio Mar, a cornucopia of shellfish in a garlic-powered broth ($10.75). The garlic-strewn T-bone steak with french fries ($11) will assure you a wide berth at a movie theater afterward. Perhaps the best bargain is the succulent chuletas de puerco (extra-thick pork chops) smothered with onion gravy ($7.25). If you clean your plate, the strolling guitarist may dedicate "Malagueña" to you.

Rio Mar, 7 Ninth Avenue, at the corner of Little West 12th Street, is open daily from noon to 4 A.M. Telephone: 243-9015. A sister establishment, called **Riazor,** 245 West 16th, carries similar food. Telephone: 929-9782.

SARDI'S

❧ For decades Sardi's has been synonymous with the world of Broadway theater. Sadly, the food has deteriorated to an abysmal state at this once-bustling theatrical institution, so it can only be recommended as a place to stop for a drink before or after theater.

Sardi's, 234 West 44th Street, is open 11:30 A.M. to 12:30 A.M., Monday through Thursday, 11:30 A.M. to 1 A.M., Friday and Saturday, and noon to 11 P.M., Sunday. Telephone: 221-8440.

SFUZZI

❧ Sfuzzi is Italian slang for fun food. It's also the name of a diverting Italian restaurant and night spot near Lincoln Center that serves some bright and zesty pastas, salads, and entrées. The 2-level, 150-seat establishment, a branch of the Dallas original, is a zany combination of neoclassical trompe l'oeil and futuristic high tech: plaster murals are chipped and faded to reveal bare brick underneath, and columns look as if they have suffered a bazooka attack. The triangular Italian-designed chairs, constructed with steel tubing wrapped in black rubber, look as if they came out of a cockpit. They are unnerving at first, but I got used to them.

Histrionics aside, some of the food sampled is good, starting with half orders of rigatoni with cubes of roasted eggplant, strips of red peppers and mozzarella, and light and fresh lobster-filled ravioli under a saffron-edged tomato-cream sauce (both $8). Salads and pizzas are available in the $6 to $13 range.

Among entrées, salmon steak is beautifully pan-seared and served under a tangle of deep-fried leeks and a basil-lemon sauce; and a salmon special, with sautéed fennel, is equally alluring (both $21). The veal chop is exceptionally tender and tasty under its orange-tinted sage-butter sauce, with herb-flecked tagliatelle on the side ($24).

The house special drink, a frozen Sfuzzi, is a cooling combination of sparkling wine, peach schnapps, fresh peaches, and ice. The scene is lively (and rather loud), with pulsating background music, two television monitors overhead, and an animated, stylish crowd.

Sfuzzi, at 58 West 65th Street, is open for lunch, 11:30 A.M. to 3 P.M., Monday through Saturday; Sunday brunch, 11:30 A.M. to 3 P.M.; dinner, 5:30 to 11:30 P.M., Monday through Wednesday, 5:30 to midnight, Thursday through Sunday.

SIDEWALKERS'

🐚 You are hit with a blast of a familiar aroma upon entering the sprawling dining room, a blend of sea air and hot spices. All over the room, animated diners wearing plastic bibs are hammering away at mounds of steaming red crabs, sending shards in all directions. Sidewalkers', at 12 West 72nd Street, is about as close as you'll get to the eastern shore of Maryland without leaving Manhattan Island.

Its specialty is steamed and liberally spiced hard-shell crabs, the kind that make a mess of your hands, napkin, bib, the table and floor. The crabs are generally fresh, the meat snowy and sweet, and the spices just piquant enough to keep you rubbing your lips against an icy beer mug in between bites. The size of the crabs depends on availability; a dozen of the medium size cost about $25, a dozen large about $30.

The dining room has a freewheeling, down-home atmosphere conducive to such inelegant consumption—wooden plank floors, rust-colored walls, paper-covered tables, and a young good-time crowd. In addition to the hard-shell crabs, you can get nicely sautéed soft shells with tarragon butter and some of the best crab cakes in town.

Sidewalkers' is open from 5 to 11 P.M., Monday through Thursday, 5 to 11:30 P.M., Friday and Saturday, 5 to 10 P.M., Sunday. Telephone: 799-6070.

SYLVIA'S

To call Sylvia's the most popular ribs-and-fried-chicken restaurant in Harlem, if not in the entire city, would be a gross understatement. This congenial spot, operated by Mrs. Sylvia Woods and her family, is an institution where local politicians meet over braised short ribs and an ever-growing roster of celebrities from near and far stop by for some restorative soul food that has its origins in Mrs. Woods's hometown of Hemingway, South Carolina.

Sylvia's has a pleasantly appointed dining room for leisurely meals and a long bonhomous counter for those who want to eat and run—waddle is more like it—after one of these rib-sticking repasts. Friday night is braised-ribs night, and they can be ordered with peppery collard greens and moist corn bread. The congenial waitresses tend to address customers as "honey" and to encourage them to eat more than they should. Save room for the sweet potato pie, which is so good it could stop a Baptist preacher in mid-sermon. Sylvia's, 328 Lenox Avenue, between 126th and 127th streets, is open from 7:30 A.M. to 10:30 P.M., Monday through Saturday, 1 to 7 P.M., Sunday. Telephone: 996-0660.

TOMMASO

This spirited Italian restaurant, owned by Thomas Verdillo, a wine aficionado and opera lover with a stirring tenor voice (he may burst into a Verdi aria at any moment), is a diverting spot in the far reaches of Brooklyn's Bensonhurst section. The cheerful one-hundred-seat dining room is a favorite gathering place in this predominantly Italian neighborhood. I have enjoyed some lovely dishes there, including sautéed eggplant under a snowfall of crumbled goat cheese, roasted pheasant, and assorted pastas. The wine list is rich in Italian selections at good prices. The restaurant has a handsome wood-paneled room that seats up to sixty for private parties.

Tommaso, 1464 86th Street, between 14th and 15th avenues, serves lunch from noon to 3 P.M., Tuesday through Saturday; dinner, 4 to 11 P.M., Tuesday through Friday, 4 P.M. to midnight, Saturday, 1 to 10 P.M., Sunday. Telephone: (718) 236-9883.

BEER

❧ New York City is often touted today as one of the wine capitals of the world. Long before the wine boom came to this country, however, it was a mecca for beer drinkers—more than seventy breweries existed in the five boroughs at the turn of the century. That era is long gone, but there are still a good number of taverns and restaurants that stock a wide range of domestic and imported beers. Among them are:

American Festival Cafe, 20 West 50th Street, Rockefeller Plaza, 246-6699.

Empire Diner, 210 Tenth Avenue at 22nd Street, 243-2736.

First Avenue Restaurant, 361 First Avenue at 21st Street, 475-9068.

Fleming's, 232 East 86th Street, 988-1540.

Gage & Tollner, 372 Fulton Street, Brooklyn, (718) 875-5181.

Joe Allen, 326 West 46th Street, 581-6464.

Landmark Tavern, 626 Eleventh Avenue, at 46th Street, 757-8595.

Manhattan Brewing Company, 40-42 Thompson Street, at Broome Street, 219-9250. Drink this company's beer inside the brewery next to the giant copper brewing vats.

North Star Pub, 93 South Street, in the South Street Seaport, 509-6757.

Peculier Pub, 182 West 4th Street, 691-8667.

P. J. Clarke's, 915 Third Avenue at 55th Street, 759-1650.

Rathbone's, 1702 Second Avenue at 80th Street, 369-7361.

Ryan McFadden, 800 Second Avenue, at 42nd Street, 599-2226.

Peculier Pub merits special mention for beer lovers; the selection of brews here is extraordinary. Have a craving for a frosty beer on a hot summer day? How about a bottle of Kulmbacher Schweizerhofbräu from Bavaria, or Tooths Sheaf Stout from Australia, Tiger from Singapore, Chihuahua from Mexico, or EKU 28 from West Germany, billed as "the strongest beer in the world"?

These and about two hundred other domestic and imported brews can be found at a remarkable bar in the West Village called the Peculier Pub (the unorthodox spelling comes from Old Peculier Ale from England, the manager's favorite brew).

The pub, at 182 West 4th Street, is small, with eight chairs at the bar and about a dozen tables along the walls lined with bottles and cans of beer from around the world. All beers are kept in five packed refrigerators. Customers order from a two-page beer list; daily specials are listed on a chalk board. On a recent day, specials included Peking, a Chinese beer; O.B. from Korea; and Taj Majal from India.

The pub's manager, a former chemist, who identifies himself only as Tommy, is a walking encyclopedia of brewing lore. Prices range from $1.75 for domestic beers (fifteen of them) to $5 and more for special imports such as St. Sixtus Trappist Ale, a wonderfully creamy and flowery dark brew from Belgium. The Peculier Pub is strictly a burger-and-sandwiches spot, presumably to keep the spotlight on the beers.

The Peculier Pub is open from 4 P.M. to 2 A.M., Sunday through Thursday; 4 P.M. to 4 A.M., Friday; 2 P.M. to 4 A.M., Saturday.

BREAKFAST

🍴 Finding a tranquil and elegant spot for breakfast in New York is not always easy. Best bets usually are luxury-hotel dining rooms: the **Carlyle Restaurant** at the Carlyle (35 East 76th Street, 570-7192) and **Maurice** at the Parker Meridien (118 West 57th Street, 245-7788). Other luxurious choices are the **Café Pierre** in the Pierre Hotel at Fifth Avenue and 61st Street, 940-8185, the Regency Hotel's **540 Park** (540 Park Avenue, at 61st Street, 759-4100) and **Ad-**

rienne at the Hotel Maxim's de Paris (700 Fifth Avenue, at 55th Street, 903-3918).

When the thermometer plummets and steam rises from the manholes, mother's age-old plea to put "something warm in your stomach" before heading out the door seems to carry a belated aroma of logic. But even the most enthusiastic home cooks may find preparing anything more than strong coffee too much of a challenge before noon.

Residents of the Upper West Side have a pleasant solution in a cozy little café called **Good Enough to Eat,** at 424 Amsterdam Avenue, between 80th and 81st streets. It has a narrow dining room with exposed brick walls sporting copper molds and other Americana as well as baskets of dried flowers and knickknacks. The regulars who drift in when the door opens at 8 A.M. sit at small wooden tables and read their morning papers to the background of mollified pop music—the most one could handle at this hour.

The menu offers such homey fare as eggs and omelets with buttermilk biscuits, old-fashioned oatmeal with cream, brown sugar, and cinnamon toast, as well as banana-walnut pancakes with strawberry butter, pecan waffles, apple pancakes, and a combination platter called "the lumberjack," two pancakes, three strips of bacon, and two scrambled eggs. Prices are in the $5-to-$10 range.

The pancakes and waffles are made with thick, eggy homemade batter. The banana-walnut pancakes, three huge disks, are sprinkled with chopped walnuts, sliced bananas, and an orange slice. They should fortify you for any challenges in the day ahead.

If you want to butter up your co-workers, take out some of the grainy bran muffins, bulbous scones, or banana-walnut muffins. Good Enough to Eat is open from 8 A.M. to 11:30 P.M., daily. Telephone: 496-0163.

If you like your eggs sunnyside-way-up, try the breakfast at **Windows on the World.** From 7:30 to 10:30 A.M. on weekdays, an à la carte breakfast is served in the glass-fronted Hors d'Oeuvrerie high above New York harbor. Prices range from $3.95 for Irish oatmeal with honey and cream to $9.50 for smoked salmon and cream cheese. Windows on the World is at 1 World Trade Center, 107th floor. Brunch is also served from noon to 2:30 P.M. on Saturday, and from noon to 7:30 P.M. on Sunday. Telephone: 938-1111.

CHINATOWN

&. Aside from the major Chinatown restaurants that appear in the restaurant review section of the book, there are some noteworthy spots, some large and bustling, others little more than nooks, that I have enjoyed over the years. Here's a brief rundown.

Big Wong Restaurant Inc., 67 Mott Street. Two Chinese acquaintances introduced me to this humble eat-and-run spot on Mott Street, the restaurant row of Chinatown. This is a good place to keep in mind for a quick and I mean quick—wholesome lunch at incredibly low prices. If you bark your order to a waiter while scooting to a table, and have the dexterity to eat noodles in broth with chopsticks, it's possible to enjoy a savory lunch and be back on the street with three-quarters of your lunch hour left over. Try the wonton mein, a deep bowl of flavorful broth filled with thin whole-wheat noodles and pork dumplings (about $2.50). Platters of cold roast duck and chicken, as well as a house favorite, salty boiled chicken, are good accompaniments—especially dabbed with some megavolt hot sauce. Open 10 A.M. to 10 P.M., daily; entrées, $6 to $10. Telephone: 964-0540.

HSF (Chinatown), 46 Bowery, south of Canal Street. This clattering and colorful restaurant buzzes all day long, from dim sum breakfast until midnight. The dining room is a gastronomic Roller Derby where waiters spin around the room behind carts overloaded with small portions of dumplings, roast duck, shredded chicken, and all varieties of shrimp, squid, pork, fish, and pastries. Turnover is fast and furious, so the food is generally hot and fresh when you get it. The eyes-bigger-than-stomach syndrome is endemic here. Open 7:30 A.M. to 2 A.M., daily; $15 to $25 for four dim sum entrées. Telephone: 374-1319.

King Fung, 20 Elizabeth Street, south of Canal Street. This big, brassy newcomer is well suited to a large communal dinner, and there are plenty of first-rate preparations to keep everyone happy. Peking duck is a real delight, crackling outside and succulent within; other good choices are the dry scallop soup, shrimp in lemon sauce, steamed dumplings, and lobster Chinese style, served with black beans. Waiters are friendly and energetic. Open 8 A.M. to 11 P.M., daily; $15 to $25 for a three-course meal. Telephone: 964-5256.

Peking Duck House Restaurant, 22 Mott Street. The name says it all. If you are looking for a succulent rendition of Peking duck, try this unassuming and lively second-story restaurant where the art has been honed to a reliably satisfying science. A whole duck, which feeds up to six as part of a multicourse meal, costs $24. Open noon to 10:30 P.M., Sunday through Thursday; noon to 11:30 P.M., Friday and Saturday; $12 to $18 for a three-course meal. Telephone: 227-1810.

Yuet Tung Restaurant, 40 Bowery. The name "Hakka" translates roughly as "guest people," and it describes an ancient Chinese subculture, originally from the north, that exists today in the southern provinces around Canton. Not only do the Hakka have their own dialect, but they also have a distinctive cuisine characterized by various organ meats. This trim, inexpensive restaurant offers an unadulterated introduction to such specialties as crispy pork intestines, sizzling fried pork legs, pork cake with preserved fish, chicken kidneys with vegetables, and beef tripe with sour cabbage—rustic and assertive all. For the less adventuresome, there is a tasty baked, salted, shredded chicken. Open 11 A.M. to 4 A.M., daily; $15 to $20 for a three-course meal. Telephone: 608-6383.

DINING ALONE

&❧ Eating out is usually a social occasion as much as a gastronomic one; however, most of us at one time or another find ourselves looking for a place to dine alone in peace, perhaps to read a magazine or just get away from it all. Below are some suggestions. Sushi bars are usually suitable for dining alone as well.

Aurora, 60 East 49th Street, 692-9292. Elegant eating-and-drinking bar.

The Ballroom, 253 West 28th Street, 244-3005. Colorful tapas bar (Spanish snacks).

Brasserie, 100 East 53rd Street, 751-4840, 751-4841. Large rectangular eating counter; many tables suitable for one.

Cabana Carioca, 123 West 45th Street, 581-8088. Communal table arrangement.

Cafe de Bruxelles, 118 Greenwich Avenue, at West 13th Street, 206-1830. Banquettes.

Cafe des Sports, 329 West 51st Street, 581-1283. Inconspicuous small tables suitable for singles.

Cafe 212, 212 East 52nd Street, 486-0212. Wide, comfortable sushi bar.

Chez Napoleon, 365 West 50th Street, 265-6980. Inconspicuous small tables suitable for singles.

China Grill, 60 West 53rd Street, 333-7788. Long dining bars.

Hamburger Harry's, 157 Chambers Street, between West Broadway and Greenwich Street, 267-4446. Eating counter surrounding grill.

Inagiku, 111 East 49th Street, 355-0440. Large circular tempura bar.

La Bonne Soupe, 48 West 55th Street, 586-7650. Banquettes in front room suitable for singles.
Mezzogiorno, 195 Spring Street, 334-2112. Long dining bar where pizzas, pastas, and salads are served.

Oyster Bar and Restaurant, in Grand Central Station, 42nd Street and Vanderbilt Avenue (lower level), 490-6650. Expansive eating counters, animated atmosphere.

Restaurant Florent, 69 Gansevoort Street, between Washington and Greenwich streets, 989-5779. Long counter in converted diner.

The Ritz Cafe, 2 Park Avenue, at 32nd Street, 684-2122. Two large wooden eating-and-drinking bars.

Sam's Restaurant, 152 West 52nd Street, in Equitable Center, 582-8700. Large dining bar.

Terrace Five, Trump Tower, level 5, 725 Fifth Avenue, between 56th and 57th streets, 371-5030. Small tables suitable for single diners; good lighting.

Union Square Cafe, 21 East 16th Street, 243-4020. Comfortable oyster bar where full meals can be ordered.

OUTDOOR CAFÉS

Neither smog nor heat nor threat of rain nor honking traffic will stay New Yorkers from their appointed weekend rounds of outdoor cafés in warm weather—and the choices are growing every year. Stretches of Columbus Avenue, the Upper East Side, and Greenwich Village are beginning to resemble Jones Beach as umbrellas pop up on sidewalks and terraces, in gardens and plazas.

Each summer seems to spawn more sidewalk cafés, and the casual observer can easily follow their migratory patterns. Where five years ago they were considered cute attractions scattered loosely in the Village and parts of the East Side, they are now an integral part of the summer social life nearly everywhere, particularly the Upper West Side.

The familiar favorites are going strong: **The River Café** in Brooklyn's Fulton Ferry district, where drinks are served on an outdoor terrace overlooking the East River and all of lower Manhattan (see review, page 329); **Tavern on the Green** in Central Park, which has a leafy and magical ambiance in summer and early fall (see review, page 372); **The Terrace** at the American Stanhope Hotel (995 Fifth Avenue, at 81st Street, 288-5800), across from the Metropolitan Museum, and the assorted restaurants at the South Street Seaport and Pier 17, which have a number of American grill-style restaurants and lively bars that offer panoramic views of the harbor. The views surpass most of the food, though.

The following outdoor cafés are recommended for atmosphere, comfort, and service; food quality varies widely, from average to superior. Also taken into consideration is the "fume factor." All of these selections are a safe distance from the street and from the eye-burning exhaust fumes that are the bane of many urban cafés. Those who plan to go to any of the restaurants are advised to specify the outdoor café when calling for reservations.

The American Festival Cafe, at Rockefeller Center, 20 West 50th Street, occupies one of New York's most popular tourist haunts. It is also worth visiting even by those who live here. The café, offering an all-American menu, is part of a glittering three-restaurant complex that also includes The Sea Grill, a slightly more formal restaurant, which features fish grilled over charcoal, and Savories, a combination carryout, sandwich, and salad shop. The café has a dining area called the Bar Carvery, offering slices of steaming roast beef, turkey, or cold poached fish, and a wide variety of American beers.

All of the restaurants spill out into what is in winter the home of the Rockefeller Center skating rink, under the golden statue of Prometheus. Trying to figure out which outdoor tables belong to which restaurant can be a challenge, but once you settle in, you can enjoy a comfortable, fume-free meal under the red-and-pink umbrellas flanked by palm trees and potted geraniums.

The American Festival Cafe starts up at 7:30 A.M. for

breakfast, which can be lovely on a breezy summer morning, and closes at 10 P.M.; late-night supper up to midnight is planned soon. You can sample from a rainbow of frozen drinks at the outdoor bar until 1 A.M. Telephone: 246-6699.

Greenwich Village outdoor cafés tend to be cramped affairs, jutting out into narrow sidewalks crowded with pedestrians. **Caffè Vivaldi,** at 32 Jones Street, has the advantage of being on a quiet side street with a neighborhood atmosphere. There are a half dozen tables outside under an attractive canopy. You can order such tidbits as prosciutto and mozzarella or quiches. There are all sorts of exotic iced coffees, ten different teas, imported sodas, mineral waters, and a wide range of desserts.

Open 10 A.M. to 1 A.M., weekdays; until 3 A.M. weekends. Telephone: 929-9384.

Da Silvano, 260 Avenue of the Americas, between Bleecker and Houston streets, is a popular Tuscan restaurant just outside the crowded core of Greenwich Village (see review, page 137). The once-superior food has become wobbly, but the outdoor café on a wide sidewalk is still a lovely place to share a bottle of wine and assorted hors d'oeuvres. Da Silvano is open for lunch, 11 to 3 P.M., Monday through Friday; dinner, 6 to 11 P.M., Monday through Thursday, 6 P.M. to midnight, Friday and Saturday, 6 to 11 P.M., Sunday. Telephone: 982-0090.

The Fountain Café in Lincoln Center, Broadway and 64th Street, is one of the most pleasant and diverting cafés on the Upper West Side. There is always plenty of action in the broad plaza around the illuminated fountain at Lincoln Center, especially in the evening, when the opera- and concertgoers stroll by. The café tends to get crowded before performances but clears out about 8 P.M. At lunchtime, it is quiet and relaxing. A simple but competently prepared menu stresses salads, sandwiches, and pastas ($10 to $15). There is a small wine list.

Open during warm months; hours vary with performances at Lincoln Center. Telephone: 874-7000.

Le Madeleine, 403 West 43rd Street, a fine place to cool off with an iced cappuccino and a tea cake, is one of the more charming little cafés in the theater district. The restaurant, which serves simple French fare in the $10-to-$15 range at lunch, slightly more at dinner, has a small but lovely backyard garden with ivy-strewn brick walls and about a dozen tables under white umbrellas.

The café is open from noon to midnight, daily; brunch is served from noon to 3:30 P.M., Saturday and Sunday. Closed Sundays in summer. Telephone: 246-2993.

There is a massive red-granite outcropping in the garden behind **Lion's Rock,** 316 East 77th Street, a French-American restaurant. The rock is so startling, like a chunk of the Appalachian range transplanted to Manhattan's East Side, that you can't help suspect it is a masterly papier-mâché prank. But it is real, a glacial remnant that was a famous picnic spot for couples a century ago. Dramatic lighting at night makes the scene even more impressive as you sit at one of the eighteen tables in the tastefully landscaped garden.

Steaks and chops are the best bet here. The outdoor tables are generally reserved for diners in peak meal hours.

Brunch served Saturday and Sunday from 11:30 A.M. to 3 P.M.; lunch, 11:30 A.M. to 2:30 P.M., Monday through Friday; dinner, 5:30 P.M. to midnight, daily. Telephone: 988-3610.

The refurbished **Loeb Boathouse** on the lake in Central Park is one of the most serene spots in town to wind down under the open sky. Aside from two restaurants, one more a snack bar, the other more formal, there is a relaxing outdoor terrace overlooking the lake. Diners in either restaurant have the option of sitting indoors or outside. The Boathouse café is open daily in summer months from 11:30 A.M. to 4:30 P.M. for lunch and 6 to 10 P.M. for dinner. The patio is open continuously from noon to 11 P.M., daily, March through November. Telephone: 517-2233.

If you are the type who derives smug pleasure from watching others exercise while you dine and drink, **Manhattan Island,** at 482 West 43rd Street, on the roof of the Manhattan Plaza Health Club, is a fine choice for lunch or dinner. Weather permitting, good pastas, salad, and grilled entrées, as well as a variety of frozen drinks, are served at fifteen tables adjacent to the rooftop swimming pool and tennis courts. If thunderclouds threaten, you can always repair to the handsome bar-dining room or the larger upstairs room, overlooking the pool. Open noon to 11 P.M., Monday through Saturday, noon to 9:30 P.M., Sunday. Telephone: 967-0533.

If you are in the mood for just a drink or a burger, there is a landmark bar at 129 East 18th Street called **Pete's Tavern,** once frequented by O. Henry, which also has an outdoor café. Hours: 11 A.M. to 11:30 P.M., Sunday through

Thursday; 11 A.M. to 12:30 A.M., Friday and Saturday. Telephone: 473-7676.

One of the old standbys near the theater district, **Tout Va Bien,** 311 West 51st Street, has opened a small, tree-shaded courtyard in back with a half dozen large tables under green-and-white umbrellas. You will think you are going on a guided tour of the boiler room as the waitress leads you through a dim back hallway to the garden, but once you are there it is peaceful and pleasant.

Stick with the simple entrées—steak and french fries, broiled chicken, stews. Anything fancier is consumed at your own risk. Lunch is a singular bargain, with many entrées in the $7-to-$10 range. The café is open for lunch from noon to 2:30 P.M.; dinner, 5 to 11:30 P.M., Monday through Saturday, 5 to 10:30 P.M., Sunday. Telephone: 265-0190.

For those with a nautical bent, **The Water Club,** on the upper deck of a barge on the East River at 30th Street, is the place to go for before- or after-dinner drinks and snacks. You sit on directors' chairs under the summer sky and watch ships and tugs ply the river or, if you are facing landward, monitor traffic on the F.D.R. Drive. The only break in the tranquillity is the flutter of helicopters at a nearby landing pad, briefly drowning conversation at each landing and takeoff.

Food served on the outdoor deck is limited to hamburgers, hot dogs, clams, oysters, and dessert in the $3-to-$5 range.

The deck is open 4 P.M. until midnight, weekdays, and noon until 1 A.M., weekends. Telephone: 683-3333.

Ye Waverly Inn, 16 Bank Street, corner of Waverly Place, a nearly 180-year-old Greenwich Village landmark, has been known in recent years more for its nostalgic atmosphere than for its food, but its backyard garden is a charming setting for a cool drink. Among the house specials are concoctions called Peach Fizz, Lemon Mint Freeze, and iced Alaskan coffee. There are also piña coladas and daiquiris. Brunch, 12:30 to 3:30 P.M., Sunday; lunch, 11:45 A.M. to 2 P.M., Monday through Friday; dinner, 5:15 to 10 P.M., Monday through Thursday, 5:15 to 11 P.M., Friday and Saturday, 4:30 to 9 P.M., Sunday. Telephone: 929-4377.

RESTAURANT ROW

❧ The renovated block of 46th Street between Eighth and Ninth avenues had a much needed face-lift in 1986. Restaurantgoers who remember the row as far back as the 1950s will notice dramatic changes in its ethnic stockpot. In the postwar years, the street was a French enclave, owing largely to the nearby Hudson River pier where French passenger liners arrived carrying immigrants. Many French families literally walked along West 46th Street and settled in the first suitable apartments they could find. A number opened bistros, hence the genesis of the row.

Today most of the oldtime bistros are gone, many replaced by Italian, American, and Asian restaurants: The former A la Fourchette is now a spiffy Italian spot called Audrone's; the old Chambertin is being converted to a Thai restaurant; Jack's Epicure, a Continental dining room, is now the Neapolitan-style Fontana Rosa. A Chinese restaurant-carryout has taken root near Ninth Avenue, and one of the most popular spots on the block is Orso, a vibrant Italian restaurant serving individual pizzas, game, and pasta.

In recent years, Restaurant Row has had a volatile reputation, with many restaurant comings and goings. Here is a nibbler's tour of the current crop:

Audrone's, 342 West 46th Street. A crisp and cool stage built around checkerboard tiles, black banquettes, mirrors, and splashes of watercolors makes this one of the more buoyant newcomers to Restaurant Row. The food, similarly, is bright and tidy, a generally appealing blend of pastas, seafood, and good straightforward meat dishes—at Off Off Broadway prices. Even if seasonings miss their cue now and then, the food is fresh and the effort sincere. Lunch entrées are under $10 (try the pasta primavera bolstered with sun-dried tomatoes for $7.25), while three-course dinners run between $25 and $30 with a modest bottle of wine. Lunch, noon to 3 P.M., Monday through Saturday; dinner, 5:30 to 9 P.M., Monday through Thursday, 5 to 10 P.M., Friday and Saturday. Telephone: 246-1960.

Barbetta, 321 West 46th Street. If you are looking for the Big Deal dining experience before theater, complete with oversize chandeliers, bursts of spring flowers, and comforting old-world service, eighty-year-old Barbetta awaits. The food is hardly as splendid as the setting (see full review, page 79), although there are ample successes on the extensive menu to assemble a satisfying meal. Barbetta has an impressive list of Italian wines at affordable prices. The outdoor garden is a delightful place for lunch in warm weather, especially when the magnolias and wisteria are in bloom. Lunch, noon to 2 P.M., Monday through Saturday; dinner, 5 to 11:30 P.M., Monday through Saturday. Telephone: 246-9171.

Big Wok, 360 West 46th Street. This pretty little eat-and-run Chinese restaurant, specializing in Hunan and Sichuan cuisines, will be familiar to anyone who lives on the Upper West Side. Big Wok also features carryout and free delivery for an $8 minimum order. Open 11:30 A.M. to 11 P.M., daily. Telephone: 315-2770.

Broadway Joe, 315 West 46th Street. In recent years an identity crisis has plagued this steakhouse with an Italian accent. Recent visits indicate it is still trying to find its niche among the new neighbors. The dining rooms are rather lugubrious—dim, superficially renovated, and plain. The kitchen specializes in high-fire torching of steaks and chops until they are carbonized outside and medium-well inside; vegetables are unsullied by any seasonings. Lunch, noon to 3:30 P.M., daily; dinner, 3:30 P.M. to midnight, daily. Telephone: 246-6513.

Carolina, 355 West 46th Street. Carolina is not on my mind often these days when colleagues ask for dining recommendations in the theater district—unless one yearns for crab cakes, which are still first rate. Much of the Southern-style food, emphasizing hot smoked meats, chilies, and the like, has lost its Dixie bravado. On revisits, the best offerings were skewered shrimp with red peppers and brisket of beef with a cloud-light corn pudding. (See full review, page 105.)

The ground-floor main dining room with its gray banquettes, wraparound mirrors, and a skylight is still one of the classier settings on the row. Lunch, noon to 3 P.M., Monday through Friday; dinner, 5:30 P.M. to midnight, Monday through Saturday, 1 to 9 P.M., Sunday. Telephone: 245-0058.

Crêpes Suzette, 363 West 46th Street. The smiles are as genuine as they are wide when you are welcomed by the Frenchwomen who run this veteran stucco-and-brick bistro. While the food is predictable, much of it is assertively seasoned and soothing. Cassoulet, full-flavored and generous with sausage and duck, is a winner; other suggestions are rack of lamb for two, beef Bourguignon, and coq au vin.

I have sampled only one seafood entrée recently, of dubious freshness, so my instincts are to stay on the other side of the menu aisle. Beware of the deceptively inexpensive Burgundies from inferior vintages on the wine card and stick to familiar middle-of-the-road reliables. Brunch, noon to 4 P.M., Sunday; lunch, noon to 3 P.M., Monday through Saturday; dinner, 3 to 10 P.M., Monday through Thursday, 3 to 11:30 P.M., Friday and Saturday, 4 to 7 P.M., Sunday. Closed Sunday during summer. Telephone: 974-9002.

Joe Allen, 326 West 46th Street. This is one of the hot spots for people-watching along the row—frequented by the up-and-coming, the movers and shakers and wistful thespians of every sort. Stick with the simple tasty salads, grilled meats and such: chicken paillard, grilled salmon, grilled lamb chops. Beer aficionados will be delighted with the remarkable selection. The perpetually packed bar is a diverting spot to spend some time before or after the show. Open noon to midnight, daily, bar closes at 1 A.M. Telephone: 581-6464.

Lattanzi, 361 West 46th Street. The workaholics of the Lattanzi family have taken on five establishments around town. This handsome brick-lined grotto turns out an array of zestily seasoned pastas and grilled entrées. Bucatini all'amatriciana is a highlight, rich with bacon, sweet onion, and tomatoes; linguine with white clam sauce is good too. After 8 P.M., the kitchen offers what it calls "classic cuisine of the Italian Jews"—among the dishes are artichokes in olive oil and garlic, orecchiette with tomato and tuna-fish sauce, and red snapper with raisins and vinegar. Lunch, noon to 2 P.M., Monday through Friday; dinner, 5:30 to 11 P.M., Monday through Thursday, 5:30 P.M. to midnight, Friday and Saturday. Telephone: 315-0980.

La Vieille Auberge, 347 West 46th Street. Comfort and tranquillity are the two major assets of this enduring Restaurant Row institution, which is showing its mileage— the off-white banquettes have become off-off-white from years of friction. The food is unreconstructed 1950s fare. Vichyssoise is light, creamy, and brightened with chives, saucisson en croute is hearty and filling with a brown stock sauce; and for main courses, stick with roast poultry, rack of lamb with rosemary, and steak with red-wine sauce. The seafood I have sampled there was given heavy-handed treatment. Dinner is about $30 per person before tax, tip, and wine. Lunch, noon to 2:30 P.M., Monday through Friday; dinner, 5 to 9 P.M., Monday through Thursday, 5 to 11 P.M., Friday and Saturday. Telephone: 247-4284.

454

Le Rivage, 340 West 46th Street. It certainly looks authentic, this gleaming, lodgelike sanctuary of wood paneling and brick with piped-in Edith Piaf lending the mood of a 1940s French film. However, that's about as far as the fantasy goes. The assorted appetizer plate is anemic, onion soup is pale, and duck terrine is lackluster. The timidly seasoned but well-cooked filet mignon au poivre is one of the better choices, as are lamb chops. I have seen better wine lists in upscale diners. Dinner is about $30 per person before wine, tax, and tip. Lunch, noon to 2:30 P.M., Monday through Saturday; dinner, 5 to 9:30 P.M., Monday through Thursday, 5 to 10:30 P.M., Friday and Saturday. Telephone: 765-7374.

Orso, 322 West 46th Street. The clientele at this breezy Italian trattoria with a sunny skylight and animated open kitchen can be a veritable who's who of the *Playbill* set—it has long since eclipsed fatigued Sardi's as the place for theatrical types. Moreover, the food is arguably the best on Restaurant Row. If you want something quick and relatively light, get the arugula salad with hard ricotta and anchovies, followed perhaps by one of the zesty, thin-crusted individual pizzas. For more substantial fare, pastas and grilled items are usually on the mark, although quality has become erratic in the past year or two. The wine list is thoughtfully matched with the food and reasonably priced. Open 11:30 A.M. to 11:45 P.M., Wednesday and Saturday, other days noon to 11:45 P.M. Telephone: 489-7212.

The Red Blazer Too, 349 West 46th Street. Jazz combos strike up about 8 o'clock nightly (9 P.M. weekends) at this newcomer to the row. All blond wood, stained glass, and colorful murals, this spacious cabaret-restaurant is a good place to have an after-theater drink along with some of the best Buffalo chicken wings in town—crisp-skinned, moist, and coated with a fiery Tabasco-and-vinegar sauce. Some of the food sampled was humdrum, such as a dried-out roast chicken, but linguine with clam sauce is better than average, combining fresh clams with lots of garlic and herbs. Hamburgers and sandwiches are reliable. Brunch, noon to 5 P.M., Sunday; lunch, noon to 3 P.M., Monday through Saturday; dinner, 5 P.M. to 1 A.M., Monday through Saturday, noon to midnight, Sunday. Telephone: 262-3112.

UPPER EAST SIDE

Golden Tulip Barbizon Restaurant, in the Barbizon Hotel, 140 East 63rd Street, at Lexington Avenue. The wine selection may not be the grandest in town, but the setting is one of the more genteel. This renovated 1920s hotel with its long polished bar and tables facing animated Lexington Avenue is a fine place to unwind with a glass of wine or champagne. An eight-bottle Cruvinet carries mostly California and French labels, while during the holidays three kinds of sparkling wine are available.

Open noon to 2 A.M. daily. Telephone: 838-5700.

UPPER WEST SIDE

Grapes, 522 Columbus Avenue, between 85th and 86th streets. The wacky appearance of white walls sawed open to reveal brick underneath and buoyant murals depicting city scenes disguises a serious approach to wine at this Upper West Side spot. More than twenty-five wines, including champagnes and ports, are available by the glass. The restaurant serves a mixed bag of pastas, grilled fish, and roasts. Open from 3:30 P.M. to 4 A.M., Monday through Friday, 11 A.M. to 4 A.M., Saturday and Sunday. All wines half price from 5 to 7 P.M. daily. Telephone: 362-3004.

MIDTOWN

Café Europa, La Brioche, 347 East 54th Street. This is a most unlikely setting in which to find a high-tech wine bar featuring a decent international selection, a charming old-world restaurant specializing in earthy stewlike meat and seafood preparations that are served in carved-out brioche loaves the size of softballs. The colorful dining room, festooned with rustic artifacts, looks as if a team of gypsies could dash in at any moment and begin dancing on the tables. It has a tile-fronted fireplace, stucco walls, rustic wooden beams overhead, ornate brass chandeliers, and a loyal clientele that looks as if it were cast for the role. A nice option is the snack menu to accompany the wines, including rillettes of pork with French bread, garlic sausage brioche, and rabbit-duck terrine with Armagnac.

The bar serves during restaurant hours: Lunch, noon to 2:30 P.M., Monday through Friday; dinner, 5 to 10:30 P.M., Monday through Saturday. Telephone: 755-0160.

Cafe 43, 147 West 43rd Street. This is a convenient spot to meet friends for a glass of wine before or after a Broadway show. The bright and cheerful interior is in the grand café style, with lots of mirrors, deep banquettes, and a long brass-and-wood bar where twenty-six wines, including champagnes, are poured by the glass. The bottle list is impressive as well, especially the California selections. Prices are moderate. The food at this handsome brasserie has plummeted. Don't bother. Open noon to midnight, Monday through Friday, 5 P.M. to midnight, Saturday. Telephone: 869-4200.

The Drake Bar, in the Drake Hotel, 440 Park Avenue, at 56th Street. Just off the busy lobby of this swanky hotel is a cushy two-tier lounge surrounding a wood-and-marble bar. This is one of the more sedate and formal bars in the city, a good place for a romantic interlude or a tranquil business meeting. The only exception might be when a pianist starts tinkling away in the early evening, exposing you to the potential risk of a tipsy, frog-voiced conventioneer performing a painful rendition of "New York, New York." Because the Drake is owned by Swissair, the regular lineup of wines by the glass, nineteen by last count, includes a few labels from Switzerland.

Open 11 A.M. to 1 A.M., daily. Telephone: 223-2235, 223-3876.

Lavin's, 23 West 39th Street. The genial bar in this handsome, wood-paneled restaurant is one of the classiest places to sample a wide range of familiar and up-and-coming wines. Close to twenty selections, including champagnes and sparkling wines (and a dozen ports), are available. Open for lunch from noon to 2:30 P.M., Monday through Friday; dinner, 5:30 to 9 P.M., Monday through Friday. Telephone: 921-1288.

Terrace Five, Level Five, Trump Tower, 725 Fifth Avenue, at 46th Street. It may be surprising to learn that amid the hustle and bustle of this vertical shopping mall is a relaxing little oasis where you can get a good salad and simple grilled fish while sampling from about ten well-chosen wines. Prices are on the high side, but so, too, is the rent.

A small bar with an eight-bottle Cruvinet extends to the

shopping arcade, while on the other end there are little tables in a cheerful back room with a stunning view down Fifth Avenue. Desserts are most tempting.

Open for lunch, noon to 3 P.M., Monday through Saturday; tea, 3:15 to 5 P.M., Monday through Saturday; dinner, 6 to 10 P.M., Monday through Saturday; bar open throughout these hours. Telephone: 371-5030.

GREENWICH VILLAGE

Siracusa, 65 Fourth Avenue, near 10th Street. About a dozen wines, nearly all Italian, are served by the glass in this engaging little family-run spot in the downtown theater district near Astor Place.

A wonderful match to the hearty Italian red wines is the cold appetizer plate, which might include mozzarella cheese with sun-dried tomatoes, little ricotta cheese fritters, eggplant salad, fried sardines, marinated mushrooms, and broccoli pie. Open for lunch, noon to 3 P.M., Monday through Friday; dinner, 6 to 11 P.M., Monday through Thursday, 6 to 11:30 P.M., Friday and Saturday, 6 to 11 P.M., Sunday; wine bar open during restaurant hours. Telephone: 254-1940.

SOHO

I Tre Merli, 463 West Broadway, near Houston Street. A pair of Genoese importers built this dramatic wine bar in SoHo to showcase their portfolio of Ligurian wines, all of which carry three blackbirds on the label, thus the bar's name. The setting is striking, with its towering ceiling, brick walls lined neck-high with stacked bottles, a sixty-foot modular bar in a rough figure-eight pattern, and, late in the evening, pulsing pop music. In the early evening it is a soothing and relaxing spot; later, it becomes one of SoHo's more clamorous meeting places. An elevated dining area serves a mixed Italian menu.

About twenty-eight wines and seven sparkling wines are available by the glass. Italian selections are particularly well represented.

The bar is open Sunday through Thursday from noon to 1 A.M., until 2 A.M. Friday and Saturday; the restaurant serves lunch from noon to 5 P.M. and dinner from 6 to midnight, daily. Telephone: 254-8699.

SoHo Kitchen and Bar, 103 Greene Street, between Spring and Prince streets. This is about as close to an oenophile's heaven as you'll ever see. More than one hundred wines by the glass, sixteen special "flight tastings" in which patrons can sample up to eight wines of the same type side by side, seasonal wine festivals, weekly wine festivals, and much more. Aside from the first-rate list of French, Italian, and American, there are many unusual selections such as Australian cabernets and German Eiswein. Even the setting is bigger than life, with a soaring ceiling, mile-long bar, and multitiered dining areas.

The bar is open from 11:30 to 2 A.M., Monday through Thursday, until 4 A.M., Friday and Saturday; the kitchen is open from 11.00 A.M. to midnight, Monday through Thursday, until 1 A.M., Friday and Saturday. Telephone: 925-1866.

BROOKLYN

It is billed as Brooklyn's first wine bar, this cheerful and casual spot in the Park Slope section called **De'Vine Restaurant and Wine Bar.** Opened by a former actress, Susan Garrett, it serves about 45 well-chosen wines by the glass, mostly in the $3-to-$5 range. California and France are best represented, along with a smattering of German, Italian, and Australian labels. A full menu of terrines, salads, pastas, and seafood is served in this café setting with an open hearth, tile tables, and Art Deco paintings on the walls. De'Vine Restaurant and Wine Bar, 396 Seventh Avenue, at 12th Street, Brooklyn, is open for brunch from noon to 3:30 P.M., Sunday; from 5 P.M. to midnight, Wednesday through Saturday; and for Sunday dinner from 5 P.M. to midnight. Telephone: (718) 499-9861.

BEST DISHES

Angulas (Spanish-style eels)	Harlequin
Apple pandowdy	An American Place
Apple pie	The Coach House, Oyster Bar and Restaurant in Grand Central Station
Apple tart	Quatorze
Baked Alaska	The Rainbow Room
Baklava	Anatolia
Beef brisket	Carolina
Beef, cooked on stones	Kitcho
Beef, with orange	Chin Chin, Fu's, Pig Heaven
Beef, prime ribs	The Coach House
Beef ribs, grilled	Rosa Mexicano, Sylvia's
Beer	Joe Allen, Peculier Pub
Black bean soup	Arcadia, The Coach House, Union Square Cafe, Victor's Café 52
Bollito misto	Le Cirque, La Métairie (East)
Boudin blanc	Anabelle's, Café Un Deux Trois
Boudin noir (blood sausage)	Bistro d'Adrienne, Café 58, Chez Josephine, Restaurant Florent
Bouillabaisse	Ambassador Grill, Oyster Bar and Restaurant at Grand Central Station, Provence
Bourride	Provence
Brandada de bacalao	Harlequin
Brandade de morue	Bistro d'Adrienne, Chez Jacqueline, La Bonne Soupe, Provence
Bread	Montrachet, Palio
Bread, Indian-style	Bukhara, Tandoor
Bread pudding	Anabelle's, Arcadia, Lavin's
Bruschetta	Il Mulino, Union Square Cafe

Calf's liver	Brive, Il Cantinori, Man Ray, Maurice, Montrachet
Caponata	Azzurro
Carpaccio	Le Cirque, Mezzogiorno, Palio
Cassoulet	Ambassador Grill, Café 58, Chez Louis, Crêpes Suzette, Le Zinc, Man Ray, Voulez-Vous
Caviar	Petrossian
Cheesecake	Palm, Peter Luger, The River Café
Cheese plate	Le Régence, Palio, Parioli Romanissimo, The Quilted Giraffe
Chicken, fried	Jezebel
Chicken, grilled	Melrose, The Village Green
Chicken, roasted	Arcadia, Chez Louis, Lutèce, The Quilted Giraffe
Chicken, salt baked	The Nice Restaurant, Phoenix Garden Restaurant
Chicken, tandoor baked	Bukhara, Tandoor
Chicken and waffles	Jezebel
Chicken hash	Manhattan Island, "21" Club
Chicken Kiev	The Russian Tea Room
Chicken paillard	Cafe Luxembourg
Chicken potpie	The Coach House
Chili	Arizona 206, Exterminator Chili
Chinese hot pot	Great Shanghai Restaurant
Chocolate cake	Lavin's
Chocolate mud pie	Bice, Docks Oyster Bar and Seafood Grill
Chocolate mousse	Maurice
Chocolate pudding	An American Place, Arcadia
Chocolate terrine	Arcadia
Choucroute garnie	Man Ray, Voulez-Vous
Chowder, New England clam	Coastal
Coffee, Greek-style	Periyali
Coleslaw	Jane Street Seafood Cafe
Corn bread	Jezebel, Sylvia's
Corned-beef sandwich	Carnegie Deli
Couscous	La Métairie, La Kasbah

Crab cakes	Cafe Luxembourg, Carolina, The Coach House, The Four Seasons, The Odeon, "21" Club
Crabs, soft shell	Jane Street Seafood Cafe
Crabs, steamed	Sidewalkers'
Crème brûlée	Le Cirque, Le Cygne, Provence, Voulez-Vous
Crème caramel	Man Ray
Crostini	Sistina, Union Square Cafe
Dacquoise	"21" Club
Desserts, overall	Aurora, La Tulipe, Le Cirque, The Quilted Giraffe, The River Café
Dim sum	HSF, King Fung
Drinks, mixed	Peter Luger, Sparks Steakhouse
Duck, confit	Ambassador Grill, Anabelle's, Aurora, Lafayette, La Tulipe, Prunelle
Duck, grilled	Melrose
Duck, roasted	Maurice, The Nice Restaurant, Phoenix Garden Restaurant, 20 Mott Street Restaurant
Duck, Thai-style	Tommy Tang's
Duck à l'orange	Terrace
Duck breast, grilled	The Four Seasons, Le Cirque, Rakel
Dumplings, Chinese	Great Shanghai Restaurant, Pig Heaven
Empanadas	Sabor, Zarela
Enchiladas	Cinco de Mayo
English trifle	John Clancy's
Espresso	Il Cantinori, Mezzaluna
Fajitas	Zarela
Feijoada	Cabana Carioca, Cabana Carioca II
Fish, grilled/broiled	The Dolphin, John Clancy's, Periyali, Roumeli Taverna
Foie gras	La Caravelle, Lafayette, Le Cirque, Maurice, Prunelle

French fries	Lavin's, The Manhattan Ocean Club, Sam's Restaurant
Frisée aux lardons (chicory and bacon salad)	Quatorze
Frogs' legs	Le Cygne
Gazpacho	Lavin's
Gelati	Gelateria Siracusa, Positano
Gnocchi	Arquà, Remi
Goat, curried	Jezebel
Guacamole	Rosa Mexicano
Guinea hen	Lafayette
Hamburger	Hamburger Harry's, Sam's Restaurant, Union Square Cafe
Hash, fish	Pesca
Ice cream	Chanterelle, Sofi
Key lime pie	Café des Artistes, Sabor
Kidneys, Oriental-style	Shun Lee
Lamb, braised	Periyali
Lamb, navarin of	Le Cirque
Lamb chops	Peter Luger
Lamb kebab	Pamir
Lamb steak	Moroccan Star
Linguine with clam sauce	Marcello, Trastevere
Lobster, broiled or steamed	Coastal, Docks Oyster Bar and Seafood Grill, John Clancy's, La Petite Ferme, Palm, Smith & Wollensky
Lobster, grilled	Cafe Luxembourg
Lobster, smoked	Arcadia
Lobster Américaine	John Clancy's
Lobster club sandwich	Arcadia
Lobster fricassee	Windows on the World
Lobster panroast	Oyster Bar and Restaurant in Grand Central Station
Mashed potatoes	Bistro d'Adrienne, Gotham Bar and Grill
Moussaka	Periyali
Mozzarella	Azzurro, Erminia

Mussels, steamed	Palio
Mutton chops	Keen's
Napoleon	Café des Artistes, Terrace
Octopus, grilled	Periyali, Rio Mar
Octopus salad	Anatolia, Rio Mar, Roumeli Taverna
Osso buco	Il Cantinori, Positano
Oxtail, braised	Caribe
Oysters, fried	Chelsea Central, Docks Oyster Bar and Seafood Grill
Oysters on half shell	Docks Oyster Bar and Seafood Grill, Oyster Bar and Restaurant in Grand Central Station
Paella	Harlequin
Pancakes	Good Enough to Eat
Paris-Brest	Man Ray
Pasta, overall	Arquà, Azzurro, Mezzaluna, Mezzogiorno, Primola, Remi, San Domenico
Pasta all'amatriciana	Union Square Cafe
Pasta arrabbiata	Chelsea Trattoria Italiana
Pasta puttanesca	Frank's, Il Cantinori
Pasta with clam sauce	Erminia, Sal Anthony's
Pasta with lamb ragout	Toscana
Pastilla	Moroccan Star
Pastrami	Carnegie Deli
Peanut butter pie	Manhattan Island
Peking duck	Auntie Yuan, Fu's, King Fung
Pheasant	The River Café
Pierogi	Gramercy Park Bistro
Pig's foot	Café 58
Pistou (French vegetable soup)	La Mirabelle, Montrachet
Pizza	Mezzogiorno, Orso
Plantains	Sabor
Polenta	Arquà
Pommes soufflées	The Rainbow Room
Potato chips, homemade	Maxim's
Potatoes, sautéed	Maxim's
Pot-au-feu	La Grenouille, Voulez-Vous
Profiterole	Lavin's, Maxim's
Prosciutto	Felidia

Quail, barbecued	Arizona 206, Auntie Yuan, Chin Chin
Quail, grilled, roasted	Anatolia, Arcadia, La Réserve, Orso, The River Café
Rabbit	Adrienne, Lutèce
Rabbit paillard	Provence
Rabbit sausage	Huberts
Rillettes of pork	René Pujol, Restaurant Florent
Risotto	Alo Alo, Chelsea Trattoria Italiana, Palio, Parioli Romanissimo
Salads	Gotham Bar and Grill, The Health Pub, Manhattan Island, Mezzogiorno, Sofi
Salmon, grilled	The Quilted Giraffe
Salmon, sautéed	Anabelle's, Aquavit, Prunelle, Union Square Cafe
Salmon terrine	Brive, Le Cygne
Sashimi	Kitcho
Saté, chicken	Tommy Tang's
Saté, beef	Café Un Deux Trois
Scallops	Le Bernardin, Le Cirque, Trumpet's
Sea bass, crispy	Chin Chin
Sea bass in potato crust	Le Cirque
Seafood, overall	The Dolphin, John Clancy's, Lafayette, Le Bernardin, The Sea Grill
Seafood salad	Gotham Bar and Grill
Sea urchin	Le Bernardin, The River Café
Semifreddo	Felidia
Serrano (cured Spanish ham)	Alcala
Sesame noodles	Chin Chin
Shrimp, fried	Phoenix Garden Restaurant
Shrimp, grilled	Petaluma
Shrimp, grilled on sugarcane	Cuisine de Saigon
Shrimp, steamed	Sidewalkers'
Smelts, deep fried	Phoenix Garden Restaurant, Roumeli Taverna

Sole, Dover, grilled	The Dolphin, John Clancy's, La Côte Basque
Sorbet	Palio
Soufflés, dessert	Maurice
Soup	Indochine
Spanakopita	Roumeli Taverna
Spareribs, Chinese	Fu's
Spring rolls	Indochine, 20 Mott Street Restaurant
Squab, grilled	Arcadia, Arizona 206, Aurora, The River Café
Squab, in a pot	The Nice Restaurant
Squab, Oriental-style	Phoenix Garden Restaurant
Squab, roasted	Maurice
Squid, deep-fried	Alcala, Coastal, Wilkinson's Seafood Cafe
Squid, grilled	Fu's, Ozeki
Squid, steamed Oriental-style	Indochine
Squid salad	The Dolphin
Steak	Chez Josephine, Peter Luger, The River Café, Sparks Steakhouse
Steak au poivre	The Coach House, La Gauloise, La Grenouille
Steak pommes frites (steak with french fries)	Cafe Luxembourg, Chez Josephine
Steak tartare	Café Un Deux Trois, The Rainbow Room, Voulez-Vous
Strawberry shortcake	An American Place
Suckling pig	Chez Louis, The Nice Restaurant, Sabor, Texarkana
Sushi	Hatsuhana, Mitsukoshi
Sweet potato pie	Sylvia's
Sweetbreads	Aurora, Lola, Lutèce, The Quilted Giraffe, Rakel, "21" Club
Swordfish	Lavin's
Tacos	Rosa Mexicano
Tandoori fish	Gaylord
Tartufo	Dieci X
Tempura	Inagiku, Kitcho, Ozeki
Terrines, overall	The Four Seasons, La Caravelle
Tiramisù	Arquà, Dieci X, Marcello, Mezzogiorno

Tortilla, Spanish-style	The Ballroom
Trifle dessert (English)	John Clancy's
Truffles	Le Cirque
Tuna steak, grilled	Rakel, Sam's Café, Union Square Cafe
Veal chop	Anabelle's, Aurora, Le Régence, Rakel, Sal Anthony's, Violetta
Vitello tonnato	Toscana
Vegetables, grilled, roasted	Alo Alo, Chez Louis
Vegetable platters, steamed	Auntie Yuan, The Four Seasons, The Health Pub, Lavin's
Venison	Arcadia, Chanterelle, Maurice, Maxim's
Wine bar	SoHo Kitchen and Bar
Wine list, American	Oyster Bar and Restaurant in Grand Central Station, The River Café, The Sea Grill, Windows on the World
Wine list, French	La Côte Basque, Le Cirque
Wine list, Italian	Il Nido, Le Cirque, San Domenico, Sparks Steakhouse
Wine list, overall	La Côte Basque, Le Cirque, The Quilted Giraffe, The River Café, Windows on the World
Zabaglione	Il Nido, Parioli Romanissimo
Zuppa di pesce	Marcello, Trastevere

RESTAURANT INDEX

Map numbers appear in parentheses. The map section begins on page 2.